The Road to Judgment

University of Pennsylvania Press
MIDDLE AGES SERIES
Edited by
Edward Peters
Henry Charles Lea Professor
of Medieval History
University of Pennsylvania

A listing of the available books
in the series appears at the
back of this volume

The Road to Judgment
From Custom to Court in Medieval Ireland and Wales

Robin Chapman Stacey

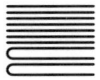

University of Pennsylvania Press
Philadelphia

Portions of this volume have been reprinted from the following works:

Robin Chapman Stacey. "Law and Order in the *Very* Old West: England and Ireland in the European Middle Ages." In *Crossed Paths: Methodological Approaches to the Celtic Aspect of the European Middle Ages*, ed. Benjamin T. Hudson and Vickie Ziegler. Lanham, Md., and London: University Press of America. Copyright © 1991.

Robin Chapman Stacey. "Ties That Bind: Immunities in Irish and Welsh Law." *Cambridge Medieval Celtic Studies* 20 (Winter 1990).

T. M. Charles-Edwards, M. Owen, and D. B. Walters, eds. *Lawyers and Laymen: Studies in the History of Law Presented to Professor Dafydd Jenkins on His Seventy-fifth Birthday*. Cardiff: University of Wales Press, 1986.

Copyright © 1994 by the University of Pennsylvania Press
All rights reserved
Printed in the United States of America

Library of Congress Cataloging-in-Publication Data
Stacey, Robin Chapman.
   The road to judgment: from custom to court in medieval Ireland and Wales / Robin Chapman Stacey.
     p. cm. — (Middle Ages series)
   Includes bibliographical references and index.
   ISBN 0-8122-3216-X
   1. Suretyship and guaranty—Ireland—History. 2. Suretyship and guaranty—Wales—History. 3. Law, Medieval. I. Title. II. Series.
KD1752.C48 1994
346.417′074—dc20
[344.170674]   93-47677
                                                                           CIP

To Bob and Will

Contents

Acknowledgments	ix
Abbreviations	xiii
Introduction	1
1. Law and Lawbooks in Medieval Ireland and Wales	11
2. Contractual Suretyship in Irish Law	27
3. The Social Context of Personal Suretyship	55
4. The Hostage-Sureties of Irish Law	82
5. The Road to Judgment	112
6. Court and Custom in Medieval Wales	141
7. Past and Present in the Law of Hywel	179
8. The Suretyship of the Gods	199
Conclusion	222
Notes	229
Bibliography	303
Index	329

Acknowledgments

This project has been a part of my life for more years than I care to count, and it gives me great pleasure finally to acknowledge the generosity and support of those who have helped along the way. As a graduate student first at Oxford, and then at Yale, I was extraordinarily fortunate in my mentors and instructors. Particularly happy and productive were my years at Oxford, where D. Ellis Evans introduced me to the rudiments of the Welsh language despite numerous more important demands on his time, and where I first learned from my fellow participants in the Welsh medieval law seminar how stimulating and inspiring collegial interaction could be. Special thanks go to Dafydd Jenkins and Morfydd Owen for their incisive comments on my work, and for their ongoing encouragement over the years. At Yale, I was privileged to work with John Boswell, who directed the dissertation from which this book ultimately emerged with the energy and intelligence for which he is well known; without his friendship and sympathetic support I doubt I would have made it through the final stages. Jaroslav Pelikan encouraged me tremendously both by his words and example, and by his willingness to read through endless drafts of a project very far from his own field of specialization. The late Warren Cowgill also gave unselfishly of his time and expertise to help a struggling novice attempt to unravel the intricacies of (among other things) the dreaded "Gwynn text."

Since leaving Yale, I have rewritten this book substantially, and there are many whose assistance has been crucial to the manner in which it has developed. Martin Jaffee, Neil McLeod, and Nerys Patterson made portions of their own work available to me in advance of publication and helped me to sort out my views on a variety of tricky issues by sharing with me their own. The History Research Group at the University of Washington patiently labored through several chapters, courteously setting aside their reservations about history written in the absence of "real" historical sources and alerting me to many instances in which I was presuming too much or too little of my readers. Patrick Ford, Joseph Falaky

Nagy, Robert Stacey, and Patrick Wormald generously took the time to read and comment on all or portions of this work. Their insights and ideas enriched this book considerably, and I am very grateful to them for their wisdom and their time.

Undoubtedly my most significant intellectual debt is to my former Oxford tutor, Thomas Charles-Edwards. It is impossible adequately to convey how much his patient, good-humored instruction has meant to me over the years, or to enumerate the occasions on which his extensive comments have rescued me from scandalous errors. He will not (and does not) agree with everything in this book, but his unstinting support of the project and its author despite this fact has been an essential factor in its completion. For his wisdom, his willingness to give of his time and himself, and his own good heart, I thank him.

And to all of these scholars goes my appreciation for saving me from numerous embarrassing errors. It seems a small, but necessary, recompense for their efforts to exculpate them entirely from responsibility for those that remain.

It is a pleasure to acknowledge also the various types of financial and technical assistance I have received in the course of this project. To the Fulbright/Hays Foundation and the British government I express my thanks for making it possible for me to study at Oxford. Crucial financial support for research was provided by the Keller Fund and by various hourly research funds administered through the Department of History at the University of Washington. I was privileged also to receive two grants from the Graduate School Research Fund here at the University, one for summer research support and one to assist in meeting publication expenses. Edmund Kamai, Byron Nakamura, Rita Stockwell, Lizz Sullivan, Margaret Paton Walsh, and Susanne Young provided important technical assistance, while Kevin Streit assisted me greatly in the production of the bibliography. The patience and diligence exhibited by my editors at the Press were nothing short of remarkable; I am grateful to them for saving me from many inconsistencies and errors. My thanks also to the editors of *Cambridge Medieval Celtic Studies*, University Press of America, and the University of Wales Press for their willingness to allow me to reprint portions of my previously published work in this volume.

Finally, to those friends and family members who have suffered with me in my struggles with this work I express my love and warmest thanks. My father and brother remained encouraging even in the most difficult moments, which was not an easy task. Rosemarie Zagarri will never know how much strength I have drawn over the years from our extensive chocolate research and compensatory jogs in New Haven, Haarlem, and elsewhere. And Kathy Leech Bentson has been an important part of my life for twenty years. But my greatest debt is unquestionably to my husband, whose relief at having this finished may well exceed my own. To him, and to my son, I dedicate this work with my gratitude for teaching me what actually matters most.

List of Abbreviations

ALW	*Ancient Laws and Institutes of Wales*, ed. Aneurin Owen (London, 1841). References are to book.chapter.paragraph unless otherwise noted.
AM	*Audacht Morainn*, ed. Fergus Kelly (Dublin, 1976).
AU	*The Annals of Ulster (to A.D. 1131)*, ed. Seán MacAirt and Gearóid Mac Niocaill (Dublin, 1983).
BAR	British Archeological Reports
BB	*Bechbretha: An Old Irish Law-tract on Bee-keeping*, ed. T. M. Charles-Edwards and Fergus Kelly. Early Irish Law Series vol. 1 (Dublin, 1983).
BBCS	*Bulletin of the Board of Celtic Studies: Bwletin y Bwrdd Gwybodau Celtaidd*
BDC	*Bretha Déin Chécht*, ed. D. A. Binchy. *Ériu* 20 (1966): 1–66.
Bleg	*Cyfreithiau Hywel Dda yn ôl Llyfr Blegywryd*, ed. Stephen J. Williams and J. Enoch Powell (Second edition, Cardiff, 1961). References are to page.line unless otherwise indicated.
Bleg	*Llyfr Blegywryd* (The Blegywryd Redaction)
Br. Crólige	*Bretha Crólige*, ed. D. A. Binchy. *Ériu* 12 (1934): 1–77.
Bürgschaft	*Die Bürgschaft im irischen Recht*, ed. R. Thurneysen. *Abhandlungen der preussischen Akademie der Wissenschaften* 2, Phil.-Hist. Klasse, Jahrgang 1928 (Berlin, 1928).
CA	*Cáin Adamnáin: An Old-Irish Treatise on the Law of Adamnán*, ed. Kuno Meyer. *Anecdota Oxoniensia*, Medieval and Modern Series 12 (Oxford, 1905).
C. Aicillne	*Cáin Aicillne*, ed. R. Thurneysen in "Aus dem irischen Recht I. [1. Das Unfrei-Lehen]." *ZCP* 14 (1923): 336–394.
Cáin Śoerraith	*Cáin Śoerraith*, ed. R. Thurneysen in "Aus dem irischen Recht II. [2. Das Frei-Lehen]." *ZCP* 15 (1925): 238–260.

CCF	*Cóic Conara Fugill: Die fünf Wege zum Urteil*, ed. R. Thurneysen. *Abhandlungen der preussischen Akademie der Wissenschaften* 7, Phil.-Hist. Klasse, Jahrgang 1925 (Berlin, 1926).
CD	*Cáin Domnaig*, ed. Vernam Hull. *Ériu* 20 (1966): 151–177.
CG	*Críth Gablach*, ed. D. A. Binchy. Mediaeval and Modern Irish Series vol. II (Dublin, 1941; reprinted, 1979). References are to lines unless otherwise noted.
CGH	*Corpus Genealogiarum Hiberniae*, ed. M. A. O'Brien. Vol. I (Dublin, 1962; reprinted, 1976).
CIH	*Corpus Iuris Hibernici*, ed. D. A. Binchy. 6 vols. (Dublin, 1978). References are to page.line unless otherwise noted.
C. Lánamna	*Cáin Lánamna*, ed. R. Thurneysen in *SEIL*, pp. 1–80.
CLP	*Celtic Law Papers Introductory to Welsh Medieval Law and Government: Studies Presented to the International Commission for the History of Representative and Parliamentary Institutions* 42, ed. Dafydd Jenkins (Brussels, 1973).
CMCS	*Cambridge Medieval Celtic Studies*
Col	*Llyfr Colan*, ed. Dafydd Jenkins (Cardiff, 1963). References are to numbered sentences unless otherwise noted.
CU	*Coibnes Uisci Thairidne*, ed. D. A. Binchy, *Ériu* 17 (1955), 52–85.
Cyfn	*Llyfr Cyfnerth* (The Cyfnerth Redaction)
DC	Dál Caladbuig tract, ed. J. G. O'Keeffe in "Dál Caladbuig and Reciprocal Services between the Kings of Cashel and Various Munster States," in *Irish Texts*, ed. J. Fraser and others. 5 vols. (London, 1931–1933), vol I, pp. 19–21.
DIAS	Dublin Institute for Advanced Studies
DIL	Royal Irish Academy, *(Contributions to A) Dictionary of the Irish Language*, (Dublin, 1913–1976; compact edition, 1983).
DwCol	*Damweiniau Colan: Llyfr y Damweiniau yn ôl Llawysgrif Peniarth 30*, ed. Dafydd Jenkins (Aberystwyth, 1973). References are to numbered sentences unless otherwise noted.

ECI	*Early Christian Ireland*, by Kathleen Hughes (Ithaca, 1972).
EHR	*English Historical Review*
EICL	*Early Irish Contract Law*, ed. Neil McLeod (Sydney, Australia, 1992).
EJ	"The Epistle to Jesus," ed. J. G. O'Keeffe in "*Cáin Domnaig*: I.—The Epistle concerning Sunday." *Ériu* 2 (1905): 189–214.
FF	*Frithfolaid* texts, ed. J. G. O'Keeffe in "Dál Caladbuig and Reciprocal Services" (see DC above).
GC	*Gúbretha Caratniad*, ed. R. Thurneysen in "Aus dem irischen Recht III. [4. Die falschen Urteilssprüche Caratnia's]." *ZCP* 15 (1925): 302–370.
GEIL	*A Guide to Early Irish Law*, by Fergus Kelly. Early Irish Law Series vol. 3 (Dublin, 1988).
GOI	*A Grammar of Old Irish*, by Rudolf Thurneysen. Translated from the German by D. A. Binchy and O. Bergin (Dublin, 1946; reprinted, 1975).
HMSO	Her/His Majesty's Stationery Office
IER	*Irish Ecclesiastical Record*
IHS	*Irish Historical Studies*
IK	*Die irische Kanonensammlung*, ed. H. Wasserschleben (Leipzig, 1885).
Ior	*Llyfr Iorwerth*, ed. Aled Rhys Wiliam (Cardiff, 1960). References are to paragraph/sentence unless otherwise noted.
Ior	*Llyfr Iorwerth* (The Iorwerth Redaction)
Irish Kings	*Irish Kings and High-Kings*, by Francis John Byrne (New York, 1973).
LAL	*Lawyers and Laymen: Studies in the History of Law Presented to Professor Dafydd Jenkins on His Seventy-fifth Birthday*, ed. T. M. Charles-Edwards, M. Owen, and D. B. Walters (Cardiff, 1986).
LTMW	*The Law of Hywel Dda: Law Texts from Medieval Wales Translated and Edited*, by Dafydd Jenkins (Llandysul, 1986).
LTWL	*The Latin Texts of the Welsh Laws*, ed. Hywel Emanuel (Cardiff, 1967). References are to page.line unless otherwise noted.
MGH	*Monumenta Germaniae Historica*

PKM	*Pedeir Keinc y Mabinogi*, ed. Ifor Williams (Cardiff, 1930; reprinted, 1978).
PPCP	*Pagan Past and Christian Present in Early Irish Literature*, by Kim McCone. Maynooth Monographs 3 (Maynooth, 1990).
PRIA	*Proceedings of the Royal Irish Academy*
RC	*Revue Celtique*
SD	*The Settlement of Disputes in Early Medieval Europe*, ed. Wendy Davies and Paul Fouracre (Cambridge, 1986).
SEIL	*Studies in Early Irish Law*, ed. R. Thurneysen, D. A. Binchy, and others (Dublin, 1936).
TRHS	*Transactions of the Royal Historical Society*
UR	*Uraicecht na Ríar: The Poetic Grades in Early Irish Law*, ed. Liam Breatnach. Early Irish Law Series, vol. 2 (Dublin, 1987).
WEMA	*Wales in the Early Middle Ages*, by Wendy Davies (Leicester, 1982).
WLW	*The Welsh Law of Women: Studies Presented to Professor Daniel A. Binchy on His Eightieth Birthday, 3 June 1980*, ed. Dafydd Jenkins and Morfydd Owen (Cardiff, 1980).
WML	*Welsh Medieval Law*, ed. A. W. Wade-Evans (Oxford, 1909; reprinted Darmstadt, 1979). References are to page.line unless otherwise noted.
ZCP	*Zeitschrift für celtische Philologie*

Introduction

The study of the early history of Ireland and Wales is still in its infancy. Few perhaps will mourn this cold hard truth; rare indeed is the historian whose sympathies are greatly stirred by what has been termed in another context the "unrewarding gyrations of vagrant tribes." And one can, to a certain extent, understand this lack of enthusiasm for what might appear an intensely obscure field of endeavor. Ireland, and to a lesser degree Wales, did stand outside many of the political and religious developments that shaped the future of Western Europe. It was, for example, only in the twelfth century, long after the opening shots in the struggle between the papacy and the empire had been fired on the continent, that the Irish church adopted a systematized network of territorial dioceses, and it is characteristic of the archaizing tendencies of the Irish learned class that the model for this ecclesiastical reorganization was the suggestion made by Gregory the Great to Augustine of Canterbury in 601.[1] Neither Ireland nor Wales shared extensively in the general medieval trend toward feudalization, urbanization, or monarchical consolidation, although these developments were common to the emerging European states around them.[2] In all fairness, the Celtic lands could not be counted on the cutting edge of European historical development, and their presence outside the normal scholarly curriculum might not seem thus to constitute much of a threat to the natural order of the academic world.[3]

To measure the significance of Irish and Welsh history according to such variables is, however, to indulge in the worst sort of Whiggery, for the Celts were not irrelevant, merely different, and their political sophistication was of another kind. Unlike most of Western Europe, Ireland was never subject to Roman occupation; tribal institutions and pagan rituals that disappeared or were modified in the rest of Europe survived and continued to develop in Ireland after the fall of Rome. Traditions associated with sacral kingship, for example, many of them possibly Indo-European in origin, were preserved by the Irish schools of sacred and secular learning long after they had been abandoned by the Germanic tribes and by

Rome itself.[4] Later these same sacral perceptions, resituated within a Christian context, found their way from Ireland into the writings of the sophisticated theoreticians of kingship of the Carolingian Renaissance; clearly, the Irish contribution could be of importance even in a world on the march to Christian empire.[5] Wales was more extensively acquainted with Roman traditions and institutions, though the extent of Roman influence varied greatly from region to region. Here too, Celtic customs and attitudes survived to influence other more "advanced" European countries; the outcome of King Alfred's educational and propagandistic campaigns, to cite but one example, might have been quite different had Asser not accepted the call from Saint David's.

Quite apart from such cross-cultural influences there are the Celtic sources, which are spectacularly rich and varied. Whereas few demonstrably pre-eleventh-century sources survive from Scandinavia, another important non-Romanized culture, Irish historians dispose of huge numbers of tales, law codes, genealogical tracts, annals, and saints' lives, many of which can be dated on linguistic grounds to the seventh through ninth centuries. The genealogical collection, most of which relates to the period between 450 and 750, contains some 13,000 names,[6] and Richard Sharpe's recent study of medieval Irish saints' lives has added at least nine hagiographical texts to the number of Latin lives known to date to the period before 900.[7] Irish annalistic sources become contemporary by at least the seventh century and continue without significant gaps for centuries after the arrival of the Normans in 1170;[8] and the laws, undoubtedly the most important of the Irish sources, fill six volumes in the modern edition.[9] Wales has preserved fewer indisputably early sources, though there, also, a significant genealogical and legal corpus has survived, and Wendy Davies's research in *The Book of Llandaff* has uncovered several important early Latin charters. As at least twenty of these charters date from before 600 and demonstrate the continuity of Roman landowning units and of a Latin charter tradition into the sixth century, they must be considered significant even in a general European context.[10]

Many of these sources were, furthermore, composed in the vernacular and were at least in part the product of a highly literate academic tradition unique in Western Europe. A distinctive learned class had existed among the Celts from a very early period, as Caesar's description of the druidic schools of the continental Celts makes clear,[11] and a strong tradition of oral learning remained in Ireland and Wales for centuries after the introduction of Christianity.[12] We still have much to learn about the manner in which the poets and jurists who were the representatives of the old oral legal tradition responded to the literate culture of the monastic schools, though it is clear that the contact between these two intellectual traditions produced something remarkable indeed. T. M. Charles-Edwards and Fergus Kelly have recently argued that in seventh-century Ireland secular lawyers were composing texts in writing that were intended to be read rather than heard and were learning their craft via literate means of instruction in non-monastic schools.[13] Their belief in the existence of such secular law-schools has certainly not gone unchallenged; indeed, the majority of recent studies have tended to emphasize the ecclesiastical, rather than the pre-Christian, element of the laws.[14] However, it is clear that at least some literate laymen were involved in the production of important legal texts, and the significance of this should not be overlooked.[15] Of all the other European lands, only Anglo-Saxon England preserves any significant amount of early vernacular material, and many medievalists would still argue that even there literacy did not extend far outside the ecclesiastical context.[16] If Charles-Edwards and Kelly are right, the intellectual tradition represented by the early Irish texts has no clear parallel elsewhere in medieval Europe.

All of this serves to underline what must surely be the central paradox of Celtic historiography: the Irish and Welsh sources together represent the largest body of pre-twelfth-century vernacular material extant from anywhere in Western Europe, and yet they remain essentially unknown to the vast majority of early medieval historians.[17] The reasons for this are complex and have much to do with the very different manner in which Celtic and European medievalists have traditionally approached their subjects. Celticists have for years written largely for one another, and Irish historians particularly have worked from a philological standpoint that their medievalist colleagues find mystifying and dull. It should be said that the various grammatical perversities of the Old Irish language have left them little choice. The fourteen noun declensions, the conjugated prepositions, the infixed and suffixed pronouns, the complicated system of initial mutations—all fall more or less within the range of normal human linguistic capacity. But it takes a dedicated philologist to look with equanimity on the Irish system of stress, which can reduce a verbal stem to the initial consonant of the root syllable, or even to zero, and which dictates two different verbal forms for every person of every compound verb. And because of the various phonological changes that affected the Irish language between the fourth and the seventh century (syncope, apocope, lenition, the reduction of certain consonant clusters), many words are not always easily identifiable as forms of the same verb. Few persons unacquainted with the rudiments of the Old Irish language would, for example, automatically associate *ad-cota*, "he obtains," with *-éta*, its prototonic form. It is therefore neither surprising nor inappropriate that Irish historical writing should have assumed such a philological bent; indeed, many of the most important sources remain unedited and untranslated even today. And while the Welsh texts do not present such linguistic difficulties, they too pose serious problems of dating and textual affiliation that can be sorted out only by specialists in the field. Many a general medievalist, faced with the relative inaccessibility of Celtic sources and scholarly work, has had to withdraw from the lists in quiet frustration.

But the problem is not simply a matter of the scholarly methods with which historians of Ireland and Wales have had to approach their sources, although these methods have served to emphasize rather than to diminish the gap between them and their colleagues. At the heart of the matter lies an assumption that has proved curiously appealing to Celticists and general medievalists alike—that Ireland and Wales were nations on the historical periphery of Europe, and as political and social entities were so fundamentally different from the European lands around them that historians specializing in one field would not necessarily find it helpful to read extensively in the other. It is true that Ireland and Wales were distinct in many ways from the rest of Europe. Scholars familiar with the continental records who approach the Irish and Welsh sources with questions drawn from their own historical literature will be surprised at what they do and do not find. Much of what they take for granted will seem simply not to exist; there will be many kings but few signs of royal administration,[18] many large settlements but no real towns.[19] Bishops there will be in numbers, with clear pastoral and administrative responsibilities, but with no clear monopoly of ecclesiastical authority and no settled hierarchical structure within which to work.[20] And some of what they see will appear archaic and unfamiliar, such as procedures for legal fasting,[21] for example, or sick-maintenance,[22] or *dadannudd*, an ancient method of claiming an inheritance.[23] The differences are striking—so striking indeed that the presumption that the Celtic and other European lands had little in common in the early medieval period has shaped scholarship on both subjects for many years.

But it is one thing to acknowledge difference and quite another to dwell on it. Ireland and Wales were in many ways dissimilar to their

European neighbors, but difference was not all there was. Scholarly perception of Celtic "otherness" may owe as much to differences in the nature and stylistic qualities of the sources as it does to the historical reality of the institutions those sources describe.[24] Certain types of evidence common in European medieval scholarship simply do not survive from Ireland and Wales, and this, combined with the rhetorical and archaizing style that often characterizes the Celtic texts, can make things seem more dissimilar than they actually were. In Richard Sharpe's excellent study of dispute settlement in medieval Ireland, for example, Irish institutions may appear primitive and vague when compared to continental and English procedures.[25] The institutions Sharpe describes are, however, recognizable and important within the general European context; their "otherness" is exaggerated by the fact that the Irish sources do not permit the sort of case-law approach to which the other essays in the collection are devoted.

Ireland and Wales did not, after all, exist in a historical vacuum. There were regular contacts between the Celtic and non-Celtic European lands even in this early period; their peoples traded with one another, consulted one another on important matters, and educated one another on theological and political issues. Many of the social and political challenges they faced were in essence the same. In all of these societies were the respective claims of kinship and lordship being slowly sorted out, centralized political authorities beginning to emerge, and the church and the world working to define their rights and prerogatives. The differences that seem so striking to historians might seem to argue otherwise, but they all belonged, in name and in deed, to the same Western European world. Celticists and medievalists have more to say to one another than either has so far realized, if only because the larger historical questions that they seek to answer are much the same.[26]

It is in the spirit of bringing these fields somewhat closer together that the present work, a study of a legal and social phenomenon at once peculiarly Celtic and irrefutably universal, is offered. Personal suretyship, an office through which one man guaranteed, by virtue of his personal strength or with his liberty or property, the eventual fulfillment of a legal obligation by another, is one of the most ubiquitous institutions known to students of comparative law. It has been found in almost all societies, ancient and contemporary, tribal and non-tribal.[27] It is not irrelevant even to our own legal situation; those who today post bail to guarantee that another will appear in court, or who co-sign a loan in order to ensure that a debt will be repaid, are acting in a manner their ancestors would surely understand. But the origins of this venerable institution lie not in contemporary concerns and mores, but rather in the uncertain relationship between the state and the local legal process that so often characterizes societies at an early stage of their political development.

In societies like our own, it can be argued that social order is virtually synonymous with written law. It is law that defines and regulates relations within our communities and law that determines how contentions that arise should be addressed. Our concept of order essentially presumes the existence of a state that can create and enforce the regulations by which its citizens live; order is for us an externally generated quality, one imposed on society from above by agencies charged with acting impersonally toward the individuals whose interests they collectively embody. For societies like those of early medieval Europe, on the other hand, in which such states were only just beginning to emerge, the question of order was much more difficult. There, no powerful impersonal entity existed to define and enforce the obligations to which men were subject. Individuals and communities had instead to look within themselves, to the social structures and relationships that gave them shape, to establish and maintain the limits of acceptable behavior. In a world in which the failure of even one individual to meet his obligations could put communal prosperity at risk, institutions like suretyship represented nothing less than the means by which chaos might be averted and order achieved.

That historians of both Celtic and non-Celtic-speaking cultures will be familiar with the circumstances that made suretyship and other institutions like it so important to the developing nations of Western Europe is obvious. Less evident, however, may be the fact that suretyship and indeed the whole question of legal enforcement in stateless societies can be approached in a particularly fruitful manner through the Irish and Welsh sources. In part this is a reflection of the extremely—indeed unusually—important role sureties played in the legal processes of those lands. Because of the relatively unhurried pace at which royal administration developed in Ireland and Wales, private officers of law long remained the norm in those areas and experienced little interference from their more public colleagues. Even as late as the ninth century in Brittany, for example, sureties still enjoyed an unusually powerful role in legal enforcement.[28] And so essential was suretyship in its heyday in Ireland and Wales that the language and images associated with it were frequently used to describe relationships that other societies conceptualized in an entirely different manner. Thus was the promissory oath said, for example, to be backed by the "suretyship" of God,[29] and the financial and supervisory liabilities of one kindred member for another termed the "suretyship" of the kindred.[30] Even Biblical stories were conceived of in such terms: the Old Irish "Gospel of Thomas" uses the image of the *ráth*-surety to evoke Christ's redemption of mankind,[31] and the legal text *Di Astud Chor* gives as an example of an inequitable, but nonetheless non-rescindable, contract that made by Adam, who knowingly sold the whole world for a single apple.[32] It is not always the case that an institution prominent in the law tracts turns out to be important in everyday life; in this instance, however, there seems little room for doubt.

If the prominence of suretyship as an institution in medieval Irish and Welsh society is one reason a legal phenomenon of such universal interest might best be pursued through these sources, it is not the only one. An essential, and not unrelated, consideration is the richness and variety of the available source material. Extant today are Irish and Welsh tracts on the subject, both of which preserve a significant amount of demonstrably early matter. And unlike the contemporary Germanic accounts of suretyship that tend, where they exist at all, to be terse and allusive and interspersed with other matters, the Celtic treatments are detailed and informative, as befits the work of professional legal scholars. To remark that they represent the fullest medieval treatment of the topic is no exaggeration. In terms of precision, length, and extended use of figurative detail, they stand completely apart from other contemporary treatments.

Moreover—and this is a crucial point—the nature of this material itself casts considerable light on what have traditionally been for English and continental historians some of the darker corners of early medieval life. Not only have the scholarly instincts of the jurists preserved for us what purport to be the exact formulas and rituals by which voluntary obligations were established and fulfilled, but the approach taken by these specialists toward their material makes it possible for us to trace the gradual movement of suretyship and other classic institutions of "private" law into the curial domain. Also important is the unusually descriptive and analytic character of Irish and Welsh law, for through this we can look beyond the range and functions of the individual sureties themselves to the sociological and ideological assumptions that sustained them in their work. After all, guarantors were exchanged not by strangers, but by individuals linked together in a community of shared belief. Communal perceptions of what was right and what was wrong, of who was honorable and who was not, even of what an individual's proper relationship to the spiritual world should be—these formed the backdrop against which such institutions of early law developed and flourished.

To study the mechanisms by which men were held to their obligations is to watch extremely sophisticated social processes at work, processes that operated at all levels of society, domestic and intertribal. This study thus attempts to look at the social and ideological context of suretyship as well as at the institution itself. If we can, through the Irish and Welsh texts, come eventually to understand something of the manner in which an essentially stateless society—any stateless society—with few enforcement mechanisms of its own, could define and protect the transactions on which its prosperity depended, we will have accomplished something of value.

And it is any such society that is at issue here. The issues raised by this study are as meaningful for the Germanic-language kingdoms as they are for early Ireland and Wales, for behind the specific matter of suretyship lurks the larger question of the nature of social order itself. It is true that one can trace in the Germanic sources the gradual growth of royal involvement in the enforcement of justice and see in the various innovations of late Carolingian and Anglo-Saxon states the beginnings of a system of centralized law and order. But the manner in which persons were held even in these societies to the expectations of the community in which they lived is still only vaguely understood. Recent research has made clear the extent to which even such incipient royal institutions drew on the sociological framework within which they operated.[33] Procedures like feud, for example, long thought to be part of the problem of social disorder, are now viewed as an important part of the solution instead.[34] Justice remained for centuries among the Germanic peoples what it was for inhabitants of the Celtic-speaking regions of Europe: an essentially local and personal process that had as much to do with communal perceptions and beliefs as with the implementation of written law. Those who would understand the origins of order in early medieval society would do well to look at the example provided by the Irish and Welsh texts.

I turn now to the terminology employed in this study and to the manner in which it has been organized. In the discussion that follows, I will make limited use of the terms "private" and "public" law. By "private law" I refer to legal actions and procedures taking place largely outside of the professional or curial context—in other words, outside of the control of authorities who claim, by virtue of their official position or professional training in the law, the right to interpret or enforce "public" standards in disputes arising within the community. "Public law" thus includes procedures or disputes conducted under the supervision of jurists employed by kings or princes on behalf of individual tribes or communities; it also includes disputes submitted voluntarily for arbitration by private individuals to professional jurists not employed by the community, since the law these jurists are interpreting is the "official" and "public" law of the legal schools. Quarrels submitted for resolution to those who are not professionally trained in the law, however, are treated as instances of "private" jurisdiction, since the decisions rendered in such situations will not necessarily be grounded in the "public" law of the schools.

I use these terms because they are current in the scholarly literature and because no better terms exist to describe the progression "from custom to court" that lies at the heart of this work. However, I use them reluctantly and am aware of the essential artificiality of the distinction I evoke. The opposition between "private" and "public" is a heuristic device employed to describe two ideal forms of human legal organization, neither of which existed in its pure state in any medieval society with which I am familiar. Indeed, then as now, it was very common for disputes that had their origins in the "private" sphere to make their way eventually into the "public" arena when other attempts at resolution had failed (or vice versa). In terming a given procedure "public" or "private," therefore, I wish merely to situate it with respect to these two polar ideals; I do not mean to suggest that any individual transaction ought to be, or even can be, considered purely public or purely private in nature or application.

A word now about the organization of this book. The foregoing has made clear the unusual extent to which the study of Irish and Welsh legal institutions cannot be separated from the study of the sources themselves. This fact has helped to determine the manner in which the work proceeds: I have, to a certain extent at least, "taken the jurists at their word" and allowed their priorities and concerns to guide me in my presentation. As they treat individually each type of surety in turn, so I have done as well; Chapters 2, 4, 6, and 8 all take as their starting point a particular type of guarantor and the arrangements he secured. Much of my discussion in these chapters is necessarily descriptive and reconstructive in nature: as will be evident from the texts quoted in this study, the Irish and Welsh sources do not yield their secrets easily. But just as the jurists sought to look beyond the functions of the legal personalities they described to the context within which they operated, so I have done as well. Chapters 1, 3, 4, 7, and 8 attempt to recover something of the social, political, and conceptual background of medieval justice, while Chapters 5, 6, and 8 chart the passage of "private law" procedures and personalities into the curial domain—a progression that is a major theme of this book.

Although I cannot claim to be following the jurists in my attempt throughout the work to elucidate the manner in which their own professional concerns shaped the material they bequeathed to us, the exercise is one of which they, as proper intellectuals, would surely have approved. All of this has produced a work with an undeniably kaleidoscopic quality to it, a study that may seem to address a variety of questions from constantly changing vantage points. This book has only one real aim, however, and that is to explore the potential of the sources on which it is based. The Irish and Welsh lawbooks are stubborn, irascible texts with a will of their own. They often will not go in the direction that one wishes they would, and there is no historical carrot to dangle enticingly before them. But if they are allowed to wander, to choose their own direction, they can return a tidy profit. I have tried in this work to follow where the texts would lead. My hope is that my readers will forgive the wandering if it distracts them and consider the sights along the way.

1. Law and Lawbooks in Medieval Ireland and Wales

It is ironic that a study of the quintessentially social process that was medieval justice should be rooted in the inhumanly static phrases of the lawbooks.[1] In a sense this is a hazard of the discipline: professional historians must daily reconcile the rigidity of the texts before them with the individuality of the past. Conjuring movement out of stillness is very much their job. But historians of legal institutions in particular may find it difficult to get beyond the letter of their sources to the spirit that inspired them. The modern definition of law as a body of regulations declared by the state and enforced impersonally by its agencies is a compelling one. But it is in the end a paradigm constructed entirely from our own experience, one which defines law by the institutions we use today to create and enforce it. There are many reasons for which laws can be written down that do not require a state to enforce them, and many forms of law that would not be recognized by candidates for the Bar. Medieval lawbooks particularly have their own agenda, their own reasons for existing, that transcend contemporary notions of ordinance and statute, and these are the terms on which we must seek to understand them.

Medieval historians generally are convinced of the importance of the legal texts to their work. What they do not yet agree on, however, is what exactly should be made of them and how they should be treated. Most controversial have been the law codes of the early Germanic West.[2] The traditional approach to these sources was that espoused by scholars of the influential German legal schools of the last century. Historians like Bluhme, de Salis, Zeumer, Boretius, and Brunner saw the early codes through the eyes of their own age, as a body of statutes deriving from the customary law of the folk and impersonally enforced by the relevant state authorities. Taking the legal sources essentially at their word, without probing too deeply into the whys and wherefores of their creation, the German *Rechtsschule* constructed huge compendia of early medieval social and institutional history that scholars still today consult.[3]

Modern historians have only somewhat improved on this state of affairs, for while they have more fully elucidated the ambiguities of these troublesome texts, they have come no closer to a consensus on how to use these sources in a manner that will resolve the doubts they have about them. J. M. Wallace-Hadrill voiced the doubts of many when he observed that the "immediate practical use" of the codes seemed to have been to record "just that fraction of custom that seemed enough to satisfy royal pride in legislation." "The fact of their existence as books," he wrote, "was what mattered most." And although he eventually concluded that the laws could be used "with caution, to illustrate social structures," Wallace-Hadrill remained uneasy about the ability of historians to distinguish the real from the fictional in what he called the "whole mass of barbarian custom."[4]

Wallace-Hadrill's pupil, Patrick Wormald, elaborated on his tutor's suspicions in a provocative article published in 1977. Wormald addressed what he called the "paradox" of early medieval written law. There exists, he remarked, "a considerable quantity of legislation, much of it implying its relevance to the preservation of law and order; yet the texts themselves have features which, taken together, do argue against their applicability, and there is remarkably little evidence for their application."[5] What Wormald termed the "warts on the face of barbarian legislation" suggested to him that the majority of early medieval lawbooks were never intended to be used, in our sense at least, in formal legal procedure. Codes were too selective in the topics they chose to cover, impractically organized for use in a curial setting, and written in Latin to boot. Much of what they said was demonstrably inaccurate—either wildly archaic, as with references to the payment of *wergild* in codes pertaining to twelfth-century England, or linguistically absurd, as with the Bavarian provision, *coitu ictu quolibet*.[6] Only the Southern European texts, those associated with what would become the *pays du droit écrit*, showed evidence of having actually been regularly consulted in a proper judicial setting.[7] The value of the others lay primarily in their existence as royally sponsored lawbooks designed to enhance the image and the functions of the king who had ordered them to be written. As a reflection of barbarian society and custom, they were at best "indirect"; as evidence, however, of the ambitions and priorities of kings and their publicists, they were unparalleled.[8]

Wormald based his argument primarily, though not exclusively, on the Germanic codes, and his views have not gone unchallenged.[9] But the general questions he raises must be put to the Irish and Welsh sources as well. His insistence on the ideological value of early legal sources must surely be right; King Alfred's laws, which begin with quotations from Old Testament legislation and end with the laws of his West Saxon predecessor Ine, are an obvious example. And although the Irish and Welsh lawbooks, unlike the Germanic codes, do not represent royal legislation, they also are not free from ideological considerations. The northern Welsh text of *Llyfr Iorwerth* intentionally reinforces the ascendency of the kingdom of Gwynedd in its remarks that only the king of Aberffraw can receive gold as the price of his *sarhaed*, "insult payment."[10] Nor could such concerns have been far from the mind of the tenth-century Welsh king Hywel Dda, to whose influence the first collection of Welsh law is generally attributed.[11] Indeed even in Ireland, where the lawbooks were the product of legal schools rather than royal chanceries, *Uraicecht Becc*'s confident assertion that the "king of Munster is chief over kings"[12] might suggest that the question of royal image was not entirely irrelevant even to this tract's composition.[13]

Wormald's concern about the applicability of early medieval law, however, is what strikes the most telling blow at the Irish and Welsh lawbooks. Celtic scholars have long entertained serious doubts about the realism of their sources, that is, about the purposes for which they were intended and the uses to which they were put. The Irish and Welsh lawbooks are laden with archaisms,[14] mired in rhetoric,[15] and fantastically selective. Many of their provisions are contradictory,[16] and some are so formalistic as to defy belief.[17] Furthermore, recent research has made clear the extent to which the ostensibly secular Irish law tracts draw on Biblical and canonical texts, a fact that must raise the question of their relationship to contemporary legal practice.[18] Clearly some caution has to be exercised.

To these objections must be joined other, more fundamental doubts about the workings of law in stateless societies. Anthropologists have for years debated the relevance of statute law to the actual legal process.[19] Ever since 1926, when Malinowski issued his challenge to the prevailing orthodoxy regarding the nature of law in tribal communities,[20] scholars have argued about whether order in such circumstances can be said to derive more from law and legal institutions or from the social context in which those institutions operate. Some have stressed the manner in which the law establishes a normative framework within which legal decisions can be made,[21] while others have focused instead on the social processes underlying disputes and their resolutions.[22]

This debate will undoubtedly continue for some time yet, but already the "truth" seems likely to lie somewhere in between these two positions.

Max Gluckman's studies of the Barotse, for example, revealed a people who perceived themselves to live by a code of law, and who had recourse in their judgments to what Gluckman called "traditional legal propositions," but whose actual judgments were grounded in perceptions of relative social status and mutual obligation. A man might have a legal "right" to a certain payment, but if he had earlier failed to live up to the obligations imposed on him by his own social standing, he could lose his case, even if his own defaults had nothing to do with the actual matter before the court. Thus, Gluckman argued, the essential property of tribal law was its flexibility—its ability to encompass such abstract concepts as respect and disrespect, responsibility and irresponsibility, duty and the neglect of duty.[23] Justice in stateless societies would appear, therefore, to be both a personal and a normative process, one that draws as much from the associations and perceptions regulated by communal norms as from those norms themselves.

It is evident that such arguments, if correct, must pose a serious challenge to the historian who has nothing but lawbooks with which to work. And it must be said that, at first glance, the early Celtic legal sources seem peculiarly susceptible to such anthropological reservations. Unlike the neighboring Germanic lands, where details of individual legal cases are frequently preserved in *placita*, chronicles, charters, capitularies, or, occasionally, in the codes themselves,[24] in Ireland and Wales there is little left to show how the law was actually applied. Ireland particularly is notorious for its lack of those types of subsidiary documents that might bring life to the ponderous aphorisms of the legal texts. There are few early charters and only one actual documentary record.[25] Also, only a few leading cases, like the story of the bees that blinded Congal Cáech and thereby put him out of the kingship of Tara, survive, and most of these are fragmentary and obscure.[26] The annals lack the exuberant love of gossip that makes Gregory of Tours so valuable, and although there is something of value to be found in the hagiographical material, we still know little about the actual workings of law in early Ireland.[27]

Welsh historians are in a slightly more advantageous position, if only because many of the *damweiniau*, "eventualities," and *cynghawsedd*, "pleading[s]," incorporated into the lawbooks seem actually to reflect twelfth- or thirteenth-century practice and thus give these scholars more of a toehold on reality.[28] The Llandaff charters are also important,[29] and the saints' lives also are full of interesting and revealing details. Unfortunately, however, few of these sources are particularly early, and it is difficult to determine with certainty to what period individual details might belong. Furthermore, as every historian of medieval Wales knows all too well, there are virtually no documentary legal records extant from the period before the late thirteenth century.[30]

When one considers all of these difficulties, it is not surprising that so few readers, casual or professional, have actually perused the Irish and Welsh lawbooks. But it would be wrong of us to dwell exclusively on what these texts are not and on what they cannot tell us. For despite their "warts," they must be counted as important, at least in part because medieval people themselves thought so highly of them.[31] Our task must be to judge them on their own terms rather than on ours, and this is challenging indeed. Irish law particularly may seem odd and unapproachable to those who come to it fresh from the perusal of a modern civil code. What survives today is a bewildering conglomeration of old and new, text and commentary, plain prose and obfuscatory verse.[32] The uneven texture of the laws may be partly attributable to their origin in the various legal schools of early Ireland. Scholars generally agree that the Irish laws reflect, at least in part, an oral tradition stretching from the druidic schools mentioned by Caesar to the poetic classes into whose custody law, like other branches of historical learning, fell at some time in the prehistorical period. And legal knowledge would appear to have remained the monopoly of these poet-jurists until the emergence of law as a specialized field within the poetic schools themselves.[33]

The advent of literate Christianity, however, clearly transformed both the laws themselves and the schools in which they were studied and preserved. How and to what extent it did so is quite uncertain. Many of the texts display differences of style or language that suggest the existence of schools of particular geographical regions or types; in some tracts the influence of the poetic schools is dominant,[34] while in others the Church has had the greater impact.[35] Scholars have traditionally taken such stylistic variations as indicative of greater or lesser proximity to native oral tradition. Particularly poetic or rhetorical tracts have been associated with schools in which poetry and law had yet to be differentiated from one another, while the verse passages cited so frequently in the tracts have been seen as direct quotations from the oral teaching of the native schools.[36] This may yet be true in a general way: legal instruction clearly was oral in pre-Christian times. But recent studies have considerably complicated the equation of oral and poetic with native and traditional. It is now clear that there were extensive contacts between "native" and Christian literati during the period the tracts were composed and that clerics of the eighth century were not only capable, but desirous, of composing legal verse in the archaic oral style for their own particular purposes. What these purposes were, and how our understanding of them should affect how we read and use these tracts, are questions which are only just beginning to be explored in the literature.[37]

Despite the unsettled state of current scholarship on the origins and nature of the extant Irish tracts, however, there can be no doubt but that some of the practices described in them were venerable indeed—perhaps even archaic at the time the jurists wrote about them. Most of the extant texts seem to have been composed in writing somewhere between 650 and 750,[38] but even within a tract that is itself datable to the eighth century, old passages frequently lurk side by side with later bits; such, for example, is the sick-maintenance passage of *Críth Gablach*.[39] What is perhaps strangest of all, however, is that eventually the foundation within which these legal "fossils" were embedded became fossilized itself. The very act of committing these texts to writing seems to have crystallized them, and the widescale composition of new tracts appears to have ceased around the middle of the eighth century.[40] The classical texts became set in stone, copied and recopied, and expounded on time and time again. Succeeding generations of jurists composed fantastically inaccurate glosses on tracts that had become largely irrelevant to their own society and that were written in a language that they themselves could only partially understand.[41] "It is as though," Binchy wrote, "the great Roman *iurisprudentes* of the classical period had confined themselves to transcribing and expounding the surviving text of the Twelve Tables without so much as a hint of the changes that had revolutionized Roman law in the interval."[42]

Welsh law appears at first glance more familiar and more comforting to those accustomed to the law codes of other societies. Attributed to Hywel Dda and, in the case of the northern codes at least, encouraged by the princes of Gwynedd,[43] the Welsh laws preserve the fiction of royal sponsorship, although they can in no way be considered officially promulgated statutes. And Welsh law was still very much "living" law in the twelfth and thirteenth centuries when the lawbooks were redacted; many of the *damweiniau*, "eventualities," and *cynghawsedd*, "pleading[s]," incorporated into them represent legal practices contemporary or nearly so with their composition.[44] "This [particular type of] plea (*cynghaws*)—there is no judgment in the lawbooks about it, and since there is not, it is necessary to give judgment about it here," remarks one thirteenth-century text.[45]

And although the most likely purpose of the Welsh lawbooks was to act as textbooks for apprentices in legal schools,[46] some manuscripts at least were consulted and quoted by judges in actual legal cases.[47] Welsh law thus appears to be considerably more straightforward and more realistic than its Irish counterpart.

And this it is, in some ways, but its accessibility is deceptive. The Welsh lawbooks suffer from what must be one of the most complicated textual traditions known to any field of study. There are three principal vernacular redactions of the lawbooks, *Llyfr Cyfnerth, Llyfr Iorwerth*, and *Llyfr Blegywryd*, and five extant Latin versions, of which one, Latin C, is incomplete.[48] Each of these redactions is represented by several manuscripts that can vary significantly in content, detail, and organization from one another. The manuscripts of *Llyfr Cyfnerth* are generally agreed to reflect a much looser textual family than do, for example, the manuscripts of *Llyfr Blegywryd*; this is because *Llyfr Cyfnerth* is likely the oldest of the principal redactions, dating probably to the last quarter of the twelfth century, and its manuscripts are therefore the furthest removed from their archetype. The prominence accorded in *Llyfr Cyfnerth* to the kingdom of Deheubarth in southern Wales suggests that this redaction had its origins in that region. *Llyfr Iorwerth*, by contrast, is associated with the northern kingdom of Gwynedd and was probably redacted in the reign of Llywelyn ap Iorwerth, who died in 1240.[49] The third vernacular version of the lawbooks, *Llyfr Blegywryd*, is closely tied to the Latin tradition. For the most part it represents a translation of Latin D, a redaction probably to be dated to the second half of the thirteenth century that derives, like *Llyfr Blegywryd* itself, from southwest Wales.[50] Of the other Latin lawbooks, Latin A (thirteenth century) is usually associated with South of Wales, and Latin B and Latin E (thirteenth and fourteenth century, respectively) with the North. Latin C, a Gwynedd production, does not contain the suretyship tractate and will not be considered here.

Moreover, as if this textual tradition were insufficiently complicated, each of the Welsh lawbooks comprises several tractates, short texts on specific topics that are, like the Irish legal tracts, primarily descriptive, rather than prescriptive, in nature. Many of these tractates may have circulated independently prior to their inclusion in a given lawbook; not all tractates in a book necessarily shared the same line of development.[51] What is most striking about these texts, and what indeed brings Welsh law quite close to that of its Celtic neighbor, is that much of the material contained in them is very, very old. None of the Welsh legal manuscripts is earlier than the thirteenth century, but some of the passages in them more closely reflect conditions and priorities of the early Middle Ages than of the period in which the lawbooks were compiled. As in Irish law, archaic customs are frequently placed side by side with twelfth-century practices and thirteenth-century corrections.[52] In both traditions it is, alas, very much a case of *caveat lector*.

Of all the qualities of Irish and Welsh law it is undoubtedly this melding of the present with the past that has proved the most unsettling to those whose training has been rooted in the source material of traditional medieval history. For those accustomed to looking forward in time, the frequent backward glances of the Irish and Welsh jurists can be a disorienting experience. Indeed, the intellectual vertigo induced by such sudden shifts in focus must be counted an important aspect of the distance that has for so long separated these fields. For the very adherence to archaism that is to non-Celtic historians the greatest liability of the Irish and Welsh lawbooks has until only very recently been viewed by Celticists as their most significant asset. Linguists discovered in the nineteenth century that they could reconstruct from existing linguistic fragments elements of the protolanguage from which the various modern Indo-European tongues derive. Since that time, students of comparative law and mythology, Celticists foremost among them, have made that methodology their own. From the historical and lexical fragments that remain, many of which are preserved only in the Irish and Welsh lawbooks, these scholars have attempted to reconstruct the customs and institutions of the Indo-European society presumed to have used this protolanguage.[53]

Some suggestive discoveries have been made. Convincingly parallel institutions have been found on opposite ends of the Indo-European world. Horse-sacrifices are associated with kingship rituals in India and Norway as well as in Ireland;[54] institutions like sick-maintenance and distraint are found in Germanic and Hindu as well as Irish law.[55] Fasting against recalcitrant debtors is a method of legal enforcement known both in Ireland and in India,[56] and the Hindu *Dharmasutras* contain a list of marriages very similar to the Welsh *Nau Kynywedi Teithiauc*.[57] Not everyone will agree that such legal phantoms should be pursued, and it is true that the sort of relative certainty with which historians are most comfortable is impossible to attain. But fasting is not an obvious legal remedy, and a common origin for the Indian and Irish practices is at least as likely as any other explanation. For us it is enough to note that the backward-looking nature of the Irish and Welsh lawbooks has inspired scholars at least to attempt a history that cannot be learned elsewhere.

Hunting for the Indo-European ancestors of legal institutions is, by its very nature, an elusive and highly controversial enterprise. One of the benefits of the search, however, has been to call attention to the existence of a Common Celtic legal heritage that cannot be denied. Still visible in the archaic subtext of the thirteenth-century Welsh lawbooks are concepts, institutions, and legal personalities that have clear parallels in early Irish law. That these similarities are more than coincidental is evident from the existence of a legal terminology that must be Common Celtic in origin.[58] Many cognate terms and concepts exist; the Irish *díles*, for example, "immune from claim," appears in Welsh as *dilys* and in Breton as *dilis*.[59] The *macc ingor*, "undutiful son" (literally the "unwarm son"), of Irish law has its exact parallel in the Welsh *mab anwar*, and the Irish *macc*, "enforcing surety," its counterpart in the Welsh *mach*.[60] Sometimes Welsh law preserves an ancient term that has almost disappeared in Irish, as with Welsh *deddf*, "enacted law," (Irish *deidme*), and Welsh *amod*, "contract," which survives in Irish in the phrase *ben imtha*, "a woman of contract."[61] Other linguistic and institutional similarities abound.[62] The existence of this common legal heritage has had tremendous implications for Celtic scholarship, since it has convinced historians that the Irish and Welsh legal texts can, and indeed should, be treated together whenever possible, despite the many centuries that separate the manuscripts that contain them. Often intricacies of one tradition have served to illuminate the obscurities of the other,[63] and Irish and Welsh historians both have benefited from the exchange.

The methodological problems raised by the attempt to recover Indo-European or even Common Celtic legal forms are evident. Differentiating old from new is a complicated proposition at the best of times. Historians interested in pursuing such phenomena must distinguish that which is archaic and outdated in their sources from that which is contemporary. That compilers intent on demonstrating the timelessness of their product occasionally change the older material they have before them to disguise its incompatibility with contemporary custom does not help at all.[64] Fortunately, there are some signposts that help to mark the route. The historical development of the Old Irish language is sufficiently well known at this point to allow scholars to date individual passages with some accuracy, although Liam Breatnach's arguments on the continuing composition of *rosc*-style texts must make us wary of presuming the archaic nature of such passages in the absence of other dating criteria.[65] But in a general way, while one might not be able to assign a text to its proper decade, one can hope to distinguish seventh- from eighth-century, and eighth- from ninth-century, material.

Welsh law is not susceptible to such linguistic analysis, and Welsh historians must take another route. Occasionally old material can be discerned stylistically, by its "ancient and fishlike smell," as Dafydd Jenkins calls it, although this method (like most fish stories) is necessarily speculative and uncertain.[66] Legal developments can sometimes be traced within the laws themselves; both Irish and Welsh law show evidence of an evolution in the contractual capabilities of women, for example.[67] But perhaps the best method to isolate the archaic from the contemporary in these lawbooks may be to compare Welsh with early Irish law. For, as one scholar has remarked, often "what appears as a fossil in a Welsh text can be recognised in its living form in an Irish one."[68] Such comparisons do not allow us to date archaic Welsh practices with any degree of certainty, but they give us a way to attempt to distinguish what is old from what is not. And through the *cynghawsedd* of the northern Welsh texts, which reflect to some degree the opinions and experiences of lawyers contemporary with the tracts themselves, we can see something of the manner in which the law evolves. Even sources as reluctant to acknowledge change as are the Irish and Welsh lawbooks betray themselves eventually.

The reconstruction of ancient institutions has proved a fruitful field of inquiry for Celticists and historians of comparative law alike, and there is much work of this nature that could yet be done. But for those whose interests lie more in medieval institutions and practices than in their Indo-European antecedents, the questions raised by the conservatism of the Irish and Welsh law tracts are obvious and troubling. It cannot simply be presumed that texts that seem to focus so unblinkingly on the past will speak to us as well about their present. The concerns voiced by Wormald and others about the likely relevance of written legal texts to contemporary social practice are, if anything, rendered even more urgent by the archaizing nature of the Irish and Welsh sources. We need to know more about how to read these tracts, about the purposes for which they were compiled and the circumstances in which they were composed, before we can say anything of value about the law as lived. Only then will we be able to use the lawbooks as reflections of things present as well as of things past.

It seems somehow appropriate that it is by posing yet another question that we can best begin to address such doubts. That this question is, in a sense, so obvious that it is rarely asked is confirmation not of its insignificance but rather of the truly fundamental nature of the issues that it raises: why do the Irish and Welsh lawbooks preserve as many archaisms as they do? Until only recently, scholars pressed for an explanation of this phenomenon would likely have pointed to the vast herds of antiquarian instincts presumed to roam at will among the Celtic learned classes. Not that such an explanation should be dismissed out of hand—Caesar's account of the druidical schools would suggest that the oral transmission of ancient material was a priority in all the Celtic lands, and the tales of the Irish Ulster cycle, with their emphasis on head-hunting, chariot warfare, and the champion's portion, certainly convey more of the ethos of the early Iron Age than of medieval Ireland.[69] But antiquarianism per se is an inadequate explanation for what is surely a more complicated intellectual stance.[70] There are, after all, many reasons archaisms might be preserved, including concerns both practical and textual in nature; by so reducing the matter one runs the risk of seriously underestimating the true complexity of the process.[71]

Furthermore—and this is a crucial point—to label a particular approach "antiquarian" is almost by definition to divorce it from its true intellectual context. But the jurists did not work in isolation from their learned colleagues in other fields. Rather, they were part and parcel of an intellectual elite, a "mandarin caste of churchmen, scholars, jurists, canon lawyers, historians and poets" who modeled themselves consciously on the Levite class and who knew and drew on each other's work.[72] Recent research is beginning to make clear the enormous debt owed by the Irish jurists to the exegetical concerns and techniques of their ecclesiastical colleagues.[73] The Welsh lawyers similarly were profoundly affected by the no less exegetical methods of the twelfth and thirteenth-century Italian legal schools.[74] It is likely, in other words, that the archaizing of the Irish and Welsh lawbooks owed as much to the contemporary emphasis on the preservation and elucidation of ancient texts as to the cultural antiquarianism to which it has usually been attributed. Moreover, just as exegesis itself can speak as much to contemporary as to historical concerns, so too did the archaizing of the Irish and Welsh jurists. It is an error to assume that the antique can have no real meaning in a contemporary context; indeed, in some cases its significance is political and direct.[75] To look behind is not always to look backward.

These are observations of considerable importance for the study of

Irish and Welsh law; we can begin to enlarge our understanding of the nature and intent of these laws by appreciating something of the intellectual milieu from which the texts emerged. Much more than methodology is at issue; at stake is the fundamental question of what the jurists saw themselves as doing. We classify the documents before us as legal tracts, and the questions we ask about them reflect our own conceptions of what law ought to do and be. But the variety of disciplines and approaches adopted by the jurists in explicating their material suggests that the scope of the endeavor in which they perceived themselves to be engaged was wider than we might imagine. For the scholars of Ireland and Wales, no hard impenetrable barrier separated the disciplines of history, literature, and law. The lawbooks were historical as well as legal texts, literary as well as political documents. This was history in the *senchas* tradition, a field in which chronological accuracy mattered rather less than did the situating of the visible present within the confines of a predictive past.[76] Neither the authority of the *Féni* nor the wisdom of Hywel Dda was restricted to the age in which they themselves had lived. The past was "proof" of the present, and the ability to cite with confidence the opinions and practices of venerable ancestors itself a marker of professional expertise. Small wonder then that the jurists expended such energy preserving and manipulating the material before them, old and new, in a manner designed to demonstrate the authority of a tradition of which they were themselves the guardians. Law was part of the tangled web of *senchas*, and the jurists its beneficiaries.

For if the jurists were academics, they were also gainfully employed. Unlike the Germanic law codes, some of which had their origins in the incipient royal chanceries of the barbarian kings, the Irish law tracts were composed in legal schools that existed to expound and to perpetuate the sacred mysteries of the law. And the students of these schools were the future advocates and judges of their day. Indeed, education was one of the means by which one advanced through the legal ranks from advocate to judge.[77] Moreover, the texts from which we presently work were the very books from which younger jurists learned their craft.[78] What remain to us today, in other words, are tracts composed both by and for practicing members of the legal profession; in fact Liam Breatnach has recently argued that the Nero A vii version of the Irish tract *Bretha Nemed* was compiled by three kinsmen, one of whom was a judge.[79]

Although we know little directly about the role these texts played in the judicial process, it is apparent that those who wrote them perceived them to be relevant to the "practical" as well as to the academic aspects of their profession. *Uraicecht Becc* is not the only text to indicate that "truth" could be established only through the *roscaid* and *fásaige*, the "maxims" and "precedents" of the lawbooks.[80] Now it is true that these texts more than most reflect the interests of the men who wrote them. It may be that the extent to which these highly trained individuals controlled the legal process in early Ireland was somewhat less than the tracts suggest, and it is possible, as I will suggest below, that the lawbooks themselves were part of the process by which native jurists consolidated their authority within the judicial sphere. There is no reason to doubt, however, the essential accuracy of the procedures they describe nor to question the jurists' knowledge of the legal structures of the society in which they lived.[81] Whatever the role played by non-specialists in the legal process, it is clear that law as learned and law as lived were intimately intertwined in early Ireland.

In Wales also, those who redacted the lawbooks were directly involved both with the teaching of law and with the administration and practice of justice in the localities.[82] There, as in late medieval Ireland, such matters tended to remain within the families of professional hereditary jurists; Iorwerth ap Madog and Cyfnerth ap Morgenau, with whose names the lawbooks of *Llyfr Iorwerth* and *Llyfr Cyfnerth* are generally associated (accurately probably only in the case of *Llyfr Iorwerth*), were both members of the family of Cilmin Droetu, one of the most prominent legal families in Wales. Many of the members of this family were, furthermore, judges (*ynaid*) as well as jurists, including Cyfnerth himself, Morgenau his father, and Madog Goch Ynad, his first cousin once removed. More remarkable still was the career of Cynyr ap Cadwgan, whom we know to have been a redactor of a version of the laws and to have acted as judge on at least one occasion. When Cynyr died he left his lawbook to his two sons, both of whom were judges in Powys.[83]

Professional judges of the *ynad* type seem to have been confined primarily to the North of Wales, but even the amateur *brawdwyr o fraint tir*, "judges by virtue of land tenure," who predominated in the South were expected to be knowledgeable in all aspects of Welsh law. Indeed, it was clearly in their own interest to know the law, since their verdicts could be appealed to legal specialists, and since they could be penalized for any false judgments they rendered.[84] And although we do not know the extent to which these judges, amateur and professional, actually relied on these lawbooks in their judicial activities, we do know that this is what they saw themselves as doing. Judges occasionally made specific reference to the lawbooks in their judgments, and judicial verdicts could be appealed if they seemed to contradict the law.[85] It looks very much as though judges were, in rendering their verdicts, acting as the lawbooks constantly pleaded with them to act—*herwyd kyfreith*, "according to the [written] law."

Herein lies the paradox of these texts, as well as the challenge that they pose to historians who would work with them. They were both contemporary and archaic, practical and outdated. The men who composed them were in regular contact with the vicissitudes of the legal process, but when they wrote about the law they portrayed it as eternal and unchanging. To us, accustomed as we are to the tenacity with which modern lawyers cling to the precise legal prose of their statute books, such inconsistencies seem troublesome in works of serious law. In the presence of such obvious "warts" we are reluctant to accord to such sources a historical authencity that is anything more than symbolic in nature. But to hold the Irish and Welsh lawbooks to such standards is fundamentally to misunderstand the nature of the enterprise, and this is precisely what we must appreciate if we are to overcome the professional doubts we have about them. For these were not statute books, and they were not intended to be strictly and uniformly applied to every case that came within their purview. Indeed, such a concept would be quite alien to early medieval society, as we will later see. Even the Welsh lawbooks, which were edging in the thirteenth century closer and closer to something we might recognize as a written "code" of law, remained at heart a collection of distinctly nonstatutory tractates.[86]

These texts rather were teaching texts, possessed of all the qualities and ambiguities normally associated with educational materials. Thus they sought to analyze as well as to describe,[87] to convey the principles that lay behind the legal process as well as the regulations that gave it structure. They spoke not just of norms, but of exceptions to norms, not just of institutions, but of the systems of perception and belief and status within which those institutions functioned.[88] It is no accident that so many of the Irish and Welsh tracts are centered on the very structures and associations on which anthropologists lay such emphasis. The jurists were well aware of the complexities of the process they were attempting to communicate. Even in their most schematic moments, they never lost sight of the social context that gave their work its meaning; only in such a manner could students learn to think for themselves about the profession they had chosen. This finally is the reason why the tracts have such value for present-day historians: modern as well as medieval students can benefit from the lessons that they teach.

But if these tracts were educational, they were also texts of law. The jurists were lawyers as well as literati, and their writings spoke to both aspects of their profession. We must not lose sight of this important fact, for it urges on us a question that will recur throughout this work. It is easy to assume, from the blemishes in our extant sources, or from our doubts about the level of literacy in early medieval society, that the gap between written law and social order must have been very great indeed; easy, too, to be suspicious when a medieval legal text enjoins its use. But the close connection that apparently existed in Ireland and Wales between law as learned and law as lived must give us pause: might not the relationship between written law and social order be much more subtle than we have hitherto imagined? Perhaps we are wrong to assume that the only way to "use" a written lawbook is to apply its provisions literally to every incident that arises. For the experience of the Irish and Welsh lawbooks would suggest that these texts were consulted not merely for specific rules that could be applied to the case at hand, but rather for a general understanding of how things ought to be. This is surely why, for the jurists as for Gluckman's Barotse, it was not important that the lawbooks be entirely shorn of their anachronisms. Deliberately "elastic" concepts like duty and the neglect of duty, status and the absence of status, could be continually reinterpreted in the light of contemporary standards and expectations. Rooting out the old, or resolving every inconsistency, was simply not a pressing need. There was life in the old law yet.

In this we mark the peculiar value of the Irish and Welsh legal sources, for what they offer us is unique in the historiography of the medieval West. No other body of early source material allows us to observe lawyers educated and alive to the nuances of their profession in the process of thinking and writing about what they did. These texts are not perfect, and the challenges they pose are real. What we are reading is not "law," but writing about the law, not "truth," but somebody's version of the truth. And the stance from which these jurists wrote was hardly a disinterested one. The very act of writing law was an exercise in authority, and not merely because the presence of an actual written text might induce litigants to accept more quickly the word of the man who held it.[89] Scholarship is itself an assertion of mastery and control, a claim that by prudent shaping, pruning, and grafting one can realize the "natural" contours of the plant. It is evident that even the most well-intentioned of interventive techniques will change the look of the product that results, and there is evidence to suggest that in this instance the jurists' involvement was anything but disinterested. They were concerned not merely to record or represent the law but also consciously to enhance their own stature as those charged with interpreting and preserving it. The legal tradition, both in its literary and its practical manifestations, had its own momentum, its own internal needs. Complex indeed are the sources of legal change, and there can be no better proof of this than the literate legal traditions of early Ireland and Wales.

But though these obstacles are real, they are not insuperable. Some scholars might go so far as to argue that image is all we can ever hope to see—that social constructs of the sort we see in the Irish and Welsh lawbooks are reflections merely of the systematizing instincts of the learned legal classes. The reminder that the human intellect is capable of creating a system where none before existed is a useful one, and one particularly relevant to these tracts, as we shall see. We must not forget, however, that the position of the jurists who wrote the tracts was dual: they were lawyers and judges as well as academics, teachers of law as well as scholars of jurisprudential doctrine. And while they certainly shaped their raw material, sculpted it into forms amenable to their purposes, they did not entirely invent it. Their passion as scholars for precision and detail, their interest as lawyers in the niceties of procedure, must indicate that the task of reconstructing at least certain aspects of medieval legal life is not entirely beyond us. Furthermore, the simultaneously practical and educational nature of these texts affords us the opportunity to recreate the environment that sustained and nurtured such institutions. Even the self-consciousness of the juridical classes can be turned to our advantage, for through it we trace the manner in which the internal priorities of a legal tradition themselves help to shape the course of legal development.[90] What we have in these sources is nothing less than the chance to bring the past alive. It is this potential—and these liabilities—we must remember as we begin our study of suretyship in early Ireland and Wales.

2. Contractual Suretyship in Irish Law

The Irish jurists were certainly not above the disingenuous use of the rhetorical, but in ranking the dissolution of contracts up with plague and war as a principal source of global instability they were saying no more than what they perceived to be the truth.[1] Just as natural disasters rendered weak and uncertain the communities through which they passed, so also, in the view of the jurists, did the dissolution of contracts make vulnerable the network of political and economic alliances on which Irish society was based. Arrangements made for sale or hire, agreements regulating joint-farming or clientship relationships—voluntary obligations of this sort were the key to individual prosperity and advancement. Moreover, the potential repercussions of such agreements extended far beyond the personal and financial interests of the parties to the original transaction. A man who promised to sell an ox to another and then did not fulfill his promise injured not only the person with whom he had made the agreement, but also the neighbor with whom that man had agreed to farm after obtaining the ox. And if this default in turn prevented the neighbor from meeting his financial obligations to his lord, the consequences could be serious indeed. In the small face-to-face communities of the early Middle Ages, to jeopardize the financial standing even of individuals was to undermine the very structures on which lordship itself was based. Small wonder then that the legendary king Conn Cétchathach was appalled to learn that the jurist Caratnia had allowed a contracted ploughing partnership to be dissolved.[2] If men could not be held to the agreements that they made, the social and economic cooperation that was the basis even of princely power might simply cease to exist. In such a direction, as the jurists rightly observed, did madness lie.

It must be stressed, however, that the Irish belief in the sanctity of contract was neither obvious nor inevitable. For while all societies recognize the need for some degree of economic collaboration, not all rely on contract to achieve this goal. There are many communities that operate solely by exchange or barter, many in which the notion of future obligation implied in contract does not obtain. Some, like the Zuni, do not focus on the specific transaction at all, but rather on the social network of which the exchange is a part.[3] Given the crucial role played by contract in contemporary financial affairs, such reticence on the part of older or less commercially-minded societies to accept the concept of the binding promise might seem difficult to understand. But contract itself, as a legal idea, embodies certain social and political assumptions with which not all are likely to agree. Peoples for whom sharing and gift-exchange is a primary method of distributing goods and services may find ideologically abhorrent the principles of formality and obligation entailed in contract. Gifts are, by definition, voluntarily given and received, even when their giving might reasonably be anticipated by custom or precedent. The unforced nature of the exchange is both symbol and guarantor of the permanence and reciprocality of the relationship between the parties involved. Contract, by its very nature, erects a barrier of necessity and obligation between donor and recipient that gift-giving cultures may perceive as counterproductive. Certainly the idea that contractual arrangements are a necessary, or even desirable, part of complex financial interaction is not a universal apprehension.

But the ideology of contract is only one of the possible obstacles to its reception as a legal practice. Serious practical problems will, of necessity, confront any state or judicial system attempting to extend official recognition and protection to agreements made in a private setting. Knowing precisely what has been agreed on by parties to a given transaction, and ensuring that the goods or services promised are eventually delivered are difficulties that, though likely to be most pressing in societies in which state mechanisms of legal enforcement and discernment are only just beginning to develop, would challenge any legal system. Furthermore, given the limited resources that individual communities can bring to bear on the panoply of legal problems that confront them, it may simply not be possible to support all agreements in the same manner and to the same degree. Some determination must be made as to exactly which arrangements merit, and which do not merit, communal intervention and protection. Not all promises are made with equal solemnity of intent; not all transactions are equally beneficial to the individuals and groups most directly affected by them. A society may not wish to accord to offhand or impetuous gestures of goodwill the rigor and respect afforded more formal undertakings, and it may not wish to intervene in exchanges that it views as unprofitable or unwise. Even those agreements not perceived as positively harmful might be of such limited consequence as to render official involvement superfluous and unnecessary. The very acceptance of the principle of contract is, in other words, an exercise in discretion; communities must select and define agreements they wish to protect and distinguish them from those to which public recognition will not be accorded. That the impact of such choices will be considerable for the individuals whose financial dealings are regulated by these decisions is evident. Less obvious, though no less important, is the manner in which the institutionalization of social and legal priorities previously unspoken or unacknowledged can act to shape the contours of society itself.

Nowhere is the severity of the difficulties associated with the making and breaking of private promises more evident than in the Roman law of contract, which one legal historian has called "the most original . . . and . . . admired" part of "the most innovative and most copied system in the West."[4] It would be difficult to overestimate the impact that Roman contractual conventions have had on the successor civilizations of the West: we ourselves are heir to many of their classifications and perceptions. But remarkably, even in Rome, in this most sophisticated of ancient legal systems, a true theory of contract never really developed. The verbal *stipulatio*, which could easily have been expanded into a flexible contractual instrument, instead remained for centuries an intensely limited undertaking that gave participants little opportunity for maneuver or review. Neither party could stray from the precise words in which the obligation had been couched. The individual who offered the *stipulatio* was obliged to fulfill only those obligations to which he had committed himself and nothing more; the person receiving it had no responsibilities in the matter at all because the formula as recited was unilateral. This extreme attachment to the literal form of the agreement prevailed, moreover, in all stages of the transaction. Even if coercion, fear, error, or bad faith were later proved to have played a role in the making of a contract, the arrangement could not be renegotiated. Consent, even if fraudulently obtained, was judged to be consent. Other contracts that did assume good faith on the part of the participants eventually arose in Roman law, but even these were defined by function (e.g., sale, deposit, hire) rather than by form. As such, they were clear exceptions to the general Roman rule that private agreements did not in themselves create obligations that merited recognition in law.[5]

This is precisely why the Irish evidence is so valuable. Ireland did not directly participate in the legal inheritance of Rome, so its methods for creating and securing voluntary obligations were unique. Not all of these methods were contractual in nature, as we will later see; certain types of exchanges specifically did not make use of the formalities associated with the "full-dress" Irish contract, and indeed the mere conveyance of goods seems in itself to have established a presumption of entitlement and obligation on the part of the parties to the transaction. But the jurists' emphasis on contract as the principal means of securing voluntary obligations, and the intricacy of the contractual system they describe, render the Irish experience of particular interest to historians of legal development.

Like the *stipulatio*, the Irish oral contract (*cor mbél*) was a highly formal arrangement initiated by the recitation of specific formulas outlining in detail the dues and obligations of the parties to the transaction. In this respect it was, like its Roman counterpart, distinguished by its form rather than by its function. But unlike the *stipulatio*, Irish contracts were reciprocal; both creditor and debtor had responsibilities to which they publicly committed themselves in the course of the ritual by which the contract was created. Furthermore, the strict adherence to form that characterized Roman contractual relations seems not to have obtained to the same degree in Irish law. Irish contracting parties were, for example, assured of rights outside of the promises that had actually been exchanged. Agreements made through coercion or in bad faith could be abrogated or renegotiated through the intervention of a judge; errors made unwittingly could be corrected. Contracts were essentially private matters, but they existed within a network of public safeguards. In this sense were Irish contracts more flexible and pragmatic even than their classical equivalents.

The special sanctity accorded contractual relations in Irish law is most evident in the elaborate procedures through which such relations were established and protected. We are fortunate in knowing a great deal about such matters from two remarkable legal tracts that address themselves specifically to these concerns.[6] *Di Astud Chor*, a tract that has been dated by its editor to the eighth century, is a composite text extant, or partially extant, in a relatively large number of manuscripts.[7] Curiously, perhaps, this tract is primarily concerned not with the creation or implementation of oral contracts but rather with what might be termed their judicial aftermath. The tract is divided into two parts: the first affirms the basically binding nature of all contractual agreements, and the second treats of the exceptional circumstances (e.g., fraud, error, or defective consideration) in which such agreements might have to be renegotiated or rescinded. Extended Biblical metaphors and images are employed throughout the text;

it may have been composed either in an ecclesiastical environment or by an individual with contacts in the ecclesiastical sphere.[8] Since many of the legal concepts embodied in these metaphors are, however, expressed in more prosaic terms elsewhere in Irish law, it seems likely that the composer of this tract was recasting practices of native origin into Christian terms rather than engaging in the "levitical modeling" characteristic of certain other ecclesiastically oriented texts.[9]

The second text of interest is the legal tract on suretyship known as *Berrad Airechta*, literally, "the Shearing of the Court," which contains a uniquely detailed account of the various stages through which a contract passed.[10] This tract did not form part of the great legal collection known as the *Senchas Már*, and it has been preserved only in the early sixteenth-century manuscript H 3. 18 of Trinity College, Dublin; it was known in the legal schools, however, and cited twice by name in the lawbooks.[11] It is unquestionably a composite text,[12] and the language of its latest stratum would suggest a date of about A.D. 700 for its compilation.[13] Some sections, however, have syntactical features that suggest a date of composition considerably prior to this time. Most notable is the heavily glossed *Córus Fíadnaise*, "Law of Witnessing,"[14] but the two portions of the tract that treat of the contracting parties (the *fechemain*) and the *aitire*-surety respectively, also have an archaic—or archaizing—core, centered as they are on the oral formulas through which sureties and their contracts were bound.[15] Even the latest sections of the text, which focus on the "immune transactions" of Irish law and on the *naidm*-surety, incorporate quotations from and references to the early legal material known as *Fénechas*.

Despite the composite nature of *Berrad Airechta*, there can be little doubt but that it was intended by its compiler to be read as a single piece. Occasionally he refers back to subjects considered earlier in the work,[16] and the etymological glosses that he added to passages originally independent of *Berrad Airechta* seem deliberately designed to ease the transition between them and the main body of the text.[17] There are, moreover, strong indications that the compiler deliberately reworked his sources in order to structure his tract on procedural lines.[18] Certainly, the organization of the tract as it remains to us today cannot be accidental, for it replicates in its structure the successive stages of a contractual relationship. The first surviving section of the tract acts, in essence, to "set the question" by distinguishing contractual from non-contractual transactions,[19] while the second treats of the *naidm*, the surety whose appointment bound the contract itself. The third section is devoted to the binding and repayment of the obligation by the contracting parties, and the fourth to the witnesses whose task it was to testify to the terms of the agreement should questions later arise. The fifth part describes the *aitire-* and *ráth-*sureties, whose duty it was to discharge debts in the case of default by the original debtor. And the tract closes with several rhetorical remarks enjoining the preservation of rightful contracts and the renegotiation of those that prove inequitable. Such a consciously procedural structure seems likely to have been deliberate, reflective in some degree of the compiler's interests and ambitions for his work. What these ambitions were, and how they might affect our understanding of the subject, are questions we will return to later in this study; first we must attempt to look beyond the constructs of the jurists to the nature and implications of the rituals they describe.

To do this is to be struck by the enormously sophisticated manner in which Irish contractual procedure confronted the difficulties inherent in the making and securing of private agreements. Certain of these difficulties will be obvious to us even from our own experience. Determining whether an obligation can be said to exist, and if so, what the nature and limits of that obligation might be is a challenge faced by all societies in which the principle of contract is accepted. Similarly, some method must be provided to ensure the proper behavior of creditor and debtor. Those who owe must be prevented from denying or evading their contracted obligations, while those entitled to payment must neither exaggerate their claims nor deny receiving what is owed them once it has been paid. In our own society, we rely for the resolution of such questions primarily on the use of writing. When we make a formal covenant, or promissory agreement, we put everything on paper; we thus know that a contract has been made and the proper procedure followed, that both parties have agreed to the arrangement, and that the terms of the arrangement are as they are recorded in the document. Once the agreement has been fulfilled, a receipt is issued that protects the debtor against a false claim by the creditor. And if objections are later raised by either party, it is to the written agreement and receipt that the courts will look in forcing the miscreant to meet his obligations. Documents serve for us, therefore, as the oracles to which we repair in moments of uncertainty.

In early Ireland, by contrast, the legal process remained almost entirely oral, despite efforts by Romanized churchmen to popularize the written contract from a very early period.[20] All of the problems that in our system are resolved by the existence of written documents had therefore to be addressed in some other fashion. Other difficulties, inherent in

Ireland's essentially acephalous political structure, existed as well. Most notable was the absence of police or other law enforcement agencies, for in such circumstances other mechanisms for the protection of the contract and the indemnifying of the creditor had of necessity to prevail. Moreover, given the serious manner in which lengthy or unresolved disputes could disrupt the network of alliances on which the prosperity of Irish society depended, it was essential that such mechanisms be free from suspicions of favoritism or coercion. Authority of all kinds was in question.

The Irish answer to these problems was procedural: the rituals through which contracts were made and implemented, and the legal personalities to whose care agreements were entrusted, served simultaneously as oracles and avengers. Every step in the contractual process was designed to anticipate and facilitate the eventual resolution of difficulties that could arise.[21] At the heart of the process lay an elaborate series of oral performances—intentionally theatrical presentations designed both to inform and to engage the response of the community within which they were enacted. For those unaccustomed to the methods by which individuals within oral cultures structure and regulate their affairs, the concept of performance may seem an odd issue to raise in a discussion of law and legal relationships. In fact, it is anything but. Even in our own society the dramatic ability of counsel can determine the outcome of a case; in the small, principally non-literate cultures of the early Middle Ages, performance was the primary means by which legal arrangements were created, proclaimed, implemented, and finalized. Some of the most theatrical of such spectacles incorporated elements of humor or the burlesque into their presentations, often to make a point about the subversive or inappropriate behavior of the individual being mocked.[22] But other, less histrionic dramas were enacted as well: the public perambulation of the boundaries of a contested estate, the grasping of a *festuca* to signify consent to a judicial decision, the throwing of earth on a person rendered liable for a kinsman's offense.[23] And of course no play on Broadway could easily outdo the judicial ordeal for showiness and sophisticated staging.[24]

Many of the theatrical elements of the rituals by which contracts were created and enforced in early Ireland will be readily apparent even to those unaccustomed to looking at legal procedures in such a way. Less obvious, however, is the sophisticated manner in which the fact of performance itself was keyed—that is, the method by which a dramatic framework was constructed that served simultaneously to advise the "audience" that a performance was imminent and to provide for them a context within which to interpret the messages conveyed by that performance.[25] Students of performance theory have isolated several types of communicative devices by which productions and their meanings can be keyed in different cultures. Particularly important is the use of specific styles or types of language in alerting onlookers to the significance of the performance taking place before them. We cannot be entirely certain that the formulas preserved in *Berrad Airechta* reflect the actual words spoken by the parties to a given contractual arrangement; indeed, it would be unwise to presume that every Irishman in the throes of such an agreement would have repeated these words verbatim. Direct quotation is certainly not impossible, however, especially in a legal culture like that of the Irish, which placed great emphasis on memorization. All in all, it seems most likely that these formulas reflect, in general character at least, language actually in use in the community—extended and systematized by the jurists as was their wont.[26] If this is true, it is important, for the language of these formulas suggests that linguistic "cueing" devices of this sort may have been in use in early Ireland as well. Parallelism, repetition, alliteration, and the use of fixed phrases or expressions are constant features of the *Berrad Airechta* formulas,[27] and all of these are devices deemed important by performance theorists.[28] It is even possible that these formulas—if not in fact archaic—were deliberately phrased in archaic style in order to evoke associations with the oral poetic style of the early juristic schools.[29] At the very least, this language must have served to establish the boundaries of the performance—much as does a curtain in a modern play.

At the center of this contractual drama lay its most prominent actor—the principal Irish surety, the *naidm*. This surety was much more than just a guarantor of the agreement. He was, in a very real sense, its public representative, a constant and vital reminder within the community that a pact had been made and that payment was expected. His special status is clear even from the procedure by which the terms of the contract itself were bound. The creditor there repeated the following words to the debtor:

> gaib fort laim fiach dam-sa huait dia laithiu airchiunn isind forus. . . . cona focal ocus a dilsi. . . . im seilbh-si nó a seilb nech doas mo gnimu. . . . Gaib it laim, nach airm na taire a llaa-sin, reithith a trian nairi dind fiach nascar ann. . . . fiach fir bíí eter da cobhach beoa, na airberna éc raithe na feicheman na fir nadanaisc nad for nascar.[30]
>
> Take on your hand that [this] debt [will be paid] to me by you on [such and such] a future day, in this place appointed for payment. . . . with it[s quality] having been tested and its immunity from claim [guaranteed]. . . . into my possession or into the possession of the person who "kindles" my affairs. . . .

Take into your hand that, should you not come on that day, as a consequence one-third of the debt that is here bound "runs" [i.e. becomes an additional debt].... [Let it be] the debt of a living man between two living contracting parties, [a debt] that the death of a *ráth*-surety or of a contracting party or of the man who binds [the obligations][31] or of [the man] on whom they are bound[32] does not diminish.

After the recitation of this formula, the *naidm*-sureties[33] to the agreement repeated a shortened version of it to the debtor, who answered simply *aicdiu*, "I appoint."[34] Thurneysen translated this response as *Ich stelle Garantien*, "I give guarantors," and surmised that the contract was bound through these words, and that the appointment of *naidm*-sureties to the contract would shortly have followed.[35] But *aicdiu* is from *ad-guid*, a verb that is used specifically in the legal texts for the appointment of *naidm*-sureties, and it should be translated here in its proper technical sense: "I appoint *naidm*-sureties." There is no need then to envisage a separate binding ritual for the *naidm*, for this was the moment at which both surety and contract were bound. Even in his name is the true significance of this guarantor revealed, for the literal meaning of the word *naidm* is "binding": the binding of the *naidm* was the binding of the contract, because the two were one. What Thurneysen called *der Vertrag in Person* was exactly that—the dramatic human embodiment of a contractual reality.[36]

Naidm-sureties were appointed not just by the debtor but by the creditor as well. Indeed, *lethnadmen*, "one-sided *naidm*-sureties," were specifically prohibited from enforcing their suretyship in Irish law.[37] The practice of joint appointment was crucial to the protection of the agreement. It eliminated in the first instance a potential cause of future friction between creditor and debtor, thus considerably minimizing the chances of the agreement ending in hostility and dispute. It also gave both parties a voice in the selection of the sureties, a step that dramatically increased the likelihood that actions taken by these guarantors in the course of the transaction would be accepted by all sides. Even if a party were to wish later to dispute the testimony or the actions of the *naidm* appointed to him, he could no longer do so on the grounds that the guarantor was inherently biased or unsuited to his position. The symbolic significance of this action should not be overlooked. Joint appointment established the surety's responsibility for the contract as a whole: in this simple action did the *naidm* move from player to director, a transformation designed both to anticipate and to close off avenues by which the production could be disrupted.

The dramatic form of the appointment ceremony also worked to ensure that the contract would go forward as agreed. We are nowhere told specifically how the creditor signaled his acceptance of the *naidm* appointed to him, but the evidence of Welsh law, where the creditor, the debtor, and the surety all joined hands at the undertaking of the contract, would suggest that the first words of the Irish formula, *gaib fort/it láim*, "take onto/into your hand," should be taken at face value. The grasping of hands to signal the appointment of a guarantor is a practice found in many other cultures,[38] and we still rely today on the handshake to convey our acceptance of the terms of an agreement. But whereas this gesture is for us primarily a symbol of good faith, for the early Irish it was a theatrical and potent guarantee that the transaction would be remembered by those who witnessed it. The physical joining of creditor, debtor, and surety created a strong visual image that was likely to impress itself on the mind.[39] But the mnemonic appeal of the Irish binding ceremony was not limited to the visual sense alone; four of the five human senses were actively involved in the confirmation of the pact. *Di Astud Chor* speaks directly of the four "gages" that establish the immunity of every contract in Irish law: the eye, the ear, the hand, and the tongue. The tongue recites the terms of the agreement while the ear listens to them; the hands touch to confirm those terms while the eye watches and records the event.[40] Every aspect of the appointment process, from the fact of its existence to the manner in which it was done, was designed to have the greatest possible impact on those who witnessed and participated in it.

Furthermore, the structure of the binding ritual itself guaranteed that there would be many who did witness it. Contracts were reciprocal in Irish law; the creditor also had his responsibilities in the matter, and these had also to be bound on him by the debtor to whom they were due in a similarly theatrical ceremony. The relevant formula is never quoted directly in *Berrad Airechta*, but we know its substance from the words that the creditor recited when he came to receive the payment of his debt: *Atrogath macu be coir airitin ocus dingbalae, [sláin]*[41] *ocus frettechtae tairis, acht rombe fiach*,[42] "I have appointed *mac*-sureties[43] that I will behave correctly with respect to receiving and removing [the payment] and [with respect to a declaration of] freedom from loss and renunciation [of any further claims on the debtor], provided that the debt has been paid to me." We must infer from the perfect tense *atrogath* that after the debtor had given his sureties to the creditor and the creditor had accepted them, the creditor would then have appointed *naidm*-sureties of his own to the debtor to guarantee that he would behave properly when collecting the debt.

Assuming that these guarantors also could not have been one-sided, the debtor must have had to approve them, presumably again by joining hands with them. In a simple one-sided debt, therefore, there must have been at least two *naidm*-sureties involved. And if both parties were debtors to each other, as must often have been the case in the sale of an animal, for example, there would have been at least four sureties in the affair; each contracting party would give one surety to guarantee the payment of his own obligation, and another to insure that he would properly receive the payment made by the other party.

In most cases, however, the matter would not even have ended there. The contract between the creditor and the debtor would have been perceived as binding after the performance of the ceremony described above. In normal circumstances, however, the creditor would want additional guarantees from the debtor, and it was at this point that the Irish paying surety, the *ráth*, would enter into the transaction. The *ráth* had also to be publicly bound to the responsibilities of his office, although not before the debtor had bound himself to compensate the *ráth* for any expenses that he might incur as a result of the debtor's delay or default. Both of these "bindings" were also done through *naidm*-sureties. The formulas recited by the debtor to guarantee that the *ráth* would be compensated for his losses, and by the *ráth* to confirm that he would fulfill the obligations of his office, are cited in *Berrad Airechta*, and like the formulas exchanged by the principals, employ many of the performative "keying" devices mentioned earlier.[44]

To remark, then, that the "full-dress" Irish contract was a deliberately public affair seems a serious understatement. One ought perhaps to speak rather in terms of community collaboration or audience participation: a reciprocal debt in which both parties gave both types of sureties to one another could involve as many as eight *naidm*ships, two *ráth*ships, and any number of witnesses. That many of these individuals would be known to each other and to their audience—perhaps even bound to one another by relationships of kinship or clientship—is highly probable. Such widespread participation in the contract assured creditor and debtor constant access to its terms and stipulations, and vested those around them with a degree of responsibility for its eventual fulfillment.

This high level of public performance was equally characteristic of the later stages of the transaction. The *naidm*, as befitted his special status as a living symbol of the contract, witnessed or participated in each subsequent phase of the transaction, and his testimony prevailed over that of ordinary witnesses if there were conflicting memories of the event.[45] If no challenges were issued, and nothing occurred after the binding of the contract to invalidate it before the date set for repayment of the debt, the payment would be brought by the debtor on the appointed day to the creditor or his agent.[46] At this exchange as well, the *naidm* would usually have been present,[47] acting both as witness for the specific action taken (e.g., for the delivery of the goods) and as supervisor and guardian of the contract as a whole.

But the *naidm*'s participation was but one aspect of the publicity attendant on the successive stages of the transaction. Each new development was marked by the public recitation of formulas that specified precisely what had just transpired and how the fact of its occurrence had changed the status of the contract. If, for example, the debtor paid and the creditor received payment in accordance with the guarantees that each had given, the contract was complete, although it could, in certain circumstances, be invalidated even after the exchange of goods.[48] The formulas exchanged on this occasion probably served to absolve the debtor publicly from further liability.[49] If only one of the contracting parties appeared at the appointed place and time, that individual would formally announce his fulfillment of the obligations to which he himself was committed and would declare his future intentions with respect to the contract.[50] And in cases where a *ráth* had paid the debt on behalf of a defaulting debtor, both the debtor and the *ráth* would ask the creditor to swear that the surety's payment had been made in a lawful manner and had extinguished the obligation.[51] Each successive act in the contractual drama, from the creation of the obligation to its ultimate fulfillment, was marked by the maximum degree of publicity and formality.

So far we have explored how the personalities and rituals of Irish contractual procedure acted to anticipate, and thereby attempt to avoid, the many problems that could arise in the course of an ordinary agreement between two individuals. But even the best of precautions cannot always be successful, and the prospect that a debtor might refuse to meet his contracted obligations loomed always on the horizon. Once a debtor had defaulted, public pressure might in itself have been sufficient to return him to the paths of lawful behavior; in a small community, shame and the possible loss of economic and social collaboration are highly potent guarantees.

But the Irish did not rely entirely on such relatively intangible methods for the enforcement of their contracts. Instead, the two contractual sureties, the *naidm* and the *ráth*, worked together in a manner that in most cases guaranteed that the contract would be fulfilled even if the debtor attempted to default. The two had very different duties. If a debtor failed to meet his obligations, fines amounting to one-third of the value of the debt would be immediately added to the original sum due from him.[52] If the *naidm* had witnessed the debtor's default,[53] the surety was required to try to force him to pay the debt. The *naidm* was permitted to use force against a recalcitrant debtor and was considered exempt from all fines and sick-maintenance that would ordinarily have been due from a man who had wounded another.[54] He was also allowed to deprive the debtor of his liberty for an unspecified period of time,[55] or to distrain against him, which was probably the most common method of enforcement at the time of the compilation of *Berrad Airechta*.[56] Only certain well-defined legal exemptions,[57] or intervention by a dignitary of the tribe on behalf of the debtor,[58] could protect the defaulter from the *naidm*'s zeal. And if the *naidm* proved unable to force the debtor to meet his obligations, the *ráth* would have been summoned to act. Even if this happened, however, the *naidm* would not have been freed from his duties of enforcement until the debt had been paid.[59]

If the debtor simply could not be found, or was totally insolvent (a contingency for which none of the enforcement procedures mentioned above allow), the *ráth* would have been required to make payment for the defaulting debtor. Once he had done this, the creditor's claim was considered to have been extinguished,[60] although the *ráth* then had a clear claim for restitution and damages against the debtor. As the debtor had earlier managed to resist the enforcing efforts of the *naidm*, however, the difficulties in collecting the amount the *ráth* was entitled to could be considerable. Irish law met this challenge by subjecting the recalcitrant debtor to increasing physical and psychological pressure. The first step was to try once again to get the debtor to meet the creditor's claim:

> Mad ic urslucuth indisi ria ndiriuch tíí feichem, asren fadesin (ocus) a colainn feich ocus a smachta riasiu asria rath tara cenn; ocus asren boin do raith inna imloth ocus in naurslucud a indisi; Ar at se laa deac imme-roloith[61] rath; miach cach laithe do di[diu] tar heisi ind imloid,[62] bo do samlaith; is ed is [s]lan nurslicthi indise in so. Os [s]lan nurslictho iar ndiriuch. caide son? ma 'scomrae rath tar cend, co ndecomrastar a indes airi, logh a enech iarna míad. is ed [a] slan, ocus gert ocus indoth ocus fuillim ocus colainn feich.[63]
>
> If it happens that the debtor comes at [the time of] the opening of the milking enclosure [but] before the stripping, he himself pays the principal of the

debt and its fines before the *ráth* pays on his behalf, and he pays a cow to the *ráth* for his disturbance and for the opening of his milking enclosure. For there are sixteen days during which a *ráth* is "disturbed": he receives then a sack every day after that for the disturbance—he thus receives a cow. This is the compensation for the opening of a milking enclosure. And the compensation for the opening [of the *ráth*'s milking enclosure] after stripping—what is that? When a *ráth* has paid on [the debtor's] behalf, so that his milking enclosure has been stripped to his disadvantage, his compensation is his honor-price according to his rank together with cattle by-products and the young [of his cattle] and interest and the principal of the debt.

The affair thus proceeded in stages of payment and compensation, and with each passing phase, the stakes got higher and the pressure more intense. In the first stage, the debtor was made aware that the *ráth*'s milking enclosure had been opened in some unspecified manner,[64] but the surety did not yet have to pay the claim. The debtor then had sixteen days in which to pay the debt and its fines, and even if he paid within this time, he owed a additional cow to the *ráth* as compensation for the trouble to which the surety had been put.[65] During this sixteen days, enforcement efforts continued as the *ráth* worked in conjunction with the *naidm* and the creditor to try to force the debtor to meet his obligations.[66] Since all three of these individuals were likely to be known, and some perhaps even related, to the debtor, the pressures on the debtor must have been social as well as physical, psychological as well as material.

If the debtor had not paid by the end of this period, the *ráth* would himself be obliged to pay the debt on the debtor's behalf, and the second stage would begin. Immediately the debtor's debt rose considerably, for although he no longer owed anything to the creditor, he now owed a substantial sum to the *ráth* in compensation, including the surety's honor-price, the by-products (milk and dung) and the calves of any animals with which the *ráth* had had to part, restitution of the debt, and an unspecified amount of interest.[67] The problem, as always, was to get the debtor to pay what he owed the *ráth*, for although there was a *naidm* specifically charged to enforce the *ráth*'s claim against the debtor, there was no guarantee that this *naidm* would prove any more successful than had the last. This problem was addressed by sharply increasing the financial pressures on the debtor, as a highly rhetorical *Bretha Nemed* text suggests:

Slanadh soráthusa sluinnter iar néiric in ndaghlaithibh dlighidh; Dleghar fiach, fodhbaither cosmhailsi máir, [is] (n)etaim cuigedh colla feich fedhair fri mís.[68] máraighidh saoghlonna. soilbhech beitheach la lógh niomsaotha im airchenn eallamh, no séd i muin araile ar lá go noidhche, go tresi do sédaibh la logh n-enech neallamh fir bes a séd serbthar.⁶⁹

The indemnifying of a good *ráth*ship—let it be declared [as having been completed] after [the] payment [of compensation] in the good days of law. A debt is owing, let the equivalent of the large amount (i.e. the principal of the debt) be obtained; a fifth of the principal of the debt is the *etaim*—let it be calculated at a month. A sage exalts. A cow in good milk with the price for disturbance [is given] for a speedy resolution, or [one] *sét*⁷⁰ in addition to another [is given] for [every] day and night until three days [worth] of *séoit* [have been given], along with the ready honor-price of the man whose property is led astray.⁷¹

This passage is difficult to interpret—its author was clearly more interested in displaying his poetic skills than in conveying what he knew about the compensation of the *ráth*—but some aspects of it are decipherable. The cow given for a "speedy resolution" of the debt we recognize from *Berrad Airechta* as this is the amount that an unforfeited *ráth* would receive from his principal in compensation.⁷² Presumably, the resolution of the crisis is perceived as "speedy" in the sense that the debt has been paid before the surety has had to pay it himself. Compensation after payment by the *ráth* entails restitution (the "large amount"), the surety's honor-price, an unidentified payment called the *etaim*, and the three days worth of *séoit*. The three days of *séoit* are not paralleled in *Berrad Airechta*, but this must have been a period of sharply mounting interest designed to encourage the debtor to pay what he owed as soon as possible. The days in question were presumably the first three days after the *ráth* made payment, and it should be noted that the incentive for the debtor to pay during these three days was considerable, since the liability incurred here represents a cow every twenty-four hours, which was a substantial sum.

Intense financial pressure was thus put on the defaulting debtor immediately after the surety made payment on his behalf. This was not, however, the only financial pressure to which the debtor was subject. If he did not pay within those three days, the debt continued to increase over the long term at the rate stipulated here for the *etaim*. The exact meaning of the word *etaim* has yet to be determined. It seems, in some contexts, to refer to a type of gage, but it is glossed at least once in the legal tracts with *smacht*, "fine."⁷³ What little is known about it suggests only that an *etaim* was something that could fall due to a person in certain ill-defined but often punitive circumstances. We would probably, therefore, have remained completely in the dark about its meaning in the passage cited above had not one of the Irish canons commented on the question of the *ráth*'s compensation in similar terms:

> De modo, quo debet reddere debitor solutum ratae. In definitione ejusdem Sinodi (Hib.): Debitor reddat, quantum rata solvit et quantum fatigatus fuerit; si autem humanus fuerit, rata non quaeret usuram, nisi tantum quod solvit rata, et quantum fatigatus fuerit; sin vero inhumanus fuerit, uno anno crescit usura, et omne debitum reddat, et quintam partem debiti in omni mense unius anni.[74]

> Of the manner in which a debtor ought to repay the payment of a *ráth*. According to the definition of the aforesaid (Irish) synod: let the debtor pay as much as the *ráth* has paid, and as much as he may have been disturbed. If he has been merciful, however, a *ráth* should not seek interest, but only as much as the *ráth* has paid and [compensation] for the extent to which he has been disturbed.[75] If, however, he has been merciless, the interest grows for one year, and let him (the debtor) pay the entire debt and a fifth part of the debt for every month of one year.

The *etaim* of the *Bretha Nemed* passage must then refer to the interest paid by a defaulting debtor to his forfeited surety, which increased month by month at the rate of a fifth of the debt per month until the end of a year. Thus was a recalcitrant debtor subject to both short- and long-term financial pressures. Immediately after the *ráth* was called on to pay the debt began a period of three days during which the debtor's fines increased very rapidly. After this three-day period had ended, a debtor who had still not paid the *ráth*'s compensation could expect to see his debt increase monthly until the interest on the debt was more than twice the amount of the principal.[76]

The safeguards that protected Irish contracts were thus considerable. Their greatest security lay in the sureties appointed to guarantee them. Every step of the contract, from the formal public ceremony in which the debt was assumed to the payment of the *ráth*'s compensation, was witnessed and guaranteed by sureties. The *naidm* was himself the "binding" that united the contracting parties; he pledged his honor that the contract he symbolized would not be broken.[77] To fulfill this charge, he supervised the contract from its inception to its conclusion and, when the occasion warranted, acted as policeman for the affair. The *ráth* provided additional security for both the contract and the creditor. His participation in the matter guaranteed that the creditor would be paid even if the debtor proved resistant to the *naidm*'s efforts. And while it would not always have been easy for the *ráth* to obtain the compensation to which he was entitled, this part of the contract also was hedged about with safeguards. The defaulting debtor was subject to a constant series of deadlines; each deadline he ignored rendered him liable to further increases in his financial obligations. Since a debtor's property could always be distrained against by the relevant *naidm*, it is unlikely that a debtor would have ignored his increasing debts for any substantial length of time. Thus did the prerogatives of one guarantor support the efforts of the other.

The force that could be brought to bear against a defaulting Irish debtor by the individuals and penalties ranged against him was therefore quite remarkable. To fully appreciate the complexity of the Irish system of contractual suretyship, however, we must not overlook the subtle procedural guarantees to which such arrangements were also subject. Private agreements are troublesome precisely because they are private; the confidential nature of the circumstances in which they are made and implemented is itself a frequent source of hostility and misunderstanding. Irish contractual procedure deliberately undermined that privacy by turning every agreement into a public spectacle. The performative aspects of the rituals by which contracts were created ensured that they remained a part of the collective memory of the audience for which they had been enacted. Thus did the physical presence of the actors within the community act as a uniquely tangible reminder that a contract existed and had not yet been fulfilled. And the large number of individuals joining in the agreement made its deadlines and stipulations impossible to forget.

Procedural pressures worked as well to guide agreements toward fulfillment. The formal stages of waiting and of payment through which all transactions passed gave every obligation a psychological structure of its own. Normal contracts progressed at an even and unhurried rate, while defaulting debtors saw deadline follow deadline with mounting intensity and speed. Presumably, the effects of this pacing were not merely individual. The passing of each deadline must have heightened communal anxiety about the outcome of the affair, while the formal declarations that marked each new development urged on all the growing need for resolution. But if pacing created this increasing sense of pressure, it also structured it; disputes proceeded in a manner that was predictable and controlled. Remedies were provided, but on their lawful day and time: thus were tempers cooled and hostilities guided into channels that could contain them. In the intimate atmosphere of an early medieval community, even the subtle pressures of time and place could act as guardians of the peace.

The personalities and procedures we have been looking at will seem a far cry from those with which we are ourselves familiar. And this they are: suretyship is in many ways the quintessential institution of "private" law. This is not, of course, to suggest that what is public can be entirely distinguished from what is private. In societies in which state institutions are only beginning to develop, even the most "public" of verdicts may be reached only after extensive "private" negotiation.[78] And, as is evident from the discussion above, rituals of private law often invite or presume community collaboration. Indeed, in that the *naidm* wagered his reputation against the prospect of default, the effectiveness even of this private legal officer was vested in community perceptions of his status. But though the boundary between public and private is in no sense hard and fast, the essentially non-public nature of the formal Irish contract is indisputable. The procedure was, in all its most fundamental aspects, virtually self-contained. There was no need for an outside legal authority to supervise its progress or intervene in its enforcement, and there was no appeal to public coffers if the debtor did default. The system functioned on its own, within a framework that it had itself constructed. In this sense, then, were contracts in essence matters of private, rather than of public, policy.

At least by the time of the compilation of the Irish legal tracts on suretyship and contract, however, and perhaps even earlier,[79] the situation had become more complicated. Procedures and institutions that were, in their nature and origins, essentially private matters had become embedded in a larger network of public judicial safeguards. The principles governing this network are spelled out in detail in the lawbooks: agreements judged to have violated acceptable standards of equity and fairness were to be renegotiated or rescinded. Contracting parties were perceived to have, in the words of the Irish tracts themselves, a natural "entitlement" (*dliged* or *cert*) to a fair and equitable bargain.[80] Those who believed themselves to be naturally "entitled" to more than they had received could seek a remedy for contractual defects from a judge, and in this case, as *Berrad Airechta* tells us, "there is a time when entitlement is more to be respected than a *naidm*, [and] another time when the *naidm* is more to be respected, [and] another time when both are to be respected equally."[81]

The question as to which was the more to be respected in any specific instance depended entirely on the manner and circumstances in which the contract had been made. Three considerations in particular were fundamental—whether the agreement had been warranted by sureties, whether the parties to the contract had known at the time of the unfair nature of the exchange, and (a stipulation presumably not limited to contractual transactions) whether the goods and services promised were ever actually delivered. Contracts made with sureties took clear precedence in the law, and in general such agreements would not be rescinded. *Di Astud Chor*, our main source on the process of renegotiation, tells us directly that "second thoughts [about the wisdom of making the contract] do not prevail after [the] involvement of the honor of *mac*-sureties and a *ráth*."[82]

This rule did not hold in every situation; if a person had been forced into the agreement by fear, coercion, or fraud, the contract was completely rescindable.[83] But as a general principle, the fact that sureties had been involved ensured that the contract would be renogotiated in the presence of a judge rather than canceled altogether. Plaintiffs could claim the "pouring away of the over-full [or the] filling up of the over-empty," so that the exchange would be an even one.[84] Only if the defrauded party was mentally and legally competent, and had known of the defect at the time he made the contract, would the inequity hold completely, for in such cases "a *mac*-surety . . . pierces [natural] entitlement."[85] Adam, Lucifer, and Judas are cited in *Di Astud Chor* as examples of this principle—individuals whose "contracts," though clearly disadvantageous, were held to be legally binding because they realized at the time the nature of the bargain they were making.[86] Contracts in which the considerations promised never changed hands were also rescindable: *Ar is naidm fás cach naidm cen folud*,[87] "every surety without consideration[s] is an empty surety."

Equity could thus require that any specific contract be renegotiated or rescinded. It is important to realize, however, that this is an indication of the strength, and not the weakness, of the law of contract as a whole. The insistence on fair play and equal exchange in contractual transaction merely underscores the special role such arrangements played in the ordering of Irish society. Preserving equitable agreements that had been undertaken in good faith and according to the proper form was the clear priority of the norms by which these arrangements were governed. But what then of agreements that had not been undertaken in this manner—arrangements made without the sureties and rituals that were the hallmark of the Irish formal contract? Were they also to be perceived as binding? This question may appear a simple one, but the issues that it raises go to the very heart of the nature of contractual obligation itself. Neil McLeod has recently argued, primarily on the basis of the testimony of *Di Astud Chor* and related commentaries, that while guarantors and contractual rituals were *important* to the contract in that they provided a means by which it might be enforced, they were not in any sense *necessary* to the establishment of an individual's right to specific goods. Contracts made without sureties would not be rendered void by their absence, though they might well be rendered unenforceable. The sureties and rituals through which such arrangements were bound were not, in other words, the true basis of contractual obligation: that lay, presumably, in the actual exchange of promises and goods by the parties in question.[88]

The question is a complicated one, and it is truly fundamental. Perhaps the greatest challenge to any society in which the notion of contract is accepted lies in determining whether an obligation can be said to exist from the legal point of view. That this is a problem even in contemporary jurisprudence is evident from the doubts and controversies that beset the modern law of contract. The boundary between binding and non-binding promises is a tricky one to draw. Indeed, the concept of "binding" itself is ambiguous; questions about the validity and permanence of an agreement can arise at several points in the transaction, and in each case the degree to which the contract is to be considered "binding" may be defined in different terms. For the Irish jurists, two stages in the proceedings seemed particularly vulnerable to claim or challenge: the point at which a promise had been made but not yet fulfilled, and the point at which a promise had been made and the goods and services promised had been delivered. In the first instance, the issue was the existence or non-existence of the contract itself—whether, in other words, a contractual entitlement (*dliged*) to goods or services had been established, and if so, what the terms and limitations of that contractual entitlement were. In the second instance, the fact that an agreement had been made was not in question; the issue was rather the wisdom and legitimacy of the agreement or the quality and value of the considerations that had been exchanged as a result of it. Here the jurists spoke of the "immunity" of the exchange to claim (*dílse*), a term that referred, in essence, to the extent to which either the terms or existence of the agreement could be renegotiated or rescinded if challenged.

That there might be many different degrees of immunity will be evident. Objects exchanged might be deemed completely irretrievable, in which case an agreement would be considered "completely immune" to claim (*ruidles, dílsem*). Or items and agreements might be regarded as immune to rescission (*díles*) but subject to renegotiation if defects in them later became apparent. Moreover, not all agreements would likely have been regarded as equal in the extent of their renegotiability: exchanges could be deemed "partially immune" in the sense that even after renegotiation the surplus would not be evenly distributed. Entitlement and immunity are, in a sense, two sides of a single coin; indeed, as we have seen, entitlement (though not contractual entitlement[89]) was the basis on which inequitable exchanges were renegotiated. But though not entirely separate, they are at least separable, and our tracts speak to both. We must confront them on their own terms if we are ever to make our way through the intricacies of Irish contractual theory.

The first question to be considered, then, is the issue of contractual entitlement. On what basis, and in what circumstances, would one individual's promise to another give rise to an entitlement that would be recognized in law? Here the evidence of *Berrad Airechta*, as of most of the other tracts that raise the question, would suggest that the appointment of guarantors in a formal binding ritual was crucial to the establishment of an acknowledged obligation.[90] This equation of suretyship and contractual entitlement is perhaps clearest in *Berrad Airechta*, though it is found as well in *Cóic Conara Fugill*.[91] Suretyship was, for the compiler of *Berrad Airechta*, the means by which Irish contractual relationships were created, defined, and framed. Indeed the point is made literally in the organization of the tract itself: this is surely the rationale that lies behind its consciously procedural structure. The *naidm* was more than an enforcer of the arrangement; he was, in every sense, the literal bond that linked the contracting parties to one another and to their obligations. So closely indeed was he identified with the contract he was appointed to secure that the renegotiation of an unsatisfactory agreement is depicted in that text as a judicial confrontation between the *naidm*, acting as the guardian of the contract, and *dliged*, "fairness" or "natural entitlement."[92] Of the extant tracts that speak to the subject, only *Di Astud Chor* implies that promises made in the absence of guarantors would necessarily have had legal consequences for their participants. For the others, the source of contractual obligation and entitlement seems to have lain in the formal enunciation and binding of terms in the presence of sureties.

But what then ought we to make of the testimony of *Di Astud Chor*? According to this tract, even promises made in the absence of sureties could not be entirely rescinded unless defects of which the buyer had been unaware were later found in the goods that he had received. This would imply that an obligation could be contracted merely by one person promising another that goods would be delivered or services performed, even if that promise was never formally bound and witnessed by guarantors. Now it must be said that the language of much of this text is highly allusive and rhetorical, and its provisions on such matters far from clear.[93] If its editor is correct, however, in understanding the word *comnaidm* to refer to any mutual promise, whether formally undertaken or not, then *Di Astud Chor*'s testimony is interesting indeed. For the idea that even unwarranted agreements might be afforded public recognition and protection must challenge our notions of the foundations on which the jurists perceived contractual obligation to rest.

To understand the testimony of *Di Astud Chor* we must determine what served for the compiler to validate a *comnaidm* exchange. It is noticeable that the text mentions *comnaidm* transactions only in the context of exchanges that have been perceived as inequitable and have been challenged on this basis. Since such a challenge must, of necessity, happen *after* the goods are exchanged and found to be wanting, it might be objected that the recipient's entitlement was understood to derive not from any promise that had been made but rather from the fact that goods had actually changed hands.[94] *Di Astud Chor* says only that it is *fri enec cor comnadma*[95] that the exchange cannot be rescinded altogether. McLeod emends the manuscript reading *cor* to *cur* here, and translates "on account of honor in a contract involving the mutual exchange of promises." If he is correct in so doing, the "honor" of which the text speaks must be that of the parties who gave their word that their agreement would be fulfilled; in other words, it must be to the promise itself, and not to the exchange, that the passage refers.[96] The reference later in the tract to transactions whose security proceeds *do nadmannaib rath*,[97] "on the basis of the bindings of sureties," may even be intended to set up a contrast between such transactions and *comnaidm* exchanges based on "honor." Thus, if McLeod is correct, there would seem for the compiler of *Di Astud Chor* to have been *two* ways in which an obligation could be established: by the binding of a contract through sureties and by a mutual promise in which sureties were not involved.

Even for the compiler of *Di Astud Chor*, however, the entitlement established through an unwarranted agreement was a distinctly lesser degree of entitlement. This is most clearly visible in the provisions contained in that text and others on the renegotiation of unsatisfactory transactions. All of the jurists agreed that the mere exchange of goods was not in itself enough to establish that the items handed over would remain entirely immune to claim or challenge; the presence or absence of sureties at the making of the agreement made a tremendous difference to how a transaction, once challenged, would proceed. Sureties, in effect, rendered exchanges "immune from claim"; only in the extreme cases of fraud, coercion, or the failure of considerations could agreements bound through sureties be rescinded. This is not to say that agreements bound through sureties would prevail as originally bound in every instance. As we have seen, "justice" (*dliged*) could require inequitable contracts, even those effected through sureties, to be renegotiated. But even in such cases, the participation of guarantors would lend added security to the arrangement. If parties to a transaction in which sureties had been involved later discovered defects in the considerations they had received—defects of which they had previously been unaware—the agreement would be renegotiated so as to allow them to recoup at least some of their losses. If no sureties had been involved in the arrangement, the exchange could be canceled altogether.[98] Formally bound and completed agreements were, in other words, perceived as "more immune" and "more binding" than were exchanges that had not been warranted by guarantors.[99] Suretyship was, then, together with the exchange of *folad* itself, a principal basis of contractual immunity; for most of the jurists, it was the source of contractual entitlement as well.

It is the similarities between our tracts rather than the discrepancies that should, however, most impress us. And indeed it would be difficult to overestimate how unusual all this evidence really is. That we should know what we know about Irish contract law for any culture would be surprising and important; that we should know it for an early medieval people is nothing short of remarkable. Contractual theory is not a field frequently traipsed on by historians of the early medieval West. But the fact that our two principal sources on Irish contract seem to disagree on such a crucial point as the origins of contractual entitlement must give us pause; if nothing else, it brings us sharply up against a fact we might otherwise overlook. Neither *Berrad Airechta* nor *Di Astud Chor* is a transparent historical source; both are works of literature as well as works of law. The lawyers who composed them must be counted as authors by any standards—in their use of imagery, in their careful selection and presentation of material, in their setting of the scene and structuring of the "plot."

This is not to say that all we read is fictional. We have no cause to believe, for example, that *Berrad Airechta*'s compiler actually invented the binding formulas around which his tract is structured; there are, as we have seen, considerable linguistic reasons to conclude that he did not. And *Di Astud Chor* contains a poem on the adjustment of a contractual surplus that ought probably to be dated on the basis of its style of composition to the early seventh century and that cannot, therefore, have been composed by the author of the tract itself.[100] But if these are not short stories, full of wondrous fabrications, no more then are they objective records devoid of purpose and perspective. These tracts existed as texts, not just as textual frames for material otherwise independent of their compilers, and we must not lose sight of this fact. What we see as truth is no more than a presentation of the truth, one which has been guided, both consciously and not, by the perceptions and perspective of the presenter.

This is a point of some importance to the question we have been discussing, the nature of contractual obligation in Irish law. For while we cannot hope to distinguish clearly at this distance the exact methods and motives of the compilers of these tracts, we can at least avoid being taken unawares by the assumptions on which their work is predicated. The question as we have posed it is very much a lawyer's question. Outside the professional legal context, the categories implicit in the terms of our discussion—entitled or not entitled, binding or not binding, immune or not immune—have very little meaning. In a system of purely private law, promises made will either be fulfilled or they will not. Those that are not fulfilled and that cannot be enforced will cease to have any effective existence. And while communities may devise complex means to ensure that agreements made will proceed as planned—guarantors, public rituals, and so on—promises made in the absence of such formalities are unlikely to be voided on this basis alone if they are in fact fulfilled. Neither the category "binding but unenforceable" nor "enforced but not binding" has any real significance in such a world. This is not to say, of course, that difficulties cannot arise. Bargains made by incompetent individuals, or exchanges perceived by the family of a buyer to be inequitable, might occasion renegotiation or feud. But even if this happens, community perceptions of what is "just" in such a case are likely to be based on a wide variety of factors, not all of which are "legal." The social and economic alliances of the participants may be as important in this respect as are the actual circumstances in which the obligation was undertaken. Social as well as legal priorities will establish the terms on which the dispute will be resolved.

Once a degree of public legal jurisdiction has been established, however, matters can change dramatically. Definitions and categories previously only loosely imagined or defined can take on an existence of their own, at least in part because the process of adjudication itself is so often built around them. With the development of a professional legal class, moreover—individuals whose function it is to preserve and explicate the distinctions on the basis of which legal verdicts are reached—such categories are likely to be even further refined and developed. Often indeed they begin to be seen as fundamentally exclusive of one another. Agreements made without guarantors may come to be viewed as no longer merely insecure, but as actually non-binding, because in a world of exclusive categories, that which is inherently "non-binding" cannot also be "binding." And even in less relentlessly rigorous systems, in which categories are not perceived as entirely exclusive of one another, degrees of exclusiveness can be quantified and defined—usually by the creation of yet further categories. Plaintiffs seeking the adjustment of contractual surpluses, for example, might receive different amounts of money back depending on the combination of categories into which they fall: surety or non-surety, defect known in advance to seller or not, defect known in advance to buyer or not, and so on.[101] Thus would the degree to which their agreements were "binding" or "non-binding" be defined and quantified by the process of public adjudication itself.

My point is not to suggest that the perceptions and priorities put forward in *Berrad Airechta* and *Di Astud Chor* are invented or unreal. I am confident that they derive from the compilers' observations of and experiences with Irish contractual procedure. That the tracts agree on so many basic issues is evidence of their being well-grounded in the realities of Irish legal procedure. But I would argue that the very process of translating what were, at least in origin, procedures of private law into the vernacular of the professional legal class gave rise to distinctions and categories that had previously existed in an entirely other form. It is obvious that the question of which agreements would, and which would not, be recognized in law was a matter of great moment to the jurists who had to adjudicate disputes arising from such issues. *Berrad Airechta* and *Di Astud Chor* both are concerned with this problem, although they tackle it in slightly different ways. It is highly significant that the fundamental criteria established, or at least recorded, in both these tracts for contractual validity are essentially the same: procedures and personalities that had originally developed to ensure the enforcement of contracts in a private legal setting functioned in the public sphere as the main determinant of public recognition and validity. The appointment of sureties in what was originally a private binding ritual was for both compilers, in other words, the principal method by which promises to which full public recognition was extended were distinguished from those to which it was not. What had originally been merely "secure" had become that which was inherently "binding."

But as interesting as the similarities between these two tracts are the subtle differences that separate them. The appointment of sureties was undoubtedly, in the private legal setting in which the binding ritual originated, the means by which agreements made could be rendered most secure. Nevertheless, it is unlikely that all agreements made were made in this manner. Promises must frequently have been given and fulfilled without the pomp and ceremony attendant on the formal Irish contract, either because the amount involved was so small, or because the parties to the contract were so closely related as to make such formalities unnecessary between them,[102] or for other reasons. We know from *Di Astud Chor*'s reference to such unwarranted promises (assuming McLeod to be correct in his interpretation of *comnaidm*) that these types of agreements were still being made at the time our tracts were compiled. And it seems likely that such arrangements were a frequent source of dispute; this is in fact very much the context in which they are mentioned. But whereas the compiler of *Di Astud Chor* would appear to have acknowledged that such agreements would exist and have a claim to be adjudicated, the author of *Berrad Airechta* did not mention them at all. *Di Astud Chor* certainly qualified the support it extended to unwarranted promises, and in its complicated system of percentages of restitution awarded to plaintiffs, exalted formally bound contracts above those made without sureties. It did not, however, exclude the latter altogether. To judge from *Berrad Airechta*, on the other hand, unwarranted promises, apart from the few exceptional transactions that it names,[103] would simply not have been acknowledged in the eyes of the law. The elaborate showcasing of suretyship and procedure to which this tract was dedicated acted, in essence, to imply the existence of a legal situation that *Di Astud Chor* would suggest did not obtain.

We cannot hope from our vantage point entirely to sort out these differing points of view. Nor can we reasonably expect to reconstruct precisely the reasons and motives that lay behind them. It is possible that the apparent discrepancies between these two tracts reflect variations in regional legal practice, but as we have no indication that these tracts originated in different regions of the country, and no means of identifying the provinces from which they might have come, such ideas remain a matter of speculation. That we have extant two tracts on contract may suggest that the manner in which private agreements were to be adjudicated in a public setting was actually in the process of being worked out at the time the texts were compiled.[104] Indeed, the process of incorporating an essentially private legal ritual into a public system of adjudication is implied even in the title of *Berrad Airechta* itself. O'Brien suggested long ago that

Berrad Airechta should be translated as the "Abridgement of the Court" and that the tract was intended to serve as a sort of procedural abstract or handbook by which judges might be instructed in the proprieties of contractual behavior.[105] *Di Astud Chor*, on the other hand, was very clearly aimed at helping lawyers acting in a more or less public capacity to achieve a durable settlement in matters already gone awry. In this sense, the two tracts would appear to be considering the issue from very different perspectives and to be addressing discernably different sets of juridical anxieties. Whereas the compiler of *Berrad Airechta* chose to stress, in the selection and presentation of his material, the prevention of the legal and social entanglements that could arise from breaches of contractual convention, the compiler of *Di Astud Chor* looked principally toward a cure. It is possible that such differences in perspective could account for the manner in which each compiler approached the problems that lay before him.

Perspective is not, however, a necessarily neutral force. Literature, even that which is educational in nature, can be written to persuade as well as to inform, and it seems most likely that what we are watching here are the disputations and debates that lie behind the process by which law itself is created. *Berrad Airechta*'s emphasis on contractual procedure, for example, may well betray a personal conviction that attempting to adjudicate agreements made in the absence of public rituals and guarantors was an inherently futile undertaking. By presenting the binding ritual as a legal fait accompli, its compiler may have hoped both to advertise its availability and, in implying a unanimity of practice that did not in fact obtain, to make more likely its use.[106] Similarly might the compiler of *Di Astud Chor* have been arguing a personal stand in his willingness to adjudicate unwarranted arrangements, although the manner in which he treated them showed that his interest also lay in minimizing their impact and popularity. His intricate calculations of the various degrees of restitution owed to victims of inequitable contractual arrangements may also have been a construct of his own devising. Certainly, the fact that other percentages are found elsewhere would suggest that the question was at best unsettled. Priorities personal and professional in nature can lie behind even the most objective-seeming of historical sources. What appears to read as an authoritative account of legal practice might be only one jurist's view of what legal practice ought to be. If we are not alone in perceiving it as we do that is very much the point; thus can perspective and experience, confidently asserted, begin the process of turning custom into law.

Speculations of this nature are always risky and uncertain, and at a certain point in time one must decline to follow further the circles within circles that such reasoning represents. But this much can be said with confidence: at the heart of Irish contractual procedure stand two very different legal personalities—the sureties through whom formal contracts were created and enforced and the lawyers who wrote about them. To place our principal sources side by side is to be reminded forcefully of the extent to which a legal tradition itself can act to shape and to limit our knowledge of legal practice. But even in acknowledging this fact, it is important to recognize how extraordinary the opportunities afforded us by this legal tradition actually are. Through the work of the Irish jurists we can trace the outlines of a system of contractual suretyship of remarkable complexity, a system that rivaled, in its flexibility and effectiveness, even that of Rome itself. The many levels of security afforded Irish contracts are an excellent indication of the sophistication with which a private legal system can function to initiate and secure even the most complicated of transactions. And equally valuable—certainly more rare—is the glimpse we obtain through the Irish sources of the passage of such private legal rituals into a more public sphere of jurisdiction. Whether considered from the public or the private point of view, both the tracts themselves, and the procedures they outline, are important and distinctive. If the jurists were right to maintain that the binding of every person in their contracts could deflect the "madnesses of the world," the early Irish would seem to have had relatively little to fear.

3. The Social Context of Personal Suretyship

The extraordinarily detailed picture of suretyship and contract presented in the Irish tracts has no parallel in any other medieval legal source. And yet it is, in its own way, quite misleading. One would be forgiven for concluding from these accounts that contracts were, by their very nature, entities unto themselves—discrete transactions separately bound and enforced, involving people unrelated to one another in any long-term way. But this view of contractual agreements as creatures apart, acts in some sense isolated from the environment in which they were created and fulfilled, is an illusion fostered by the legal tradition itself. The jurists' focus on procedure, their need as educators to communicate to their students the intricate rituals by which contracts were bound and implemented in early Ireland, should not be allowed to obscure the larger context within which individual transactions themselves progressed. Arrangements made by persons in small communities are by definition part of a larger network of social obligation and responsibility. To understand the "law of contract" one must know something of the "rules" of social order to which that law was subject.

That autonomous contractual arrangements between independent principals existed in early Ireland is not in question. Any of the various contracts mentioned in Irish law in which sureties were involved—deposits, gifts, gages, sick-maintenance fees, sales, to name but a few—could have been undertaken by unrelated persons acting strictly on their own behalf.[1] And such agreements may well have become quite frequent in the late seventh and early eighth centuries, when joint farming between kinsmen became less common than it once had been.[2] But although such transactions may have been more frequent in early Ireland than they were among Gluckman's Barotse,[3] for example, they were almost certainly still the exception rather than the norm. Most Irish legal arrangements would have been made by people who were already united in some type of social or legal relationship. Many would have involved kinsmen; in *Cáin Aicillne* it is stated that

> Coru cach comsa, cach focrec, cach crec, cach rec, cach cunnrud, cach cor, cach ceilsine, cach giallnu, cach fognum fri fine teachta iar comfocus coibfine. . . .[4]
>
> Every agricultural partnership, every rent, every sale, every purchase, every exchange, every contract, every [agreement of] clientship, every [agreement of] unfree clientship, every service is more properly done with a kinsman [who is] lawful according to the nearness of the relationship. . . .

Neighbors involved in joint-ploughing or other legally recognized neighborhood partnerships, fosterers and their fosterchildren, and men and their lords were also likely to conduct business with one another on a regular basis. And although such relationships themselves might have little to do with the terms of a specific contract, the perquisites and obligations associated with them could have a tremendous effect on the way a given transaction might proceed. Even when parties to an exchange had no direct relationship to one another, the social or familial hierarchy of which they were each independently a part could determine the future and shape of the arrangement. Just as men moved within the constraints imposed on them by their associations and alliances, so too did the agreements that they made. Contracts were part of an interlocking network of social obligation, and this is the context in which they should be studied.

Under normal circumstances, such details would be difficult, if not downright impossible, to resurrect from the tantalizingly allusive passages of early medieval law. And for Irish law the tracts that focus specifically on contract are less helpful than one might wish. Fortunately, however, these are not the only available sources. The lawbooks preserve a number of detailed treatises devoted entirely to the social relationships and associations that bound men and women to one another. *Cáin Aicillne* and *Cáin Sóerraith*, which deal with clientship, *Cáin Lánamna*, which outlines the "Law of Couples," and *Córus Béscnai*, the "Regulation of Good Behavior," which treats of the relationship between the church and the laity, all date to the classical period of Old Irish law.[5] None of these tracts is concerned exclusively with contract, but questions of contractual capacity figure with varying degrees of prominence in all of them. To overestimate the importance of these texts to our study would be difficult, since they allow us, even at such a distance, to recreate something of the social and political context of contractual obligation.

What these texts make clear is that all persons, regardless of status, gender, age, or economic standing, moved within a complex matrix of interlocking affiliations and alliances. The nature of these associations varied greatly, and individuals were likely to find themselves in more than one relationship—and in more than one *type* of relationship—at any one given time. Some relationships were inherently subordinating in that they exalted or depressed the status of at least one of the participants. One of the most common types of subordinating association during the period in which the law tracts were composed would have been that of unfree clientship, but there were others—the relationship between husband and wife, for example, or that between father and son. Some associations were maintained by persons of essentially (or at least potentially) equal status—kinsmen,[6] for example. Many were intended to be temporary, as was the connection between teacher and pupil, whereas others were expected to endure over a long period of time, as were clientship and marriage. Some, like the bonds between kinsmen, were not the outcome of specific agreements, but were involuntary and envisaged as basically permanent. Yet despite their differences, all of these relationships were reciprocal, and all were grounded in common economic or social interests. This is an essential point. Each of the parties to the association owed services and obligations to the other: this was as true of the lord committed to protecting his client's rights as it was of the rent-paying client himself.[7]

The necessary corollary to such reciprocity was that the social or economic transactions of one partner directly affected his associate as well. Legal commitments, as *Bretha Nemed* says in characteristically rhetorical fashion, "overleap the two of them as a pair."[8] The common interests that were the basis of the relationship between the two parties gave each rights in the contracts of the other that derived not from the conditions of the specific transaction itself, but rather from the nature of the more general obligations and responsibilities that bound them together. In a subordinating relationship, for example, an agreement made by a dependent party could actually threaten the status of that person's guardian or lord, since the extent to which a man was considered noble depended on the number of clients that he had.[9] Similarly, in a relationship between persons of equal status who owned property in common—what the tract on water mill rights, *Coibnes Uisci Thairidne*, calls *comthus cacha lánamna*, the "joint economy of every pair"[10]—an imprudent transaction could jeopardize common holdings. Both sides had therefore to have some means by which they could control and direct such affairs; consequently, people did not act alone in their social and economic dealings, even when they appeared to do so. Every additional commitment that they made, every new obligation to which they bound themselves, had the potential to change the fabric of the various relationships that controlled their lives. Contracts did not stand discrete from the general social context: they were very much a part of it.

The manner in which the responsibilities implicit in such associations could influence contractual arrangements is most easily visible in the provisions that treat of those incapable of acting independently in law.[11] There were two types of legally dependent individuals recognized in Irish law: those who were fully incompetent (who had no independent legal capacity at all) and those who were restricted only by virtue of their relationship to other people. In both instances the primary responsibility of the subordinate party was to uphold the social and economic integrity of his principal by remaining, as *Berrad Airechta* puts it, "properly subordinated so that he controls neither foot nor hand."[12] His guardian was in turn obliged to protect his dependent against those who would take advantage of him. These reciprocal obligations were the cornerstone of the general relationships that bound those fully independent in law to their subordinates; because all specific transactions came within the purview of the rights and responsibilities inherent in the larger relationship, they were expected to conform as well to these basic principles.

Mutual expectations of this sort affected Irish contractual capacity most obviously in the case of those who were regarded as fully legally incompetent. These were people who were completely dependent, both economically and socially, on their legal guardians. The reasons for such wide-ranging legal incompetence ranged from real mental deficiency and a consequent inability to make sound decisions to an individual's nonexistence as a legal personality; some had no property or fixed residence through which they could be held to their obligations, and some had no recognized ability to distribute that property on their own authority. *Berrad Airechta*'s list is fairly representative:

> Ceist, cid dia nepir: ni crie ni ria de doraith? naidm son for doeru . . . amal naidm for cétmuintir, for druith, for dochund, for dasachtaigh, for deorad—ar fofuataigh-side dia sasar fair, for murchorthai. a commut for cach diaraig. . . .[13]

> Query: why is it said: "thou shouldst not buy from, thou shouldst not sell to, a legal incompetent?" That refers to a *naidm*-binding on unfree persons . . . for instance a *naidm*-binding on a chief wife, on a fool, on an imbecile, on a lunatic, on an exile—for the latter moves his residence if something be enforced against him—on a man cast ashore by the sea. Likewise for every person who cannot be bound. . . .

In keeping with the obligations inherent in their lowly status, such people could not make valid contracts without the approval of their superiors.[14] This approval process, called *forngaire* in the texts, was done by the immediate superior (in Irish usually the *cenn*, literally "head") of the person involved. Many texts refer to this procedure; *Berrad Airechta* even calls its incompetents *áes forngaire*, "people of supervision."[15] *Forngaire* was in essence an expression of a guardian's ability and obligation to protect his own. In this manner, he signaled both his formal acceptance of the existence and the terms of the contract and his willingness to suffer any financial consequences that might result from it. His approval did not have to be conveyed in a formal ceremony, a fact that is a potent reminder of the very small size of the community in which such transactions were expected to occur. If an arrangement was made in a guardian's presence and he did nothing to hinder it, or if a guardian did not repudiate an agreement within a certain period of time (even though he had not actually been present at the time it was made), he was considered to have approved it and he lost thereby his ability to reconsider its terms.[16]

As a general rule, however, any contract made by one of these incompetents, even if it had been bound with *naidm* and *ráth* sureties, could be canceled by their guardians even after the relevant goods and services had been exchanged, *ar immusfuachat a cenna cona segar forro . . . ar cacha nadmann techtait beolu iarna cul*,[17] "for their superiors annul [their contracts] so that they are not enforced against them . . . in the face of every *naidm*-binding, they possess lips behind their backs." Such a cancellation could have serious consequences for individuals careless enough to deal with one of these people, for while the goods given by the incompetent person to the other before the intervention of the former's guardian were returned to the possession of the guardian's kindred, goods received by the incompetent remained in his guardian's control.[18] It was apparently the responsibility of the competent individual to ensure that the contract had been concluded with the knowledge of the incompetent's superior; lurking behind this provision is the assumption that those likely to deal with incompetents would be in a position to recognize their legal incapacity, another indication of the small size of the community envisaged.[19]

The canceling of a contract that had been bound by *naidm* and *ráth* sureties was a serious matter. "It is then that excrement goes upon the [face] of the guarantor, when contracts are dissolved against the honor of men,"[20] one text solemnly states. That contracts could nevertheless be dissolved, despite the weighty nature of the matters put thereby at risk, is a potent indication of the extent to which individual contractual arrangements were themselves governed by the rules of social behavior. A guardian's duty was to protect and defend his dependent; a subordinate's was to remain within the confines of his proper status so as not to injure his guardian. And even persons who stood outside this relationship had a duty to protect the proper hierarchy of the community in which they lived by respecting the restrictions placed by that society on certain of its members. Implicit in the tersely worded, in some places almost formulaic, provisions in the lawbooks are ideas much larger than the concept of legal incompetence per se. The "rules" of contract were directed toward the maintenance of such cherished social principles as responsibility, duty, and, indeed, the idea of hierarchy itself.

Not all subordinating relationships were as complete and as one-sided as those pictured above. The ties that, for example, joined a man to his lord or a teacher to his pupil also placed certain restrictions on the legal capacity of the inferior partner in accordance with the principles guiding the larger relationship between them. It did not, however, affect that individual's general competency in law. The subordinate partner in such relationships was legally dependent because he was to some extent economically or socially dependent; he was not, however, legally incompetent. The responsibilities inherent in these types of associations—protection by the greater, and submission by the lesser partner—were essentially the same as those that characterized the bond between an incompetent and his guardian. But the stakes were higher, and the choices considerably less clear. Because the subordinate partner retained some degree of economic and social independence, the range of action in which his principal could exert his authority was necessarily reduced. The boundaries of his influence in individual transactions were set, in fact, by the needs of the relationship itself.

Cáin Lánamna is a tract entirely devoted to these types of relationships.[21] One of the most complicated of these arrangements is clientship, for it is in the relationship between man and lord that the boundary between independence and subservience is most difficult to define. The basis of base clientship was both social and economic. The lord invested his capital, in the form of an animal fief, in return for specified food renders and personal service from his client. In addition to the fief, the lord gave his client a payment, equivalent to the client's honor-price, and obtained thereby the right to receive a percentage of any compensation paid to his client for homicide or theft. By this payment, called the *séoit turchluide*, literally "chattels of submission," or "submission price," the lord apparently purchased part, but not all, of his client's independence in law.[22] Despite the subordination of the client, however, the association was a voluntary one. Either party was free to terminate the relationship at any time, although the financial penalties for doing so could be especially burdensome for the client.[23] And both parties were obliged to respect the rights and behavior of the other; if either showed disrespect for the other by unilaterally breaking off the relationship without just cause, he was required to redeem the injured party's honor.[24] Clientship was, therefore, both a subordinating and a voluntary relationship: the traditional obligations of protection and submission still obtained, but the boundaries were far from clear.

The extent to which a lord was allowed to intervene in contractual arrangements made by his client is nowhere spelled out precisely in the lawbooks. Certain passages seem to suggest that lords could dissolve their client's contracts if they wished:

> Ar at e teora nadmand aspa inn sin naiscaidtear la Féniu[:] cor for meamra eacalsa cor for fognamthe flatha cor for faenleagachaib fine ar doinntai flaith ocus fine ocus eaclais cach cor na toltnaigter. . . .[25]

> For those are the three useless *naidm*-bindings that are bound in Irish law: a contract [made] with members of the church, a contract [made] with servants of a lord, a contract [made] with absconders from kindred [obligations], for the lord and the kindred and the church overturn every contract to which they do not consent. . . .

But though this triad might appear to intimate that lords enjoyed privileges with respect to their clients' contracts similar to those enjoyed by the guardians of the totally legally incompetent, it cannot be made to bear the burden such an interpretation would place on it. The passage gives no indication to what type of "servants" it refers; *fognamthe* is a general term that can be used of anyone in service to a lord, whether that person be a subordinate person capable of withdrawing himself from service or a slave incapable of acting independently in law at all.[26] The sentence that immediately preceeds this one and that addresses a similar question refers among other things to a *mug*, or slave—in other words, to a completely unfree person.[27] Similar passages seem also to accord extensive rights of intervention and repudiation only to lords of completely dependent individuals.[28] In short, there is no indication that lords of base clients were allowed to intervene in all contracts entered into by their subordinates.

It seems most likely that in this case also the limits of the lord's authority in individual transactions were determined by the boundaries and priorities of the clientship relationship itself. For lords were permitted to dissolve certain types of contractual relationships. If a client contracted a second base clientship relationship without the approval of his original lord, the first lord had the right to dissolve this second relationship out of hand. Even if the lord chose later to accept the arrangement, he was entitled to compensation, because the two lords would then have to share the services of their common client.[29] The lord who exercised such authority almost certainly did so because the contracted second clientship impinged both on his interests and on the original relationship between himself and his client.

Similarly, a passage in H 3. 18 prevents individuals from entering into contracts, purchases, or sales of land without the permission of others with an interest in the property—including, in this case, the secular or ecclesiastical lord or kindred of the person concerned.[30] Only contracts that were clearly advantageous to the subordinate party (*sochor* as opposed to *dochor*) were immune to lordly intervention.[31] This is not to say that only those contracts directly affecting the lord's property or relationship with his client were judged to fall under his purview. The obligation of every principal in a subordinating relationship to protect his dependent, for example, might occasionally have led lords to interfere when they thought their clients had been coerced into something they did not wish to do.[32] Even so, however, the basic premise remains the same. The larger relationship established the parameters within which all individual transactions would proceed, and while particular contracts might strictly speaking fall outside the ambit of the lord's authority, they could not escape the scrutiny of the relationship itself.

This principle is very clearly visible in the provisions governing the contractual capacity of women. It is now clear that the chronological stages outlined by Binchy do not necessarily represent successive phases in the development of the ability of women to act independently in law.[33] The differing degrees of contractual capacity to which he points are, however, real and significant. The determining factor would seem to have been the amount of property contributed by each spouse to the marital relationship. Within relationships in which the contributions of the male partner were the most significant, women seem generally to have been treated as completely legally incompetent. A passage from the Old Irish tract on *Díre* expresses their position most succinctly:

Messom cundrada cuir ban. Air ni tualaing ben roria ní sech oen a cenn. Adagair a athair imbe ingen. Adagair a cetmuinter imbi be cetmuintere. Adagairet a mmecc imbi be clainne. Adagair fine imbi be fine. Adagair eclais imbi be eclaise.[34]

> The worst of transactions are the contracts of women, for a woman is not capable of selling anything without [the permission of] one of her superiors: her father hinders her when she is a daughter, her husband hinders her when she is the wife of a husband, her sons hinder her when she is a woman with children, her kindred hinders her when she is a woman of the kindred, the church hinders her when she is a woman of the church.

There were, however, other types of marriages, most notably the *lánamnas comthincuir*, the "union of mutual portion," a relationship where both parties contributed in fairly equal measure to the movable wealth of the household. In such relationships, married women were not only capable of making advantageous contracts without hindrance from their husbands, they were allowed to dissolve any disadvantageous contracts he might make as well.[35] Women who were not economically dependent on their spouses increased their capacity in law; factors within the marital relationship itself, in other words, determined the rights enjoyed by spouses in specific transactions. Undoubtedly, the most potent example of this principle is another type of union to which *Cáin Lánamna* makes reference. The *lánamnas for banthinchur*, literally the "union on woman-portion," was a form of marriage in which the wife contributed the bulk of the property. The husband in this relationship was quite literally said to go "in the track of the woman"; because of his unequal standing within the relationship, his honor-price was established according to that of his wife, and he became incapable of making contracts without his wife's supervision.[36] The circle of contractual capacity had come full turn.

Perhaps the most complicated of all the subordinating relationships recognized in Irish law was that which bound a father to his son. The *mac béoathar*, literally the "son of a living father," found his way onto almost every list of legal incompetents given in the Irish lawbooks. At times he kept rather strange company, considering the relatively inoffensive nature of his disability; *Córus Béscnai* places him in the same category of incompetency as captives, male and female slaves, exiles and thieves.[37] The reality of the son's situation was, however, much more complex than these relatively simplistic lists would suggest. His position with respect to his father was unique among subordinating relationships because it was, by its very nature, destined to change over time as the son matured. Whereas totally incompetent people would never acquire the economic and social independence necessary to enable them to act unsupervised in financial transactions, sons could expect to reach this level of contractual capacity eventually. Moreover, sons would expect to acquire also the privileges granted to all adult members of a given kindred, including the right to keep their portion of the family inheritance intact and unimpaired by the unwise financial decisions of their relatives.

Three different aspects of a son's relationship with his father determined his status in that relationship and, in turn, his capacity in law: his age, his personal wealth, and the extent to which he had fulfilled his filial obligations. Many sons would have been put into fosterage until the age of fourteen,[38] and until that age would presumably have been subject to the authority of their fosterfathers. After coming out of fosterage, a son was considered to be in a period of transition between childhood and full adult status; the lawbooks even refer to him as a *fer midboth*, a "man of middle huts," a man who, in other words, still resides on his father's land. *Críth Gablach* distinguishes two stages of *fer midboth*, one beginning at age fourteen and ending at age seventeen, and another beginning at seventeen and ending at twenty; at that age men of sufficient property apparently became eligible to take on the status of full adult freemen. Such a distinction is not made elsewhere in the lawbooks, however, and the ambiguities of the *fer midboth*'s position make it likely that the reality of the situation was more involved even than *Críth Gablach* suggests.[39]

What must have mattered most at this point in a male's life was the amount of independent property he could acquire through inheritance or by his own industry, and this would have differed greatly from person to person. A son whose father had died young could contract immediately to take on a respectably sized fief, even if he could not attain freeman status until the age of twenty. But a son whose father lived on into his son's old age, and who did not have a craft whereby he could earn his own living, remained a *fer midboth* despite the number of his years.[40] And even if a male whose father was still alive managed to acquire enough property to function independently of his father, he was still not entirely free of the relationship. Though economically independent, he was still bound by his filial obligations to maintain his parents in their old age and to submit to his father's authority in important matters.[41] There were then certainly many different types of *fer midboth*, even more in fact than *Críth Gablach* suggests, but age was only one of the characteristics that distinguished one type from another.

The rules that govern the contractual capacity of these sons themselves reflect the ambiguous nature of their status. All indications are that sons under the age of fourteen (e.g., those who had not yet completed fosterage) and sons who had not yet acquired any amount of individual personal wealth had no significant independent contractual capacity.[42] *Berrad Airechta* directly contrasts two types of dutiful son, one of whom has already been fostered and has learned or is learning a craft, and the other who, while properly subordinate to his father, has no control yet "over foot or hand." The former is capable of being economically independent and is therefore allowed to make any contract up to the amount of his honor-price that does not diminish his status or inheritance, but the latter is either still in fosterage (i.e., underage) or still economically dependent on his father, and therefore cannot make valid contracts at all independent of his father.[43]

Significantly, even otherwise independent sons were restricted to some degree by their ongoing economic and personal relationship with their fathers.[44] Fathers were allowed to annul disadvantageous contracts made by their otherwise "emancipated" sons, although they were not permitted to cancel agreements that were advantageous to the sons's holdings (they could, however, formally object to and thereby disassociate themselves financially from such transactions). As the *Heptads* indicate, sons who contract to rent land, join in profitable neighborhood relationships, or make a worthy marriage may make these arrangements without the consent or supervision of their fathers *ar is mo torbud na cor-si oldas a ninnruidiu*,[45] "because the profit of these contracts is greater than their wrongs." The only apparent exception to this rule is that sons who had not lived up to the obligations of their relationship with their fathers were not permitted to make a valid contract even if they were old enough and wealthy enough to do so under normal circumstances.[46] Sons enjoyed similar rights of intervention and objection with respect to contracts made by their fathers. But whereas dutiful sons were allowed to annul any disadvantageous contracts their fathers might make, impious sons had no authority over either their own or their father's transactions.[47]

These "rules," while confusing and occasionally contradictory, are far from arbitrary. They are confusing because they attempt to describe, in the stationary language of law, a relationship that is constantly subject to change, and this is obviously a difficult task. But still visible in all of these intricate provisions is their ultimate goal—the preservation and perpetuation of the larger relationships involved. Thus, while it is desirable that persons in close economic or personal relationships with others not be allowed to act alone in contractual affairs, they are permitted to do so in cases where the arrangements made would advance the communal interests of both, where the profits "are greater than the wrongs."[48] The needs of the relationship, in other words, take clear priority over the norms that would customarily obtain in such instances.

The lawbooks are not, however, concerned merely with the relationship between the boy and his father. Both the provision that provides for profits greater than wrongs and that which permits sons to annul the disadvantageous contracts of their fathers reflect the eventual economic independence of sons and their full reception by the kindred; since they would ultimately inherit from their father a portion of the family lands, sons had a right to block any transactions that threatened their inheritance and to add to that inheritance if they could. Similarly, since unwise agreements entered into even by dutiful and "emancipated" sons could compromise the joint holdings of father, son, and kindred, fathers retained the right to intervene in such arrangements. Perhaps the clearest indication, however, of how the needs of the larger relationship determined the outcome of arrangements made by parties to that relationship are the regulations concerning the pious and impious sons. The filial obligations implicit in *goire* had little to do directly with the existence or terms of any particular contract, but the extent to which a son had fulfilled these obligations directly affected his ability to make valid legal arrangements with others. The norms that governed contractual capacity were thus only a small part of a larger network of rights and responsibilities that bound father to son, and son to kindred.

The argument of the foregoing pages can best be summarized by a look at the procedures that regulated the making of contracts within the most prominent non-subordinating relationship known to Irish law, that between kinsmen of equal status.[49] Even here the needs of the relationship could take precedence over an individual's normal contractual rights; even here a fully adult, fully economically independent male could find his commitments overruled by his relations. The basis for such intervention was much the same as in other, subordinating relationships. Every kinsman had an obligation to protect the others: *im-dich cach corp a memru.... [is] corp caich a fine*,[50] "each body protects its members.... The body of each [person is] his kindred." And because all competent kinsmen could expect to share in the common inheritance, each had a clear responsibility to maintain and to protect their joint holdings. Individual kindred members could, therefore, intervene in any agreement that threatened their common property, because *us treise in da teangaid .x. dia tindtug oldas in aenteanga dia hasdadh*,[51] "twelve tongues are stronger for canceling [an agreement] than is the one tongue for binding it."

Many different types of transaction are specifically cited in the law-books as being agreements in which a kindred might lawfully intervene, including gifts of land, bequests, the adoption of a stranger into a kindred, and the undertaking of monastic or secular clientship.[52] If a kindred completely repudiated an agreement and refused to accept the goods of the other party, the contract did not diminish any of the kindred's property, although in certain cases at least the disappointed party could claim a small fee in compensation.[53] Contracts that did not directly involve the common holdings of a kindred could not be actually annulled, though they could be objected to. In such circumstances, kin-members would not be held liable for any compensatory or interest payments that came due because of their kinsman's default; they would be responsible, however, for the restitution of anything paid under the terms of the agreement.[54] But for the repudiation of a given contract to be recognized in law the objecting kinsmen had to be *sognimach, sobesach . . . sofoltach*,[55] "lawful in deeds, lawful in customs, [and] lawful in property." Those who had failed in their family responsibilities or in their obligation to preserve the family inheritance intact were not allowed to intervene in the contracts made by their relations.[56]

Often, of course, a kindred would have chosen to support a contract made on their behalf by one of their members. Such consent by the kindred was called *aititiu*, "acknowledgment," and it automatically committed the kindred to share in any losses that might be incurred in the transaction. The kin were considered to have acknowledged any contract of which they were cognizant, but which they did not specifically repudiate;[57] once they had either directly or indirectly acknowledged a transaction and the goods had changed hands, they could not later renege on their consent. *Cáin Aicillne*'s emphasis on the rights of the individual kinsman makes it sound as though any lawful kinsman could intervene to approve or reject a contractual arrangement that involved him. In practice, however, the consent of the kindred would probably often have been communicated—at least in the case of particularly important undertakings—by the presence of the designated kindred leader at the making of the contract and by his supervision (*forngaire*) of the terms: *ar ni techta nach foessam arna tegat ratha fine ocus nad forngara aige fine ar dichenglaiter cach chor cen raith la Féniu*,[58] "for no adoption is legally valid for which *ráth*-sureties of the kindred have not undertaken suretyship, and which the head of the kindred does not supervise, for every contract without a *ráth*-surety is dissolved in Irish law."

Several texts remark on the kindred leader's role; *Cáin Aicillne* even defines him as the man in every kindred who is most worthy, noble, and *treisi fri imfoichid*,[59] "strongest at impugning [the bad contracts of his kinsmen]." *Aititiu*, the consent of a kindred to the existence and terms of a contract, was a larger term than was *forngaire*, the supervision through which *aititiu* must often have been conveyed. The terms were obviously closely related to one another and were occasionally linked together or even confused with one another in the lawbooks.[60] Both signified that, even in a relationship that was in theory non-subordinating, an individual's freedom in contract could be restricted by the intervention of others.

The principles at stake in all of these associations, subordinating and non-subordinating, were therefore much the same. Any behavior that affected the partnership affected both parties involved in it, and people accordingly did not act alone in their contractual arrangements. Even apparently minor transactions were subject to the scrutiny of a number of interlocking and often overlapping relationships, and failure in any one of these associations could significantly restrict an individual's capacity in law. A man could be of proper standing within his kindred, and of lawful custom within his marriage, and still have his contracts overturned by the father whom he had failed to maintain. The public perception of what was profitable in an association and what was not, and who was dutiful in their obligations and who was not, could also directly affect the outcome of a specific transaction. Truly then it was the desire to preserve these relationships, rather than a unreasoning adherence to customary or written norms, that held people most firmly to their legal obligations. That this was the jurists' intent as well cannot be doubted; it is no accident that most of what we know about contracts we know from treatises on clientship, marriage, and social obligations within the tribe. All worked together to reinforce the social network that was for both the jurists and those who consulted them the essence of law in action.[61]

The discussion has centered to this point on the relationships between individuals—man and lord, husband and wife, father and son. But these associations did not themselves exist in a vacuum. Each of these partnerships was part of a social network still larger than the one we have considered so far. Kindreds and lords particularly had a clear responsibility to ensure that their members adhered to the moral and legal expectations of their community. It was the *tuiseach cacha fine aranithead feib ocus bescna*,[62] the "leader of every kindred who took responsibility for the substance and behavior [of his kinsmen]," as one legal tract admonishes. Many of the obligations envisaged in this particular passage were the "public" dues owed to Church and king, which would have been enforced by kindred or secular lords on their subordinates. *Córus Béscnai* speaks of lords forcing their clients to meet religious obligations of baptismal dues and charitable gifts,[63] and *Críth Gablach* reveals that this would usually have been done through a gage given by the lord to the appropriate authorities.[64] Both kindred and lord acted then as enforcing and paying "sureties" for their subordinates to guarantee that the public obligations they owed would be met.

But the term *béscnae*, translated above as "behavior," had moral and ethical as well as legal implications, and a kindred's responsibility to the community did not end with the fulfillment of its public commitments to king and church. The true interest of kindred and lord lay in assuring the propriety of their members with respect to *all* of their obligations, public and private. To do any less was to impugn their collective honor and to risk the restructuring of their own position within the community. Certainly, ignoring societal norms could have serious economic consequences. *Elothaig urraduis*, people who absconded from their commitments in tribal law, were counted among the "fools among the *Féni*" with whom it was considered unwise to have social or financial dealings. And kindreds or lords who sheltered these unworthy individuals could find themselves similarly penalized.[65] Exclusion from the basic economic life of the community was a serious matter—a state of affairs which no lord or kindred could afford to risk. Like the other associations we have studied so far, the relationship between kindreds and the community in which they lived was a reciprocal one: those who did not live up to its obligations were denied its privileges as well.

The preservation of this network of mutual obligation and prerogative was thus crucial to those who lived within it. Kindreds and lords had to be able to guarantee that their associates would live up to the obligations they had contracted. This they did by intervening as guarantors in the contracts made by their kinsmen and clients. Kindred leaders and lords must frequently have been appointed as *naidm*-sureties for their subordinates, since the moral and physical pressure they could bring to bear on them promised swift fulfillment of the obligation. And while the subordinate partner in a given relationship could not act as a *naidm*-surety for his principal during the period of his subordination to him,[66] he could still be appointed by a person of his own social rank to act in this capacity. Although many later glosses suggest that a *naidm*-surety should be of the lordship grades,[67] *Críth Gablach* mentions *naidm*ship as a possibility for all of the plebeian grades, and *Berrad Airechta* seems to regard the freeman *naidm*-surety as the most usual type.[68] In the early period, when most men farmed in common with their kinsmen, it is probably to the kindred that they would have looked for sureties; once this kindred system weakened, however, the non-kinsmen neighbors with whom they now conducted their affairs must well have filled the void.[69]

But because kinsmen and lords had such a high personal stake in the lawful behavior of their associates, they were allowed to force these people to meet their legal obligations even when not specifically appointed to do so. *Berrad Airechta* uses the terminology and images of suretyship to express the privileges and responsibilities of lord and kindred:

> Atat nadmann tra seghdae gnimu ceni airgistar. . . . Naidm dano fir fine forsan aile, athair fora mac, fithir fora fealmac, ap fora manchu, flaith fora ceile. Cach cend fora memru corai . . . as de ata: segar a nad aic[d]ither.[70]

> There are *naidm*-sureties then who fulfill the responsibilities [of their office] though they may not have been appointed as *naidm*-sureties. . . . A *naidm*-suretyship moreover of (i.e. performed by) one man of a kindred as against another, a father for his son, a teacher for his pupil, an abbot for his *manaig* (monks and monastic tenants), a lord for his client. Every "head" for his proper "limbs" . . . therefore is it said: "[A claim] is enforced and [a *naidm*-surety] is not appointed."

Lords and kindred leaders could enforce claims made against their subordinates even without permission from those individuals, because they themselves stood to lose so much in the affair. The additional security they thus afforded to uneasy creditors was likely to have been considerable. These "unappointed *naidm*-sureties" were, in a very real sense, the physical embodiment of the social pressures that are so often the basis of order in stateless communities: to refuse a claim urged by a kinsman or lord was to risk the relationship that defined one's life.

Injustice, however, was potentially a two-way street. All of these "sureties" would also have been expected to protect the legal interests of their associates and dependents, many of whom would of course have been incapable of acting in law on their own behalf.[71] They appear therefore to have been permitted to enforce claims against *both* contracting parties, even though they had not been appointed by either of them. Kinsmen particularly had a direct financial interest in seeing their relatives receive what was due to them; enforcement of payments owed was, according to the tract on distraint edited by Binchy, one of the prerogatives of the kin.[72] Women especially were vulnerable to fraud, and it is probably not coincidental that the one case of outside enforcement mentioned in the laws is that of a kindred enforcing a dowry payment due to them.[73] The ability of kinsmen and lords to enforce a claim against people with whom they had no official connection is significant, because it shows clearly that their relationship with the community in which they lived was not perceived to be one-sided. *Each* owed the other propriety in legal matters; this was as much of an obligation for the community as it was for the individuals who inhabited it. The preservation of the social equilibrium was so important that it took precedence over the normal right of a individual to limit enforcement to a surety he had chosen. Once again the boundaries of a specific transaction were drawn by the larger network within which it been made.

Lords and kin members could thus act as enforcing sureties for their kinsmen and clients. The extent of their financial liability—their *ráth*ship as it were—for the misdeeds of their associates is less clear. The kin did bear liability for at least some of the offences committed by its members,[74] and kindred leaders served as de facto *ráth*-sureties for the public obligations of their subordinates, as we have already seen. The liability of lords and kin-members for contractual obligations incurred by their associates is, however, a more complicated issue. Usually losses arising from contracts bound in the conventional manner would have been paid by the *ráth*-surety specifically appointed for this purpose at the time of the agreement. Given the financial connections that bound kinsmen and lords to one another, it is likely that often these officially appointed *ráth*-sureties would have been chosen from within the kindred itself. Kin-based suretyship certainly functioned elsewhere in medieval Europe as a means by which a kindred could publicly resign its interest in a given property, or communicate its consent to arrangements that affected its interests or common holdings.[75] And the passage on adoption cited earlier from *Coibnes Uisci Thairidne* speaks of such arrangements being warranted by *rátha fine*, "*ráth*-sureties of the kindred."[76]

The lawbooks, however, seem not to be unanimous in their views on kindred liability in cases where no *ráth*-surety had ever been officially appointed in a given contract or where a surety had been appointed but had failed to pay the debt. *Berrad Airechta* remarks directly that the family of a defaulting contracting party would not have been considered liable *ar cuir bél doerdae ni fuichit fine*,⁷⁷ "because ordinary oral contracts do not injure the kindred." But basic familial liability for contractual default seems to be presumed elsewhere in the lawbooks. We have seen that kindreds who did not repudiate contracts made by their members were held to have acknowledged them and were therefore considered liable for the payments owed by their defaulting kinsman. And even kindreds who disavowed, but did not actually repudiate, a contract made by one of their members were liable for restitution. Indeed, family obligations in this respect seem to have been perceived to derive from their responsibility to the community within which they lived: *Cáin Aicillne* speaks of sustaining the *cinta ocus ratha ocus curu*, the "crimes and *ráth*ships and contracts," of one's relatives as though it were a necessary qualification for good standing within the tribe.⁷⁸ Certain evidence suggests that kindreds may even have designated one or more of their members specifically to act in such cases. One of the *Heptads*, for example, mentions a *ráth forngartha fine*, a "*ráth*-surety commanded by his kindred," who is said in one of the ninth-century glosses in H 3. 18 to be entitled to compensation for what he has had to pay on his kindred's behalf despite the fact that he was never specifically appointed to act in the transaction in question.⁷⁹

It is difficult to know how to sort out these seeming contradictions. It is always possible that the extent of the kindred's liability in contract had lessened by the time *Berrad Airechta* was compiled. *Cáin Aicillne* certainly stresses kindred solidarity more than any other extant legal tract, and it is undeniable that the unity of the kindred was no longer by the eighth century what it once had been. It seems more likely, however, that what determined familial liability was the extent to which a given contract impinged on the relationship between a man and his kindred. Independent contracts made for small amounts by lawful individuals out of their own property may well have been judged to fall outside the realm of family control and liability. But contracts that did impinge on the relationship between a man and his kindred—either in their size, in their likely impact on family holdings, or in the nature of the obligations they entailed—had to be acknowledged by the kindred, and approval of such arrangements entailed liability. This is why after the death of a client, the heirs owed two months of service to the lord,⁸⁰ and why the adoption of a stranger into the kindred would not go forward if the kindred did not agree to accept the obligation. Kindred leaders, acting much like *naidm*-sureties, and "*ráth*-sureties" of the kindred, whether officially designated or not, would be expected to warrant all contracts that might directly involve their interests or reputation. Whether the paying sureties involved were standing sureties and, if so, what their relationship was to the *aire coisring* is in a sense immaterial.[81] The point is simply that a kindred's obligations to the community in which they lived required them to stand behind the claims in which they were themselves involved. Kinsmen and kin leaders were both permitted and expected to intervene as "sureties" for their associates even in situations where their intervention had not been sanctioned by the contracting parties in the usual manner. The priorities and responsibilities incumbent on the relationship between kindred and community superseded the norms by which contractual arrangements were customarily governed.

The neatly bound contractual arrangements described in such detail by *Berrad Airechta* were therefore only a small part of a much larger social network of status and obligation. But perhaps the clearest indication of the range and power of this network is the role it played in the creation and fulfillment of non-contractual commitments.[82] Both Irish and Welsh law recognized certain types of transactions that were not contractual in origin but that were as unassailable as any lawful contract made in Irish law. The nature of these arrangements, and the rationale and sanctions that lay behind them, reveal a great deal about the nature and operation of law within a tribal society. Their existence is relatively well documented. Several of the legal tracts mention these "immunities," as they were called, since the items handed over were considered totally "immune" from claim or challenge even though no guarantors had been appointed to secure them. *Berrad Airechta* actually begins its study of contractual relationships with an account of these specifically non-contractual transactions:

> Atait dano ruidlesa tuaithe la Féniu. . . . ruidles donach tacoir naimd [sic] na rrath oca ruidhilsiguth, acht rope toga aruiltin folad foib ocus doratatar fiad fiadhnaibh[83]

> There are, moreover, transactions within the tribe [which are] entirely immune from claim in Irish law. . . . [A transaction] for which neither a *naidm*-surety nor a *ráth*-surety is appropriate to render [the transaction] entirely immune from claim is, nevertheless, entirely immune from claim, provided that the values of those things that are due [from the other side to each bargain] in respect of them (e.g. the transactions) be complete, and provided that they have been given in the presence of witnesses.

Exactly what the various types of exchanges the text then lists had in common apart from their immunity from claim is not, however, immediately apparent; included are payments made for the fostering of young children, the fees of doctors, lawyers, poets, and other professionals, food-rent and fief exchanges between client and lord, gifts given to the church, and goods exchanged by allied tribes to settle feuds between them.[84] Lists extant in the *Heptads* and in *Coibnes Uisci Thairidne* add to this group gifts made to or by bishops and kings;[85] fees paid for making tools, breaking in horses, or doing handwork such as weaving or sewing; and the *comthus cacha lánamna*, translated by Binchy as the "joint economy of every pair."[86] Other scattered references are to be found elsewhere in the law-books; one of the ninth-century glosses in H 3. 18, for example, states that free clientship, with all its attendant dues and services, is to be bound not through normal contractual means but rather through *fuisitiu*, "assent," or *aititiu*, "acknowledgment."[87] Elsewhere in the same manuscript it is said that land divisions between kinsmen are immune from challenge, even though no guarantors have been involved in their establishment.[88] A full enumeration of the immunities would encompass some of the most important and most frequent transactions occurring in Irish society.

Unfortunately, however, the nature of the claims made for these transactions is our only clue to their common rationale. They were, first of all, exchanges in which guarantors were not simply unnecessary to render the goods immune from claim, but actually inappropriate[89]—a rather unusual proviso. Also unusual are the restrictions that are placed on them. Religious dues were immune from claim only if the church or the priest to whom they were given lived a properly Catholic life;[90] a poet's fee was valid only if the poem he uttered reflected truth and propriety.[91] The immunity of the earnings of an axe or a smith's tongs or a fishing net was guaranteed only if the payment had been given "in return for sweat," that is, as compensation for hard work.[92] And a teacher's salary was judged secure only if the instruction in question was free from defect.[93] Now on one level these restrictions are comprehensible in that they seek to ensure that the goods and services due from each party to the other (Old Irish *folad*) have been completely delivered or performed.[94] But as the manner in which they are phrased speaks as much to the quality as to the quantity of performance, the strict equality of the items exchanged may not be the only issue here. The matter may not be as transparent as it seems at first.

Of all of the characteristics of these transactions, the most striking is the fact that the recipient's entitlement to the payment was considered to be greater than all other claims that could be made against it. Food-rent paid to a lord in the context of a clientship arrangement could not, for example, be reclaimed by anyone unless the lord himself were guilty of wrongdoing, because his right to receive and consume the renders in question—his "entitlement" to the goods, in other words—was perceived as paramount. But we cannot understand these immunities without knowing whence this entitlement derived, and here a comparison with transactions in which guarantors and contractual rituals were considered appropriate is instructive. As we have seen, the evidence of *Berrad Airechta* suggests that in such transactions, an individual's entitlement to specific goods or services was established by the public binding of the guarantors and the contracting parties to the terms and conditions of the agreement. The presence of a surety did not in itself guarantee that the arrangement could not be challenged or emended; *dliged* or *cert* ("natural entitlement," "justice") could overrule the specifically contractual entitlement established by the involvement of a guarantor. But this contractual entitlement itself was perceived to derive from the formal enunciation and binding of the agreement, and transactions effected in the absence of such rituals were particularly vulnerable to annulment or emendation.[95] Sureties established an individual's entitlement to specific assets, even though they could not entirely protect this entitlement against every challenge that might be made against it.

This would appear then to be at least one of the rules to which the immunities were an exception: individuals became entitled to particular goods even without the intervention of guarantors. Furthermore, although many of the same restrictions on the immunity of the assets exchanged would presumably obtain in these transactions as well (goods and services exchanged would have to be complete, for example), it is apparent that assets changing hands in this manner were in some senses even more secure from challenge than were assets exchanged in the presence of guarantors. All of the texts that mention them mark their special status in some manner. In the *Heptads* they are said to be *dílsem*, "most immune from challenge," while *Coibnes Uisci Thairidne* terms them *úasalch[ui]r*, "noble contracts," thus distinguishing them from ordinary transactions (*cuir*).[96] *Berrad Airechta* calls them *ruidlesa*, from *ro-díles*, exchanges not merely "immune from claim," but "entirely immune from claim."[97]

That the distinction being made here is real is evident from the extent of the immunity of the assets. As long as the recipient himself fulfilled the obligations of his position, the goods exchanged in the context of one of these immunities could not be recalled from him by anyone.[98] Even if the items were subsequently proved to have been stolen, the recipient's right to the goods would take precedence over the right of the true owner to reclaim his stolen property.[99] In a formal contract, by contrast, the transaction would be annulled by the revelation of the theft and the items exchanged would be returned to their rightful owner.[100] The entitlement established in the context of these immunities would seem, therefore, to be more extensive and more potent than that established by guarantors. Two things, therefore, specifically distinguished the immunities from other contracts and exchanges: the special degree of their immunity from claim, and the fact that sureties were considered somehow "inappropriate" in their formation. Clearly a fresh approach is needed to explain both the nature and the idiosyncrasies of these mysterious transactions.[101]

As seems so often to be the case in Irish legal studies, the work of Daniel Binchy is a fruitful place to begin. Binchy argued, in his edition of *Coibnes Uisci Thairidne*, that the economic proximity of members of the legal pairs mentioned in that text would render sureties unnecessary in transactions between them, and that it was for this reason that the "joint economy of every pair" was counted an immunity.[102] Binchy said nothing about those immunities that did not fall into this category, but by focusing on the relationship within which the exchange occurred rather than on the exchange itself, he pointed us in what I believe to be the right direction. Again the contrast with contractual relationships is instructive. One cannot read through any of the relevant Irish tracts without being struck by the extreme precision with which contractual obligations were defined by the rituals that created them. The formulas by which the terms of the agreement were set specified not only the exact time, place, circumstances, and possible recipients of the payment, but also what was to be done if one of the parties failed to appear on the proper date, or died, or could not pay the debt when it was due.[103] And the detail with which the goods themselves were defined almost defies description; a sample contract found in H 3. 18 makes the point most clearly:

> Aic maccu a cairaich slan noicc ninnraic sochraid solomrad alahuan no treas uan . . . nip brisc a croiceann, nip forfind no forofinn, ma[d] dub no lachtna; . . . nip daintach . . . nip ladarach, nip letheirlach. . . . [104]

> Appoint sureties [to guarantee the delivery of] a whole, perfect, honorable, seemly sheep, excellent of fleece, a second or third lamb . . . let its hide not be brittle, let it not be too white or much too white if it [is supposed to be] a black or gray [sheep] . . . let it not be given to biting . . . let it not be splayfooted, let it not be leathery. . . .

Now it is true that finding the perfect sheep is not as easy as one might think. But the point of the passage is not to ensure the delivery of Plato's ideal sheep but rather to establish precisely the nature and characteristics of the animal that was expected. The emphasis in all of these texts is on demarcating boundaries and circumscribing transactions in a manner that publicly proclaims that no promise of future involvement between the two parties is implied. An obligation was established, but it was an obligation with both a beginning and an end. In the words of the formulas themselves, the repayment of the debt entailed the "death" not only of the obligation but also of all necessary connection between the parties involved.[105] (This is not to say that the two parties would never have had further relations with one another—merely that they would not be committed to doing so by virtue of their having participated in the transaction in question. Indeed, the precision with which the obligation was defined was undoubtedly intended at least in part to ensure that hostilities arising out of a particular contract would impinge as little as possible on such future relations as the contracting parties might have with one another.)

In this respect the contrast with the immunities could not be greater, and it is through this contrast that we can begin to understand the rationale and the sanctions that lay behind them. All of the immunities involved specific payments made in the context of social relationships that were by their nature long-term affiliations. Kinship and lordship bonds, political alliances, neighborhood connections, relations between churches and their parishioners—it was in the context of such associations that the immune transactions mentioned in our texts (payment of food-rent, baptismal fees, fosterage fees, and so on) occurred. Even professional fees, which might seem at first not to fit in with the rest, were, I would argue, perceived in this manner. Common sense suggests that kindreds would establish in the course of their lives regular contacts with the tribal professionals; wood, healing and the ability to engage in legal suits were surely year-round necessities, as were of course poetry and fish.

But in this instance we have something more than common sense to help us understand the nature of these arrangements. *Críth Gablach* tells us, in a passage that has not hitherto attracted much notice, that each kindred leader, called in that text the *aire coisring*, the "noble of binding obligation," customarily gave what would appear to be a standing gage on behalf of his kindred to constrain them to the authority of "king and synod and people of crafts" (*óes cherdd*).[106] Binchy was uncertain what to make of this reference to craftsmen and suggested that it might pertain to poets who had, in his words, "a semi-public status."[107] I would suggest, however, that the text can be taken literally: the purpose and effect of the *aire coisring*'s gage was to establish a relationship between kindreds and tribal professionals similar to the one they enjoyed with political and ecclesiastical authorities. And this relationship, like the others envisaged in the lists of immunities with which we began, was viewed by the participants as both reciprocal and long-term.

The distinction between short-term and ongoing relationships is, I suggest, the rationale that lies behind the Irish immunities. It helps us as well to understand the peculiar characteristics of these exchanges. For although guarantors could be used to warrant such transactions, the long-term nature of the obligations implicit in the larger relationships made such finite guarantees "inappropriate." Unlike contractual exchanges, which specifically did not imply involvement between the principals after the conclusion of the contract, exchanges made in the context of long-term relationships not only envisaged, but entailed, future links between them. Payments made by clients to lords, by parishioners to their church, and by individuals to the professionals whose services they used were the means through which the relationship between them was established, defined, enhanced, and perpetuated. This fact more than any other explains the immunity of these transactions. For once a payment had been made, it was unlikely to be reclaimed by the individual who had paid it, since to do this would be to terminate the relationship. Only if the recipient himself had not lived up to the obligations inherent in the relationship might the immunity of the payment be challenged. If, for example, fostering was badly done, or instruction muddled, the exchange became vulnerable because the relationship itself was vulnerable. The validity of any individual exchange, in other words, would be determined by the manner in which the parties themselves adhered to the obligations and behavior implicit in their partnership.

But as we have seen, the immunity of these particular exchanges was in some ways more real and more extensive than the immunity of goods exchanged in a more formal manner, and in this we look beyond the transactions themselves to the principles and priorities of the legal system within which they occurred. The Irish evidence makes clear the extent to which social relationships of the type we are discussing functioned both as determinants and as guarantors of lawful behavior. The expectations of the social network within which individuals operated set the standards for their conduct, while the fact that people had to rely on relationships such as lordship and kinship for their social and economic well-being ensured their adherence to these norms. What we see in the reluctance of the Irish jurists to impugn the immunity of exchanges made in the context of the associations mentioned is a reflection of the crucial significance such affiliations held for the community. Even in cases of theft, exchanges had to remain immune from challenge by parties external to the relationship—immune even to the rightful owner of the goods involved. For whereas contracts could be annulled in such circumstances because there was nothing larger at stake, the forced return of assets exchanged within the terms of a known relationship put the relationship itself in jeopardy. At risk was nothing less than the social network through which law and order were themselves effected.

The glimpse afforded us of the social sanctions that lay behind the immunities invites us also to think about the manner in which debt and obligation themselves served to bind men to one another and to the community in which they lived. This is an idea long been familiar to anthropologists, but one that medievalists are only beginning to explore. We tend to think of debts as things to be paid off, preferably as quickly as possible, and preferably by somebody else. In many societies, however, the termination of an obligation is often deliberately deferred as a means of expressing and perpetuating a bond between the individuals involved. Even as late as the 1930s in county Clare, for example, farmers would remain intentionally in debt to shopkeepers for years, paying off their obligations completely only if they had decided to change their associations or move out of the community altogether.[108] The paucity of charter material makes it difficult for us to judge the extent to which similar relationships might have existed in early Ireland, although the passage in *Berrad Airechta* in which a debt is postponed for a year when the creditor fails to appear on the appointed day to receive his payment, certainly suggests that deferred debts might not have been uncommon.[109]

What we learn from the immunities, however, is that the general concept of debt as social bond was one familiar to the Irish. For what else lies at the heart of clientship, and maintenance arrangements, and neighborhood relationships, if not an extended state of indebtedness on the part of one or both of the parties involved? Certainly the jurists conceived of the relationship between the church and its parishioners in exactly these terms. *Córus Béscnai*'s use of contractual language in its enumeration of the dues owed by the church to the laity (e.g., baptism, communion, masses for departed souls) and by the laity to the church (e.g., tithes, first fruits, and legacies of the appropriate size) would strike a modern-day churchgoer as nothing short of bizarre; only in a culture in which debt was an expression of ongoing affiliation does such language make sense.[110] Similar language is used to describe tribal relationships in the *Frithfolaid* tracts,[111] and, if I am correct about the manner in which kindreds were bound to the professionals of the tribe, the use of a standing gage in this context is a clear indication that this relationship also was perceived as one of extended obligation. Debt for us is frequently an occasion for isolation and withdrawal; its function in early medieval society was quite different.

The foregoing has made clear the extent to which even seemingly self-contained legal institutions like suretyship and contract cannot be understood apart from their social context. But the realities of social order in early Ireland must have been more complicated even than this brief sketch would seem to imply.[112] Many cases would not have been at all simple to sort out. Balancing the many conflicting claims of entitlement that could be brought to bear on a particular dispute must often have proved difficult to do, given the many different levels on which entitlement could operate. A son was subject to his father, to his fosterfather, to his tutor, to his kindred, to his lord, to his king, and to his church; it is not unreasonable to imagine that occasionally these various claims on his resources would come into conflict. And while the boundaries between these various authorities can be drawn somewhat with the aid of the schematic outlines presented in the lawbooks, they must have proved in practice a great deal more fluid. If this same son had been dutiful to his father but negligent in his relations with his kindred, and then concluded a mutually profitable contract with his lord, the proceeds of which he wished to donate to his local church, it is difficult to know what decision might have been reached. Even when one claim seemed to have clear priority over another, such as, for example, the entitlement of a kindred to land that a kindred member had given to his church in excess of the amount he was allowed to give, the matter would be less clear if the party with the weaker claim was also the one with the greater status. It seems safe to suggest that established relationships would take precedence over associations into which a party was attempting to enter—a kindred could probably expect to be able to invalidate an unwanted adoption, for example, or block a kinsman's attempt to enter into an unsuitable clientship—but there are few other guidelines one can point to with confidence.

The assumption behind all of these provisions, however, is that such things can be known and judged—that it is possible to determine whether a contract is profitable or not, or whether a tutor has properly instructed his pupil, or whether a church's entitlement to offerings outweighs the right of a kindred to protect itself from poverty. No doubt the manner in which such questions were adjudicated would appear markedly inconsistent to modern eyes, but this is because our priorities are different. When a man trips over a rake in another person's yard today the identity of the victim is irrelevant to the legal suit that ensues; in medieval law the outcome would hinge directly on the relationship of the victim to the injured man. It is tempting for modern readers to view medieval lawbooks as though they were twentieth-century legal codes and to mistake thereby individual legal provisions for the principles that lay behind them. But this is a failure of the imagination on our part. The Irish jurists reduced principle to provision in order to render comprehensible and predictable the complexities of the social network in which men really operated. They did not intend for us to mistake the endless enumeration of apparently unrelated enactments for law. What they intended to convey were the principles that lay behind the provisions, the fact that who could make what contract was ultimately less important than the context in which the transaction occurred. That we can still do this after eleven hundred years is a tribute to the solidity of their work and the subtlety of their thought.

4. The Hostage-Sureties of Irish Law

Many of the concepts outlined in the previous chapter may seem strange or unfamiliar to us. With the hostage-surety, however, we enter a world that is sadly simultaneously archaic and modern. The practice of holding individuals hostage for the fulfillment of specific legal or political obligations is referred to in Roman law as early as the fifth century B.C.E., when the law of the Twelve Tables allowed creditors to hold their debtor in captivity for sixty days before (perhaps literally) dividing him between themselves in the market square.[1] Hostages were as well the usual guarantors of the political pacts of Republican Rome and its successor states, and in Ireland they remained the primary vehicle through which political alliances or subordination were expressed throughout the twelfth century. Indeed, most societies have, at some point in their history, engaged in this venerable practice. One might wish it otherwise, but the fact that hostage-taking is so prominent a feature of the modern political scene is testimony both to its effectiveness and longevity as an institution.

Irish law of the classical period recognized two different types of hostage-sureties, the *aitire* and the *gíall,* and although the distinctions between them seem gradually to have disappeared after the ninth century, it is the boundaries between their respective spheres of activity that have quite properly preoccupied those who have written on the subject. Thurneysen, in his study of the Irish hostage-sureties incorporated into his 1928 *Die Bürgshaft im irischen Recht*, concluded that the differences between the *aitire* and the *gíall* lay in the nature and responsibilities of the offices that they exercised, and his assessment of this relationship has remained the definitive one.[2] More is known now, however, about the nature of early Irish law than was known at the time Thurneysen wrote and it seems therefore a good point at which to look again at the subject. The differences between these guarantors may have lain not so much in what each actually did, but rather in what each symbolized to those who made use of them. The relationship between the *aitire* and the *gíall* both derived from and reflected, I would argue, the complex structures that governed domestic and political relations in early Ireland; it mirrored not only the reality of Irish polity, but the perceptions and priorities of those who wrote about it as well.

Thurneysen's *gíall* was a standing hostage-surety who originally would have acted only in intertribal affairs, but who, by the time of the compilation of the Old Irish tract on hostage-suretyship, *Di Gnímaib Gíall*, "On the Actions of Hostages," could be appointed to act on behalf of his kindred or tribe in any unexpected legal difficulty, whether between tribes or within the tribe itself.[3] *Gíall*-sureties (plural *géill*) would have been appointed not for specific legal obligations, but rather *ein für allemal*, "once for all occasions," and their obligation to act in any matter that involved their principals distinguished them significantly in Thurneysen's eyes from *aitiri* (singular *aitire*). For *aitiri*, although also hostage-sureties, would have been appointed by contracting parties to handle particular legal or political obligations; after the agreement for which they had been appointed had been fulfilled, *aitiri* would have had no further obligations to the person or tribe who had initially invoked them.[4] Binchy essentially agreed with Thurneysen's assessment in his influential legal glossary to *Críth Gablach*, adding further that *aitiri* might originally have represented an adaptation of the *gíall* to private contractual affairs.[5] Thus, for both Thurneysen and Binchy, the differences between the two Irish hostage-sureties were firmly rooted in the nature of their offices. The *gíall* was originally a political standing surety later adapted for use within the tribe, while the *aitire* was a specifically contractual surety whose responsibilities did not extend beyond the terms of the specific agreement he guaranteed.

Thurneysen's work on the hostage-sureties was grounded in certain textual and historical assumptions, some of which can be challenged on the basis of recent scholarship on the laws. His assessment of the *gíall* relied heavily on the enthusiastic but often ill-informed commentaries of the later Irish jurists, and his dependence on these frequently untrustworthy texts led him to accept certain ideas about the *gíall*'s office that are in some instances contradicted by the testimony of earlier, more reliable sources. It is unlikely, for example, that *géill* were required to pay only a portion of the normal seven *cumal* ransom fee at the end of their period in captivity as he claimed, since that same fee formed part of their compensation.[6]

Thurneysen's reliance on the later jurists, however, affected much more than just his views on specific aspects of the *gíall*'s office. The commentaries seem also to have shaped his entire approach to the subject and to have determined the questions he would and would not ask of his material. His work on the *aitire* did not rely as much on the assertions of the later commentators, but in this case also his conclusions were influenced by certain historical assumptions about the *aitire*'s suretyship that were not imposed on him by the early sources. He never seriously questioned, for example, the commentators' assertion that both the *gíall* and the *aitire* participated in matters of personal obligation within the tribe, although in fact the amount of old evidence for their role in such affairs is minimal.[7] And his picture of the *aitire* as a surety appointed to guarantee specific contractual obligations is difficult to reconcile with the extant sources. A new approach, one less dependent on the work of the later jurists, suggests a rather different picture both of these sureties themselves and of the relationship between them.

It must be admitted at the outset that the sources on this issue are difficult even by the exacting standards of early Irish law. The lone tract on the *gíall* has the distinction of being incomplete, imperfectly preserved, and almost impenetrably obscure. There are two "exemplars" of what remains of this text, the longest and most detailed of which is preserved in a section of manuscript that Binchy has termed "possibly the most unsatisfactory of all the legal vellums."[8] The other surviving version, in manuscript H 3. 18, is little more than a jumble of disembodied fragments and is of interest primarily because of the early (ninth-century) glosses that accompany it.[9] Fortunately, these two manuscripts contain what appears to be roughly the same section of the original tract, although a quick perusal of the whole will convince even the most ardent aficionado of the Irish legal sources that there are greener pastures to be had elsewhere.

The tract appears to be bipartite in structure: the first section concerns the duties and compensation of hostages taken into custody and the second addresses questions arising from the unlawful prosecution of a claim by a plaintiff. There is no indication in the text as to whether the hostage in question would have been a standing surety appointed prior to the commission of the offense; such is the normal pattern of hostage-suretyship, but one of the H 3. 18 glosses implies that the *gíall* might not have been appointed until after the lord had received notification of the offense.[10] The identity of the individual who appointed the hostage or the social unit on behalf of which the *gíall* in question was supposed to act is also unclear. Both text and glosses mention a *muire*, "chief" or "lord," who according to the glosses appoints the *gíall*, and the glosses then further equate this *muire* with the *flaith* or "lord." These terms are, however, themselves ambiguous. *Flaith* is used throughout the lawbooks (*Cáin Aicillne*, for example) to describe the local lord of the kindred, but the *márflaith*, "great lord," mentioned at the beginning of the hostage-surety tract is almost certainly a king.[11] Similarly, though *Cáin Adomnáin* speaks of a *muire* who seems to be at best a local dignitary, the *muiredach* mentioned in the text *Slán nAitire Cairde* is the chief tribal representative in cases of intertribal treaty violations.[12] Elsewhere also the word *muire* (or *muiredach*) itself refers to men of royal rank.[13]

Di Gnímaib Gíall does spell out some of the details of the *gíall*'s office. Hostages taken into custody because of offenses committed by another could be held in captivity by the plaintiff for thirty days. After this period they could release themselves by paying compensation for the offense as well as, if the Old Irish glosses are correct, the usual seven *cumal* ransom fine of the normal Irish freeman. Compensation for the *gíall*'s imprisonment then consisted of at least a cow for every night that he had been detained;[14] the H 3. 18 glosses state further that *géill* could expect to receive with these thirty cows the seven *cumal* ransom fee, and twice the amount they had had to pay to settle the offense. The text also notes that certain (here unspecified) penalties would be charged to plaintiffs who prosecuted their claims unlawfully, and one of the old glosses suggests that such plaintiffs would thereby forfeit their claim to compensation.[15]

One of the most pressing questions raised by this (admittedly fragmentary) tract is whether we have any basis to conclude, or indeed even to suspect, that *géill* ever acted to guarantee personal obligations within the tribe. The late commentaries on which Thurneysen based much of his understanding of the *gíall*'s office speak of his participation in private matters, but the text itself does not. In fact, the opening sentence of the tract, with its unambiguous references to "great lords" and the "tribes" in service to them, must refer to a specifically political and intertribal hostage.[16] Certainly the payments envisaged in the text as the appropriate compensation for a forfeited hostage seem more applicable to a tribal rather than to an individual offense: thirty cows is roughly equivalent to ten *cumala*, and even the *aitire* forfeited as the result of a violation of an intertribal peace treaty received only the seven *cumal* ransom fee and twice the amount of the original obligation.[17] And while it is true, as Thurneysen pointed out, that save for the opening sentence neither the glosses nor the text itself speak in terms of more than one tribe being involved, the evidence is so fragmentary that such an omission cannot be considered of great significance.

The answer to this question is inextricably entangled with the issue of the identity of the *flaith* and the *muire* who are said in the glosses to supervise the procedure. If they were local dignitaries, the *gíall* might indeed have acted in matters of private personal obligation. If, on the other hand, they were tribal officers, or local officers acting on behalf of their kindred in intertribal affairs, then the suretyship of the *gíall* could easily have been confined to the realm of tribal and intertribal obligations.[18] The *flaith* and the *muire* are mentioned together elsewhere as the supervisors of intertribal regulations known as *cánai* (singular, *cáin*) to which tribes committed themselves; in *Cáin Domnaig*, the "Law of Sunday," for example, *flaithi* and *muirig* receive half of the fines paid as the result of a violation of the law.[19] And since we know from elsewhere that the penalties in *cáin* law "advance to the double," as the fines are also said to do in the hostage-surety tract, this seems most likely to be the true context of the tract.[20] In other words, the evidence of this text gives us no reason to believe that *géill* acted in any circumstances other than those deriving from the public and political obligations for which they were primarily known.

Indeed, the only instance in the law tracts in which the *gíall* clearly appears as a guarantor for private personal obligations serves in fact to confirm the essentially political nature of his office. At least by the time of the compilation of the classical law tracts, base clientship did not require a surety to guarantee its mutual conditions and responsibilities.[21] But the Irish word for this relationship, *aicillne*, the verbal noun of *ad-gíallna*, contains as its root the now familiar term *gíall*. This alone might suggest that clientship had once involved the giving of a hostage by a base client to his lord, but there is other evidence also to support this idea. *Críth Gablach* speaks of a *fer gill do gíal(d)naib*, a "man of security for [the king's] base clients," whom Binchy thinks to be a holdover from a period when every client would have confirmed his obligations to his lord by the giving of a hostage.[22] Another law tract mentions a *fer gíallna*, a "man of clientship," who is defined in the late glosses as a guarantor for a contract of clientship, and one of the Old Irish glosses in H 3. 18 remarks that when a client fails to pay the required food-rent to his lord, the *gíall* may make restitution on the client's behalf.[23]

This last text is especially interesting, since it suggests that the relationship between the *gíall* and *aicillne* was still apparent to the jurists of the ninth century. But while it may seem tempting to generalize from the particular here and conclude that because *gíall*-sureties once guaranteed contracts of clientship they must also have acted in other personal obligations as well, such a conclusion would not be warranted. For clientship was not an ordinary private relationship. It was, above all, a relationship of personal and political subordination, one that entailed a loss of personal status for the client, and that enhanced the social and therefore the political standing of the lord. On such a level what seems personal must more rightly be termed political: there is no evidence that the *gíall* was anything other than a surety for the public and political obligations of his principals.

Thurneysen's work on the *gíall* was affected by the late and untrustworthy texts on which he relied; his work on the *aitire* was similarly influenced by the preconceptions with which he approached the study of this guarantor. Thurneysen presumed that because the Old Irish tract on suretyship, *Berrad Airechta*, dealt mostly with the role of sureties in private contractual affairs, the *aitire* must therefore have been one of these contract-sureties, and his suretyship must closely have approximated that of the more conventional *naidm* and *ráth* sureties. It is, however, difficult to reconcile this picture of the *aitire* with the evidence presented in *Berrad Airechta*, as Thurneysen himself seemed in some places to realize.[24] Thurneysen's *aitire* was a *Zahlbürge*, a surety liable for the payment of the debt on the default of his principal. Unlike the other Irish contract-sureties, however, the *aitire* was a hostage-surety; at the conclusion of the contract he swore an oath, the text of which is quoted in *Berrad Airechta*, to surrender himself to the creditor upon the default of the debtor, and to remain in captivity for a set forfeiture period. If at the end of this time the debtor had not yet discharged the debt, the *aitire* ransomed himself, paid the amount owed, and collected his compensation from the defaulting debtor.[25]

Binchy modified this assessment somewhat, maintaining that the archaic binding formulas quoted in *Berrad Airechta* showed the *aitire*'s role as *Zahlbürge* to have been a relatively late development, roughly contemporaneous with the compilation of the tract itself. Because, according to Binchy, this new responsibility of financial *Haftung* eventually rendered unnecessary the *aitire*'s role as a hostage-surety, the *aitire* evolved finally into the much more familiar *ráth*.[26] Both Binchy and Thurneysen agreed, however, that the major difference between the *aitire* and the other two types of Irish surety was the different manner in which they provided security for a contracted debt. The *naidm* used force to compel the debtor to meet his obligations, while the *ráth* paid the debt to the creditor after the debtor had defaulted. The *aitire*, by contrast, pledged his person to secure the contracted debt—an action that encouraged the debtor to pay by threatening to involve him in huge compensation payments—and, by the classical Old Irish period at least, paid the debt himself if the debtor did nevertheless default.

And yet there is something odd about the *aitire*. The legal sources clearly distinguish between the *naidm* and *ráth* sureties on the one hand, and the *aitire* on the other. The phrase *naidm ocus ráth*, which replaced the earlier *mac ocus ráth*, occurs quite frequently in the laws, and it is clear that normally these two sureties would have acted together in a given transaction.[27] They provided in this manner double security for the debt, since if the *naidm* proved unable to force his principal to obey the terms of the contract, the *ráth* would himself discharge the debtor's obligations. The *aitire*, however, stood quite apart; only rarely is he mentioned together with them in the legal sources.[28] Even in the very old *Córus Fíadnaise* tract that has been incorporated into *Berrad Airechta*, where *naidm* and *ráth* sureties are both cited as normal witnesses to contractual arrangements, the *aitire*'s name is conspicuously absent.[29] Binchy attributed the differences between them to their origins; the *naidm* and the *aitire* were, he suggested, the descendants of two very different types of Indo-European personal surety.[30] His hypothesis is intriguing, although it does not explain why the *naidm* and the *aitire* were kept apart in the sources when the *naidm* and the *ráth*, whom he says evolved from the *aitire*, were not. And it does not in any case seem a sufficient explanation for the continuing distinctions made in the laws between the *aitire* and his ostensible contractual colleagues.

The special status of the *aitire* is also apparent in the binding oath (*lugae, luige*) through which he committed himself to his suretyship. The *aitire* was the only surety to bind himself to his obligations through an oath; the *naidm* was appointed and bound directly by the contracting parties, and the *ráth* undertook his suretyship by appointing *naidm* sureties to the debtor.[31] The substance of the *aitire*'s oath is particularly revealing:

> toing do dia fondfiad-sa . . . gnimu aitire hi taig frim-sa ocus frisin fer-so. . . .
> Tossimmuirr techta cirt[32] coir di oghi in gnima inntindnaigh cach ara thaig,

co saigith ocus inmbleogain . . . co nic cen dichell, co noige neich inothasa a rreir brithemon asberam . . . cia sa cia dam i ndiul[33] co scor. Toing do dia nach focre fondotcerthar[34] . . . nach dal nach aidbden . . . dosnimmuir do nirt. . . . sed taurbuith do bais no galair no thaulnaidmand tuath. . . . Toing do dia doindraigi snadhugud cleirich no laich co hairm i neipertar frit do dal . . . na digentar dít munas denu-sa nó muna déna mo fer dala conmeisur. Toing do dia neime, nach airm indra indermill do gnimu co agae notgeibhi[35] . . . besaib aitire[36] degmosaigi degmoferae fir, nad ela, dechmoheiren.[37]

Swear to God that you will fulfill[38] . . . the responsibilities of the *aitire*-suretyship into which you enter, as against me and as against this man. . . . That you will compel them according to what pertains to proper justice, [fulfilling] completely the responsibilities that each person for whom you act as surety gives [to you], by enforcing [the claim], and "milking,"[39] . . . by making payment without neglect, by fulfilling any [responsibility] that "reaches" you according to the decision of the judge that we appoint . . . whoever may enforce [the claim], whoever may acknowledge [judgment?], by payment [of the debt, thus] "unyoking" [the contract]. Swear to God that any summons by which you may be summoned . . . any meeting [and] any arrangement . . . that you will enforce them with your strength . . . except [if you are prevented by] a legal exemption [accorded to you] because of your death or your sickness or [your obligation to perform the duties associated with] an immediate *naidm*-suretyship of tribes.[40] . . . Swear to God that you will undertake the safe-conduct of a cleric or a layman to the place in which your [legal] meeting is announced to you . . . [that] it (the responsibility of your office?) will not be removed from you unless I remove it or unless my legal agent, whom I will appoint, should remove it. Swear to God of heaven [that] wherever an obligation[41] may "reach" your responsibilities [as surety] until [the end of the established] time period, you will undertake it . . . in accordance with the customs of an *aitire* who best enforces, who best carries out what is just, who does not evade [his responsibilities and] who best pays.

What is most noticeable about this oath and what distinguishes it dramatically from the formula recited to the *ráth* at the undertaking of his suretyship is the complete absence of references to the specific places, times, and people of the contract. There is no mention of the date on which payment is to be made, nor of the place to which it should be brought.[42] Indeed, the oath above suggests that the *aitire* could expect to receive more than one summons and that such a summons might come at any time.[43] The *aitire* did swear to act as surety until the end of a fixed period of time, but nothing in the text suggests that this period coincided with the ending of a particular obligation or debt. Even more puzzling is the uncertainty regarding the contracting parties with respect to whom the *aitire* would be expected to undertake his suretyship. The preposition *fri*, "against," is used primarily in the suretyship texts with reference to the "creditor" of the transaction, while the preposition *ar*, "for," is used with reference to the "debtor."[44] The oath above would seem therefore to envisage two "creditors" ("as against me and as against this man," and possibly, "judge that *we* appoint") and an unspecified number of "debtors" ("each person for whom you act as surety"). What is most curious, however, is that neither the identity of the "debtor" nor of the eventual enforcer of the contract seems to be known ("cleric or layman," "whoever may acknowledge," "whoever may enforce"). This markedly ambiguous terminology does not seem appropriate for the binding oath of a surety guaranteeing a particular obligation; nothing in these passages necessarily indicates that *aitiri* would have involved themselves in private contractual arrangements at all.

Clues to the identity of the *aitire* of *Berrad Airechta*—called in that text the *aitire luigi*, "the *aitire*-surety of an oath," because of his binding formula—lie in those legal texts that treat of the *aitire* who stood surety for the fulfillment of specifically intertribal obligations. One of these texts, *Slán nAitire Cairde*, "The Immunity of *Aitire*-sureties of *Cairde*-treaties," was edited and translated along with *Berrad Airechta* by Thurneysen in his *Bürgschaft*. This short tract describes the *aitire* appointed by his own tribe or kindred to guarantee compensation for any breaches committed by them of an intertribal peace treaty, known technically as a *cairde*. *Slán nAitire Cairde* tells us that the *aitiri* who enforced these pacts had been appointed prior to any breaches of the treaty, and it therefore seems likely that they would have been sworn to their duties by the overking and the tribal king at the time the treaty itself was concluded.[45]

Responsibility for the prosecution of claims arising from violations of the treaty lay first of all with the *muiredaig* (singular *muiredach*), enforcing officers who, like the *aitire*, had apparently been designated prior to the commission of the offense. Each of the tribes bound by the *cairde* had at least one such enforcing officer.[46] Once the treaty had been broken by the criminal actions of one of the members of another tribe, the *muiredach* of the injured tribe would enter the territory of the offender and seek out the *aitire chairdi*. He would inform the *aitire* of the crime, and then he and his men, accompanied by the *aitire*, would go to the guilty kindred or kindred-member and demand compensation for the offense. If the guilty parties agreed to make payment, all would be settled. If they refused to provide suitable compensation, the *muiredach* would take the *aitire* hostage in pledge for the debt. The *aitire* would then remain in the custody of the *muiredach* until the end of a set forfeiture period, the length of which is not defined in this particular text.[47] If at the end of this period the debt had not yet been paid, the *aitire* then lapsed like any inanimate gage and thus became the personal "property" of the *muiredach*. The *aitire* could regain his freedom by giving a gage for his seven *cumal* ransom fee to the *muiredach*; once freed, the *aitire* had then to pay this ransom fee and the full amount of the original debt. He became thereby entitled to collect twice the amount of the debt and his seven *cumala* from the guilty kindred.[48] If, however, the surety had himself been negligent and had failed to take action after having been notified two or three times of a breach of the *cairde*, he would have to redeem his own forfeited suretyship.[49]

Slán nAitire Cairde says nothing about any further compensation beyond the payment of the ransom fine and the doubling of the original debt that a defaulting kindred might owe to the *aitire*. There are, however, two short passages from the H 3. 18 glosses that suggest that additional compensation might be due to the aggrieved surety:

> Slan cairde .i. ma dollece nech forsin aitaire fiachu cairdi do er[aic] (?) dia chinn, is rath cin athchor sin forsan fine mana errither fo cétoir cona meth coir, nibi rath for ceile a meth-sin[50] ond flaith.[51]

> The compensation of a *cairde*—that is, if anyone should cause the *aitire* to pay the fines [for a breach of] a *cairde* on his behalf, that [becomes] a fief [for which food rent is due from] the kindred[52] that is not (cannot be) returned unless [the fines are] paid immediately with their proper doubling-fine; that doubling-fine [itself] is not [considered as] a fief on a client from the lord.

This passage is remarkable for its use of the legal terminology of clientship.[53] *Rath* here has its specifically legal meaning of "fief," a grant of stock given by a lord to his client in return for which food-rent is due. The gloss would seem therefore to impose additional penalties on a debtor who defaulted on the original debt and then delayed payment of the compensation due to his *aitire*. Once the *aitire* had paid his own ransom fee and the debt, the offender was obliged to pay the ransom fine, the debt, and the doubling-fine immediately to the *aitire*; if he delayed, the payments that had been made by the *aitire*, with the exception of the doubling-fine itself,[54] were treated as if they were a grant of stock that had been made by the surety to the defaulting debtor, and for which the debtor would now owe food-rent to the *aitire*.⁵⁵ The fact that the clause disallows the *athchor*, "return of a fief without financial penalty," shows that it is to a fief of unfree clientship that this clause refers, since the unpenalized return of a fief was possible only in free clientship.⁵⁶

The existence of such a fief is supported also by another gloss from the H 3. 18 manuscript:

> Rath naitire .i. aitire cairdi son bis tar cenn thuaithi iarna aitite ocus iarna tabuirt a slain sed bid aitire techtae. Cadead-side? ni anse, tanusi tuisig son du a⁵⁷ natamar dano tanisi la tuaith uili; ni didiu icas-[s]ide fri cach is⁵⁸ rath fair ocus ni athcuirither a frithise.⁵⁹

> The fief of an *aitire*, i.e. that is [the fief] of an *aitire chairdi* who [acts as surety] on behalf of his tribe, [which fief is given] after he has been acknowledged, and after he has been given his compensation, provided that he is a proper *aitire*. What are those [fiefs]? Not difficult, that is [the fief] of the tanist⁶⁰ of the chief [of the tribe] where he is acknowledged, moreover, as tanist by all the tribe; anything then that that person pays in respect of each person is a fief upon [the offender] and [cannot] be returned.

Thurneysen suggested that one should read *ría*, "before," or *cen*, "without," for *íar*, "after";⁶¹ such an emendation is not, however, necessary if one understands that the payment made by the *aitire* was treated as a fief even after he had received his compensation because the offender had previously delayed the payment of that compensation.

Perhaps the most interesting aspect of this particular gloss is the information it provides on the identity of the *aitire chairdi*. The tanist would be a particularly effective intertribal guarantor; he was likely wealthy enough to be able to pay the fines demanded of him, and his importance within the tribe would encourage even the most recalcitrant of debtors to pay up as quickly as possible. It is perhaps significant that the prior, the steward, and the cook, individuals of comparable importance in any medieval monastery, are named in *Cáin Adomnáin* as the *aitiri* for a chief-church.⁶² The high status of the *aitire chairdi* is further suggested by an early poem on the rights and privileges of the Airgialla federation. The Airgialla were originally a group of unrelated tribes living in the region of what is now counties Londonderry, Armagh, Fermanagh, and Monaghan. These tribes had, at an early period, been subject to the Ulaid, but when the Uí Néill drove the Ulaid from Emain Macha into the northeastern part of Ireland, probably in the fifth century, the Airgialla accepted the change of overlordship. A new genealogy was invented for them by which they were proclaimed to be of royal descent, equal in blood to their overlords the Uí Néill, but barred from the kingship by their part in an ancient kin-slaying. This is the relationship described in the poem, at a period sometime after C.E. 600 but before the end of the eighth century.[63]

The poem does not actually use the term *cairde* in its account of the relationship between the Airgialla and the Uí Néill, but it does refer to the month-long period granted in *Críth Gablach* for the enforcement of claims within a *cairde*, and the arrangement is guaranteed through *aitiri*.[64] The men named in the poem as *aitiri* were all early kings of the Airgialla tribes—Bécc mac Cúanu of the Uí Thuirtri, Cairpre Dam Aircit of the Uí Chremthainn, Eógan mac Níalláin of the Uí Níalláin sept of the Airthir, and Máel Bressail mac Máel Dúin of the Mugdorna.[65] Most of them are sixth-century figures, but there is nothing to indicate that the poet was working from a genuinely archaic source. Most significant is the poet's assumption that the position of *aitire* was likely to have been occupied by a member of the royal family and his confirmation of what the second of the H 3. 18 glosses suggests, that the *aitire chairdi* exercised his suretyship on behalf of his tribe and not merely on behalf of his kindred.

The *aitire chairdi* of these texts seems therefore very similar to the *aitire* of *Berrad Airechta*. Both helped to enforce the claim, surrendered themselves as hostages on default, and ransomed themselves after a set forfeiture period by the payment of the ransom fine. Both paid the amount owed and became thereby entitled to collect twice that amount in compensation from the debtor. And most importantly, both could be called on at any time to act for any of the people on whose behalf they had undertaken their suretyship; this must be the explanation for the frequent meetings referred to in the oath of the *aitire* quoted in *Berrad Airechta*. It should not be surprising that these two *aitiri* seem as similar to one another as they do, for the *aitire chairdi* was an *aitire luigi*: the compiler of *Berrad Airechta* remarks, in an important historical aside, "it is in respect of a *cairde* that there first was an *aitire luigi*."[66]

Whether the compiler's claim that the *aitire chairdi* was the first type of *aitire luigi* is historically accurate is not the issue; more significant is the fact that his remark suggests that the *aitire chairdi* was not the only type of *aitire luigi* known to him at the time he was writing. In other words, the *aitire luigi* must, by the time of the compilation of *Berrad Airechta*, have occurred in situations other than those related strictly to *cairde-*

treaties. The original difficulty thus remains; if we understand the *aitire luigi* to be a surety of private contractual arrangements as Thurneysen and others have done, we still have to explain the special status of the *aitire* in the legal sources and the peculiarities of his binding oath. If, on the other hand, we reject the notion of such a contract-*aitire* because of these difficulties, we have still to explain in what circumstances other than claims arising from the violation of a *cairde* an *aitire luigi* might have been used.

To understand the *aitire* of *Berrad Airechta* it is necessary to turn to yet another type of *aitire* and to yet other sources. These are the *cánai* (singular *cáin*), secular or ecclesiastical ordinances pledged by overkings on tribes subject to them.[67] Since a *cáin*'s authority within a given tribe derived solely from the king's pledge to abide by it, it is likely that normally it would have been valid only for the period of that king's rule.[68] *Cánai* were in this respect quite different from provisions of customary law, although their validity could be and often was extended by periodic renewals. Unfortunately, only two ecclesiastical *cánai* survive.[69] *Cáin Domnaig*, the "Law of Sunday," is a tract from the first half of the eighth century that sets out in detail the regulations and penalties associated with the observance of the sanctity of Sunday. Closely related to it is the "Epistle of Jesus," which also deals with sabbatarian matters. The "Epistle" is said to have been brought from Rome to Ireland by Conall mac Coelmáine, a sixth-century abbot of Inis Coel, although the text as we have it is probably to be dated to the first half of the ninth century.[70] The other extant *cáin* is the famous *Cáin Adomnáin*, a tract that, as it stands now, seeks to protect clerics, women, and children from violence. The language of the first half of this text is relatively late, but the last half of the text, which is generally regarded as the original law of Adomnán, has no linguistic forms that would be inconsistent with the year 697, the date at which it is first mentioned in the Irish annals.[71]

Both of these *cánai* were guaranteed primarily through *aitiri*, although in neither text is the enforcement procedure clearly outlined. *Cáin Adomnáin* says virtually nothing about the duties associated with the office of the *aitire*, remarking only that he acted on behalf of his kindred.[72] *Cáin Domnaig* is more forthcoming, although the density of its prose makes it difficult to reconstruct the procedure involved. This *cáin* depended at least partly for its enforcement on private individuals who, in the course of their own legitimate activities, observed others in violation of the law.[73] There may have also been officers appointed specifically to enforce the *cáin* who acted alongside these private individuals. Common sense alone would suggest this, since *Cáin Domnaig* allocates half of the fines collected to various unidentified *flaithi*, "lords," and *muirig*, and these lords would presumably have had some way to guarantee that they would eventually receive the sums due to them. Both *Cáin Adomnáin* and the "Epistle of Jesus" mention *rechtairi*, "stewards"; the "Epistle" actually refers to them as the *rechtairi na cána*, "stewards of the law," so they must have been appointed specifically for the occasion.[74] *Cáin Domnaig* does not mention such stewards by name, but it is conceivable that the *fir thobaig*, "men of levying," appointed by the tribe from every kindred to prosecute claims arising from *Cáin Domnaig* are identical with these *rechtairi*.[75] Their name links them also with the *áes tobaig*, "people of levying," who are mentioned in the "Epistle," but the "Epistle" does not say whether the *rechtairi* were considered to have formed part of this group.[76] One would expect that at least some of these *rechtairi* would have been men from outside the tribe, since the overking under whose authority the *cáin* had been accepted would certainly have expected a share of the profits arising from it.

Once a transgression had been "identified" by a private individual or by the *rechtaire*, the accused man was, according to *Cáin Domnaig*, required to give a gage immediately for payment of the four-heifer fine if he did not wish to contest the charge. If he denied the charge and demanded judgment, the "identifer" of the violation then bound him before a secular or clerical judge of the tribe, or in the presence of an overking, to answer the accusation made against him.[77] Those who were to prosecute the claim would then seek out the *aitire*, and all would go afterward to the accused man.[78] If the accused was present when they arrived, he was obliged either to give a gage to guarantee that he would submit to judgment or else to allow the *aitire* to be seized and maintenance charges to begin. If he was not present, and the *aitire* had been taken after midday, maintenance charges would not begin until the following day. Once the accused man had given his gage, judgment would be passed on him immediately, unless either he or the *aitire* preferred that judgment be delayed. Either was entitled to a respite of three days, but in such a case the *aitire* was taken hostage, and the accused man became liable for his surety's maintenance charges. The prosecutors also were entitled to a three day delay if they wished the time to obtain evidence to support their charge, and then the final verdict would be given on the fifth day, and the fines would have to be paid by the tenth.[79]

Of the fines collected, half would go to the prosecutors, half to the aforementioned lords, and one-seventh from the whole to the *aitiri*. If the offender refused to meet his legal obligations, the *aitire* was obliged to pay the fine, to pay any maintenance charges, and to "pledge."[80] Although the gradual forfeiture of an *aitire* of a *cáin* is never mentioned in either of these texts, our experience with the surety of *Berrad Airechta* and of *Slán nAitire Cairde* would suggest that this "pledge" was for the seven *cumal* ransom fine.[81] If indeed the *aitire* had to make any such payments, his compensation was twice the amount of his loss, which is the same as the compensation associated in other texts with the *aitire luigi* and the *aitire chairdi*. If, on the other hand, an *aitire* defaulted on his own suretyship, the prosecutor had the choice of pursuing the claim through distraint, a "cross," a *gíall*, or through a "kinsman" *aitire* chosen by the *muire*.[82]

The *aitire* of these *cánai* thus seems very similar to the other *aitiri* we have encountered. All helped to enforce the claim, acted as hostages for the amount owed, paid the claim for the defaulting offender, and received twice what they had paid as compensation. The major difference between them would seem to be the group on whose behalf they undertook their suretyship; the *aitire* of a *cáin* acted on behalf of his kindred, the *aitire* of a *cairde* on behalf of his tribe. This picture of the *aitire* of a *cáin* suggests an obvious solution to our original question: the nature of the office undertaken by the *aitire* described in *Berrad Airechta*. For if the *aitire luigi* to which the text refers is an *aitire* for a *cáin*, the references in the text to several different judicial "meetings" and to the several different "contracting parties" would be easily comprehensible. The "two men" with respect to whom the *aitire* undertook his office would in this case have been the overking and the tribal king in a secular *cáin*, or the overking and the synodal official in an ecclesiastical *cáin* (or the kindred leader and these various officials), and these would presumably have been the lords to whom the revenues arising from the *cáin* would have gone. The otherwise obscure references to the *aitire*'s "immediate *naidm*ship of tribes" would refer to the *aitire*'s duty to enforce the *cáin* on behalf of both his own tribe and the tribe of the overking. And the fact that the *aitire* would act only with respect to transgressions against a *cáin* or a *cairde* would explain why the legal sources consistently distinguish between the *aitire* and the other contractual sureties. If it is to the *aitire* for a *cáin* that *Berrad Airechta* refers, *aitiri* need not have operated in private contractual matters at all.

There is, however, another possibility. The *aitire* might indeed have acted, as Thurneysen and others have suggested, as a guarantor for private contractual obligations. Certainly, such a surety would better fit the context of *Berrad Airechta*, since the rest of the text is devoted to such transactions. If so, however, he cannot have been the sort of surety described by Binchy and Thurneysen, a surety given by a debtor to a creditor at the time of the creation of a contractual obligation. He must have been rather a standing officer, nominated by his kindred and appointed by his tribal king to represent his kindred in affairs for which no surety or other guarantee existed. Only in this manner can one understand the frequent judicial meetings and the unidentified claimants mentioned in his oath.

Such an interpretation would also explain the distinction made in the law tracts between the *aitire* and the other personal sureties. For the *naidm* was a true contract surety; he was appointed to handle one specific contract only, and he himself was the sole supervisor and the ultimate witness of the agreement. The *aitire*, by contrast, would have responded to claims arising out of unexpected deeds or occurrences, situations in which the terms and amounts of the obligation would not have been known in advance and in which the participation of an arbitrator or tribal judge might therefore have been required. Claims arising from accidental or intentional wounding, for example, where the fines might need to be established or where the offender might wish to protest the charge made against him, would seem particularly suited to this type of suretyship; it is significant that the *aitire* is associated with exactly these offenses in other law tracts.[83] In claims of this "unexpected" nature, one of the *aitire*'s most important duties would presumably have been that of accompanying his principal to the place of judgment, and these are exactly the functions we find him fulfilling both in *Berrad Airechta* and in *Cóic Conara Fugill*.[84] That a distinction would be made in the sources between transactions that did or did not require the involvement of legal professionals might seem unlikely, and perhaps even anachronistic, because of the idea of a tribal "judicial system" it presupposes; it is, however, a distinction that *Berrad Airechta* itself makes consciously and clearly.[85]

Thurneysen's original assessment of the two Irish hostage-sureties must therefore be revised. It is still possible that *gíall*-sureties acted to guarantee private obligations other than those arising from the inherently "political" relationship of clientship, but there is no early evidence to support this suggestion. And even if one accepts, with Binchy and Thurneysen, that the *aitire* did operate in private contractual affairs, one cannot accept their picture of a guarantor who stood surety only for those specific agreements for which he had been appointed. Rather, the *aitire*, like the *giall*, must have been a standing surety who engaged himself through his oath to act in any unexpected claims made against his principals. In fact, the basic nature of the offices exercised by the *aitire* and the *giall* would appear to have been exactly the same, which must raise again the question of the differences between them.

Thurneysen's implicit solution to this dilemma, that the *giall* was a standing surety and the *aitire* was not, now seems unlikely. And Binchy's suggestion that the *aitire* was a type of *giall* adapted for use in private obligations is similarly unsatisfying. Not only is it premised on the assumption that the *aitire* did in fact act in private matters, it also cannot explain why the *aitire* should ever have replaced the *giall*, if *géill* could themselves operate in the private realm, as Binchy also thought they once had done. Nor is it clear why the *aitire* should be the guarantor to act to guarantee the very public, very political *cairde* treaty. The solution must lie elsewhere, outside the responsibilities associated with the respective offices of *aitire* and *giall* and outside any division between the tribal and intertribal spheres of endeavor.

Since *aitire* and *giall* sureties most frequently appear in the intertribal context, it is to the intertribal pacts discussed above that we should turn for a possible solution to the mystery. The exact nature of the Irish *cairde* has long eluded historians, not least because of the potential ambiguities inherent in the term. *Cairde*, literally "kinship, friendship," cognate with Welsh *kerennyd*, is an abstract noun formed from the common Old Irish word *carae*, "kinsman," and it can sometimes be difficult to distinguish the more general meaning from the technical legal term.[86] It is usually translated as "peace treaty," although as Binchy noted, this translation can itself describe a wide range of relationships, from the simple armistice referred to in *Críth Gablach* to a much more substantial alliance.[87]

There are, however, two (admittedly propagandistic) texts that purport to describe the arrangements made between allied tribes that may give us some insight into the manner in which this elusive compact was conceptualized. The poem on the Airgialla tribal federation, to which reference has already been made, was written on behalf of the Airgialla to affirm the high status that the Airgialla claimed to possess and to outline the privileges due to them from their overlords, the Uí Néill, in virtue of their status.[88] In this poem the Airgialla agree to provide military service to the king of the Uí Néill, but they limit this service to a period of three fortnights once every three years, and in the third fortnight they incur no liability for whatever mischief they might do. They provide entertainment for an Uí Néill king who passes through their territory unless his company "extends to hundreds," but they claim a *cumal* in compensation for any night an Uí Néill army camps in their territory. And although they agree to "rise before" (in order to honor) the kings of the Uí Néill, they are careful to emphasize that the Airgialla and the Uí Néill are "equal in nobility of race."[89]

Similar privileges are claimed by the kings of three Munster tribes, the Uí Fidgenti, the Eóganacht Locha Léin (Irluachair), and the Eóganacht Raithlind, in a probably early ninth-century *frithfolaid* tract.[90] This text actually uses the term *cairde* in its description of the relationship between these three tribes and the king of Cashel, and the relationship itself accords in almost every detail with the agreement outlined in the Airgialla poem.[91] The three Munster kings agree to "rise before" the king of Cashel, and to participate with him in hostings but only against Munster's traditional enemies, Leinster and the North, in order to "defend the honor of Munster." Indeed the king of Cashel must pay seven *cumala* to them or to their heirs after the hosting in return for the services that they had provided. And if they accept a fief of property from the king of Cashel, they must pay rent for it for as long as they hold it, but they are free to return it at any time they wish.[92]

The similarity between the relationships described in these two sources, and the nature of the obligations and privileges of which these associations were composed, suggest that it is to relationships of tribal "free clientship" that both of these texts refer. Early Irish polity mirrored the domestic relations between clients and lords; just as clients stood in privileged (free) or unprivileged (base or unfree) relationships with their lords, so tribes were said to stand with respect to their political overlords.[93] The analogy is conscious and explicit in many Irish texts. The genealogies themselves refer frequently to "free" and "unfree" tribes, and even to *aithech-thúatha*, "rent-payer, plebeian-tribes."[94] The Airgialla poem speaks directly of their "clientship" with the Uí Néill (§23), and the obligations owed by them to the Uí Néill and by the Munster tribes to the king of Cashel are precisely those owed by a free client to his lord—personal military service, rent on the fief, and "rising."[95] Even the terminology employed in the *frithfolaid* tract is the technical legal terminology of clientship; the Munster tribes claim the privilege of *athchor*, the unpenalized separation from a lord allowed only to free clients.[96] Such then was the nature of the relationship between free client tribes and their overlords, and it is important to note that, as in free clientship, the high status of both participants was in no way diminished by the terms of the clientship.

To remark that the free clientship relationship enjoyed by these tribes was to some extent at least defined or enhanced by the *cairde* that existed between them is not, of course, to demonstrate conclusively that the *cairde* was the means by which such privileged relationships would be achieved. It does, however, raise the possibility that such might have been the case—an interpretation that would accord very well with the general genealogical principle that the degree of "freedom" possessed by a given tribe derived from their genealogical proximity to one of the major royal lineages of Ireland. (As has been noted already, the literal meaning of the word *cairde* is "kinship.") One of the many prose passages in the Book of Leinster collection states the principle directly:

> Ic Cund trá fodlaiter sáerchlanna Síl Chuind et it fortuatha Síl Chuind cach óen nach berar genelach co Cond eter nóebu ocus rígu amal atát Lugni ocus Delmna ocus Galenga ocus Cianachta. . . . Ic Ailill Olom fodlaiter sáerclanna Muman ocus cach óen nád berar genelach co Ailill Olom it fortuatha Síl nEchach Múmo amal atát hÉraind ocus Ciarraigi et cetera.[97]

> At Conn then are the free tribes of Síl Chuind divided, and each one whose genealogy is not brought back to Conn, both saints and kings, are the alien (unfree) tribes of Síl Chuind, as are the Luigne and the Delbna and the Gailenga and the Cianachta. . . . At Ailill Olom are the free tribes of Munster divided, and each one whose genealogy is not brought back to Ailill Olom—they are the alien tribes of Síl nEchach of Munster, as are the Érainn and the Ciarraige, etc.

The *cairde*, "kinship," claimed by the Airgialla with the Uí Néill was certainly close; they were "cousin" tribes, descended directly from Conn Cétchathach and Cairpre Liphechar (see Diagram 1). Similarly, the kings of the Eóganacht Raithlind and of the Eóganacht Locha Léin claimed descent from Conall Corc, the direct ancestor of the king of Cashel, while the Uí Fidgenti took their genealogy back to the Eógan Már from whom the royal tribes of Cashel took their name (see Diagram 2). Sometimes one can even catch the genealogists in the act of manipulating their pedigrees in order to ensure that a "free" tribe will have the proper descent, as when they shamelessly attach the Síl mBairr, one of the "free tribes" of the

Diagram 1: THE AIRGIALLA AND THE UÍ NÉILL*

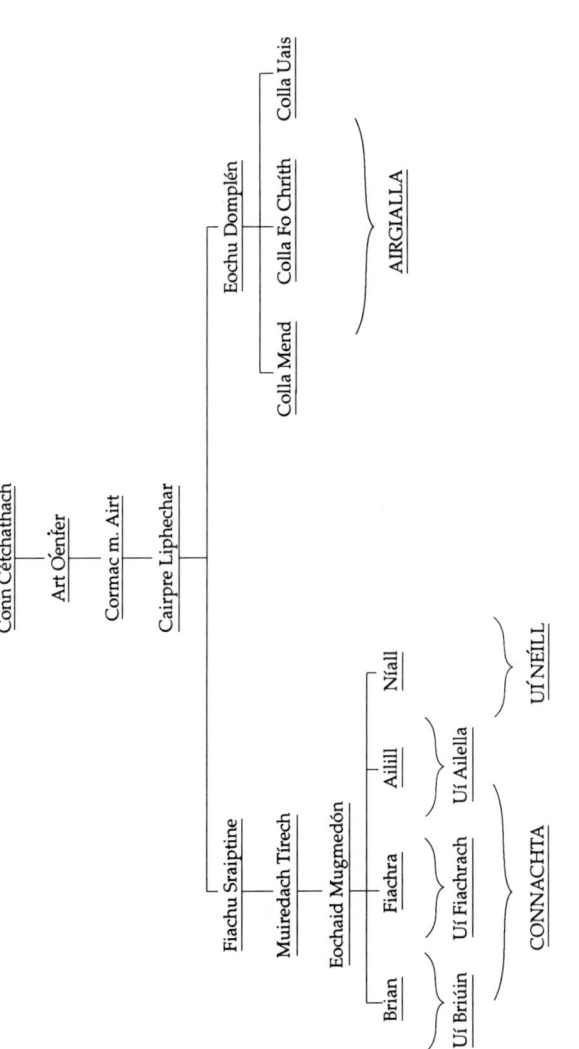

*Source: CGH, pp. 130-131; and see also Irish Kings, p. 280.

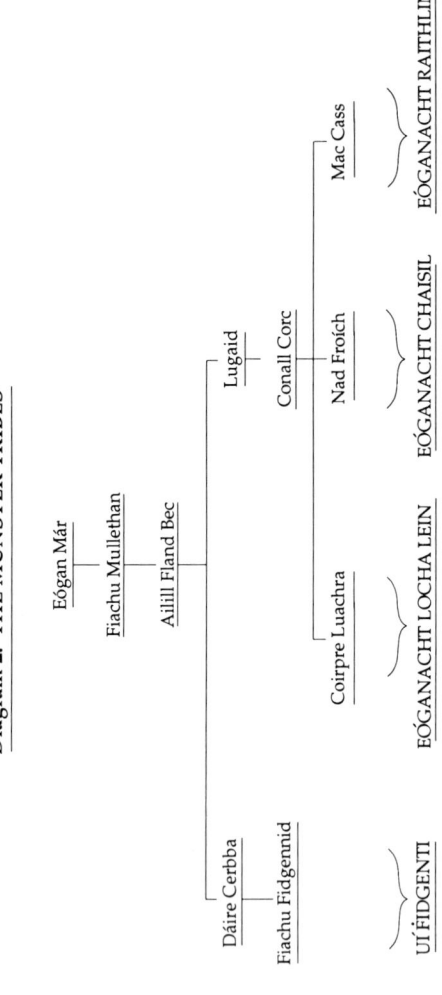

Diagram 2: THE MUNSTER TRIBES*

*Source: CGH, pp. 195-196; and see Irish Kings, pp. 291-296.

Loíchsi, to the ruling royal line (see Diagram 3).⁹⁸ A *cairde* could thus express not only the free and privileged relationship between two tribes, but the genealogical reasons for which such a relationship was appropriate as well. And whether or not it was *cairde* that actually established the relationship of tribal free clientship, it seems that the relationship enjoyed by tribes allied by virtue of such treaties was one characterized by privilege and high status.

If *cairde* was the technical legal term for the pact that cemented an agreement of tribal free clientship—or if such treaties were at least normal components of such relationships—then tribal base clientship may have been similarly associated with (and perhaps even created by) the secular intertribal ordinances known as *cánai*. The phrase *cáin ocus cairde* is a commonplace in the legal texts;⁹⁹ often the sources speak of *cáin* or *cairde*, as if they were two complementary but mutually exclusive political relationships in which a tribe might expect to find itself.¹⁰⁰ The ambiguity of the term itself complicates matters, however, for *cáin* is one of the most elusive words in an already elusive language. Historians who have written on the subject have invariably had to accept two separate definitions for the term, one of which is, quite simply, "law." This is probably its meaning in *Cáin Adomnáin* and *Cáin Domnaig*, religious or moral ordinances promulgated by overkings in consultation with the church. The term can also apply to non-legislative Irish law. Many of the most important tracts of native law use the term in their titles: *Cáin Aicillne*, the "Law of Base Clientship," *Cáin Sóerraith*, the "Law of Free-Fief," *Cáin Lánamna*, the "Law of Couples," and *Cáin Íarraith*, the "Law of Fosterage" are all examples of this type of usage. This general use of the word seems to have no relationship either to *cairde* (as above in the stereotyped expression *cáin ocus cairde*) or to base client relationships.

The second definition is potentially more relevant to our inquiry. It is usually given by historians as "tax" or "tribute,"¹⁰¹ but the examples on which this definition is based cover a wide range of situations, almost all of which carry connotations of the domestic or political subordination that was the essence of the base clientship relationship. In the tract on the exploitation of water rights the word *cáin* is used to describe certain legal "servitudes" from which heirs could not free themselves because their fathers and grandfathers had acknowledged them.¹⁰² The tract on honor-price, *Díre*, refers explicitly to the *cáin* of base clientship; the relationship between fosterfathers and fostersons is similar, it says, *fri cain flatha ocus a celi. ocus fri cain neclaise ocus a manac*,¹⁰³ "to the *cáin* of a lord and his

Diagram 3: THE LOÍCHSI AND THE SÍL MBAIRR[1]

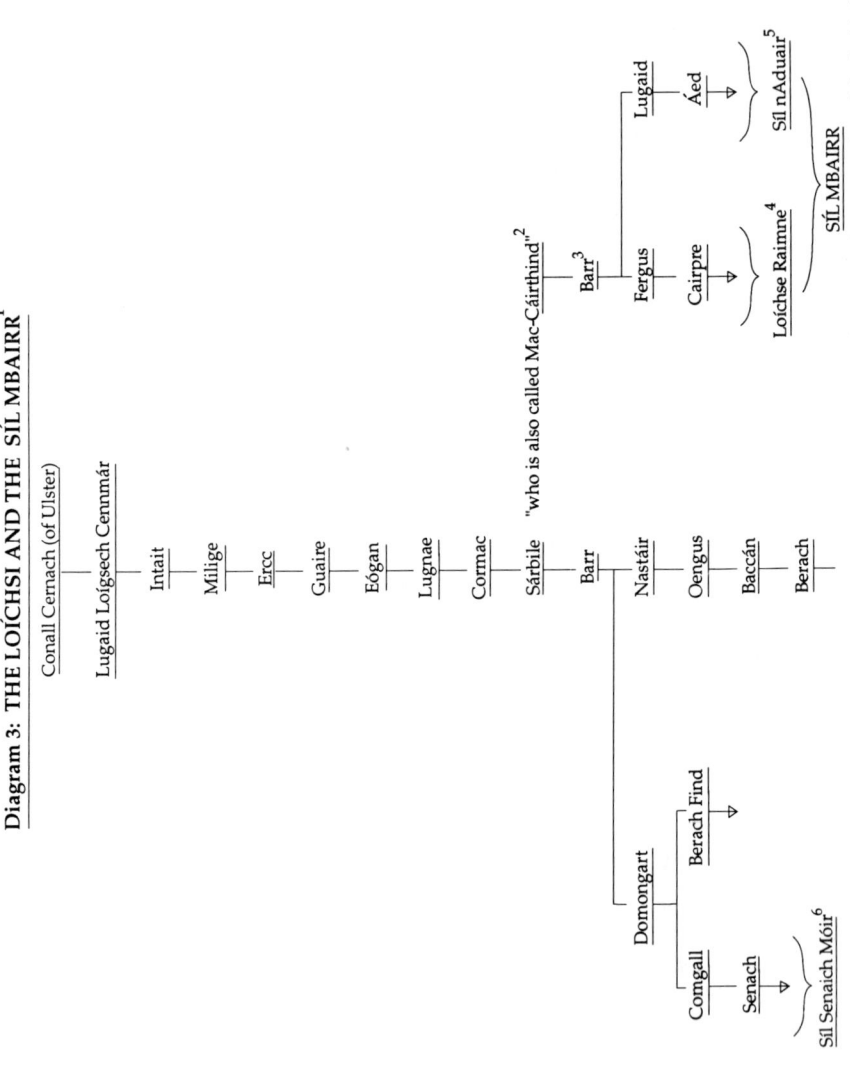

Diagram 3: THE LOÍCHSI AND THE SÍL MBAIRR (cont'd)

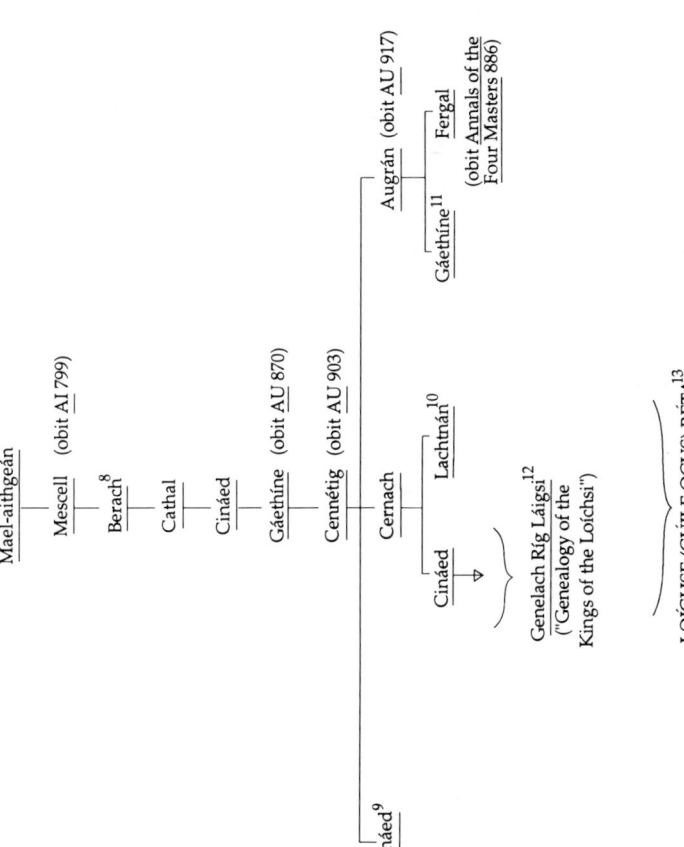

Please refer to pp. 300–301 for Diagram 3 notes 1–13.

base client, and to the *cáin* of a church and its [unfree] monastic client." In documents dealing with intertribal affairs the term is clearly associated with political subordination. The propagandistic "saint's document" known as "MacArddae's Synod," for example, which Francis John Byrne has dated to the first half of the ninth century, depicts the beleaguered king of the Eóganacht Locha Léin being informed by the formerly subordinate Ciarraige that he must [re?]-impose his *cáin* over four other west Munster tribes before the Ciarraige will consent to send their hostages to him.[104] The genealogical origin legend of the Loíchse Réta, though suspiciously similar to the origin tale of another Leinster tribal federation, the Fothairt, claims that the Loíchse Réta are *cen cháin*, "without *cáin*," with respect to the overking of Leinster.[105] Because the Loíchse Réta had, with their military skill, defended Leinster against a Munster threat at some point in prehistory, they claimed to have won Mag Réta for themselves and their heirs, and *arin fochun-sa dlegait na sóere-se*,[106] "for this reason they are entitled to this freedom."

It is significant that in these political contexts, *cáin* is often associated directly with many of the duties and obligations that characterize base clientship. The Loíchse Réta claim the right to take from the seven Loíchsi tribes of Leinster *a fecht ocus a slógad, a cáin ocus a cobach, a cís ocus a mbés*,[107] "their military service and their hosting, their *cáin* and their tribute, their tax[es] and their food-rent." According to the *Genemain Aeda Sláine* preserved in the manuscript *Lebor na hUidre*, "Tara of the kings" held the *cána ocus smachta ocus císa*,[108] "*cánai* and tributes and taxes," of all of the men of Ireland. And in the late story "The Siege of Druim Damhghaire," the oppressive druids of Cormac mac Airt are said to have subjugated the men of Munster by their magical arts, levying their *císa ocus a c(h)ána*,[109] "taxes and their *cánai*." Examples of this association of *cáin* with other terms associated with base clientship are numerous.[110] It may be that *cánai* were in fact the tributary ordinances through which relationships of base clientship were actually established; even if this is not the case, however, it is evident that the term *cáin* has, in many of the contexts in which it appears, strong implications of political subordination.

Turning once again to the question of the relationship between the *aitire* and *gíall* sureties, it is apparent that many of the characteristics that distinguished the *cairde* from the *cáin* are applicable as well to these two hostage-sureties. The *aitire*, whose name comes from the preposition *eter*, "between," and literally means the "between-man,"[111] is never associated in any classical Old Irish text with political subordination; as we have seen, whenever a context is specified for the *aitire* it is invariably one of high status and prestige. For the *gíall*, on the other hand, such subordination appears to have been the essence of his suretyship. The tract on hostage-sureties remarks that it is through *gíall*-sureties that tribes are constrained to the rule of their overlord, and the annals make it clear that the *gíall*-surety was, throughout the medieval period, the primary means through which overlordship was expressed.[112] Similarly, while the Airgialla were quite willing to appoint *aitiri* to the Uí Néill, they would concede only *comgíalla*, "joint-hostages," to them. A mutual exchange of hostages was required also by the free tribes of the Munster *frithfolaid* tract with respect to the King of Cashel and by the rebellious Ciarraige of "MacArddae's Synod" with respect to the Eóganacht Locha Léin.[113] *Gíall*-sureties are frequently associated in political and legal texts with *cís, cáin,* and other terms of tribute, and one law tract even equates the taking of hostages with the ability to claim royal rank: *Ni rig laisna biad geill i nglasaib. dona tabar chis flatha. dona eirenedar feich cana,*[114] "He is no king who does not have hostages in fetters, to whom the tax[es] of lordship are not given, [and] to whom the penalties of a *cáin* are not paid."

(One-sided) exchanges of hostages (*géill*) seem thus to have enlarged the status of one participant and diminished the status of the other in a manner that the giving of an *aitire* did not. It may therefore be significant that although Thurneysen implied the opposite, *aitiri* seem to have had more privileges in their suretyships than did *géill*.[115] Their period of captivity may have been shorter, depending on whether one wishes to place any trust in the commentators' assertion that the *aitire* could be held for only ten days.[116] *Aitiri* seem also to have been allowed to remain at home until they were summoned for a specific claim—clearly the *aitiri* of both *Cáin Domnaig* and *Slán nAitire Cairde* are at home at the time the plaintiff notifies them of the offense. *Géill*, on the other hand, could be taken immediately to the court of the king to whom they had been appointed.[117] Usually, no doubt, unforfeited *gíall*-sureties would have been treated quite honorably at court, as they clearly are in the king's court pictured in *Críth Gablach*. But forfeited *géill* could be held in chains, and while several texts mention this grim possibility for the *gíall*,[118] chains or fetters are never associated with the *aitire*.

The differences between the *aitire* and *gíall* sureties with respect to status and privilege seem, therefore, to correspond closely to the differences between the two intertribal pacts *cáin* and *cairde*. And a passage from *Di Chetharslicht Athgabála*, the tract on distraint, links these guarantors and ordinances even more closely: *It .iiii. arag fris tobngiter na ceithri aurrathas aithgabail fri brata cai giall fri cain aitire fri cairddi. gell fri neimthiu*,[119] "There are four bindings through which the four native laws are enforced—distraint for the *Bratha Cai*, a *gíall* for a *cáin*, an *aitire* for a *cairde*, a gage for dignitaries." In this text, the "privileged" surety the *aitire* is directly associated with the "free" pact the *cairde*, while the subordinating surety the *gíall* is linked to the tributary ordinance the *cáin*. And although the political reality of such arrangements was undoubtedly more complex than this schematized passage implies, the general principles expressed here are supported by other sources. Customary law (*Bratha Cai*) was usually enforced by distraint, and gages were often used to guarantee the dues of high status personalities or institutions.[120] *Aitiri* were without question the normal guarantors for *cairde* relationships, as *Berrad Airechta*, *Slán nAitire Cairde*, the H 3. 18 glosses, the Airgialla poem, and other sources clearly demonstrate.[121] And *géill* are certainly associated frequently with *cánai* in the legal and political sources, as we have seen.[122]

But although there are numerous examples of this link between the *gíall* and the *cáin*, the ecclesiastical *cánai* at which we have already looked might seem to cast some doubt on such an association, for it is clear that they were guaranteed primarily through *aitiri*.[123] The evidence of these two ecclesiastical ordinances is not, however, an adequate basis on which to reject the possibility that *gíall*-sureties were intimately associated with subordinating secular *cánai*. The word *cáin* has, as we have seen, (at least) two different definitions and is almost certainly used in *Cáin Adomnáin* in its primary sense of "law" rather than in its secondary sense of "tribute." *Cáin* as "law" is often equated with *rechtgai* (singular *rechtgae*), royal pronouncements or legislative ordinances that were, according to *Críth Gablach*, most often declared to counter tribal emergencies or make certain beneficial arrangements for inhabitants of the tribe.[124] *Cáin Adomnáin* refers to itself as a *rechtgae*, and *Críth Gablach* knows it as the *recht Adamnán*.[125]

Moreover, despite the fact that these benevolent *cánai* were pledged by overkings on subordinate tribes, neither the word *rechtgae* itself nor the word *cáin* in the sense of *rechtgae* seems to carry any implications of subordination or unfree status.[126] *Rechtgae* is in fact never found with *cís, cobach*, or any of the other exactions demanded of subordinate tribes. Indeed the ecclesiastical *cánai*, though undoubtedly tremendous propaganda tools that dramatically increased the prestige of the king and abbot who proclaimed them, cannot have been construed as expressions of direct political overlordship, since otherwise Fland Febla, "sage-bishop" of Armagh, would not have been the first signatory to *Cáin Adomnáin*, which was sponsored by his chief rival Iona.[127] Given the prominence of Fland Febla's name and the high moral purposes for which this *cáin*, like the other ecclesiastical *cánai* known to us, was declared, it seems likely that those who drafted *Cáin Adomnáin* intended to portray it as something that would enhance the stature even of those who merely subscribed to it. This would in turn explain the choice of the *aitire* as guarantor. Only for subordinating *cánai* would political hostages likely have been thought appropriate; ordinances viewed as elevating the moral standing of the tribes who assented to them would quite naturally involve guarantors whose presence symbolized nobility and prestige rather than political subservience.

The distinction between the *aitire* and the *giall* may thus have been based less on what each did or did not do than on what each did or did not symbolize. The obligations for which the *giall* stood surety were those associated with subordinating political relationships that were conceptualized, both on the domestic (*aicillne*) and intertribal level, as forms of base clientship, and that therefore entailed a certain loss of independent status for the client or client-tribe involved. *Géill* may no longer have been exchanged in the course of domestic base-clientship arrangements by the time the classical law tracts were composed, but the *giall*'s association with political subordination was not forgotten. By contrast, the *aitire* seems to have carried no such connotations of unfreedom. Not only does the evidence suggest that the contractual *aitire*, if indeed such a guarantor ever existed, might have been viewed as particularly appropriate in cases where the parties involved were of unusually high status, the political pacts for which the intertribal *aitire* stood as surety did not in any way depress the stature of the *carait*, "kinsmen," involved in them. *Berrad Airechta* may well be correct in its assertion that the *aitire luigi* originated in the context of the *cairde*, although it is impossible to say at this point. What is perhaps more clear is that the *aitire* developed out of a need for a hostage-surety who could stand "between" tribes or kindreds of relatively equal status—who could, in other words, guarantee the terms of relationships in which political subordination was not to be implied.

With the passage of time, the differences between these two types of hostage-surety seem to have become obscured. Already by the tenth century the terms were frequently confused with one another;[128] the Annals of Ulster for 1015, for example, report that Maelsechlaind mac Domnaill "plundered Leinster, and brought away a large tribute and the *aitiri* of Leinster with him." It is likely that the roots of this confusion lie in the rapid political consolidation that was so much a feature of Irish polity in the seventh through tenth centuries. During this period, many formerly independent tribes either disappeared altogether or were absorbed into political federations organized on the dynastic principle. Byrne and others have viewed these changes as representative of an actual shift in the nature of Irish polity. The Uí Néill, abjuring the exceedingly limited tribal monarchy espoused by idealistic law tracts like *Críth Gablach*, enunciated by their example a new, dynastic principle of rule that was quickly taken up by others. Soon the provinces of an Ireland in which tribal feeling was rapidly disappearing were wracked by intense dynastic competition and consolidation.[129] The argument is intriguing, although since dynasties are visible in the earliest records of Irish history, there is no real reason to believe that dynastic polity was invented by the Uí Néill. The proliferation of dynastic septs and the corresponding diminution in the numbers of independent tribes may speak more to the Uí Néill's success in consolidating what they conquered than to their innovations in the realm of political theory.[130]

But one does not have to accept all of Byrne's interpretation to agree that the phenomenon to which he refers was real. What Byrne sees as a shift in the nature of Irish polity can, at the very least, be conceptualized as a shift in the balance of free and unfree tribes. The decline in "tribal feeling" to which Byrne makes reference must surely have had its origin in the loss of tribal independence. The fate of the Airgialla was that of many, for the privileges that they claimed in the poem were destined to be short-lived.[131] Even before the decisive battle of Leth Cam in 827, the Cenél nEógain had begun to exercise direct control over certain branches of the Airgialla. After Leth Cam, however, Cenél nEógain control over certain constituent tribes was so great that some lost their independent status altogether. The king of the Uí Chremthainn of the Airgialla, who had been consistently styled *rex* or *rí* in the annals until 827, is called only *leth-rí*, "joint-king," at his obituary in 833. Half a century later another Uí Chremthainn leader, Maelcere, is styled only *dux*.[132] And although some small tribes survived even into the twelfth century with their royal status still intact, many were not as lucky.[133]

In this rapidly shifting political balance lies the likely explanation for the changing nature of Irish hostage-suretyship. As more and more tribes passed under the control of the large dynastic federations, the complex network of free alliances and unfree tributary relationships in which the *aitire* and the *gíall* had played so crucial a role was transformed. The boundary between "free" and "unfree" became substantially more difficult to determine, as degrees and types of "unfreedom" multiplied. Later genealogists created elaborate fictions to demonstrate that "free" and "unfree" were still what they always had been: certain tribes were labeled noble by birth and ancestry but tributary by virtue of the unfree land onto which they had moved.[134] But the lengths to which these writers went themselves give the lie to the immutability of the distinction they were trying to preserve. The relationship between the *aitire* and the *gíall*, embedded as it was in the system of status and subordination that lay at the heart of Irish social structure, could not remain unaltered. As the system itself evolved, the institutions in which it was grounded were destined to change as well.

In the end what is perhaps most astonishing is not that such changes should have occurred, but rather that traditional images of power and rule should have hung on as tenaciously as they did. "Free" and "unfree" remained the terms in which polite political discourse was conducted long after the distinction between these two states had become unclear; the voluntary association of clientship remained the model according to which kingship was conceptualized even after coercion and direct rule had become the standard practice of the day. Even the fact that we can today distinguish between two extremely similar types of hostage surety— indeed, that we would even *care* to do this for reasons other than those antiquarian in nature—is itself testimony to the longevity and appeal of such myths. If nothing else, the *aitire* and the *gíall* are salutary reminders of a basic reality of the historian's craft: we see those we study through lenses constructed by and for themselves.

5. The Road to Judgment

It is axiomatic that the complexities of human social interaction can never be entirely textualized: the written word cannot possibly contain the multivalent elements of communal life and thought. The Irish lawbooks, with their focus on the priorities and relationships that gave medieval law its force, permit at least a glimpse into the complicated context within which legal affairs progressed. Even more remarkable, however, is the view they afford of the means by which that context itself was shaped. Such was not the jurists' intent; hardly themselves disinterested parties, they tended, whenever possible, to stress immutability and tradition over radical social change. And yet, as we have seen, the world in which they lived was altering rapidly. Traditional views of kinship, of relationships between peoples, indeed of the nature of rule itself, were being refined, reshaped, and recast in terms appropriate to the political discourse of the day. Authority was becoming streamlined, jurisdiction affirmed. Justice itself was not immune: the evidence speaks to a process of jurisprudential reformulation as profound as that occurring in the political sphere. In this process both suretyship itself and the jurists who described and shaped it had an important role to play.

The study of early Irish law has changed profoundly over the past few years, as is evident from what has already been said. That this should be so is surprising indeed. Twenty years ago no one would ever have predicted that a field for which the terms "conservative," "archaic," and "Indo-European" seem almost to have been coined would ever itself experience the winds of radical change. Certainly, the notion that one might find anything other than the null set occupying the intersection of the concepts "revolutionary" and "Old Irish legal studies" will take some getting used to. But such is the way the ground now lies. Recent studies by Breatnach, McCone, Breen, and Ó Corráin have challenged some of our most venerable beliefs about the nature and origins of Old Irish law. It is now disconcertingly apparent that passages long thought to be oral in origin were in fact composed in writing, that tracts assumed to be secular in nature and inspiration were actually ecclesiastical products, and, perhaps most alarmingly, that linguistic features associated with the *rosc* style are less reliable guides to an early date of composition than had previously been supposed.[1]

That similar arguments are being advanced with respect to other early legal traditions assures us that we are at least moving in the right direction; most Judaic scholars would now agree, for example, on the fundamentally literary nature of the "Oral Torah,"[2] and certain historians of early Scandinavia have argued that the differences separating the archaizing rhetorical Swedish laws from the "plain prose" Norwegian and Icelandic texts are stylistic in nature and not indicative of an earlier date or closer proximity to the oral tradition.[3] Such parallels may seem of scant comfort to Irish historians who find themselves suddenly revising ideas previously central to their work. Fortunately, however, progress, like virtue, has its own rewards, and the quantity and quality of recent publications on Irish law suggests that in this case the rewards are great indeed.

Among the questions that have attracted the most attention is that of the nature and origins of the laws themselves and of the juristic class that produced them. All would now agree that ecclesiastical influence on the law tracts was pervasive, though not everyone would go as far as Breatnach does in assigning the writing of the vernacular corpus as a whole to a strictly clerical environment. Opinions are still divided on the extent of the clerical contribution to the composition of the tracts: some would stress the ecclesiastical, and some the secular, elements of the laws, as we have seen.[4] The issue is a difficult one and unlikely to be resolved definitively in the near future. At least as interesting as the question itself, however, are its potential implications. For at stake in this debate is not merely the existence or non-existence of substantial lay literacy—although this is an important issue in itself[5]—but rather the nature of the legal tradition as a whole. What *do* these laws represent? Are they in fact the culmination of literally centuries of native thinking and teaching about the law, of active participation in the adjudicatory process by professionals of long-standing authority within the community? Or are they in essence an edifice constructed (dare one say "created?") by Christian clerics in the course of the seventh and eighth centuries? Are we witnessing through these laws the confrontation and reconciliation of two highly developed legal traditions, each with their own long history and priorities, or ought we to be thinking rather in terms of the molding of legal practices of disparate origin into a coherent body of custom under the direction of the church?

The evidence on suretyship per se does not allow us to tackle such questions directly. But the use made of suretyship in the laws calls our attention to a critical aspect of the topic that has not as yet attracted much scholarly notice: the means and processes by which a legal tradition can be constructed, and by which—if it is not too much of a contradiction in terms—its antiquity can be established. What these texts suggest is that the emergence of law as a specialized field of endeavor was as much the result of jurists attempting to consolidate their authority over the history and application of legal knowledge as it was the inevitable outgrowth of centuries of previous oral existence. Remarkably, something of the priorities and methods of these professionals are still visible in the law tracts today.

Essential to this question is the information that remains to us about early Irish "court" procedure, for it is in the passage from "private" law institutions like suretyship to the more "public" realm of curial practice that we can most easily trace developments taking place within the legal tradition as a whole. Undoubtedly, the key text on such matters is *Cóic Conara Fugill*, the "Five Paths of Judgment," two recensions of which were edited and translated by Rudolf Thurneysen in 1926.[6] *Cóic Conara Fugill* is what one would politely have to term a "difficult" text; it is, however, absolutely crucial as well. For in it, and *only* in it, are the five procedural "paths" or pleas by which Irish litigants pursued and resolved disputes in the presence of a judge enumerated and explored.[7] As is usual in Old Irish legal studies, the importance of the tract is inversely proportional to the ease with which it can be understood; not only is its textual history more than ordinarily convoluted, the language is, or at least appears, old as well.

The earliest of the three extant recensions, RE, is written primarily in *Fénechas* style,[8] the one exception being a few plain prose sentences near the beginning of the tract that Thurneysen thought might have been additions made early in the commentary tradition.[9] Since the passages in question are written in reasonably standard Old Irish, treated as text by all three recensions,[10] and glossed accordingly, this is not a conclusion to which we can cling with any security, given recent work on the dating of the language. It does serve admirably, however, to underline the inherent difficulty of the tract. All three versions are heavily glossed and commented upon, and in the two latest, U and H, the line between commentary and text is particularly difficult to draw.[11] Even in focusing primarily on the "base" text of the RE recension to isolate as far as possible the intentions of its original compiler, one must be conscious of the extraordinary chronological jumble within which the whole has been preserved.

If the task is a difficult one, however, it is nonetheless worthwhile. The tract is deceptively simple in format: five procedural paths are enumerated in turn, each of which is followed by a list of the types of disputes to be pursued on the path in question. Next under each path appear the names of the guarantors or securities—called "bindings" in the text—by which parties in dispute warrant that they will abide by the verdict reached by the judge. And that, as they say, is that, except for a brief quote from *Aí Cermna*, the "Lawsuit of Cermna," a lost legal text about which nothing further is known;[12] a citation that occurs also in *Di Chetharslicht Athgabála*, the principal tract on distraint;[13] and an excerpt from a rhetorical poem, the rest of which can be found in H 3. 18, where a marginal note attributes it to Cormac.[14]

The structure of the tract is simple, but the nature and origin of the procedures it describes are anything but. The importance of this text to the history of early Irish jurisprudence would be difficult to overestimate. Because of the age, or apparent age, of the language in which it is written, it would be natural to infer that the legal practices it details were old even at the time they were written down. In its compact and allusive phrasing, its marked use of alliteration, verb-final construction, and the second-person instructional style,[15] the tract seems to speak directly of connections with the distant oral past. And the names of the paths in question—all abstract legal nouns like *fír*, "truth," or *cert*, "justice," which are found elsewhere in the law tracts in a variety of contexts—hint at the existence of jurisprudential distinctions possibly centuries old. Certainly Thurneysen interpreted the text in this manner; *Cóic Conara Fugill* was for him a window onto an archaic curial tradition the original contours of which had long since been lost.[16] Obscure it may be, but this text would appear to present modern scholars with a truly unique opportunity: the chance to reconstruct something of the priorities and perspectives of the earliest Irish jurists.

There are many questions to be asked of *Cóic Conara Fugill*, not the least of which is what exactly a path represents. One must imagine that some sort of formalized procedure or plea was intended, though no formulas are ever cited and there are no indications anywhere in the tract as to the manner in which cases prosecuted on one path might differ from those pursued on another. The plain prose sentences that open the tract demonstrate that, at least from the point of view of the author of the passage, there are "right" and "wrong"—or at least "better" and "worse"—paths for parties in dispute to select depending on the nature of their case. Fines are to be assessed, presumably by the judge, both for "not recognizing" (*nemai[t]hne*) the proper path before beginning a suit and for changing in the middle of the suit from one path to another.[17] Another curious element in the tract are the gages and guarantors through which the verdict was ultimately to be secured. The giving of such securities is, of course, a commonplace in early medieval law; what is unusual is for each plea to require its own particular type of surety. Welsh law, for example, stipulates the appointment of a *mach ar gyfraith*, "*mach*-surety to abide by law," in court cases, but nowhere suggests that other types of security (*amodwr, briduw*) ought, or indeed even might, be offered instead according to the nature of the plea being presented.[18]

The nature and number of the paths themselves are, however, what is most mysterious. The categorizing of procedure in this manner would seem to presuppose the existence of a rationale appropriate to each category. Each path, in other words, must have, or once have had, a perceptual unity to it, a common principle that united the cases assigned to each category in some manner one to the other. Unfortunately, in one instance only is such a rationale ever enunciated; otherwise the nature of the disputes associated with each path is our only clue. Equally unclear is the framework of the whole. We are nowhere told why there are five paths or, to put the matter slightly differently, why there are four paths, since it is evident that the fifth path was in some manner construed as a culmination of the other four.[19] These, then, are the issues we must confront if we would understand the nature and origins of Irish curial procedure.

What I wish to propose is that the five paths to judgment were based not on abstruse jurisprudential distinctions, shared legal issues, or even categories of law—for example, kinship law, neighborhood law, and the like—but rather were constructed around the guarantors and securities through which dispute resolutions would customarily have been secured and, in many cases, engineered in a precurial age. *Cóic Conara Fugill* is, I suggest, a tract on court procedure through which the outlines of a thriving and still essentially "private," or non-court oriented, legal system can clearly be traced. Its framework mirrors, in large part, that of the Irish surety system itself, and this holds true whether it is interpreted as having five or four procedural paths. Just as *Berrad Airechta*, the Old Irish tract on suretyship, speaks of the five securities that protect against the evasion of a legal obligation by an offender—*naidm, ráth, aitire*, gage, and the religious ritual known as *celebrad*—so *Cóic Conara Fugill* distinguishes five separate paths by which litigants resolve their disputes before a judge and assigns a separate guarantee to each—*naidm, ráth, aitire*, and two different types of gage, one of which is given to warrant the performance of a religious ritual.[20] And just as the *aitire* of *Berrad Airechta* can be considered, because of the nature of his suretyship, very much a "summary" guarantor, so also is the fifth and final path of *Cóic Conara Fugill*—the one with which the *aitire* is associated in that text—viewed as a path which encompasses the other four.

The guarantees enumerated in *Cóic Conara Fugill* were not, in other words, assigned to existing jurisprudential categories as they might appear; rather they were, with the exception of the first path, *fír*, themselves the basis on which those categories were fashioned. It is worth noting that modeling of this type is surely what the equation of paths with "bindings" would in itself suggest. For had these paths actually been constructed around jurisprudential distinctions now obscure to us, it is inherently unlikely that each would be paired with a surety unique to itself, or that the range of "bindings" mentioned would encompass every security known to Irish law. Given the position traditionally accorded this tract in the history of Irish legal procedure, the implications of such modeling are significant indeed.

The first path is that of *fír*, "truth," a name that led Thurneysen to suggest that *fír*, in its familiar and oldest sense of ultimate "truth" or "justice," was the bedrock on which this path had been constructed. The question to be put to the judge in such disputes was, he proposed, "is this according to truth, or is it not?"[21] This is the sense *fír* appears to have in *Uraicecht Becc*, the only other tract to envisage the concept in procedural terms,[22] but there are some difficulties with this view as well. In the first place, this question can be said to be implicit in *all* legal decisions, for the Irish as for ourselves. Moreover, such an explanation does not advance us toward an understanding of why the cases assigned to *fír* are perceived to fall under its rubric. For they are a motley collection indeed: included are cases of "shameless denial," presumably of legal accusations (*lia do fír . . . fri sena nanbal*); cases which are very difficult to resolve (lit. "great difficulties"—*fri aincessa mara*); disputes over property divisions between kinsmen (*fri derbranna brathar*); disputes involving the property of a kin-group or individual for which or whom there are no obvious heirs (*fri ascnam ndibaid*); and controversies over claims to lordship (*fri flaith fri airitin*) and the prerogatives of leadership, of what is unclear (*fri dliged tuise*).²³ At first glance, there would seem to be no logical connection among these cases; the matters mentioned range broadly over the entire spectrum of Irish law, from kinship and lordship matters to criminal accusations, and it is difficult to see how they could ever have been conceived of as a unit. Furthermore, the name of the "binding" by which disputes pursued on *fír* are to be guaranteed, *fírgille*, "truth-gage," seems almost to have been invented for the purpose of proving its relevance to the path in question.²⁴ There is no indication as to what a "truth-gage" was, what role it might have played in the proceedings, or why it, and it alone, was deemed appropriate for such matters. The rationale that must once have existed for this path is anything but obvious.

Some clues are to be found, however, in the name by which it is known. *Fír* has a technical meaning in the law tracts that, while related to its broader sense of "truth," is independent of it: "ordeal," the ritualized appeal to the supernatural by which communities sought closure in difficult legal matters.²⁵ Ordeals, whether by cauldron, duel, poison, hot iron, or lots, were very common in Irish law, and a glance back at the cases enumerated under *fír* suggests that this path encompassed disputes for which resolution by ordeal was envisaged. As is widely known, ordeals were most frequently used in early medieval law for cases in which proof was difficult to obtain or not forthcoming at all, or for controversies that had the potential to be particularly disruptive of social order.²⁶ "Shameless denials" and difficult cases are obvious examples of the first of these categories, as are disputes over the property of extinct kin-groups. Indeed, property divisions as a whole involving forms of the ordeal are relatively well attested in Irish law. Lots were especially common in such matters, since they were often used between litigants of similar status or reliability. One of Caratnia's "false" judgments was to have granted precedence in dividing an inheritance to one heir over another without the casting of lots.²⁷ Lots are mentioned also in conjunction with inheritance disputes in the *Collectio Canonum Hibernensis* and were, according to recension H of *Cóic Conara Fugill* itself, a normal part of the procedure followed when a kin-group became extinct.²⁸ Tírechán's *Collectanea* even speaks of two brothers settling a dispute over the division of their inheritance by a battle ordeal.²⁹

Ordeals for disputed claims to leadership—clear instances of the type of divisive or dangerous dispute for which ordeals were often also used—are not as well attested in the sources, but they are certainly not unknown. The *Collectio Canonum Hibernensis*, citing biblical sources, speaks of lots as a means of deciding the succession to an abbacy or to kingship, and casting lots for kingship are mentioned also in later legal commentary.[30] The most compelling evidence for an association between *fír* and the ordeal is, however, a heptad on the judicial duel that, though couched in very different language from that used in *Cóic Conara Fugill*, corresponds in almost every important detail to the framework that tract establishes for *fír*. Duels, it says, are to be fought about "uncertain matters" only (*im aimbeachta*), such as oaths of denial or false accusations (*im dindis duine-taide, im gutuidmhe*), contentions over the ownership or possession of an estate (*im cosnum selbe*), and controversies over the exaction of lordly tribute from kindreds or tribes (*im dingbail cisa dia tuaith ocus ciniul*).[31] The similarities could hardly be more marked: the unity of the path that was *fír* was rooted in the ordeal, and it was a unity both symbolized and achieved by the delivery of the gages, now revealed as "ordeal-gages," by which resolution and reconciliation were ultimately assured.

The nature of the second path, *dliged*, "entitlement," appears at first glance reassuringly simpler to determine; in fact it is dishearteningly more complex. Only one type of case, the oral contract, is listed under *dliged*, and only one type of binding, the *naidm*, is viewed as appropriate. Since the *naidm* is the principal Irish contractual surety, the inference could hardly be more clear: *dliged* is the path on which disputes arising out of contracts should be pursued.[32] Unfortunately, however, the simplicity of this equation is an illusion, as one has only to glance at the third of the paths enumerated to understand. *Cert*, "justice," is the only one of the five paths for which a legal issue is directly enunciated. When goods exchanged are later found to be unequal in value, aggrieved parties have, we are told, the right to sue on *cert* for restitution of their loss unless they had themselves knowingly taken less for their goods than they were worth.[33] The difficulty is that while many of the specific exchanges listed under *cert* are not contractual in nature—gifts exchanged by people united in a *lánamnas* relationship, for example, which would be counted in *Berrad Airechta* as an immunity—some of them clearly *are*.[34] In other words, the distinction between these two paths cannot be merely that one was appropriate for contractual, and the other for non-contractual, exchanges.

The question is further complicated by the fact that while the existence and fairness of a given contract are indeed intellectually separable issues, an actual *procedural* division between *dliged* and *cert* appears to be unique to *Cóic Conara Fugill*. *Cert*, used in the technical sense of plea or procedural path, occurs nowhere else in the law tracts with which I am familiar. *Di Astud Chor*, a text Charles-Edwards has suggested may reflect in its bipartite structure the distinction between *dliged* and *cert*,[35] makes no mention of *cert* (even in its section on unequal exchanges) but speaks rather of *fir*.[36] And neither *Berrad Airechta* nor *Uraicecht Becc*, the only tracts apart from *Cóic Conara Fugill* to delineate specific paths to judgment, refer to *cert* at all. Indeed, *dliged* is envisaged in *Berrad Airechta* as encompassing all of the issues that in *Cóic Conara Fugill* were assigned to both *cert* and *dliged* and more. Questions of contractual validity and equity, disputes over the ownership of a forfeited gage, claims between persons united in kinship or lordship relationships to one another, controversies over the payment of professional fees, and suits over wounding in self-defense—all were, according to *Berrad Airechta*, to be pursued on *dliged*; in fact, *dliged* is the only path mentioned in that text.[37] One has always to keep in mind the possibility of variations in regional custom, but the fact that the distinction between *dliged* and *cert* is unparalleled elsewhere in the tracts, even in those where one would most expect to find it, must make one suspicious about it.

Such suspicions are heightened by the fact that though *dliged* and *cert* are presented in *Cóic Conara Fugill* as two entirely separate "paths," it is evident from the sources that from the procedural point of view, the legal question implicit in these two paths was exactly the same. Cases themselves might certainly vary: one might query the binding or non-binding nature of a contractual arrangement, and another seek to determine whether an individual had been deprived of his rightful due in the course of an exchange. Ultimately at issue in both, however, was the question of entitlement, *dliged*, or, to put things in their most basic form, "is so-and-so entitled to such-and-such, and if so on what basis?" The artificiality of a procedural division between *dliged* and *cert* becomes particularly visible when one considers how disputes of this type would be resolved. Contracts could be challenged on a variety of different grounds, but in only a very few instances would they be canceled altogether; in most cases, the deal would be renegotiated to even out any inequities that had occurred. In other words, the likely resolution to a suit pursued on *dliged* was the very process *Cóic Conara Fugill* assigns to *cert*. Similarly, in suits that did not seek to overturn a transaction altogether, but that looked only to equalize the value of the objects conveyed—cases of *cert*, in other words—the issue of whether the contract as a result of which the goods had been exchanged had been a binding one was absolutely vital. The presence or absence of a valid contractual *dliged* would determine the outcome of a suit pursued on *cert*. *Cóic Conara Fugill*'s distinction between *dliged* and *cert* is not one that procedurally would be easy to affect. And yet insofar as it appears to be unique to the tract in question, it must be deliberate, and we must look elsewhere for an understanding of the rationale according to which it was done.

If the division between these two paths does not originate in any discernable judicial imperative, then it may derive from the author's desire to realize the intellectual framework on which his tract was based. It is significant, I think, that while *cert* is secured with *smachtgilli*, "penalty-gages," *dliged* is said in the text to be "bound on a *naidm*, and it is not undertaken on a gage."[38] This highly unusual phrasing—and this is the only place in the tract where we are told that something is one thing and it is not another—suggests that the author wished to incorporate both *naidm*-sureties and gages into his procedural schema and fashioned his paths accordingly. An association between *naidm*-sureties and contractual entitlement is a natural one: *naidm*-sureties are, as we have seen, virtually synonymous with oral contracts in the legal sources; in most texts they are the sine qua non of contractual obligation. Gages, meanwhile, are one of the most common forms of security for payments owed, and although we are not specifically told that they would customarily have been offered in situations of unequal exchange, it is reasonable to suppose that they were. Certainly, *naidm*-sureties were *not* viewed as appropriate guarantees in such circumstances, at least if the exchange in question had originated in a contractual arrangement. *Berrad Airechta* tells us this quite directly in a clause that seems curiously the reverse of the sentence cited above from *Cóic Conara Fugill*: "[a revised claim] is enforced and [a *naidm*-surety] is not appointed."[39] What we may be seeing, therefore, in the separation of *dliged* and *cert* is not the procedural embodiment of distinct juridical issues, but rather the creation of procedural categories on the basis of a framework provided by existing legal forms and personalities. The distinction between *dliged* and *cert* may both presume and exemplify a process of abstraction that is in many ways the essence of jurisprudence: from *naidm* to *dliged*, from gage to *cert*, from social fact to legal category.

This same process appears to underlie the construction of the other paths as well. We are told that the fourth path, *téchtae*, "propriety," concerns issues of "perpetual origin," by which is meant, to judge from the examples given, disputes that relate in some manner to the servile or semi-servile status characteristic of *bothaig*, *fuidri* and *senchléithe*.[40] It is unclear from the text whether the fact of dependent status is itself at issue, or whether any claim brought against a highly dependent individual would be pursued on *téchtae*.⁴¹ What is clear, however, and what is most confusing about this path, is that dependancy is not the only issue prosecuted on *téchtae*. Also included is what is called in the tract *sensmúr cinad*, the "old rust of crime," an expression generally, and, I think, correctly, taken to refer to offences committed at a time considerably prior to the bringing of the claim.⁴²

Needless to say, the conceptual link between these two legal problems is not evident. Thurneysen suggested that the connection might derive from the fact that issues of ancestry and past events were likely to arise in such cases and necessitate the testimony of *senchaide* ("custodians of the past") as to the historical background of the dispute.⁴³ This is possible, although historical knowledge and testimony would have played a major role also in many of the cases listed under *fír* as well (e.g., inheritance or leadership disputes) and, moreover, *senchaide* are never mentioned by name in the text. Another possibility is that the "old rust of crime" refers here to one of the ways in which free individuals could lose their independent status. We know from the *Fuidir* tract that the inability to render satisfactory compensation for crimes committed could result in an offender's entering the service of the person who made payment on his behalf.⁴⁴ But this explanation too has its difficulties. The expression "old rust of crime" seems, where it occurs elsewhere in the law tracts, definitely to refer to claims advanced long after the commission of an offense rather than to the long-term consequences of criminal activity. Moreover, while the commission of a crime was one of the ways one could become a *fuidir*, it was neither the only nor, to judge from the *Fuidir* tract, the most important one.⁴⁵ Nor was it, as far as we know, connected with *bothach* status at all, although this may simply be a gap in our evidence. The problem is a difficult one.

Nevertheless, I would suggest that the *ráth*, the guarantor associated with this path, was the kernel around which the path was fashioned. At first glance this may seem unlikely. The *ráth* was the paying surety of Irish law, a guarantor who pledged to make good a contracted debt should his principal default. And since the individuals mentioned under *téchtae* were so limited in their legal capacity that they could neither offer nor accept guarantors of this or any other sort, it is difficult to see what relevance such a surety might have. But the contractual context is not the only context in which the *ráth*'s name appears in the legal sources. Because his liability for the trespasses of his principal was so marked, *ráth*ship is used frequently in the law tracts as a metaphor for the responsibilities enjoined on kindreds and lords for the doings of their subordinates. Thus is the *aire coisring*, for example, said to bear "*ráth*ship" for the legal obligations of his kin.[46] This is, I suggest, the key to this particular procedural path, and also the reason for which individuals of servile or semiservile status only are named in the text. For unlike base clients, who retained much of their independant legal capacity, *fuidri*, *bothaig*, and *senchléithe* possessed no legal independence at all. Their lords were entirely responsible for any and all offenses committed by them or their families; these lords were, to use the metaphor of the tracts themselves, their *ráth*-sureties.[47] The association between this type of lordship and *ráth*ship is one that would come naturally to a jurist familiar with the conventions and images of the tracts, and it is, I suggest, the association that lies at the heart of the path called *téchtae*. The author's desire to incorporate the *ráth* into his procedural schema led him to invoke, as the basis of the path he was constructing, the non-contractual aspect of that surety's office most familiar to him—contract itself having already been addressed earlier in his work.

Liability may also be the key to the mystery of the "old rust of crime." *Sensmúr cinad* is glossed at least once in the H recension of *Cóic Conara Fugill* as referring to crimes committed by the father or grandfather of an individual rather than to offenses for which he himself was responsible.[48] If this gloss is correct, *Cóic Conara Fugill* may simply be invoking here another familiar aspect of the *ráth*ship metaphor—the liability of the kindred for the misdeeds of their relatives.[49] If the gloss is wrong, however, there is another characteristic of the *ráth*'s office that would have been well known to the composer of *Cóic Conara Fugill* that might account for the inclusion of *sensmúr cinad*. The *ráth*'s suretyship was, unlike that of the other Irish guarantors, hereditary; the debts he secured were passed on to his heirs, just as they were to the heirs of the original debtor. And he was, again unlike the other sureties of Irish law, allowed to take action against the heirs of his principal as well as against the principal himself.[50] In other words, the association between *ráth*ship and inherited or antiquated claims and issues was a natural one. Explanations of this sort may seem farfetched to those not accustomed to the schematizing of the law tracts, but they do have the merit of explaining what otherwise cannot be explained. To accept that the *ráth* is what links these types of dispute is to proclaim that a rational solution exists, however strange or artifical that solution might seem; to reject such a connection is to consign the whole to the dustbin of irrationality.

The last of the five "paths," *coir n-athcomairc*, "suitability of inquiry," or "proper inquiry," is in many ways the most interesting of the lot, as well as being the most revealing of the intentions and methods of the author.[51] It is depicted in the sources as a "catchall" category: each of the other four paths have their own identity and cases assigned to them, but no specific disputes are associated with *coir n-athcomairc*. The only requirement for this fifth path is that the cases in question be "speedy" and "well-bound" with sureties, a peculiar stipulation the significance of which will be discussed shortly. Fergus Kelly suggests that *coir n-athcomairc* was the path on which disputes not covered under the other four paths were to be pursued, and this seems likely to be right.[52] This does not, of course, mean that the converse was equally true: the fact that *coir n-athcomairc* encompassed claims not treated on the other four paths does not mean that disputes that did fall onto one of the other four paths were inappropriate to *coir n-athcomairc*. Indeed, as a passage from *Di Chetharslicht Athgabála* cited twice in the tract remarks, "*coir n-athcomairc* is a [name] common to them all."[53]

This is important, for it reveals that in this instance also the scope and rationale of the path in question were determined by the nature of the office of the guarantor assigned to it. The *aitire*, the surety associated with this path, was very much a "catchall" guarantor. Unlike the other sureties of Irish law, he was a standing surety, a guarantor not linked to any specific contract or transaction but obliged rather to ensure that his principal answered any and all claims made against him during the period of his suretyship. Once summoned, the *aitire* was expected to accompany his principal to any and all meetings connected with the resolution of the claim. The obligations for which *aitire*-sureties tended to be summoned most frequently were, accordingly, those of an unexpected nature—claims arising out of negligence, or unplanned violence, or the like. They were thus obligations linked not by their subject-matter or type, but by the circumstances in which they arose and were prosecuted.[54] These are, I suggest, the very claims to which *coir n-athcomairc* refers, and this is why they also are not joined by specific type. Indeed, it would be possible to argue that *coir n-athcomairc* refers not to a separate plea or procedure, but rather to a stage through which *all* claims pursued in a curial setting would progress. A claim was made, an *aitire* was invoked to guarantee the defendant's appearance in court. At that point the proper path was chosen and the appropriate guarantors exchanged, while disputes that did not fall on one of the other four paths continued on *coir n-athcomairc* with the *aitire* as guarantor. The use of the surety system as a framework around which to construct the five paths of judgment could hardly be more visible than it is in this case.

To argue that the author of *Cóic Conara Fugill* modeled his paths on existing procedures and institutions is not, of course, to explain the significance of such an action, and this question returns us to the observations with which this chapter began. One of the most exciting things about recent scholarship on Irish law is the sense of fluidity and movement it has introduced into sources known previously mainly for their amberlike preservation of fossilized institutions. The law tracts stand now revealed not as dispassionate recitations of petrified custom, but as a series of conversations, often quite animated, between legal traditions and individuals. Joseph Nagy has called our attention to the jurists' concern with the issue of authority, with the manner in which Christian and pagan, written and oral, intersect, overlap, justify, and contain one another. As he points out, nowhere is the complexity of these exchanges more evident than in the origin legends attendant on the *Senchas Már* itself, in which the oral traditions of the pagan past are gathered together, purged of their unacceptable elements, and resituated within a literate Christian environment.[55] But the issue of authority is not a matter for origin legends alone. The continuing composition of *rosc* shows just how deep such waters can run. For if, as traditionally has been argued, we ought to think of *rosc* as an originally oral genre, what we have in the law tracts are passages composed in and committed to writing, possessing authority because of their oral appearance within a literate tradition of instruction for jurists whose own authority in the practice of law was rooted in oral performance. Truly there is a great deal here that needs to be sorted out.

But though we have been willing enough to acknowledge movement within this relatively theoretical sphere, we have done little yet to illuminate the equally protean nature of the practice of law itself. In our focus on the relationships between traditions, we have overlooked the possibility of developments taking place within "native tradition" as a whole. And yet precisely the same processes of definition, consolidation and, I suggest, relocation of authority are occurring here as well. *Cóic Conara Fugill* is a tract about authority and, specifically, about jurists consolidating their jurisdiction over local legal affairs. There has been much discussion of late about early Irish dispute settlement. Particularly controversial has been the extent to which kings were involved in judgment, although with the recent publication of Fergus Kelly's edition of the *Airecht* text on court procedure a consensus might at last be emerging. Verdicts on cases brought before the court were reached by judges, but they were proclaimed by or in the presence of kings and sanctioned, therefore, by royal authority.[56] This brings Irish curial procedure somewhat closer to its analogues elsewhere in medieval Europe, but one crucial difference remains: the existence of a professional judiciary in whose hands dispute settlement would appear to have lain since the days of Caesar and beyond. In no other European land did anything approaching these professional judges exist,[57] and yet our evidence for the important role they played in the adjudicatory process in Ireland appears conclusive. Saint Patrick mentions them—indeed he bribes them[58]—and there are frequent references in the law tracts to the intervention of the *brithem túaithe*, the "tribal judge," in a wide range of legal matters.[59] Whether rendering judgment from their houses, as we find in some texts, or from the tribal *airecht*-court itself,[60] these judges, whose authority in disputes derived as much from their professional status and specialist training as from the willingness of parties in dispute to bring their case before them,[61] appear to have been a regular and essential feature of the Irish legal process.

Or so the law tracts tell us. It is worth reminding ourselves, however, of what else the law tracts tell us, for matters may have been more complicated, and authority in disputes more diffuse, than the *Airecht* tract implies. Richard Sharpe has already pointed to the large number of procedural pressures urging claimants toward a "private" or non-curial resolution of their difficulties.[62] The very texts from which we glean our information on judges make it clear that many non-professionals also participated in dispute settlement. Neither of the two disputes for which we have extant accounts involved such judges.[63] *Bretha Cróilige* indicates that judges might be called on to decide whether an individual was or was not entitled to sick-maintenance but makes it clear that in normal circumstances the affair would proceed entirely under the direction of the physician, the wounded man's lord, and guarantor-witnesses.[64] In *Bretha Comaithchesa*, a trustworthy neighbor, not a professional judge, assesses the extent of reparations due for damages caused by trespassing cattle. *Bechbretha* seems similarly to envisage neighbors onto whose lands an unidentified swarm of bees ventures making the decision themselves as to how it will be divided.[65]

It is likely, moreover, that individuals who stood in a lordship or supervisory capacity to others would frequently have acted as arbiters in the disputes of their subordinates. The *aire coisring* has already been mentioned; *Cáin Aicillne* speaks of a lord passing judgments on his clients, and an unedited tract on judgment suggests that disputes might in some circumstances go first to the lord before passing on to the king.⁶⁶ There is reason to believe that craftsmen of recognized ability might have served in a similar capacity to their apprentices and, perhaps, to others in the crafts community. This has long been presumed for poets and assumed to be a special privilege deriving from their earlier custodianship of the law. But it may have been more widespread than this. *Uraicecht Becc* declares the distraints (*athgabála*) and judgments (*ríara*) of craftsmen over their pupils "free" (*saer*), that is, appropriate and free from liability. And a well-known passage from *Bretha Nemed* says specifically that every *nemed* is to have his authority (*ríar*), and every craft its entitlement (*cach dán a dliged*).⁶⁷ Clearly we need at the very least to think in terms of widescale non-specialist participation in the dispute settlement process.

It is possible that we should broaden our thinking even further. There are hints that even the status of "professional" judges was more varied and ambiguous than we tend to assume. By this I refer not to divisions existing within the law—secular, ecclesiastical, poetic—but to variations in background and training of a much more fundamental nature. Some judges may have been, to paraphrase Orwell, considerably more equal than others, and in many cases the line between "professional" and "non-professional" judges may not always have been as sharp as we have tended to infer from the tracts. Is it entirely clear, for example, that the judge in *Uraicecht Becc* who renders judgment for craftsmen on the "valuation and measuring and fashioning and remuneration of every product" is an expert in law rather than in the crafts for which he adjudicates?⁶⁸ If particularly respected craftsmen did act as mediators or judges in the disputes of their subordinates or colleagues, then the gulf between such craftsmen and *Uraicecht Becc*'s "professional" judge may not have been very great. This may even be why some cases are said to have gone to a "judge's" house rather than to the *airecht* itself. Parties requiring outside intervention in their disputes might well have sought out individuals who, though not specialists in law, were acceptable to them because of their special skills or reputation.⁶⁹

Even the word *brithem* itself may not be as transparent as it seems. There are a few instances in the law tracts where people who are demonstrably *not* professional judges but who are acting in an adjudicatory capacity are referred to as *brithemain*: *Bretha Crólige*, for example, uses the term both for the person who estimates the worth of a woman's handiwork when she has been injured and for the physician who tends her.⁷⁰ When claimants speak, in other words, as they do in *Berrad Airechta* of "the judge that we appoint," we may not be justified in assuming that the individual referred to was necessarily a specialist in legal lore.⁷¹ Certainly when Patrick mentions giving bribes *illis qui iudicabant*, "to those who rendered justice," in the regions that he visited, we cannot simply presume that it is to a professional judiciary that he refers—indeed, his use of the circumlocution instead of the common noun *iudex* may suggest that many of the recipients of his gifts were *not* perceived by him as professionals.⁷²

None of this is to say that the professional judges for which early Ireland is so famous in historical circles did not exist. The evidence on that point is clear. Nor would one wish to imply a necessary opposition between "public" and "private" forms of dispute resolution: the two coexisted happily side by side in many early medieval communities, with the former serving frequently as a resource to which disputes not resolved by private means could be channeled. But it is to observe that even in the period of the law tracts the legal process did not revolve entirely around the jurists—many disputes were apparently resolved without judicial intervention. And it is above all to question the extent to which historically the juristic class had involved itself in daily dispute settlement in the localities.

Let me be clear what I am arguing here. I am not seeking to challenge the historical existence of an intellectual class that both viewed itself and was viewed by others as possessing ultimate authority in matters of the law. What I wish to raise rather as an issue is the historical applicability of the view of the judicial "process" that emerges from our seventh and eighth-century tracts. Leaving aside for the moment our tendency—indeed obligation—as historians to question the extent to which the jurists' schematized vision of the *brithemain túaithe*, like the other schemas to which they were prone, corresponded to the reality of the period in which the lawbooks were compiled, how justified are we in reading this information backward into time? We know very little about the juristic schools before the ninth century, when they first appear in the annals. How pervasive and numerous *were* professional judges in local legal affairs in the period before written law? How many small or outlying communities would have had access to such a person on anything approaching a regular basis? Ought one to imagine the early legal schools as similar in influence to the established church, capable of fielding large numbers of representatives and ubiquitous in all matters pertaining to their expertise? Or were the jurists more of an intellectual elite whose authority in legal matters was manifested primarily in high-status or visibly performative venues and whose involvement in minor disputes was minimal? Indeed, if Binchy and Charles-Edwards are right in arguing that legal matters had originally fallen under the purview of poets and druids, how well developed was the practical side of law at all in this era?[73] Academic and practical law are, after all, separate, or at least separable, disciplines, as Campion's account of the sixteenth-century Irish law schools indicates.[74] To infer from the existence of a juristic class in the eighth century a historical pattern of systematic involvement in local legal matters may be unwarranted.

Questions of this sort are unlikely to be definitively answered. Even Caesar's well-known account of the Gaulish druids—dubious testimony anyway to conditions in early medieval Ireland—leaves the matter quite murky.[75] Other sources are, however, somewhat more suggestive. *Cóic Conara Fugill* implies that many of the practical aspects of the legal profession were actually being worked out at the time this tract was composed. Indeed, curial procedure itself seems still to have been in its infancy: the curial categories outlined in *Cóic Conara Fugill*, if not in fact the work of the author himself, seem unlikely greatly to predate the composition of the text, since time would otherwise have obscured the rationale according to which they had been constructed. Moreover, both *Berrad Airechta* and *Uraicecht Becc* demonstrate a similar interest in the formulation of curial procedure and, significantly, the solutions they advance are different from those set forth in *Cóic Conara Fugill*. *Berrad Airechta* envisages but one curial path, that of *dliged*, on which all cases brought before the *airecht* would apparently proceed.[76] *Uraicecht Becc*, on the other hand, outlines three separate categories: *dliged*, which handles oral contracts and therefore corresponds quite closely to the *dliged* of *Cóic Conara Fugill*; *aicned*, "nature," a path the purview of which is uncertain; and *fír*, the most general of the three, closest perhaps in character to *Berrad Airechta*'s *dliged*.[77]

Not only do these various visions of curial procedure conflict with one another—and this despite the fact that *Cóic Conara Fugill* and *Uraicecht Becc* are thought to have originated in the same law school[78]—but it is noticeable that only one of *Uraicecht Becc*'s categories is clearly constructed around a particular type of case. Of the others, the nature of *aicned* is unclear, while the character of *fír* is defined only in terms of the types of evidence or legal precedent that might be offered in support of an eventual verdict. Since similar standards and types of testimony must have entered into disputes pursued on *dliged* and *aicned* as well, it is difficult to resist the conclusion that *Uraicecht Becc*'s three paths, like those of *Cóic Conara Fugill*, may stem more from the categorizing instincts of the jurists than from the complexities of an existing or historically rooted curial process. Even more tellingly, the *Airecht* tract itself, a text that focuses specifically on court procedure, mentions no pleas or paths at all. It is possible, of course, that such differences may merely reflect variations in local terminology and practice. But they may also be testimony to something much more significant and profound: a growing interest on the part of the jurists in the curialization of Irish justice. Perhaps we ought to think less in terms of immutable legal tradition than of change and movement, deliberately channeled and engineered.

To remark on the development, or at least visible elaboration, of curial procedure is not necessarily to show that it was only in the wake of such changes that the jurists came to be thoroughly integrated into local processes of dispute settlement. Juridical authority in Ireland seems always to have been grounded more in specialist training than in the locale within which judges exercised their craft: neither an elaborate curial procedure nor a formal "courtroom setting" is a necessary part of an effective adjudicatory process. The curial structure articulated in *Cóic Conara Fugill*, however, suggests that in this instance the enlargement of curial procedure may indeed have been linked to a desire on the part of native jurists to expand the scope of their jurisdiction in everyday legal matters.

In this context it is instructive to return for a moment to what has already been observed about Irish dispute settlement and, specifically, to the role of suretyship in the process. The Irish system of suretyship was unusually complex, as those familiar with the institution as it existed elsewhere in early medieval Europe will already have remarked. Like many other Irish practices, it was structured in a manner intended as much to anticipate and prevent disputes as to resolve them once they had occurred. As the sources also show, however, sureties in Ireland had long been involved in the settlement of disputes as well. *Naidm*-sureties were not merely the guarantors of contractual agreements; they were the persons through whom such obligations were created, interpreted, supervised, and concluded. And since the role of *naidm* was frequently filled by the lords of the parties involved, their authority in such matters was close to absolute.[79] Similarly, *aitire*-sureties may have helped to negotiate settlements as well as to guarantee them,[80] and if I am right in identifying the *ráth* of the text with the liability of lords and kin toward their associates, these individuals also would clearly have had a role in dispute resolution.

The ordeal is a somewhat different matter, but it also raises the possibility of the widespread settlement of disputes outside the supervision of the jurists. For although many ordeals would doubtless have been performed under the auspices of a professional, the few sources we have suggest that they did not have to be. *Berrad Airechta*'s account of sureties drawing lots to decide which of them should enforce a claim makes no mention of judicial or clerical supervision.[81] Nor are any such individuals mentioned by Tírechán in his description of the battle ordeal fought by two brothers over their inheritance; the two decide, after a little saintly interference, to submit their dispute to Patrick, but to that point there is no indication of any other outside authority being involved.[82] Similarly, while some of the ordeals described in the late Old Irish text *Echtra Cormaic* are concluded under druidical supervision, many are not.[83] The efficacy of the ordeal, like that of suretyship itself, was rooted in oral performance—the public enactment of legal rituals in an authoritatively communal setting.

It is, I suggest, precisely the authority of such procedures that *Cóic Conara Fugill* is seeking to embrace. In modeling his curial paths on suretyship and the ordeal, the author of the tract may be attempting to bring under the purview of the court disputes historically settled without recourse to professional intervention. For the text nowhere challenges the manner in which authority in legal affairs was customarily expressed: sureties remain at the heart of the process by which claims are articulated and enforced. But *Cóic Conara Fugill* quite deliberately resituates these traditional performers and rituals within the dramatic setting of the court; they are placed quite literally under new direction, as the instructions with which the tract begins on the tone of voice to be used in court remind us.[84] Not that such claims would have been in any way inconsistent with traditional assertions of juristic supremacy in legal affairs; authority in matters of law would presumably always have been regarded as vested ultimately in the products of the schools. Other types of authoritative personalities and procedures were recognized as well in these communities, however, and *Cóic Conara Fugill*'s removal of these entities to a distinctively curial setting may thus represent an attempt to translate into procedural terms the ascendancy traditionally accorded to the jurists in theory.

Perhaps an instructive parallel in this regard is the process by which Germanic kings first began to turn their assertions of authority over law and law-giving into something approaching real jurisdiction in legal affairs. In these societies also, performative rituals to which communities had traditionally accorded significance—the conveyancing of a clod of earth, for example, or the breaking of alder twigs over a person's head—did not disappear once kings began consolidating their hold over local justice; they simply moved into court.[85] The king's aim was not, in other words, to deprive these rituals of the power they had traditionally possessed in the society within which they were enacted; his intention was rather to enhance his own authority by laying claim to theirs.

That *Cóic Conara Fugill* may have been attempting something similar must be counted a real possibility, and it is revealing in this context to look back at a passage in the text that seems to express these aims more directly than any other. As we have seen, the fifth and final path, *coir n-athcomairc*, "proper inquiry," is baffling on two counts particularly: its name—in other words the nature of the "inquiry" envisaged—and its declared interest in cases that are, in its words, "speedy" or "prepared" and "well-bound" with sureties.[86] Thurneysen suggested that the procedure envisaged here was one whereby parties who were uncertain as to which of the paths was most appropriate to their case might consult the judge for his opinion before making their plea.[87] This is certainly plausible, although it does not explain in what sense such cases could have been considered "speedy" or "well-bound"; indeed they would seem from any reasonable point of view to be likely to prove the opposite. "Well-bound" may refer instead to the fact that an *aitire* had been summoned to act in the dispute, although the word used here, *sonaisc*, is not generally applied to this surety.[88] If this interpretation is correct, the claim would presumably have been regarded as "speedy" in that no further guarantor had then to be appointed.

An even more intriguing possibility, however, and one which accords well with the manner in which the passage is phrased, is that the cases referred to are "speedy" and "well-bound" in that they have *already been resolved*. What *Cóic Conara Fugill* may be claiming here is the right to ratify, or reauthorize, if one prefers, arrangements previously negotiated in a private setting. In this sense, then, would the parties appropriately "seek from the judge," not necessarily advice on how to proceed with their case—already prepared and "well-bound" with sureties—but rather his verdict on the issue.[89] For there can be no mistaking the principal emphasis of the passage: *coir nathcomairc doeclannar im cach solam sonaisc acht [i]ar dloma[d] deruisc firfoglamma fiss*,[90] "*coir n-athcomairc* is selected concerning every speedy, well-bound [case] but [only] according to[91] a declaration of a verdict [based on the] true-learning of knowledge." Knowledge and learning are here portrayed as the sine qua non of judicial legitimacy; only professional expertise can provide the necessary foundation for a truly authoritative resolution. And lest a claim to reauthorize decisions already reached seem an odd or unlikely one for jurists to make, it is worth noting that exactly such a privilege is claimed directly in the late H recension of the tract, which refuses the title of *fuigell*, "judgment," to settlements reached by the parties themselves in the absence of lawyers and judges.[92]

We do not know the date of composition for *Cóic Conara Fugill*. Its language and *Fénechas* style would appear to mark it as early, but our confidence in such criteria can no longer be considered great. It is suggestive that the text uses the later word *naidm* for the principal contractual surety instead of the earlier term *mac*, and that this term is confirmed by alliteration.[93] *Mac* is the word used most frequently in the oldest stratum of the laws, especially in poetic or formulaic contexts like that of *Cóic Conara Fugill*;[94] if the tract is actually as early as it has been assumed to be, the occurrence of the word, though not linguistically impossible, is at least surprising.[95] *Cóic Conara Fugill* may be, in other words, like other legal tracts commented on recently by Breatnach and McCone, deliberately *archaizing* rather than truly *archaic*. And if this is true, it is significant, for in a culture like that of the Irish in which antiquity was a sign of authoritative discourse, the cultivation and fostering of an appearance of age is frequently an attempt to disguise its opposite.

But if the date of *Cóic Conara Fugill*'s composition remains uncertain, the context in which it was produced is much less so. It is but one of a number of tracts that seek to resituate what had been essentially "private" legal processes within a curial setting. In this it is not alone: Richard Sharpe has already commented on the heavy emphasis laid on curial authority in the tract on distraint, surely the ultimate in "self-help" procedures.[96] Moreover, the title of *Berrad Airechta*—which is, after all, a tract on suretyship—"Abridgement of Court [Procedure]," speaks to exactly the same process, as we have seen. Indeed, the jurisdictional "conflict" between curial and private is actually expressed in that text as a confrontation between "judge-law," *dliged*, on the one hand, and private procedure, symbolized by the *naidm*, on the other.[97] It is no accident that *Berrad Airechta* presents the *naidm*, a surety whose authority over contractual agreements in an earlier age would likely have been absolute, as superior to other witnesses but secondary in authority to the court. Nor is it coincidental that the *Airecht* tract on court procedure depicts him as a witness to be interrogated by the court and then dismissed.[98] Precisely the same developments occur in Welsh law at a similar stage in the evolution of curial procedure, and for precisely the same reasons.[99] In both Ireland and Wales, the expansion of public jurisdiction was both marked and engineered by—at least in part—lawyers seeking to subsume under curial authority the stature and effectiveness of private law.

A markedly curial perspective is revealed in other, more subtle ways as well. Procedural innovations were not the only method by which jurists could bring under their purview the network of rituals and relationships through which legal affairs were conducted and resolved. Abstraction and categorization are processes frequently associated with increasing jurisprudential sophistication; they are in many ways the most visible hallmarks of a developing legal tradition. What is perhaps insufficiently realized, however, is the extent to which they can themselves serve as agents for the consolidation of curial authority. It was argued earlier that the immunities of Irish law—those exchanges deemed immune to claim or challenge even though no sureties had been given to warrant them—derived their special status and identity from the peculiar importance and closeness of the social relationships within which they had been conveyed. It is important to realize, however, that the conceptualizing of relationships in this manner betrays a distinctly curial perspective. The abstracting by the jurists of the legal category *ruidlesa*, "immunities," from the social circumstances in which sureties were considered inappropriate speaks to a setting in which judges or others external to a dispute might be called on to determine the justice of an individual claim. This is not to say that the convention itself by which sureties were avoided in such instances was not a real one, but rather that labels like "immune" or "not immune," "valid" or "invalid" have meaning principally from a curial vantage point. It is primarily in such a context that the links between poets' fees and clients' fiefs become visible and significant. Similarly, *Berrad Airechta*'s implicit insistence (against the evidence of *Di Astud Chor*) on the need for sureties to ensure the validity of a given contractual arrangement betrays a distinctly adjudicatory stance. Like "immunities," the categories "binding" and "non-binding" have meaning primarily outside the private context of negotiation and feud.

To become aware of the curial perspective enshrined in the jurists' groupings is valuable in itself. It is, however, merely a first step in understanding the complex process of procedural consolidation to which the law tracts bear witness. For abstractions such as these are more than simply the random by-products of jurisprudential activity. Categorization is not a politically neutral act: to define a category is implicitly to claim authority over its application and extent. In including certain exchanges and excluding others from the categories they constructed, the jurists were, whether consciously or not, privileging certain relationships and situations over others. Exchanges between close associates took precedence over the right of an owner of stolen goods to recover his lost property; transactions between client and lord superseded in importance and durability those between independent contractual principals. Similarly, promises made in the context of a formal and public binding ritual were accorded more security and respect than those made with equally serious intent but fewer formalities.

We cannot know whether the priorities expressed through these abstractions were actually realized in practice. Nor can we judge the extent to which the jurists' theoretical constructs reflected, rather than reshaped, the circumstances of the community in which they lived. It is likely that the relationship between law as lived and law as defined was far more fluid than such a query might imply. There is no reason to think that even with the textualization of the law the relationship between social order and jurisprudence was a static one: the two must have intersected at many points, like oral and written versions of a tale, forming and reforming one another in accordance with factors both human and intellectual. What seems likely, however, is that the jurists were, in giving shape to these groupings, laying claim to be their sole and rightful interpreters. *Cóic Conara Fugill* was but one step in the process by which the jurists sought to bring under curial jurisdiction structures and affiliations that had for so long been crucial to the private settlement of disputes.

But if developments of this nature were indeed occurring in the period of the lawbooks—if the practical side of law was in some sense "under construction" at the time the tracts were written—what then was the historical context that lay behind these changes? Recent work on the *brithem túaithe*, "tribal judge," and his royal connections raises the possibility that the elaboration of curial procedure might be linked to the consolidation of kingship that is so marked a feature of the seventh and eighth centuries in Ireland. An increasing interest in channeling disputes into assemblies presided over by a king or his representative is certainly a phenomenon familiar to historians of English or continental traditions as a symptom of consolidating royal power. And although there is nothing in *Cóic Conara*

Fugill itself to suggest a specifically royal connection, the *Airecht* tract describes the king, together with the tribal bishop and chief poet, as "the cliff which is behind the courts for judgement and for promulgation" and accords him the dominant position in the court.[100] The possible appeal of a Roman or continental-style judicial assembly to the rulers of, for example, the Uí Néill or the Uí Briúin, both of whom were dramatically increasing the extent and depth of their rule in this period, ought not to be overlooked.[101]

An even more likely context for an increasing interest on the part of the jurists in the expansion of curial procedure, however—though one that is not, to my mind, in any way contradictory to the possibility articulated above—are changes taking place in juristic circles themselves. Whatever degree of collaboration came eventually to obtain between native jurists and the ecclesiastical intelligentsia that emerged in Ireland after the conversion to Christianity, relations between these two groups and the traditions they represented were unlikely always to have been harmonious. Competition and, on the part of native jurists, fear of displacement must have been prominent responses as well, especially in the critical early centuries of the Christian advance. After all, the Church possessed a formidable history and elaborate jurisprudence and procedure of its own, and its legal tradition was sanctioned not only by long usage, but also by Scripture—God's law made manifest in written form. That the native jurists were uneasy about their ability to maintain the credibility of their own legal past in the face of such competition is evident from the prologue to the *Senchas Már*. That they were equally uncertain about retaining their personal authority over that past is also likely, especially if their stature in legal matters was still intimately linked to their role as pagan religious leaders.[102] One has only to recall the provision in the "First Synod of St. Patrick" ostracizing Christians who have recourse to secular rather than to ecclesiastical judgment to understand that the threat posed to the authority of native jurists by their priestly counterparts was serious indeed.[103]

An attempt to curialize "native" justice in such a context would be of particular significance. The prospect that native law and the prerogatives of its traditional custodians might simply be absorbed by the Church was a real one. Charles-Edwards has argued that the *Collectio Canonum Hibernensis* itself was intended by its compilers to regulate secular as well as ecclesiastical affairs within the Christian community, and held thus the potential to displace its native rivals altogether.[104] In order to survive, native jurists may have found themselves having in essence to redefine both the nature of their authority and their relationship to the tradition of which they had for so long been the guardians. The "professionalization" of the discipline, an increasing emphasis on the practical and non-religious aspects of the legal craft, would likely have seemed a logical response to such a challenge. By formulating a distinctively curial procedure, the jurists may have hoped not only to bring more disputes under their own jurisdiction but also to establish a formal venue for the exercise of a specifically "secular" justice—one that would underscore, in its intricacy and ritual, the authority and special knowledge of those charged with interpreting its regulations. If pagan ceremonial had in fact played a role in earlier forms of Irish justice, the construction of procedures deriving their sanction from specialist training in law rather than from a perceived association with religious ritual is precisely what one would expect. One would not want, of course, to exaggerate the degree of conflict obtaining between native jurists and the Church; there is a great deal of evidence to suggest sustained and fruitful contacts between these two groups, as we have seen. Cooperation does not preclude competition, however: the emergence of law as a practical discipline, like the lawbooks themselves, may have its origins in the desire of those in authority to maintain the stature traditionally accorded them.[105]

To this point, we have looked at the question of authority primarily from the procedural point of view. It is important to realize, however, that the concern with curial prerogative evinced in texts like *Cóic Conara Fugill* and *Berrad Airechta* is but one aspect of an even larger process visible throughout the legal *corpus* as a whole—the elaboration and enlargement of the legal tradition itself. In grounding their paths in traditional ideas and concepts like *fír* and *dliged*, the jurists may have been seeking in part to claim for their curial innovations the respectability of age. But this was not their only aim. The schema they presented was of more than merely procedural interest. It had, and was intended to have, jurisprudential significance as well, as is evident from the manner and terms in which it is discussed: "In what is judgment (*brithemnas*) established in the [legal] language of the *Féni*?" ask the opening words of *Uraicecht Becc*. "Not difficult," comes the response, "[in] truth (*fír*) and entitlement (*dliged*) and nature (*aicned*)."[106] *Cóic Conara Fugill* speaks in equally universal, if slightly more rhetorical, terms of the "five roads that are ridden to the house of the judge;"[107] as we have seen, the names it gives to these "roads" are also abstract terms for "justice." Such phrasing is not accidental. In giving institutional form to such abstract legal entities, the compilers were, in effect, asserting the existence and antiquity of a network of independent jurisprudential perceptions that encapsulated, and thereby validated, the legal tradition as a whole. *Fír, dliged, aicned, cert,* and *téchtae*: each was rendered tangible by its procedural manifestation, and each bore potent witness to the frame of which it was itself a part. What we are witnessing here is nothing less than the creation of a highly systematized jurisprudence, a virtual cosmology of law.

To say this is not to deny the existence of a native jurisprudence. *Fír* is an ancient concept for which there are direct analogues in Welsh tradition, as the use of the cognate term *gwir* in the *Surexit* memorandum clearly shows,[108] and *fír flathemon*, the "king's justice," is a principal theme in *Audacht Morainn* and other wisdom texts dealing with sacral kingship.[109] But if the antiquity and origins of *fír* are beyond question, the historical pedigree of the concepts with which it is paired in these tracts is far less certain. Certainly the terms were not initially equal in their range and implications; there is reason to believe that *fír*, conceived of in its broadest sense, is what originally underlay the whole. *Dliged* does appear to have had an independent existence before the composition of the tracts, to judge by the frequency with which it is mentioned in them. But even so it is a markedly juridical, rather than jurisprudential, concept: *dliged*, "entitlement," is, in other words, guaranteed by judgments rendered in accordance with *fír*, "truth." Furthermore, to judge from the all-encompassing nature of *dliged* as it is presented in *Berrad Airechta*, both *Cóic Conara Fugill* and *Uraicecht Becc* have, in restricting *dliged* to the realm of oral contracts, narrowed its (original?) range and purview—perhaps deliberately in order to add *cert* and *aicned* to their schemas. *Cert* and *téchtae* are found frequently in the tracts in a variety of contexts, but there is nothing to indicate that either had specific jurisprudential significance prior to the formulation of the framework articulated in *Cóic Conara Fugill*.[110] Like *dliged, cert* and *téchtae* were originally aspects of, or guaranteed by, *fír*, rather than the other way around. Only in the schemas proposed by *Cóic Conara Fugill* and *Uraicecht Becc* do the terms acquire something approaching equality. For in the newly elaborated systems of jurisprudence they outline, *fír* is merely one component in a schema created by the proliferation of its own constituent parts.

Equally revealing of the process of jurisprudential development is the inclusion in *Uraicecht Becc* of *aicned*, "nature," or *recht n-aicnid*, "natural law," as it is more commonly termed in the lawbooks. Neil McLeod has argued that a concept of "natural order," with which he would identify the *recht n-aicnid* of the tracts, was implicit in early Irish jurisprudence. Judgments rendered were believed to have a direct impact on their natural surroundings; thus did Sencha's wrongful decision on the procedure to be followed by women in claiming land raise blisters on his cheeks that only Brig's more righteous verdict could cure.[111] McLeod's vision of a "natural order" revealed through tradition and precedent is well supported by the evidence, although in light of what has been said above, it is important to point out that according to the lawbooks, what lay at the heart of this natural order was *fír*. Truth both ensured and was revealed by a properly ordered universe; falsehood destroyed it.[112]

Despite the existence of native ideas about the relationship between justice and natural order, however, both the term and the concept *recht n-aicnid*, "natural law," were forthrightly associated by the jurists more with the writings of Saint Paul than with pre-Christian tradition. Indeed, *recht n-aicnid* is used most commonly in the tracts to situate native secular tradition with respect to the Christian dispensation that succeeded it.[113] In other words, whatever native beliefs may have been incorporated into the jurists' conception of *recht n-aicnid*, many of the ideas that term was intended to invoke—and perhaps the term itself—were ecclesiastical in nature. The obvious conclusion is difficult to resist: Irish jurisprudence was actively under construction during the period the law tracts were composed. The very expression used by the jurists to convey the timelessness of the tradition within which they worked itself reveals the extent to which that tradition was changing.[114]

The expansion of Irish procedure to which *Cóic Conara Fugill* speaks so eloquently was paralleled, therefore, by a comparable extension in the jurisprudential sphere. Moreover, the motives that inspired both of these developments were likely much the same. Even today the grounding of legal activity in the abstrusities of an intellectual tradition is a way for lawyers and judges to assert their jurisdiction in legal matters. It would hardly be surprising if the deliberate complicating of native Irish tradition to which the tracts bear witness was similarly motivated. Only thus could the jurists ensure the monopoly in legal affairs to which their extensive training and background entitled them; only thus could "rude, ignorant, and paltry folk" be successfully "scared away" from the business of litigation.[115] Binchy has suggested that professional advocates (*aigneda*) first developed to guide litigants through what he called the "shoals and quicksands of the law of distraint."[116] It is equally likely that these shoals and quicksands themselves originated in the desire of jurists to be the ones to guide claimants through them. This is in part what the textualizing of law itself was all about: the more inaccessible the procedures and the more involved the jurisprudence, the more securely could legal matters be situated within the custodianship of a learned legal class. And while we do not know if the jurists were successful in their claims, it is clear that the importance of textualized knowledge remained a theme in juristic writings long after the period during which the majority of tracts were composed. It is certainly no accident that the late text *Urchuilte Bretheman*, in listing the subjects with which judges should be familiar, refers mostly to the titles of written tracts.[117]

None of this is to say that Ireland lacked a native legal tradition. It is, however, to point to the growing self-awareness of that tradition and to the increasingly speculative attitude taken by the jurists toward the Irish legal past. In composing tracts like *Cóic Conara Fugill*, *Uraicecht Becc*, and *Berrad Airechta*, the jurists were seeking not merely to define and delimit what had been, but to resituate it with respect to what they wished to be. Thus could they attempt to consolidate their own authority in a manner that transformed the past without repudiating it. This should not surprise us: it has already been noted how much closer such a view brings Ireland to the Western European experience as a whole. Elsewhere also was authority an issue; elsewhere also were oral performances and performers absorbed within the dramatic setting of the court. Similarly, royal claims to jurisdiction in other European lands were rooted in increasingly grandiose visions of the jurisprudence that had in theory inspired them.[118] Those occasionally frustrated by the frequency with which the words "except for Ireland" appear in general works on law should perhaps take heart.[119] The process we are witnessing in the Irish lawbooks is in some sense universal: the attempt to transfer procedures and perceptions associated with "private" law to an authoritatively "public" setting. Even for the Irish jurists, the road to judgment was anything but a straight and narrow "path."

6. Court and Custom in Medieval Wales

Historians do not always know the ending to the stories that they tell. Questions rather than answers ultimately remain to us from our study of *Cóic Conara Fugill*. In the absence of charters or dispute settlements, it is impossible to determine how native jurists fared in their bid for jurisdiction and authority.[1] Nor can we reasonably hope to outline the manner in which the curial environment itself might have helped to reshape or transform the legal practices it absorbed. Later sources tell us little, either about the fate of the sureties themselves or about the changing social context within which they operated. Even our confidence in the increasing depth and intrusiveness of royal administration in the centuries immediately preceding the arrival of the Normans is not matched by a sense of the effects of such changes on local customs and relationships.[2] We may be able to trace the beginnings of the tale, but of its ultimate denouement, and of the destiny of its principal characters, we know relatively little.

It is specifically for this reason that comparisons between the Welsh and Irish lawbooks are so valuable. Let me be clear at the outset on precisely what such comparisons do and do not imply. Few historians today would deny the necessity for treating institutions and customs within their proper historical context. Wales is not, and was not, Ireland, nor was the thirteenth century the same as the eighth.[3] The Welsh *mach*-surety, though almost certainly descended from the Common Celtic **makkos* and similar therefore in many ways to its Irish cognate the *naidm* (earlier *mac*),[4] nevertheless did not mirror it completely. Nor did the systems as a whole correspond in every respect: there was no Welsh equivalent to the Irish *ráth*, nor any Irish equivalent to the Welsh *gorfodog*- or *amodwr*-sureties. Welsh guarantors, like the people that they served, existed and functioned within their own milieu, and it is thus that they must be studied.[5] As Ó Corráin has remarked, "inheritance is not the only and not always the most important" of the determinants of social structure.[6]

That said, however, it is clear that a knowledge of one tradition can considerably enrich and enlarge our understanding of the other. As in everything else, caution and attention to contextual detail is the key. It would be futile, for example, to speculate which of two practices might be the closest to a Common Celtic original in the absence of evidence as to the origin and dating of legal change. In Irish society, both parties to an agreement appointed guarantors to the other, regardless of whether the debt contracted was a mutual one; in Wales, there is no evidence to suggest that in one-sided debts, more than one surety would ever have been offered. To argue then from this that the Irish was the original form, and that indeed the Welsh *amodwyr*, "contract-men" were, because they acted in groups,[7] the true descendants of the Common Celtic enforcing surety rather than the *mach* (despite the semantic evidence to the contrary), would presume too much on the one hand and ignore contemporary Welsh evidence for a recent origin for the *amodwr* on the other.[8] It may seem an obvious point, but it is an important one as well: knowing "what happened" in Ireland does not entitle one simply to assume that events transpired in a parallel fashion in Wales.

But if such direct correspondences are unwise to presume, more careful comparisons are nevertheless worthwhile. Texts of one tradition can be used to flesh out fragmentary or allusive passages in another, or to delineate the likely direction of legal development where there is evidence within a tradition that changes have occurred.[9] Because, for example, the Irish *naidm* was an enforcing surety who bore no financial liability for the obligation, it would be unwise automatically to assume that the Welsh *mach* also had originally borne no responsibility for the debt, especially since the *mach* was clearly, by the time of the composition of the lawbooks, a paying as well as an enforcing surety. Since evidence within the Welsh lawbooks themselves suggests that the *mach*'s primary responsibilities in the agreement had shifted over time from enforcing to paying, however, the Irish parallels at once lend credence to this argument and enlarge considerably our understanding of developments in Wales in the period of the lawbooks. Similarly, *Llyfr Iorwerth*'s labored efforts to "explain away" a provision forbidding women to give sureties to others are best understood in light of the Irish evidence as an attempt to incorporate into contemporary law the textual remnants of earlier Welsh practice.[10] If it is prudent to treat with caution such parallels as may appear, it is equally imprudent to ignore them altogether.

Moreover, although the Welsh lawbooks tell us nothing about Ireland per se, they do provide a stance from which to examine some of the key theoretical issues raised by the Irish evidence. For in few places was the question of authority more central, or the curializing of private disputes more intently pursued, than in Wales on the eve of the loss of its independence. Wales in the thirteenth century was a hodgepodge of competing claims and jurisdictions. English, Marcher, and native lords jostled one another anxiously for authority and recognition, and law was without question an essential element in this struggle.[11] Law and national identity were intimately, and intentionally, linked: *Cyfraith Hywel* served both to rally the Welsh against their English enemies and to bolster Gwynedd's assertion of authority over the other native principalities.[12] The customs of the March were consciously invoked to support that region's claims to a distinctive identity of its own. And Edward's magisterial—though partial—"reauthorizing" of Welsh law in the 1284 statute of Rhuddlan articulated his claims to supremacy in that region no less clearly than Patrick's "reauthorizing" of Irish law in the prologue to the *Senchas Már* claimed Ireland and Irish tradition for Christianity.[13]

As important as law to the political struggles of the period was the application of law. The precise relationship between the legal texts themselves and the consolidation of princely power is uncertain. No extant lawbook is explicitly attributed to a particular ruler (apart from Hywel himself, of course), although the prologues to many redactions of the lawbooks seem likely to have been composed during the reigns of particularly powerful princes.[14] And it is clear that local communities retained an important role in the settlement of disputes into the thirteenth century and beyond.[15] The effects of the legal renaissance in England on the political power of the rulers of that country had not gone unnoticed in Wales, however, and lords sought increasingly from the twelfth century on to expand their role in legislation and the administration of justice.

Justice and the profits deriving from it were particularly critical to the success of the Welsh principate, and the political ambitions that characterized the age of the Llywelyns mandated significant changes in judicial administration. Llywelyn ap Iorwerth's attempts to strengthen his control over the lesser lords of *pura Wallia* and to expand the scope of his jurisdiction in his native Gwynedd resulted in the establishment of a high court, over which the prince and his chief justice, an "*ynad llys* writ large," presided.[16] This court could respond directly to suits for land by vassals of the prince, and could even adjudicate appeals from the local commote courts in certain types of cases. By the thirteenth century at least, a regular pattern of princely commotal courts existed throughout native Wales, and more and more cases that would earlier have been resolved in an extracurial setting came now within the purview of the lord's court.[17] One of the few extant dispute settlement records reveals how complicated these overlapping patterns of jurisdiction had become by the early thirteenth century. A land claim prosecuted at Llandinam in Arwystli was referred for resolution to men from the local community; however, the court session in which it was heard was presided over by a local ruler and representatives of the prince.[18]

Wales thus offers us the opportunity to study in greater depth many of the social and political processes visible in inchoate form in the Irish texts. One can imagine no more suitable venue from which to observe the curializing of "private law" personalities and practices than this essentially "early medieval"[19] society, propelled, by the pressure of political competition, into a world of increasingly seigneurial jurisdiction under the watchful eye of a literate and historically-minded juristic tradition. As always, it is important not to overestimate the extent to which "private" and "public" overlapped, or to insist on a dichotomy between the two that the evidence does not support. Davies's work particularly illuminates the extent to which curial and extracurial forms of dispute settlement coexisted in pre-Conquest Wales, where even "official" judges frequently resolved disputes by private arbitration.[20] The key issue, however, as in Ireland, was authority—or, at the very least, aegis in the process of becoming authority. In a society struggling to come to grips with lordship as it was understood and practiced in thirteenth-century Europe, it was inevitable that the removal into a curial context of previously extracurial procedures would eventually reshape both these processes themselves and the social structures on which they were based. The intersection of court and custom was very much at hand.

Again as in Ireland, suretyship lay at the heart of the changes taking place. Few other institutions could so effectively claim to straddle the divide between legal past and present. In origin and general structure, Welsh suretyship was "early medieval" in every sense of the term: as we shall see, the Welsh *mach* shared much more with his Irish counterpart the *naidm* than his Common Celtic name. Furthermore, despite the status and visibility of contemporary English law, Welsh contractual procedure remained relentlessly oral, a reflection both of the small-scale nature of the transactions taking place and of the essentially "preliterate"[21] nature of the society within which they occurred. But if there is much that is old about the Welsh *mach*, there is much that is new as well. Nothing can be clearer from the sources but that suretyship was, and remained throughout the fourteenth and fifteenth centuries, an active area of the law. All of the principal complete redactions of the lawbooks (*Llyfr Cyfnerth*, *Llyfr Blegywryd*, *Llyfr Iorwerth*, and Latin A, B, D, and E) contain extensive tractates on the subject, and while the existence of these texts need not in itself imply a continuing interest in the provisions they contain, it is evident that parts of *Llyfr Iorwerth* particularly had been revised in accord with the latest trends in legal writing. Its tractate opens with an elaborate narrative setting forth the manner in which suretyship could be denied in court—a passage that not only reflects great familiarity with contemporary pleading tactics, but that must have been, to judge from the much briefer descriptions of the same process contained in other versions of the lawbooks, deliberately rewritten by the compiler to highlight appropriate curial procedure in such cases.[22] Furthermore, suretyship was, along with theft and land-law, one of the three usual topics for *cynghawsedd*, a sophisticated genre of legal writing that developed in Gwynedd in the twelfth century and spread southward in the course of the fourteenth and fifteenth centuries.[23] In fact, two post-Conquest manuscripts (F and G) contain a collection of *cynghawsedd* devoted almost entirely to suretyship.[24]

It may at first appear odd that such an ancient institution should attract the energy and attention of contemporary-minded jurists. Cases of theft and disputes over land have the potential to infringe on seigneurial prerogative in many and evident ways; that lords should seek to acquire dominion over the resolution of such claims is not surprising. Contracts made by individuals, however, many of them involving sums no larger than a single lamb or colt, might seem a less consequential matter altogether. After all, thirteenth-century English justice declined even to involve the royal court in cases of the sort envisaged in the Welsh pleas.[25] But it would be a mistake to equate the size of the amount in dispute with the significance of the rights being claimed. In a society in which lordship remained, despite the best efforts of both the Welsh and English princes, a largely piecemeal affair, and in which political boundaries fluctuated wildly according to the vagaries of war, jurisdiction exercised—on however small a scale—was at once an assertion and a confirmation of supremacy. For if the Irish evidence has anything to teach us about the Welsh situation, it is that medieval suretyship was not merely, or perhaps even principally, a financial matter. To regulate contractual associations between individuals was implicitly to direct the course of a wide variety of relations between peoples and groups. Certainly the Bishop and Chapter of St. Asaph's recognized the political implications of such actions when they complained of Llywelyn ap Gruffudd having inappropriately attempted to assert his seigneurial authority over hitherto private contracts of betrothal and loans.[26] In truth, there was much at stake.

The removal of custom into court was much more than just a matter of geography. As *mechni* and other older mechanisms of social control were gradually absorbed within the increasingly seigneurial world of the twelfth and thirteenth centuries, they were, inevitably, transformed.[27] What we know of the early *mach* suggests that his primary functions were similar to those performed by his Irish counterpart, the *naidm*.[28] Like the *naidm*, the *mach* participated in the hand-in-hand binding ritual by which the obligation was undertaken; the evidence suggests that the public and performative aspects of this ceremony not only retained their importance in the twelfth and thirteenth centuries, but had actually crystallized by that time into something approaching a legal technicality.[29] The *mach* served also as chief witness for the transaction. In many texts he appears as one of the nine *tafodiogion* of Welsh law, men whose testimony under oath would prevail against all challenges.[30] Furthermore, again like the *naidm*, his witnessing extended to more than just the details of the agreement; a *mach* was not allowed to begin to enforce the claim until he had seen for himself the debtor's public declaration that he did not intend to pay what he owed.[31] And the *mach* was as well the chief enforcer of the obligation. By the time of the composition of the lawbooks, the *mach* had become primarily a paying, rather than an enforcing, surety, but there can be little doubt but that this was a secondary development;[32] many texts define his office primarily in terms of enforcement.[33]

More striking even than these similarities in function is that the early *mach*, like the *naidm*, was regarded in the community not only as the supervisor of the agreement between the two contracting parties, but as the living symbol of the bond uniting them as well. This is indeed an ancient idea, one that speaks directly to the intimate and precurial nature of the environment within which contractual "dramas" had originally been enacted in early Wales. Only once is the unity between *mach* and claim expressed directly in the lawbooks: according to a passage in the *Llyfr Iorwerth* tractate, claimants who refused law in the presence of a judge lost their *mach* and thereby their case, *cane phara e haul namen hyt tra parhao e mach*,[34] "since the claim lasts only while the *mach* lasts." But the special status of the *mach* is also visible in the imagery of many of the rituals attendant on his office. What we know about the binding procedure, for example, suggests that creditor and debtor did not themselves join hands with one another but were united only by the *mach*, who stood between them and clasped the hands of both. If one of the parties failed to join hands with the *mach*, that part of the bargain would not hold: if, for example, the *mach* joined hands with the creditor, thus pledging him his faith that he would enforce the claim, but did not join hands with the debtor, the *mach* became liable himself for the debt, since he was bound to the creditor even though the debtor was not. Similarly, and most tellingly, if the creditor did not take the *mach*'s hand in his, no debt was owed even if the debtor had conscientiously performed his side of the ritual. In other words, if the *mach* did not bind the two parties to one another, nothing did; the image offered in the texts is that of a buckle that, if fastened, holds the two ends of a strap together against all opposition, but that if loose, easily gives way.[35]

Nor was the binding procedure the only ritual associated with the *mach* in which his symbolic identification with the contract found tangible expression. Men who wished to deny a claim urged against them did so by denying neither the fact of the debt nor the accuracy of the plaintiff's accusations, but rather the person of the *mach* himself. Indeed, once a defendant had indicated his desire to deny the obligation, the plaintiff dropped out of the process altogether, and the matter proceeded between the defendant and the *mach*.[36] And while it might be argued that a defendant's ability to deny a *mach*, and thereby his debt, was itself a relatively late development, reflective perhaps of the decreasing intimacy of the community within which such transactions occurred,[37] it is striking nevertheless that the perceptions and priorities of an earlier age are so clearly preserved in this curialized procedure. Certainly other provisions also speak to the special authority of the *mach* in the agreement. A triad preserved in *Llyfr Cyfnerth* and in the Latin lawbooks not only forbids the creditor to distrain directly against the debtor, but prohibits him even from granting the debtor additional time in which to meet his obligations without the *mach*'s permission.[38]

We are less fully informed about the social context within which early *mechni* operated. There is evidence that many of the perceptions governing the functioning of suretyship in early Irish society obtained in some fashion as well in early Wales. Persons existing in subordinating relationships with others might, for example, find their actions with respect to contractual arrangements circumscribed by those relationships. Welsh law preserves a list of those incompetent to act as sureties to others, and although the *Llyfr Cyfnerth* and Latin versions of this list were borrowed into

Welsh law from the Irish *Collectio Canonum Hibernensis*, the *Llyfr Iorwerth* version, which seems to reflect archaic practice in forbidding such incompetents even to give sureties on their own, probably reflects native Welsh custom.[39] Similarly, the reciprocal obligations enjoined on at least certain kindred leaders (*dux generis*) and the community in which they lived meant not only that such persons were expected to be consulted when the seizure of one of their dependents was imminent, but also that they would ensure the continuing captivity of the offender until the dispute had been resolved.[40] People whose dealings with others had been improper might find their rights in unrelated legal situations curtailed,[41] and a triad found in *Llyfr Cyfnerth*, *Llyfr Blegywryd*, and the Latin lawbooks implies that the concepts of public honor and shame were operative in ensuring that those who undertook suretyship would fulfill the responsibilities of their office.[42] But perhaps most suggestive of the social context underlying the rules regulating *mechni* are the *da dilis diuach*, "goods immune from claim without a surety," mentioned in *Llyfr Cyfnerth*, *Llyfr Blegywryd*, and the Latin tradition. For if, as appears to be the case, the principle at work in these fragmentary texts is the same as that operative in the Irish immunities, then in Wales also had ongoing affiliations of extended indebtedness once been marked off from ordinary transactions of short-term duration by the presence or absence of sureties.[43]

It is important not to overestimate the similarities between the Irish and Welsh sureties nor to focus so intently on the parallels that the differences between them go unnoticed. Dissimilarities in structure have already been mentioned. Irish transactions involved several sureties but Welsh agreements only one, a fact that has led Charles-Edwards to suggest that the Welsh contract was an altogether less formal affair. As he argues, this may even be the reason why Welsh law permitted a debtor to deny a surety by compurgation, a possibility that is never mentioned in the Irish texts. Alternatively, the ability of a debtor to disown his obligation may reflect the decreasing role played by personal lordship and kinship in the enforcement of legal liabilities. If a man's lord or kindred leader acts as his surety for specific contractual obligations, the chances of him wishing—or being permitted to—deny his debt are exceedingly slim. If, however, the surety is a person less involved with or well known to his debtor, then a defendant's ability to deny an accusation of debt affords him important protection against fraud.[44]

Of all the differences separating the Welsh *mach* from the Irish *naidm*, however, the most striking is that the *mach* had become, at least by the period of the lawbooks, primarily a paying surety—a guarantor liable, in other words, for the obligation of his principal on that person's default. That the financial liability of the *mach* represented a development over time, and was not a feature of the early *mach*'s office, is relatively certain.[45] It is possible even to trace in the lawbooks various stages of his evolution from enforcing to paying guarantor. All of the principal lawbooks (*Llyfr Iorwerth* particularly) contain provisions requiring *mach*-sureties who do not fulfill the characteristic duties of their office (*teithi*) to pay the debt themselves. Since this is clearly viewed in the texts as a penalty for inadequate performance, the presumption must be that at the time these provisions were written, the surety in question would not normally have had to pay the debt.[46] Similarly, a provision in *Llyfr Iorwerth* speaks of a *mach* who has had the misfortune to go surety for a debtor who is subsequently banished; in such cases the debt is divided into two, and *talu o'r mach e neyll hanner e'r haulur, canys hager yu talu o'r mach kubel ac ef en wyreon, ac nat tegach colly kubel o'r haulur yr credu ohonau ew y mach*,[47] "the *mach* pays the one-half to the claimant since it is unfair that the *mach* should pay all and he innocent [of the default], and it is not more fair for the claimant to lose all on account of having trusted in the *mach*." Clearly the *mach* of this passage, though on his way to becoming a *Zahlbürge*, did not yet bear full financial liability for the debt.

By the thirteenth century at least, however, the *mach* had become a true paying surety, certainly in the South of Wales and probably in the North as well. It is surely no accident that Latin B and Latin E's versions of the provision cited above on the exiled debtor envisage either the lord or the *mach* meeting the obligation in full.[48] The reasons underlying the *mach*'s transition from enforcing to paying surety are complicated and will probably never be fully understood. Wales was experiencing significant economic change in the twelfth and thirteenth centuries: in both native and Anglo-Norman regions, new lands were being brought under cultivation, urbanization was proceeding apace, and commerce and trade were developing rapidly. Currency was circulating widely for the first time in many areas, and it would not be surprising if the increasing sophistication of the Welsh economy was reflected in more complex arrangements for credit and debt.[49]

But what is perhaps most odd about the *mach*'s new role is not that such a surety would have appeared, but rather that he should apparently have developed as late as he did—late enough, in other words, for the transition to be still visible in the lawbooks. After all, paying guarantors had existed for centuries in many other European lands, including Ireland, where the *ráth* was well established by the time *Berrad Airechta* was compiled around 700. It is possible, of course, that the solution is a textual one—that passages like those cited above on *teithi* and on exile derive from a date far removed from that of the texts in which they have been preserved, and that paying sureties had existed for a while in southern Wales particularly before they were recorded in the laws. It is at least worth noting, however, that the transformation from enforcing to paying surety was not the only change taking place in *mechni* at the time the lawbooks were composed. From the thirteenth century on, suretyship was dramatically reshaped by the curial environment within which it increasingly operated. The change in emphasis from an executory to a financially liable *mach* may well be only one aspect of a broader spectrum of change—a transformation political as well as economic in nature.

For there can be no doubt but that the expansion of seigneurial authority in legal affairs had considerable impact on older, precurial methods of social control. The *mach* who had been, in an earlier period, the ultimate guardian and living symbol of individual contractual arrangements became instead a type of plea—one method of claim among many, subject increasingly to the authority, records, and even willingness to enforce, of the lord and his court. Suretyship was not the only ancient institution to experience such changes: *dadannudd*, a very early method of claiming land by the public uncovering of the hearth of a proprietor ancestor, had become by the thirteenth century only one of several court approved pleas by which one could pursue a claim to land.[50] Interestingly, both *dadannudd* and *mechni* retained in their curial manifestations much of the imagery and language of the earlier period. In many ways it is this interaction between old and new that is most striking about the process: in absorbing the authority of the *mach*, the court implicitly redefined its own. But if the rhetoric remained the same, the legal relationships originally expressed through this language were altered considerably. The ancient notion of the unity of surety and contract that had in many ways encapsulated the duties and status of the early *mach* could not long withstand his removal to a setting in which ultimate jurisdiction resided elsewhere.

The process by which the lord's court gradually absorbed the functions prerogatives of suretyship is evident throughout the lawbooks. Often, seigneurial jurisdiction was simply imposed on already existing structures. Lords claimed the right, for example, to prosecute offenses (and thereby collect fines) in cases arising out of *mechni*, even in situations where the matter remained at least nominally under the surety's control. According to *Llyfr Cyfnerth*, claimants unwise enough to take distraint from a debtor without consulting their surety became liable for a fine to the king or lord.[51] Similarly, *Llyfr Iorwerth* mentions lords pursuing charges of perjury against debtors who attempted unsuccessfully to deny sureties brought against them,[52] and charges of theft against the person at fault when an item purchased turned out to belong to someone other than the seller.[53] Lords[54] also claimed special privileges exempting them from strictures normally observed in the prosecution of a claim of suretyship. According to *Llyfr Iorwerth* and later *Llyfr Blegywryd* traditions, for example, gages given by sureties or lords had no need of further sureties to guarantee their immunity from claim by third parties, a warranty that was required of others.[55] War or other varieties of seigneurial "business" could delay the pursuit of a claim arising out of suretyship,[56] and goods given by lords to their men were considered items for which no sureties need be exchanged.[57]

But though the privileging of lords with respect to claims arising out of suretyship is one measure of the extent to which seigneurial authority was making itself felt in the period of the lawbooks, it is in the actual transfer of duties previously performed by *mach*-sureties to officers of the court that we can most clearly see the impact of the curial environment within which such claims were increasingly being pursued. As we have seen, the principal responsibility of the early *mach* had been that of enforcement. But the enforcing surety is a creature of a precurial age; not surprisingly, therefore, this aspect particularly of the *mach*'s office was affected by the growing prominence of the court. Enforcement remained part of the rhetoric of the later legal texts, but the emphasis tended increasingly to be placed on the financial liabilities to which the *mach* had newly become subject: *kyfreith mach yv pan adefho y vechniaeth talu neu gymell*,[58] "the law regarding a surety is that when he may acknowledge his suretyship, [he is either] to pay or to enforce."

Moreover, it is evident even in the lawbooks that sureties attempting to enforce the obligations for which they had been appointed were at this point acting frequently under the supervision of the lord. Texts found in all traditions show that the early *mach* had exercised authority over the taking of distraint or a gage from the debtor.[59] Indeed, as has been noted, claimants could not themselves even extend the due date of a debt without the surety's permission.[60] By at least the thirteenth century, however, the lord was becoming more and more often the arbiter of such matters. *Ior*

62/12–13 requires a surety to seek the lord's permission before taking an outsize gage from a debtor who has nothing to offer as a gage except a costly item that he does not wish to surrender. And a similar provision, included in the *Damweiniau* of manuscripts D, G, and *Llyfr Colan*, allowed a lord to divide communal property in order to permit a *mach* to take a gage the immunity of which could not be challenged by the former co-owners of the goods.[61] Most striking of all, however, is the textual confusion surrounding the identity of the person whose permission must be sought so that a creditor might distrain against his debtor. In some lawbooks, it is the surety who is in charge; in others it is the lord. A few texts attempt to split the difference: Latin E2/E4 and *Llyfr Blegywryd* preserve both traditions side by side, while in *Llyfr Cyfnerth*, authority is retained by the *mach*, but a fine is paid to the king if a transgression occurs.[62]

What would appear then to be reflected in the lawbooks is a transitional phase in the history of Welsh contract law in which authority in matters of enforcement was shifting from the *mach* to the lord. The possibility of regional variation makes it difficult to be positive about such a conclusion, but lords were, at the very least, taking an active interest in the manner in which contractual claims were enforced, and it is reasonable to assume that their enthusiasm grew more, rather than less, intense over time. It is evident indeed from some of the texts that the lord himself sometimes acted as *mach*. This may have been a tradition of long standing; in early Ireland a man's personal lord or kindred leader often stood surety for his subordinates, and this may have obtained also in early Wales. Certainly by the time *Llyfr Iorwerth* was compiled at least, the lord could inherit the suretyship of a *mach* who died without an heir and become thereby entitled to enforce the claim against the defendant as if he himself had originally been appointed as surety of the obligation. Furthermore, both *Llyfr Iorwerth* and *Llyfr Cyfnerth* (following *Llyfr Iorwerth*) remark directly that the lord should act as surety for all acknowledged exchanges that do not already have a surety assigned to them.[63]

To say that the lord sometimes acted as automatic surety for acknowledged transactions, however, may be only to say that Wales had by this period developed political authorities capable of enforcing law. Indeed, one fourteenth-century manuscript casts the lord's responsibilities in precisely such terms: among the authorities that exist to enforce obligations, it says, are a surety with respect to his suretyship and an *arglwydd y gymell pob peth ny bo mach arnaw or a ddylyer o cyfreith*,[64] "a lord to enforce everything owed by law for which no *mach* exists." Late sources mention lords enforcing claims brought before them by a variety of methods, including direct distraint and prison.[65] Ironically, seigneurial enforcement of suits for land, and perhaps for other types of claim as well, often involved a special kind of paying *mach*. In origin probably a cross between the contractual *mach* and the ancient appearance surety, this *mach ar gyfreith*, "*mach*-surety to abide by law" had, by the thirteenth century, been adapted to the changing political circumstances of the day. The principal duty of such sureties in the period of the lawbooks was to guarantee that the parties to a suit would pursue in good faith the claims and counter-claims they submitted to the court and abide by the verdict eventually given by the judge. No longer involved in the enforcement of the claim, they were, in essence, living pledges, held in the custody of the lord until the case had been concluded, and amerced if their principals failed in their obligations.[66]

Ultimately even contracted *mechni* came to rely principally on the court in matters of enforcement. Manuscript H, of the fourteenth century, acknowledges quite openly the manner in which the prosecution of claims arising out of suretyship had changed since the days of Hywel:

> Ynghyfreith Hywel dda ydd oedd y fach gymell y fechni o nerth ac na allei neb fot un fach eithyr a gymellei ay fodd ay o anfodd; ac anawd oedd hynny rhac na allei rei hynny. Sef gwnaethbwyt gwedy, y fach ac y bawb y gymell a chroes a chosp am danei os torrir; sef yw hynny naw ugein.[67]

> In the law of Hywel Dda a *mach* enforced his suretyship by strength, and no one could be a surety except one who could compel [another to meet his obligations] whether he wished to do so or did not so wish; and that was difficult, because some could not do that. This was later enacted: that a *mach* and everyone would enforce by means of a cross, with a penalty for breaking it. This is that [penalty], 180 [pence].

Placing a wooden cross on property in dispute was a method, particularly popular in the fourteenth and fifteenth centuries, of laying claim to that property; the possessor of the goods or land in question had either to answer the claim in court or pay a substantial fine—here 180 pence—to the lord for contempt of the law.[68] "Private" enforcement, in other words, now turned on "public" power. But even more striking is what this passage implies about the personal background of those likely to be appointed in this period as sureties. Not only was the *mach*'s status with respect to the obligation diminished by his removal to the curial sphere, so potentially also was his social status. With enforcement becoming the province of the court, the powerful lords and kindred leaders to whom contracting parties would naturally have gone in the earlier period were no longer necessarily involved. The essential qualifications would now appear to have been solvency and a willingness to serve—qualities which passages in *Llyfr Iorwerth* and manuscript H suggest might not have been so common at this point that parties could take them for granted.[69] And although the lawbooks provide no specific information on this point, it seems a reasonable inference that the widening social gap between lord and *mach* might well have served to reinforce the former's already expanding authority in contractual matters.

The diminishing social status of the *mach* may also be a factor underlying another of the changes occurring in *mechni* in this period. As we have seen, the early *mach* was considered a *tafodiog*, a person whose special status as a witness to the transaction is most clearly expressed in *Llyfr Iorwerth*:

> o byd mach adeuedyc a dyweduet o'r neyll bot e uechnyaeth ar peth maur a'r llall paneu ar beth bychan, canes adeuedyc e mach, credadue yu ef pahar e rodet. . . .[70]
>
> if there be an acknowledged *mach*, and one party says that his suretyship is for a large amount and the other [says] that it is for a small amount, since the *mach* is acknowledged [by both parties], he is to be believed as to the amount for which he was given. . . .

There are, however, clear signs in Latin E and other later texts that the special status of the *mach*'s testimony was coming already by the thirteenth century to be no longer universally accepted. Increasingly, passages are included in the legal sources that anticipate problems arising about the impartiality and accuracy of the *mach*'s evidence. Sureties who declared the debt to be a greater amount than either the defendant or plaintiff had acknowledged, for example, are said in some sources to become liable for the difference;[71] similarly, sureties who asserted an amount less than either party acknowledged might also be obliged to make payment themselves.[72] Guarantors who simply did not remember the size of the debt are treated in some texts as liable for the amount in dispute, and in others as apparently immune from financial involvement.[73] And in cases where one *mach* agreed with the statement of the claimant and the other with that of the defendant, the sources also disagree, some requiring the larger, and some the smaller, amount to be paid.[74] Indeed, what is in many ways most interesting about these provisions are the many discrepancies between them.

The issue was obviously in the process of being worked out in the period in which these passages were written, despite the fact that testimony of this nature would surely have been received with considerable skepticism even in an earlier age. That cases of this sort would have been sufficiently common by the thirteenth century to merit frequent mention in the sources probably reflects, at least in part, the increasing social distance between *mach* and debtor. But it is likely too that environment also played a role: many of these provisions may seem to reflect little more than common sense, but it is common sense exercised in a distinctively curial setting.

Strictly speaking, the doubts outlined in the provisions above do not in themselves demonstrate that the *mach*'s testimony had lost all of the prestige it had once possessed, although they do represent a departure from his early status as *tafodiog*. The surety seems still in these passages to have been regarded as the primary witness of the transaction, as his testimony was questioned only when he could not remember the amount for which he had been appointed or was obviously wrong about it. There are, however, other texts that make it clear that the *mach*'s role as chief witness had changed significantly by the late thirteenth century and that these developments were related to larger changes within *mechni* itself. *Llyfr Cyfnerth* manuscript V and *Llyfr Blegywryd* remark that

> Tri mach hagen yssyd ac ny cheiff vn ohonunt dwyn y vechniaeth ar y l6 e hunan kyt g6atto ran ac adef ran arall o'e vechni: nyt amgen, dyn a el yn vach y g6yd llys a mach diebredic a mach talu. Beth bynhac a tygho y kyntaf, y llys a dyly tygu ygyt ac ef neu yn y erbyn; y deu ereill beth bynhac a tygho, ar y seithuet o'e gyfnesseiueit y t6g; kanys tala6dyr uyd pop vn ohonunt.⁷⁵

> Three *mach*-sureties there are nevertheless who are not allowed to bear their suretyship on their own oaths, though [they] deny one part and acknowledge another part of their suretyship—namely, a man who becomes a *mach* in the presence of the court, and an inefficient *mach*, and a paying *mach*. Whatever the first may swear, the court must swear together with him or against him. The two others, whatever they may swear, they must swear as one of seven of their closest kin, since each of them is a debtor.

This passage is interesting on several counts. For one thing, the transition from enforcing to paying surety had dramatically decreased the *mach*'s credibility as witness. As an enforcing surety, the *mach* could have no motive to testify inaccurately about the amount for which he had been appointed; as a potential debtor, however, the *mach* could be considered no more reliable on this point than was the defendant. Even more striking is the subordination of the *mach*'s testimony to the record of the court, for this marks a clear break with practices of the past. The increasing professionalism with which court records were kept, and the growing role played by the court in matters of suretyship, must have been important elements in the loss of the special status once accorded to the *mach*.[76] Indeed, even *Llyfr Iorwerth*, which generally upholds the *mach*'s traditional status as *tafodiog*, reveals the manner in which the balance of authority had shifted. In cases where the contracting parties disagree on the amount of the debt, the judge is to declare that the *mach*'s verdict is to prevail: in other words, the *mach*'s status as *tafodiog* was now to be reauthorized by the court.[77] It is a sign of how far the once unchallengeable *mach* had fallen that some texts envisage that sureties suspected of partiality in the matter of the debt might be disqualified (*llyssu*) like any other witness brought into court to testify,[78] and that others instruct a debtor who claimed to have paid part of his debt already to prove his assertion *ae trvy vach, ae trvy dynyon ereill ny aller na llys nac amheu ar nadunt*,[79] "either through a *mach*, or through other men against whom no disqualification or doubt [can] be alleged."

Court involvement in suretyship also had its effect on denials of *mach* and *mechni*. In early law, the debtor had been permitted (and privileged) to deny his debt, and a *mach* his suretyship, through a seven man compurgation.[80] There are hints in the later sources, however, that already by the thirteenth century these rights of denial were coming to be significantly curtailed. According to the fifteenth-century *Llyfr Blegywryd* tradition manuscripts P and Q, neither a *mach* given to guarantee the payment of a judge's fee nor one given by a lord or his servants for any purpose could be denied at all.[81] And sureties appointed in certain public places were similarly treated:

> Tri lle y rodir mach yndun ny dyly y 6adu: kyhoedogr6yd pl6yf; a gorsed gyfreitha6l; neu rac bron argl6yd: 6rth vot y tri lle hynny yn tri kyhoedogr6yd kyfreitha6l, ac nat oes dim a6neler ygkyhoedogr6yd a dylyir y 6adu.[82]

> In three places is a *mach* given where he cannot be [subsequently] denied: the public place of a parish, a legal assembly, or before the lord; because those are the three lawful public places, and nothing done publicly ought to be denied.

Manuscript S goes on to say that while a debtor cannot deny such a *mach* at all, a surety given in one of those places can himself deny his suretyship *euthur leu perthyno kof llys*,[83] "except where the record (literally, the "memory") of the court pertains." And while these cases are presented in the lawbooks as anomalous, transactions exceptional in their setting and participants, evidence suggests that the curtailment of privileges they imply was becoming more widespread. Certain pleas contained in the book of *cynghawsedd* extant in manuscripts G (fourteenth century) and F (fifteenth century) envisage witnesses being brought against a debtor to prevent his denial.[84] And although other *cynghawsedd* contained in the same manuscripts ardently defend the right of a surety to present a compurgation of denial, their detailed descriptions of a plaintiff's attempt to bring witnesses against the *mach* suggest that the *mach*'s right to denial also was under attack. Indeed, the whole issue of whether witnesses could be brought against a surety seems to have engendered considerable debate in legal circles of the period. Many texts stress that even an attempt to bring testimony against a *mach* will lose a plaintiff his case.[85] Other passages, however, seem almost to take it for granted that this might be done: *Ior* 60/7, for example, encourages a plaintiff to obtain witnesses to testify to a *mach*'s acknowledgment of his suretyship, lest the *mach* seek to withdraw from his office at a later date. And the notion that a surety might be disqualified from acting as a witness because of partiality (*llyssu*) presumes that testimony could be adduced against the *mach* in support of the person objecting. It is probably no accident, therefore, that while some texts allow this, others explicitly forbid it.[86]

The *mach*'s removal into the curial domain thus had a dramatic effect both on the responsibilities he was expected to fulfill and the status he possessed in the transaction. His primacy as enforcer and chief witness of the obligation was under fire, and many of his most distinctive functions and privileges were gradually being assumed by the officers and records of the court. But there were other developments as well—changes less tangible in nature, perhaps, but no less fundamental, arising from the increasingly legalistic environment in which contractual claims were being pursued. Whereas early visions of the *mach*'s office had highlighted the unity between surety and contract, equating the existence of the debt with that of the *mach* himself, in later practice this notion was almost entirely obscured by changes taking place in the procedures governing the prosecution of debts. The *mach* remained, it is true, crucial to the binding of the contract even in the later period; as we have seen, many otherwise contemporizing sources rigorously insist that the hands had actually to touch in order for the bond between creditor and debtor to exist. But this rigid adherence to the form of the old law, to flesh pressing flesh, disguised the fact that the legal relationship of which it was a symbol could no longer be taken for granted. The obligation had now an existence of its own: the *mach* may still have been important to the binding of the debt, but he was longer its literal bond.

These developments are most clearly visible in the remarkable book of *cynghawsedd* devoted principally to suretyship and contract extant in manuscripts G and F. The sample pleadings included in this collection show that, procedurally, the *mach*'s role in the claim had changed dramatically since his precurial days, both with respect to the manner in which plaintiffs pursued their claims and to the options exercised by debtors in defending themselves against such charges. The book begins with a series of provisions focusing first on the manner in which a surety can become *yn dilv ac un di dadyl*,[87] "oathless and released from the case," despite the fact that he acknowledges his suretyship (*ALW* VIII.i.12–VIII.iii), and secondly on the procedural errors by which a claimant will automatically lose his case, however sound it may be (*ALW* VIII.iv–vi). From the first section particularly we learn a great deal about how plaintiffs pursued their claims and about the role played by sureties in the process. And one of the most striking lessons in this respect, especially to those acquainted with the office of the early *mach*, is that sureties had no longer necessarily to be involved in the proceedings. Whereas the *mach* had previously been the conduit through which all actions associated with the obligation had had to pass, the later *mach* was in essence a type of "plea"—one only of a number of alternatives available to a plaintiff intent on recovering what was owed to him. A claimant could sue the debtor, or he could sue the *mach* as a debtor, if he had reason to believe that the surety was the more likely to pay. If he chose the debtor, and the debtor acknowledged the obligation but refused to pay up, either because of bankruptcy or recalcitrance, the claimant could then seek the debt from the *mach* unless the surety was successful in forcing the debtor to meet his responsibilities. If he chose the *mach*, that surety again would have either to enforce, pay, or deny.[88]

In much of this, there is nothing particularly surprising: the *mach* appears in either case to be summoned to fulfill his by this point customary duties of *talu neu gymell*, "paying or enforcing." But the matter is more complicated than the brief summary above might imply. It is unclear from the sources whether the claimant was required to press his claim first against the debtor before attempting to collect what he was owed from the *mach*. One of the pleadings voices the sentiment that the debtor ought

Court and Custom in Medieval Wales   159

to be approached before the surety, because *kyntaf abyd kyfnewit rvg yr havlvr ar kynnogyn ac y gadarnhau y gyfnewit y gvneir y mach ac y gymhell ac y talu y lle y dylyho*,[89] "first is the exchange between the creditor and the debtor, and the *mach* is given to confirm the exchange, and to enforce and to pay where he ought;" but other texts suggest that the claimant's choice might be rather less directed than this passage indicates.[90]

What is clear from the pleadings in G and F, however, is that claimants unfortunate enough to pursue a debtor who subsequently declared his intent to deny the charge could lose the use of their surety altogether. Once a plaintiff had made his claim against the defendant, and the defendant responded that he planned to deny the claim,

> Tystet y mach yna yr vynet yr havl y arnav ef abot yn gyfreith yr havlvr dewissav y havl ae ar y mach ae ar y kynnogyn ar dewyssav o honav y havl ar y kynnogyn, ar vynet yr havl y arnav ef or ford honno ac uelly y dyly y mach y vot yn dilv ac yn di dadyl, ac yn adefedig gantav y vechniaeth.[91]

> Then let the *mach* obtain witnesses as to the claim having been removed from him, [and] to its being law for the claimant to choose his claim, whether [to make a claim] against the *mach* or against the debtor, and to his having chosen to [make a] claim against the debtor, and to the claim's having been removed from him in that manner; and thus is the *mach* entitled to be without an oath [being required of him] and without a suit [being prosecuted against him, even though] he acknowledges his suretyship.

Because the plaintiff had not chosen to pursue his claim through the *mach*, the surety was released from his responsibilities, and the case then proceeded to its (here undetermined) outcome without further reference to the man who in an earlier period would have been at its heart.

A plaintiff could thus proceed with his claim with or without reference to the *mach* appointed to him in confirmation of the obligation. Even more surprising is that the defendant is pictured here denying his obligation without involving the *mach*. This is, however, exactly what seems to be suggested: the surety's release follows immediately on, and is a direct result of, the defendant's declaration that he will deny his obligation and the creditor's that he will prove the debt against this denial. The involvement of the surety in the denial of the obligation was mandatory in the early law of *mechni*, as it was the *mach* that the debtor denied, and indeed the various oaths and counter-oaths detailed in the *cynghawsedd* suggest that the participation of the *mach* was the norm in later law as well.[92] But the pleading cited above reveals that there had developed in the later period other ways for defendants to deny debts they thought unjustified. Both claim and denial could proceed without the involvement of the surety originally appointed to secure the debt.

The manner in which the two principals might conduct their suit without reference to the *mach* is not outlined in detail in this pleading, but the claimant's declaration that he and "enough with him" would prove the charge lodged against the debtor reveals that he planned to call witnesses to testify in support of his accusation.[93] This seems also to be the case in two of the components of a triad found only in Latin D and *Llyfr Blegywryd*:

> Tri lle yd ymdiueicha mach kyfadef am dylyet aghyfadef. Vn yw o diwat o'r talawdyr y mach. Eil yw o gaffel tystolyaeth o vn o'r kynnygyn ar y gilyd trwy ymhyawl yn llys. Trydyd yw o lyssu o vn ohonunt tyston y llall y mywn llys.[94]
>
> In three places is an acknowledged *mach* freed from his suretyship in a case of an unacknowledged obligation. The first is by the debtor denying the *mach*. The second is by one of the debtors bringing testimony against the other in a mutual claim in court. The third is by one of them disqualifying the witnesses of the other in court.

The second situation depicted here is that of a mutual claim, where the parties concerned are both debtors to one another by virtue of having exchanged sureties to guarantee those parts of the obligation that remain to be fulfilled. The *dadyl teithi mach*, "suit concerning the characteristic duties of a *mach*," that opens the book of *cynghawsedd* contained in F envisages a contract of sale in which, for example, the buyer guarantees that he will pay the stipulated price and the seller guarantees that the animal sold is free from defects.[95] The triad in *Llyfr Blegywryd* and Latin D seems then to suggest that the sureties guaranteeing these promises would be released from their duties if the parties chose to pursue their respective claims and denials through witnesses instead of through sureties. The third member of the *Llyfr Blegywryd* triad appears to refer to a situation similar to the one described in the pleading from F and G. The plaintiff would attempt to prove his charge through the witnesses he had with him. If a defendant could disqualify them (*llyssu*), the claimant's charge would collapse; if he could not, the plaintiff would win his suit and become thereby entitled to collect the amount of the debt from the defendant. In either instance, the participation of the *mach* would no longer be necessary.

That the debtor's denial might proceed without reference to the *mach* is particularly revealing, since the compurgation presented in an earlier age by a defendant against the *mach* was itself an expression of the symbolic unity of surety and claim. Unlike early law, where a *mach* stood surety *ar e keynnyauc dywethaf mal ar e gentaf*,[96] "for the last penny as for the first," the surety of the *cynghawsedd* could be released from his responsibilities even before the suit was resolved. Nor is this the only instance in which this was true. F and G offer us another case in which the surety's connection with the contract was severed before the claim itself had been resolved. A debtor there claims in response to a creditor's suit that although he had originally owed what the creditor is alleging, he had subsequently paid back part of that amount and is therefore liable only for a reduced sum. The creditor then charges the debtor to prove this assertion, which is viewed in the text as a charge now brought by the debtor against the original plaintiff (who thus becomes the defendant in the suit), and the case then proceeds according to this claim.

> A chany dylynir y mach yny dadyl honno, ac na bu gyghavsset yr ydav [ef] aneb, namyn yrvg yr havlvr ar amdyffynvr y barn kyfreith ar gyghavssed yr havlvr ar kynnogyn; ac y bernir bot y mach yn ryd. Ar eil lle yv hvnnv y barn kyfreith vot mach yn dilv ac yn di dadyl, ac yn adefedic gantav y vechniaeth.[97]
>
> And because the *mach* is not proceeded against in that suit, and there has been no pleading between himself and any one [else], only between the claimant and the defendant, the law judges on the basis of the pleadings of the claimant and the debtor; and the *mach* is judged to be free. And that is the second case where the law judges the *mach* to be without an oath [being required of him] and released from the suit, and his suretyship [nevertheless] acknowledged by him.

The pleading does envisage that the debtor might *choose* to prove his claim through the surety; in this case, presumably, the *mach* would not have been freed from his obligation in the manner outlined above. But should the debtor choose instead to use as his witnesses *dynyon ereill ny aller na llys nac amheu ar nadunt*,[98] "other men against whom no disqualification or doubt can be [proved]," the surety had no longer to be involved. The ancient bond between surety and contract had been irreparably broken.

Mechni was thus experiencing significant change in the course of the thirteenth and fourteenth centuries. For several of these developments it is not difficult to find an explanation. The *mach*'s role as supervisor and primary witness of the transaction was compromised by his financial liability and was increasingly subordinated to the records of the court, while his position as enforcer of the obligation was gradually subsumed under the authority of the state. One need look no further than Wales in the period of the lawbooks to understand something of the manner in which personalities of "private" law can pass into and be absorbed by the public domain. When one comes to consider the causes underlying some of the other developments noted, however, particularly the rupture of the traditional connection between *mach* and claim, one is brought sharply up against a point otherwise easy to overlook. The curial process itself has the potential to reshape dramatically the customs and institutions subjected to it. As anyone familiar with the workings of modern justice will realize, professionals working within a system of rules that, though not closed in the sense of refusing absolutely to countenance innovation, is nevertheless suspicious of it, will find other ways to stretch the parameters of those rules. To put the matter more directly: lawyers like to win their cases and will do what it takes to secure the result they desire. And since what works will be repeated, experimentation itself enhances the likelihood of change. Legislation and statute are not the only sources of legal innovation; law can be created in unconscious as well as conscious ways.

Nowhere was this more true than in Wales during the period in which the *cynghawsedd* were composed. The existence of a highly professional legal class has been extensively documented.[99] And lawyers were already by this point actively committed to stretching the limits of their craft: as Charles-Edwards has argued, the transition from the count (*narratio*) of the early common law to the type of sophisticated pleading visible in F and G may have occurred even earlier in Wales than in England.[100] Indeed, the original purpose of the book of *cynghawsedd* must have been both to encourage ambitious lawyers to "try one on" in the pursuit of their goal and to provide them a model by which success might ultimately be theirs. Inevitably, attempts by these professionals to manipulate rules and procedures in favor of their clients had a profound impact on institutions governed by those rules.

Suretyship was no different in this regard. Few of the important changes wrought in suretyship during this period were, as far as we can determine, intentional or commanded by statute. No law mandated that sureties no longer be identified with the contract they had bound; no lord declared that the office of *mach* henceforth not be coterminous with the existence of the debt. These developments, significant as they were in helping to reshape the contours of early *mechni*, were the result not of legislation, but of expediency. As S. F. C. Milsom has observed of English common law, lawyers "thinking about nothing beyond the immediate interest of each client" focused their attention on how the system within which they worked might be turned to their own particular use and "never looked up to consider as a whole" the substantive law they were in the process of creating.[101]

The breaking of the bond between surety and contract was one of the most visible results of the subjection of *mechni* to the process of legal pleading. Not that every aspect of this complex development can be traced to this specific cause: the (presumably deliberate) absorption by the lord of the *mach*'s supervisory and executive responsibilities must also have played a substantial role in distancing the surety from his transaction. There can be no doubt, however, but that the rules of curial procedure were themselves instrumental in effecting change. The structure of claim and counter-claim itself laid the groundwork for this transformation. In the process envisaged by the *cynghawsedd*, the plaintiff's representative (*cyngaws*, "pleader") first presented his claim (*hawl, cyngheusaeth*, or *arddelw*[102]) and offered proof of same. The defendant's representative had then either to acknowledge the charge, deny it, or offer an *arddelw*—in essence a counter-claim or assertion of new facts intended to refine the issue to reveal more clearly the actual point in contention. Were the defendant's *cyngaws* to acknowledge the claim, the plaintiff would win his case; were he to deny it, the plaintiff would have the chance to bring forward his witnesses and thereby win his case. Were the defendant to respond to the plaintiff's charge with an *arddelw* of his own, however, the burden would then fall back on the plaintiff, who would accordingly either acknowledge the defendant's *arddelw*, deny it, or respond with a new position phrased again in *arddelw* form. In most (though not all[103]) cases the advantage would fall to the party who was ultimately permitted to bring forward his witnesses in support of his claim, and this was therefore the position into which parties and their representatives tried to maneuver themselves.[104] One other principle seems also to have governed the proceedings: claimants could use their *arddelwau* to refine or modestly reshape their positions, but they were not allowed to renew the suit on a totally new basis after proof on one claim had failed.[105]

The structuring of pleading between claimant and defendant was an important factor in the developments taking place in *mechni* during this period. As we have seen, the evidence suggests that plaintiffs were required in their initial claim to choose the *arddelw* they thought had the best chance of success—in this case, to decide whether to sue the debtor or the *mach*. This is significant, for the necessity to choose between these two types of *arddelw* in the initial stages of the lawsuit had the effect of potentially freeing the *mach* altogether from involvement in the affair. Were the claimant to choose the debtor, the charge then became the debtor's to acknowledge, deny, or refine. If the debtor acknowledged but could not pay the debt, the *mach* would still be involved; in any other situation, however, the *mach*'s services would be required only if the parties wished them to be.[106] Nor could the claimant change his *arddelw* once proof on one claim had failed: if he first chose the debtor, and the debtor subsequently denied the obligation, the creditor could not later renew his suit against the *mach*, even if the *mach* had acknowledged his office in the context of the debtor's denying the charge. Once a debtor had denied his surety, there existed no surety to sue; and once a claimant had sued one debtor over a given contract, he could not attempt the same charge against another (e.g., the surety in the guise of debtor).[107]

In the particular case of a defendant successfully denying his obligation, the procedure outlined in the *cynghawsedd* had the effect of merely reinforcing older law. As far as we know, sureties denied by their debtor did not become liable for the debt even in the period before pleading of this sort became common. We have seen, however, that the necessity to select one's *arddelw* at the beginning did make it possible for a *mach* to be freed from a suit if the debtor chose not to make use of him in his response to the claimant's charge. Furthermore, there is at least one case in the lawbooks where the mutually exclusive nature of (provable) *arddelwau* may have in essence "created" substantive law, or at least justified a particular stance on a controversial issue. *Ior* 63/2 says that no one should accept a person who is both surety and debtor,

> kanys dev ardelw ynt ac na cheyff entew namyn dewys y ardelw: os o vechny e dewys y ardelw nyt oes kynnogyn; os o kynnogyn e dewys nyt oes vach; ac wrth henny ny eyll vn dyn sevyll en vach kynnogyn.

> for they are two legal roles (*arddelw*) and that person must choose his role: if he chooses to put himself forward as a surety there is no debtor; if he chooses to put himself forward as a debtor there is no surety; and because of that no man may act as both surety and debtor.[108]

Llyfr Colan's version of this passage does not mention *arddelw* specifically, but is particularly concerned about the plaintiff's difficulties in securing the enforcement of his claim. Manuscript G's reservations are even more simply stated: *ny diga6n un dyn seuyll yn vach kynnogyn, cany dylyir barnu un ura6t am deu acha6s*,[109] "a single man cannot stand as a surety-debtor, since a single judgment ought not to be adjudged for two cases."

What makes all this especially interesting is that we know from other sources that self-suretyship was permitted in certain parts of Wales by the thirteenth century.[110] *Llyfr Iorwerth*'s preoccupation with the categorizing of legal roles, and with the exclusive nature of those categories, leads it to dissent (or else justifies its dissent) from legal norms elsewhere. And while the context is not sufficiently detailed for us to determine whether *arddelw* is being used in this passage in its technical sense of a plea made in court, clearly the setting envisaged in G is a curial one, and *Llyfr Iorwerth*'s concern with the issue implies some interest in how judges will decide such disputes. Certainly, those interested in the development of judicial procedure will find the idea of fashioning curial pleas—for example, *mechni*, "suretyship," or *kynnocnaeth*,[111] "debtorship"—around the privileges and responsibilities of "private" law personalities strikingly reminiscent of the process visible in *Cóic Conara Fugill*. We may have in these texts a glimpse of how certain curial pleas at least were originally conceptualized and created.[112]

The intricacies of curial procedure may thus themselves have helped to reshape contractual suretyship. Equally important were the means by which lawyers working within these complex procedures attempted to manipulate them toward the end they desired. As we have seen, rules regarding the denial of *mach* and *mechni* seem to have been somewhat in flux in the period of the *cynghawsedd*. Although compurgations of denial are the norm for both debtor and surety in the lawbooks, the *cynghawsedd* often mention plaintiffs attempting to bring witnesses against both in an effort to prevent them from denying their obligations. This practice seems to have been generally well accepted by the early fourteenth century (the period to which G dates) for testimony against the debtor. The debtor in the case outlined in *ALW* VIII.i.12–15, for example, does not even attempt to assert his right to a compurgation of denial in response to the creditor's claim but allows the case to continue in its normal sequence of claim/denial/proof. And the surety in another case asserts his right to denial with the remark that his privilege (*breint*) is greater than that of the debtor's, as he has the right to prove his denial through compurgation—a statement that implies that the debtor's entitlement was in doubt.[113]

But if dissent over the prospect of testimony against a debtor was limited or non-existent by this period, such was not the case with respect to the prospect of summoning witnesses to testify against the *mach*. We have seen that there was considerable disagreement on this issue; and this is important, for what we may be witnessing in this debate is a clash between professional expediency and the perceptions of a precurial age. The right of a litigant whose claim (*arddelw*) is denied to produce conclusive proof of his position is the basic presumption on which pleadings in the book of *cynghawsedd* are structured. Earlier court procedure envisaged both parties calling witnesses in support of their claims, but the advent of the type of sophisticated pleading evident in G and F resulted in the adjudging of this right to only one of the parties involved. In attempting to bring witnesses forward in support of their contractual claims, therefore, the plaintiffs of the *cynghawsedd* on suretyship were acting fully in accordance with the established procedural norms of their day. To judge from the lawbooks at least, however, debtors and sureties of an earlier period would both have had the right to present compurgations of denial. It is possible, therefore, that the apparent loss of this right represents a change in the law deriving not from legislation but from claimants and their lawyers invoking newly altered norms of curial procedure to circumvent the possible nullification of their claims.

For defendants specifically this is not, it must be said, a necessary conclusion: it is conceivable that even in the pre-*cynghawsedd* period debtors would not have been allowed to present compurgations of denial in instances where impartial witnesses existed to support the creditor's claim. Nothing is said to this effect in the lawbooks, but as an approach to legal problem-solving, it does have the merit of common sense. Furthermore, in the very earliest period, denials of this sort would presumably not have occurred at all, since the authority and status of the *mach* would have inveighed against any such attempts; the fact that the lawbooks even allow a debtor to deny his obligation through compurgation is already a sign of the diminishing significance of the surety in the transaction and the increasing importance of the lord's court in legal matters.[114] In this sense, then, testimony against the debtor was not necessarily a new thing in the period of the *cynghawsedd*, and while the acceptance of the practice of calling witnesses against the debtor *may* reflect a change in previous custom arising out of the manipulation by litigants of new procedural norms, such a conclusion can not be proven.

On the question of testimony against the *mach*, however, the matter seems more certain, for here the conflict is evident. There is no hint in the earlier sources that witnesses might ever have been brought against the *mach*; indeed, the evidence indicates quite the opposite. As we have seen, the earliest strata of the lawbooks stress the complete authority of the surety in all matters pertaining to the agreement. And yet plaintiffs in the *cynghawsedd* are clearly attempting to invoke against the *mach* the relatively novel right of litigants to produce conclusive proof of their claim once the opposing party has denied it. One of the plaintiffs in a case of suretyship outlined in F and G states his case with reference to the general legal principle of "one tongue urging and another denying":

> Tauaut vyfy yn gyrru ac arall vit titheu yn gvadu; a rac ar kahel gvat o honat ti, y dugum inheu tystolyaeth arnat ti: kanys muryedic yg kyfreith [y6] yny lle ny bo namyn tauavt yn gyrru ac arall yn gvadu kaffel gvat or gvadvr ony byd ae gvyppo a rac y gvadu o honav ynteu y dugum inheu tystolyaeth; ac vrth hynny ny dylyaf inheu colli vyn dadyl namyn y chaffel kanys yssit im ae gvyppo y dylyu.[115]

> I am one tongue urging [a claim] and you are another denying [it]; and lest you deny [the claim], I brought testimony against you: since it is established in law, that in a case where there is but one tongue urging and another denying, the denier secures his denial unless there be those who may know [the facts of the matter]; and lest he (sic) deny, I brought testimony; and because of that, I am entitled not to lose my suit but to win it, since I have [persons] who know what I am due.

The creditor here is claiming the right to apply to suretyship the recognized procedural principle that while a claim unsupported by evidence ("one tongue urging") will fail if the defendant denies it ("one tongue denying"), a charge proved through witnesses will prevail over the defendant's denial, and the plaintiff is entitled to present such witnesses if he has them. The contrast with the older procedure outlined in *Llyfr Iorwerth*, in which the conflict between "one tongue urging" and "one tongue denying" is resolved by the judge's declaration that the surety has the right to present a compurgation of denial, could not be more striking.[116]

To present an argument is not, of course, necessarily to win it. The pleading outlined above is presented as unsuccessful—or at least a response is provided in the text that seems intended to be determinative. Sureties are to remind the plaintiff that they have greater status than do debtors and that they are entitled to be immune to testimony and to present a compurgation if they wish. Furthermore, they are to argue that since the claimant has gone against established law in attempting to bring witnesses against a *mach*, he automatically loses his case because *na dyly kyfreith nys gvnel*,[117] "he is not entitled to law who does not act in accordance with it" (literally: "who does not do it"). Which position ultimately prevailed is impossible to say. The pleadings in F and G consistently uphold the immunity of the *mach* from testimonial affronts, but in the frequency with which they discuss the issue they implicitly acknowledge the seriousness of the threat: it is difficult to avoid the conclusion that claimants were attempting this approach with some regularity. And as we have seen, the passage in the *Llyfr Iorwerth* pleading on denial leaves one room to doubt that the *mach*'s special status in this respect was everywhere observed.[118]

The response suggested to the surety is, however, in many ways as instructive as the claim itself. We are witnessing here the reconceptualization in curial terms of a "fact" of early law, one that derived originally from circumstances now irrelevant to those charged with interpreting its remains. The authority of the early *mach* over the contracts he guarantees has become in these later texts an unexplained privilege to be invoked against aggressive lawyers and the claimants they represent. One is reminded anew of Milsom's apt formulation of the process by which law so often develops in the type of curialized setting these texts presume:

> Change has for the most part been indirect. All that the practitioner can do for one hit by a rule, whether yesterday's taxing statute or some entrenched result of circumstances long dead, is to look for a way round it. If he succeeds, the rule is formally unimpaired. If the route that the special facts of his client's case enabled him to take can be exploited and broadened by others, the result in the real world may be reversed, but the rule remains. Even when it is formally abolished or finally forgotten, its shape will be seen in the twisting route by which it was circumvented. And the ideas involved in the circumvention will prove their own strength. The first resort to them may have been artificial; but their natural properties will assert themselves, and consequences may follow as far-reaching as the ecological disturbances produced by alien animals or plants.[119]

In such a manner also was the shape of early *mechni* preserved. The lengths to which the lawyers went to circumvent the traditional privileges of the *mach* reveal the past history of his office as clearly as does the newly proverbialized assertion with which those privileges were defended against attack. And while the outcome of this particular legal struggle may be obscure to us, the process itself bears witness to the generative potential of the conflict between old and new.

To this point our study has focused entirely on the *mach* and on how the office of this quintessentially "private law" guarantor was transformed by the political and economic developments occurring in Wales during the period of the legal manuscripts. But the *mach* is not the only contractual guarantor mentioned in the lawbooks, nor are the changes in his role the only indication of the increasing prominence of seigneurial jurisdiction.

Also of interest is the surety known as the *amodwr*, literally "contract-man," short accounts of whose office are attached to the main suretyship tractates in *Llyfr Iorwerth, Llyfr Colan*, and *Llyfr Cyfnerth* manuscript W. The *amodwr* is an enigma: like the *mach* and yet separate from him, a surety whose duties seem in many ways merely to duplicate those already performed by others and yet who seems from the evidence of the later manuscripts to have maintained a separate legal identity of his own. Many of the mysteries surrounding his office will probably never be solved, as the evidence is scanty. Yet he is almost certainly a product of the period and processes we have been considering. Indeed, as will be argued here, his very existence is eloquent testimony to the fact that the broadening of the "public" sphere in Wales was accomplished in many different ways.

Perhaps the easiest place to begin is not with the question of who the *amodwr* likely was, but rather with who he almost certainly was not. Binchy argued in his article on Celtic suretyship that the *amodwr* was a descendant of the same Indo-European enforcing surety that had, in his opinion, also given rise to the Irish *naidm*; indeed Binchy implied even that the characteristics of this ancient surety were in some respects continued to an even greater degree in the office of the *amodwr* than in that of the *mach*.[120] Most would not at this point concur with Binchy's argument: his position presumes an enforcing function for the *amodwr* that the texts do not support and implicitly minimizes the executory responsibilities of the *mach*.[121] And while it is true, as Binchy argues elsewhere, that the Welsh word *amod*, "contract," is very old and has its Old Irish parallel in the expression *ben imtha*, "woman of contract," it does not follow from this that the *amodwr* was old as well, since the term *amod* is at least by the time of the lawbooks one of general application.[122] Even the distribution of the evidence on the *amodwr* raises doubts about Binchy's suggestion. For of the three vernacular legal traditions, only *Llyfr Iorwerth* discusses the *amodwr* in detail; *Llyfr Cyfnerth* manuscript W's treatment of his office derives directly from a *Llyfr Iorwerth* account, and the only evidence for his existence in the *Llyfr Blegywryd* or Latin traditions are a few brocards of text that are patently later additions.[123] Recent scholarship has tended to postulate a later origin for the *amodwr*, and this seems likely to be right.[124]

But if the *amodwr* was not a descendant of an Indo-European enforcing surety, his true identity still remains a secret. Those who wrote the lawbooks conceptualized him as a form of contractual guarantor similar to the *mach*, even though there were evident differences in the duties those sureties performed. Certain aspects of the *amodwr*'s office must originally have been patterned after *mechni*, a phenomenon visible also in juristic treatments of *briduw* and *gorfodogaeth* and another indication of the relatively late date at which the *amodwr* must first have appeared. Both *Llyfr Iorwerth* and *Llyfr Cyfnerth* manuscript W append their brief sections on the *amodwr* to their main suretyship tractates, and both stress the similarities in the procedures by which a debtor might deny *mach* and *amodwr*.[125] *Llyfr Iorwerth*'s account implies that the *amodwr* might have participated in the hand-in-hand binding ceremony between creditor and debtor, although it is nowhere explicit about the actual role that he played.[126] And the later legal texts clearly envisage the *amodwr* together with the *mach* and *briduw* as forms of *cadernid*, "security," for promises made and items exchanged.[127] His name is frequently coupled with these two other forms of guarantee in a that shows that, like them, he also took on ultimately the characteristics of a plea in court.[128]

Despite these similarities, however, there were also important differences between the *amodwr* and the *mach*. Neither of the two major functions associated with the *mach*, *talu* or *cymell*, formed any part of the office of the *amodwr*. The *amodwr* bore no financial liability in the transaction, nor was he involved in enforcing the obligation against a recalcitrant debtor. Indeed, such strong-arming as had to be done is stated explicitly in the texts to be the responsibility of the lord. The *amodwr*'s principal function (aside from any role he might have had in the binding of the debt) seems to have been witnessing the contract and providing testimony to the details of the obligation in cases where questions later arose.[129] In *Llyfr Cyfnerth* and certain texts of the Latin tradition, his name is even added to the list of unchallengeable witnesses (*tafodiogion*) recognized in Welsh law.[130] *Amodwyr* seem frequently to have acted in groups,[131] a phenomenon again not associated with the *mach*, and the extent to which they might also have served as supervisors and living symbols of the contract for which they were appointed is uncertain. Only the *amodwr*'s role in the denial procedure even hints at such a notion, and the blatant patterning of his office after that of *mechni* renders this evidence suspect. It is not even clear that it was the *amodwyr* that the defendant denied in such instances: *Llyfr Iorwerth* and *Llyfr Colan* both depict the *claimant*, not the *amodwyr*, taking the leading role in the defendant's compurgation.[132]

We appear to have here then a mystery—a legal personality whose office is frequently equated in the sources with contractual suretyship but whose duties seem more closely to approximate those of the Welsh *tyst*, "witness." Yet even the latter comparison is inadequate, since the lawbook passages on the *amodwr*—by far the fullest treatments of his office—distinguish very carefully both between *amodwyr* and *tystion* and between pacts made in the presence of those two individuals. The word *amod* is only once used in these texts to refer to agreements made in the absence of *amodwyr*, and then in a context that stresses the inherent insecurity of such arrangements.[133] By contrast, the words used to describe pacts made before *tystion* are always *adau* or *emadau*, "promise" or "mutually promise"; the term *amod* is notable principally by its absence.[134] Some texts even state directly that without *amodwyr* there can be no *amod*, and given the role possibly played by *amodwyr* in the formation of the contract—a prospect never mentioned for *tystion*—this is hardly surprising.[135]

Amodwyr are also distinguished from *tystion* in the effect their presence has on the security of the contract. All of the sources are agreed that where *amodwyr* have been present at the making of the agreement, the defendant must present a compurgation of denial in order to free himself from his obligation. And all are in accord as well that promises made in the absence of witnesses of any kind can be denied with a single oath. But whereas *Llyfr Iorwerth* and *Llyfr Cyfnerth* manuscript W would also uphold pacts made in the presence of *tystion* only until such witnesses "fail" (*pallu*), presumably either by being disqualified or by failing utterly in their duty to testify, *Llyfr Colan* declares such arrangements as vulnerable as those made entirely in private.[136] *Llyfr Colan*, in other words, recognizes as legally enforceable only those agreements confirmed by *amodwyr*, *meichiau*, or *briduw*. And even in *Llyfr Iorwerth* and *Llyfr Cyfnerth* manuscript W a distinction is made between the security provided by a *tyst* and that afforded by *amodwyr*. For as is made clear elsewhere in the lawbooks, ordinary witnesses can be disqualified relatively easily, presuming that witnesses can be found to testify to their partiality; compurgations of denial, however, such as are required to countermand the evidence of the *amodwyr* are much more serious and solemn affairs that defendants would find difficult to engineer.[137] What these distinctions may suggest is that *amodwyr* were actually "designated witnesses"—persons specifically chosen by the parties involved who were not only present at the initiation of the agreement but actively focused on it. *Tystion*, by contrast, may have been thought of as much more casual observers, passers-by perhaps, whose attention and knowledge of the transaction taking place in their vicinity was limited at best. *Llyfr Cyfnerth* certainly implies that *tystion* might be found retroactively according to the plaintiff's need.[138]

But for what purposes then might the *amodwr* have been invented? What advantages might there be to employing a "designated witness" in a given transaction rather than a *mach*? In these questions we reach at last the heart of the mystery surrounding the *amodwr*, for a deliberate creation he must have been, given the careful manner in which he is distinguished from the *mach* and the *tyst*. Furthermore, he was more than just a figment of the jurists' imagination: the documents cited by R. R. Davies in his article on the law of the March make it clear that the *amodwr* was a living legal form in the fourteenth century.[139] Certainly, there are advantages to this form of suretyship that are missing in ordinary *mechni*. Dafydd Jenkins points out that individuals might have been more willing to act as *amodwyr* than as *meichiau*, given that they could not in this capacity be held as liable for the debt.[140] The fact that the lord was charged with enforcing the agreement and that the *amodwr*'s duties were not heritable unless the heir wished to assume them might also have made the office of *amodwr* seem easier and less burdensome than that of the *mach*.[141] But although observations of this sort help to explain why persons might prefer to serve as one rather than the other, they do not advance us particularly toward an understanding of the *amodwr*'s origins. It is difficult to believe that jurists would invent a legal office strictly for the convenience of those who might potentially fill it, and even harder to imagine a specialized category of this sort arising ex nihilo from the ground up, as it were. Witnesses and sureties both serve specific purposes, the advantages of which will be evident to all parties involved in a contractual situation; "designated" witnesses, on the other hand, who bear neither financial nor executory liability in the transaction are another matter altogether.

One possible explanation is that *meichiau* and *amodwyr* guaranteed different types of arrangements, and that this was the essential difference between them. Many sources seem to support such an idea. The *Damweiniau Colan*, for example, are not alone in conceptualizing the relationship in this manner:

> Pvy bennac a holo da o kyfnewyt, holet truy uach. Puy bennac a holo da truy edewyt, holet truy uryduu. Puy bennac a holo da truy amot, holet truy amotwyr.[142]
>
> Whoever may claim goods on the basis of an exchange (*cyfnewid*), let him claim [them] through a *mach*. Whoever may claim goods through a promise, let him claim [them] through *briduw*. Whoever may claim goods through a contract (*amod*), let him claim [them] through *amodwyr*.

In many other sources also is the *amodwr* associated specifically with the *amod* and the *mach* with the *cyfnewid*;[143] moreover, even texts that do not name the guarantors appropriate for these two types of agreements often differentiate between them.¹⁴⁴ Nowhere in the lawbooks, however, is the distinction between *cyfnewid* and *amod* specifically spelled out. The examples of *amodau* cited in the lawbooks are certainly suggestive: the *Damweiniau Colan*, for example, envisage one *amod* between fishermen as to who will get the first, and who the last, fish caught, and another between a guest and his host as to who will keep the by-products (milk, dung, etc.) produced by the guest's animals during his stay.¹⁴⁵ And *Llyfr Iorwerth* and *Llyfr Colan* are rife with references to *amodau* made between ploughing partners in the context of their joint endeavors; parties may contract to work together longer than would otherwise be customary, or to allow one partner to yoke the ox of his companion without his permission, or to prevent one partner from ploughing an area the other does not wish ploughed.¹⁴⁶

The evidence suggests, then, that the term *amod* was frequently used in the lawbooks to denote short-term and highly personal arrangements of entitlement or service, whereas *cyfnewid* might be presumed to refer to the sale, purchase, or exchange of specific goods.¹⁴⁷ This theory has many merits, not the least of which is that it helps us to understand many of the stipulations attached to these agreements—why *amodau* were not hereditary, for example, and why one person could not make an *amod* on another's behalf. It might also seem to explain the identity of the guarantors assigned to these various pacts in the sources: plaintiffs seeking money or property from their debtors would naturally prefer the economic security offered by the *mach*, while persons looking to ensure the fair division of a catch of fish would find the financial liability of their guarantor a less pressing concern.

Unfortunately, however, the issue is probably not that simple. There is much to suggest that the distinction between *amod* and *cyfnewid* was not as definite as the sources cited above would lead us to believe. Certainly, the semantic range of the word *amod* is much broader than the *Damweiniau Colan* imply: *amod* is in fact the general Welsh word for contract and appears frequently in this generic sense in a wide variety of legal and literary sources.¹⁴⁸ That certain jurists would choose to restrict its meaning in specific contexts to pacts made in the presence of "designated" witnesses only (as in the lawbook accounts of the *amodwr*'s office) is so at odds with the bulk of the evidence that it in itself reveals the artificiality of the enterprise. The only pact mentioned in the sources that is always and invariably associated with the *amodwr* is the *amod deddfol*, the "legal *amod*"—and the only thing we know about it is that it is always linked to the *amodwr*.[149] Needless to say, this fact does not advance us appreciably in our quest: a more circular definition would be difficult to imagine.

Moreover, even if one were to concede that the links between *mach* and *cyfnewid*, and *amodwyr* and short-term negotiated arrangement were generally valid, there is nothing to suggest that they ought to be regarded as ironclad rules. There is no inherent reason why a *mach* could not have been involved in his enforcing and supervisory capacity in any of the *amodau* detailed above; none of the passages that describe these arrangements mention any guarantor at all. Nor is there any reason to believe that *amodwyr* could not have acted in contracts of sale or property exchange. Indeed, some sources mention *amodwyr* in what would appear to be precisely such a context.[150] It may be generally true that witnesses were frequently summoned to guarantee the types of short-term agreements called *amodau* in the lawbooks and that *meichiau* were preferred in contracts of debt or sale, but this tells us only under what circumstances each might have been used. It does not entitle us to conclude that the distinction between *amod* and *cyfnewid* is the key to the origin of the *amodwr*.

It might be useful to step back from the evidence momentarily and consider the context in which the groupings *amod*/*amodwr* and *cyfnewid*/*mach* were likely to have originated. It is unlikely that such differences as existed between these two types of agreement could ever have been so visible on the local level as to have prompted the creation of an entirely new form of guarantor. Contracting parties might well differentiate between agreements on the basis of the identity of the person with whom they were made; kinsmen or lords, for example, might be treated in a manner others were not.[151] Locals would surely also recognize circumstances in which witnesses would be more appropriate and easier to obtain than enforcing or paying guarantors. However, that such persons would then further subdivide the category of "witness" into "designated" and "non-designated" classifications—*amodwyr* and *tystion*, respectively—is almost inconceivable. "Designated," like *deddfol*, is not a notion that has much meaning in such a setting. The solution to the enigma of the creation of the *amodwr* seems more likely to be found in the inner workings of the legal mind than in the localities in which contractual agreements were made and enforced.

Almost certainly, therefore, it is within a juridical context that the matter ought most properly to be viewed. If one imagines judges confronted in court with the difficult task of determining which contracts ought to be regarded as valid and deserving of seigneurial backing, and which ought not to be so privileged, one begins to gain some insight into the process by which *amodwyr* must originally have come into being. Some disputes will be thankfully easy to resolve; arrangements made in a formal, public fashion through *meichiau*, for example, will seem relatively straightforward to confirm or deny. But agreements made in the absence of such fanfare, negotiated in private circumstances without the involvement of a specific surety, will be infinitely more difficult to prove or disprove. Ought such arrangements (which are, by the way, precisely the sort of private accords frequently termed *amodau* in the lawbooks) also to be considered adjudicable and enforceable?

The matter is not at all clear-cut. A variety of stances are possible on the issue. Judges might choose, for example, to regard only those contracts made through *meichiau* as legally enforceable. Alternatively, they might incline toward a slightly broader view and choose to uphold contracts made without sureties, but in the presence of impartial witnesses. Implicit in this latter position, however, is another troubling problem: what exactly constitutes an acceptable witness to an agreement? It is not at all obvious that the testimony of a mere passer-by, a person, for example, whose presence was unplanned and participation in the pact minimal at best, ought to gain the credibility of the court. And what of those accords for which no witnesses exist—ought unsubstantiated charges of this nature to have a claim on the lord's attention?

These are the questions to which, I suggest, *amodwyr* were the answer. In a sense, we have been here before: the Irish jurists also wrestled with this problem, generally inclining, as we have seen, toward the relatively conservative position of privileging contracts made with sureties over those for which no guarantors had been appointed. But the logic and variety of the Welsh response is particularly striking. Welsh lawyers seemed in general willing to uphold private contracts as long as it was clear that those who witnessed them had truly been involved in the agreement and were knowledgeable about its details. Hence, the *amodwr*—not a separate class of guarantor at all, but rather a "designated" witness, the nature of whose participation in the transaction met the criteria established by the judges of the court. And hence, also, the *amod deddfol*, the only pact invariably linked to the *amodwr*. *Amod* was probably in origin a very general word for contract, one which denoted a promissory agreement of any sort; its frequent association with *amodwyr* in the legal sources likely reflects the desire of lawyers to clarify and promote the use of that office once it had come into existence.

A semantic history of this nature would account both for the generic use of the term and for its apparently much more narrow range of meaning in passages like the one cited from the *Damweiniau Colan*.[152] The word *amod* itself, however, carries no implicit guarantee of the sort of legal recognition the presence of *amodwyr* would ensure. Contracts might well be considered morally binding but be viewed nevertheless as legally unenforceable—in the words of one lawbook, a *iaón dylyet heb gedernyt heb praóf arnaó*,[153] "a just obligation [but] without security [and] without proof," that could be denied on the defendant's oath alone. When the jurists wished to stress, therefore, that only *amodau* made in a particular manner would receive the backing of the court, they added the adjectives *deddfol* or *cyfreithiol* to make their point.[154] Of course, as we have seen, not all texts agreed even so on exactly what made an *amod* "*deddfol*." *Llyfr Iorwerth* and *Llyfr Cyfnerth* manuscript W (following *Llyfr Iorwerth*) reasoned that the presence of non-designated witnesses (*tystion*) ought properly to throw the burden of proof onto the defendant in such cases. Until and unless a defendant could impugn the testimony offered by the plaintiff, the agreement would be regarded in law as binding.[155] *Llyfr Colan*, however, took a much more conservative view, as did various other lawbooks: a defendant could conclusively deny any obligation made without *amodwyr* or other form of security on his single oath alone.[156]

The interest of the *amodwr* is much broader, therefore, than the details of his office might suggest. What we are witnessing in the lawbook accounts of *amodwyr* and *tystion* is an attempt by the Welsh lawyers to confront and resolve the difficulties inherent in adjudicating private agreements. Moreover, the significance of this attempt is as much jurisdictional as it is juridical. There are many legal systems that are neither capable nor desirous of embroiling themselves in disputes arising from promises made by individuals in private circumstances. The "creation" of the *amodwr*—or, rather, the privileging for curial purposes of certain types of testimony over others—is a good indication that curial jurisdiction may already have come by the time Ior was compiled to encompass more than just the type of public, formal arrangements associated with *meichiau*.

Alternatively, it may mean merely that lawyers and lords wished it thus. For there are distinctly political aspects to the *amodwr* that ought not to be overlooked. To claim the right to adjudicate and enforce accords negotiated in a private setting is implicitly to assert jurisdiction over the activities of the individuals involved. What two people take as their right to decide between themselves may appear otherwise to those charged with the resolution of disputes. That this should happen in Wales in the period of the lawbooks should not surprise us: the bringing of informal or ill-publicized agreements under the authority of lord and court is frequently a characteristic of consolidating political jurisdictions. That it should engender controversy or resistance amongst those affected should not surprise us either. St. Asaph's *gravamina* against Llywelyn ap Gruffudd centered on contracts secured by *meichiau* (Latin *fideiussores*) rather than by *amodwyr* (Latin *convenciatores*), but they are revealing as an indication of the methods and priorities of that prince and of the resentment he inspired:

> Item, penam appositam in sponsalibus de futuro, et super usurarum solucione, si fideiussores intervenerint, ratione fideiussionis huiusmodi compellit ad pene solucionem huiusmodi contrahentes.[157]
>
> Moreover, a penalty having been established [by the contracting parties] in [cases of] betrothal and regarding the payment of interest [for a debt or loan], if sureties were involved, he [Llywelyn] would compel contracting parties of this sort to the payment of the penalty by reason of such suretyship.

If St. Asaph's complaints were justified, not only was Llywelyn asserting ultimate jurisdiction over individual contracts of betrothal or debt, but he was implicitly laying claim to the institution of suretyship itself. If sureties had been exchanged, a contract had been made, and if a contract had been made, it was Llywelyn's prerogative as prince to implement and enforce it, regardless of the wishes of the parties originally involved. Llywelyn's efforts were, in this sense, parallel in many ways to the more or less contemporaneous attempt by the Church to secure authority over the making of private marriages. Over aristocratic unions, the Church was able to exert some degree of control from the twelfth century on; it was not until the Council of Trent in the sixteenth century, however, that the Church had consolidated its position sufficiently to require the presence of a parish priest at all marriage ceremonies. In asserting the right of the lord to intervene in private agreements, and in constructing from these "private" agreements the beginnings of "public" power, the Welsh lawyers and princes were acting in a manner fully comprehensible to their canonical counterparts.

And in the end, it is probably the *amodwr*'s association with the sphere of "public" jurisdiction that stands out as the most distinctive aspect of his office. For whereas the *mach* came ultimately to rely on the lord for help in ensuring the completion of the contracts he guaranteed, the *amodwr* seems by contrast to have functioned from the beginning within a curial environment. His very existence presumes the presence of a public authority capable of holding individuals to their legal obligations, since it is the lord, not the *amodwr*, who is explicitly charged with enforcing what he attests. Even more significantly, it is the convenience of the court that has, in a very direct sense, dictated the "creation" of the *amodwr*'s office by imposing new standards on the testimony henceforward to be offered in court on contractual matters. Indeed, in the curial associations of the *amodwr* we may have a reflection of the frustration lords such as Llywelyn experienced in attempting to absorb traditionally "private" guarantors like the *mach* within the ambit of seigneurial authority. Like the changes taking place in *mechni* during the centuries in which the lawbooks were written, the *amodwr* may be very much a product of his time—at once cause and consequence of the expansion of lordly dominion in medieval Wales.

7. Past and Present in the Law of Hywel

Few would dispute the value or rarity of the insight the Welsh sources provide into the process by which a system of law dependent primarily on extracurial perceptions and relationships can be brought under the aegis of court and lord. The passage of custom into court is not an easy one to trace in other contemporary legal traditions: English historians have found it immensely difficult to bridge the procedural gap between the unofficial legal compilations of the late Anglo-Saxon and early Norman period and the common law as it had developed by the age of Glanvill and Bracton.[1] But the interest of these texts is even greater than one might automatically assume, for they urge us to reflect, not merely on the fact of legal change, but on the consequences of it and attitudes taken toward it by those charged with preserving and interpreting the tradition as a whole. The lawbooks were anything but disinterested accounts of legal developments within the milieu in which they were composed. Not only were the aspirations of the professional class that produced them practical as well as intellectual, the texts themselves were written in a period in which the future of the tradition represented by that class was very much in doubt. It may be true that the Welsh lawbooks were not the work of particular kings or princes; both in content and in form, however, they reproduce the political circumstances in which they were composed.

It would be difficult to overestimate the seriousness of the threat with which Welsh lawyers found themselves confronted in the tumultuous period that was to prove the final century of native rule. Welsh law had become a rallying cry in the struggle against the English crown—eloquent testimony to a national identity predating by at least a century the arrival of the Normans in what became their land. But the very qualities that made Welsh law so appealing to partisans of the native cause attracted also the attention of its enemies. R. R. Davies has convincingly chronicled the ideological wars waged by Edward and Llywelyn over the conflict between royal prerogative and Welsh legal independence; that Welsh law would emerge somewhat bowed and bloodied from this conflict was inevitable in the wake of the English victory. Certainly Archbishop Pecham's well-known invective against the defects in virtue and righteousness he regarded as rife in Welsh custom did little for its reputation. Furthermore, as has recently become evident, Welsh law faced serious challenges not merely from without but from within as well. Even the most nationalist of Welsh princes frequently changed, or rejected outright, individual customs of the law they cited in support of their political ambitions. And while Edward's commission of 1281 was hardly an impartial inquiry, it did reveal that lesser Welshmen also were turning increasingly to the procedures of the common law. Ambivalence rather than unwavering allegiance was the hallmark of even native attitudes toward the legacy of Hywel.[2]

In defense of an embattled legal tradition of which they frequently found themselves the most loyal proponents, the compilers of the lawbooks stressed tradition and the past. This was unquestionably their strongest card, and they played expertly. The model lawbook from which the extant versions ultimately derive may actually have originated in the time of Hywel, as Charles-Edwards has recently argued.[3] What is even more certain, however, is that the link between Hywel and the law, whether real or not, was deliberately embellished and exploited by the jurists in their efforts to further the cause and prospects of the legal tradition he had come to represent. Huw Pryce has recently examined the various prologues to the extant lawbooks, placing their date of composition in the twelfth and thirteenth centuries, precisely the period when the challenge to Welsh law became most acute. As he points out, the elaborate story of Hywel's assembly at Tŷ Gwyn was fashioned to reassure critics and adherents alike of the law's morality, legitimacy, and historical authenticity. Particularly interesting is the jurists' determined assertion of a connection between the law and Hywel's authority as king, a phenomenon by no means restricted to the prologues. If law became for the Welsh princes a means by which to authorize their rule against a hostile English king, royal backing in the form of Hywel's sponsorship became for the authors of the lawbooks a means by which to vindicate the legal tradition from the criticisms levied against it.[4]

This is all well known. What have not yet been explored, however, are the difficulties posed by change and innovation to a legal tradition that seeks self-consciously to authorize itself by reference to the distant past.[5] The Welsh lawyers were, to put the matter bluntly, in a monumental bind. It was essential that Welsh law be perceived as part of a cultural tradition spanning the centuries—the noble inheritance of an ancient past, as indeed in fact it was. And yet the period of the lawbooks was precisely the period in which changes in all spheres of activity—political, social, and economic—were at their greatest height. Furthermore, the exposure of the Welsh to the modern and, in some cases, seemingly more efficacious procedures of the common law made it all the more important for native lawyers to keep pace with the latest trends. Many of the (admittedly partisan) submissions to Edward's 1281 commission unfavorably contrast the "law of Keverith"—compurgation—with the "truth" that procedure by inquisition could reveal.[6] And many of the legal perceptions and practices of the Welsh were indeed "old law," as has already been observed. Herein, then, lay the challenge. To sanction their work, the lawyers needed to retain and perhaps even to embellish what was old; to ensure its use, however, they needed to convince practitioners, especially lords, of its relevance and effectiveness in a rapidly changing world.

None of these problems is, of course, unique to the Welsh. Most legal traditions draw to some extent on their past, and there is no inherent reason why innovation ought to be impossible even within an historically minded legal tradition. But where few alternative authorizing devices exist, change has the potential to be particularly disruptive. The Welsh were not strangers to the prospect of, for example, innovatory legislation: new or "improved" laws are attributed in the lawbooks to Bleddyn ap Cynfyn, prince of Gwynedd and Powys, who died in 1075, and to Rhys ap Gruffudd, ruler of much of southern Wales until his death in 1197, among others. But royal decree, which served in many contemporary legal cultures to validate particular texts or procedures, does not seem to have carried as much weight in Welsh legal circles as it did elsewhere. The authors of the lawbooks seem often to regard the legislative changes they record with some ambivalence; sometimes they accept them, sometimes they explicitly reject them, and sometimes they imply that the issue was still confused.[7] At least once they indicate that a person may choose the custom by which he prefers to be judged.[8] Indeed, the fact that the laws are consistently attributed to Hywel rather than to any of the contemporary princes with whose reigns modern scholars have linked the composition of all or portions of the lawbooks (most notably Rhys ap Gruffudd and Llywelyn ap Iorwerth) is itself revealing.[9] In a period when jurisdiction was fragmented and the longevity of a particular prince's rule uncertain, the sanction of an historical ruler whose authority could no longer be challenged was a much safer bet.

Perhaps what is most interesting, however, is that the jurists themselves realized that the conflict between old and new posed a potential threat to the authority of the tradition they represented. The composer of a passage in manuscript G concedes that one of Bleddyn's legal innovations had largely been adopted by his own time, but takes great care to distinguish legislative improvement from actual "law," to which he accords a fundamental primacy: *Eissoes nyt kyfreith un or awnaeth Bledyn namyn llunnyeith da canyt oes namyn un kvfreith herwyd Kymry o dadyl uyt sef yó honno kyfreith Hywel*,[10] "Nevertheless, the [improvement] made by Bleddyn was not law, but a good ordinance, for there is ever but one law according to the Welsh for legal cases [and] that is the law of Hywel." Within a legal tradition sanctioned by a royal authority centuries old, the legislation of contemporary princes enjoyed in juristic circles at best an ambiguous status.[11] It was essential that the law of Wales remain the law of Hywel, no matter how frequently Hywel and his successors seemed to disagree, and no matter how many of the practices associated with his reign seemed no longer to obtain.

The manner in which the Welsh lawyers attempted to reconcile their need for the past with the vicissitudes of contemporary life is impossible precisely to outline. No single stance is taken in the lawbooks on the relationship between old and new; at best one can speak in terms of a range of approaches governing the disposition of awkward or potentially contradictory material. On the level of the tradition itself, however, the connections between past and present came eventually to be articulated in a specific vision of the law, one which rooted innovation in the apparent immutability of former custom. Into the thirteenth century, *Cyfraith Hywel*, the name given in the sources to the legal tradition as a whole, was perceived as primarily oral in nature. As the lawbooks increased in popularity and use, however, written law came more and more to the fore, and this created difficulties for contemporary-minded lawyers looking to incorporate into this tradition the practices of their day. For in an oral setting, innovation leaves no trace: as Charles-Edwards has remarked, what is right is viewed as traditional, and what is traditional must needs be right.[12] A written text, by contrast, reveals immediately the gap between the two. To emend the canon in a principally literate environment runs the risk of undermining the authority of the tradition thereby improved.

The authors of the manuscripts of the principal redactions responded to this problem in somewhat different ways. In *Llyfr Cyfnerth, Llyfr Blegywryd*, and the Latin redactions, new material tended to be incorporated directly into the existing lawbooks; these texts thus remained "within a tradition in which all of Hywel's law was expounded within Hywel's Book."[13] By contrast, in *Llyfr Iorwerth* and many of its associated manuscripts, while new material was also integrated into the lawbook itself, the most striking vehicle for innovation were two entirely new compositions appended to the work as a whole. These compositions, the *Llyfr y Damweiniau*, "Book of Eventualities," and the *Llyfr Cynghawsedd*, "Book of Pleading," differed from "Hywel's Book" in being unified by form rather than by subject matter, and in displaying an absence of structure rather than the pattern by that point associated with Hywel.[14] They were, in other words, perceived as separate from the lawbook to which they were attached: even in *Llyfr Iorwerth* manuscripts was a dichotomy maintained between those sections of the written law taking the form believed original to the law of Hywel, of which the extant versions of the lawbooks are our best exemplars, and those perceived as additions made over time to Hywel's work.

That this was a deliberate dichotomy intended specifically to preserve the integrity of Hywel's book cannot be doubted. For while it reflects in part the circumstances in which the relevant texts were composed and transmitted, as the *Llyfr y Damweiniau* and *Llyfr Cynghawsedd* were essentially new compilations, while behind the redactions lay a lawbook prototype associated with Hywel, it is important to realize that matters did not have to be thus. There is no inherent reason why the pattern of the model lawbook could not have been continually expanded to accommodate new material just entering the tradition. Indeed, *Llyfr Iorwerth* does alter the layout of the lawbook prototype, creating a third section, the *Llyfr Prawf Ynaid*, or "Judges' Test Book," which it appends to the Laws of Court and Country found in earlier versions of the lawbook. This is, however, very much the exception that proves the rule. Much of the material found in this "Test Book," the aim of which seems to have been to gather together and update information particularly important to practicing lawyers, is found in other traditions dispersed throughout the lawbook proper. Moreover, the Test Book, like *Llyfr Iorwerth* itself, is organized into tractates, unified by subject matter rather than by form, and actually begins with tractates that in other versions appear within the Laws of Country. Unlike either the *Llyfr y Damweiniau* or the *Llyfr Cynghawsedd*, then, the Test Book was envisaged as part of the frame that was *Cyfraith Hywel*—another indication that the distinction between Hywel's book and what Owen called the "Anomalous Laws" was neither necessary nor accidental.[15]

But if this dichotomy was deliberate, there must then have been reasons for which it was established and maintained. Significantly, the evidence suggests that those writing about these sources conceptualized their relationship to the tradition in very different ways. To the redactions only is accorded the authoritative name of *Cyfraith Hywel*; material outside the versions is referred to principally by its form or genre: *llunyeithiau*, "ordinances," *damweiniau*, "eventualities," *cynghawsedd*, "pleading." When a thirteenth-century manuscript of *Llyfr Cynghawsedd* makes mention of the *llyuyr Hywel*, "Book of Hywel," it refers not to itself, but to one of the principal redactions (in this case *Llyfr Iorwerth*).[16] Even more tellingly, manuscript U of *Llyfr Cyfnerth* remarks, at the end of its version of *Cyfraith Hywel* and the beginning of the *Llyfr y Damweiniau* appended to it, that now "it is turning from law, *cyfraith*, to customs, *defodau*."[17] Nor is U unique in refusing to accord the name *cyfraith* to material external to the principal versions: as we have seen, manuscript G draws a similar and equally self-conscious distinction between Bleddyn's *llunnyeith da* and the body of *Cyfraith Hywel*. These differences in terminology, while seemingly minor, are significant, for they suggest that the lawyers wished to portray the dichotomy between the versions and the subsidiary texts as one of substance as well as form.

And yet this is a patently artificial distinction. The three redactions themselves contain many examples of both *damweiniau* and (*Llyfr Iorwerth*) *cynghawsedd*. Furthermore, the compositions appended to the redactions, like the ordinances they cite, certainly state "law"; indeed some of what is contained in the *Llyfr y Damweiniau* may be older and more genuinely "traditional" than many passages in the versions.[18] There are several texts in the redactions that cannot have had much of a history behind them, including the pleading on the denial of *mach* and *mechni* incorporated into *Llyfr Iorwerth*. The distinction between the versions and the other legal collections is not, in other words, one forced on the compilers of the lawbooks by the nature of their material. Rather it reflects the desire of the lawyers to retain the authority of antiquity while making room for procedural and legislative change. The distribution of singular and plural itself makes the point: *cyfraith* bespeaks an ancient and immutable legal tradition, while *damweiniau* and *llunyeithiau* are but additions made separately to that tradition at points subsequent in time. By remaining true to the pattern to which it was heir, *Cyfraith Hywel* the book retained the authority of the past; by making room for innovation without forfeiting its roots, *Cyfraith Hywel* the tradition retained its appeal in an increasingly competitive legal world. Quite literally were the possibilities of the future appended to the authority of the past.[19]

The matter may be even more complicated than this. For by the thirteenth century, the Roman law distinction between written law (*lex*) and oral custom (*consuetudo*) was well known and much discussed in European legal circles.[20] Bracton in fact begins his lawbook with some musings on the subject, for it was a point on which the English were particularly vulnerable; following Glanvill, who had earlier been confronted with the same dilemma, he argued that although English customs were unwritten, royal sanction gave them the stature of true law. It is likely, although impossible to prove, that the Welsh lawyers also were familiar with the distinction between *lex* and *consuetudo*, as they unquestionably were with other Roman law concepts.[21] The dichotomy established in the lawbooks between *cyfraith* and *defodau* may, then, draw to some extent on the Roman idea: in the redactions is preserved the written legacy of Hywel, in the anomalous material, the previously unwritten customs of those following in his wake. And just as law takes precedence over custom (except, apparently, in the case of England), so also does *cyfraith* both confirm and authenticate later accretions to the tradition it represents.[22]

An association of this sort between the Welsh and Roman law ideas, if true, would have important resonances in the political context in which the Welsh lawbooks were written. Not only would it help us to understand the somewhat ambiguous status accorded by the jurists to princely legislation, likely by its nature to be oral, it would speak as well to the manner in which partisans of Welsh law sought to promote their cause in the face of the threat posed by common law procedures. For Welsh law was written law and had been since the time of Hywel, or such at least was the inherent claim of the prologues. English law, by contrast, was not *lex* but *consuetudo*: inferior, in other words, both in stature and in form. Charles-Edwards is surely right to remark that, from the point of view of content, *Llyfr Cyfnerth* manuscript U's distinction between *cyfraith* and *defodau* is a false one.[23] But from the point of view of the manner in which the Welsh lawyers had come to conceptualize their tradition, authority within that tradition, and its relationship with other contemporary forms of legal discourse, *Llyfr Cyfnerth*'s "false distinction" may be very much to the point.

The level of tradition is not the only one on which the jurists confronted the difficulties inherent in authorizing their work. Their concern with legal change also shaped the manner in which they conceptualized and presented individual customs old and new. In a sense, the groundwork for such an endeavor had already been laid by the time the redactions of the lawbooks first appeared. For if ever an era had existed when *cyfreithiau* rather than *cyfraith* had been viewed as the outcome of the assembly at Tŷ Gwyn, that time had long since passed. To paraphrase the words of a historian of another ancient legal tradition in the process of (re)construction, whereas once this or that specific tradition was envisaged as stemming from Hywel, "now tradition as such was linked to him." And with the increasing professionalism of the lawyers themselves, "[t]radition itself, under the pressure of the systematic concerns of jurisprudence, [became] a subject of reflection as well as a body of knowledge, a text to be interpreted as well as a medium of discourse."[24]

The business of reinterpreting the "text" of tradition to bridge the gap between past and present was a task lawyers appear to have undertaken with tremendous enthusiasm. Offices and institutions, new and old, were reconceptualized in a manner that created a tie, whether historically accurate or not, between contemporary practice and earlier custom. The patterning of relatively recent institutions after their predecessors, for example, established a continuity that, though in actuality more apparent than real, performed the valuable function of disguising the unsettling fact that change had occurred. The modeling of curial pleas on formerly authoritative legal personalities like the *mach* has already been discussed. And while the *amodwr*'s duties may have been tailored in every way to meet the needs of the curial environment in which he had originated, the novelty of his office was effectively obscured by the deliberate modeling of his role on that of the *mach*. Nor was the placement of *Llyfr Iorwerth*'s discussion of his office (immediately following the tractate on suretyship) in any sense accidental. Even his name, which drew directly on the terminology traditionally employed in contractual contexts, invoked connections with the past that a critical assessment of his actual duties would suggest did not exist.

Ironically, patterning also served as a means by which older practices and institutions could be brought up-to-date and incorporated into an increasingly systematized jurisprudential structure. Especially vulnerable to such "reinterpretation" were customs that appeared, by the thirteenth century, obscure or eclectic in some way or that posed a potential challenge to the jurisdiction of the seigneurial court. *Briduw* and *gorfodogaeth* both were repatterned after *mechni* in precisely the same way the *amodwr* had been, although for rather different reasons. Both were probably relatively old forms of suretyship, less well known and less accessible than their contractual counterparts; reshaping them in the image of *mechni* enabled the jurists to bring them into a curial setting without cutting their ties to the past that authenticated them.

Briduw will be discussed separately in the following chapter, but *gorfodogaeth* makes the point just as well. All indications are that the *gorfodog* was not in origin a contractual guarantor of any kind. Rather, much like the Irish *aitire chána*, he was an attendance surety who guaranteed that his principal would provide compensation to an injured party once an offense had been committed. The *gorfodog*'s ultimate origins lay probably in kin-based hostageship,[25] and the context in which he would originally have been most likely invoked was one in which a violent or unexpected crime had occurred.[26] By the time of the lawbooks, however, a *gorfodog* could be demanded of anyone whose behavior was suspicious or status and connections uncertain.[27] His function was quite literally to substitute himself for the person on whose behalf he acted as guarantor: if a *gorfodog*'s principal were to commit a crime during the *gorfodog*'s period of service (defined in most texts as a year and a day[28]), and the surety proved unable to force the offender to come to law, he automatically became liable for the penalty his principal would have incurred.[29]

What makes the *gorfodog* particularly interesting is the manner in which his office was assimilated in the sources to standard *mechni*, presumably to facilitate his absorption within the curial context. For it is apparent from the later legal texts that the *gorfodog*, like the other Welsh sureties, functioned increasingly over time within the confines of the seigneurial court. In his curial manifestation, the *gorfodog* took on the characteristics of a *mach ar gyfraith* for criminal affairs.[30] The parallels between the *gorfodog*'s duties and curial *mechni* are very clearly articulated in the sources. Already in *Llyfr Blegywryd*, he is actually called a *mach goruodawc*, a designation that becomes common in later texts, where he also appears frequently as a *mach ar heddwch*, a "*mach* to guarantee peace."[31] *Llyfr Iorwerth* and *Llyfr Colan* both attach their short tractates on his office to their discussion of *mechni*, and in the Latin texts also the few brocards of information relevant to his duties are incorporated into the main suretyship tractate. Most revealing of all, however, is *Llyfr Iorwerth*'s statement that *gorfodogaeth*, like *mechni*, is to be bound with three hands.[32] This is a provision that makes little sense in the context of *gorfodogaeth* itself. Three hands are indeed the norm in normal contractual suretyship—those of the *mach*, the creditor, and the debtor. In *gorfodogaeth*, however, the identity of the plaintiff is not known at the time the office is undertaken. Indeed, given the length of time that the *gorfodog* was expected to serve, a truly unfortunate surety could find himself confronting several plaintiffs. The requirement that entering into *gorfodogaeth* be accomplished by the clasping of three hands is most easily comprehensible within the context of the deliberate reshaping of that office along the lines of its much more familiar counterpart *mechni*.[33]

Another method used by the jurists to connect legal past and present was the recasting of specific customs or practices into familiar and inherently authoritative forms of presentation. Of these forms the best known is undoubtedly the triad, a mnemonic device with a long history behind it in the circles of oral learning that were the foundation for the written legal tradition of the twelfth and thirteenth centuries.[34] One would be a long time indeed trying to list all the examples of "triadizing" in the lawbooks; *Llyfr Cyfnerth*, *Llyfr Blegywryd*, and the Latin lawbooks contain entire sections devoted to this form, and many examples of it appear as well in the *Llyfr y Damweiniau*. What is perhaps more interesting and profitable to contemplate are the circumstances in which material tends to be recast into triadic form.

It will probably come as no surprise to those familiar with Welsh or Irish legal tradition to find that the triad was often used in later manuscripts to lend the authority of apparent age to practices that in actuality were not at all old. Provisions appearing in two fifteenth-century manuscripts, for example, ostentatiously recast the reality of seigneurial and curial privilege into venerable triadic form. One lists three possessors of *tafodiog* status among the Welsh—the lord, the judge and the *mach*.[35] And another passage in the same manuscript makes use not only of the triad, but of one of the old proverbs of Welsh law as well. The saying *amot a tyr ar dedyf*, "an *amod* cuts through the law," appears in several places in the lawbooks, including *Llyfr Iorwerth*'s and *Llyfr Cyfnerth*'s mini-tractate on the *amodwr*. In the triadic version preserved in manuscripts Q and P, however, three things are listed that *tyrr ar kyfreith* ("cut through law"), of which one is an *amod*, and another a "lord who improves upon [the letter of the?] law in pursuing truth or displaying mercy."[36]

Obviously, it is impossible to be certain at this distance of the motives for which any specific item of "new law" might have been recast in triadic form. After all, mnemonic devices are useful even in primarily literate settings. But the authenticating of innovation is not an unlikely explanation, and it is perhaps significant that in Anglo-Saxon and Scandinavian tradition also, "oral" devices like alliteration are often more a feature of later rather than early law. Equally interesting, though even more uncertain, is its apparent opposite—the recasting of old material originally not phrased in this form into triads for use in a contemporary context. The Welsh evidence suggests that triads served often as a way to preserve for posterity customs that though discernably early, were endangered in some manner. At least occasionally they were used to perpetuate the memory of customs no longer current or understood. It seems likely, for example, that the lawyers no longer understood the circumstances that lay behind the *da dilis diuach*, "goods immune from claim without a surety," mentioned in *Llyfr Cyfnerth, Llyfr Blegywryd*, the Latin lawbooks, and manuscripts S and Q.[37] No rationale is offered for these unusual transactions, and it would be hazardous indeed to assume that the provisions found in the lawbooks represented thirteenth-century practice on such matters. Their special status is simply asserted, in triadic form, and left at that. If, as has been argued, these transactions preserve the remnants of a social order that no longer obtained at the time the lawbooks were compiled, the triadic form in which they are presented may be significant. Triads may have been used by the jurists as a type of "fixative," a vehicle through which to preserve the memory of customs that, though recognizably "old law," could no longer be explained within a contemporary context. Rather than allow such conventions simply to disappear (a prospect not to be taken lightly in a tradition so grounded in the past) the lawyers chose to perpetuate them in a structure that necessitated no elaboration.

The authoritative terseness of the triad may have proved particularly useful within the newly curial context envisaged in the *cynghawsedd*. For, as we have seen, implicit in the imaginative manipulation of legal procedures is the potential for random and seemingly limitless innovation. In such an atmosphere, change is difficult to resist: outmoded perceptions and institutions stand little chance against the logic of procedural precedent. Triads are, however, by their very nature almost impossible to refute, since they neither require explanation nor tolerate argument. That which they assert simply is, and cannot be argued away. These are qualities that must have been of enormous value to litigants attempting for reasons of their own to stem the tide of legal change. Indeed, we have already looked at precisely such a case: the immunity of the *mach* from testimony brought against him derived from his earlier supervisory role in contractual obligations—a status that no longer obtained at the time the *cynghawsedd* on suretyship were written. But plaintiffs of the period cared more about the payment of what was owed them than about the historical privileges of the *mach* and therefore tried their best to undermine the surety's status in this regard. Significantly, the response suggested to the surety in the *cynghawsedd* is phrased in triadic form; the *mach* is to respond that bringing witnesses against a surety is one of the three procedural errors in Welsh law that causes a plaintiff automatically to lose his case.[38] In this one statement, present and past are intricately linked. An ancient privilege is updated by being rephrased in terms more conducive to the curial setting in which it was deployed; the arguments of contemporary-minded pleaders are silenced by the logic of tradition. Not even the most articulate of advocates can overcome the rhetoric of a structure that does not permit debate.

The reconceptualizing of the legal tradition itself and of individual elements within that tradition bears eloquent testimony to the jurists' continuing concern with the relationship between legal past and present. A common thread runs through the lawbooks as a whole; for these compilers, confronted with a need for both permanence and change, the past became a frame within which innovation could occur. But while the relative positioning of old and new is an issue that resonates generally throughout the lawbooks, it is apparent from the sources that not all the jurists experienced their legacy in precisely similar ways. Within the confines of Hywel's book are visible a variety of degrees of awareness of the problem of legal change. Indeed, the redactions themselves differ markedly from one another, both in content and approach. In some the richness of tradition is evident, while in others it is cloaked; some embrace substantive change, while others seem almost to resist it. These differences are revealing, though obviously difficult to gauge: traditions probably varied widely in the regions in which the lawbooks were composed. This may in itself, however, be more of a question than an answer. In the balancing of old and new may be revealed something of the priorities and concerns of the juristic circles in which these texts originated.

Of the principal versions of the suretyship tractate contained in *Cyfraith Hywel*, probably the most broadly dissimilar are those of *Llyfr Iorwerth* and the Latin and *Llyfr Blegywryd* traditions.[39] For although the earliest manuscripts of these traditions date to precisely the same period (the early to mid-thirteenth century), in vision, style, and origins these books are worlds apart. The Latin lawbooks form one of the loosest of textual families in that the tractates contained in these redactions frequently vary significantly one from the other. In the case of the suretyship tractate, a single Latin original would appear to lie ultimately behind all of the extant Latin texts and, therefore, also behind *Llyfr Blegywryd*'s version as it is principally a translation of Latin D (it draws also on a *Llyfr Cyfnerth* text or sources). Latin A is the shortest of the tractates in question, and the least visibly influenced by other versions of *Cyfraith Hywel*; it is likely therefore to be most reflective of the original Latin prototype. Latin B is a poorly edited and organized hodge-podge of material from a variety of sources, and Latin E is the fullest and most comprehensive of them all, having been greatly influenced by a text of the *Llyfr Iorwerth* tradition. The prototractate lying behind these versions almost certainly originated in the South: Latin A, Latin D, *Llyfr Blegywryd*, and indeed the Latin tradition as a whole have clear associations with Deheubarth, and even Latin B and Latin E, compiled as lawbooks in the North, betray at their core a southern point of view.[40]

Sensible persons will be reluctant to generalize about sources as complex and varied as these redactions seem to be. To judge at least from Latin A, however, the Latin prototype would seem to have contained very little material that would have struck its compilers as necessarily archaic. This is not to say that no discernably "old law" occurs in this text. Two provisions deriving ultimately from an eighth-century Irish canon collection are included in Latin A and are for the most part reproduced in the other Latin texts.[41] But though these texts are demonstrably old in origin, there is no evidence to suggest that they would have been regarded by this period as outdated or irrelevant or that the compilers knew of their origins and valued them principally for their connection to the past. One passage deals with persons who were forbidden to act as sureties because of their inferior social or legal status; the inclusion in *Llyfr Iorwerth* of a similar provision deriving not from the Irish canon but from a Welsh original suggests that we are at least in the presence of a native custom, quite possibly one of continuing application.[42]

It is possible to be even more specific about the relevance of the other Irish canon. This is a text dealing originally with the Irish paying surety the *ráth* who, as we have seen, was in existence in Ireland already by the eighth century, if not before. Paying suretyship would seem to have come later to Wales than it did to Ireland, to judge from the continuing references in the lawbooks to enforcement as the primary duty of the *mach*. We know, however, that the practice was known in Wales at least by the time of the composition of Latin A, because that text includes other less ambiguous references to the custom.[43] Though this passage may have stemmed originally from an early Irish canonical collection, then, it was nonetheless directly relevant to the situation obtaining in southern Wales at the time the lawbooks were composed. Indeed, it is even possible that the circulating of this text in southern Welsh legal circles actually inspired the transition from enforcing to paying surety: *Llyfr Iorwerth* is completely silent on the matter of paying sureties, and the Irish canons do not appear to have circulated in the North, where *Llyfr Iorwerth* was compiled.[44]

Thus while the Latin and *Llyfr Blegywryd* versions of the tractate do contain some clearly old material, one is not entitled to presume from this that the primary interest of these passages for those who compiled and used them was historical rather than practical. One need not look as far as the American Constitution for an example of how the law of an earlier age can be rendered applicable to more contemporary situations. In any case, it is impossible to know whether the compilers were aware of the ultimate origins of their material: unless old and new come directly into conflict, which by and large is not the case in the Latin and *Llyfr Blegywryd* texts, change can be very difficult to discern.[45] It is, however, notable that "old law" does not occupy much space in the Latin and *Llyfr Blegywryd* versions of the tractate. Even more striking—indeed, perhaps the most prominent aspect of this version of the tractate—is that the compilers showed no hesitation about incorporating into it provisions of substantive law that were probably relatively new at the time the prototype was compiled.

Llyfr Blegywryd and the Latin redactions are the only principal versions of the lawbook to refer in absolutely unambiguous terms to a native paying surety. *Llyfr Cyfnerth* incorporates its own rendition of the Irish canon into its tractate but contains no other reference to the subject, and *Llyfr Iorwerth*, as has already been observed, is silent on the matter altogether. The Latin texts, by contrast, including Latin A, not only discuss the practice openly but make frequent use of the Roman law term *principalis debitor*. *Llyfr Blegywryd* and the Latin texts are also the only versions to acknowledge that a person might stand as surety for himself, a practice expressly forbidden in *Llyfr Iorwerth* and *Llyfr Cyfnerth*, and one that almost certainly reflects the increasingly active economic climate of the period in which the lawbook was first compiled.[46] This willingness to accomodate innovation seems, moreover, to continue over time. Redactions subsequent to Latin A, for example, show ample evidence of the increasing prominence of seigneurial jurisdiction.[47] The only aspects of contemporary legal life that appear to be absent from these traditions are the procedural and jurisprudential developments visible in *Llyfr Iorwerth* itself and in the *cynghawsedd* appended to it.[48] In most other respects, the *Llyfr*

Blegywryd and Latin tractates seem to reflect the circumstances in which they were composed and not to dwell particularly on the past.

In contrast to this stands the *Llyfr Iorwerth* version of the suretyship tractate. *Llyfr Iorwerth* generally is thought to be the most up-to-date of all the lawbooks in terms of its contents and approach.[49] And this in many ways it is: no other tradition contains the extended juristic reasoning, elaborate pleadings, and frequent references to judge and lord that are so characteristic of this book. The *Llyfr Iorwerth* tractate is particularly receptive to the procedural innovations of its day. It replaces what was probably in origin a short statement on the denial of suretyship by a debtor with a verbatim account of the curial procedure to be followed in such cases, and it quotes a plea on the *mach ar gyfraith* that captures very realistically the machinations and misapplied quotations inherent in the pleading process.[50] Jurisprudentially it is also quite sophisticated. Whereas *Llyfr Cyfnerth*, *Llyfr Blegywryd*, and the Latin texts show little interest in the variety of legal opinions held by jurists of the period, *Llyfr Iorwerth* frequently acknowledges differing points of view, often prefacing its own resolution to the problem with the remark that while *rey a deweyt*, "some say" a particular practice is right, *e keureyth a deweyt eyssyoes*, "nevertheless the law says" otherwise. It is impossible to read through the *Llyfr Iorwerth* tractate without getting a sense of highly professional minds at work—persons involved in and knowledgeable about the legal issues of their day.

And yet, as has recently been pointed out, *Llyfr Iorwerth*'s tractate also contains a higher proportion than do any of the other traditions of what would appear to be discernably "old" substantive law. Its provisions on legal incompetency, for example, return us to a very early era in legal development. It says nothing about a paying surety, even though a financially liable *mach* was almost certainly known in northern Wales by the thirteenth century.[51] Indeed, it even includes in its tractate a passage on the surety's paying half for an exiled debtor that probably represents a transitional stage in the development from enforcing to paying *mach*.[52] *Llyfr Iorwerth* is aware of the practice of self-suretyship but forbids it, and also takes a conservative stand on the question of whether the heir of a dead surety ought to be allowed to deny his father's obligation.[53] Furthermore, it consciously incorporates into its tractate a provision on women's dependent status that is not only very old but that is recognized by the compiler as something quite out of keeping with the customs of his day. That the compiler of Latin E also had access to a version of this provision and yet chose neither to include it in his tractate on suretyship nor to confront the difficulties it presented, is quite telling. *Llyfr Iorwerth*'s compiler went to great lengths to reinterpret this provision in a manner consistent with the practices with which he was familiar. He was clearly uncomfortable, therefore, with the fact of legal change; the prospect of omitting from his lawbook part of the textual legacy bequeathed to him, however, discomfited him even more.[54]

These facts are revealing, for they may suggest something about the attitude and materials with which these compilers approached the task in which they were engaged. The *Llyfr Iorwerth* tractate is remarkable for its all-inclusive nature. It is notable as well for its commitment to working out the jurisprudence of the whole: as has already been noted, only *Llyfr Iorwerth* involves itself extensively in the debates that are in many ways the hallmark of a living legal tradition. Procedurally also is it the most sophisticated of the versions, reflecting the developments in pleading and legal argument current in the juristic circles of its day. And yet *Llyfr Iorwerth* incorporates into its tractate items of substantive law that clearly no longer were applicable to the period in which it was written. Furthermore, in terms of its approach to substantive innovation, *Llyfr Iorwerth* appears to be quite conservative. If its compiler knew of the paying *mach*, he took no steps to ensure that the practice would be recorded in his tractate. And he explicitly rejects many of the contemporary innovations of which he was aware. Even the inclusion of the passage on the *amodwr*, which might seem to be an exception, in fact supports the rule, for the *amodwr* is, in essence, a procedural innovation—a privileging of certain kinds of testimony over others for the convenience of the court rather than a substantively new type of guarantor. The Latin prototype, by contrast, would appear to have been relatively contemporary in terms of the substantive law that it contained. If its compilers had access to much old material, they made little use of it. In terms of jurisprudence and procedure, however, both it and its successor redactions lag very far behind, demonstrating little interest in the issues so compelling to the compilers of *Llyfr Iorwerth* and almost no awareness of the procedural changes taking place amongst their colleagues to the North (this is somewhat less true of Latin B and E, both of which were compiled in the North).

The question, of course, is why. These differences may reflect little more than variations in regional custom; certainly, there is no reason to believe that practices were uniform throughout the country as a whole. Part of the answer may lie in the nature and extent of the material from which these compilers were working. *Llyfr Iorwerth*'s authors may well have had access to older traditions not available to those involved in the composition of the Latin and *Llyfr Blegywryd* tractates.⁵⁵ To advance such arguments is not, however, entirely to resolve the dilemma. That procedure was advanced in one region and not in another, or that the North tended to resist substantive changes to the lawbooks while the South embraced them, are questions in themselves. Moreover, the survival of old material in one area but not in another itself makes one wonder about the reasons for which this might have occurred. What all of this points to is suggestive of real differences in the longevity, professionalism, and approach of the legal traditions associated with these two regions.

To a certain extent regional differences of this sort have long been recognized—even in the thirteenth century Gwynedd was acknowledged to be the primary center of legal activity and debate. But they have not generally been linked to another distinction documented recently between northern and southern legal practitioners (specifically judges).⁵⁶ As R. R. Davies has made clear, Gwynedd was the home of the *ynaid*, professional and highly trained judges who remained peculiarly characteristic of the region throughout the high and late Middle Ages. It was to the North that those who would learn the law of Hywel made their way for specialist training; it was in the North that the professional order of *ynaid*, similar in many ways to that of the poets, was based. In the South, by contrast, amateur or semi-professional doomsmen were the rule and professionals the exception. All who owned land could expect to serve as *brawdwyr*, "judges," and if judges of the *ynaid* type had ever existed there in any numbers, they had virtually disappeared by the thirteenth century.⁵⁷ Moreover, it was in the South that the sort of legal interactions between native Welsh and Marcher or English lords that must lie behind the production of the Latin redactions were most frequent and sustained. Obviously the lawbooks, both northern and southern, were composed by professionals. It stands only to reason, however, that differences in the training and orientation of the judiciary of these regions might be reflected in lawbooks originating in these areas. For as anyone who has ever written anything for public consumption will immediately recognize, the audience for whom a work is intended can shape that piece as directly as does the author himself.

In the association between author and audience we may have the beginnings of an answer to our question, as well as a sense of the attitudes towards legal innovation current in juristic circles of the period. The *Llyfr Iorwerth* tractate was quite clearly produced by, and directed at, a professional legal class, one highly conscious of its responsibility toward the tradition it both embodied and perpetuated. On the one hand this responsibility entailed the faithful preservation of the legacy of the past. If a tradition existed in written form, it would not be jettisoned; if a new tradition was created, it would be regarded with suspicion until affirmed by prolonged usage. Legal castes are, after all, notoriously conservative on the question of admitting new substantive material to the tradition of which they perceive themselves to be the guardians. On the other hand, it is no accident that *Llyfr Iorwerth* is quite receptive to procedural innovation nor that much of the evidence for the substantive changes occurring in *mechni* over time comes from the *Llyfr Cynghawsedd*. The manipulation of procedures is particularly common in otherwise conservative legal environments, providing practitioners with room for maneuver while appearing not to threaten the tradition of which they are a part. Substantive change may in fact occur, but it will be difficult to discern by those involved in the procedural machinations that produce it. And those whose business it is to notice and record legal change are likely to become aware of the manner in which procedural strategems threaten to reshape the contents of tradition only when practitioners find themselves appealing to the past in defense of their case—defending a surety against testimony brought against him, for example. *Llyfr Iorwerth*'s apparent reluctance to sanction substantive change is not at all at odds with its general enthusiasm for procedural innovation. The *Llyfr Iorwerth* tractate is as conservative as it is in terms of contents precisely *because* the legal tradition that produced it was so active and jurisprudentially aware. For these jurists particularly, the past was the foundation on which the future would be built.

The Latin and *Llyfr Blegywryd* prototype speaks to an entirely different atmosphere, one in which judicial priorities were likely much more practical than theoretical. For those who are not professionals—or who are not native—need primarily to know the content of the law, not the historical and theoretical rationales in which it is grounded. Furthermore, while in such a setting the legacy of the past is important, contemporaneity is also a virtue. Indeed, if the texts of the Latin and *Llyfr Blegywryd* traditions did play a critical role in the actual transmission of legal knowledge, it is probably no accident that it is in the South that written lawbooks seem first to have found their way into court. Nor is it surprising that the Latin and *Llyfr Blegywryd* redactions should be so relatively receptive to substantive innovation. Those for whom this tractate may have been primarily composed would have no stake in preserving the seamlessness of tradition: substantive change poses little threat to those who see their task as administering in fairly pragmatic fashion a body of written and oral custom. While substantive change may be more willingly acknowledged, however, procedural innovation is much less likely to occur. Non-professional judges are less likely to appreciate intricate strategems of the sort reflected in the *cynghawsedd*. Moreover, relative flexibility on the part of the substantive canon would probably render procedural maneuverings less necessary and less effective.

To maintain that the distinction between North and South was in any sense hard and fast would be unwise. Redactions spread from one region of Wales to another within only a short period of their composition. There are southern manuscripts of *Llyfr Iorwerth*, and northern manuscripts of the Latin texts—indeed, both Latin B, of the mid-thirteenth century, and Latin E, of the early fifteenth century, have clear northern connections, as we have said. Judicial environment may, however, have played a role in shaping the earliest versions of these lawbooks. And it is possible that focusing on the nature and training of judicial personnel may help us to understand in a general way the manner in which trends in popularity shifted over the course of the Middle Ages away from the *Llyfr Iorwerth* and toward the *Llyfr Blegywryd* tradition. There can be no doubt of *Llyfr Iorwerth*'s enormous and continuing prestige; one has only to look at the extensive borrowings from *Llyfr Iorwerth* evident both in the fourteenth-century *Llyfr Cyfnerth* manuscripts V and W and in Latin E to realize the respect *Llyfr Iorwerth* continued to engender in regions of Wales other than that in which it had originally been composed.

That which is jurisprudentially sophisticated and historically inclusive is not, however, always the most practical text from which to work in court. The Latin and *Llyfr Blegywryd* redactions, pithier, more accessible, and in some ways more contemporary—especially once fleshed out with useful material from the *Llyfr Iorwerth* tradition (and in their most popular late medieval manifestation *Llyfr Blegywryd* appropriately "clericized")—may have seemed much more usable.[58] It may even be significant that although highly trained judges of the *ynaid* type certainly continued to exist in the post-Conquest period, they seem to have become over time more localized and more peripheral to the actual administration of justice.[59] If, as has been argued, the Latin and *Llyfr Blegywryd* redactions originally had been designed to respond to the needs of a relatively non-professional judiciary, it would stand to reason that the popularity of this tradition might increase as the number and importance of highly trained specialists declined. Certainly, it is suggestive that the majority of legal manuscripts the origins of which can be determined were commissioned by gentry occupying official positions of some kind.⁶⁰ The principal need in such an environment, as perhaps also in the setting in which the Latin and *Llyfr Blegywryd* traditions originated, was the communication of basic legal knowledge. The fact that this could be done in both Welsh and Latin could only have added to the attraction of these redactions in an increasingly anglicized world.

Both the problem and the fact of legal change would seem, therefore, to permeate the legal tradition as a whole. Even more compelling is the related matter of authority. Huw Pryce is right to argue that the authors of the lawbook prologues crafted their visions of royal and religious sanction in a manner designed to secure for their tradition the often wavering loyalties of native lords and princes.⁶¹ And while the prologues are probably the most blatantly fictive sections of these works, the frequent references to lord and court, the sophisticated pleadings, and the elaborations of existing institutions (e.g., *mechni* and the *amodwyr*) that are so characteristic of these texts may not have been merely reflective of the circumstances in which they were composed. Such features, like the existence of *Llyfr y Damweiniau* and *Llyfr Cynghawsedd*, may have been intended to persuade lords of the innovatory potential and contemporary appeal inherent in Welsh law, just as the invocation of Hywel and recasting of new material into traditional forms reminded them of the venerable tradition to which they were heir. Even more interesting is the support that a consideration of the issue of legal change would seem to lend to another of Pryce's suggestions—that the authors of the lawbooks were as much concerned with challenges from inside their own legal community as they were with threats from outside. Most of the ideas and processes we have examined here (the methods used to disguise or sanction innovation, for example, or the shaping of traditions around their anticipated audience) would appeal primarily to those already immersed in the tradition. Only those in a position to recognize the pattern of Hywel's lawbook would appreciate the fact of its remaining essentially intact; only those who viewed themselves as successors to a historical tradition would find meaningful the attribution of the lawbooks to jurists well known within that tradition.⁶² Lawyers themselves may have worried more about change than the secular rulers who brought it about. For these persons particularly, it was essential that past and present come together in the law of Hywel.

8. The Suretyship of the Gods

That lords and lawyers in medieval Wales were concerned with potential challenges to their own authority is clear from what has already been said. That they were sufficiently concerned as to attempt to bring acts of God as well as man within their sphere of jurisdiction is equally evident from the lawbooks. Long before the composition of the Welsh legal texts in the thirteenth century, the gods had played an important role in the regulation of human delictual and contractual affairs. Divine intervention was not always perceived as a necessarily good or just thing; one of the Greek philosophers remarked rather sourly that legal oaths were better sworn by the constant elements of nature than by the temperamental and irascible gods.[1] But welcome or not—and the philosopher's reservations were more the exception than the rule—the gods were involved. It is difficult for modern historians to write sensibly about the place of the supernatural in early societies. Indeed it is with reluctance that we give credence to the concept at all, having ourselves been taught to regard the supernatural as simply that which has not yet been understood. We are made uncomfortable by the presence of "irrational" belief, by the faith of peoples not as removed as we from the miracles of the Old and New Testaments, from the "*passio* [which] abolished time."[2] It is not surprising, therefore, that we should find it difficult to bridge the gap between ourselves and those for whom the natural and the supernatural were equally real, equally objective forces. What we have learned to distrust in ourselves we certainly do not wish to find in our ancestors.

And so we scurry through the rituals of early law, glancing hurriedly from left to right, pausing only to confront undeniably supernatural institutions like the oath and the ordeal. Conscious that we can no longer resort to traditional terms like "primitive," or "superstitious," labels our predecessors used to separate themselves from the rudest of their forebears, we look for new ways to explain what we do not comprehend. Recent anthropological studies have made us sensitive to the manner in which man's appeal to the supernatural was suited to the psychological, ceremonial, and social needs of the community in which he lived.³ But even in this understanding we run the risk of investing religious ritual with overtones of functionalism, of portraying belief as something one can pick up or leave off as one needs it, rather like a hammer.⁴ When we choose, for example, to emphasize the fact that the ordeal was reserved primarily for cases in which human methods of proof had proved inadequate, we say as much about ourselves as about the people we study. To pose the question in these terms is to reveal our own desire to define and to isolate the supernatural, and perhaps, unconsciously, generously to impart to our ancestors the rationality we ourselves so prize.⁵ In this, as in other respects, we seem to study faith primarily in order to circumscribe it. But we are in danger of missing the point; medieval persons invoked their saints and martyrs even when they did not have to. The supernatural was incorporated into every aspect of their lives, into every stage of the legal process. If we dwell exclusively on the boundaries between the rational and the mystical, on the dramatic institutions that cannot be ignored, we will never see the whole.

In few places was the boundary between the sacred and the secular less clear than in the Celtic lands, where the natural beauty of the place was matched only by the relentless meddling of the supernatural beings that inhabited it. It would not be easy to reconstruct from this distance the religious life of the average Celt, and it is fortunate that such a monumental enterprise lies outside the purview of this study. We have only to remark, as did Hoebel to the Sunday Supplement writer who asked him for a description of the love-life of Neanderthal man, that "he undoubtedly had one."⁶ But the role of the supernatural in the contractual law of Ireland and Wales is a far more feasible area of inquiry. Both the Irish and the Welsh lawbooks testify to the existence of a type of supernatural guarantee that is likely very old indeed, and that is unfamiliar, at least in such terms, to the rest of medieval Europe. The "suretyship of God," known in Welsh as *briduw*, and in Irish by a variety of different names (the *naidm/ aitire/ráth* of God, the saints, or the Gospels) seems by all accounts a remarkably ancient institution. Binchy saw in it the earliest form of suretyship, the model, perhaps, for the Indo-European enforcing surety: "Perhaps the earliest additional security was the invocation by one or both parties of supernatural powers as guarantors of the engagement, an expanded form of the oath which would give these powers a direct interest in the performance of his promise by the party who had invoked them and would expose him to punishment at their hands if he broke it."⁷ Similar invocations are known from ancient Egypt, from Greece, and from Rome, where Jupiter was summoned as both witness and enforcer of the terms of the agreement between Rome and Alba, *nec ullius vetustior foederis memoria est*, "and there is no more ancient memory of a pact."[8] In the Welsh *briduw* and its Irish equivalent, we have then, at least in Binchy's view, a "vestigial survival" of an ancient time.

Binchy's theories on the origins of contractual suretyship as an institution are interesting and plausible and are supported in this instance by a recent study of the oath in ancient Greece.[9] And while it would be impossible to prove that a common Indo-European ancestor lies behind the ancient invocations of Greece, Rome and the institution known in thirteenth-century Wales as *briduw*, the similarities are suggestive. A number of references exist in early Irish literature to persons invoking what would appear to be pagan deities as guarantors in broadly contractual contexts. Indeed, the "suretyship of the elements," traditionally assumed by scholars to be a precursor of the Christian institution, is a commonplace in the Irish sagas. The manifold death of the historical king Lóegaire mac Néill at the hands of his supernatural guarantors is told and retold: the earth swallowed him, the sun burned him, and the wind (his breath) left him after Lóegaire violated the guarantee he had given in their name never again to collect the *bóruma* tribute.[10] The subject-tribes of Ireland guaranteed their allegiance to Tipraite Tírech and his descendants with the *ráth*-sureties of "heaven and earth, moon and sun," and a similar story is told about Tuathal Techtmar.[11] Personalities as diverse as Pope Gregory the Great and the pagan god the Dagda found themselves subject to supernatural guarantees.[12] Other examples abound elsewhere.[13] Even oaths taken in the name of tribal gods, similar to those common in ancient Greece, are found as well in the Irish sagas.[14]

But though the evidence for the existence of a form of supernatural suretyship among the pre-Christian Celts seems overwhelming, in fact it is extremely difficult to use. None of the texts cited above are particularly early, and we know nothing about the dates or compositional context of the tales themselves. And while it is true that Irish literature often preserves archaisms no longer extant elsewhere, it cannot be assumed that every institution depicted in the sagas has one foot in the Iron Age. What we would like to see as a reflection of an earlier time may be nothing more than that most permanent of mirages, the literary cliché. Indeed, as Ó hUiginn has argued with reference to the numerous oaths sworn by tribal gods that appear in these tales, some of these passages may be the work of archaizing Christian literati rather than genuine remnants of an inherited tradition.[15] The late prologue to *Cáin Adomnáin*, which was redacted under ecclesiastical auspices and yet makes reference to the *rátha* of sun, moon, and elements, is certainly an example of this phenomenon.[16]

For whatever else the suretyship of the elements might have been, it was an excellent pseudo-historical device. All of the arrangements envisaged in the literary sources were, without exception, long-term relationships of subordination or alliance. By using the elements as guarantors the pseudo-historians emphasized the permanence of the arrangements they described. The terms were, quite literally, woven into the fabric of nature; they would last, as one text says, *céin maras muir im Érinn*, "as long as the sea remains around Ireland."[17] An early poem on the Airgialla makes the point most clearly: the specific terms of the treaty between the Uí Néill and the Airgialla federation were warranted by *aitiri*, and the terms of the hosting by human *rátha*, but the perpetual alliance between the two was guaranteed by guarantors of nature and of Heaven.[18] The suretyship of the elements was a useful literary tool; whether it also reflected a historical Indo-European reality is a more difficult question.

Unfortunately, this tension between the historical and the literary, between reality and make-believe, is all too typical of the subject as a whole. Most of the Irish evidence hails from the literary camp, where vengeful saints and self-righteous relics keep order with considerable ferocity. In the Welsh sources exactly the opposite obtains: there are few literary examples, but the legal account is relatively full. The invoking of religious persons or objects as contractual guarantors is, however, attested in the Irish lawbooks as an actual historical practice—in other words, it seems to have been more than just a literary conceit.[19] And the Welsh custom of *briduw* is almost certainly older than the thirteenth-century lawbooks in which it is most thoroughly discussed.[20] Moreover, while there is no Common Celtic term for this form of contractual guarantee, implicit in the manner in which it is discussed in both Irish and Welsh tradition are strikingly similar assumptions (see below on *bri*). The evidence is sketchy and difficult to use, but the likelihood is nevertheless that Binchy was correct in his suggestion that supernatural suretyship was a Common Celtic phenomenon, one which was continued in both Welsh and Irish tradition in Christianized form.[21]

It may even have been a distinctively Celtic phenomenon, at least phrased in such terms. Promissory oaths on weapons or saints were common among contemporary Germanic peoples, but the practice of a debtor offering to his creditor the "suretyship of God" as a warrant for their agreement was not.²² The only close parallels to Welsh and Irish practice in the early medieval world come from Brittany—a principally Frankish land, as its most recent historians have argued, but one with clear Celtic connections²³—and from Alfred's law code, where the passage probably represents a borrowing from or remnant of early Welsh law.²⁴ Such differences may, of course, be reflective more of divergent metaphors or patterns of conceptualization than of variations in actual practice, and one would not want to draw hard and fast lines between Celtic and Germanic expectations of the deities they invoked. Societies in which guarantors acted as both bond and enforcer of individual transactions might find the image of suretyship a particularly potent means of expressing the promise and threat implicit in divinely sanctioned agreements, whereas cultures in which sureties were regarded primarily as substitute debtors might not find the metaphor nearly so appropriate. The most the evidence allows one to say is that the image itself, and likely its ceremonial implementation as well, would appear to have been part of the Common Celtic legacy, and this is significant. *Briduw*'s inclusion in the the thirteenth-century Welsh lawbooks affords us the rare opportunity to trace the passage of an ancient, and perhaps originally even pagan, custom into the ambit of medieval Christian lordship.

The place to begin is by determining what exactly the suretyship of the gods was supposed to be and what was expected of it. By the time of the compilation of the Welsh lawbooks in the thirteenth century, it was an established institution and a plea in court.²⁵ It is presented in the Welsh texts entirely within the context of suretyship, as an agreement in which *Duu a kemeruet en lle mach*, "God was taken [as a surety] in the place of a [human] *mach*."²⁶ But *briduw* may have had its origins in the sacred promissory oath, as Binchy and others have suggested. Certain of the Irish terms for it—the *naidm*ship of the Gospels or of the saints, most notably—seem to reflect the divine beings and holy objects on which such oaths would have been sworn.²⁷ And although it is true that *naidm* status was not generally conferred through an oath (*naidm*-sureties were "invoked" or "appointed" in the process outlined earlier in Chapter 2), *aitire* status was, and there is a reference in one text to the *aitire Dé*, the "*aitire*-ship of God."²⁸ On the other hand, *Coibnes Uisci Thairidne* speaks of the "men of heaven" (*fir nime*) and the "Gospel of Christ" being "invoked" as guarantors, and the term it uses for this process, *ad-guid*, is the one normally used in the appointment (not by oath) of human sureties.²⁹ The conceptual leap from promissory oaths sworn on religious personalities or objects to the invoking of those persons or things as guarantors is a natural one, and it may be that attempting to distinguish too precisely between these is unrealistic. Regardless of whether this type of guarantee had evolved originally from the sacred promissory oath, however, the conceptual "leap" from oath to suretyship (frequently undertaken by oath, and perhaps representing, as Binchy suggests, an "expanded" form of it) had already occurred by the period of the Irish lawbooks.

The Welsh sources also leave unresolved the relationship between *briduw* and the promissory oath, although for entirely different reasons. Williams and Powell suggested, and Dafydd Jenkins accepted in his notes to *Llyfr Colan*, that the term *bri Duw* (as it appears in most of the texts that discuss it and in *Llyfr Cyfnerth*, likely our earliest version[30]), derived originally from an oath sworn [*myn?*] *bri Duw*, "by the honor of God," through which the pact in question was concluded.[31] This is not an unlikely oath, although it does not occur in the one (admittedly literary) description we have of a *briduw* pact. When Pryderi and Rhiannon disappear from the court at Arberth as a result of the enchantment laid over Dyfed by Llwyd fab Cil Coed, their spouses, Cigfa and Manawydan, are left alone together in the court:

> Pann welas Kicua, uerch Gwyn Gloew, gwreic Pryderi, nat oed yn y llys namyn hi a Manawydan, drygyruerth a wnaeth hyt nat oed well genti y byw no'y marw. Sef a wnaeth Manawydan. . . . "Mi a rodaf Duw y uach it, na weleisti gedymdeith gywirach noc y keffy di ui, tra uynho Duw it uot uelly. . . . E rof a Duw," heb ef, "titheu a gey y gedymdeithas a uynych y genhyf i, herwyd uyg gallu i. . . ."[32]

> When Cigfa, the daughter of Gwyn Gloew, the wife of Pryderi, saw that there was no one in the court except herself and Manawydan, she lamented that to live was to her not better than to die. This is what Manawydan did. . . . "I give God as a *mach*-surety to you that you have not seen a companion more true than you will find me, as long as God pleases that you be thus. . . . Between me and God," he said, "you will have the companionship that you desire from me, to the extent that I may be able. . . ."

Manawydan thus confirmed his promise to Cigfa with what appears to be a type of oath—*e rof a Duw*, "between me and God"—but the words *bri Duw* do not occur here, and in general the passage seems more commensurate with what we know about the appointment of *mach*-sureties than with the promissory oath per se.[33] Indeed the expression *bri Duw* itself, if in fact it is old, suggests that such arrangements must have been conceptualized as a form of suretyship from a reasonably early period, regardless of their original relationship to the oath. For *bri Duw* means, literally, either the "honor of God" or the "strength of God," and both of these speak directly to assumptions implicit in ordinary *mechni*.[34]

Whatever the nature of the original connection between *briduw* and the oath, however, it is likely that by the time the Welsh lawbooks were compiled, the gap between these two forms of agreement was, from the lawyers' perspective at least, very small. Certainly by the thirteenth century, as Huw Pryce has observed, there was little to distinguish, in terms of form or usage, *briduw* from the pledging of one's faith (Latin *fides*, Welsh *ffydd* or *cred*), despite the fact that the two had very different origins. Indeed, as Pryce argues, the lawyers' attempt to explain *briduw* as *fides*, together with the uncomprehending manner in which *briduw* is treated in the southern lawbooks, are important arguments for its being an ancient (and now obscure) form of contractual guarantee. Similarly, *fides* and the promissory oath itself were also being increasingly amalgamated by the jurists.[35] This blurring of the boundaries between what had presumably been originally independent forms of obligation is evident throughout the lawbooks. The *Damweiniau Colan*, for example, refer to *briduw* as a means of obtaining goods *truy edewyt*, "through a promise."[36] And Welsh law allowed any baptized person, male or female, who had reached the age of seven and had submitted himself to the authority of a confessor, to give *briduw*. Considered strictly within the context of suretyship, this provision would mean little, especially since a female child of this age would have had limited legal and commercial abilities; however, it was at the age of seven that children of both sexes became eligible to give oaths.[37] It is probably impossible to determine at this point, therefore, whether *briduw* had originally evolved out of the promissory oath, or even whether such oaths still played a role in the thirteenth-century institution. All one can say with certainty is that a number of divinely sanctioned pacts were recognized in Wales in the period of the lawbooks, and that at least one of these, *briduw*, was conceptualized as a form of suretyship. Attempting to compartmentalize these various agreements further into neatly defined categories is likely to prove a fruitless exercise.[38]

As elusive as the history and form of such arrangements are the expectations they generated in those who made use of them. Divine suretyship may well have had its origins in the "no-man's-land" separating magic from religion, for in envisaging a deity whose honor could be impugned or whose strength could be summoned to bear on a particular human pact, it assumed a deity whose power could be manipulated by human means. In this sense it represented, in Malinowski's terms, a "ritualization of man's optimism" rather than of his uncertainty.[39] That such perceptions may have survived in some form the transition to Christianity seems quite likely. Certainly the man who lauded Patrick for staging a successful hunger strike against God and for cursing a cleric who refused to perform a miracle seems not to have been overly concerned in his own oaths with preserving the omnipotence of the deity.[40] On the other hand, matters may well have looked rather different to the sophisticated clerics of thirteenth-century Wales, where the dangers of the "controlled miracle" were becoming obvious to all.[41] God, while ultimately just, was not always proximately so, and some may have found it increasingly prudent to regulate their commercial transactions in accord with this knowledge.

But while it may seem tempting to see in the changes that take place in the suretyship of God between the eighth century in Ireland and the thirteenth century in Wales a progression from greater to lesser "magic," the issue is not that simple.[42] Obviously we are dealing here with an area of the popular imagination for which there can be no sources; an individual's expectations of supernatural suretyship, or of the ordeal, or even of the Mass itself, are his or her own. No one can reasonably hope to measure the "magical" content invested by the race of Cynaythuy in the Gospels of Gildas, for example, which were said to shorten the life of any man of that lineage who committed perjury upon them.[43] As Keith Thomas so aptly pointed out, one man's supplication is another's attempt to manipulate, and the line between them can be very hard to draw.[44]

What the lawbooks make clear, however, is that regardless of changes in the "magical" content invested in *briduw* by those who made use of it, the most critical factor in determining the shape taken by this practice in the thirteenth-century lawbooks was the legal community itself. The unambiguously jural procedure outlined in the sources had come a long way from the ritual from which it had originally derived. The jurists were, in effect, deliberately "institutionalizing" *briduw* to bring it into line with the legal and political realities of their own day. Our information on *briduw* is preserved in two principal versions: a southern tradition represented by *Llyfr Cyfnerth*, Latin D, and *Llyfr Blegywryd*, and a northern tradition represented by *Llyfr Iorwerth*, *Llyfr Colan*, and Latin B and E (Latin family texts but originating in the north). The southern tradition particularly tells us little about *briduw* itself. *Llyfr Cyfnerth's* reference occurs almost as an afterthought to a passage concerned principally with the denial of *mechni*, although the text shows that the denial process used for *briduw* has reshaped that of *mechni* as well as the other way around.[45] And Latin D and *Llyfr Blegywryd* muddle the matter altogether, stating that it is the *mach* who denies *briduw*, a confusion that must mean, as Pryce has observed, that they no longer understood the institution to which they were referring.[46]

It is in the northern Welsh lawbooks of *Llyfr Iorwerth* and *Llyfr Colan* that we find the fullest exposition of *briduw*.[47] Here also do we get a clear sense of the jurists' priorities, as well as our first glimpse of how *briduw* was evolving in the period of the lawbooks. For the most striking aspect of the northern tradition's treatment of *briduw* is the very deliberate manner in which the lawyers strove to assimilate it, both textually and procedurally, to standard *mechni*. The textual parallels are particularly strong: not only does *Llyfr Iorwerth* append its discussion of *briduw* to the suretyship tractate (as it does also with its passages on the *gorfodog* and the *amodwr*); it patterns its account structurally on the *mechni* tractate as well. *Ior* 68/1 corresponds to *Ior* 58/1–3; *Ior* 68/2–6 on the denial of *briduw* to *Ior* 58/4–61/4; *Ior* 68/7 on differences between creditor and debtor as to the amount of the obligation to *Ior* 61/5; and *Ior* 68/9 on enforcement to *Ior* 62 (and compare *Ior* 68/10 with *Ior* 63/1–2). That such patterning was intentional can hardly be doubted: by assimilating the mini-tractate on *briduw* to their more formidable and inherently authoritative work on the *mach*, the compilers carved out for *briduw* an unassailable niche within the tradition of *Cyfraith Hywel*.

The procedural remodeling in which the northern compilers engaged is more difficult to trace since, as was remarked earlier, *briduw* seems to have been conceptualized as a form of *mechni* from a fairly early period. It is possible that the binding procedure for *briduw* was patterned on that of ordinary *mechni*. *Ior* 68/8 (*Col* 130) states that *nat bruduu ene keuarfo e llau a'e gylyd*, "it is not *briduw* until one hand meets another," and hand-in-hand binding is, as we have seen, the manner in which *mach*-sureties were usually appointed. It should be noted that patterning is not a necessary conclusion, since the joining of hands may always have played a role in the formulation of *briduw* pacts. But the early *Llyfr Iorwerth* manuscripts C, E, and A share a common reading requiring the meeting of *three* hands, a confusion that does seem most likely to have resulted from the attempt to model one institution after the other.[48]

The assimilation of *briduw* to *mechni* is even more clearly visible in the changing nature of the procedure through which *briduw* pacts were denied.[49] In the southern traditions represented by *Llyfr Cyfnerth* and, secondarily, by Latin D and *Llyfr Blegywryd*, the suretyship of God was to be denied by the defendant's own oath given on seven different altars.[50] The northern versions of *Llyfr Iorwerth* and *Llyfr Colan*, on the other hand, stipulate denial through compurgation in the manner of ordinary *mechni*.[51] It is conceivable that such differences reflect nothing more than variations in local custom; it is not unusual for the southern traditions of *Llyfr Blegywryd* and *Llyfr Cyfnerth* to differ significantly from the northern texts of *Llyfr Iorwerth* and *Llyfr Colan*. The question is somewhat complicated, however, by the fact that both Latin B and Latin E agree with *Llyfr Iorwerth*'s formulation of the procedure for denial.[52] The paragraph in which these references occur is unique to Latin B and E, and did not, therefore, form part of the Latin core tractate. Nor does it represent a mere borrowing on the part of the compilers of the Latin texts from *Llyfr Iorwerth* itself, since the differences between these passages are more significant than they would be in such a case. They must therefore represent, as Pryce has remarked, evidence independent of *Llyfr Iorwerth* for the existence by the thirteenth century of the practice of denying *briduw* through compurgation.[53] It is unclear whether the change from oath to compurgation represents the introduction by the compilers of Latin B and E of a northern custom into the Latin tradition or, alternatively, a reshaping of an earlier practice obtaining originally throughout all Wales (e.g., denial through oath) initiated by the northern compilers and later adopted by their colleagues elsewhere. What matters most is that deliberate reshaping has clearly occurred and that its aim was unquestionably to remake *briduw* in the more familiar image of *mechni*.

There is some evidence outside the Welsh lawbooks that is potentially relevant to this question. The Anglo-Saxon laws of Alfred are the only other early medieval source in which a *briduw* type of arrangement is clearly mentioned:

> Gif hwa oðernes godborges oncunne and tion wille, þaet he hwelcne ne gelaeste ðara ðe he him gesealde, agife þone foreað on feower ciricum, and se oðer, gif he hine treowan wille, in xii ciricum do he ðaet.[54]

> If anyone should accuse another [of a breach] of a "God-suretyship," and wishes to complain that he (the defendant) has not fulfilled any of those [promises] that he (the defendant) gave to him, let him (the plaintiff) give the fore-oath[55] in four churches, and let the other, if he wishes to exculpate himself, give that [oath of denial] in twelve churches.

Although this provision does not accord in every detail with the account contained in *Llyfr Cyfnerth*, the similarities are striking. Neither the word

Godborg, nor the concept of divine suretyship itself occurs anywhere else in the Anglo-Saxon sources, and given the close contacts obtaining between Wales and Wessex in this period, the possibility that Alfred borrowed this idea from Welsh custom must be counted a strong one. It is also possible that in *Godborg* we have the remnants of an institution native to the Britons of the Southwest that was incorporated into the West-Saxon kingdom at a very early date. In either case, Alfred's laws provide evidence for the altar form of denial that predates even the reign of Hywel Dda himself. One still cannot rule out the possibility of regional variation, since Alfred's relations with the South were much closer than his relations with the North. However, the preponderance of evidence suggests that the oath was the original denial procedure, and that it was ultimately replaced by the jurists as part of their effort to assimilate *briduw* to *mechni*.[56]

This conclusion is borne out by other passages in the lawbooks in which the process of repatterning the denial of *briduw* seems almost visible. In manuscript H, of the fourteenth century, a triad is used to assimilate *briduw*'s denial procedure to that of *mechni*: *briduw* appears in that text together with *amodwyr* and *mechni* as one of the three places in which one swears alternately in the course of denial (*gwers tra gwers*).[57] (Triads were, as we have seen, frequently used as vehicles for perpetuating or authorizing provisions of uncertain provenance or applicability, a fact of obvious relevance for *briduw*, a procedure that Latin D's compiler at least seems no longer to have understood.) Manuscript S, of the fifteenth century, also groups *briduw*, *amodwyr*, and *mechni* together, remarking that *dróy reith ossodedic y góedir pob vn o honynt*,[58] and "through [the] established compurgatory *raith* is each one of them to be denied." And in *Ior* 65/10–11, the repatterning of *briduw*'s denial after that of *mechni* even leads that text to contradict one of its most established principles. *Ior* 65/10 allows a woman who has given an ordinary surety to deny him with a compurgation of seven men, since the surety she denies is male. *Ior* 65/11 adds to this that if it is *briduw* that she denies, she is entitled to deny it with a compurgation of seven women. The reasoning in *Ior* 65/11 thus exactly follows that of 65/10. *Briduw* is here treated as a type of self-suretyship; the woman in question is allowed to deny the obligation with a compurgation of women because it is perceived that the person whose suretyship she denies is herself. This contradicts, however, Iorwerth's clearly stated rule that a woman is not allowed to be a surety (*Ior* 65/8).

Rituals of denial were not the only procedural aspects of *briduw* to be deliberately modeled on *mechni*. *Briduw* appears relatively infrequently in the "anomalous" legal texts, but when it does, it is almost always in conjunction with *mechni*. In many passages it is classified (together with *mechni* and *amod*) as one of the "bindings" (*rwym* or *ymrwym*) of Welsh law, and manuscript H states clearly that any type of property transfer that can be pursued through *mechni* can be done through *briduw* as well, including gifts, loans, deposits, and exchanges. In fact, H is particularly forthcoming on the subject of *briduw*, including it in a number of its provisions on the rules and exemptions of *mechni*.[59] Like *mechni*, *briduw* also may be enforced by the placement of a cross, and the giver of *briduw*, like an acknowledged *mach*, is permitted to state definitively for what amount he is obligated.[60] *Mechni* and *briduw* are also treated together in H's provisions on *arddelwau* and the procedural errors that parties may allege in defense of their position in a claim.[61] And *briduw* itself gives shape to the denial ritual of another type of claim, *tyllwedd*, "concord."[62]

The repatterning of *briduw* after *mechni* is thus pervasive throughout the lawbooks. Moreover, the motives that underlay the lawyers' efforts in this regard were likely both procedural and textual in nature, as were the changes themselves. The procedural assimilation of *briduw* to *mechni* must have served first to clarify the nature of this ancient institution for those who, like the compiler of Latin D, were no longer certain of its meaning and purview. It must also have facilitated the integration of *briduw* pacts within the increasingly curialized world of thirteenth-century justice. *Briduw* is in fact regarded as a curial plea in the later lawbooks—as a method, in other words, not only by which goods might be claimed, but by which goods might be protected against claims brought by others.[63]

Some sense of the thoroughness with which *briduw* and institutions like it came ultimately to be integrated into the setting of the court (and into the tortuous world of juristic pleading) can be gotten from a remarkable case preserved in manuscripts Q and K, both of the fifteenth century. The plaintiff in the case brings a complaint of *sarhaed*, "insult" or, here, "assault," against another, who then denies the charge on the grounds that he was not striking him, but rather pledging his faith to him (*rodi cret arnaó*). To this unusual response, the claimant asserts that the pledging of faith is to be done by touching hand to hand, not by striking the shoulder or breast, and that what he (the defendant) had done was *sarhaed*, not the giving of *cred*. Perhaps not surprisingly, given the nature of the defendant's response, the prosecution is upheld as justified.[64] Strictly speaking, of course, this case involves the pledging of faith, rather than *briduw* per se.[65] The boundaries between these types of agreement were, however, quite uncertain, as we have seen. This blurring of the boundaries between *briduw, fides*, and the promissory oath (Welsh *llw*) may even itself reflect a desire to assimilate *briduw* to other, more familiar types of social pact. In any case, the use of such pacts in manipulative pleading is a good indication of the familiarity with which they came eventually to be regarded in judicial circles.

The textual assimilation of *briduw* to *mechni* is also quite striking and presumably played a similar role in identifying and authorizing a procedure that for many may have seemed obscure, troublesome, or possibly even presumptuous in its claims on God's attention. Worth noting also is the extent to which both the reshaping of *briduw* and its distribution within the lawbooks confirms what was suggested in the previous chapter about attitudes toward innovation on the part of northern and southern jurists. *Llyfr Cyfnerth* preserves only a trace of the procedure—had *Llyfr Iorwerth*'s account not survived we would know nothing substantive about it at all. Latin D and *Llyfr Blegywryd* are completely mystified by it, and Latin B and E probably obtained their information from a northern source. *Briduw*, then, did not form part either of the core Latin tractate or, to judge from Latin D and *Llyfr Blegywryd* at least, of living law in the South.

In the North, by contrast, not only is *briduw* preserved, but it is institutionalized and adapted for use in a curial setting by its assimilation to *mechni*. As was the case with *mechni* itself, the curializing of ancient procedures, rather than the simple substitution of new practices for old, allowed the compilers to make room for innovation while not relinquishing the past. That they were endeavoring in their work to quell the doubts not just of the princes whose political support they sought but of their professional colleagues as well is clear from the nature of the changes they made. The textual parallels outlined above would mean little to those not already immersed in the forms and language of *Cyfraith Hywel*. The fact that an ancient institution like *briduw* should exist within the tradition may already have seemed embarrassing to some professionals; the idea that it should be retained in a period in which that tradition was under attack must have struck many as incomprehensible indeed.

But the jurists were speaking to lords, as well. As striking as the curializing of *briduw* in the lawbooks is the emphasis placed on seigneurial authority over its implementation. Lords were depicted as intimately involved in the enforcement of *briduw* pacts, acting in concert with representatives of the church. Ior 68/9 specifies that *Er egluys a'r brenhyn a dele kemell bruduu, canys Duu a kemeruet en lle mach, ac urth henne er eglues byeu e wahard am uruduu a'r brenhyn e kemhell*, "The church and the king are obliged to enforce *briduw*, since God is taken in the place of a [human] *mach*, and because of that, it pertains to the church to "prohibit" in *briduw*, and to the king to enforce." *Col* 131 also requires the church to "prohibit," and the lord to enforce, but completely omits the first two clauses of the *Llyfr Iorwerth* version. The *gwahard*, "prohibiting," to which the church is committed is never clearly defined in the texts, but assuming that *gwahard* is intended to be seen as an aspect of *cymell*, "enforcing," it must have here its technical legal sense of "forbidding" a person to make use of an object in dispute until its ownership can be determined by law.[66] A "prohibition" issued by the church would presumably forbid an offender to participate in the sacraments or other religious rites, and be tantamount in some cases at least to excommunication.[67]

It is impossible to determine with any certainty whether the role of the lord in enforcing *briduw* pacts represented a continuation of the enforcement procedure that obtained in the period before the lawbooks were compiled. It is certainly consistent with the integration of sacred and profane that was so characteristic of the early Middle Ages, a period in which Christianized sacral kingship was regarded as the ideal form of human government. Early Irish law, however, seems from what little information we possess to have left the earthly enforcement of such suretyships to religious personalities, most notably the mysterious *déorad Dé*, the "exile of God." Like the "holy man" of Syria described by Peter Brown,[68] the *déorad Dé* was an outsider, a pilgrim who, though not possessing any discernible ecclesiastical rank, was regarded as being particularly close to God.[69] Neither fully human nor fully divine, he was the miracleworker, the "oracle," the spiritual powerbroker of the community; difficult legal decisions were to be referred to him because it was thought likely that God would reveal the truth of the situation to him.[70] And because of his special relationship with the "men of Heaven," he acted on their behalf in divine suretyships:

> ní i n-aiccditer fir nime ocus soscéla[e] Críst, ar dlega[i]r do cach déorad dé saigid a nadma[e] amal adrogesta[e] ind no do-dic[h]sed a chelebrad aire.[71]
>
> [Not to be dissolved is] a thing for which the men of heaven and the Gospel of Christ are invoked [as sureties], for every exile of God is obliged to enforce their suretyship as though he himself had been invoked for it or as though his celebration [of religious rites][72] had guaranteed it.

It is possible that the *déorad Dé* was only one of several types of holy man who might be called on to act in such cases. He is the only such character mentioned in the Irish legal sources, but several Welsh charters suggest that oaths at least might often have been enforced by the authorities of the church who owned the relics on which they had been sworn.[73]

Ireland's experiences were of course quite different from those of Wales, and it is possible that Welsh lords and princes may always have participated in the enforcement of *briduw*. Cooperation rather than confrontation between secular and ecclesiastical authorities is certainly the hallmark of many of the arrangements described in the Welsh lawbooks.[74] The distinction articulated in *Llyfr Iorwerth* between *gwahard* and *cymell* has a somewhat artificial look to it, however, and it is possible that seigneurial claims to jurisdiction in such cases were relatively novel, or at least that a degree of uncertainty obtained in many circles as to where the proper boundaries of the sacred and the secular sphere ought in such instances to be drawn.[75] Certainly, the rustic who cheerfully perjured himself before the king in a case of theft but then confessed, terrified, when he discovered that he had given his oath in the presence of what he took to be Saint Cadog's knife seems to have considered the enforcement of spiritual obligations to be more properly the province of ecclesiastical rather than secular authorities. The presence of the king (*regulus*) did not apparently concern him, but the presence of a relic wielded by the sexton of Llancarfan, Cadog's principal monastery, was an altogether different matter.[76] It might not always have been easy for lords to get themselves taken seriously in such cases.

From the point of view of the lawyers, however (and presumably of the lords whose support they hoped to attract), it was natural that the secular arm of a Christian state should be an agent of the divine will. *Briduw* was subject to the authority of the lord precisely because it was a sacred procedure, *canys Duu a kemeruet en lle mach*,[77] "because God was taken in place of a [human] surety." In this it was not alone: the Welsh lawbooks are full of instances in which the lord asserted his right to act on God's behalf, whether by imposing a fine for perjury, claiming sole authority over the placement of a legal cross, or preventing a man who had committed a crime while carrying relics from claiming their protection.[78] What makes all this so striking is that such claims were distinctly out of keeping with the post-Gregorian context in which the lawbooks were compiled. Elsewhere in Europe, church courts claimed jurisdiction over matters of perjury, *fides*, and the oath.[79] The assertion that the lord's court was the proper forum for *briduw* disputes was thus a very deliberate one, and one made in direct contravention to prevailing ecclesiastical desiderata. Regardless of whether the lord was or was not originally involved in the enforcement of *briduw* pacts, the fact of his claim, and the directness with which it was articulated, were not simply remnants of the early medieval understanding of the relationship between the temporal and spiritual spheres.[80] As both Gregory VII and Henry IV discovered to their cost, the reassertion of traditional roles in a period of rapidly changing perceptions can itself constitute a distinctly radical act.

It is probably as an issue of jurisdiction that we ought to understand the change from the altar form of denial to denial through compurgation—as also the other transformations occuring in *briduw* in the wake of its repatterning after *mechni*. Dafydd Jenkins speaks in contrast to this of the "secularization" of *briduw*, but such an approach sets up a dichotomy between *mechni* and *briduw* that would be easy to overemphasize.[81] To the modern mind particularly, accustomed as it is to isolating the sacred from the profane, *briduw*'s most distinguishing characteristic will seem its appeal to the supernatural. But to draw a sharp distinction between the "sacred" procedure of *briduw* and its "secular" counterpart *mechni* is greatly to underestimate the "sacred" quality inherent in ordinary *mechni*.[82] Oaths were used throughout the suretyship procedure; no stage in the process was exempt. A surety who wished to testify to the amount involved in the transaction supported his testimony with an oath,[83] and a creditor whose surety died offered an elaborate public compurgation over the grave of the deceased.[84] *Ior* 64/5–9 acknowledges but rejects a similar graveside oath for a son of a dead surety who wishes to deny his father's suretyship.

The point is made most clearly, however, by the dramatically structured ritual through which *mechni* was denied. The first oath was taken on relics and before a judge who solemnly abjured the parties not to perjure themselves: "the protection of God against [perjury by] you, and the protection of the Pope of Rome, and the protection of your lord—do not enter into a false oath."[85] *Nawdd*, the term used here for "protection," is the technical legal term for the "sanctuary" offered by the church and others to criminals; the judge's formula thus deliberately threatened the would-be perjurer with the withdrawal of both secular and supernatural support. If the surety chose to counterswear against the debtor, he was to do it as the debtor put his lips to the relic, the symbolic moment at which the realms of the spiritual and secular made contact. And if both parties completed these oaths without hesitation, the debtor was required to give a compurgation of seven men in church on the Sunday following. He made his oath before the spectators in the church at the moment the *eulogia* were distributed among the congregation at the conclusion of the

Mass;[86] in other words, the "secular" office of *mechni* could only be denied through a ceremony associated with one of the most solemn sacraments of the Christian Church.

The distinction between "religious" and "secular" suretyship is thus a false one. Religious language and symbolism were as much a part of *mechni* as they were of *briduw*; the two differed not in that one was secular and the other sacred, but in that one involved a human surety and the other did not. Moreover, it would be a mistake simply to presume from our personal skepticism about the likely reliability of the deity as a commercial guarantee that in medieval Ireland and Wales human sureties would necessarily always have been preferred. Jenkins expressed great doubt about the extent to which *briduw* would have been used after its "secularization" in the thirteenth century, especially since a man who acknowledged giving *briduw* to another could not be challenged in his testimony as to the amount involved.[87]

But to phrase the issue in such terms may underestimate the range and appeal of this complex procedure. *Briduw* could well have been viewed as highly suitable, for example, in circumstances in which persons without family or friends in a given area found themselves in need of guarantors. Dorothy Whitelock suggested that the Anglo-Saxon *godborg* would have been especially useful to traders, and Pryce has noted parallels to *briduw* in Edward I's 1285 statute regarding London merchants.[88] Latin B's language certainly situates *briduw* within a distinctly commercial context.[89] For the English king Henry III, who invoked God as his surety (*Deum posuimus in plegium*) in his famous Oath of Bromholm, the issue was probably one of status; no one but the deity could hope to enforce against the king.[90] And Manawydan may well have confirmed his promise to Cigfa by taking God as surety simply because there was no one else left in the court to use.[91] There is no indication, however, that the creditor who not long before the coming of the English to Ireland accepted a cross in Dublin "and it alone, as the witness and surety of a certain contract" had no other options available to him.[92] Like all other legal procedures, the suretyship of God was likely invoked whenever the parties involved felt it to be the most appropriate form of security to use. It did, after all, offer a flexibility lacking in a completely human guarantee: a *mach*-surety could only be expected to enforce the terms of the contract for which he had been appointed, but God could see the justice of the situation as a whole.

We probably tend to underestimate the potency of the guarantee provided by a supernatural surety. Religious suretyship did not exist in isolation; it was but one aspect of a much larger network of supernatural sanctions and assumptions. The boundaries of this world are easiest to trace in Ireland, where learned intellectuals created an elaborate mythological reality that intruded into even the most resolutely sober of historical sources. Masters of the art of historical manipulation, Irish pseudo-historians left no natural phenomenon, no political truth unexplained, anticipating by a millenium and more Hugh Kenner's characterization of the people as a whole: "not a "poetic" people; no, a ruthlessly logical people, who invent whole worlds to fit new kinds of reason."[93] A quick perusal of almost any saint's life, or of the fabulous stories collected by Giraldus during his stay in Ireland, will explain every regional idiosyncrasy: every stone, every tree, every stream has its reason for being what and where it is. From the *Tripartite Life of Patrick* one can learn why the stones of Uisnech are unfit for human use, why there are cheese-shaped stones in the territory of the Fir Rois, why only the eastern half of the river Búall is barren of fish, and why two salmon reside in a well in Achad Fobair. One will learn a great deal as well about secular and ecclesiastical politics: why Armagh has a claim to the churches of Caill Uallech and Immliuch Sescainn, and why the Cenél Conaill will prosper always.[94] All of nature, indeed all of life, had for both composers and consumers of these tales a mythological component—and a uniquely tangible mythology it was, not at all remote and distant, a mythology of the everyday, of the commonplace.

Significantly, the instruments with which the pseudo-historians constructed this vision of reality were the very saints on whose powers those invoking supernatural guarantees must frequently have called. Peter Brown has written at length about the warmth and intensity of the late-antique relationship between man and the "very special dead," an association that owes much to the late Roman concepts of friendship and patronage.[95] But while post-classical men regarded their saints with affection and respect, the Irish frequently did not. Irish saints had fallen heir to an entirely different tradition, that of the malevolent poet, a man whose powers commanded respect, but whose moral character was far more ambiguous than what we normally think of in a saint. Saints could be arrogant, narrow-minded, and extremely dangerous: Patrick was said by one of his biographers to have tried to run over a hostile bishop with his chariot and to have actually killed his own pregnant sister in this manner. Finian of Clonard was little better, and tangling with even "saintly" saints like Columba was likely to result in one's hurried demise.[96] To be sure, not all Irish saints partook of this tradition, and the exaltation of saintly rancor became more common after the writing of the *Tripartite Life*, circa C.E. 900. But Giraldus considered vindictiveness to be a peculiar and distinctive characteristic of the Irish saints, one that impressed him greatly, and one that several English soldiers experienced to their cost.[97]

Such was the context in which the suretyship of God must have functioned, and such therefore was its sanction. And although we cannot prove that similar perceptions were widespread as well in medieval Wales, Giraldus does seem to imply that Welsh saints inspired many of the same reactions.[98] One has only to remember the poor rustic cringing in anguish before what he thought was Saint Cadog's knife to think that he might be right. Certainly the tale of how Saint Cadog caused two of his most holy disciples to be drowned because they had forgotten to bring with them on a journey a book that he had requested has its own peculiar moral.[99] The sources from which these examples are taken are, of course, largely literary and written from the point of view of the monastic house of which the saint in question was a patron. But they may also have been well known; the *Tripartite Life* itself was "almost certainly intended for preaching to the public on the three days of Patrick's festival."[100] And while not everyone would have believed these tales—indeed one wonders sometimes how many Irishmen might have shared a laugh at Giraldus's expense—it is not the content of any individual story that matters most. Rather, it is the assumptions underlying this mythology, and particularly the proximity of the natural and supernatural worlds that is so fundamental to these tales, that provide the foundation for *briduw* and other institutions like it.

We have, to this point, concentrated exclusively on *briduw* and its Irish counterpart. The supernatural was, however, an important part of the whole of Irish and Welsh law.[101] No aspect of law, no stage in the legal process was without its appeal to a higher authority. Proof is of course an area of early medieval law well known for its reliance on supernatural appeals like the oath, the ordeal, and the sworn testimony of witnesses,[102] and the process of exculpation likewise. Even a quick perusal of the Welsh regulations on proof and denial will convince one that the relic was one of the cornerstones of Welsh legal process.[103] Almost every oath offered in Welsh law was taken on relics, and almost every type of case had the potential to involve an oath. Relics were obviously expected to be readily available for legal purposes; indeed one passage allows an offender a maximum of three days to obtain the necessary relics, and this because he was a foreigner and was required in this case to use relics from his own particular locality. Similarly, close relatives of an impoverished murderer who wished to force other family members to contribute to the *wergild* of the victim went with relics to other members of the kin and forced them either to pay their share or to deny their relationship to the offender. Presumably, such persons were not expected to have difficulties obtaining relics for this purpose.[104] Relics were as necessary to the legal process as were judges themselves.

But proof and denial were not the only stages of the legal process to rely on the appeal to the supernatural. They are perhaps the most obvious, because in such matters circumstances could easily progress beyond the capacity of "secular" law, but supernatural procedures were also used in other capacities, even when they did not have to be. The suretyship of God was not, for example, the only "supernatural" method of binding a valid obligation in Irish law. A cleric could also bind an agreement through a liturgical rite known as *celebrad*, "celebrating," a procedure that unfortunately is never specifically defined. The word originally referred to the celebration of the canonical hours, but seems more likely in the legal texts to refer to the celebration of the Mass itself.[105]

Through *celebrad* binding legal agreements could be made; a *déorad Dé* was required to enforce this type of arrangement *amal ad-rogesta[e] ind no do-dich[h]sed a chelebrad aire*,[106] "as though he himself had been invoked [as surety] for it or as though his celebration [of religious rites] had guaranteed it." *Berrad Airechta* lists *ceilebrath* as one of "five [things] that exist [in order to protect] against the evasion [of a claim]," a group that includes the *naidm*, *ráth*, and *aitire* sureties as well as the gage.[107] And Giraldus notes with evident disapproval one of the ways in which the Irish made their treaties:

> First they make a treaty on the basis of their common fathers. Then in turn they go around the church three times. They enter the church and, swearing a great variety of oaths before relics of saints placed on the altar, at last with the celebration of Mass and the prayers of the priests they make an indissoluble treaty as if it were a kind of betrothal. For the greater confirmation of their friendship and completion of their settlement, each in conclusion drinks the blood of the other. . . . [108]

Solemn covenants had to be expressed in solemn terms, and there was no better way to stress the importance of an agreement than to invest it with the history and special gravity of the Christian sacrament. And while there is no evidence to suggest that a similar binding ritual was recognized as well in Wales, the confirming of land grants through solemn ecclesiastical rituals is a recognizable tale type in the Llandaff charter material.[109]

The Irish *celebrad* could be used in the enforcement of a claim as well as in its binding. As a method of enforcement it seems to have resembled somewhat the archaic Irish practice of *troscad*, "fasting," a manner of obtaining legal redress the sanctions for which were almost certainly supernatural in nature. *Troscad* was probably no longer used very often by the time of the compilation of the classical legal texts, but its memory remained.[110] *Bretha im fuillema gell* actually classes the two together:

> Techte fuillema gill cach comgrad di gradaib ecalsa otha cetgradaib co ruicce cruimther rosuidiged for trib setaib . . . la log a tomalta mani rochestar troscud no chelebrad aire. . . . [111]
>
> The propriety of the interest of the gage [given by] everyone equal in rank in the hierarchy of the church, from the bottom-ranks up to the priest, is established at three *séoit* . . . in addition to the price [established for] consuming [the by-products of the gage] unless fasting or celebrating be endured for it. . . .

Like fasting, *celebrad* was an elaborate public ritual that threatened an offender who ignored it with certain, but undefined, supernatural consequences. But like similar rituals found in Africa, it was presumed to be effective only when the claim was just;[112] the "celebrating" of a man "for whom swearing to truth and to falsehood were the same" is listed as one of the seven "enforcements" (*tobaig*) that can lawfully be ignored.[113]

It is in the Welsh laws that we find the fullest account of yet another supernaturally sanctioned procedure intended to secure the enforcement of a claim. In both Irish and Welsh law the placement of a cross was used to proclaim that an item or claim was in dispute and could not, therefore, be used until the claim had been resolved. By the time of the compilation of the Welsh lawbooks, jurisdiction over the procedure was claimed entirely by the lord; only in cases where haste was necessary to preserve an owner's claim to land was a man allowed to place a cross without seigneurial consent.[114] In Ireland, such permission was of course unnecessary, but it is significant that here too the cross was a remedy available apparently to laymen as well as to clerics. *Cáin Domnaig* allows a man who detected and then prosecuted a violation of the sanctity of Sunday to choose how he should enforce his claim if the *aitire* appointed for that purpose evades his prosecution. Most of the options listed are the standard "secular" techniques of legal enforcement—a hostage, distraint, a kinsman *aitire*—but it is stipulated that he may use a cross if he wishes.[115] In Wales the cross could be used to enforce many different types of claims, including *briduw*, *mechni*, and *wergild*,[116] and it is possible that it had such a range in early Ireland as well, although it is mentioned specifically only in the two (obviously ecclesiastical) laws of Sunday. The disputes for which a cross might have been employed were thus, at least in Wales, "secular" as well as ecclesiastical in nature. And although we do not know anything specific about the sanction that was perceived to lie behind the placement of a cross, the symbol itself suggests that it was supernatural in origin. If so, it is significant that *Cáin Domnaig* at least envisages that a man might choose it as a way to pursue his claim, rather than the more usual and, for us, seemingly more tangible forms of enforcement available to him.

These are but a few of the ways in which the appeal to the supernatural was woven into the fabric of what we would classify as essentially "secular" law. There are others, but to discuss them thoroughly would require a book in itself.[117] It is enough now to observe that for the people by and for whom these lawbooks were composed, such appeals were not merely rituals of last resort. They were, rather, part and parcel of the entire legal process, and their effectiveness as procedures was rooted in the common beliefs and assumptions uniting the community in which they operated. The desire of Welsh lords and jurists to assure princely jurisdiction over the implementation of supernaturally sanctioned procedures is itself eloquent testimony to the strength of their appeal. The supernatural was a part of law because it was a part of life itself.

The mingling of the natural and supernatural worlds that lies at the heart of procedures like *briduw* is a perception most frequently associated with the early Middle Ages. That Irish law should rely so visibly on such practices is therefore no surprise. Welsh law, on the other hand, occupies a more ambiguous position in the developing relationship between the sacred and secular spheres. Peter Brown has already chronicled the transformations taking place in this relationship in the twelfth and thirteenth centuries, a shift he attributes to the changing nature of the societies in which supernatural rituals like the ordeal were enacted. The newly open communities of the twelfth century, he argues, had less need to resort to mystical devices to contain the violent impulses that had once so seriously threatened their earlier, "face-to-face" existence.[118] There is much wisdom in this observation, although medieval people themselves would probably have been uneasy with its quintessentially modern premise that religion is an instrument of man, rather than the other way around.

Perhaps what was actually lost in the rapid social expansion of the twelfth century was not the need for the supernatural, but a firm consensus on its relationship to the community as a whole. The Welsh lawbooks, in their attempt to curialize *briduw*, are evidence not merely of the tenacity of traditional beliefs about the relationship between the gods and men, but of post-Gregorian anxieties about the nature and purview of secular rule as well. The sacred and the profane no longer moved as obviously together as they once had done. Boundaries were now to be drawn where few had previously existed, and the experts did not always agree on where. Clerical rejection of the ordeal in 1215 and the essentially contemporaneous institutionalization of *briduw* were, above all else, attempts to reformulate a relationship whose original outlines had somehow been lost. The process of reformulation took centuries to complete, and in many ways we are still heirs to its uncertainty. But of the many familiar institutions and rituals that were fated eventually to disappear in the shuffle, one remained. The promissory oath remains with us today, ultimate proof of the truly timeless efficacy of the suretyship of the gods.

Conclusion

The suretyship of the gods is a concept whose shadowy origins can be guessed at, speculated about, but never known. And in many respects, the questions raised by the inclusion of such a potentially ancient practice in thirteenth-century lawbooks are those raised by the Welsh and Irish legal sources as a whole. It would be difficult to imagine a more stark juxtaposition of old and new, "private" and "public," than the chapter on *briduw* included in *Llyfr Iorwerth*. I hope the preceding has made clear, however, that to focus only on the eccentricity and archaism of this procedure is to risk overlooking the meaning it possessed in the curial and seigneurial context within which *Llyfr Iorwerth*'s account was written. It is also to deny historians of other medieval societies access to the lessons *briduw* has to teach. Issues like the growth of public jurisdiction, the drawing of boundaries between the sacred and the profane, indeed the process of legal change itself, are far from being the unique domain of Celticists.

And what is true of *briduw* is surely true also of "Celtic" historiography as a whole. Archaism and the lack of "real" historical sources have for so long been identified as the primary characteristics of this field that its wider potential has been shrouded from view. And yet our foray into suretyship has revealed a legal world that, in most of its essentials, would be immediately recognizable to historians of other medieval European societies. Like Davies and Fouracre's recent volume on European dispute settlement,[1] this study has emphasized the extent to which legal personalities and rituals like those visible in the Irish and Welsh lawbooks cannot be separated from the community in which they occur. Suretyship was far from being a simple matter of one man forcing another to meet his obligations. The elaborate public rituals through which contracts were effected, with their special language, gestures, and pronouncements, were designed in the first instance to inform the community of the special nature of the events taking place.

But their appeal was likely much broader, and their summons to community action more urgent, than even the above would imply. All contractual transactions had the potential to transform or reshape the identities and relationships on which communal stability was built. Individuals became debtors or creditors to one another; neighbors were transformed into sureties entitled to use force against those who were otherwise their social equals. The dramatic form of the binding ceremony rendered tangible these important social transformations, directly engaging the attention and participation of the community within which they were enacted. Sureties, often characterized as "private officers of law," were in fact as deeply embedded in the social structure of the community as *briduw* itself must have been in the belief system of the society in which it originated.

Suretyship may also have functioned within such communities as a form of communication and alliance. Wendy Davies has suggested that in ninth-century Brittany acting as surety for another served "as . . . part of a local, small-scale pattern of alliance-making that is largely hidden from the records."[2] The description of the procedure as it occurs in the Irish and Welsh lawbooks lends credence to such an idea. Functioning as a guarantor for another must have enhanced or refined the relationship between the individuals concerned. Equally suggestive is what the lawbooks have to say about transactions in which sureties were not involved. Not requiring a surety in instances where one might otherwise have been expected, as in the case of the immunities, for example, communicated as much about the relationship and status of the people involved as did the appointment of guarantors in the normal manner. Similarly, the Airgialla's insistence on giving *aitiri* rather than one-sided *géill* to their Uí Néill overlords made clear to others the manner in which they wished their dependency to be construed. Even the process of intervening in disadvantageous contracts made by another person could function as a communicative device, in this case as a way to proclaim the common economy and interests of the pair. It might not even be too far-fetched to imagine that such intervention would sometimes have been used intentionally as a vehicle through which to assert or maintain status within a relationship: a wife whose property exceeded her husband's, for example, might choose to repudiate a doubtful contract made by him in order to publicize her status to the community.

As intriguing as the workings of justice within these communities is what happens to legal perceptions and personalities of this nature once they are translated into a more recognizably "public" domain of jurisdiction. This again is an area of research in which the Irish and Welsh lawbooks are particularly valuable. Most Germanic-language societies did not develop a professional legal class to reflect on such matters until relatively late in the game; in Wales particularly, however, this class not only existed but survived the transition from a (more or less) precurial to a (more or less) curial system of justice. What is perhaps most striking about the Irish and Welsh evidence is the extent to which it suggests that emerging curial systems tend to absorb, rather than displace or supersede, the mechanisms of "private" law. Old forms or procedures are used as building blocks for the new: sureties become pleas in court and their presence in a given arrangement the primary criteria of its "public" validity. Personalities and rituals originally devised to fill particular purposes within the local setting in which they function take on entirely new characters. Norms on who can or cannot intervene in a particular contract, for example (norms concerned originally not with contract at all, but rather with the relationships they were designed to protect) become "rules" to be adjudicated. Procedures like hand-in-hand binding, designed originally to inform and engage onlookers to the contract, are transformed by the process of public scrutiny into legal technicalities. And categories like "valid" or "invalid," "binding" or "non-binding," are created out of earlier, more fluid characterizations like "enforceable" or "unenforceable." What we are watching is nothing less than part of the complex process by which "custom" passes into "law"—the manner in which mechanisms of social order, removed from the local framework within which they originated, are recast within the curial setting as universal standards of behavior.

Another important aspect of this issue illuminated by the lawbooks, and one with which legal historians have traditionally been much concerned, is the process of legal change. Milsom's observations on the extent to which the antics of wily practitioners can themselves change or create "law" are certainly borne out by the Welsh texts. The clash between existing norms or privileges and attempts by lawyers to find ways around those norms was, for the Welsh law of suretyship, a fruitful process indeed. We do not know whether the *mach*'s traditional privilege to deny his suretyship by compurgation ever entirely disappeared; however, it looks very much as though the debtor's privilege in this regard was ultimately overcome by the exigencies of the pleading procedure. The machinations of aggressive lawyers were not, of course, the only source of legal change. Environment too played a role: thus were the *mach*'s witness and enforcing functions absorbed by the court into which he was removed. Many changes seem to have been entirely unintentional; such, for example, was the loss of the *mach*'s stature as the literal bond of the obligation for which he stood surety. All in all, what is most striking in these texts is the lack of emphasis on actual legislative change. Seigneurial power lurks always in the background, of course; indeed it is the sine qua non without which none of the other changes mentioned above would ever have taken place. But legislation per se seems at least in Wales to have played relatively little role in the process. Even the *amodwr*, an innovation probably contemporary with the composition of the lawbooks, seems more likely to have originated in the court itself, for the convenience of judges ruling on difficult cases, than in any specific act of "law."

Legal innovation does not, of course, go unnoticed by those charged with custodianship of the tradition in which it occurs. Within traditions that authorize themselves by reference to the past, a visible discordance between old and new can inspire doubt, on the part both of practitioners themselves and of those making use of their services. The threat is particularly severe when a rival system exists by which the original might be displaced, for in such circumstances, discrepancies that might otherwise go unnoticed take on a new and ominous significance. And when the preservation of the original lies in the hands of a particular profession or class of individuals that perceives its prerogatives endangered by the prospective change of leadership, some type of response is inevitable. The Irish and Welsh lawbooks provide rare insight into the anxieties experienced by professional jurists during such periods of rapid legal flux. Their attitudes toward the challenges with which they were faced were very similar: sometimes they acknowledged change, sometimes they disguised it, always they attempted to resituate it within the confines of the familiar.

But there were differences also in their reactions. Irish jurists, fearing the moral authority of ecclesiastical tradition to be greater than their own, expended a great deal of energy integrating native jurisprudence and procedures into the Biblical schema. Welsh lawyers, on the other hand, bolstered perhaps by the lack of historical sanction enjoyed by their rivals but plagued by the perception that their tradition was insufficiently up to date, simultaneously modernized their procedures and played the Hywel Dda "card" for all it was worth. In both cases, however, seamless, "intact" tradition functioned both as a badge of professional authority and as a link to the authorizing past. It may seem paradoxical, but the preservation, indeed cultivation, of archaism to which these sources speak so eloquently was for both cultures a means of allaying anxieties distinctly contemporary in nature.

It is a measure of the strength of these two great legal traditions that matters worked the other way as well. So expertly did canon lawyers in Ireland learn to mimic the native legal vernacular that it is only recently that their work has been recognized for what it is. And no less an Englishman than Edward I himself made use of Hywel Dda's name—and some of "his" laws—in his campaigns to win jurisdiction over that king's successors. Much of this "exchange" was not, of course, particularly positive or productive; much of it, however, was, is, or still has the potential to be.[3] It is the ultimate hope of this book that the productive aspects of this "interaction between traditions" will come ultimately to prevail in the historiographical arena also.

One would not wish, of course, to downplay entirely the very real differences that separated Irish and Welsh experiences in the Middle Ages from those of their Germanic-speaking neighbors. Rome comes quickly to mind (particularly with respect to Ireland), and the presence in Wales and Ireland of a professional learned class must also be counted as a factor distinguishing those societies with a "typically Celtic stamp" from those without.[4] But as Patrick Wormald has reminded us, historians are truly the prisoners of their sources; what we take as the "reality" of a given culture may in fact be nothing more than a reflection in a mirror of that culture's own devising.[5] That kingship and law are two of the areas in which the Roman-inspired model of the Germans clashed most visibly with the much more diffuse and less centralized model of the Celts must be taken seriously into consideration.

For even if it is true that the Celtic and Germanic "mirrors" differed from one another in many significant ways, the traditional response to these differences does both fields a disservice. Distance, however respectful and mutually preserved, is still distance, and as such is counterproductive. One may not be able to transfer information or conclusions directly from one field to another, but restoring Ireland and Wales to their proper European context offers historians of both traditions the opportunity to enlarge their sense of what was possible in this world so intrinsically foreign to their own. Celticists have already begun to reap the benefits of such an approach. Many of the most important recent discoveries in the field have stemmed from historians conversant with the patterns and priorities of non-Celtic societies combing their sources for parallels that logic would suggest must be there. This why we now know that "even in Ireland" kings were involved in justice and law, collected taxes, and exercised rule in a manner familiar to their continental counterparts,[6] or that the image of a relentlessly "monastic" church that has for so long shaped our understanding of the ecclesiastical situation in pre-Norman Ireland is fundamentally misguided.[7] Similarly, it is now apparent that not only did the transition from "count" (*narratio*) to pleading occur in medieval Wales, but it happened earlier in Wales than in the English Common Law tradition with which it has usually been associated.[8] The fruits of comparative reading have been plentiful indeed.

But such lessons can be valuable in the other direction as well. It is true that the Irish and Welsh sources can never offer continental medievalists the specific charter or documentary evidence that is the backbone of their own historical research. I hope I have demonstrated in this book, however, that what the lawbooks have to say about issues like the workings of medieval justice, or the evolution of "law," or the consolidation of curial authority will likely be of interest to more than just Celticists. It is paradoxical, startling, and yet probably true, for example, that the image of medieval justice one obtains from the Irish lawbooks is in many ways more accurate for most Germanic societies than is the uneasily "Roman" picture one gets from the codes produced by those societies. A knowledge of how norms actually functioned in the small, intimate communities of early Ireland—communities not at all unlike those envisaged in English and continental legal sources—may even suggest a new way of reading the troublesome Germanic codes. As in Ireland, such texts may have functioned less as collections of universally enforceable "laws" in our sense than as principles or guidelines on which parties in dispute might, or might not, choose to draw in the resolution process.[9] Reading the law codes for the principles and priorities they express, instead of the statutes they enumerate, may allow historians to again make use of sources on which it might otherwise be tempting to give up entirely.

Indeed, the more broadly one reads in early medieval scholarship, Celtic and non-Celtic, the more affinities one is likely to find. There is no clear parallel in the Germanic legal sources to the feverish attempts by the jurists to redefine and preserve their tradition in the face of the threat posed by the appearance of a powerful rival. The process, however, by which a professional class makes room for change while simultaneously asserting the timelessness and historical authenticity of the tradition it represents is highly reminiscent of the efforts of Roman intellectuals to accommodate, and yet disguise, the advent of barbarian kingship and the disappearance of Rome. Similarly, the tenacity with which the Irish literati clung to traditional images of rule against what must have been substantial evidence to the contrary raises many of the same questions as does the production of texts like *The Battle of Brunanburh*, and perhaps even *Beowulf* itself,[10] in the atmosphere of late Anglo-Saxon rule. Even the adherence to archaism that has for so long isolated Irish and Welsh sources from the mainstream has its close parallel in Latin literacy that, as Janet Nelson has shown, served similarly in Carolingian circles to establish the identity and prerogatives of a "ruling cadre" of professionals.[11] Again, it is important not to minimize the differences between these societies and particularly between the images they constructed for themselves. What may be in the end most striking, however, is not how different they actually were, but rather how different they contrived to look. The road "from custom to court" traversed by the jurists of medieval Ireland and Wales, like other historical highways and byways, may have been more familiar to their European contemporaries than it has seemed to us to date.

Notes

Introduction

1. Even Gilbert of Limerick's influential *De statu ecclesiae* drew on ninth-century Frankish sources like the treatises of Amalarius of Metz: John Watt, *The Church in Medieval Ireland* (Dublin, 1972), 12–13.

2. The best histories of medieval Wales are *WEMA*; Wendy Davies, *Patterns of Power in Early Wales* (Oxford, 1990); R. R. Davies, *Conquest, Coexistence, and Change: Wales, 1063–1415* (Oxford, 1987); and David Walker, *Medieval Wales* (Cambridge, 1990). Ian Jack outlines the source material in *Medieval Wales* (Ithaca, N.Y., 1972). For Ireland, see Gearóid Mac Niocaill's *Ireland before the Vikings* (Dublin, 1972; reprinted, 1980); Donnchadh Ó Corráin's *Ireland before the Normans* (Dublin, 1972); *Irish Kings*; and Michael Richter, *Medieval Ireland: The Enduring Tradition*, trans. Brian Stone and Adrian Keogh (originally published in German in 1983; translation published in New York in 1988). Ó Corráin discusses the emergence of a protofeudal society in the eleventh and twelfth centuries in his "Nationality and Kingship in Pre-Norman Ireland," in *Nationality and the Pursuit of National Independence*, ed. T. W. Moody (Belfast, 1978), 22–35.

3. This work focuses very deliberately on Ireland and Wales, but a word must be said about Brittany and Scotland, two "Celtic" lands that do not find much of a place here. Their position is an anomalous one, both in the discussion that follows and in historical scholarship as a whole. Scottish institutions might well be expected to shed some light on Irish and Welsh practices, but there is so little relevant evidence extant from early Scotland that the comparison is not in fact helpful. Brittany, on the other hand, preserves a large number of early sources, many of which pertain to suretyship, the principal topic of this book. While there are, however, many aspects of Breton society that are arguably "Celtic" in nature and origin, the peculiarly hybrid character of Breton culture makes it impossible to characterize this as a distinctly Celtic—or Roman or Frankish, for that matter—society. Certainly its most recent historians have shown themselves reluctant to situate Brittany within a Celtic context: Wendy Davies, *Small Worlds: The Village Community in Early Medieval Brittany* (Berkeley and Los Angeles, 1988), 142, note 35, and p. 211, especially; W. Davies, "Suretyship in the *Cartulaire de Redon*," in *LAL*, 85–87; and see also Julia Smith, *Province and Empire: Brittany and the Carolingians* (Cambridge, 1992). Patrick Wormald's astute observation that it may have been the learned classes in Ireland and Wales that gave those societies their distinctively "Celtic stamp," and that this might be the reason regions like Brittany, in which such experts seem not to have existed in any numbers in the historical

period, differ so markedly in their culture and institutions from the typically "Celtic" pattern, is another argument in favor of treating Ireland and Wales on their own: Patrick Wormald, Review of *LTMW* and of *LAL, CMCS* 16 (Winter 1988): 99.

4. *Irish Kings*, 16–18; *PPCP*, 107–121.

5. The tract *De duodecim abusivis saeculi* was used by both Jonas of Orleans and Hincmar of Rheims in their treatises on kingship and may have been written in Ireland: *AM*, pp. xv–xvi; and M. L. W. Laistner, *Thought and Letters in Western Europe A.D. 500–900* (London, 1931; revised edition London and Ithaca, N.Y., 1957), 144–146.

6. F. J. Byrne, "*Senchas*: The Nature of Gaelic Historical Tradition," *Historical Studies* 9 (1971): 138–139; and see David Dumville's "Kingship, Genealogies, and Regnal Lists," in *Early Medieval Kingship*, ed. P. H. Sawyer and I. N. Wood (Leeds, 1977; reprinted, 1979), 72–104.

7. Richard Sharpe, *Medieval Irish Saints' Lives: An Introduction to Vitae Sanctorum Hiberniae* (Oxford, 1991). See also previous discussions in *ECI*, 219–247; J. F. Kenney, *Sources for the Early History of Ireland: Ecclesiastical. An Introduction and Guide*, with addenda by Ludwig Bieler (New York, 1966); and Michael Lapidge and Richard Sharpe, *A Bibliography of Celtic-Latin Literature, 400-1200* (Dublin, 1985).

8. *ECI*, 99–159; Alfred Smyth, "The Earliest Irish Annals: Their First Contemporary Entries, and the Earliest Centres of Recording," *PRIA* 72 C (1972): 1–48; John Bannerman, "Notes on the Scottish Entries in the Early Irish Annals" in his *Studies in the History of DalRiada* (Edinburgh, 1974), 9–26; and *AU*, pp. ix–xii.

9. *CIH*, on which see the editor's comments in D. A. Binchy, "*Corpus Iuris Hibernici*—incipit or finit amen?," in the *Proceedings of the Sixth International Congress of Celtic Studies, 1979*, ed. G. Mac Eoin (Dublin, 1983), 149–164. An earlier edition is the *Ancient Laws of Ireland*, published with translation in 6 vols. (Dublin, 1865–1901), but many of the translations it contains are inaccurate and cannot be relied on.

10. The Welsh source material is outlined in *WEMA*, 198–218. On the Llandaff charters, see text in *Liber Landavensis: The Text of the Book of Llan Dâv*, ed. J. Gwenogvryn Evans and J. Rhys (Oxford, 1893; reprinted Aberystwyth, 1979), and discussion in Wendy Davies, *The Llandaff Charters* (Aberystwyth, 1979); W. Davies, *An Early Welsh Microcosm: Studies in the Llandaff Charters* (London, 1978); and K. L. Maund, *Ireland, Wales and England in the Eleventh Century* (Woodbridge, Suffolk, 1991), 183–206.

11. Caesar, *The Gallic War; with an English Translation by H. J. Edwards (De bello gallico)* (Cambridge, Mass., 1917; reprinted, 1979), VI.14; and see also "The Celtic Ethnography of Posidonius," trans. J. Tierney, *PRIA* 60 C (1959–1960): 189–275.

12. We know less about Welsh oral tradition than we do about the Irish because the sources are so much scarcer. That there was a strong oral tradition maintained in Wales is not in doubt, although Mac Cana suggests that the tradition

of narrative prose may not have been as well refined and preserved in Wales as it was in Ireland: "Conservation and Innovation in Early Celtic Literature," *Études Celtiques* 13 (1971): 81–82. Works important for the nature and transmission of early Welsh tradition include: *Trioedd Ynys Prydein*, ed. Rachel Bromwich (Cardiff, 1961; reprinted 1978); *Cyfranc Lludd a Llefelys*, ed. Brynley Roberts (Dublin, 1975), which is thought by some scholars to embody the remnants of an ancient Celtic and possibly even Indo-European myth; *The Mabinogi and Other Medieval Welsh Tales*, ed. Patrick Ford (Berkeley and Los Angeles, 1977); *The Poetry of Llywarch Hen: Introduction, Text, and Translation*, ed. Patrick Ford (Berkeley, Los Angeles, and London, 1974); *Astudiaethau ar yr Hengerdd: Studies in Old Welsh Poetry*, ed. Rachel Bromwich and R. Brinley Jones (Cardiff, 1978); *Early Welsh Poetry: Studies in the Book of Aneirin*, ed. Brynley Roberts (Aberystwyth, 1988); and *The Arthur of the Welsh: A Collaborative Study of the Arthurian Legend in Medieval Welsh Literature*, ed. Rachel Bromwich, A. O. H. Jarman, and Brynley Roberts (Cardiff, 1991). A recent study with implications for Breton oral tradition is Caroline Brett, "Breton Latin Literature as Evidence for Literature in the Vernacular, A.D. 800–1300," *CMCS* 18 (Winter 1989): 1–25.

13. T. M. Charles-Edwards, "The *Corpus Iuris Hibernici*," review article in *Studia Hibernica* 20 (1980): 141–162; *BB*, pp. 36–38; and *GEIL*, 231–236.

14. The most important of these studies are: Donnchadh Ó Corráin, Liam Breatnach, and Aidan Breen, "The Laws of the Irish," *Peritia* 3 (1984): 382–438; Liam Breatnach, "Canon Law and Secular Law in Early Ireland: the Significance of *Bretha Nemed*," *Peritia* 3 (1984): 439–459; Kim McCone, "Notes on the Text and Authorship of the Early Irish Bee-Laws," *CMCS* 8 (Winter 1984): 45–50; McCone, "Dubthach Maccu Lugair and a Matter of Life and Death in the Pseudo-Historical Prologue to the *Senchas Már*," *Peritia* 5 (1986): 1–35; *PPCP*, 84–106; Liam Breatnach, "The Ecclesiastical Element in the Old-Irish Legal Tract *Cáin Fhuithirbe*," *Peritia* 5 (1986): 36–52; and Breatnach, "Lawyers in Early Ireland," in *Brehons, Serjeants, and Attorneys: Studies in the History of the Irish Legal Profession*, ed. Daire Hogan and W. N. Osborough (Blackrock, co. Dublin, 1990), 1–13. See also more generally: Donnchadh Ó Corráin, "Nationality and Kingship," 18–20; Proinsias Mac Cana, "The Three Languages and the Three Laws," *Studia Celtica* 5 (1970): 62–78; Gearóid Mac Niocaill, "Christian Influences in Early Irish Law," and Donnchadh Ó Corráin, "Irish Law and Canon Law," 151–156 and 157–166, respectively, of *Irland und Europa: Die Kirche im Frühmittelalter/Ireland and Europe: The Early Church*, ed. Próinséas Ní Chatháin and Michael Richter (Stuttgart, 1984); and Donnchadh Ó Corráin, "Irish Vernacular Law and the Old Testament," in *Irland und die Christenheit: Bibelstudien und Mission/Ireland and Christendom: the Bible and the Missions*, ed. P. Ní Chatháin and M. Richter (Stuttgart, 1987), 284–307.

15. Breatnach argues that the Nero A vii text of *Bretha Nemed* was compiled by three kinsmen—a bishop, a poet, and a judge: "Canon Law and Secular Law," 441–445, 459.

16. At least in the seventh and eighth centuries, when the most important Irish legal and literary texts were composed: Patrick Wormald, "The Uses of Lit-

eracy in Anglo-Saxon England," *TRHS* 5th series 27 (1977): 95–114, and his more recent views in *SD*, 161–162. There are signs that this consensus might be changing: see discussion below in Chapter 1. Literacy may well have been important to the late Anglo-Saxon state: James Campbell, "Observations on English Government from the Tenth to the Twelfth Century," in Campbell, *Essays in Anglo-Saxon History* (London and Ronceverte, 1986), 157–158; and Simon Keynes, "Royal Government and the Written Word in Late Anglo-Saxon England," in *The Uses of Literacy in Early Mediaeval Europe*, ed. Rosamond McKitterick (Cambridge, 1990), 226–257.

17. Historians have for years essentially excluded the Celtic-speaking lands from their accounts of the development of the medieval West. None of the textbooks currently in widespread use in the United States for the teaching of medieval history to undergraduates, for example, discusses Ireland or Wales in any detail, and even Roger Collins's otherwise excellent *Early Medieval Europe, 300-1000* (New York, 1991) treats Ireland and Wales only when developments in those regions affect other, more "mainline" European kingdoms.

18. At least until the eleventh and twelfth centuries: Ó Corráin, "Nationality and Kingship," 26–30. Patrick Wormald makes an interesting case for a more administratively complex Celtic kingship than has hitherto been acknowledged (and, incidentally, proves himself an exception to the usual reluctance of non-Celtic scholars to venture into the Celtic material) in his "Celtic and Anglo-Saxon Kingship: Some Further Thoughts," in *Sources of Anglo-Saxon Culture*, ed. Paul Szarmach with Virginia Oggins (Kalamazoo, Mich., 1986), 151–183.

19. Urban life appears to have centered on the monasteries in Ireland, and the same may have been true in Wales as well: Charles Doherty, "The Monastic Town in Early Medieval Ireland," and Leo Swan, "Monastic Proto-Towns in Early Medieval Ireland: The Evidence of Aerial Photography, Plan Analysis and Survey," 45–75 and 77–102, respectively, of *The Comparative History of Urban Origins in Non-Roman Europe: Ireland, Wales, Denmark, Germany, Poland and Russia from the Ninth to the Thirteenth Century*, ed. H. B. Clarke and Anngret Simms, BAR International Series 255 (i) (Oxford, 1985); Nancy Edwards, *The Archaeology of Early Medieval Ireland* (Philadelphia, 1990), 99–131; Lisa Bitel, *Isle of the Saints: Monastic Settlement and Christian Community in Early Ireland* (Ithaca, N.Y., 1990), 17–82; and *WEMA*, 57–58.

20. The classic study is Kathleen Hughes's *The Church in Early Irish Society* (London, 1966; reprinted, 1980), but recent studies, particularly by Richard Sharpe, have revolutionized our understanding of the early Irish church: Richard Sharpe, "Some Problems concerning the Organization of the Church in Early Medieval Ireland," *Peritia* 3 (1984): 230–270; Sharpe, "Churches and Communities in Early Medieval Ireland: towards a Pastoral Model," in *Pastoral Care before the Parish*, ed. John Blair and Richard Sharpe (Leicester, 1992), 81–109; and Huw Pryce, "Pastoral Care in Early Medieval Wales," 41–62 of that same volume; Hughes, "The Celtic Church: Is This a Valid Concept?," *CMCS* 1 (Summer 1981): 1–20; Wendy Davies, *Early Welsh Microcosm*, 139–159; and W. Davies, *Small Worlds*, 24–28.

21. Rudolf Thurneysen, "Das Fasten beim Pfändungsverfahren," *ZCP* 15 (1925): 260–275; D. A. Binchy, "Irish History and Irish Law," *Studia Hibernica* 15 (1975): 7–36, and 16 (1976): 7–45, esp. vol. 15, pp. 24–26; Binchy, "Distraint in Irish Law," *Celtica* 10 (1973): 34–35; and *GEIL*, 182–183.

22. *Br. Crólige* is the principal tract on the subject; see also D. A. Binchy, "Sick-Maintenance in Irish Law," *Ériu* 12 (1934): 78–134; and *GEIL*, 130–133.

23. *LTMW*, 101–104, 261–262. A similar Irish procedure is *tellach*, on which see *GEIL*, 186–189, and T. M. Charles-Edwards, "Boundaries in Irish Law," in *Medieval Settlement: Continuity and Change*, ed. P. H. Sawyer (London, 1976), 83–87.

24. A point made recently by Patrick Wormald in "Celtic and Anglo-Saxon Kingship," 152–158.

25. Richard Sharpe, "Dispute Settlement in Medieval Ireland: A Preliminary Inquiry," in *SD*, 169–189.

26. Happily, there are signs that things have begun to change in this respect. Recent works include *Ireland in Early Mediaeval Europe: Studies in Memory of Kathleen Hughes*, ed. Dorothy Whitelock, Rosamond McKitterick, and David Dumville (Cambridge, 1982); *Irland und Europa*; *Irland und die Christenheit*; *LAL*; *SD*; *The Uses of Literacy*; and *Pastoral Care before the Parish*. *GEIL* and *LTMW* are also aimed at both specialist and non-specialist readers. Earlier studies are Nora Chadwick's *Celt and Saxon: Studies in the Early British Border* (Cambridge, 1963); Kathleen Hughes's "The Celtic Church and the Papacy," in *The English Church and the Papacy in the Middle Ages*, ed. C. H. Lawrence (London, 1965), 3–28; and Aubrey Gwynn's many articles on the European aspects of the Irish church reform in *IER* 57 (1941): 213–232; *IER* 57 (1941): 481–500; *IER* 58 (1941): 97–109; *IER* 59 (1942): 1–14; and *IHS* 8 (1953): 192–216.

27. As is evident from the series on personal suretyship issued by the *Societé Jean Bodin: Les sûretés personnelles, Recueils de la Societé Jean Bodin pour l'Histoire Comparative des Institutions* 28–30 (Brussels, 1969–1974). Beyerle devoted one of his most famous pieces to the subject: *Der Ursprung der Bürgschaft, Zeitschrift der Savigny-Stiftung für Rechtsgeschichte* 47, germanistische Abteilung (1927): 567–645.

28. Wendy Davies, "Disputes, Their Conduct and Their Settlement in the Village Communities of Eastern Brittany in the Ninth Century," in *The Discourse of Law*, ed. Sally Humphreys, *History and Anthropology* 1, part 2 (1985): 301–302; W. Davies, "Suretyship in the *Cartulaire de Redon*," *LAL*, 85–87; W. Davies, "People and Places in Dispute in Ninth-Century Brittany," in *SD*, 76–78; and W. Davies, *Small Worlds*, 58 and 152–154. Davies is reluctant to overemphasize the Celtic aspects of the Breton sureties, but their unusual policing powers and prominence in local legal enforcement seem most easily explained in this manner.

29. *CU*, 66–67, §7, for example, and see Chapter 8 below.

30. *CU*, 66–67, §6, for example, and see Chapters 3 and 5 below.

31. *The Poems of Blathmac Son of Cú Brettan together with the Irish Gospel of Thomas and a Poem on the Virgin Mary*, ed. James Carney, Irish Texts Society vol. 47 (Dublin, 1964), 102, §39.

32. *CIH* 351.27–28 = *EICL*, 164–165, §33.

33. *SD*, 214–240; John Bossy, *Disputes and Settlements: Law and Human Relations in the West* (Cambridge, 1983); and W. Davies, "Disputes, Their Conduct and Their Settlement."

34. Max Gluckman, "The Peace in the Feud," in Gluckman, *Custom and Conflict in Africa* (Oxford, 1955; reprinted, 1963); and J. M. Wallace-Hadrill, "The Bloodfeud of the Franks," in Wallace-Hadrill, *The Long-Haired Kings* (London, 1962; reprinted Toronto, 1982), 121–147.

Chapter 1. Law and Lawbooks in Medieval Ireland and Wales

1. Parts of this chapter are reprinted from Robin Chapman Stacey, "Law and Order in the *Very* Old West: England and Ireland in the Early Middle Ages," in *Crossed Paths: Methodological Approaches to the Celtic Aspect of the European Middle Ages*, ed. Benjamin T. Hudson and Vickie Ziegler (Lanham, Maryland, and London, 1991), 39–60. I thank University Press of America for their permission to reprint portions of this essay.

2. A distinction fundamental to the work of recent scholars is that between "primary" and "secondary" legislation, as Patrick Wormald remarks in his groundbreaking study "*Lex Scripta* and *Verbum Regis*: Legislation and Germanic Kingship, from Euric to Cnut," in *Early Medieval Kingship*, ed. Sawyer and Wood, 109–110.

3. Brunner's *Deutsche Rechtsgeschichte*, 2 vols. (Leipzig, 1887–1892; third edition with C. F. von Schwerin, Berlin, 1961) is the classic example of this genre.

4. J. M. Wallace-Hadrill, *Early Germanic Kingship in England and on the Continent* (Oxford, 1971), 37.

5. Wormald, "*Lex Scripta* and *Verbum Regis*," 123. The preeminence of *verbum regis* over *lex scripta* is also a major theme of two other important articles by Wormald: "The Uses of Literacy in Anglo-Saxon England and its Neighbours;" and "Aethelred the Lawmaker," in *Ethelred the Unready: Papers from the Millenary Conference*, ed. David Hill, BAR, British series 59 (Oxford, 1978), 47–80.

6. Wormald, "*Lex Scripta*," 113–117. On the issue of language, see Susan Kelly, "Anglo-Saxon Lay Society and the Written Word," in *The Uses of Literacy in Early Mediaeval Europe*, ed. Rosamond McKitterick (Cambridge, 1990), 57–58; and Stacey, "Law and Order in the *Very* Old West," 43.

7. Wormald, "*Lex Scripta*," 124. Wormald's forthcoming book on early law will strengthen the case for regional differences in the use of written codes in court. It is worth noting, however, that what Wormald classifies as the "southern European" Burgundian code contains some of the most archaic provisions known to Germanic law, including one reminiscent of the Iron Age bog burials discussed by P. V. Glob in his book *The Bog People: Iron-Age Man Preserved*, trans. Rupert Bruce-Mitford (New York, 1969; reprinted, 1977): *Leges Burgundionum*, ed. R. de Salis, *MGH, Legum* Sectio I, *Leges Nationum Germanicarum*, vol. 2, part 1 (Hannover, 1892; reprinted 1973), §34.1, and see also §§97 and 98. I am very grateful to Patrick Wormald for making papers relevant to my study available to me in advance of publication and for his excellent advice generally on matters of early law.

8. Wormald, "*Lex Scripta*," 135–138. Wormald's most recent work makes clear that his original argument has been frequently misunderstood by subsequent scholars and that he did not intend in "*Lex Scripta*" to denigrate the sophistication or effectiveness of early medieval government, nor to drive too deep a wedge between written and enforced law. In general, however, his view of the relationship between written law and law as practiced in Northern Europe remains similar: the northern codes are to be regarded as primarily "symbols of a people's identity or of a judge's office" rather than "precise guides to legal practice" ("*Lex Scripta* and *Verbum Regis*: A *Retractatio*?," unpublished paper made available by the kind offices of the author).

9. Rosamond McKitterick argues that some of the Frankish legal manuscripts show signs of having actually been used in the administration of justice by royal officials: McKitterick, "Some Carolingian Law-books and their Function," in *Authority and Power: Studies on Medieval Law and Government presented to Walter Ullmann on his Seventieth Birthday*, ed. Peter Linehan and Brian Tierney (Cambridge and New York, 1980), 22–25; and see also McKitterick's *The Carolingians and the Written Word* (Cambridge, 1989), 23–75. Other challenges or modifications to Wormald's views include Dafydd Jenkins, "The Medieval Welsh Idea of Law," *Tijdschrift voor Rechtsgeschiednis* 49, numbers 3–4 (1981): 323–348; Simon Keynes, "Royal Government and the Written Word in Late Anglo-Saxon England," in *The Uses of Literacy in Early Mediaeval Europe*, 228–246 especially; and Stacey, "Law and Order in the *Very* Old West." Works advancing interpretations similar to Wormald's views include Hanna Vollrath, "Gesetzgebung und Schriftlichkeit: das Beispiel der angelsächsischen Gesetze," *Historisches Jahrbuch* 99 (1979): 28–54; Hermann Nehlsen, "Zur Aktualität und Effektivität germanischer Rechtsauzeichnungen," in *Recht und Schrift im Mittelalter*, ed. Peter Classen, Vorträge und Forschungen 23 (Sigmaringen, 1977): 449–502; and see also two important essays by Janet Nelson, "Legislation and Consensus in the Reign of Charles the Bald," in *Ideal and Reality in Frankish and Anglo-Saxon Society: Studies presented to J.M. Wallace-Hadrill*, ed. Patrick Wormald with Donald Bullough and Roger Collins (Oxford, 1983), 202–227; and "Literacy in Carolingian Government," in *The Uses of Literacy in Early Mediaeval Europe*, 258–296.

10. *Ior* 3/4–5 (see note 48 below on the system of references employed in this book). T. M. Charles-Edwards examines the relationship between law and political authority in *The Welsh Laws* (Cardiff, 1989), 38–43. An earlier study is J. Goronwy Edwards, "The Royal Household and the Welsh Lawbooks," *TRHS* fifth series 13 (1963): 163–176.

11. *The Hywel Dda Millenary Volume, Aberystwyth Studies* 10 (1928); J. Goronwy Edwards, "Hywel Dda and the Welsh Lawbooks," *CLP*, 135–160; J. Goronwy Edwards, "The Laws of Hywel Dda," in *Wales through the Ages*, ed. A. H. Roderick (Llandybie, 1959), 67–73; Huw Pryce, "The Prologues to the Welsh Lawbooks," *BBCS* 33 (1986): 151–187; Charles-Edwards, *The Welsh Laws*, 73–76 on pre-Norman elements in the laws and 83–85 on the attribution to Hywel; and *LTMW*, xi–xx.

12. *CIH* 1617.33. This tract has been translated by Eoin MacNeill in "Ancient Irish Law: the Law of Status or Franchise," *PRIA* 36 C (1923): 272–281. A new

edition is forthcoming from Christopher McAll in the DIAS series on early Irish law.

13. Traditional accounts assign kings little role in the early Irish judicial process: D. A. Binchy, *Celtic and Anglo-Saxon Kingship* (Oxford, 1970), 15–19; Proinsias Mac Cana, "The Three Languages and the Three Laws," 76–78; and Richard Sharpe, "Dispute Settlement," *SD*, 186–187, note 83. Recently, however, the consensus appears to be changing: Neil McLeod, "Parallel and Paradox: Compensation in the Legal Systems of Celtic Ireland and Anglo-Saxon England," *Studia Celtica* 16/17 (1981–1982): 36–39; McLeod, "The Concept of Law in Ancient Irish Jurisprudence," *The Irish Jurist*, 17 (1982): 356–358, esp. notes 3 and 4; Fergus Kelly, "An Old-Irish Text on Court Procedure," *Peritia* 5 (1986): 74–106; Marilyn Gerriets, "The King as Judge in Early Ireland," *Celtica* 20 (1988): 29–52; *GEIL*, 18–26; and *PPCP*, 85, 126. Ó Corráin's suggestion that jurists might often have been recruited from the "politically unsuccessful segments of ruling dynasties" is particularly interesting in light of this shift in opinion: "Nationality and Kingship," 18–20, 22–23.

14. D. A. Binchy, "Ancient Irish Law," *The Irish Jurist* 1, no. 1 (1966): 84–92; Binchy, "Linguistic and Legal Archaisms in the Celtic Law-Books," *CLP*, 109–120; and *GEIL*, 231–232, 240–241.

15. *Bretha Nemed* is well known for its obscure and rhetorical style: D. A. Binchy, "*Bretha Nemed*," *Ériu* 17 (1955): 4–6; Breatnach, "Canon Law and Secular Law;" and "The First Third of *Bretha Nemed Tóisech*," ed. Breatnach, *Ériu* 40 (1989): 1–40. Welsh law also delights in "rhetorical images" that lend what R. R. Davies has called an "air of unreality" to the whole: "The Status of Women and the Practice of Marriage in Late-Medieval Wales," *WLW*, 94.

16. D. A. Binchy, "The Legal Capacity of Women in Regard to Contracts," *SEIL*, 207–234; and Stacey, "The Archaic Core of Llyfr Iorwerth," *LAL*, 21–27.

17. For example, the Irish status tract *Críth Gablach*, which details to the last cooking pot the possessions expected of the various social ranks (*CG* 171–247). The Welsh laws also define to the penny the value of items owned by each grade (e.g., *Ior* §§139–145).

18. See references in note 14 above of the Introduction and, for a different perspective, Mac Niocaill, "Christian Influences in Early Irish Law;" *GEIL*, 231–241; and T. M. Charles-Edwards, "Early Irish Law," which paper was made available to me in advance of publication by the author, to whom I am very grateful.

19. The works of P. J. Bohannan, "Anthropology and the Law," in *Horizons of Anthropology*, ed. S. Tax (Chicago, 1964; second edition, 1977), 290–299; Sally Falk Moore, *Law as Process: An Anthropological Approach* (London, 1978), 214–256; Simon Roberts, *Order and Dispute: An Introduction to Legal Anthropology* (New York, 1979); John Comaroff and Simon Roberts, *Rules and Processes: the Cultural Logic of Dispute in an African Context* (Chicago, 1981); and Sally Humphreys, "Law as Discourse," in *The Discourse of Law*, ed. Humphreys, 241–264, outline the literature in some detail. Also helpful is Michael Gagarin, *Early Greek Law* (Berkeley and Los Angeles, 1986), 1–17.

20. Bronislaw Malinowski, *Crime and Custom in Savage Society* (London, 1926; reprinted New Jersey, 1972), 122–123.

21. For example, A. R. Radcliffe-Brown, "Primitive Law," *The Encyclopedia of the Social Sciences*, vol. 9 (New York, 1933), 202–206; Ian Schapera, *A Handbook of Tswana Law and Custom* (London, 1938); K. N. Llewellyn and E. A. Hoebel, *The Cheyenne Way* (Norman, Okla., 1941); Radcliffe-Brown, *Structure and Function in Primitive Society* (London, 1952); Leopold Pospisil, *Kapauku Papuans and their Law* (New Haven, 1958); Ian Hamnett, *Chieftainship and Legitimacy: An Anthropological Study of Executive Law in Lesotho* (London, 1975); and Hamnett, "Introduction," *Social Anthropology and Law*, ed. Hamnett (London and New York, 1977).

22. See, for example, Malinowski, *Crime and Custom*; E. E. Evans-Pritchard, *Witchcraft, Oracles, and Magic among the Azande of the Anglo-Egyptian Sudan* (Oxford, 1937); V. Turner, *Schism and Continuity in an African Society* (Manchester, 1957); P. H. Gulliver, *Social Control in an African Society; a Study of the Arusha: Agricultural Masai of Northern Tanganyika* (Boston, 1963); and Gulliver, *Neighbours and Networks: the Idiom of Kinship in Social Action among the Ndendeuli of Tanzania* (Berkeley and Los Angeles, 1971).

23. Max Gluckman, *The Ideas in Barotse Jurisprudence* (New Haven and London, 1965), 17, 22, 25; Gluckman, *The Judicial Process among the Barotse of Northern Rhodesia* (Manchester, 1955); and Gluckman, *Politics, Law and Ritual in Tribal Society* (1965; reprinted Oxford, 1977).

24. For example, *L. Burgundionum*, §§51 and 52; and Tassilo's judgment from the *Capitulare Franconofurtense: Capitula Regum Francorum*, ed. Boretius, *MGH, Legum* Sectio II, vol. 1 (Hannover, 1883; reprinted, 1984), §28. On *placita*, see *SD*, 273.

25. Wendy Davies, "The Latin Charter-Tradition in Western Britain, Brittany and Ireland in the Early Mediaeval Period," *Ireland in Early Mediaeval Europe*, 258–280; Sharpe, "Dispute Settlement," *SD*, 170–178; and *GEIL*, 238–241.

26. *BB*, 68–73, §§31–35. Others are translated by Myles Dillon in "Stories from the Law Tracts," *Ériu* 11 (1932): 42–65, and see *GEIL*, 238–240.

27. For example, Librán's filial obligations detailed in *Adomnan's Life of Columba*, ed. A. O. Anderson and M. O. Anderson (London, 1961), Book II, chapter 39. Many of the Irish charters mentioned by Davies in her article come from saints' lives: W. Davies, "The Latin Charter-Tradition," in *Ireland in Early Mediaeval Europe*, 271–274.

28. Charles-Edwards, *The Welsh Laws*, 49–69.

29. For example, *Liber Landavensis*, §233 (127)—dated by Davies to ca. 905 in *The Llandaff Charters*, 123, and numbered according to the system articulated in that work—which contains a provision on the insult-payment due to a bishop similar to that established in *Llyfr Blegywryd* for the kings of Dinefwr and Aberffraw (*Bleg* 3.17–4.6 and note 48 below).

30. Wendy Davies is forced to rely on post-eleventh-century saints' lives in *WEMA* (see her discussion of this on pp. 207–208), and R. R. Davies must base his studies of Welsh marriage law and judges on the post-1284 court rolls: "The Status of Women and the Practice of Marriage in Late-Medieval Wales," *WLW*, 93–114; and "The Administration of Law in Medieval Wales: The Role of the *Ynad Cwmwd* (*Judex Patrie*)," *LAL*, 258–259.

31. Stacey, "Law and Order in the *Very* Old West," 39.

32. *GEIL* is an excellent introduction and reference guide to early Irish law. Additional bibliography can be found in Liam Ronayne's "*Seandlithe na nGael*: An Annotated Bibliography of the Ancient Laws of Ireland," *The Irish Jurist* 17 (1982): 131–144. Older works include Rudolf Thurneysen, "Celtic Law," *CLP*, 49–70; and D. A. Binchy, "The Linguistic and Historical Value of the Irish Law Tracts," *CLP*, 71–107.

33. Binchy, "*Bretha Nemed*," 5–6; P. Mac Cana, "The Three Languages and the Three Laws," 66–72; *GEIL*, 47–49, 231–238; T. M. Charles-Edwards, "Early Irish Law"; Liam Breatnach, "Lawyers in Early Ireland," 3–5; but compare *PPCP*, 85–86.

34. Binchy, "*Bretha Nemed*," 5–6; Binchy, "The Date and Provenance of Uraicecht Becc," *Ériu* 18 (1958): 44–54; and *GEIL*, 246.

35. Ó Corráin, Breatnach, and Breen, "The Laws of the Irish;" Breatnach, "*Cáin Fhuithirbe*"; and *PPCP*, 84–106. *GEIL* discusses the law-schools on 242–263.

36. Charles-Edwards, "The *Corpus Iuris Hibernici*," 146–147, 153–155; *BB*, 24–25.

37. See references in note 14 of the introduction above; McCone, "Dubthach Maccu Lugair," 27–28; and Charles-Edwards, "Early Irish Law." A balanced survey of the "nativist" controversy and its implications for the study of Old Irish literature is Máire Herbert, "The World, the Text, and the Critic of Early Irish Heroic Narrative," *Text and Context* (Autumn 1988): 1–9.

38. Charles-Edwards, "The *Corpus Iuris Hibernici*," 153–155; and *GEIL*, 225–232.

39. *CG* 52–62.

40. Exceptions include the H 3. 18 glosses on the *Senchas Már* (*CIH* 877.4–924.31); "The Distribution of *Cró* and *Díbad*," which was printed by Kuno Meyer in his "A Collation of *Críth Gablach*, and a Treatise on *Cró* and *Díbad*," *Ériu* 1 (1904): 214–215; *Urcuilte Bretheman*, printed by Thurneysen in "Aus dem irischen Recht V," *ZCP* 18 (1930): 362–364; and recension H of *CCF* (pp. 26–61 of that text). See *GEIL*, 249–250.

41. Philologists have traditionally classified Irish after the year 900 as Middle, rather than Old, Irish: Thurneysen, *GOI*, p. 1, §1.I.1a.

42. Binchy, "Archaisms in Celtic Law-Books," *CLP*, 113.

43. See above, notes 10 and 11; introduction to *Col*, pp. xxiv–xxvi; and Dafydd Jenkins, *Cyfraith Hywel* (Llandysul, 1970), 1–12.

44. Charles-Edwards concludes that *damweiniau* may go back into the twelfth century, while *cynghawsedd* ought primarily to be associated with the thirteenth: *The Welsh Laws*, 49–69.

45. *ALW* VIII.x.5.

46. *Col*, pp. xxii–xxiii; Dafydd Jenkins, "The Lawbooks of Medieval Wales," in *The Political Context of Law: Proceedings of the Seventh British Legal History Conference, Canterbury 1985*, ed. Richard Eales and David Sullivan (London and Ronceverte, 1987), 4–5; and Charles-Edwards, *The Welsh Laws*, 51–53.

47. *Medieval Welsh Society: Selected Essays by T. Jones Pierce*, ed. J. Beverly

Smith (Cardiff, 1972), 383–384. It is noticeable that these texts (manuscripts P, Q, and S), exclude much of the archaic matter that characterizes other Welsh legal manuscripts.

48. *Llyfr Cyfnerth* manuscript U was edited by Owen in *ALW* (the "Gwentian Code"); manuscript V (with additions from W) was edited by A. W. Wade-Evans in *WML*. *Llyfr Iorwerth* was also edited in *ALW* (the "Venedotian Code"), but the most frequently cited scholarly edition is by Aled Rhys Wiliam. *Llyfr Blegywryd* was also included in *ALW* (the "Dimetian Code"), but the standard edition is by S. J. Williams and J. E. Powell. The Latin texts do not appear in *ALW*, but were edited by H. D. Emanuel in *LTWL*. The following conventions and abbreviations have been used throughout this book: the titles of individual redactions of the lawbooks (e.g., *Llyfr Cyfnerth, Llyfr Iorwerth, Llyfr Blegywryd*, Latin A) have been spelled out in full in the text, but appear in abbreviated form (Cyfn, Ior, Bleg, Lat A) in the notes for reasons of economy. Titles of *particular editions* of these redactions are designated in the manner outlined in the "List of Abbreviations" (e.g., *WML, Ior, Bleg,* and *LTWL*, Lat A). *Ior* 60/2 is thus a reference to paragraph 60, sentence 2 of Wiliam's edition of the *Llyfr Iorwerth* (Ior) redaction of the lawbooks. Other versions of the lawbooks include *Llyfr Colan*, essentially a revised version of Ior dating to the late thirteenth century, and *Llyfr Cynog*, which is only partially extant. The relationship between these various texts is outlined in detail in *WLW*, 2–3; Charles-Edwards, *The Welsh Laws*, 16–48; and Huw Pryce, *Native Law and the Church in Medieval Wales* (Oxford, 1993), 1–14, and the discussion that follows is based primarily on those accounts.

49. There is good evidence to suggest that legal procedures varied greatly from region to region even within Welsh-speaking Wales: *Medieval Welsh Society*, 380–383. But while the general equation of Ior with the North and Cyfn and Bleg with the South is a useful one, reality was more complicated. Lawbooks influenced one another extensively, and individual manuscripts of a particular redaction could originate in different parts of Wales: Charles-Edwards, *The Welsh Laws*, 17–22, 25–48, 68–93.

50. H. D. Emanuel, "The Book of Blegywryd and MS. Rawlinson 821," *CLP*, 161–170; *LTWL*, 70–72. The compiler of Bleg also made use of a version of Cyfn: Charles-Edwards, *The Welsh Laws*, 20–21.

51. Compare, for example, the tractates on women and suretyship: T. M. Charles-Edwards, "Relationship of the Tractates in Latin Redactions A and B to those in Llyfr Iorwerth and Llyfr Cyfnerth," *WLW*, 180–185; and Stacey, "The Archaic Core of Llyfr Iorwerth," *LAL*, 15–46. See also Charles-Edwards, *The Welsh Laws*, 45–46; and J. Enoch Powell, "Floating Sections in the Laws of Howel," *BBCS* 9, part 1 (1937): 27–34.

52. *LTWL*, Lat B 245.17–246.16, for example, corresponds to §§2–16 of the *Canones Wallici* edited by Ludwig Bieler (*The Irish Penitentials, Scriptores Latini Hiberniae* vol. 5 [Dublin, 1963; reprinted 1975], 136–159, esp. 136–139), and dated by Fleuriot to the sixth century in "Un fragment en Latin de très anciennes lois brétonnes armoricaines du 6ᵉ siècle," *Annales de Bretagne* 78 (1971): 601–660. David Dumville modifies this dating in "On the Dating of the Early Breton Lawcodes," *Études Celtiques* 21 (1984): 207–221. See also T. M. Charles-Edwards, "The

Seven Bishop Houses of Dyfed," *BBCS* 24 (1970–1972): 247–262; Huw Pryce, "Early Irish Canons and Medieval Welsh Law," *Peritia* 5 (1986): 107–127; Stacey, "The Archaic Core of Llyfr Iorwerth," *LAL*, 15–46; and Charles-Edwards, *The Welsh Laws*, 73–83. The composite nature of the lawbooks is well illustrated by Dafydd Jenkins's reconstruction of the lost manuscript of Llanforda: "Llawysgrif Goll Llanforda o Gyfreithiau Hywel Dda," *BBCS* 14 (1950–1952): 89–104, esp. p. 98. On the nature of the laws see also generally Morfydd Owen's "Y Cyfreithiau—(1) Natur y Testunau," and "Y Cyfraith—(2) Ansawdd y Rhyddiaith," in *Y Traddiodiad Rhyddiaith yn yr Oesau Canol*, ed. G. Bowen (Llandysul, 1974), 196–244; and her "Functional Prose," in *A Guide to Welsh Literature*, vol. 1, ed. A. O. H. Jarman and G. R. Hughes (Swansea, 1976).

53. Much of the work on law and legal institutions has centered on the Proto-Indo-European lexicon itself: Émile Benveniste, *Le Vocabulaire des Institutions Indo-Européenes*, 2 vols. (Paris, 1969); and Calvert Watkins, "The Indo-European Origin of English," and "Indo-European and Indo-Europeans," *American Heritage Dictionary of the English Language*, 19–20 (1975): 1496–1502, and end papers. Many non-Celtic historians have relied on the Irish laws in their work on comparative legal institutions such as, for example, Franz Leifer, "Zum römischen *vindex*-Problem," *Zeitschrift für vergleichende Rechtswissenschaft* 50 (1935): 5–62; and J. H. Michel, "Réflexions sur quelques traits généraux du cautionnement archaïque à la lumière de l'ancien droit irlandais," *Les sûretés personnelles* 29, part 2 (1971): 383–397. On the methodology itself, see A. Meillet, *The Comparative Method in Historical Linguistics*, trans. G. Ford (Paris, 1967); C. Scott Littleton, *The New Comparative Mythology: an Anthropological Assessment of the Theories of Georges Dumézil* (Berkeley and Los Angeles, 1966; reprinted, 1973); and *Myth in Indo-European Antiquity*, ed. G. J. Larson, C. Scott Littleton, and Jaan Puhvel (Berkeley and Los Angeles, 1974).

54. Franz Schröder, "Ein altirischer Krönungsritus und das indogermanische Rossopfer," *ZCP* 16 (1927): 310–312; *Irish Kings*, 17–18; H. R. Ellis Davidson, *Myths and Symbols in Pagan Europe: Early Scandinavian and Celtic Religions* (Syracuse, N. Y., 1988), 53–56; and *PPCP*, 117–120.

55. See references in note 22 of the Introduction above, and see Calvert Watkins, "Sick-Maintenance in Indo-European," *Ériu* 27 (1976): 21–25; "A Text on the Forms of Distraint," ed. D. A. Binchy, *Celtica* 10 (1973): 72–86; Binchy, "Distraint in Irish Law;" and *GEIL*, 177–182. An Indo-European origin has also been proposed for suretyship: Binchy, "Celtic Suretyship, A Fossilized Indo-European Institution?" in *Indo-European and Indo-Europeans: Papers Presented to the Third Indo-European Conference, 1966*, ed. G. Cardona (Philadelphia, 1970), 355–367 (reprinted in *The Irish Jurist* 7 [1972]: 360–372).

56. See references in note 21 of the Introduction above.

57. Charles-Edwards, "*Nau Kynywedi Teithiauc*," in *WLW*, 23–39.

58. Which would seem to date, in other words, to the Common Celtic period (ca. 1000 B.C.E.): *GEIL*, 231–232. An early study is Sir D. Brynmor-Jones, "The Brehon Laws and their Relation to the Ancient Welsh Institutes," *Transactions of the Cymmrodorion Society* (1904–1905): 7–36.

59. *LAL*, 342–343.

60. Binchy, "Archaisms in Celtic Law-Books," *CLP*, 115–116; Binchy, "Celtic Suretyship," 360–361, 366, note 16; Stacey, "The Archaic Core of Llyfr Iorwerth," *LAL*, 16–17; and *GEIL*, 172. It may also be a component of the Breton *machtiern*, although Eric Hamp takes a different view in "Varia. XVIII. Mech Deyrn," *Études Celtiques*, 21 (1984): 137–140. See, on the *machtiern*, *LAL*, 349; W. Davies, *Small Worlds*, 138–142; and J. G. T. Sheringham, "Les machtierns," *Memoires de la Societé d'histoire et d'archéologie de Bretagne* 58 (1981): 61–72.

61. D. A. Binchy, "Archaisms in Celtic Law-Books," *CLP*, 114–115.

62. D. A. Binchy, "The Linguistic and Historical Value of the Irish Law Tracts," *CLP*, 94–95; Binchy, "Archaisms in Celtic Law-Books," *CLP*, 113–120; Thurneysen, "Celtic Law," *CLP*, 66–68; Binchy, "Some Celtic Legal Terms," *Celtica* 3 (1956): 221–231; and *GEIL*, 231–232, esp. note 19, and 240–241.

63. A more detailed consideration of the methodological issues raised here is presented in Chapter 6 below; particularly important are Ó Corráin's reservations expressed in "Law and Society—Principles of Classification," in *Geschichte und Kultur der Kelten/History and Culture of the Celts*, ed. Karl Horst Schmidt with Rolf Ködderitzsch (Heidelberg, 1986), 234–240; and Wormald's observations on Breton law in his review of *LTMW* and of *LAL*, 99.

64. As has happened in the Welsh laws on women: Stacey, "The Archaic Core of Llyfr Iorwerth," *LAL*, 24–27.

65. Breatnach, "Canon Law and Secular Law," 452–459. Fergus Kelly outlines some of the relevant linguistic criteria in *AM*, pp. xxix–xl; Thomas Charles-Edwards uses similar criteria in his "The *Corpus Iuris Hibernici*," 153–155. Breatnach's work affects the dating of *Fénechas* style passages only.

66. Dafydd Jenkins, "Legal and Comparative Aspects of the Welsh Laws," *Welsh History Review*, Special Number of 1963 devoted to the Welsh Laws, 56.

67. Binchy's argument in "The Legal Capacity of Women in regard to Contract," *SEIL*, 207–234, is problematic, as Neil McLeod points out in *EICL*, chapter 3.5, although his general outline of a progression from lesser to greater capacity may still be correct, if the glosses and commentaries he cites are representative of later legal practice. For Welsh law, see Stacey, "The Archaic Core of Llyfr Iorwerth," *LAL*, 21–27.

68. *LTMW*, xxxiv. The chronology of the corresponding Irish institutions is suggestive: Stacey, "The Archaic Core of Llyfr Iorwerth," *LAL*, 43, note 117, and see discussion below in Chapter 6.

69. Caesar, *The Gallic War (De bello gallico)*, VI.14; Kenneth Jackson, *The Oldest Irish Tradition: A Window on the Iron Age* (Cambridge, 1964); and see now *Aspects of the Táin*, ed. J. P. Mallory (Belfast, 1992); and "Focus on the Origins of the Ulster Cycle," *Emania: Bulletin of the Navan Research Group* 10 (1992).

70. As Máire Herbert shows with reference to "The Preface to *Amra Coluim Cille*," in *Sages, Saints, and Storytellers: Celtic Studies in Honour of Professor James Carney*, ed. Ó Corráin, Breatnach, and McCone, (Maynooth, 1989), 67–75. See also Ó Corráin, "Historical Need and Literary Narrative," *Proceedings of the Seventh International Congress of Celtic Studies*, ed. D. Ellis Evans, John G. Griffith, and E. M. Jope (Oxford, 1986), 141–158; and, on the use made by later medieval lawyers of Old Irish law, Gearóid Mac Niocaill, "Aspects of Irish Law in the Late Thir-

teenth Century," *Historical Studies* 10, ed. G. A. Hayes-McCoy (Galway, 1976), 25–42; Mac Niocaill, "Notes on Litigation in Late Irish Law," *The Irish Jurist* 2 (1967): 299–307; Nerys Patterson, "Brehon Law in Late Medieval Ireland: "Antiquarian and Obsolete' or "Traditional and Functional'?," *CMCS* 17 (Summer 1989): 43–63; and Máirín Ní Dhonnchadha, "An Address to a Student of Law," in *Sages, Saints and Storytellers*, 159–177.

71. Jones Pierce suggested long ago that the Welsh jurists retained references to the clearly archaic *galanas*, "wergild," payments because of their relevance to other, still vital, legal institutions: *Medieval Welsh Society*, 22. The preservation of archaisms might also be dictated by textual or political considerations: Stacey, "The Archaic Core of Llyfr Iorwerth," *LAL*, 31–35; and see below, Chapter 6.

72. Ó Corráin, Breatnach, and Breen, "The Laws of the Irish," 394. The expression is now current in the historical literature, although as Máire Herbert points out, the images it embodies are, to say the least, mixed: "The World, the Text, and the Critic," 8, note 21.

73. Herbert, "The Preface to *Amra Coluim Cille*," *Sages, Saints, and Storytellers*, 67, 73. Charles-Edwards shows how deeply influenced the jurists were by the techniques of the Latin schools in "The *Corpus Iuris Hibernici*," 147–152; and see references in note 14 of the Introduction.

74. *LTWL*, 24–40; and Charles-Edwards, *The Welsh Laws*, 63–67.

75. Herbert, "The Preface to *Amra Coluim Cille*," *Sages, Saints, and Storytellers*.

76. On the Irish tradition of *senchas*, literally "tales about the past," see: Byrne, "*Senchas*"; Kathleen Hughes, *The Early Celtic Idea of History and the Modern Historian* (Cambridge, 1977); John Kelleher, "Early Irish History and Pseudo-history," *Studia Hibernica* 3 (1963): 113–127; and Kelleher, "The Pre-Norman Irish Genealogies," *IHS* 16 (1968–1969): 138–153. The distinction we perceive to exist among the purely literary, the purely legal, and the purely historical is an arbitrary one, as is evident often from the textual context in which legal sources are found. Thus the wisdom text *Audacht Morainn* may have originated in the same poetical-legal school that produced the *Bretha Nemed* tracts (Binchy, "*Bretha Nemed*," 6) and may once have been contained in the now lost manuscript *Cín Dromna Snechta* along with the genealogical and literary texts for which that manuscript is primarily known: *AM*, pp. xxv–xxvi; *GEIL*, 235–236, 284. Similarly, the Welsh Book of Llandaff contains saints' lives in addition to its famous charters (Davies, *The Llandaff Charters*, 15–16).

77. *CIH* 896.19–41 (edited and translated by Liam Breatnach in "Lawyers in Early Ireland," 11–12); D. A. Binchy, "*Féchem, Fethem, Aigne*," *Celtica* 11 (1976): 26–30; and Sharpe, "Dispute Settlement," *SD*, 183–184.

78. *GEIL*, 51–57, 232–238, 242–250. The "textbook style" of many of the Irish legal tracts is significant in this respect: Charles-Edwards, "The *Corpus Iuris Hibernici*," 146–156.

79. Breatnach, "Canon Law and Secular Law," 441–445, 459. Another of these kinsmen was a bishop, and it is suggestive that in the ninth through twelfth centuries, high-ranking clerics often served as judges: Ó Corráin, "Nationality and Kingship," 14–16.

80. *CIH* 634.26. See also Gerriets, "The King as Judge," 48–51; Sharpe in "Dispute Settlement," *SD*, 185, note 74; and Charles-Edwards, "The *Corpus Iuris Hibernici*," 155–156.

81. *GEIL*, 237–241.

82. Dafydd Jenkins, "The Lawbooks of Medieval Wales," 4–5, 8–9; *LTMW*, xviii–xx; R. R. Davies, "The Administration of Law," *LAL*, 264–265; Charles-Edwards, *The Welsh Laws*, 23–24, 49–67, 90–93; and David Stephenson, *Thirteenth-Century Welsh Law Courts*, Pamffledi Cyfraith Hywel (Aberystwyth, 1980). This is the generally accepted view, but see also Alan Harding, "Regiam Majestatem amongst Medieval Law-Books," *Juridical Review* (1984): 110–111; and Harding, "Legislators, Lawyers and Lawbooks," *LAL*, 237–257.

83. Dafydd Jenkins, "Iorwerth ap Madog: gwr cyfraith o'r drydedd ganrif ar ddeg," *National Library of Wales Journal* 8 (1953–1954): 164–170; and Jenkins, "A Family of Medieval Welsh Lawyers," *CLP*, 121–133, especially the genealogical chart on p. 124.

84. R. R. Davies, "The Administration of Law," *LAL*, 261–262, 267; *Bleg* 98.28–99.6 on the various types of judges; and *Bleg* 100.22–30 on the penalties imposed for false judgments.

85. *Medieval Welsh Society*, 383–384; R. R. Davies, "The Administration of Law," in *LAL*, 261, 267; and *LTMW*, xxxiv–xxxv.

86. Charles-Edwards, *The Welsh Laws*, 1–24.

87. T. M. Charles-Edwards terms *Críth Gablach* "one of the few outstanding pieces of social analysis in early medieval Europe" in "*Críth Gablach* and the Law of Status," *Peritia* 5 (1986): 73.

88. The classic "exceptions" text in Irish law is *GC*. Exceptions of this sort occur in Welsh law also, although sometimes in a form that is difficult to untangle without the help of Irish parallels; see, for example, on the *da dilis diuach*, R. C. Stacey, "Ties That Bind: Immunities in Irish and Welsh Law," *CMCS* 20 (Winter 1990): 50–57.

89. Dafydd Jenkins, "The Medieval Welsh Idea of Law," 345; and see P. Wormald's review of *LTMW* and *LAL*, 99.

90. An important aspect of legal change, as Dafydd Jenkins reminds us in his review of *SD*, in *CMCS* 15 (Summer 1988): 89–92.

Chapter 2. Contractual Suretyship in Irish Law

1. *CIH* 350.26–27, and cf. also *EICL*, 166–167, §34. I am grateful to Neil McLeod for making his edition of *Di Astud Chor* available to me in advance of publication.

2. *CIH* 2192.16–17 = *GC*, 308–309, §3.

3. E. A. Farnsworth, "The Past of Promise: An Historical Introduction to Contract," *Columbia Law Review* 69 (1969): 579–580.

4. Alan Watson, *The Evolution of Law* (Baltimore, 1985), 4.

5. See Watson, *The Evolution of Law*, 3–42, on the development of these contracts, and see also W. W. Buckland, *A Textbook of Roman Law from Augustus to*

Justinian (Cambridge, 1921; third edition revised by Peter Stein, 1963; reprinted with additions and corrections, 1975), 405–603; Farnsworth, "The Past of Promise;" and Gy. Diósdi, *Contract in Roman Law from the Twelve Tables to the Glossators* (Budapest, 1981).

6. Other texts that contain material of interest to Irish contractual procedure are *Córus Iubaile* and *Do Tuaslucud Rudradh* (*GEIL*, 277–278, §§55–56). A good introduction to the subject is *GEIL*, 158–163, 167–176.

7. *EICL*, 94–122.

8. For example, *CIH* 1350.22–24; 1352.26–1353.1; and 1356.32–34 = *EICL*, 128–129, §4; 138–141, §§13–14; and 164–165, §33, respectively.

9. Lucifer and Adam are used in the passages cited above as examples of the principle that competent persons who are aware that they are being cheated in a transaction cannot expect to have their losses redressed at a later time; however, this same concept is expressed elsewhere in Irish law in more traditional fashion (*CIH* 593.14–16 = *Bürgschaft*, 10, §31). On "levitical modeling," see Ó Corráin, Breatnach, and Breen, "The Laws of the Irish," 384–412.

10. The standard edition of this tract is Thurneysen's *Bürgschaft*. An English translation is available in Robin Chapman Stacey, "*Berrad Airechta*: An Old Irish Tract on Suretyship," *LAL*, 210–233. References are given below both to *CIH* and to *Bürgschaft*. Because the paragraphing of the English translation follows that of Thurneysen's edition, it is not cited separately here.

11. *CIH* 896.29 (called there simply *Berrad*), and 973.13–14.

12. The majority of it is written in what has been called the "textbook" style of Old Irish prose, characterized by etymological glosses, the question/answer format, and the frequent use of enumeration: Charles-Edwards, "The *Corpus Iuris Hibernici*," 147–152.

13. Pretonic *to-* and *di-* are found in compound verbs throughout the tract (*GOI* §§831 and 855B: *CIH* 592.33; 593.12; 593.17; 594.4; 595.23; and 597.33), and final *-th*, instead of the more usual *-d*, is a constant feature of even the latest sections (*GOI* §130.2: *CIH* 591.10; 594.11; 594.20; 594.30; 595.18; and 597.32). The independent dative is also used occasionally (*GOI* §251: *CIH* 595.17; 597.32; and 597.33).

14. Listed by *GEIL* as a separate text: 281, §72. The copulative conjunction *ocus*, first attested in the mid-seventh-century Cambray homily, does not appear in this portion of the text, and Binchy has suggested that the absence of *ocus* is an indication of an early date (*BDC*, 3–4). There is one instance of the old conjunction *sceo* (*CIH* 596.23), and a possible example of enclitic *-ch* in *CIH* 596.21–22 (although cf. D. A. Binchy, "Indo-European *Q^we in Irish," *Celtica* 5 (1960): 81–82). The archaic verb-final constructions known as Bergin's Law and tmesis are represented as well (*GOI* §513: *CIH* 596.9; 596.13–14; 596.14; 596.15; and 596.24–25). Breatnach has recently found examples of Bergin's law, tmesis, and the omission of *ocus* in prose which he dates to the eighth century (Breatnach, "Canon Law and Secular Law," 452–453), so it is possible that we are mistaking an archaizing style for the genuinely archaic. Since chronological explanations are, however, at least as likely as are stylistic explanations, especially in the absence of any indication that the reconciliation of native and Christian traditions was a priority for the author, I have here analyzed the texts in the traditional manner.

15. Examples of possible archaisms in this part of the tract include the old plural *nadmen* (*CIH* 598.27), the masculine form *tre*, which is found as well in the Cambray homily (*GOI* §385: *CIH* 598.32), and the old form of the second person possessive pronoun *to* (*GOI* §439: *CIH* 598.23).

16. *CIH* 593.22–23 = *Bürgschaft*, II, §34, although the compiler has forgotten that the *rath tar arrdigh*, the "fief [given] for extra services," had not previously been mentioned.

17. *CIH* 596.3–6 = *Bürgschaft*, 19, §58 and 597.4–5 = *Bürgschaft*, 22, §64, though it is uncertain whether *Córus Aitire* was originally an independent text. It does have a title, like the unquestionably independent *Córus Fíadnaise*, and this may be significant, since these are the only two parts of the text for which separate titles are provided.

18. If the provisions on the *ráth* were originally part of *Córus Aitire* (on which see Stacey, "Berrad Airechta," *LAL*, 232, note 86), it is possible, given the stylistic similarities between the binding formulas used by the contracting parties and those used by the parties involved in binding the *ráth*, that all of these formulas stemmed originally from the same source. If so, that source was probably *Córus Aitire*, and it probably contained the binding formulas for the intertribal *aitire*-surety, the *ráth* (i.e., the *aitire fóisma*), and the contracting parties. These last formulas would presumably have been contained in a section now no longer extant on the *aitire nadma*, "the *aitire* of binding" (referred to on 597.6), which the compiler excised because he had discussed the *naidm* earlier in his work.

19. The fact that the first sentence of the tract incorporates the word *dano*, "moreover," suggests that we do not have extant the work in its entirety.

20. W. Davies, "The Latin Charter-Tradition," *Ireland in Early Mediaeval Europe*, 268–269; *GEIL*, 163; and Jane Stevenson, "Literacy in Ireland: the Evidence of the Patrick Dossier in the Book of Armagh," in *The Uses of Literacy in Early Mediaeval Europe*, 28–32.

21. Sharpe, "Dispute Settlement," *SD*, 180–181.

22. Nerys Patterson, "Honour and Shame in Medieval Welsh Society: A Study of the Role of Burlesque in the Welsh Laws," *Studia Celtica* 16/17 (1981/1982): 73–103.

23. *SD*, 271, on the *festuca*. On the throwing of earth (Frankish *chrenecruda*), see *Lex Salica*, ed. K. A. Eckhardt, *MGH, Legum* Sectio I, *Leges Nationum Germanicarum*, vol. 4, part 2, (Hannover, 1969), §58.

24. Peter Brown, "Society and the Supernatural: A Medieval Change," *Society and the Holy in Late Antiquity* (Berkeley and Los Angeles, 1982), 302–332; Paul Hyams, "Trial by Ordeal: The Key to Proof in the Early Common Law," in *On the Laws and Customs of England: Essays in Honor of Samuel E. Thorne*, ed. Morris Arnold, Thomas Green, Sally Scully, and Stephen White (Chapel Hill, 1981), 90–126; and Robert Bartlett, *Trial by Fire and Water: The Medieval Judicial Ordeal* (Oxford, 1986).

25. Gregory Bateson, *Steps to an Ecology of Mind* (New York, 1972); Jurgen Ruesch and Gregory Bateson, *Communication* (New York, 1968); Erving Goffman, *Frame Analysis: An Essay on the Organization of Experience* (New York, 1974; reprinted 1986); Richard Bauman, "Verbal Art as Performance," in *Verbal Art as*

Performance, ed. Bauman (Prospect Heights, Ill., 1977), 3–58; and Richard Bauman and Charles Briggs, "Poetics and Performance as Critical Perspectives on Language and Social Life," *Annual Review of Anthropology* 19 (1990): 59–88.

26. The formulas are presented in the text as direct quotations rather than as indirect speech, and the one other example of a specific contractual arrangement that remains to us is very similar in aspect to *Berrad Airechta*'s phrasing: *CIH* 675.13–17; and see also 900.29–33; and 920.3–4.

27. For example, *CIH* 595.3–4 = *Bürgschaft*, 15–16, §51a; *CIH* 598.17–18 = *Bürgschaft*, 26–27, §74a; *CIH* 598.26 = *Bürgschaft*, 27, §74d; *CIH* 598.32–33 = *Bürgschaft*, 28–29, §76a; *CIH* 675.14–16; 900.30–32; and cf. 920.3–4. I discuss this issue in more detail in my forthcoming article "Legal Drama in Early Ireland."

28. Bauman, *Verbal Art*, 15–24. The Navaho make use of such language in certain narrative contexts: J. Barre Toelken, "The "Pretty Language" of Yellowman: Genre, Mode, and Texture in Navaho Coyote Narratives," *Genre* 2 (1969): 211–235.

29. Calvert Watkins examines the various forms of "marked" and "unmarked" discourse delineated in the early Irish *Auraicept na n-Éces* in his "Language of Gods and Language of Men: Remarks on Some Indo-European Metalinguistic Traditions," in *Myth and Law Among the Indo-Europeans: Studies in Indo-European Comparative Mythology*, ed. Jaan Puhvel (Berkeley and Los Angeles, 1970), 8–17.

30. The entire formula can be found on *CIH* 595.2–15 = *Bürgschaft*, 15–16, §51. Texts cited from *CIH* appear here *without* normalization as printed, although abbreviations have been silently expanded, and I have occasionally restored missing letters for ease of comprehension (square brackets). Endnotes have been given to important emendations; manuscript 7 appears throughout as *ocus* and manuscript ł as *nó*. Unless otherwise indicated, translations are my own. Material in square brackets indicates words or phrases not actually present in the Irish original but necessary for its translation; material in parentheses represents explanations or suggestions of my own regarding the meaning of the text. I am grateful to the University of Wales Press for their permission to reprint *Berrad Airechta* translations from *LAL*.

31. The creditor.

32. The debtor.

33. It is clear that there would often have been more than one *naidm*-surety involved in a given transaction: *CIH* 598.15 = *Bürgschaft*, 26, §74; *CIH* 598.27 = *Bürgschaft*, 28, §75; and *CIH* 599.12 = *Bürgschaft*, 29, §77.

34. Such an order of events is to be inferred from *CIH* 595.15 = *Bürgschaft*, 15–16, §51d and, by analogy with the *ráth*'s binding procedure, from *CIH* 598.27–30 = *Bürgschaft*, 28–29, §§75 and 76, and *CIH* 599.12–14 = *Bürgschaft*, 29, §77.

35. Or at least such is the implication of his remarks about the missing binding formula of the *naidm*: *Bürgschaft*, 60.

36. A different view of the *naidm* is taken by McLeod in his introduction to *EICL*, chapter 1. T. M. Charles-Edwards points out to me a bit of canonical wordplay in *IK*, 169, XLII.27, where *vincula* probably refers to the *naidm*.

37. *CIH* 593.2–5 = *Bürgschaft*, 10, §27. The only exception recognized here is

inge ma frisroirsetar [*leg. frisrairsetar* with Thurneysen] *folaith*, "unless the considerations have been counter-bound." The meaning of this is unclear, but Thurneysen observed (*Bürgschaft* 10, §27, note 2) that a verb with similar meaning, *fris-naisc*, was used in the legal sources to describe the relationship between a lord and his client and suggested that this was the situation to which the clause referred. However, there is probably no need to limit this exception to clientship arrangements only, since all of the "immune transactions" discussed in *Berrad Airechta* were "counter-bound" in the manner described below in Chapter 3. The "one-sided *naidm*-sureties" to which the text refers here were probably either the senior partners in the relationship or kindred *naidm*-sureties who would intervene to help their kinsmen obtain dues to which they were lawfully entitled.

38. It is referred to in Talmudic, Greek, ancient Egyptian and even Babylonian law: *Les Sûretés personnelles*, vol. 28 (1974): 174–176, 229, and 239.

39. See *EICL*, 23–24.

40. *CIH* 990.33–38; 991.27; 993.25; and 993.31–35 = *EICL*, 142–143, §16; 146–147, §20; and 162–163, §§29–30, respectively. Similarly, *Berrad Airechta* stresses the importance of the senses of sight and hearing when offering testimony on a matter before a judge: *CIH* 596.20–25 = *Bürgschaft*, 20, §60.

41. Manuscript: *airitin ocus dingbal aeslam* (*CIH* 595.22). I have accepted here Binchy's proposed emendation: *CIH* 595, notes l and m–m.

42. *CIH* 595.21–23 = *Bürgschaft*, 17, §52.

43. *Mac* is an earlier term for *naidm*: see Chapter 5 below.

44. *CIH* 598.16–29 = *Bürgschaft*, 26–28, §§74–75; and *CIH* 598.31–599.14 = *Bürgschaft*, 28–29, §§76–77.

45. *CIH* 593.18 = *Bürgschaft*, 10, §32.

46. *CIH* 595.4 = *Bürgschaft*, 15, §51a.

47. *CIH* 594.23–25 = *Bürgschaft*, 13, §44.

48. See discussion below.

49. These formulas are not preserved, but one can infer both their existence and their content from the formulas exchanged on all other occasions where obligations were repaid. The debtor, for example, would ask the creditor to swear that the *ráth*'s payment had extinguished the obligation (*CIH* 595.31–33 = *Bürgschaft*, 18, §55), and the *ráth* would ask the creditor to swear that he had paid the debt in a lawful manner (*CIH* 595.35–36 = *Bürgschaft*, 18, §56).

50. The repayment process is described in full in *CIH* 595.23–29 = *Bürgschaft*, 17–18, §§53–54.

51. *CIH* 595.30–36 = *Bürgschaft*, 18, §§55–56.

52. *CIH* 595.5–6 = *Bürgschaft*, 15–16, §51b.

53. This is how I interpret the *naidm*'s cryptic statement of *CIH* 594.23–25 = *Bürgschaft*, 13, §44.

54. *CIH* 7.9 and 9.5.

55. This seems to be the implication of *CIH* 239.37; see *Bürgschaft*, 56–57.

56. *CIH* 397.35–36; see *Bürgschaft*, 56–57.

57. For example, hosting, the building of a burial mound for a lord, the death of a man of the debtor's household, or a party of high-ranking guests: *CIH* 898.28–33 = Binchy, "A Text on the Forms of Distraint," 80–81, §§12–13.

58. A king, a bishop, an *ollam*-poet, a church, and a man of *ánsruth* status

within the tribe could offer sanctuary to a defaulting debtor, although *Berrad Airechta* implies that this would have been done only when the debtor wished to dispute the justice of the claim: *CIH* 594.22–31 = *Bürgschaft*, 13–14, §§44–45. *CIH* 594.31–34 = *Bürgschaft*, 14, §§46–47 outlines the alternatives available to a *naidm* when a debtor sought sanctuary from one of these people. On the *ánsruth*, see *Bürgschaft*, 14, §45, note 2.

59. *CIH* 598.11–12 = *Bürgschaft*, 26, §73.

60. *CIH* 595.4–5 = *Bürgschaft*, 15, §51a; and *CIH* 595.30–596.2 = *Bürgschaft*, 18, §§55–57.

61. Thurneysen's emendation of MS. *immen olrath*: *Bürgschaft*, 25, §70, note 1.

62. Thurneysen's emendation of MS. *isim log*: *Bürgschaft*, 25, §70, note 2.

63. *CIH* 597.37–598.6 = Bürgschaft, 25–26, §§70–71.

64. Thurneysen suggested that the surety's enclosure was open in the sense that an animal had been removed from it and given to the creditor as a gage to guarantee the eventual payment of his debt. If the debtor failed to redeem the *ráth*'s gage during the sixteen-day period, the surety himself redeemed it by paying the debt: R. Thurneysen, "Aus dem irischen Recht V. Nachträge zur Bürgschaft," *ZCP* 18 (1930): 376–378. This is plausible, but it is also possible that the milking enclosure was perceived as "open" in the sense not that something had been taken from it but in that it had been rendered vulnerable by the debtor's default. Usually an animal would not have been given as a gage (although the tract on gage-interests shows that they could be: *CIH* 465.29–31 and 470.21–31). More often, an item of real or symbolic value to the person offering it would have been given in gage (*CG*, pp. 94–95, and *GEIL*, 164–165). Furthermore, no animal by-products are mentioned in the surety's compensation until *after* he had had to pay the debt, and one would expect these if an animal had previously been removed from his enclosure. Nor does the surety's compensation seem high enough to compensate him adequately for his disturbance, reward him for his services, and cover the interest on a gage.

65. One of the Irish canons extended the payment period over a greater period of time: *IK*, 122–123, XXXIV.4. And see Thurneysen, "Aus dem irischen Recht V. Zu der Etymologie von irischen *ráth*, 'Bürgschaft,' und zu der irischen Kanonensammlung und der Triaden," *ZCP* 18 (1930): 369–370, and also "Nachträge zur Bürgschaft," 377–378.

66. *CIH* 598.11–12 = *Bürgschaft*, 26, §73 and *CIH* 2194.29–30 = *GC*, 327, §18, with Thurneysen's corrected interpretation of this passage in "Nachträge zur Bürgschaft," 377.

67. Thurneysen suggests that *fuillem*, "interest," is here an error for *fuilled*, "filling up, doubling [of the debt]": *Bürgschaft*, 26, §71, note 3. See also *C. Aicillne*, 346, 365–366, and 377.

68. The punctuation here is my own.

69. *CIH* 1122.27–31. The text was published as "The Advice to Doidin," ed. Roland Smith, *Ériu* 11 (1932): 66–85. Thurneysen knew only a few phrases of this paragraph: *Bürgschaft*, 45.

70. An amount equal to a young heifer, or approximately half a milk-cow, at "normal" Old Irish exchange rates: *CG*, pp. 105–106; and on currency generally,

see *GEIL*, 112–116, and Marilyn Gerriets, "Money in Early Christian Ireland according to the Irish Laws," *Comparative Studies in Society and History* 27 (1985): 323–339.

71. A verb **serbaid* is unattested, but there is an infrequently attested noun *serbad*, which could be the verbal noun of a denominative verb of the a-conjugation formed from the adjective *serb*, "bitter, hurtful" (*DIL* s.v. *serb*). I am grateful to T. M. Charles-Edwards for this suggestion.

72. Although in *Berrad Airechta*, the cow compensates the surety both for the opening of his milking enclosure and for his disturbance, whereas here the cow is paid in addition to an unspecified sum for disturbance. Thurneysen translates *la* here as "inclusive of" so that the two texts might agree exactly (*Bürgschaft*, 45, and note 3), but I have retained its more usual meaning of "with, along with."

73. See Stacey, "*Berrad Airechta*," *LAL*, 230, note 39; *CIH* 1238.29.

74. *IK*, 123, XXXIV.5, and see also Thurneysen, "Etymologie," 370–371. On the relationship between the Latin *ratae* and the Irish *ráth*, see "Etymologie," 364–368.

75. The identity of this "merciful" *ráth* is open to dispute. Thurneysen saw him as the *ráth airnisi*, the "bound *ráth*," whose compensation did not go over a fixed amount: *CIH* 789.25–26; *Bürgschaft*, 52; and Thurneysen, "Etymologie," 371. The old glosses in H 3. 18 explain the *ráth airnisi* differently (*CIH* 906.26–27), but a gloss in the *Heptads* supports Thurneysen's interpretation: *CIH* 61.15–16. What may have happened in the passage above is that the Irish synod has simply rearranged the usual procedure for the compensation of a *ráth* in order to discourage the charging of excessive interest. In their hands, the usual compensation for a surety who has not been rendered forfeit becomes the compensation demanded by a non-usurious surety, while the payment given to a forfeited surety is transformed into the compensation of the "merciless" surety.

76. This may be one of the reasons (in addition, of course, to the obvious similarity between the words themselves) why *fuillem*, "interest," and *fuilled*, "filling up, doubling," are so often confused in the legal texts.

77. *Bürgschaft*, 60–61.

78. *SD*, 228–240. As outlined above in the introduction, "public" is used here to imply the official involvement of kings or jurists in a given arrangement and should not, therefore, be taken as a synonym for "communal."

79. See discussion in Chapter 5 below.

80. The law tracts are not consistent here in their terminology. The word *dliged* refers in *Berrad Airechta* to this idea of "natural entitlement," or "fairness," that is, that to which a person is entitled because his claim is considered inherently "just." In other texts, however, like *Cóic Conara Fugill* and *Uraicecht Becc*, *dliged* refers to specifically "contractual entitlement," that is, that to which a person becomes entitled by virtue of having made a contract involving a promise of future action with another. In *Cóic Conara Fugill*, *cert* serves as the term for "natural entitlement": see discussion in Chapter 5 below. The distinction between "natural entitlement" and "contractual entitlement" is an important one; *dliged*, "contractual entitlement" is not necessarily synonymous with *dliged*, "natural entitlement, fairness," as is evident from the fact that "fairness" may force a renegotiation of what a given party would have been "entitled" to under the strict terms of the

contract. See Stacey, "Ties That Bind," appendices one and two particularly. Procedurally, on the other hand, contractual and natural entitlement would be very difficult to distinguish from one another—see Chapter 5 below.

81. *CIH* 593.8–10 = *Bürgschaft*, 10, §28. The *naidm* here represents the contract as it was originally negotiated and bound.

82. *CIH* 1354.31 = *EICL*, 150–151, §23, and see chapters 2.2 and 3.1.

83. *CIH* 593.18–20 = *Bürgschaft*, 11, §33; *CIH* 593.39–40 = *Bürgschaft*, 11, §37; *CIH* 599.21 = *Bürgschaft*, 30, §80; *CIH* 599.25–27 = *Bürgschaft*, 30–31, §81; and *CIH* 988.9–24. The contract was also rescindable if legally incompetent individuals had participated in it without the permission of their guardians: see Chapter 3 below.

84. *CIH* 2201.11–12 = *CCF*, 19, §11; and see *CIH* 599.15–16 and 599.26–27 = *Bürgschaft*, 29–31, §§78 and 81.

85. *CIH* 593.14–16 = *Bürgschaft*, 10, §31; and see also *CIH* 521.13–14. The process by which contracts were renegotiated was a complicated one. It is evident that in such cases the "surplus"—that is, the amount by which the goods obtained by one party exceeded in value the goods obtained by the other—would be divided between various of the parties to the contract. But the texts themselves disagree on how precisely this would be done. *Di Astud Chor* envisages the surplus being divided in various proportions (according to the circumstances) between creditor and debtor, while *Córus Béscnai* in one instance divides it in half between the *ráth* and witnesses (*roach*) on the one hand and the contracting party who has received the surplus on the other: *CIH* 520.31–32. The most detailed treatment of the renegotiation of contractual surpluses is to be found in *EICL*, chapter 2 and references.

86. *CIH* 1352.26–1353.8 = *EICL*, 138–141, §§13–15.

87. *EICL*, 182–183, §49 = *CIH* 987.20–21. *Naidm* can also mean "binding" here, but in either case the sense of the passage is the same.

88. *EICL*, chapters 1 and 2. McLeod suggests that the basis of Irish contractual obligation lay not in the *naidm* or in the rituals through which the contract was bound, but in the exchange of obligations (*feich*) and in the buyer's "contractual entitlement" (*dliged*) to the goods and considerations promised in the contract (*folad*). See discussion below, and Stacey, "Ties That Bind," 42–45 and 57–59, from which part of what follows has been reprinted. I am grateful to *CMCS* for permission to reprint this material.

89. See note 80 above.

90. With the exception, that is, of the "suretyship of God," discussed below in Chapter 8, and of the immune transactions discussed below in Chapter 3, which are clearly viewed as exceptions to the normal rules governing contracts and conveyances.

91. *CIH* 2200.34–35; 2201.4–5 = *CCF*, 18, §§8–9; and see below, Chapter 5.

92. *CIH* 593.8–23 = *Bürgschaft*, 10–11, §§28–34. McLeod presents an alternative view in *EICL*, chapter 1, especially 1.7. However, *dliged* cannot refer in this context to "contractual entitlement," as he says, since it is precisely that (e.g., the terms of the contract) which is being emended. The *naidm* represents "contractual entitlement" here and is placed in opposition to the *dliged*, "natural entitlement" in accordance with which the contract will be renegotiated.

93. The precise nature of the exchange that is termed in Old Irish *comnaidm*, "joint binding," is unknown, although McLeod understands it to refer generally to mutual promises made in the absence of sureties: *EICL*, 150–151, §23 and notes on pp. 214–215. Kindred-suretyship seems to me also a possibility, since we know that kindred leaders or lords could serve as "unappointed" *naidm*-sureties for the people under their authority: *CIH* 592.32–36 = *Bürgschaft*, 9, §§23–24. On *comnaidm* as conveyance, see below.

94. That is, entitlement would derive from conveyance rather than from contract. Given the emphasis placed in Irish law on the exchange of *folad*, "considerations," it would not be at all unlikely that the conveyance of goods would in itself be perceived as establishing the recipient's right to at least part of the goods in question: see *CIH* 987.20–21 and 988.41–989.4 = *EICL*, 182–183, §49 and 194–195, §56; and 599.26–27 = *Bürgschaft*, 30–31, §81, for example.

95. *CIH* 1355.8 (also 992.21–22).

96. *EICL*, 152–153, §24. For the sake of argument, I have accepted McLeod's general interpretation of *Di Astud Chor*'s stance on the issue of unsecured contracts, both because fluidity of this sort makes sense to me in the historical milieu within which all of this is taking place and because, as McLeod himself points out, common sense would indicate that sureties were unlikely to have been used in instances where the amount involved was very small: *EICL*, 18. His is not, however, a necessary interpretation of the passage cited above. If one were to retain the manuscript reading *cor* (genitive plural), and translate "on account of the honor of contracts of *comnaidm*," then it would be possible to perceive the honor of the parties becoming engaged only after an exchange had been made. In other words, *cor comnadmae*, the actual "putting" of goods or services, could then be contrasted with *cor mbél*, the "putting" of the mouth (e.g. a promissory agreement). I am grateful to T. M. Charles-Edwards for his help in sorting out this issue.

97. *CIH* 992.41 = *EICL*, 156–157, §26.

98. *EICL*, chapter 2.2–2.3 provides the best discussion.

99. With the exception of the "immunities" mentioned in *Berrad Airechta* and the *Heptads*: see discussion in Chapter 3 below, and *EICL*, chapter 1.2.

100. *EICL*, 217.

101. *EICL*, chapter 2.3.

102. *EICL*, chapter 1.2, and see discussion below in Chapter 3.

103. Two sets of oppositions govern the opening pages of the tract: that between non-surety and surety transactions, and that between "entirely immune" and "immune" exchanges. Paradoxically, it is the non-surety transactions that are deemed "entirely immune," but the tract quickly makes clear that these transactions are exceptional in being both (entirely) immune and made without sureties. The evident presumption lurking behind this passage is that ordinarily non-surety transactions could not be considered binding at all.

104. See Chapter 5 below.

105. O'Brien, "Varia," *Ériu* 11 (1932): 88–89. Meroney suggests "*summa*" as an alternative translation: Meroney, "The Titles of Some Early Law-tracts," *Journal of Celtic Studies* 2 (1958): 189–192. See also below, Chapter 5.

106. See Chapter 5 below.

Chapter 3. The Social Context of Personal Suretyship

1. See, for example, *CIH* 20.13–15; 25.13–15; 462.30–31; 675.13–17; 2301.15–16 = *Br. Crólige*, 44–45, §55; *CG* 52–62. Also mentioned are adoption (*CIH* 459.12–14 = *CU*, 66, §6); fasting (*CIH* 367.6–7 = "Das Fasten beim Pfändungsverfahren," 262, §6); the legal procedure called *tellach* (*CIH* 23.10); marriage (*CIH* 47.21–23); fines for distraint (in the H 3. 18 glosses: *CIH* 900.29–33); and clientship (also in the H 3. 18 glosses: *CIH* 918.25–28).

2. See T. M. Charles-Edwards's note in *ECI*, 61–64.

3. Gluckman, *Barotse Jurisprudence*, 151, 171–176.

4. *C. Aicillne*, 372, §34 = *CIH* 490.1–3.

5. *Cáin Aicillne*, *Cáin Sóerraith*, and *Cáin Lánamna* have all been edited and translated by Thurneysen (*Cáin Lánamna* in *SEIL*, 1–75). *Córus Béscnai* (*CIH* 520.1–536.27) has unfortunately not yet been translated (but see excerpts in Ó Corráin, Breatnach, and Breen, "The Laws of the Irish," 384–412). Also useful are the two tracts on status, *Críth Gablach* and *Uraicecht Becc*. The former was edited by Binchy (*CG*), and the latter is forthcoming in the DIAS Early Irish Law Series from R. C. McAll. Both were translated by MacNeill in his "Ancient Irish Law: the Law of Status or Franchise."

6. Kinsmen were not necessarily of equal status—indeed the law tracts show a marked preference for kinsmen-lords: *CIH* 490.1–2 = *C. Aicillne*, 372, §34; and T. M. Charles-Edwards, "Kinship, Status and the Origins of the Hide," *Past and Present* 56 (1972): 17–21 and 32–33.

7. See, for example, the *aire désa*, "lord of vassalry," of *CG* (339–340) who protects "his clients with respect to damages arising from contract, *cáin*, and a peace treaty."

8. *CIH* 2220.34.

9. *CG* 328–331.

10. *CU*, 66–67, §7 = *CIH* 459.25; see also Thurneysen's note on *comthus* in *SEIL*, 17–18.

11. On contractual capacity and legal incompetency, see *GEIL*, 68–98 and 159–163, and *EICL*, 25–26 and 55–83.

12. *CIH* 593.30–31 = *Bürgschaft*, 11, §36.

13. *CIH* 592.26–29 = *Bürgschaft*, 9, §22.

14. Or perhaps even at the "command" of their superiors—the precise content of *forngaire* is unclear. McLeod regards it as a form of agency: *EICL*, 58–62.

15. *CIH* 593.35 = *Bürgschaft*, 11, §37. See also *CIH* 17.4–5 and 17.16–17; 45.17–18; *CIH* 491.32–35 = *C. Aicillne*, 376, §39; *CIH* 521.20–21; and 522.1–4.

16. *CIH* 1348.34–35 (where the time period is defined as a month) and 1351.35–36 (cf. 1961.23–25) = *EICL*, 124–125, §1, and 132–133, §7, respectively, with discussion on pp. 58–62; and see also *CIH* 521.20–21; and *GEIL*, 159, note 10, on *aititiu*, "acknowledgment."

17. *CIH* 592.26–31 = *Bürgschaft*, 9, §22.

18. *CIH* 491.12–15, 491.24–26 and 491.32–36 = *C. Aicillne*, 374–376, §§37–39, which also makes clear that if a contracting party refused to return the goods given to him by a legally incompetent individual, the goods were considered to have been stolen, and the recalcitrant was charged the penalty for theft.

19. In cases where a person was not inherently incompetent but had become so by virtue of shirking the responsibilities implicit in his status, a proclamation of incompetence would be issued by the kin. Contracting parties would be expected to be aware of this proclamation: see discussion below and *CIH* 491.13–15 = *C. Aicillne*, 374, §37.

20. *CIH* 2056.10–11. There is a play on words here: *enech*, "honor," is also the Old Irish word for "face," and both are obviously in question in this case. See also *CIH* 522.28–29, and discussion in *EICL*, chapter 2.

21. None of the couples discussed in *Cáin Lánamna*—a lord and his unfree client, a church and its unfree monastic tenant, a father and his daughter, a sister and her brother, a son and his mother, a fosterson and his fostermother, a teacher and his pupil, and a husband and his wife—involve persons of equal status within the relationship; they are all subordinating associations.

22. *CIH* 1780.9 = *C. Aicillne*, 342, §4; *CG* 85–86 and note on pp. 96–98. On base clientship see Nerys Patterson, "Material and Symbolic Exchange in Early Irish Clientship," *Proceedings of the Harvard Celtic Colloquium* 1, ed. Doan and Buttimer (Cambridge, Mass., 1981): 53–61; Marilyn Gerriets, "Economy and Society: Clientship according to the Irish Laws," *CMCS* 6 (Winter 1983): 43–61; and *GEIL*, 26–32.

23. *CIH* 498.1–5 and 499.20–21 = *C. Aicillne*, 387–388 and 390, §§53 and 56.

24. *CIH* 499.20–21, 499.25–29, 500.32–33, and 501.12–16 = *C. Aicillne*, 390–392, §§56–57 and §§59–60 respectively. This penalty was not exacted if the separation occurred because the client was too poor to maintain the food-renders required of him—a clear indication that clientship was not a purely economic relationship: *CIH* 501.25–27 and 502.3–4 = *C. Aicillne*, 392, §61.

25. *CIH* 220.4–7.

26. *DIL* s.v. *fognum* and *fo-gni*.

27. *CIH* 220.1–4.

28. For example, *CIH* 988.6–24 = *EICL*, §§53–54 (as McLeod's notes to these paragraphs make clear, *manach* must refer here to the ecclesiastical equivalent of the *fuidir* or *bothach*). It is possible, but unlikely, that the people called *dóer* in *CIH* 593.35 = *Bürgschaft*, II, §37, and in the triad reprinted by Binchy ("The Legal Capacity of Women," *SEIL*, 212, §5) are base clients. *Dóerchéile* is the Irish word for unfree client, but the adjective *dóer* can be used to describe any type of unfree person, including slaves, *bothaig*, *fuidri*, and *senchléithe*, and this is likely the type of person to which the passage refers: *GEIL*, 162.

29. *CIH* 493.31–33 and 494.17–19 = *C. Aicillne*, 381–382, §§44–45.

30. *CIH* 591.3–5.

31. *CIH* 1374.18–21. On *sochor*, see Rudolf Thurneysen, "Sochor," in *Féilsgríbhinn Eóin Mhic Néill*, ed. John Ryan (Dublin, 1940), 158–159; *GEIL*, 158–163; and *EICL*, 34–39.

32. Contracts of coercion, fear, or fraud are mentioned in the lawbooks as "rescindable" transactions (e.g., *CU*, 66–67, §5, gloss 1, with Binchy's note on 79–80), and it is only logical to assume that it would sometimes have been the individual's lord that stepped in to protect his client. Whether the lord could actually *annul* such disadvantageous transactions—as opposed to merely registering his disapproval of them (Ir. *fo-éigi*)—is unclear.

33. *EICL*, 71–80. Christopher McAll, "The Normal Paradigms of a Woman's Life in the Irish and Welsh Law Texts," *WLW*, 11–15, generally follows Binchy, and see also *GEIL*, 75–78. I also thank Nerys Patterson for sharing with me her insights on this issue.

34. *CIH* 443.29–32 = *Díre*, ed. by R. Thurneysen in *Irisches Recht, Abhandlungen der preussischen Akademie der Wissenschaften* 2, Phil.-Hist. Klasse, Jahrgang 1931 (Berlin, 1931): 35–36, §38. Binchy cites other similar passages in "The Legal Capacity of Women," *SEIL*, 211–215.

35. *CIH* 507.16–18 = *C. Lánamna*, 27, §8; and *CIH* 505.35–506.26 = *C. Lánamna*, 18–19, §5. For the composer of *Cáin Lánamna*, this type of relationship was clearly the norm: Binchy: "The Legal Capacity of Women," *SEIL*, 224–228; and McAll, "The Normal Paradigms of a Woman's Life," *WLW*, 11–15.

36. *CIH* 515.23 = *C. Lánamna*, 57, §29; and see Binchy, "The Legal Capacity of Women," *SEIL*, 226–227; and *CIH* 426.35–427.6 and 427.17–18 (translated by Binchy in *SEIL*, 215). The verb used here to describe the authorization given by the wife to her husband's contracts is *for-congair*, from which the noun *forngaire* is derived.

37. *CIH* 536.23–24; *CIH* 29.9–13; 522.1–4; 593.24–40 = *Bürgschaft*, 11, §§35–37; and passages A 3, 4, and 5 in Binchy's "The Legal Capacity of Women," *SEIL*, 211–212. See also discussion in *GEIL*, 80–81, and *EICL*, 62–71.

38. This is the age given in *Críth Gablach* (*CG* 30–34) and in *Berrad Airechta* (*CIH* 591.35–36 = *Bürgschaft*, 7, §10), but *Bretha Crólige* puts the age at seventeen (*CIH* 2288.6–8 = *Br. Crólige*, 8–9, §7), as does the commentary to the tract on fosterage, *Cáin Íarraith* (*CIH* 1766.17–18). *Cáin Íarraith* itself also implies that seventeen was the proper age: *CIH* 1768.32 and 1769.1–2. See *GEIL*, 86–90.

39. *CG* 23–46; 63–86; and discussion, pp. 89–90; *GEIL*, 82; and Neil McLeod: "The Two *Fer Midboth* and their Evidence in Court," *Ériu* 33 (1982): 61–63.

40. *CG* 67–70.

41. These filial duties are known as *goire*, literally "warming," but are usually translated as *pietas: CG*, p. 98 and, for another view of the origin of the word itself, Warren Cowgill, "The Etymology of Irish *guidid* and the Outcome of *g^wh in Celtic," in *Lautgeschichte und Etymologie*, ed. Mayrhofer, Peters, and Pfeiffer (Wiesbaden, 1980), 62–63. Some idea of the responsibilities involved in the maintenance of aged parents can be obtained from the story of Librán told in *Adomnan's Life of Columba*, Book II, Chapter 39.

42. *Críth Gablach* does allow one of its *fir midboth* to take on a very small fief: *CG* 71.

43. *CIH* 593.32–34 = *Bürgschaft*, 11, §36; *CIH* 2040.33–34; and see also 2325.18–20.

44. McLeod argues that father and son formed a legal couple (*lánamain*) even after the son's economic "emancipation": *EICL*, 62–71.

45. *CIH* 45.17–46.18; and see also *CIH* 2193.5–6 = *GC*, 311, §7; and *CIH* 536.1–3.

46. If the father had proclaimed him to the community as being *ingor*, "impious": *CIH* 536.12–15; and 593.27–29 = *Bürgschaft*, 11, §36.

47. *CIH* 536.1–15; 227.7–10; and cf. 593.27–29 and 593.32–34 = *Bürgschaft*, II, §36. One heptad permits an "emancipated" son to make even disadvantageous contracts to the amount of his honor price without fear of intervention from his father, except for secular or monastic clientship, or anything that defiles his kindred's land: *CIH* 2040.33–34.

48. This is also true both of the relationship between husband and wife, where the only contract one can make without the other's authority is one that profits the joint household (*CIH* 506.1 = *C. Lánamna*, 18–19, §5), and of the relationship between kindreds and secular and ecclesiastical lords and their subordinates (*CIH* 1374.18–21).

49. *GEIL*, 12–16, 100–105, and 159–163; *EICL*, 80–87.

50. *CIH* 488.25–26 = *C. Aicillne*, 369, §§30–31.

51. *CIH* 247.24–25. *Cáin Aicillne* links this privilege directly to the fact that kinsmen are responsible for liabilities incurred by one another: *CIH* 489.8–27 = *C. Aicillne*, 370–371, §§32–33.

52. *CIH* 222.6; 222.20–21; 247.24–25; 459.1–3 = *CU*, 64–67, §§4–6; and *CIH* 534.20–21. Even if a man brought additional property into the kindred he was required to leave a certain percentage of this acquired wealth to the kindred, and was not, therefore, completely free in his bequests: *CIH* 532.28–30 and 533.17–20. A man who substantially diminished the kindred's holdings was not capable of making any bequest at all: *CIH* 532.20.

53. *CIH* 491.12–15 = *C. Aicillne*, 374–375, §37; *CIH* 459.1–3 = *CU*, 64–67, §4.

54. *CIH* 492.11–12 and 492.33–36 = *C. Aicillne*, 377–378, §§40–41.

55. *CIH* 488.25–26 = *C. Aicillne*, 369, §30.

56. *CIH* 229.9; 489.16–27 and 490.16–19 = *C. Aicillne*, 370–371, §33, and 373, §35; and see *CIH* 2195.19–20 = *GC*, 331, §23, on lords or kindred leaders deemed to be *anfoltach* toward their subordinates, that is, disqualified by virtue of not having fulfilled their obligations to them.

57. *CIH* 490.30–34 = *C. Aicillne*, 373–374, §36; *CIH* 521.20–21; and 492.34–36 = *C. Aicillne*, 378, §41.

58. *CIH* 459.12–14 = *CU*, 66–67, §6.

59. *CIH* 488.34–35 = *Cáin Aicillne*, 369, §31; and see also *CIH* 222.6; 222.20; 443.10–11; and *DIL* s.v. *forglid, forglide*.

60. For example, *Córus Béscnai: forngaire cach natmaithi*, "everything acknowledged is authorized" (*CIH* 522.16). Compare also *CIH* 924.30–31 with *CIH* 459.13 = *CU*, 66–67, §6.

61. A condensed version of the foregoing argument, together with a discussion of parallel perceptions in Anglo-Saxon law, can be found in Stacey, "Law and Order in the *Very* Old West," 46–48 particularly.

62. *CIH* 227.29.

63. *CIH* 524.11–12; 524.22–25; and 525.1. The mutual obligations of ecclesiastical and lay grades are set out more fully in *CIH* 529.20–26 and 530.32–532.12.

64. In this case, the *aire coisring*, or kindred leader: see *CG* 277–294, and Stacey, "Ties that Bind," 59. The *Heptads* also speak of a gage given by the kindred leader (*CIH* 32.4 and 33.30–32), and *Córus Béscnai* mentions a gage given to guarantee church dues, although here the gage is given by a lord (*flaith*) on behalf of

both his kindred and his unfree clients (*aicillne*): *CIH* 526.20–21. Kings similarly pledged intertribal obligations on their tribe(s): *CIH* 526.20–23; *CG* 514–524, and cf. *CIH* 914.9–10 on the *muire* of the kindred.

65. A person giving shelter to a proclaimed son became liable for any crime he might commit, but lost his entitlement to any legacies left by, or legal fines due to, that individual. The same penalties were incurred by a man who protected his unlawful kinsman against legitimate legal claims: *CIH* 2123.30–2124.7.

66. *CIH* 592.22–25 = *Bürgschaft*, 9, §21; *CIH* 1007.35–37.

67. For example, *CIH* 223.30 and 225.4.

68. *CIH* 594.10–12 = *Bürgschaft*, 12, §41; and *CG* 26; 43; 128; 137; 165; 207; 264; and 295 (including ranks likely included only for the sake of schematization).

69. For example, *CIH* 214.11–12, and see *ECI*, 61–64.

70. *CIH* 592.32–36 = *Bürgschaft*, 9, §§23–24.

71. *CG* 339–340 and 411–413; and *CIH* 488.25–26, and 489.8–9 = C. Aicillne, 369, §30, and 370, §32.

72. *CIH* 898.16 = Binchy, "A Text on the Forms of Distraint," 80–81, §9.

73. The *fine derb ocus inderb*, "close and remote kindred," enforce this payment (called here the *slabrae mnaí*): *CIH* 592.32–33 = *Bürgschaft*, 9, §23; and cf. *CIH* 795.25–31; and 443.21–25, esp. gloss 2.

74. The most detailed explication of kindred liability in criminal matters is to be found in the late tract *Do breitheamhnus forna huile chin doní gach cintach*, on which see *GEIL*, 273, §40. See also on this topic: *CIH* 1711.34–35; 411.22–23; 489.25 = C. Aicillne, 370–371, §33; Binchy, "Distraint in Irish Law," 33, and 45–47; and *GEIL*, 12–15.

75. W. Davies, "People and Places in Dispute," *SD*, 77; W. Davies, "Suretyship in the *Cartulaire de Redon*," *LAL*, 83.

76. *CIH* 459.12–14 = *CU*, 66–67, §6.

77. *CIH* 594.33–34 = *Bürgschaft*, 14, §47.

78. *CIH* 489.25–27 = C. Aicillne, 370–371, §33.

79. *CIH* 61.9–10 and 790.4, with gloss on 906.28–29. The gloss calls him a *ráth forsaidi fine*, "a standing *ráth*-surety of the kindred"; that he had never been specifically appointed as surety is to be inferred from the fact that his compensation had not been bound by the contracting parties (the binding of compensation being part of the ritual by which the surety himself was appointed). See *GEIL*, 169, note 89.

80. However, they were not responsible for fines or penalties that the lord had, through his own negligence, failed to collect from their dead relative: *CIH* 486.31–33; 487.4–7; and 487.16–19 = C. Aicillne, 364–366, §§24–26.

81. The *aire coisring* was responsible for some of the public debts incurred by his relations; indeed, some commentaries refer to his duties as a *ráth*ship (e.g. *CIH* 708.12–16 and 1231.18–21). The *Heptads* make it clear that both suretyships operated through gages, although the amount of compensation due the kindred *ráth* differed from that assigned the *aire coisring* (at least in *CG*): *CIH* 61.10–11; 62.29–34; and *CG* 284–294.

82. Much of what follows has been reprinted from Stacey, "Ties That Bind."

83. *CIH* 591.9–11 = *Bürgschaft*, 6, §1.

84. *CIH* 591.9–592.21 = *Bürgschaft*, 6–8, §§1–20; 593.22–23 = *Bürgschaft*, 11, §34.

85. The syntax is ambiguous, and both meanings are possible: *CU*, 80.

86. *CIH* 24.11–25.5; and *CIH* 459.12–460.2 = *CU*, 66–69, §§6–7. Item eight in the *CU* heptad, "a thing for which the men of heaven and the gospel of Christ are invoked [as sureties]" (Binchy's translation), is probably an addition to the original group that does not in fact fit the category. Transactions of the sort to which this passage refers do involve guarantors, albeit guarantors of a spiritual and intangible nature. See *CU*, 80–81, and Chapter 8 below.

87. *CIH* 902.15.

88. *CIH* 753.34–754.5. This is clearly the original intent of the passage, but the version which appears in H 3. 17 has mistaken its meaning; land use there is not to be bound *without mac* or *ráth* sureties: *CIH* 1961.31–32.

89. *ruidles donach tacoir nai[dm] na rrath oca ruidhilsiguth*: *CIH* 591.9–11 = *Bürgschaft*, 6, §1.

90. *CIH* 591.25–27 = *Bürgschaft*, 7, §6. *Bretha Nemed* mentions also that misdeeds could deprive churches of their standing in law and of their right to keep offerings made to them: *CIH* 2211.27–2212.3.

91. *CIH* 591.27–29 = *Bürgschaft*, 7, §7; and see also *CIH* 2192.20–21 = *GC*, 309–310, §4.

92. *CIH* 592.10–12 = *Bürgschaft*, 8, §13.

93. *CIH* 592.12–13 = *Bürgschaft*, 8, §14.

94. Incomplete or insufficient *folad*, "considerations," were, as mentioned in Chapter 2 above, grounds for the emendation or cancellation of a contract unless the injured party had known in advance that what he was receiving was worth less than what he was giving. These calculations are worked out in detail in *EICL*, chapter 2, and see also *CIH* 986.31–33; 599.15–16 = *Bürgschaft*, 29–30, §78; and, on the renegotiation process, *CIH* 593.8–21 = *Bürgschaft*, 10–11, §§28–33.

95. Even according to *Di Astud Chor*, the entitlement established by unwarranted promises, while lesser than that established by an exchange of sureties, was not actually "immune" to challenge: see Chapter 2 above.

96. *CIH* 24.11; and compare *CIH* 459.23–25 with 459.11–14 (= *CU*, 66–69, §7, with §§5 and 6 of that same text).

97. *CIH* 591.9–10 = *Bürgschaft*, 6, §1. *Ro* is the intensifying particle here—hence "*entirely* immune from claim."

98. Binchy calls them "irretrievably alienated" in his notes to *CU*, 80.

99. *CIH* 591.15–17 = *Bürgschaft*, 6, §2; and *CIH* 592.13–15 = *Bürgschaft*, 8, §16. Only if a lord knew that the food-rent being paid to him had been stolen would the goods be considered retrievable by the rightful owner. (The provision on theft is attached to only two of the immunities mentioned in the text, but the phrasing of the passage might suggest that it applied to the rest as well.) For *ruidles* in non-contractual contexts, see *BB*, 84–85, §49 and note to *óenruidles* on 158.

100. *CIH* 25.13–14 and 987.15.

101. McLeod points to the important role played by status in some of these exchanges (*EICL*, 38–39, and see also *GEIL*, 162–163). McLeod also argues (pp. 18–21) that the fact that sureties do not participate in service contracts can be under-

stood by reference to modern law, in which courts refuse to adjudicate contracts involving them in "the constant supervision of the level of performance." That modern courts are reluctant to supervise such arrangements does not, however, explain why medieval guarantors living in close proximity to the parties involved would have been similarly hesitant. The restrictions placed on the immunity of these transactions suggest that some assessment of the quality of the work performed was not only possible but expected. Despite my reservations about this particular argument, I am grateful to Neil McLeod for a very fruitful exchange of views in correspondence.

102. *CU*, 80.

103. *CIH* 595.2–596.2 = *Bürgschaft*, 15–18, §§51–57; and 598.16–599.14 = *Bürgschaft*, 26–29, §§74–77.

104. *CIH* 675.13–17.

105. *CIH* 595.31 = *Bürgschaft*, 18, §55; and 598.24 and 34 = *Bürgschaft*, 27–28, §§74c and 76a respectively.

106. *CG* 277–294. Lines 293–294 imply that the *aire coisring*'s gage was a standing gage—a gage that would normally have been kept in a receptacle in the *aire coisring*'s custody, though it would not have been usable by him: see Stacey, "Ties That Bind," 59, Appendix III.

107. *CG*, p. 70, and see also *GEIL*, 48.

108. Conrad Arensberg, *The Irish Countryman* (New York, 1950), 168–176; and C. Arensberg and S. T. Kimball, *Family and Community in Ireland* (reprinted Gloucester, Mass., 1961), 295–297 and 313–314. Peter Brown documents similar sentiments in the Syrian villages of late antiquity: Brown, *Society and the Holy*, 128–129. Both the general concept of debt as social bond and the Irish example are discussed by Gluckman in *Barotse Jurisprudence*, pp. 265–266.

109. *CIH* 595.23–28 = *Bürgschaft*, 17, §53. If both fail to appear, the year is split in two between them, and the debt falls due again in six months: *CIH* 595.29 = *Bürgschaft*, 17–18, §54.

110. *CIH* 529.20–26 and 530.32–532.11. The terminology used in these passages is exactly that of contractual law: see, for example, *dliged túaithe i neclais* (529.20), and *coir ecalsa ó túaith* (530.32).

111. "*Dál Caladbuig* and Reciprocal Services between the Kings of Cashel and Various Munster States," ed. J. G. O'Keeffe, in *Irish Texts*, ed. J. Fraser and others, 5 vols. (London, 1931–1933), I, 19–21. Note especially the terms *dliged*, *frithfolaid*, and the terminology of clientship: *rath* and *athchor*. For the modeling of political relationships between tribes on the institutions of base and free clientship see Marilyn Gerriets, "Kingship and Exchange in Pre-Viking Ireland," *CMCS* 13 (Summer 1987): 39–72.

112. Some of what follows is reprinted from Stacey, "Law and Order in the *Very* Old West," 48–49.

Chapter 4. The Hostage-Sureties of Irish Law

1. *Remains of Old Latin*, ed. E. H. Warmington, 4 vols., (Cambridge, Mass., 1935–1940), vol. 3, 424–515, Table 3. Table 3.6 is open to many different

interpretations. Ancient commentators interpreted it quite literally as meaning that creditors were allowed to cut the defaulting debtor to pieces in the market square; however, as W. W. Buckland points out, there is no record of this ever having actually been done: *Text-Book of Roman Law*, 619–620.

2. *Bürgschaft*, 61–83, especially 82–83. For more recent discussions, both of which draw heavily on Thurneysen's study, see *GEIL*, 172–176, and *EICL*, 17.

3. *Bürgschaft*, 77, and 82 on *gíall*-sureties being held only by kings. *GEIL*, 278–279 outlines the texts relevant to hostage suretyship.

4. *Bürgschaft*, 67–68, 82–83. The differences outlined above are significant and implicit in Thurneysen's discussion of both guarantors, but they do not form part of the list given on 82–83 (summarized in *GEIL*, 175).

5. Binchy, "Celtic Suretyship," 363; and see *CG*, pp. 74–75, 95–96.

6. *Bürgschaft*, 83; *GEIL*, 175; and see the ninth-century gloss in H 3. 18 (also included in the H 3. 17 version of the tract): *CIH* 901.17–18, and 1756.18–20. At the "standard" rate of exchange, one *cumal* was equal to three cows: *CG*, pp. 81–82, and 105–106; *GEIL*, xxiii.

7. Although he did raise the question of why the first sentence of the hostage-surety tract referred to political affairs when the rest of the tract, in his opinion, obviously did not: *Bürgschaft*, 76–77.

8. D. A. Binchy, "Bergin's Law," *Studia Celtica* 14/15 (1979–1980): 41. The manuscript in question is H 3. 17: *CIH* 1755.17–1759.5 (*GEIL*, 279, §65).

9. *CIH* 901.14–33.

10. *CIH* 901.22.

11. *CIH* 901.14–15; and see *Bürgschaft*, 82–83.

12. *CA*, 32–33, §51. *Slán nAitire Cairde* was edited by Thurneysen in *Bürgschaft*, 32–33 (*GEIL*, 279, §63).

13. See *CIH* 1517.23–24; 1416.38–40; and compare also "Advice to a Prince," ed. Tadhg O'Donoghue, *Ériu* 9 (1921–1923): 45, §3, with *CIH* 219.5.

14. On the grammar of this provision, see David Greene, "Archaic Irish," in *Indogermanisch und Keltisch*, ed. Karl Horst Schmidt (Wiesbaden, 1977), 25; Binchy, "Bergin's Law," 41; and cf. *BDC*, 36–37, §23.

15. *CIH* 901.29–30, but cf. 1757.27–28.

16. *Bürgschaft*, 76–77, 79–82; *CIH* 901.14–15.

17. So argues Binchy, "Celtic Suretyship," 363, although he also adds the *aitire*'s honor-price (see also *GEIL*, 173). Thurneysen was less certain about the addition of the honor-price, since none of the sources actually mention it, but he did remark that since the *ráth*-surety received his honor-price if he had had to pay, the mention of the *aitire*'s honor-price might have simply been omitted from *Berrad Airechta* by mistake: *Bürgschaft*, 70. *Slán nAitire Cairde* and *Cáin Domnaig* (*CD*, 166–167, §6, lines 55–56) make it sound as though the *aitire* would receive double of everything that he had paid, including the ransom fee, although this seems a very high amount. *Berrad Airechta* does not double the ransom fee, though it does grant the *aitire* an unspecified amount for his activity: *CIH* 597.26–28 = *Bürgschaft*, 24–25, §67.

18. See *Bürgschaft*, 61–63; Thurneysen, "Nachträge zur Bürgschaft," 379–382; *CD*, 162–163, §2, lines 25–26; and *CD*, 166–167, §6, lines 56–58.

19. *CD*, 162–163, §2, lines 25–26; and see also *CIH* 914.8–12 on the *muire*

fine, the "*muire* of the kindred" and his responsibilities in *cáin* law. On *cánai*, see CG, p. 79; GEIL, 21–22; and discussion below.

20. CIH 965.9–10.

21. See above, Chapter 3. Base clientship was, as has been noted, a tributary relationship in that it depressed the status of the client since his lord acquired the right to share in compensation due to him for certain injuries. "Base" or "unfree" clients were not, however, "unfree" in the sense of being unable to own property or to move from the land on which they were settled: CG, pp. 96–98; GEIL, 29–32; and Gerriets, "Economy and Society."

22. CG 585–586 (the translation is Binchy's); and see discussion on pp. 38 and 96.

23. CIH 214.13 and 214.25–26; 919.2–4.

24. For example, *Bürgschaft*, 67.

25. *Bürgschaft*, 61–74.

26. Binchy, "Celtic Suretyship," 364–366. I am not convinced by this argument. It is likely that the payment of the debt was an important part of the *aitire*'s suretyship even in the period in which the archaic portions of the text were composed, since the *aitire* committed himself through his oath to "payment," and it is more likely that this refers to payment of the debt than to the ransom fee. See also the old quotation in CIH 1371.6–7.

27. For example, CIH 23.10; and 591.10; 594.5; 596.9; and 596.35 = *Bürgschaft*, 6, §1; 12, §39; 19, §59; and 21–22, §63, respectively. See also Binchy, "Celtic Suretyship," 360.

28. CIH 901.3–7, and see also the especially obscure passage from *Bretha Nemed* on CIH 2227.20–28, where the reference to "three plains" may suggest that the claim here is an intertribal one. If this is right, the *naidm* in question may be the *muiredach* mentioned in *Slán nAitire Cairde* as an intertribal enforcer, since the word *naidm* can be used to refer to anyone involved in enforcing any type of claim. The *aitire* himself is said to undertake a *tulnaidm túath* when enforcing an intertribal claim (CIH 597.14–15 = *Bürgschaft*, 22–23, §65c), and this may be the situation referred to in CIH 594.15–16 = *Bürgschaft*, 13, §42.

Another example is CIH 594.35–37 = *Bürgschaft*, 14–15, §48. The situation is the following: the *naidm* has not been able to compel the debtor to pay the debt, either because he has simply refused to pay or because he has obtained sanctuary. The text now instructs the plaintiff to go "to the *ráth* or the *aitire* if they are behind [the debtor's] back." This passage would thus appear to associate the *aitire* with the *naidm* in much the same way it associates the *ráth* with the *naidm*. But there is nothing in this text that requires us to read it in the context of a private debt and to conclude that the *aitire* must therefore have acted in contractual transactions in the way that a *ráth* would have done. The *aitire* was, like the *ceilebrath*, "celebrating," and the *gell*, "gage," mentioned in the following line, only one of several methods of guaranteeing that payments arising from any type of obligation would be made. When the compiler returns to the strictly contractual context within which he had been working, he repeats the sentence with reference to the *ráth*, but omits any mention of the *aitire*.

29. CIH 596.9; 596.30; 596.35; and 596.38 = *Bürgschaft*, 19–20, §59; 21, §62; and 21–22, §63.

30. Binchy, "Celtic Suretyship," 358.
31. See above, Chapter 2.
32. MS: *Tossimmuirtes acirt*. See *Bürgschaft*, 22, §65a, note 2, and Thurneysen, "Nachträge zur Bürgschaft," 398.
33. MS: *cia sa cia dama ndiul co scor*. Thurneysen's emendation is not necessary if one assumes that the identity of the person who will pay the debts or fines is not yet known: *Bürgschaft*, 22–23, §65a, note 4, and Stacey, "*Berrad Airechta*," *LAL*, 232, note 81.
34. MS: *fond tocerthar*. See *Bürgschaft*, 22, §65b.
35. MS: *notgeibhid*, with deletion mark under the *d*.
36. MS: *aiter*.
37. *CIH* 597.6–25 = *Bürgschaft*, 22–24, §65.
38. Thurneysen's suggestion: *Bürgschaft*, 23, §65a, note 2.
39. Thurneysen translated this "milking" as *Einstehen*, "standing-in-for," and understood it to refer to the surety's "being milked for" (paying the debt for) the defaulting debtor. In other texts the word has the meaning of "surrogate debtor, kinsman debtor," as in the text on distraint: Binchy, "Distraint in Irish Law," 33. If this is the meaning intended by *Berrad Airechta*, Binchy must be wrong in his suggestion that the *aitire*'s duty to pay was a secondary development, since the word is found here in the archaic stratum of the tract. It is possible, however, that the word here has reference to the *aitire*'s duty to enforce the claim—the verb *in-omblig* has the meaning of "levies, mulcts, exacts," and it is used once elsewhere in the tract in the active voice: *CIH* 599.9 = *Bürgschaft*, 28–29, §76d; and see Stacey, "*Berrad Airechta*," *LAL*, 232–233, notes 80 and 93.
40. See note 28 above, on the *tulnaidm túath*. Thurneysen changes this to a singular noun, "tribe": *Bürgschaft*, 24, §65c, note 2.
41. See *Bürgschaft*, 24, §65e, note 1.
42. See *CIH* 595.2–3 and 595.4–6 = *Bürgschaft*, 15–16, §51; *CIH* 598.22–23 = *Bürgschaft*, 27–28, §74c; and *CIH* 598.35–37 = *Bürgschaft*, 28–29, §76b.
43. The text refers directly to several "legal meetings": *CIH* 597.14 = *Bürgschaft*, 22–23, §65c.
44. *Bürgschaft*, 35.
45. *CIH* 892.39–40 = *Bürgschaft*, 32, §1 (although cf. *CIH* 717.20–21). The king of a subordinate tribe pledged his consent to a *cairde* by giving a gage on behalf of his own tribe to the superior king: *CG* 505–508.
46. Both manuscripts say clearly that it is the *muiredach aili*, the "other *muiredach*," who enforces the claim. It is unclear, however, whether these *muiredaig* were officers appointed specifically to enforce the *cairde*, or whether they should be understood as people within the kindred or tribe of the victim who would normally enforce claims on behalf of their subordinates. One of the two manuscripts has *muirethaig cairdi*, the "*muiredaig* of the *cairde*," which would support the first hypothesis, but the other manuscript omits *cairdi* altogether: *CIH* 574.18–19 vs. 892.39–40 = *Bürgschaft*, 32, §1.
47. Later glosses and commentaries usually put it at ten days: *Bürgschaft*, 63–65; Binchy, "Celtic Suretyship," 363; *GEIL*, 173; and *EICL*, 17.
48. *GEIL*, 173, says that it is to the plaintiff and not to the *aitire* that the

doubling of the debt is paid. *Slán nAitire Cairde* suggests the opposite, however: *CIH* 893.9–10 = *Bürgschaft*, 33, §3; *CG*, p. 75; and note 53 below.

49. By the payment of his own honor-price: *CG*, p. 75; and *CIH* 1268.3–5.

50. MS: *mech-sin*.

51. *CIH* 919.6–8.

52. Or "kindred member"; *fine* can refer to either.

53. For example, *meth*, "failure to provide food-rent" (and hence secondarily "penalty paid for same"); *athchor*, "unpenalized return of a fief to a lord"; and *rath*, "fief." On *meth* as a "doubling fine" see *CIH* 914.35.

54. This is how I interpret the final sentence of the passage. It is also possible that this sentence means only to stress that the *rath* given to an *aitire chairdi* as part of his compensation was not the same as the *rath* given by a lord to his client in clientship. If this is correct, however, no clue is provided here as to the nature of the difference between these two types of *rath*.

55. See the similar provision in *Berrad Airechta*, where a horse loaned by a father to a fosterfather to help him teach his fosterling how to ride must be returned if the boy is returned. If the horse is not returned, it becomes a *rath* on the fosterfather: *CIH* 591.36–37 = *Bürgschaft*, 7–8, §10.

56. The fief of an unfree client could also be returned at any time, but the client was liable in such cases to a financial penalty. Such a separation in unfree clientship was called *scarad* and is described in *C. Aicillne*, 383–393, §§48–61. On the *athchor* of free clientship, see *Cáin Sóerraith*, 246–248, §5 and notes.

57. MS: *dau*.

58. MS: *id*.

59. *CIH* 919.40–920.2.

60. Literally the "second," or "heir" of a king: *CG* 434–435 and pp. 107–108; Binchy, "Some Celtic Legal Terms"; Gearóid Mac Niocaill, "The "Heir-Designate" in Early Medieval Ireland," *The Irish Jurist* 3 (1968): 326–329; T. M. Charles-Edwards, "The Heir-Apparent in Irish and Welsh Law," *Celtica* 9 (1971): 180–190; and Donnchadh Ó Corráin, "Irish Regnal Succession: A Reappraisal," *Studia Hibernica* 11 (1971): 7–39.

61. Thurneysen, "Nachträge zur Bürgschaft," 381–382.

62. *CA*, 32, §53. *CIH* 789.12 glosses *aitire* with *aire désa*. McLeod suggests that *aitiri* would have been used in contracts where the parties involved were of such high status that they could not have been bound in any other way, an idea that accords well with the evidence cited above regarding the *aitire*'s own high standing: *EICL*, 17, and see also the poem by Blathmac mac Con Brettan (mid-eighth century) in which the narrator volunteers to stand as *aitire* on behalf of the Virgin Mary: *Medieval Irish Lyrics, Selected and Translated with The Irish Bardic Poet*, ed. James Carney (first published separately Dublin, 1967; new edition in one volume, Dublin, 1985), poem VII, 18–19. As will shortly become evident, I also think status to be a key element in distinguishing the *aitire* from the *gíall*.

63. *CGH*, 147–152, Rawlinson B.502 142a 15–142b 30; "A Poem on the Airgialla," ed. Máirín Ó Daly, *Ériu* 16 (1952): 179–188; *Irish Kings*, 72–74, 81, 115–117, and 219–220; and Gerriets, "Kingship and Exchange," 40–43, 47–48, and 50.

64. *CG* 359; "A Poem on the Airgialla," 180, §16; and 184, §§46–47. *Ráth*-sureties are mentioned on 182, §29, but they seem there to be the specific guarantors for the hosting itself.

65. "A Poem on the Airgialla," 188, notes 9–13; and *Irish Kings*, 116. A "sept" is a particular lineage, real or constructed, within a tribe.

66. *CIH* 597.29 = *Bürgschaft*, 24–25, §67.

67. *CG* 505–508, assuming that the term *rechtgae* refers to a *cáin*; see discussion below and *GEIL*, 21–22.

68. It is therefore significant that many of the kings and ecclesiastical princes whose names are appended to *CA* hold the status of *tánaise*: Máirín Ní Dhonnchadha, "The Guarantor List of *Cáin Adomnáin*, 697," *Peritia* 1 (1982): 178–215. I am most grateful to Máirín Ní Dhonnchadha for many helpful conversations on *CA*.

69. Also extant is *Cáin Fhuithirbe*, on which see Breatnach in *Peritia* 5 (1986): 36–52; and the *Ríagail Phátraic*, which is not the same ordinance mentioned as *Cáin Phátraic* in the *Annals of Tigernach* for 737 (edited Whitley Stokes, *RC* 16–18 [1895–1897]): see *GEIL*, 281–282, §75. *Cáin Éimíne Báin*, edited by Erich Poppe in *Celtica* 18 (1986): 35–52, and discussed by him in "The List of Sureties in *Cáin Éimíne*," *Celtica* 21 (1990): 588–592, may incorporate an old legal core and witness list, as Poppe suggests (pp. 588 and 592). In genre, however, it is much more reminiscent of a hagiographical charter preface than of an actual *cáin*, and indeed the title *cáin* is applied to it in only one manuscript ("A New Edition of *Cáin Éimíne Báin*," 35–36; "The List of Sureties in *Cáin Éimíne*," 588). Most recently on *cánai*, see Pádraig O Riain, "A Misunderstood Annal: A Hitherto Unnoticed *Cáin*," *Celtica* 21 (1990): 561–566.

70. EJ; *CD*, 152–158; Dorothy Whitelock, "Bishop Ecgred, Pehtred and Niall," in *Ireland in Early Medieval Europe*, 57–66.

71. Ní Dhonnchadha, "Guarantor List of *Cáin Adomnáin*," 179. *CA* is mentioned by name in *CG* 524, which Binchy has dated to the opening years of the eighth century. John Ryan discusses the original focus of *CA* in *SEIL*, 269–276.

72. *CA*, 32–33, §53. "Noble lords" (*ardflaith*) and "chief churches" (*primé-clais*) were also required to appoint *aitiri*.

73. Called "identifiers" (*nech ad-fíri*) in *CD* (e.g. 162–163, §2, lines 21, 25, and 27–28), and probably to be identified with the "person who strips [the offender]" mentioned in EJ, 206–207, §27.

74. *CD*, 162–163, §2, lines 25–26; *CA*, 30, §48; EJ, 208–211, §§29 and 33.

75. The passage in which these *fir thobaig* appear (*CD*, 162–163, §2, lines 26–28) can be interpreted in at least two different ways: (1) everyone in a tribe is expected to help the main witness in his prosecution of the claim, unless specific leviers (*fir thobaig*, perhaps the same thing as *rechtairi*) have been appointed to this task by the tribe; or (2) everyone who sees an offense must identify and levy the claim together with the *rechtaire* (the "person who sues and who acts as identifer") unless people have been appointed specifically from each kindred to levy any claim identified by a member of their kindred. If there are such *fir thobaig*, they would presumably be expected to work together with the original identifier and with the *rechtaire* to prosecute the claim.

76. *EJ*, 210–211, §33. Compare the division of fines outlined here with that of *CD*, 162–163, §2, lines 25–26.

77. *CD*, 162–165, §§2–3. The offender is also stripped of his apparel and belongings: compare *CD*, 162–163, §2, lines 19–20, with *EJ*, 204–209, §§23–24, 27, and 29. *CA*, 26–27, §37, remarks that its judges are to be chosen by the "community of Adamnán," in other words, by Iona, the church under whose authority the law was issued.

78. *CD*, 166–167, §6, lines 59–60. Note the four men as enforcers; five men are mentioned in *CG* 358–361, and see *CA*, 30, §48, which suggests that this figure is to be understood as the number of men legally entitled to maintenance while involved in the enforcement of a claim.

79. *CD*, 164–167, §§4–5, lines 38–46; and compare *CA*, 26–27, §38.

80. *CD*, 162–163, §2, lines 25–26, and 166–167, §6, line 55. The fact that the word *aitire* is here put in the plural is not necessarily significant, since the offender is also referred to in the plural: e.g. *CD*, 164–165, §4, line 40; and 166–167, §6, line 55.

81. Thurneysen explained this gage as one the *aitire* had given earlier on behalf of the debtor for the fulfillment of the obligation: *Bürgschaft*, 72. However, *CD* says clearly that the *aitire* is to "pledge" only *after* the debtor has evaded, and this suggests that the gage in question is the ransom gage. If this is correct, the *aitire* here would appear to have a claim to twice the ransom fee in compensation (or, alternatively, to twice the amount he lost by having the gage in the other's possession).

82. *CD*, 166–167, §6, lines 57–58. On enforcement by "cross," see below, Chapter 8.

83. See *CG* 52–62, although this passage could refer to a *cairde* or a *cáin* as well as to a general wounding within a tribe. Most tracts on sick-maintenance mention only gages (*CG*, p. 26, note 59; and Binchy, "Sick-Maintenance in Irish Law," 104), but the *aitire* is also mentioned in connection with a case of *cró*, "wounding" or "killing," in *CIH* 2227.20–28. McLeod suggests that *aitiri* might have been invoked in cases where physical retribution would likely be taken if the contract was broken, although since the breaking of any contract might result in violence, this distinction seems less helpful than his remarks on the high status of the participants (*EICL*, 17).

84. *CIH* 597.16–17 = *Bürgschaft*, 22–23, §65d; *CIH* 2202.3 = *CCF*, 23, §19.

85. *CIH* 593.8–23 = *Bürgschaft*, 10–11, §§28–34; and see Chapter 5 below.

86. *GOI* §262.4; and see *CIH* 522.34, for example.

87. *CG*, p. 80.

88. Gerriets also reaches this conclusion, although she seems more hesitant about it: "Kingship and Exchange," 42–43.

89. "A Poem on the Airgialla," §§23–24; 19 and 28; and 10 and 13, respectively.

90. Printed along with a short tract on the Dál Caladbuig in "Dál Caladbuig and Reciprocal Services," (here abbreviated FF and DC according to the conventions established by Gerriets in "Kingship and Exchange"). See on these tracts *Irish Kings*, 196–199; Liam Ó Buachalla, "Contributions towards the Political His-

tory of Munster, 450–800 A.D.," *Journal of the Cork Historical and Archaeological Society* 56, part 1 (1951): 87–90; 57, part 1 (1952): 67–86; 59 (1954): 111–126; and 61, part 1 (1956): 89–102; and Gerriets, "Kingship and Exchange," 40–42, and 49–52.

91. FF, 21, §18.

92. FF, 20, §9; 21, §17; and 21, §18, respectively.

93. *Irish Kings*, 43–46, and 196–199; and see Gerriets, "Kingship and Exchange," for an extended discussion.

94. *Aithech* is used in *CG* for "commoner": *CG*, p. 74. See also Gerriets, "Kingship and Exchange," 44–52.

95. On free clientship, see *Ireland Before the Normans*, 43; *ECI*, 50; *CG*, p. 107; and *GEIL*, 32–33. Gerriets comes to a somewhat different conclusion about the Airgialla poem specifically, which she regards as describing a relationship of base, rather than free, clientship—although she acknowledges that the two are not always easy to distinguish from one another ("Kingship and Exchange," 44–52, esp. pp. 47–50). Gerriets's principal arguments in favor of base clientship are (1) the use of the word *gialla*[*e*] in §23 of the poem; (2) the name of the Airgialla itself, which incorporates the verb *ar-gíall*[*n*]*a*, "submits by giving hostages to" or, possibly, "submits in base clientship"; and (3) (not cited by Gerriets but implicit in her argument) the use of the verb *bíathaid*, "feeds, provides food-rent for" in §20.

My own view is, however, that the prerogatives claimed by the Airgialla in this poem are more consistent with a relationship of free, rather than base clientship, and that the gist of the poem is, moreover, to claim for the Airgialla a privileged position vis-à-vis their overlords (and by implication, other, less high-status tribes subordinate to the Uí Néill). Not only is the term of military service envisaged in the poem very short and hedged about with exemptions in favor of the Airgialla (e.g. §§23–30, and 35–36), it is discernably military service also—not the manual agricultural labor associated with base clients. Moreover, while food-rent is mentioned in the poem, free clients also paid food-rent (indeed at a higher rate than did base clients), and the primary focus of the poem in any case is not food-rent but rather military service and "rising" (§13), which are the basic components of free clientship. Nor are the references to *gialla*[*e*] or to *ar-gíall*[*n*]*a* out of keeping with claims to a free clientship relationship, since both terms can be used broadly to refer to "clientship" without necessary reference to base or subordinate status. (Indeed, Gerriets herself prefers to translate *ar-gíalla* in this sense: p. 48.) Much more significant than the use of these general terms in the poem is the fact that the Airgialla claim the right to "joint-hostageship" (*comgíalla*[*e*]) with the Uí Néill—exactly the same privilege that is claimed with respect to the king of Cashel by the undoubtedly free Munster tribes: compare "A Poem on the Airgialla," §39, with FF, 21, §18, and see Gerriets on the Munster relationships on p. 49 of "Kingship and Exchange."

96. FF, 21, §18, and see note 53 above on *athchor*.

97. *CGH*, 358, LL 318c, 4–14.

98. They accomplish this by equating Barr m. Sárbile, a member of the royal Loíchsi line, with Barr m. Cáirthind, the reputed progenitor of the Síl mBairr. Unfortunately, it is impossible to know at what date this might have been done,

since the annals have no record of any of the individuals named in the Síl mBairr genealogies. Some of the genealogical texts try to smooth over the problem by asserting that Sárbile was "also called Mac-Cáirthind."

99. For example, *CIH* 526.22–23; 583.22; 1123.32–33; 2232.5–7; and *CG* 340 and cf. 342–343.

100. For example, *CIH* 477.14; 477.18; 713.2; 914.3–12; 1260.28; and DC, 19, §6. Gerriets argues in "Kingship and Exchange," 66–68, for a third category of political clientship, the tribal equivalent of extremely subordinate *fuidir* status (*sub censu*). As she notes, base and free client status could not be presumed by either side to be hereditary, in the sense that lords or kindreds wishing to continue the relationship after the death of the original client would have to make new contracts to this effect. *Fuidir* status, however, could be counted on much more readily by lords, since *fuidri* had limited economic resources and were unlikely to leave the land on which they had been settled. The presumption in the case of these extremely subordinate persons or tribes, in other words, would have been that the relationship would continue unless something unexpected occurred. If this is so, it would explain why in these cases a formal, periodic renewal of the relationship (*cáin* or *cairde*, as suggested below?) would not have been necessary.

101. Binchy suggests "tribute" as the earlier of the two meanings (*CG*, p. 79), but see M. A. O'Brien, "Etymologies and Notes," *Celtica* 3 (1956): 172, §7. GEIL offers both meanings: 305, and see p. 22. See also on *cánai* generally: Felim Ó Briain, "The Hagiography of Leinster," in *Féil-sgríbinn Eóin Mhic Néill*, 457–458; Kathleen Hughes, "The Church and the World in Early Christian Ireland," *IHS* 13, no. 50 (1962): 101–104; Thurneysen, "Nachträge zur Bürgschaft," 386–396; and *CCF*, 65–66.

102. *CU*, 68–69, §9; "rules" or "servitudes" is Binchy's translation.

103. *CIH* 440.16–17. The clients are "unfree," because the text refers specifically to their lord giving their honor-price to them.

104. The text is given by Kuno Meyer, "The Laud Genealogies and Tribal Histories," *ZCP* 8 (1912): 315–316; and see also *Irish Kings*, 216–220; Ó Buachalla, "Contributions towards the Political History of Munster," *JCHAS* 57 (1952): 78–81; and Gerriets, "Kingship and Exchange," 46–47. The tract is, as F. J. Byrne remarks, a "political manifesto" (*Irish Kings*, 219), and not an accurate reflection of what the Ciarraige could actually expect to achieve.

105. The Fothairt claimed descent from one Eochaid Finn Fuath nAirt, and they, like the Loíchsi, claimed to have been introduced into their lands as the mercenaries of the Laigin: *CGH*, 79–86, and see Alfred Smyth, *Celtic Leinster: Towards an Historical Geography of Early Irish Civilization* A.D. 500–1600 (Blackrock, County Dublin, 1982), esp. pp. 19 and 60.

106. The genealogies of the Loíchsi are found immediately following those of the Fothairt. The tract opens with the story of the origin of the name "Loíchsi" (*CGH*, 87, Rawl. B.502 126 b 13 ff.), and continues with several horizontal and vertical genealogies (*CGH*, 87–93) and brief prose passages explaining the political relationships between the seven Loíchsi tribes (*CGH*, 92–93). The Loíchsi origin legend follows these texts, on *CGH*, 94–95, and it is here that their relationship to the king of the Laigin is set out.

The early history of the Loíchsi is obscure. Adomnán mentions the Leinster bishop Columban moccu Loígse in Book III.12 of his life of Columba, and his use of the term *moccu* indicates that the Loíchsi were a tribe already at this date. Alfred Smyth suggests that the Loíchsi had been settled in Mag Réta by the Uí Failge to defend the ancient trackway *Slige Dála* against invasions from Ossory and from Munster, an idea that accords well with the Loíchsi origin legend and its memories of cross-border warfare. The Loíchsi may once have served the Uí Enechglaiss as well, at a point before the Uí Enechglaiss had been forced from their original lands onto the eastern seaboard (*Celtic Leinster*, 76–77). The Loíchsi do not become prominent in the annals until the late eighth century, when the death of a Mescill m. Mael-Aithcin, *rí Laíchse*, "king of the Loíchsi," is recorded in the Annals of Inisfallen for 799 (*The Annals of Inisfallen*, ed. Sean MacAirt [Dublin, 1951]). It is possible that Mescill's father was the same Mael-Aithcin whose death in 767 as the abbot of the important Leinster church of Clonenagh (situated in Loíchsi territory) is recorded by the Annals of the Four Masters (*Annála Rioghachta Éireann: Annals of the Kingdom of Ireland by the Four Masters, from the earliest period to the year 1616*, ed. J. O'Donovan, 7 vols. [Dublin, 1848–1851]).

It is clear, however, that the Loíchsi became important in the provincial politics of Leinster only in the mid-ninth century, when Gáethíne m. Cináed allied with the powerful king Cerball of Ossory (see *Fragmentary Annals of Ireland*, ed. Joan N. Radner [Dublin, 1978], esp. §387). From this point on, the obits of the Loíchsi kings and tanists are frequently recorded in the annals. By the eleventh century, the dominant Loíchsi family, the O'Mores, were slowly taking over lands that had formerly belonged to the Uí Bairrche and the Uí Buide, and they finally annexed these lands in the fourteenth century. A map done in the Tudor period shows at least thirteen Celtic lordships in the area associated with the Loíchsi (*Celtic Leinster*, 70, 105–106).

107. *CGH*, 93, Rawl. B.502 127 b 13 ff. Gerriets identifies many of these terms with base clientship or even lower status relationships: "Kingship and Exchange," 48–49, and see pp. 52–68 and 71–72.

108. *Lebor na hUidre, Book of the Dun Cow*, ed. R. I. Best and Osborn Bergin (Dublin, 1929), LU 52a 12–52b 4, lines 4206–4208.

109. "Le siège de Druim Damhghaire," ed. M. L. Sjoestedt, *RC* 43 (1926): 58–59, §58; see also 50–51, §51; 56–77, §57; and 114–115, §120. This is a late and literary piece and would not be in itself sufficient evidence to prove the point, but since it uses the term in a context verified by other more trustworthy sources, I include it here.

110. See *CIH* 219.5–6; *CGH*, 92, Rawl. B. 502 127 a 42 ff.; and *CGH*, 94, Rawl. B. 502 127 b 43–45; *Genealogical Tracts I*, ed. Toirdhealbhach Ó Raithbheartaigh (Dublin, 1932), 122; "Mitteilungen aus irischen Handschriften," ed. Kuno Meyer, *ZCP* 8 (1912): 108.

111. Liam Breatnach, "On Abstract Nouns from Prepositions in Irish," *Celtica* 15 (1983): 18.

112. *CIH* 901.14–15, and see *GEIL*, 173–175 for numerous other examples.

113. "A Poem on the Airgialla," §39; FF, 21, §18; and "The Laud Genealogies and Tribal Histories," 316.

114. *CIH* 219.5–6, and see also: *CIH* 1544.26–27 and 2231.40–41; *CGH*, 207, Rawl. B.502 149 b 27–29; *The O'Clery Book of Genealogies*, ed. Séamus Pender, *Analecta Hibernica* 18 (1951): 33, §441; "The Laud Genealogies and Tribal Histories," 316; and "Siège de Druim Damhghaire," 114–115, §120.

115. Thurneysen argued that the *gíall* had only to pay a portion of the ransom fine and could keep himself from captivity by giving a gage to the plaintiff: *Bürgschaft*, 83. The only evidence, however, for the *gíall* paying only a percentage of the fine comes from a late commentary, while Kelly cites evidence to suggest that the *gíall* could not free himself in such a manner: *GEIL*, 175, note 128.

116. Binchy, Kelly and McLeod accept the ten day period of the commentaries: *CG*, pp. 74–75; *GEIL*, 173; and *EICL*, 17.

117. This is clearly the case in the annals, and in most places where *gíall*-sureties are mentioned, including *CIH* 219.5; and *CG* 594–597.

118. *CG* 594–597; *CIH* 219.5 and 2231.40–41; and Kuno Meyer, "Uber die älteste irische Dichtung," *Abhandlungen der königlichen preussischen Akademie der Wissenschaften* 6 (1913): 41, §28.

119. *CIH* 412.13–15.

120. Binchy, "Distraint in Irish Law;" and *CG* 277–280, for example.

121. As did also the no longer extant text on *cairde* (*GEIL*, 279, §62): *CIH* 791.35.

122. Thurneysen's argument that *géill* were held only by kings is significant in this context: *Bürgschaft*, 82; and *GEIL*, 175.

123. Thurneysen viewed *géill* and *aitiri* as equal alternatives between which a person prosecuting a *cáin* could choose (*Bürgschaft*, 71–72 and 75, note 1, and see *GEIL*, 176), and indeed *géill* are mentioned as possible guarantors in both *CA* and *CD*. The reference in *CA* is very vague, however, and may imply that the *gíall* would have been used in exceptional circumstances only (*CA*, 32, §53), since all other *CA* passages (e.g. *CA*, 26, §39) stress that it is through *aitiri* that claims should be pursued. The *géill* in *CD* (166–167, §6, lines 56–58) appear to be "back-up" guarantors to be used only *after* the *aitire* had absconded, and this may be the situation envisaged in *CA* as well. The Middle Irish tract on *cró* and *díbad* mentions both, although since it dates to a period when the distinction between *aitiri* and *géill* was no longer clear, its evidence is difficult to use: *CIH* 601.7–11, and cf. 600.11–14.

124. *CG* 514–524. Some texts write *rechtgae ocus cairde* as if it were synonymous with the more common *cáin ocus cairde*: *CG* 341–343, and 505–508, although there are others where *cáin* and *rechtgae* are mentioned separately: e.g., *CIH* 428.33–35; 526.21–23; and 585.27. It is likely that *rechtgae* is, as Binchy says (*CG*, p. 104), a general term that can be used to describe several different types of law, including *cánai*.

125. *CA*, 30, §47; *CG* 524; and see Ó Corráin, "Nationality and Kingship," 22.

126. The Old Irish gloss in the H 3. 18 version of the hostage-surety tract mentions a "*rechtgae* [through which tribes are constrained]." But the gloss is seeking here to expand the abbreviation found in the original tract, *r-a*, which Binchy is surely correct in restoring as *rechta*, "men," rather than *rechtgae*: *CIH* 901.14.

127. Ó Briain cannot be correct in his view that the churches who subscribed to these *cánai* belonged to the *paruchia* of the sponsoring church ("The Hagiography of Leinster," 457), since CA was signed by the ecclesiastical leaders of Armagh, Kildare, Clonard, Clonmacnois, Emly, Bangor, and others. Ó Corráin places more stress than do I on the subordinating nature of these ecclesiastical *cánai*, although still less than does Ó Briain: "Nationality and Kingship," 22.

128. The *gíall* seems to have remained what he had been, while the purview of the *aitire* became much less certain (often he seems synonymous with the *gíall* in later texts). Thurneysen comments on the confusion in *Bürgschaft*, 34 and 73, and one can see it clearly in the annals, e.g., *AU*, 959 (*recte* 960); 1006 (1007); 1009 (1010); and so forth. Sometimes the *aitire* is equated with the *ráth*: *Bürgschaft*, 34 and 73; and cf. also *CIH* 2040.39 and 2103.13, where the two are discussed together.

129. Binchy, *Celtic and Anglo-Saxon Kingship*, 34–40; F. J. Byrne, *The Rise of the Uí Néill and the High-Kingship of Ireland* (Dublin, 1969); Byrne, "Tribes and Tribalism in Early Ireland," *Ériu* 22 (1971): 151–162; T. M. Charles-Edwards, "Some Celtic Kinship Terms," *BBCS* 24 (1970–1972): 117–122; and Ó Corráin, "Nationality and Kingship," 8–11.

130. Ó Corráin expresses skepticism about the extent to which the fiction of tribal non-interference was ever realized in practice: "Nationality and Kingship," 10.

131. To the extent, of course, that these privileges had ever existed in the first place. If Byrne (*Irish Kings*, 73) is right that Níall Noígíallach's epithet ("Níall of the nine hostages") derived from the hostages he received from the nine tribes of the Airgialla federation, the *cairde* claimed by the Airgialla may always have been more of a genealogical and political fiction than an accurate description of the power balance between the two groups.

132. *Irish Kings*, 114–125; *AU*, 878 (*recte* 879); and see also Ó Corráin, "Nationality and Kingship," 22–26. Similar types of changes can be documented in Anglo-Saxon society: James Campbell, "Bede's *Reges* and *Principes*," in Campbell, *Essays in Anglo-Saxon History*, 85–98.

133. "Tribes and Tribalism," 156–157. Charter IV of the charters in the Book of Kells mentions two very small tribal (and apparently geographical) groups that seem to have retained their royal status at least until 1020, the earliest date possible for the charter: "The Irish Charters in the Book of Kells," ed. J. O'Donovan, *Miscellany of the Irish Archaeological Society* 1 (1846): 127–158. Ó Corráin, "Nationality and Kingship," outlines these developments very clearly.

134. *CGH*, 138, Rawl. B.502 140 b 30 ff.

Chapter 5. The Road to Judgment

1. See discussion and references in Chapter 1 above.

2. Jacob Neusner, *Rabbinic Traditions About the Pharisees Before 70* (Leiden, 1971); Neusner, *Oral Tradition in Judaism: The Case of the Mishnah* (New York, 1987); Martin S. Jaffee, "From Literary Tradition to Oral Torah: The Effective-History of Halakhah in Tannaitic Sources," unpublished paper forthcoming from Mouton de Gruyter as "*Halakhah* in Early Rabbinic Judaism: Innovation Beyond Exegesis, Tradition Before Oral Torah," in *Innovation and Religious Traditions:*

Essays in the Interpretation of Religious Change, ed. C. Cox, M. Jaffee, and M. Williams; and Jaffee, "The *Taqqanah* in Tannaitic Literature: Jurisprudence and the Construction of Rabbinic Memory," *Journal of Jewish Studies* 41, no. 2 (Autumn 1990): 204–225. I am grateful to Martin Jaffee for making his paper on *Halakhah* available to me in advance of publication.

3. Peter Foote, "Oral and Literary Tradition in Early Scandinavian Law: Aspects of a Problem," in *Oral Tradition, Literary Tradition: A Symposium*, ed. Hans Bekker-Nielsen, Peter Foote, and A. Haarder (Odense, 1977), 47–55 (and see also pp. 116–117).

4. See discussion and references in Chapter 1.

5. It is also an issue on which considerable work has recently been done for the early Middle Ages: see the Introduction and Chapter 1 for references and discussion, and Anthony Harvey, "Early Literacy in Ireland: The Evidence from Ogam," *CMCS* 14 (Winter 1987): 1–15.

6. *CCF*. Other tracts containing information on procedure are listed in *GEIL*, 280–281, §§69–72.

7. Other texts mention specific categories of law by name, but only in *CCF*, *Uraicecht Becc* and *Berrad Airechta* do these groupings seem to have a procedural reality to them: compare with these *CIH* 2299.19–21 = *Br. Crólige*, 38–39, §47; and *AM*, 14–15, §51, for example.

8. As defined by Charles-Edwards, "The *Corpus Iuris Hibernici*," 146–147, who includes the RE recension of *CCF* in his list of *Fénechas*-style tracts: p. 154. There are significant differences between the R (Rawlinson B.502) and E (Egerton 88) versions. R is clearly the superior text: E either omits or rephrases several important (and, to judge by the language, old) clauses, including all of the stipulations on the bindings (*arach*) and the description of the types of suits appropriate to *coir n-athcomairc*.

9. *CIH* 2200.2–6 = *CCF*, 15, §2 (not in E); commentary on pp. 6 and 62, §2. Other clauses thought by Thurneysen to be later additions include *CIH* 2200.16–17 = *CCF*, 16, §3 (note on p. 8); and *CIH* 2201.31–32 = *CCF*, 21, §14 (note on p. 10).

10. Even R casts the passage in the "text script" that usually serves in the laws to distinguish the original text from commentaries and glosses made on it: *CIH* 2200.1–6.

11. A text of "intermediate" date, U, treats passages that appear in R and E as commentary as genuine text: compare, for example, *CIH* 2201.7–8 (R) with 2258.21–24 (U). H is a text of ca. eleventh-century date that mixes old and new with impunity.

12. *CIH* 2202.33–34 = *CCF*, 25, §27; and see *GEIL*, 280, §69.

13. *CIH* 2202.37–39 = *CCF*, 25, §28 (where it is attributed to the *Senchas Már*, the great legal collection of which *Di Chetharslicht Athgabála* formed a part), and cf. *CIH* 410.7–8. The clause is also cited earlier in *CCF*, where it is attached to the poem mentioned above (*CIH* 2202.10–11 = *CCF*, 23–24, §23). It is typical of the complexities of *CCF* that although *Di Chetharslicht Athgabála* is almost certainly later in composition than the earliest recension of *CCF* and cannot, therefore, be considered independent evidence for the existence of the paths, the

citation in question may well have originated there and been borrowed back by later jurists for inclusion in their commentaries on *CCF*.

14. *CIH* 2202.8–10 = *CCF*, 23–24, §23; and *CIH* 590.4–9.

15. *CIH* 2200.19 = *CCF*, 17, §4, and *CIH* 2201.4–5 = *CCF*, 18, §9; *CIH* 2200.1 = *CCF*, 15, §1; and *CIH* 2201.4–5 = *CCF*, 18, §9; and *CIH* 2200.11 = *CCF*, 16, §3; and *CIH* 2200.34 = *CCF*, 18, §8, respectively.

16. *CCF*, esp. pp. 5–6 and 11–12.

17. *CIH* 2200.1–6 = *CCF*, 15–16, §§1–2. The evidence is contradictory on this point. H 3. 18 (*CIH* 589.35–590.2) suggests that the paths were not in fact mutually exclusive of one another but could be manipulated by the lawyers involved in any way appropriate to their case. Thurneysen interprets *CCF* in accordance with this passage (pp. 11–13), but it may be significant that the H 3. 18 passage is primarily concerned with the activities of professional advocates (*aigne*), individuals whom Binchy argues developed historically later than the *fethemain* mentioned in the RE recension of *CCF* (*CIH* 2202.11 and 38, reading *fethemain* for *fechemain*; and Binchy, "*Féchem, Fethem, Aigne*," 22–24). In other words, the H 3. 18 passage may date to a period in time later than the situation envisaged in *CCF*. Alternatively, regional differences may account for the discrepancy.

18. See Chapter 7 below, and *LTMW*, 251–252, notes to 77.29–78.4.

19. *CIH* 2202.10–11 and 38–39 = *CCF*, 23–24, §23, and 25, §28; and *CIH* 410.7–8.

20. *CIH* 594.36–37 = *Bürgschaft*, 14–15, §48. On *celebrad*, "celebrating," see below, Chapter 8.

21. *CCF*, 8.

22. *CIH* 1591.13–14, together with 1591.20 and 1591.24, seem to envisage *fír* as a sort of catchall category for cases not pursued on *dliged* or *aicned*.

23. *CIH* 2200.11–17 = *CCF*, 16, §3. Thurneysen suggests that *fri ascnam ndibaid* and *fri dliged tuise* represent later additions: p. 8.

24. Thurneysen suggests that *fír* may have been added to ensure alliteration: *CCF*, 8.

25. *GEIL*, 208–213; Bartlett, *Trial by Fire and Water*, 5–6 and 48 on the Irish ordeal specifically. Thomas Charles-Edwards suggests to me that although *fír* is used commonly in its technical sense to refer to the ordeal (e.g., *fír fer, fír coiri, fír compertae noíbe*, ordeal by battle, cauldron, and holy judgment, respectively), the actual *meaning* of *fír*, even in these phrases, may be something closer to "proof," as in the phrase *fír noilled*, "proof by oath."

26. *SD*, 221–222.

27. *CIH* 2193.22–23 = *GC*, 316–317, §10.

28. *IK*, 112, XXXII.8 and 117, XXXII.23; *CIH* 1034.3–20 = *CCF*, 42–43, §§64–66.

29. *The Patrician Texts in the Book of Armagh*, ed. Ludwig Bieler, *Scriptores Latini Hiberniae* vol. 10 (Dublin, 1979), 148–149, §32.

30. *IK*, 76, XXV.2, and 131, XXXVII.1a; *CIH* 1289.7–9.

31. *CIH* 49.36–50.20.

32. *CIH* 2200.34–2201.5 = *CCF*, 18, §§8–9. This is how Thurneysen interprets the path in question: the issue to be resolved by the judge in such cases is, he

suggests, "is this a binding contract or not?" (*CCF*, 8–9). *Uraicecht Becc* also associates *dliged* with oral contracts (see below), but the commentaries accompanying *CCF* include under *dliged*'s purview many arrangements that specifically were not concluded in the presence of sureties, including several of the immunities discussed in Chapter 3: *CIH* 1281.12–25 = *CCF*, 18–19, §10, for example (and cf. *CIH* 2200.37–2201.3). In U, some of this commentary has made its way into text script: *CIH* 2258.21–24.

33. *CIH* 2201.9–20 = *CCF*, 19–20, §§11–12.

34. For example, *crece /for briathruib/ cundartha*, assuming that the interlinear gloss *for briathruib* is correct in its understanding of the original intent of the clause (*CIH* 2201.15–16 = *CCF*, 19, §11). Even if the gloss is incorrect, however, there is no reason to believe that *crece cundartha* was intended to refer specifically to non-contractual exchanges—indeed, the opposite holds true. As we have seen, purchases of this nature would normally have been concluded with all appropriate formalities, including sureties.

35. Charles-Edwards, "Early Irish Law," 31–32. Charles-Edwards is concerned primarily in his argument to demonstrate the possibility of a native, rather than a canonical, origin for the "dialectical" structure of *Di Astud Chor*. As he points out, the text is divided into two sections that seem to reproduce the division articulated in *Cóic Conara Fugill*, focusing as they do on the validity of the contract and the renegotiation of unfair exchanges respectively. Athough this is a possible explanation for the structure of *Di Astud Chor*, it is not the only one. The division between validity and fairness is not even held to consistently in the tract (see, for example, *CIH* 988.6–24 = *EICL*, 190–193, §§53–54), nor is the terminology employed similar to that used in other texts on the subject. Indeed, *Di Astud Chor* generally displays very little interest in procedural matters, either in its contents or terminology. The tract focuses rather on the reasoning according to which judges reach decisions about individual contracts or exchanges, and herein lies, I think, the most likely explanation for *Di Astud Chor*'s bipartite structure. Judges faced with the possibility of having to renegotiate particular arrangements would have first to determine their validity—the one was a logical first step for the other in judicial reasoning—and the progression visible in *Di Astud Chor* from validity to renegotiation simply reproduces this mental process. It is thus not necessary to resort either to the procedural categories articulated in *Cóic Conara Fugill* or to canonical example to understand the structure of the text. Just as *Berrad Airechta* reflects in its structure the stages involved in making and fulfilling a contract, so *Cóic Conara Fugill* reflects the stages of judicial reasoning through which contested contracts would ordinarily proceed.

36. And even here it would be difficult to argue that *fír* has in this text a specifically procedural meaning; it seems mainly, where it occurs, to refer to "truth" in its broadest sense of "natural justice": *CIH* 986.3; 986.37; 987.28; 987.37; and 993.29 = *EICL*, 170–171, §37; 178–179, §44; 186–187, §52; and 162–163, §29, respectively. Instances of *fírinne*, "truth," in the text include *CIH* 993.3 and 987.32–33 = *EICL*, 156–157, §26 and 188–189, §52. The word *cert* is used in the text, but in an entirely different (and distinctly non-curial) sense: *Imfuachar cert cidh iar nilbliadnaib*, "A right [to property which you have obtained unfairly] can be annulled

though it be after many years" (McLeod's translation: *EICL*, 174–175, §41 = *CIH* 986.24–25).

37. See discussion in Chapter 2 above; and *CIH* 591.9–592.21 and 593.22–23 = *Bürgschaft*, 6–8, §§1–20 and 11, §34; *CIH* 593.10–12 = *Bürgschaft*, 10, §29; *CIH* 593.18–21 and 599.15–20 = *Bürgschaft*, 11, §33, and 29–30, §§78–79; and *CIH* 594.1–7 = *Bürgschaft*, 12, §§38–39.

38. *CIH* 2201.4–5 = *CCF*, 18, §9. This sentence is preceded in R by *.i.*, the standard abbreviation for *id est*, the phrase commonly used in the law tracts to signal that what follows is a gloss rather than original text. It is extremely unlikely, however, that this sentence is a gloss; this is probably an error unique to R. Not only does R present the sentence in text script, the clause itself contains within it many of the linguistic features characteristic of the rest of the tract—such as alliteration and verb-final construction, including a possible example of Bergin's Law, reading *gaibther* with U: *CIH* 2258.18. Certainly Thurneysen believed it to be part of the original: *CCF*, 5.

39. *CIH* 593.20–21 = *Bürgschaft*, 11, §33.

40. *CIH* 2201.26–33 = *CCF*, 21–22, §§14–15. Roughly translated "cottiers," "tenants-at-will," and "hereditary serfs" respectively: see *GEIL*, 33–36. Two other types of people are mentioned in the text, the *aithech bunaid* and the *aithech cís*, the "commoner of origin" and the "commoner of tribute" (*CIH* 2201.31–32 = *CCF*, 21, §14). It is difficult to know what to make of these references. They would appear at first to be out of keeping with the others named, since the term *aithech* is usually used to designate base clients rather than those totally dependent in status. It is possible that these clauses represent additions made to the original text at a later stage: they do not appear in E, and Thurneysen believed this to be the explanation (*CCF*, 10). If they are original to the text, however, they ought probably to be understood as underscoring the point that *téchtae* embraces all totally dependent people, whether their status derives from their ancestry (*senchléithe*) or from their current liability to tribute (*bothaig, fuidri*).

41. The recensions disagree on this point. R says that claims *im bothus*, "concerning *bothach*-status," and *im fuidrius*, "concerning *fuidir*-status," are to be pursued on *téchtae* (*CIH* 2201.27–28 = *CCF*, 21, §14). All other recensions, however, including E, read *im bothach* and *im fuidir*, "concerning a person of *bothach*-status," and "concerning a person of *fuidir*-status": *CIH* 1281.40–41 (E); 2259.21–23 (U); and 1038.20–22 (H). R is our best text, so the issue is unlikely ever to be definitively resolved. Even R, however, continues its list with *im senchleithe*, "concerning a person of *senchleithe*-status" (*CIH* 2201.29).

42. *CCF*, 78, note 55; and cf. *CIH* 598.19 = *Bürgschaft*, 26–27, §74a.

43. *CCF*, 10.

44. *CIH* 428.11–12 = *Irisches Recht*, ed. R. Thurneysen, 65–66, §§7–8, and 77, note 3. Thurneysen argues (I think correctly) against connecting this path with the meaning *téchtae* often has in the legal tracts of dues owed to lords by their clients (*CCF*, 10). Later commentators, however, took a different view: *CIH* 2259.32–35 (U); and cf. recension H in *CCF*, 55–56, §127.

45. The severing of connections with one's kindred is given greater prominence in the tract: *CIH* 428.9 = *Irisches Recht*, 65, §7.

46. *CIH* 802.31–803.2; and see 2216.4–2217.2; Chapter 3 above; and *GEIL*, 169, note 89 on the *ráth forngartha fine*.

47. *GEIL*, 29–36; and "The *Senbríathra Fíthail* and Related Texts," ed. Roland Smith, *RC* 45 (1928): 31, §11.

48. The gloss ultimately offers both explanations: *CIH* 1038.24–25 = *CCF*, 53–54, §118.

49. Although some texts suggest that liability did not always transcend death: *CIH* 487.5–6.

50. *CIH* 599.4–9 = *Bürgschaft*, 28–29, §76d. The comparison is made most clearly in *CIH* 1030.23 = *CCF*, 33, §32. It may be in this manner that we should understand 2201.26–27 = *CCF*, 21, §14: *Techta do bithbunud biid*. *Bithbunad* must mean something like "perpetual origin or source"—in this context, perhaps "that which is eternally native to one by virtue of one's origins."

51. *CIH* 2201.38–2202.3 = *CCF*, 22–23, §§18–19.

52. *GEIL*, 192.

53. *CIH* 2202.10–11 and 37–39 = *CCF*, 23–24, §23, and 25, §28; and *CIH* 410.7–8.

54. For this view of the *aitire*'s office, see above, Chapter 4.

55. Joseph Falaky Nagy, "Talking With and About the Past," unpublished lecture given at the University of Washington in February of 1990. Nagy has written extensively about the issue of authority in medieval Irish narrative: "Close Encounters of the Traditional Kind in Medieval Irish Literature," in *Celtic Folklore and Christianity: Studies in Memory of William W. Heist*, ed. Patrick K. Ford (Santa Barbara and Los Angeles, 1983), 129–149; "Orality in Medieval Irish Narrative," *Oral Tradition* 1 (1986): 272–301; "Oral Life and Literary Death in Medieval Irish Tradition," *Oral Tradition* 3/3 (1988): 368–380; "Representations of Oral Tradition in Medieval Irish Literature," *Language and Communication* 9, no. 2/3 (1989): 143–158; "Sword as *Audacht*," in *Celtic Language, Celtic Culture: A Festschrift for Eric P. Hamp*, ed. A. T. E. Matonis and Daniel F. Melia (Van Nuys, Calif. 1990), 131–136; and "Hierarchy, Heroes, and Heads: Indo-European Structures in Greek Myth," in *Approaches to Greek Myth*, ed. Lowell Edmunds (Baltimore, 1990), 200–238. I am grateful to Joseph Nagy for generously sharing with me his considerable knowledge of this topic and for making available to me the text of his lecture and the manuscript of his forthcoming book on depictions of oral and written tradition in Irish literature. See also, on the prologue to the *Senchas Már*: McCone, "Dubthach Maccu Lugair," 5–28; and most recently John Carey, "The Two Laws in Dubthach's Judgment," *CMCS* 19 (Summer 1990): 1–18. An older view is that of Binchy, "The Pseudo-Historical Prologue to the *Senchas Már*," *Studia Celtica*, 10/11 (1975–1976): 15–28; and see also McLeod, "The Concept of Law in Ancient Irish Jurisprudence," 363–367.

56. The traditional view is that kings of the historical period were not involved in judging: Binchy, *Celtic and Anglo-Saxon Kingship*, 15–17; Mac Cana, "The Three Languages," 76–78; and Sharpe, "Dispute Settlement," *SD*, 186–187, note 83. Recent challenges to this view include: McLeod, "Parallel and Paradox," 36–39; Kelly, "An Old-Irish Text on Court Procedure," 80–81; Gerriets, "The King as Judge;" *GEIL*, 23–25; and *PPCP*, 85–86 and 126.

57. *SD*, 216–217.

58. *Saint Patrick. Confession et Lettre à Coroticus*, ed. Richard Hanson (Paris, 1978), 126–127, *Confessio* §53, and see also 124–125, *Confessio* §52, where Patrick distinguishes between kings and judges (Sharpe, "Dispute Settlement," *SD*, 186–187, note 83).

59. For example, *Br. Crólige*, 26–27, §33; *CD*, 162–165, §§1 and 3; *CIH* 1268.35–1269.20 (edited and discussed by Breatnach, "Lawyers in Early Ireland," 7–10); and see also *GEIL*, 51–56; and Gerriets, "The King as Judge," 45–52. The earliest annalistic references to *brithemain* date to the early ninth century: *GEIL*, 248–249.

60. *CIH* 2202.33–34 = *CCF*, 24–25, §27; Kelly, "An Old-Irish Text on Court Procedure," 77–82; and *GEIL*, 191–198.

61. Several texts stress the connection between judging and specialist training: for example, *CIH* 429.14–15; 432.22–23; 1377.37–41; 1612.23–26; *AM*, 8–9, §23; and the Middle Irish text known as *Urcuilte Bretheman* (*CIH* 2102.31–2103.32). Judges were paid by the parties in dispute: *CIH* 24.22.

62. Sharpe, "Dispute Settlement," *SD*, 180–187.

63. Sharpe, "Dispute Settlement," *SD*, 170–178.

64. *Br. Crólige*, 42–43, §54; 22–23, §27; 24–25, §31; and 46–47, §59. Binchy was uncertain of the identity of the *fiu-flaith fuissiten i feine fresndul*, the "worthy lord of acknowledgement (?) for attendance according to Irish law (?)" (*Br. Crólige*, 74–75, note 59), but it is probably the *aitire* to whom this passage refers. The *aitire* was, as we know from *CG*, the usual surety in cases of sick-maintenance, and his primary role was to accompany and protect the wounded individual on his way to the place of healing (*CG* 52, and cf. *CIH* 597.16–17 = *Bürgschaft*, 22–24, §65d). As Binchy points out, *foisitiu* can mean "protection"; protection and attendance are, in other words, the primary duties of the "worthy lord" of *Br. Crólige*, just as they are of the *aitire*. *Br. Crólige*'s circumlocution is almost certainly designed to render the passage alliterative: *flaith foridmbi, fiu-flaith fuissiten i feine fresndul, flatha fiadnaisi fri forgell*.

65. *CIH* 580.18–19; *BB*, 80–81, §45.

66. *CIH* 802.31–803.2; *CIH* 499.12–15 = *C. Aicillne*, 389, §55; and *CIH* 1969.26–27. See also *CIH* 635.32, and Gerriets, "The King as Judge," 37–38.

67. *CIH* 1613.22–26; *UR*, 23, lines 77–78.

68. *CIH* 1613.38–1614.4.

69. Sharpe and Kelly suggest that minor cases might have gone to the judge's house, whereas more important disputes would have been resolved at the *airecht*: Sharpe, "Dispute Settlement," *SD*, 185; *GEIL*, 192–193; and Kelly, "An Old-Irish Text on Court Procedure," 81–82, on open-air courts.

70. *Br. Crólige*, 24–25, §31, and note to §31 on pp. 63–64.

71. *CIH* 597.10 = *Bürgschaft*, 22–23, §65a.

72. *Confession et Lettre à Coroticus, Confessio*, 126–127, §53 (reading *iudicabant* with Hanson and Bieler). The word *iudex* does appear in a quotation elsewhere in the *Confessio: Confessio*, 74–75, §4.

73. Binchy, "Bretha Nemed," 5–6; Binchy, "The Date and Provenance of Uraicecht Becc," *Ériu* 18 (1958): 45; *GEIL*, 47–49; and Charles-Edwards, "Early Irish Law," 18–21. McCone takes a different view: *PPCP*, 85–86.

74. *GEIL*, 253, note 52, and on the schools themselves, 250–263.

75. According to Caesar, druids were involved in the resolution of individual disputes. Their authority was exercised, however, not through any recognizably judicial or curial procedure but through the performative and high-profile practice of banning individuals from public sacrifice. Given their religious obligations and high status, it seems likely that druids might have concerned themselves principally with cases of high visibility and importance, leaving the resolution of lesser matters to others.

76. See especially *CIH* 593.8–594.7 = *Bürgschaft*, 10–12, §§28–39.

77. *CIH* 1590.1–1591.31: "*dliged* is based in oral contracts and acknowledgement," "*aicned* is based in concession and proper arrangement (*for logud ocus cocorus*)," and "*fír* is based in legal verses and legal maxims and true testimonies."

78. Binchy, "*Bretha Nemed*," 5–6; and *GEIL*, 246; though see Charles-Edwards, "Early Irish Law," 15, especially note 62.

79. See Chapter 2 above, and Sharpe, "Dispute Settlement," 181, esp. note 50.

80. *CD*, 166–167, §6, line 59, implies the participation of the *aitire* in initial attempts at resolution.

81. *CIH* 592.40–593.2 = *Bürgschaft*, 10, §26.

82. *Patrician Texts in the Book of Armagh*, 148–149, §32.

83. Whitley Stokes, "The Irish Ordeals, Cormac's Adventure in the Land of Promise, and the Decision as to Cormac's Sword," in *Irische Texte*, ed. Stokes and Windisch, 3, pt. 1 (Leipzig, 1891), 183–229. Ordeals that do involve supervision of some kind include (by implication) the various collars of Morann (188–190, §§12–16); Sencha's lots (191, §18); Luchta's iron (192, §23); and "waiting at an altar" (192–193, §24). Ordeals in which clerics or druids do not seem to be involved include Mochta's adze (190, §17); the three dark stones (191, §20); and the cauldron of truth (191–192, §21).

84. *CIH* 2200.3–6 = *CCF*, 15, §2. This is not to dissent from Kelly's interpretation of this passage, namely, that the prohibition against litigants speaking too softly suggests the presence of large numbers of people in court ("An Old-Irish Text on Court Procedure," 81). It is, however, to point out that the primary intent of the passage is to assert the authority of the judge over the advocates and litigants appearing before him. The prohibition against speaking too loudly in court makes most sense in this context, and this is also the point of asserting the judge's right to fine advocates who attempt to change paths during the course of a suit.

85. For example, *Lex Alamannorum*, second edition by K. A. Eckhardt, *MGH, Legum* Sectio I, *Leges Nationum Germanicarum*, vol. 5, pt. 1 (Hannover, 1966), §81; and *Pactus Legis Salicae*, §60.

86. *Solam*, "speedy, ready, prompt;" *sonaisc*, "well-bound": *CIH* 2201.38–39 = *CCF*, 22, §18.

87. *CCF*, 10–11, and 79–80, note 62.

88. *Sonaisc* is from *naiscid*, "binds," and is most commonly associated with the *naidm*-surety, since *naidm* is the verbal noun of *naiscid*.

89. *CIH* 2202.10–11 and 38–39 = *CCF*, 23–24, §23, and 25, §28.

90. *CIH* 2201.38–2202.1 = *CCF*, 22, §18, accepting Thurneysen's emendation: *CCF*, 79–80, note 62 (MS: *acht ardloma deruisc*).

91. Or "after": *íar* can mean either.
92. *CIH* 1040.33–36 = *CCF*, 58–59, §138.
93. *CIH* 2201.4–5 = *CCF*, 18, §9.
94. For example, *CIH* 595.37–596.1 = *Bürgschaft*, 18, §57; *CIH* 598.16, 19, 22, 26, 31, 35, 38; 599.4; 599.10 = *Bürgschaft*, 26–28, §74 and 28–29, §76; *CIH* 596.9 = *Bürgschaft*, 19–20, §59; and *CIH* 24.11–12; 25.13–15; 1963.17, 20–21, and so on.

95. Assuming that *naidm* had already replaced *mac* by the time the text was written down, the term could have been inserted at that point into a previously orally transmitted original. If it was, however, the fact that the word *naidm* forms part of an alliterative phrase means that more than a simple substitution of one word for another was involved. The passage in question does contain a possible example of Bergin's Law, but Breatnach's work has shown that linguistic "archaisms" of this nature are not in themselves sufficient proof of a text's antiquity.

96. Sharpe, "Dispute Settlement," *SD*, 181.
97. *CIH* 593.8–23 = *Bürgschaft*, 10–11, §§28–34.
98. *CIH* 593.16–17 = *Bürgschaft*, 10, §32; Kelly, "An Old-Irish Text on Court Procedure," 86–87, §5. Sureties are assigned in the *Airecht* text to the "court apart," presumably so that neither they nor their testimony will be suborned or influenced by parties to the dispute.

99. See Chapter 6 below.
100. Kelly's translation: "An Old-Irish Text on Court Procedure," 85, §2; and *GEIL*, 193–195.
101. I am grateful to Patrick Wormald for this suggestion.
102. Charles-Edwards, "Early Irish Law," 19–20.
103. Bieler, *The Irish Penitentials*, 56–57, §21.
104. Charles-Edwards, "Early Irish Law," 19–20, and see extended comparison between the *CCH* and native law on pp. 28–33.
105. See on the lawbooks, Charles-Edwards, "Early Irish Law," 18–23, 28–33, and 37.
106. Reading *cid i naragar* with H 3. 18 (*CIH* 634.12) and Nat. Libr. of Ireland G 3 (*CIH* 2256.13). MacNeill's translation of the passage reflects (accurately, in my opinion) its deliberately jurisprudential significance: "Wherein is the Jurisprudence of the Language of the Féni found? Answer: In proof and right and nature" ("Ancient Irish Law: Law of Status or Franchise," 272, §V 2.-1).
107. *CIH* 2202.33–34 = *CCF*, 24–25, §27. This passage is presented in *CCF* as a quotation from a now lost text, *Aí Cermna*.
108. Dafydd Jenkins and Morfydd Owen, "The Welsh Marginalia in the Lichfield Gospels. Part I," *CMCS* 5 (Summer 1983): 37–66; and "Part II: The 'Surexit' Memorandum," in *CMCS* 7 (Summer 1984): 91–120, esp. pp. 99–101.
109. *AM*, xvii-xviii and 6–11, §§12–28; *GEIL*, 18–21.
110. *Téchtae* usually either refers to lordly dues or occurs in the stereotyped expression *cach techt*[*u*], "according to each propriety" meaning "according to law," or "according to whatever is due." See, for example, *CIH* 598.29 and 598.34 = *Bürgschaft*, 28, §§75 and 76a, respectively. An example of the manner in which many of these terms could be used without reference to specific procedures or institutions is *AM*, 14–15, §51.

111. McLeod: "The Concept of Law in Ancient Irish Jurisprudence," 359–360, 362–363, 367; *CIH* 209.12–23.

112. McLeod cites several examples from the tracts in "The Concept of Law in Ancient Irish Jurisprudence," 358–361. See also *GEIL*, 18–21, and *CIH* 1377.37–41.

113. The Pauline resonances of the term are particularly evident in the pseudo-historical prologue to the *Senchas Már*, where *recht n-aicnid* is contrasted with *recht litre*, the "law of Scripture." There have been many attempts in addition to McLeod's to interpret both this prologue and the concept of *recht n-aicnid* in general: see references above in note 55, and Ó Corráin, "Irish Vernacular Law and the Old Testament," 290–294.

114. The meaning and range of *aicned* continued to change in the centuries following the classical period of Old Irish law. In both recension H of *Cóic Conara Fugill* and in the Middle Irish text *Urcuilte Bretheman*, *aicned* is listed—together with *roscad*, "legal verse," *fásaige*, "legal maxims," testimony, and analogy—as one of the grounds on which judges could reach their verdicts: *CIH* 1040.37–39 = *CCF*, 59, §139; and *CIH* 2103.1–2. For discussion, see *GEIL*, 196–197.

115. This passage appears as commentary in the RE recension of *CCF* and in the H recension as part of the brief prologue with which that text begins: *CIH* 2202.12–17 = *CCF*, 23–24, §23 and *CCF*, 26, §1. The translation is Binchy's: "*Féchem, Fethem, Aigne*," 31.

116. Binchy, "*Féchem, Fethem, Aigne*," 25–26; and on the development of legal advocates see Breatnach, "Lawyers in Early Ireland," 10–13.

117. *CIH* 2102.31–2103.32.

118. This is surely the context into which the elegant philosophical musings of the Visigothic code fit most easily as does, for that matter, Alfred's prologue itself.

119. This is a sentiment voiced frequently in many excellent studies of early law. See, for example, *SD*, 212–213, 216–217, 222, and 225; Wormald, "*Lex Scripta* and *Verbum Regis*," 115; Bartlett, *Trial by Fire and Water*, 5–6, and 9; and Gagarin, *Early Greek Law*, 9–10, and 25, note 21.

Chapter 6. Court and Custom in Medieval Wales

1. Although Jane Stevenson suggests that the virtual (though not complete) absence of charter evidence from early Ireland is testimony to the amount of control secular lawyers retained over land and property transactions even after the arrival of the church: "Literacy in Ireland," *The Uses of Literacy*, 26–32.

2. The best short survey of these changes is Ó Corráin's "Nationality and Kingship."

3. A point made forcefully in Ó Corráin's "Law and Society," 234–236.

4. Binchy, "Celtic Suretyship," 366, note 16; Stacey, "The Archaic Core of Llyfr Iorwerth," *LAL*, 16–17.

5. New editions and translations of the suretyship tractates of Cyfn, Ior, and Latin E are available in *LAL*, 117–209, and editions and translations of the

Cyfn, Ior, and Latin A versions of the tractate on the law of women are available in *WLW*, 132–179. Because the paragraph and sentence numbers of the two Ior tractates as printed in *LAL* and *WLW* correspond to the paragraph and sentence numbers given in Wiliam's edition of *Llyfr Iorwerth* cited in the table of abbreviations, I have cited everything from Ior in the usual manner (e.g., *Ior* paragraph/sentence). The numbered sentences of the Cyfn and Latin A and E tractates as printed in *LAL* and *WLW* do not, however, correspond directly to the standard editions of those tractates, so I have provided references to both editions in my notes to those texts.

6. Ó Corráin, "Law and Society," 235.

7. Only rarely do the lawbooks speak of the *amodwr* in the singular: compare *Col* 132 with, for example, *Col* 133 and 136; *Ior* 69/1, 2, and 7; and *LAL*, 192–193 and 196–197, Cyfn 57 and 84 = *WML* 297.34–298.2 and *WML* 89.6–8 respectively.

8. Compare Binchy, "Celtic Suretyship," 360–363 and 365, and see discussion below.

9. See, for example, Charles-Edwards, "Nau Kynywedi Teithiauc," in *WLW*, 23–39; Stacey, "Ties That Bind," 50–57; and Stacey, "The Archaic Core of Llyfr Iorwerth," *LAL*, 15–46. A somewhat more liberal approach is outlined by Dafydd Walters in "The General Features of Archaic European Suretyship," *LAL*, 92–116; and in his *The Comparative Legal Method: Marriage, Divorce and the Spouses' Property Rights in Early Medieval European Law and Cyfraith Hywel*, Pamffledi Cyfraith Hywel (Aberystwyth, 1982).

10. See discussion below, and Stacey, "The Archaic Core of Llyfr Iorwerth," *LAL*, 21–31.

11. A good short survey of scholarship on the laws is Huw Pryce's "Medieval Welsh Law," *Newsletter of the School of Celtic Studies* 4 (December 1990): 30–34. On the multitude of laws in use in this period see R. R. Davies, "The Law of the March," *Welsh History Review* 5, no. 1 (June 1970): 1–30; R. R. Davies, *Lordship and Society in the March of Wales, 1282–1400* (Oxford, 1978); R. R. Davies, "Kings, Lords and Liberties in the March of Wales, 1066–1272," *TRHS* 5th series 29 (1979): 41–61; Dafydd Jenkins, "Kings, Lords and Princes: the Nomenclature of Authority in Thirteenth-Century Wales," *BBCS* 26 (1974–1976): 451–462; and J. Beverley Smith, "The Legal Position of Wales in the Middle Ages," in *Law-Making and Law-Makers in British History: Papers Presented to the Edinburgh Legal History Conference, 1977*, ed. Alan Harding (London, 1980), 21–53.

12. Charles-Edwards, *The Welsh Laws*, 10–13; Michael Richter, "The Political and Institutional Background to National Consciousness in Medieval Wales," in *Nationalism and the Pursuit of National Independence*, ed. T. W. Moody (Belfast, 1978), 37–55; R. R. Davies, "Law and National Identity in Thirteenth-Century Wales," in *Welsh Society and Nationhood*, ed. R. R. Davies, Ralph Griffiths, Ieuan Gwynedd Jones, and Kenneth Morgan (Cardiff, 1984), 51–69; and Huw Pryce, "The Prologues to the Welsh Lawbooks." This is not to say that individuals of a given nationality or political allegiance would invariably choose to settle disputes in which they became involved by their own law: see Chapter 7 below.

13. R. R. Davies, "The Law of the March," 1 and 11–12; R. R. Davies, "Law and National Identity," 63–69.

14. Pryce, "The Prologues to the Welsh Lawbooks," 152–165.

15. Particularly in the south, where landowner judges were the rule: R. R. Davies, "The Administration of Law," *LAL*, 261–264; and his *Conquest, Coexistence, and Change*, 131–135.

16. *Ynad llys*: "judge of a court."

17. T. Jones Pierce, "The Age of the Princes," and "The Law of Wales—the Last Phase," in *Medieval Welsh Society*, esp. 34–35 and 387–389; and R. R. Davies, *Conquest, Coexistence, and Change*, 135 and 260–261.

18. The appeal then went to *sapientes* convoked from surrounding provinces, one of whom at least was the redactor of a lawbook and a professional jurist: "Strata Marcella Documents," ed. J. Conway Davies, *Montgomeryshire Collections* 51 (1949–1950): 182–183; R. R. Davies, *Conquest, Coexistence, and Change*, 132–133 and 261; and Stephenson, *Thirteenth-Century Welsh Law Courts*, 10–14.

19. A characterization frequently applied to Welsh law: for example, *LAL*, 7; Charles-Edwards, *The Welsh Laws*, 85; and see also Dafydd Jenkins, "The Significance of the Law of Hywel," *Transactions of the Honourable Society of Cymmrodorion* (1977): 54–76.

20. R. R. Davies, "The Administration of Law," *LAL*, 259–261 and 267–268 (and see also pp. 6–7); most recent is Llinos B. Smith, "Disputes and Settlements in Medieval Wales: the Role of Arbitration," *EHR* 106, no. 421 (1991): 835–860.

21. R. R. Davies, "The Administration of Law," *LAL*, 258–259.

22. Compare *Ior* 58–61 with *LAL*, 184–185, Cyfn 1–4 = *WML* 85.4–17; and with *LTWL*, Lat A 125.34–36, 125.41–43; Lat B 217.1–3, 217.31–32, 217.34–218.2; Lat D 368.7–9, 369.1–5; Lat E 459.1–3, 459.24–35 = *LAL*, 202–205, Lat E 12–13, 20, 22–27; and *Bleg* 40.1–4, 41.9–15. On the narrative genre in question and its relationship to contemporary curial procedure, see Charles-Edwards, "The 'Iorwerth' Text," *LAL*, 164–168; Charles-Edwards, "*Cynghawsedd*: Counting and Pleading in Medieval Welsh Law," *BBCS* 33 (1986), 188–190; and Charles-Edwards, *The Welsh Laws*, 53–58.

23. Charles-Edwards, "*Cynghawsedd*: Counting and Pleading," 190 and 197. In *The Welsh Laws* (pp. 58–67), Charles-Edwards makes the point that the procedure outlined in these pleadings owes much to Roman example. For the contents and ordering of the *Llyfr Cynghawsedd* (and a transcript of the Peniarth 35 version), see A. R. Wiliam, "*Llyfr Cynghawsedd*," *BBCS* 35 (1988): 73–85.

24. Printed in Book VIII of Owen's *Ancient Laws of Wales*, and see also A. R. Wiliam's *Llyfr Cynog* (Pamffledi Cyfraith Hywel, Aberystwyth, 1990). Manuscript G (Peniarth 35) dates to the first half of the fourteenth century, and manuscript F (Peniarth 34) is probably fifteenth century: Charles-Edwards, *The Welsh Laws*, 100–102.

25. *ALW* VIII.viii and VIII.x; and for English law, see John Beckerman, "The 40-Shilling Jurisdictional Limit in Medieval English Personal Actions," in *Legal History Studies 1972: Papers Presented to the Legal History Conference, Aberystwyth, 18–21 July 1972*, ed. Dafydd Jenkins (Cardiff, 1975), 110–117.

26. *Councils and Ecclesiastical Documents relating to Great Britain and Ireland*, ed. A. W. Haddan and W. Stubbs, 3 vols. (Oxford, 1869–1878; reprinted, 1965), vol. 1, p. 515, §24; and see also Huw Pryce, "Duw yn Lle Mach: Briduw yng Nghy-

fraith Hywel," *LAL*, 68, note 78; and compare Llinos B. Smith, "The Gravamina of the Community of Gwynedd against Llywelyn ap Gruffydd," *BBCS* 31 (1984): 158–176.

27. *Briduw* will be discussed in Chapter 8, *gorfodog* in Chapter 7, and *amodwyr* below.

28. What follows summarizes in more abbreviated form the arguments made in Stacey, "The Archaic Core of Llyfr Iorwerth," *LAL*, 15–21.

29. The binding ritual is described in very sketchy terms in *Ior* 68/8; and *LTWL*, Lat B 216.26–27; Lat E 458.26–27 = *LAL*, 202–203, Lat E 6. *Bleg* 40.6–22, *LTWL*, Lat D 368.11–23, *DwCol* 462–468, and *ALW* X.vii.40–43 make it clear that it is not sufficient for the parties simply to extend their hands toward one another, or for the surety to act as a proxy for an absent debtor in conveying his faith to the creditor (although see *ALW* XII.ix, where the principal debtor does not seem to be present). Unless both parties are present, and unless contact is actually made, that part of the arrangement is deemed invalid. Even more precise is a plea extant in two fifteenth-century manuscripts (Q and K) in which the person to whom *briduw* has been given charges another with *sarhaed* ("insult") because the defendant, in giving his faith to the plaintiff, touched him on the shoulder or on the breast rather than joining hands with him: *ALW* VI.i.40. See also Daniel Melia's review of *LAL* in *Ius Commune, Zeitschrift für Europäische Rechtsgeschichte* 15 (1988): 293.

30. This special status is likely to be quite old, since the list of *tafodiogion* is found in Ior, Bleg, and the Latin lawbooks: *Ior* 56/5; *LTWL*, Lat A 124.18; Lat B 216.8; Lat D 367.4–5; Lat E 458.3; *Bleg* 38.18–20; and cf. *Ior* 61/5; *Col* 88; *LAL*, 196–197, Cyfn V 82 = *WML* 86.1–3; *LTWL*, Lat A 125.35–36; Lat B 217.2–3; Lat D 369.3–4; Lat E 459.3 = *LAL*, 202–203, Lat E 13; and *DwCol* 390, and 397.

31. *Ior* 62/5–6; *Col* 93. For a discussion of the textual difficulties attendant on this passage, see *Col*, pp. 59–60; *LTMW*, 248, note 68.33; and Charles-Edwards, "The 'Iorwerth' Text," *LAL*, 170–171.

32. The provision requiring a surety to enforce the claim against the debtor by taking distraint or a gage must be one of the oldest in the lawbooks, as it occurs in all three vernacular legal traditions. Furthermore, all redactions except Latin D and Bleg require the surety to "take the first blow" or "suffer the affliction that may come," stipulations that indicate that the *mach* might be expected to use, or to meet with, force in the course of his duties: *Ior* 62/3–4; *Col* 92; *LAL*, 184–185, Cyfn 8 = *WML* 85.23–86.1; *LTWL*, Lat A 125.16–18; Lat B 218.12–14; Lat E 460.3–5 = *LAL*, 204–205, Lat E 30–31; and cf. *LTWL*, Lat D 368.32–33; *Bleg* 41.1–3; and the triadic version in manuscript H (fourteenth century) in *ALW* XIV.xxii.8 and 10. There are a tremendous number of provisions governing the proper procedures to be followed in enforcing a claim. Charles-Edwards discusses the process itself, and the differences between the Welsh and Irish lawbooks on this subject, in his helpful notes to "The 'Iorwerth' Text," *LAL*, 169–171.

33. For example, *Col* 101; *LTWL*, Lat A 125.31–32; Lat B 218.8–9; Lat D 368.30–31; Lat E 459.12–13; *Bleg* 40.29–41.1; and *DwCol* 407.

34. *Ior* 67/2 and cf. 63/1.

35. See references in note 29 above.

36. *Ior* paragraphs 58–59, especially 58/8 and 59/1–4; *Col* 74–84; *LAL*, 190–191, Cyfn W 37–47 = *WML* 296.9–297.23; *LTWL*, Lat B 217.34–37; Lat E 459.27–31 = *LAL*, 204–205, Lat E 22–24.

37. Charles-Edwards, "The 'Iorwerth' Text," *LAL*, 169.

38. *LAL*, 184–185, Cyfn 4 = *WML* 85.12–17; *LTWL*, Lat B 217.31–32; Lat D 368.7–9; Lat E 459.24–25 = *LAL*, 204–205, Lat E 20; *Bleg* 40.1–4.

39. *Ior* 66/6–7; Stacey, "The Archaic Core of Llyfr Iorwerth," *LAL*, 21–23 and p. 40, note 52; Huw Pryce, "Early Irish Canons and Medieval Welsh Law," 108–117, especially p. 115.

40. This is phrased as a privilege claimed by the "progeny of St. Cadog," but even so is a good illustration of the principle that high status entails an even greater degree of responsible behavior within the community than is expected of men of lower status: *Vitae Sanctorum Britanniae et Genealogiae*, ed. A. W. Wade-Evans (Cardiff, 1944), 138–140.

41. For example, *ALW* XIV.xxix.3.

42. *LAL*, 196–197, Cyfn Mk 86; *LTWL*, Lat A 125.31–33; Lat B 218.8–9; Lat D 368.30–31; Lat E 459.12–14; *Bleg* 40.29–41.1.

43. See Chapter 3 above, and Stacey, "Ties that Bind," 50–57.

44. Charles-Edwards, "The 'Iorwerth' Text," *LAL*, 168–169. There is some evidence to suggest that a provision on the denial of suretyship formed part of the prototractate from which our present Ior and Cyfn tractates were penned: Stacey, "The Archaic Core of Llyfr Iorwerth," *LAL*, 31–37. I am less certain now than I once was about the ordering of the contents of this early tractate, given that Cyfn manuscripts X and Z are structured differently from V, Mk, and W. Manuscripts X and Z may well represent, as Morfydd Owen suggests in her notes to the Cyfn text, early versions of the Cyfn tractate (*LAL*, 180), and if so, Mk/V and W (following Mk/V?) must have reordered their material according to the Ior model. Alternatively, Mk, V, and W may indeed reflect, as I suggested, a skeletal tractate visible also in Ior, and X and Z (fourteenth and sixteenth century, respectively) imperfect versions of the Cyfn text. In either case, it is likely that some form of prototractate lies behind the extant Ior and Cyfn versions, since Ior and most Cyfn manuscripts, including X, contain the same basic material (outlined on pp. 32–33 of *LAL*). Manuscript Z is missing a few provisions, but all versions include the denial procedure, which may suggest that this provision predates the main period of the composition of the lawbooks.

45. The following paragraph summarizes, in somewhat more abbreviated form, the argument made in Stacey, "The Archaic Core of Llyfr Iorwerth," *LAL*, 27–31.

46. *Ior* 59/5, 60/5–6, 62/3–4, 62/10–11; *Col* 82–83, and 97; *LAL*, 184–185, Cyfn 8 = *WML* 85.23–86.1; *LTWL*, Lat A 125.16–18; Lat B 218.12–14; Lat D 368.32–33; Lat E 460.3–5 = *LAL*, 204–205, Lat E 30–31; *Bleg* 41.1–3.

47. *Ior* 64/1–3; *Col* 103; and see *LAL*, 190–191, Cyfn 31–35 = *WML* 295.12–296.6.

48. *LTWL*, Lat B 254.34–38; Lat E 460.28–35 = *LAL*, 204–207, Lat E 43–45.

49. R. R. Davies outlines these changes in *Conquest, Coexistence, and Change*, 139–171.

50. Jenkins, *Cyfraith Hywel*, 49–52; *LTMW*, 261–262; and T. M. Charles-Edwards, "Boundaries in Irish Law."

51. *LAL*, 184–185, Cyfn 4 = *WML* 85.12–17. Contrast with this provision that found in Bleg and certain manuscripts of Latin E that also requires sureties to be consulted on the taking of distraint, but which makes no mention of a fine to the lord: *Bleg* 40.1–4; *LTWL*, Lat E2 and E4 459, note 12—12 = *LAL*, 204–205, Lat E 20.

52. *Ior* 60/4; and cf. *LAL*, 194–195, Cyfn 69–70 = *WML* 108.20–109.5.

53. *Ior* 65/3–6; *Col* 112.

54. The term *arglwydd* can be used to refer to either territorial rulers or personal seigneurs: see Jenkins, "Kings, Lords, and Princes." Ior particularly seems to have the territorial ruler more in mind throughout its tractate, and this is how I have generally interpreted the term. It is possible, however, that certain provisions have more immediate reference to personal lords, although of course territorial rulers also would presumably lay claim to the prerogatives mentioned in those provisions. (The triad on immunities, for example, may well include both, given that Cyfn W uses *brenhin* here, and the Latin texts *rex*: *WML* 134.15–20; *LTWL*, Lat A 128.35–37; Lat B 243.36–39; Lat E 460.18–21 = *LAL*, 204–207, Lat E 39–40.)

55. *Ior* 66/1–4; *Col* 114–115; *ALW* X.vii.24.

56. *Ior* 63/3; *Col* 102; *LAL*, 184–185, Cyfn 7 = *WML* 85.20–23; *LTWL*, Lat A 125.19–21; Lat B 218.10–11; Lat D 368.28–29; Lat E 460.1–2 = *LAL*, 204–205, Lat E 29; *Bleg* 40.26–28.

57. Indeed, this is the *only* immunity that appears in all versions of the triad. See references in note 54 above, and: *LAL*, 184–185, Cyfn 9 = *WML* 86.11–13; *WML* 132.22 to bottom of the page; *LTWL*, Lat D 374.33–35; *Bleg* 117.7–10; *DwCol* 303; and *ALW* X.vii.48.

58. *ALW* VIII.i.8, and see also *ALW* VIII.iii.6.

59. *Ior* 62/1–6; *Col* 92–93; *LAL*, 184–187, Cyfn 4, 8, and 20 = *WML* 85.12–17, 85.23–86.1, and 87.12–13 respectively; *LTWL*, Lat A 125.6–7 and 125.16–18; Lat B 216.28–29 and 218.12–14; Lat D 368.32–34 and 369.29–31; Lat E 458.29–30, E2 and E4 459, note 12—12, and 460.3–5 = *LAL*, 202–205, Lat E 8, 20, and 30–31; *Bleg* 40.1–4 and 41.1–4.

60. See references in note 38 above.

61. *DwCol* 344; *ALW* V.ii.66; and Peniarth 35, f. 24v.

62. There are two provisions extant in the Cyfn, Bleg, and Latin traditions relevant to this issue, both of which show evidence of a textual confusion that may reflect changes in practice. The first is a triad on the three ways in which a surety may be released from his office. According to Lat B, Lat D, and some manuscripts of Lat E, distraint taken by a claimant *sine negatione* automatically frees a *mach* from his obligations; according to Cyfn, Bleg, and Lat E2 and E4, however, distraint taken *sine deliberatione fideiussoris* (Cyfn and Bleg: *heb ganhat y mach*) will free him: *LTWL*, Lat B 217.31–32; Lat D 368.7–9; Lat E 459.24–25; *LAL*, 184–185, Cyfn 4 = *WML* 85.12–17; *Bleg* 40.1–4; *LTWL*, Lat E 459, note 12—12 = *LAL*, 204–205, Lat E 20. The second provision is one that occurs only in texts of the Bleg and Latin traditions. Lat A imposes a fine of 3 cows to the lord for distraint taken *sine licentia*. In Lat B, Lat D, Lat E, and Bleg, *sine licentia* has become

inconsulta dominicali potentia (Bleg: *heb ganhat arglwydiaeth*): *LTWL*, Lat A 124.39–125.2; Lat B 216.30–32; Lat D 368.3–4; Lat E 458.28–29 = *LAL*, 202–203, Lat E 7; *Bleg* 39.29–30. Ior may also reflect a transitional period: the general presumption underlying paragraph 62 is the supremacy of the *mach* in matters of enforcement, but compare with this *Ior* 62/12–13, 63/3, and 66/1–4.

63. *Ior* 64/8–9 and 66/3–4; *Col* 106; *LAL*, 194–195, Cyfn 73 (and see note on p. 175) = *WML* 88.16–17.

64. *ALW* XIV.xv.18.

65. *ALW* X.v.9 and XIV.xxv.4.

66. *ALW* X.v.7–9; Charles-Edwards, "*Cynghawsedd*: Counting and Pleading," 188–196; and *The Welsh Laws*, 54–67.

67. *ALW* XIV.xli.12.

68. *BB*, Appendix 7, p. 204, and see Chapter 8 below.

69. *Ior* 66/6 and cf. *ALW* XIV.xxii.7–11. The presumption of a commoner *mach* may also be behind manuscript H's encouragement to *mach*-sureties to "take the first three blows" in the course of enforcing the claim—but then to bring a plaint for *sarhaed*, "insult," to the lord: *ALW* XIV.xxii.10.

70. *Ior* 56/5.

71. *DwCol* 402–403; *LAL*, 206–207, Lat E 50 = *LTWL*, Lat E 461.12–17.

72. *ALW* VI.i.65, though cf. VIII.xi.28.

73. *ALW* V.ii.63; Peniarth 35, f. 24r; and cf. *LAL*, 206–207, Lat E 51 = *LTWL*, Lat E 461.18–22.

74. *ALW* VIII.xi.29; *DwCol* 404–405; and *ALW* V.ii.68.

75. *LAL*, 196–197, Cyfn V 83 = *WML* 86.3–11; and *Bleg* 126.5–13, which has *mach kynnogyn* instead of Cyfn's *mach talu*.

76. Jones Pierce, "The Age of the Princes," *Medieval Welsh Society*, 32–33.

77. *Ior* 61/5.

78. *DwCol* 320; *ALW* V.ii.61; Peniarth 35, f. 24r. The usual grounds on which witnesses could be disqualified were kinship, feud, and disputes over land and women: *Ior* 79/12 and 80/1; *Col* 531.

79. *ALW* VIII.ii.1.

80. *Ior* 58–61. •

81. *ALW* X.vii.25. These particular lawbooks were consulted by the judges and principals in the Llwyn Gwyn case of 1540: Jones Pierce, "The Law of Wales—the Last Phase," *Medieval Welsh Society*, 383, n. 53.

82. *ALW* X.vii.26.

83. *ALW* X.vii.26 (S frequently confuses *i*, *y*, and *u*; in more standard orthography this clause would read: *eithyr le y perthyno kof llys*).

84. *ALW* VIII.i.13–14; VIII.v.2–3; and see discussion below.

85. *ALW* VIII.i.4–6; VIII.iv.1; VIII.v.1–3; and cf. XI.v.43.

86. Compare *DwCol* 320; *ALW* V.ii.61; and Peniarth 35, f. 24r with *ALW* VIII.i.6.

87. *ALW* VIII.ii.3. Both manuscripts have gaps, and G omits much of the first pleading.

88. *ALW* VIII.i.11 and 15; and XII.ix, which preserves an actual plaint brought by a claimant against a surety in his capacity as *mach kynoc*, "a debtor surety," on behalf of another (manuscripts of the fifteenth century).

89. *ALW* VIII.iii.1.
90. *ALW* VIII.i.15. There is no hint in XII.ix that the plaintiff had approached the original debtor first.
91. *ALW* VIII.i.12–15.
92. *ALW* VIII.i.4–6 and VIII.v.1–3.
93. *ALW* VIII.i.14.
94. *Bleg* 42.22–26; *LTWL*, Lat D 373.38–40.
95. *ALW* VIII.i.1–3.
96. *Ior* 61/8.
97. *ALW* VIII.ii.3 (reading *y rydav* for *yr ydav*, which must be an error).
98. *ALW* VIII.ii.1.
99. Among the best introductions to the subject are Charles-Edwards, *The Welsh Laws*; *LTMW*, xi-xxxvii; R. R. Davies, "The Administration of Law in Medieval Wales," and Alan Harding, "Legislators, Lawyers and Law-Books," both in *LAL*; and Jenkins, "A Family of Medieval Welsh Lawyers" in *CLP*.
100. Charles-Edwards, "*Cynghawsedd*: Counting and Pleading," 198.
101. S. F. C. Milsom, *Historical Foundations of the Common Law* (London, 1969), xi and 32.
102. On these terms, see Charles-Edwards, "*Cynghawsedd*: Counting and Pleading," 192–193, and *The Welsh Laws*, 59–60.
103. In the case outlined in *ALW* VIII.ii, for example, it is in the plaintiff's interest to reconceptualize the suit as a new charge brought against him by the debtor, since the debtor could conceivably fail in his attempt to support his claim that part of the debt had already been repaid, but there could exist no witnesses on behalf of the plaintiff's assertion that nothing had been given him. In most other cases outlined in the lawbooks, however, both parties are clearly desirous of being the ones to present their proof (e.g. *ALW* VIII.viii).
104. My summary of this procedure derives largely from the work of Charles-Edwards: "*Cynghawsedd*: Counting and Pleading," and *The Welsh Laws*, 53–67.
105. *ALW* VI.i.21. The case here involves a debtor who first attempts to prove that he had already paid the debt the creditor is seeking and then tries to deny the surety (and thereby the debt) altogether once his witnesses on his first defense fail.
106. *ALW* VIII.iii.1–2; *ALW* VIII.ii.1–3.
107. *ALW* VIII.i.7–15. This is my reading of this troublesome passage, although Charles-Edwards suggests an alternative interpretation. On his view, the surety in question has refused to swear the final oath required of him in refutation of the debtor's denial of his obligation (this possibility is raised in VIII.i.7). In such circumstances, according to *Ior* 59/5, the *mach* would become liable for the debt. But the *mach* in this instance cleverly eludes the plaintiff's summons by claiming that although he has acknowledged being a surety, he has not acknowledged being a paying surety (*mach talu*), and that the plaintiff has not alleged him to be a paying surety either. In other words, the *mach* here implies that the terms under which he had been originally appointed as surety did not include payment—or at least that this part of his suretyship remains unacknowledged by him (and unproven by the plaintiff). The plaintiff responds to this by reiterating his claim that the *mach* has acknowledged his *mechni* and ought thus to pay the debt. The *mach*, however, is given the final word, and asserts once again that he has not

acknowledged himself as debtor, merely as surety, and that since the plaintiff chose to lodge his claim not against him *trόy gynnocnaeth*, "through debtorship," but against *kynnogen arall*, "another debtor," and that debtor has denied the obligation, there exists now no debtor and, consequently, no surety, and he does not therefore have to act.

Both of these readings strike me as possible, although I prefer the interpretation I offer above in the text for a variety of reasons. Had the surety's response been intended to refer to the terms of his initial appointment, I would have expected this *arddelw* to be the issue on which the case then would proceed, with plaintiff or surety eventually offering evidence in support of their assertions, especially since the plaintiff did in effect sue the *mach* as a *mach talu*, or at least incorporated the assertion that payment is one of the obligations of a surety into his initial claim. Moreover, the issue of the *mach*'s having failed to live up to the responsibilities of his office in refusing to swear should have formed part of the plaintiff's plea. The arguments of both parties instead seem to focus not on the terms of the initial appointment but on other matters altogether. The surety's response seems to me to be that (1) the plaintiff did not choose to sue the surety as a debtor in the first instance, and that having now sued one debtor he cannot sue another (VIII.i.11 and cf. VIII.i.15); (2) the *mach* acknowledged suretyship in his oaths to the debtor, not debtorship, and therefore the legal adage that those who acknowledge must pay (VIII.i.10) is irrelevant to the present situation; and (3) even though he acknowledged his suretyship and it would have been possible for the plaintiff to sue the surety as a surety had the debtor simply refused to pay—and both plaintiff and *mach* admit that the law of a surety is that he should either pay or compel (VIII.i.8–9)—since the debtor has now successfully denied the obligation, there is no debtor and also therefore no *mach*.

108. Text and translation both from *LAL*, 148–149.

109. *Col* 101; G ff. 22r-23v.

110. *LTWL*, Lat A 125.22–30; Lat B 217.11–19; Lat D 369.6–14; Lat E 459.15–23 = *LAL*, 202–205, Lat E 18–19; *Bleg* 41.16–25.

111. *ALW* VIII.i.11.

112. The term *arddelw* has a complicated history, on which see the helpful note in *Col*, pp. 112–113, §381. The word itself is a compound formed from *ar*, "before, in front of" and *delw*, "image, form, shape," an etymology that may be significant in light of the suggestion made here. Could it be that certain pleas were originally conceived of as embodying the "shape" or "form" of precurial offices, procedures, or personalities?

113. *ALW* VIII.v.3.

114. Charles-Edwards, "The 'Iorwerth' Text," *LAL*, 169.

115. *ALW* VIII.v.2.

116. *Ior* 58–61, esp. 59/1 and 61/1–4.

117. *ALW* VIII.v.3, and cf. VIII.v.1. This principle is repeated frequently elsewhere in similar terms, for example, *ALW* VIII.i.6; VIII.iv.1; VIII.xi.31; and XIV.xvi.4.

118. *Ior* 60/7; *Col* 84.

119. Milsom, *Historical Foundations of the Common Law*, xi.

120. Binchy, "Celtic Suretyship," 360–363, 365.
121. Charles-Edwards, "The 'Iorwerth' Text," *LAL*, 176–177; and see *LTMW*, 252.
122. Binchy, "Archaisms in the Celtic Law-Books," *CLP*, 115–116, and see below.
123. *LAL*, 192–193, Cyfn 52–63 = *WML* 297.26–298.16 and 89.8–17 derives from *Ior* 69 (= *Col* 132–140). The only other evidence for the *amodwr* in the Cyfn tradition are the short sentences in V/Mk (*LAL*, 196–197, Cyfn 84 = *WML* 89.6–8), and *WML* 41.19–20. Latin B, Latin D, and Bleg also add the *amodwr* to their list of the nine *tafodiogion*: *LTWL*, Lat B 216.14–15; Lat D 367.24; and *Bleg* 39.10–11. Lat E does not follow Lat B here, but see *LTWL*, Lat E 505.16–18, and compare with Lat B 259.21.
124. *LTMW*, 252. Charles-Edwards tentatively suggests that the *amodwr* might represent "a form of *mach* transformed by the appearance of a greater role for the ruler in the enforcement of contracts," and this is also the approach taken here: Charles-Edwards, "The 'Iorwerth' Text," *LAL*, 176–177.
125. *Ior* 69/3–4; *Col* 134–135; *LAL*, 192–193 and 196–197, Cyfn W 54–56 and V/Mk 84 = *WML* 297.28–34 and 89.7–8. *ALW* X.xvii.24 implies that *amodwyr* could also deny their obligations in the same manner as did the *mach*.
126. *Ior* 69/1; *Col* 132.
127. *ALW* XI.v.43; and cf. VII.i.47; X.xvi.6; XIV.ii.1; and XIV.xxxvi.4.
128. *DwCol* 386–389.
129. *Ior* 69/2; *Col* 133; *LAL*, 192–193, Cyfn W 53 = *WML* 297.27–28.
130. Both in recognition of the primacy of his witnessing function and also by analogy with the *mach*: see references in note 123 above.
131. See references in note 7 above.
132. *Ior* 69/4 says that it is the claimant (*hawlwr*) who calls for judgment after the initial oaths have been sworn, and *Col* 135 makes it clear that at least in its version of the denial process, the claimant is the one to swear this initial oath and force the defendant to compurgation. Later treatments seem more thoroughly to have assimilated the two forms of denial. Manuscript H, for example, of the fourteenth century, includes the *amodwr* in its list of types of witness who must be denied by compurgation (*gwadu*) rather than merely disqualified (*llyssu*): *ALW* XIV.xvi.4, and see XI.v.43 and XIV.ii.1.
133. *Ior* 69/7; *Col* 136; *LAL*, 192–193, Cyfn W 57 = *WML* 297.34–298.2.
134. *Ior* 69/8–9; *Col* 137; *LAL*, 192–193, Cyfn W 58–59 = *WML* 89.13–17.
135. *LAL*, 196–197, Cyfn V/Mk 84 = *WML* 89.6–7; and cf. *Col* 132.
136. *Ior* 69/3–9; *Col* 134–137; *LAL*, 192–193, Cyfn W 54–59 = *WML* 297.28–298.2 and 89.13–17.
137. An interesting side-by-side treatment of the two is *Ior* 80.
138. *LAL*, 192–193, Cyfn W 57 = *WML* 297.34–298.2. This is perhaps also the implication of the *Os edeu ynteu heb neb yn y lle* . . . , "if he promises without anyone present" (literally: "in the place") phrasing of Cyfn 59 (*LAL*, 192–193 = *WML* 89.16–17).
139. R. R. Davies, "The Law of the March," 17, esp. note 63.
140. *LTMW*, 252.

141. *Ior* 69/10–11; *Col* 138–139; *LAL*, 192–193, Cyfn W 60 = *WML* 89.8–11.
142. *DwCol* 386–388.
143. *ALW* IX.xi.10; X.xvi.6; X.xvii.29; XIV.xxxvi.4; *LTWL*, Lat B 216.14–15; Lat D 367.24; *Bleg* 39.10–11; and *WML* 41.19–20. (In the Latin texts, the *amodwr* is associated with the *amot*, and the *fideiussor* with his *fideiussio*.) See also *LTWL*, Lat E 505.16–17.
144. *ALW* X.iv.3.
145. *DwCol* 26 and 112, respectively, and see also 111.
146. *Ior* 148/7; 150/8; 151/2; 152/5; *Col* 153; 166; 168; and 174.
147. This accords also with the frequency with which the lawbooks remark that the *mach* acts *ar peth*, "for a [specific] item": for example, *Ior* 58/2; 61/1; 61/5; 62/1; 64/10, etc., and cf. 64/1, *mach ar da*, "a *mach* for goods."
148. For example, *PKM*, 18; and see also *Geiriadur Prifysgol Cymru* (Cardiff 1950–), vol. I, p. 97; *LTMW*, 252; and Charles-Edwards, "The 'Iorwerth' Text," *LAL*, 176–177.
149. Sometimes, as in Cyfn 52 (*LAL*, 192–193 = *WML* 297.26), and *Bleg* 74.4–10, called *amot kyfreithawl* (Latin *per conditionem*: *LTWL*, Lat D 386.23–30).
150. *ALW* VII.i.47 and XIV.xxxvi.4.
151. See Chapter 3 above on immunities, and Stacey, "Ties that Bind," 50–57.
152. This suggestion is intended to enlarge on rather than contradict that made by Charles-Edwards in "The 'Iorwerth' Text," *LAL*, 177.
153. *ALW* X.xii.10.
154. Surely the message intended to be conveyed in, for example, *Ior* 69/1; *Col* 132; *LAL*, 192–193, Cyfn W 52 = *WML* 297.26–27; and *Bleg* 74.4–10.
155. *Ior* 69/8; *LAL*, 192–193, Cyfn W 58 = *WML* 297.34–298.2; and see also Cyfn W 67–70, *LAL*, 194–195 = *WML* 108.17–109.5.
156. *Col* 137; and cf. *ALW* IX.x and X.xii.10.
157. *Councils and Ecclesiastical Documents*, vol. 1, p. 515, §24.

Chapter 7. Past and Present in the Law of Hywel

1. Recent studies examining the issue of continuity include: Hyams, "Trial by Ordeal"; Bruce O'Brien, "Studies of the 'Leges Edwardi Confessoris' and their Milieu," (Ph.D. diss., Yale University, 1990); and Patrick Wormald, "In Pursuit of Crime: the Early English Approach," unpublished paper presented to the British Legal History Conference held at Oxford in July of 1991. The latter two works were made available to me by their authors, to whom I am very grateful.
2. R. R. Davies, "Law and National Identity"; Pryce, "The Prologues to the Welsh Lawbooks," 176–179; Charles-Edwards, *The Welsh Laws*, 9–13. The Irish experienced similar ambivalence: J. Otway-Ruthven, "The Request of the Irish for English Law, 1277–80," *IHS* 6, no. 24 (1949): 261–270. On Welsh law in the post-Conquest period, see R. R. Davies, "The Twilight of Welsh Law, 1284–1536," *History* 51 (1966): 143–164; and R. R. Davies, "The Survival of the Bloodfeud in Medieval Wales," *History* 54 (1969): 338–357.
3. Charles-Edwards, *The Welsh Laws*, 82–86.

4. Pryce, "The Prologues to the Welsh Lawbooks," 166–170, 181–182; R. R. Davies, "Law and National Identity," 54–57.

5. As will be evident from the notes, I am greatly indebted in what follows to Charles-Edwards' stimulating and highly original volume in the Writers of Wales series, *The Welsh Laws*.

6. *Calendar of Various Chancery Rolls: Supplementary Close Rolls, Welsh Rolls, Scutage Rolls* A.D. *1277–1326*, ed. H. C. Maxwell Lyte (London, 1912), 196–197, 198, 200, and so forth.

7. *Ior* 82/1–3 (where the proposed change is rejected); 115/6 (and see 115/2–3); *Col* 184, 190–191, 388, 392, 584; *ALW* VIII.xi.3–4; *LTWL*, Lat D 330.16–17; 361.35–37; 380.27–32.

8. *ALW* VIII.xi.3–4.

9. Pryce, "The Prologues to the Welsh Lawbooks," 152–165; Jenkins, "The Lawbooks of Medieval Wales," 12–15; A. D. Carr, *A Look at Hywel's Law* (Whitland, 1985).

10. *ALW* VIII.xi.3 (reading *uyth* for *uyt* as per Wiliam: *Llyfr Cynog*, 30, §15.2).

11. Although *ALW* VIII.xi.4, which envisages that a man might assert his right to choose between these two laws, reminds us that those living under a particular prince's jurisdiction might take his decrees more seriously than intellectualizing jurists.

12. Charles-Edwards, *The Welsh Laws*, 8–9.

13. Charles-Edwards, *The Welsh Laws*, 53.

14. Charles-Edwards, *The Welsh Laws*, 25–67, is the best introduction to these texts. As he there points out, the most important criteria was not the specific content of a particular text, but rather its form—that is, the extent to which it fit or did not fit the pattern linked to Hywel.

15. This is true also of the "appendages" to the Test Book that are, according to *Ior* 139/1, intended to be *ygyt a'r Llyuer Prauf*, "associated with the Test-Book."

16. *ALW* VII.i.9; Charles-Edwards, "*Cynghawsedd*: Counting and Pleading," 191–192; and *The Welsh Laws*, 58–59.

17. Charles-Edwards, *The Welsh Laws*, 26.

18. Charles-Edwards, *The Welsh Laws*, 49–53.

19. The evolution of the triad cited by Charles-Edwards in *The Welsh Laws*, 6–8, is a good example of conservatism within the principal redactions giving way to a much more liberal attitude towards innovation in the *Llyfr Cynghawsedd*.

20. On the relationship between law and custom, see the *Recueils de la Société Jean Bodin* 52, part 2 (1990); of special interest to Celtic scholars is Charles-Edwards, "Custom in Early Irish Law," on 435–443.

21. *LTWL*, 26–40, 62–67, 90–91; *LTMW*, xxxiv–xxxv; Charles-Edwards, *The Welsh Laws*, 63–67.

22. The fact that the *Llyfr Cynghawsedd* certainly, and perhaps the *Llyfr y Damweiniau* as well, were literate productions does not vitiate this argument. Individual *damweiniau* may have had a long oral history behind them, as their form would tend to suggest, and the *cynghawsedd*, despite their literate nature, present themselves as written transcriptions of oral pleadings done in court. What mat-

tered, in other words, was less the environment in which the books themselves were compiled, than how their contents were conceptualized.

23. Charles-Edwards, *The Welsh Laws*, 26.

24. Jaffee, "From Literary Tradition to Oral Torah," 27, 30.

25. Cyfn U associates the *gorfodog* with hostages: *LAL*, 196–197, Cyfn U 79 = *WML* 312.10–12. Once the *gorfodog* moves into court, the sources become concerned with protecting him, as a surety innocent of crime, from suffering corporal punishment on behalf of his principal; at this point, he is then directly contrasted with political hostages, whose fate it is to suffer what the lord might decree: *ALW* XIV.xix.10. An original link with the kindred is suggested by the fact that a *gorfodog* rendered liable by his principal was not entitled to compensation for his suffering unless he had specifically taken sureties from his principal to that effect: *Ior* 70/2–3; *Col* 142–143.

26. All of the sources except *Llyfr Colan* use the terminology of "criminal law": *llourud* (*Ior* 70/3–4); *kylus/dros y kam* (*Bleg* 41.26–31); *reus/pro malefacto* (*LTWL*, Lat D 369.16–18); and *manucaptor in causa capitali* (*LTWL*, Lat E2 and E4 additions, p. 460, note 2). *Llyfr Colan*'s substitution of more generic terms for claimant and offender (*haulur* in *Col* 142, and compare *Col* 143–144 with *Ior* 70/3–4) seems deliberate, and was perhaps intended to broaden the scope of the *gorfodog*'s suretyship. See also *LTMW*, 253, and *Col*, pp. 66–67.

27. There is no evidence to suggest that the ability to produce a *gorfodog*-type surety ever became mandatory in Wales as it did in Anglo-Saxon England (on English frankpledge, see Wormald, "In Pursuit of Crime"). Rather, it seems to have been a requirement restricted to those whose previous actions or contextual anonymity rendered them suspicious in some way. An excellent example of such a situation is to be found in the Arthurian romance *Chwedyl Gereint vab Erbin*, where Edern uab Nudd's dwarf insults and wounds a servant of Gwenhwyfar, who then seeks compensation for the insult. Gereint undertakes to bring Edern to justice and defeats him in a tournament, wounding him so severely that it is unclear whether he will survive his injuries. Edern is, nevertheless, sent back to Arthur's court to receive judgment on his case. According to Arthur's verdict, Edern is to receive medical care until it becomes clear whether he will survive his wounds; if he does, he is to give *mach*-sureties to guarantee that he will pay compensation for the insult to Gwenhwyfar. After rendering his decision, Arthur and several other worthies of the court then present themselves as *gorfodog*-sureties for Edern, to guarantee his future good behavior. In this instance, then, Edern is put into *gorfodogaeth* both because he was previously unknown to the nobles present in Arthur's court and because he has already been accused of an offense against the queen: *Llyfr Gwyn Rhydderch: Y Chwedlau a'r Rhamantau*, ed. J. Gwenogvryn Evans and R. M. Jones (Cardiff, 1973), 203, cols. 405–406 (from Peniarth 6, the oldest known version of this romance). The lawbooks also suggest that men who made threats against others might be placed into *gorfodogaeth*: *ALW* XIV.xv.16.

28. *LTWL*, Lat B 218.17–18; Lat E 460.9–10 = *LAL*, 204–205, Lat E 34; *LAL*, 196–197, Cyfn U and V 80 = *WML* 117.13–14. In *LTWL*, Lat D 369.15–18, and *Bleg* 41.26–31, this has become a period of protection for the *gorfodog*, in that

he cannot be punished within that period because it is not yet clear whether the offender will come to law. *Col* 146 and *Ior* 70/4 imply that the *gorfodog*'s period of service could be variable.

29. *Ior* 70/1; *Col* 141; *LAL*, 196–197, Cyfn V 81 = *WML* 117.10–12; and cf. *LTWL*, Lat D 369.15–18 and *Bleg* 41.26–31.

30. *Col*, p. 66. In one late text, the *gorfodog* acts as bail for his principal, freeing him from the lord's prison and becoming himself liable for the charge if the true offender leaves town: *ALW* XIV.xix.10. (Compare with this the definition of the *mach ar gyfreith* offered in *ALW* VII.i.9: "pledges of living men, and those in the hands of the servants of the lord.") The major difference was that whereas the *mach ar gyfreith* would suffer financially if his prinicipal evaded his responsibilities, the stakes for the *gorfodog* were in theory even greater, since criminals could be executed. This possibility, however, spurred the lawyers to address the issue of whether *gorfodog*-sureties ought to be given in capital cases. They uniformly answered this question in the negative: *ALW* XIV.xii.14; XIV.xix.10.

31. *Bleg* 41.26; *ALW* IX.xxxix.3; XIV.xv.16; and see XIV.xxii.11.

32. *Ior* 68/8. This clause is probably an addition made by the *Llyfr Iorwerth* tradition to a sentence that originally dealt only with *briduw*, since *gorfodogaeth* is not mentioned in *Col*'s version (130).

33. Only if one imagined the third hand to be that of the lord could such a provision ever have been implemented, and modeling still seems a more likely explanation.

34. Bromwich's *Trioedd Ynys Prydein* is the best study of this genre.

35. *ALW* X.vii.12.

36. *ALW* X.vii.18.

37. Stacey, "Ties That Bind," 50–57.

38. *ALW* VIII.i.6; VIII.iv.1; VIII.v.1.

39. The following sketch is based on the suretyship tractate only and is intended to be suggestive rather than conclusive. Whether the observations made below are relevant also to other tractates can only be determined by further study. Cyfn, which stems also from the South, appears less preoccupied with the sorts of concerns discussed in this chapter, although it also contains some relatively "late" law: see below and Stacey, "The Archaic Core of Llyfr Iorwerth."

40. Stacey, "The Archaic Core of Llyfr Iorwerth," *LAL*, 35–37 and 43–46; Charles-Edwards, *The Welsh Laws*, 41–44; and see Pryce, "Early Irish Canons and Medieval Welsh Law," 119–125, on the southern associations of the Irish canons included in the Latin and *Llyfr Blegywryd* tractates.

41. Indeed, these two provisions occur together in Latin A, where they are placed side by side with a passage on the taking of distraint that must be one of the oldest in all the lawbooks, since it is included in every extant version of the suretyship tractate. This gathering together of ancient material seems unlikely to be coincidental: assuming that Latin A was following its prototype in its placement of these passages, the compiler of the original Latin version likely was himself either working from an early written text or was in some manner aware of the age of the material before him. One cannot assume such knowledge on the part of the compilers of the other extant Latin texts, however, since apart from Latin A, they

all disperse this information throughout their lawbooks: compare *LTWL*, Lat A 125.8–18 with Lat B 217.6–10, 218.12–14, 256.26–31; Lat D 368.32–33, 369.32–37; Lat E 459.6–9, 460.3–5 and 11–17 = *LAL*, 202–205, Lat E 15, 30–31, and 35–38; and *Bleg* 41.1–3 and 42.16–21. The best discussion of these texts is Pryce, "Early Irish Canons and Medieval Welsh Law."

42. Stacey, "The Archaic Core of Llyfr Iorwerth," *LAL*, 21–23, and note 52; Pryce, "Early Irish Canons and Medieval Welsh Law," 113–117.

43. *LTWL*, Lat A 125.2–4, 6–7, 37.

44. Pryce, "Early Irish Canons and Medieval Welsh Law," 119–125. Perhaps Dyfed's early connections with Ireland (on which see *WEMA*, 87–89 and 95) were a significant factor in that region's receptiveness to Irish custom and/or texts.

45. If they were aware of its age, the attitude of at least some of the compilers toward this material was something less than sacrosanct. For while Latin B includes the canon on the paying surety in its lawbook, it places it far outside the tractate. Latin D omits it altogether, substituting instead a different schedule, composed of sentences that appear widely separated from one another in Lat B and E: *LTWL*, Lat D 368.24–27.

46. Stacey, "The Archaic Core of Llyfr Iorwerth," *LAL*, 35–37.

47. Compare, for example, *LTWL*, Lat A 124.39–125.2 (and *LAL*, 184–185, Cyfn 4 = *WML* 85.12–17) with subsequent versions in Lat B 216.30–32; Lat D 368.3–4; and Lat E 458.28–29 = *LAL*, 202–203, Lat E 7; and see also, for example, *LTWL*, Lat D 369.19–24; Lat B 254.34–38; and Lat E 460.28–32 = *LAL*, 206–207, Lat E 43.

48. Latin B and E demonstrate at least incipient awareness of some of these developments, although they nevertheless differ markedly from Ior in this respect: *LTWL*, Lat B 217.33–38; Lat E 459.26–31 = *LAL*, 204–205, Lat E 21–24 (cf. *Ior* 58–60).

49. *Bleg*, xix–xxv; *Ior*, p. xxi; and T. Jones Pierce, "The Kindred and the Bloodfeud," and "The Growth of Commutation in Gwynedd during the Thirteenth Century," 289–308 and 103–125 respectively, of *Medieval Welsh Society*.

50. *Ior* 58–60 and 67/4, respectively.

51. At least to judge from the facts that the *gorfodog* is already pictured in Ior as a paying guarantor and that *talu* is clearly viewed in the (also thirteenth-century) *Llyfr Cynghawsedd* appended to many Ior manuscripts as one of the *mach*'s chief duties.

52. Latin B and E also contain a version of this passage, but it clearly did not form part of the Latin prototype. Furthermore, both "update" it by stressing the responsibility of the lord of the exiled man to step in as (paying) surety unless a different guarantor had already been appointed (in Latin B outside the tractate): *LTWL*, Lat B 254.34–38; Lat E 460.28–32 = *LAL*, 206–207, Lat E 43 (Lat E 44 and 45 imply also that sureties would be liable for the entire amount rather than merely half).

53. *Ior* 63/2 and 64/5–8.

54. Stacey, "The Archaic Core of Llyfr Iorwerth," *LAL*, 23–27.

55. Stacey, "The Archaic Core of Llyfr Iorwerth," *LAL*, 31–37.

56. We know very little about the training of lawyers, but it seems reasonable to infer that their experiences in this respect paralleled those of judges. Certainly

the *Llyfr Cynghawsedd*, a text that clearly envisages an experienced group of pleaders, was a northern production.

57. Davies, "The Administration of Law in Medieval Wales," *LAL*, 262–266.
58. Pryce, "The Prologues to the Welsh Lawbooks," 158–164 and 179–81 on clerical influence, esp. in the Latin and Bleg families. On the trend away from Ior toward Bleg, see Charles-Edwards, *The Welsh Laws*, 90–93, and 100–102 on the large numbers of *Llyfr Blegywryd* manuscripts extant from the fourteenth and fifteenth centuries.
59. Davies, "The Administration of Law in Medieval Wales," *LAL*, 266–271.
60. Charles-Edwards, *The Welsh Laws*, 91.
61. Pryce, "The Prologues to the Welsh Lawbooks," 176–179.
62. Pryce, "The Prologues to the Welsh Lawbooks," 177–181.

Chapter 8. The Suretyship of the Gods

1. M. Chevrier, *Du Serment Promissoire en Droit Romain* (Dijon, 1921), 8.
2. Peter Brown, *The Cult of the Saints: Its Rise and Function in Latin Christianity* (Chicago, 1981), 81.
3. Good work has been done recently on the ordeal. Robert Bartlett stresses the role of lordship in the procedure in his *Trial by Fire and Water*, but see also Hyams, "Trial by Ordeal;" Brown, "Society and the Supernatural: A Medieval Change," reprinted in Brown, *Society and the Holy in Late Antiquity*, 302–332; and Rebecca Colman, "Reason and Unreason in Early Medieval Law," *The Journal of Interdisciplinary History* 4 (1974): 571–591. John Baldwin chronicles the campaign against the ordeal, which he regards as part "of a general movement towards more rational legal procedure" (p. 614), in "The Intellectual Preparation for the Canon of 1215 against Ordeals," *Speculum* 36 (1961): 613–636; and John Roberts looks at the statistical and anthropological aspects of these rituals in "Oaths, Autonomic Ordeals, and Power," in *The Ethnography of Law*, ed. Laura Nader, Special Publication of the *American Anthropologist* 67, no. 6, part 2 (Wisc., 1965): 186–212.
4. "The holy [is] an enabling device carefully (if unconsciously) ground into a tool to resolve otherwise unbearable human conflicts": Brown, "Society and the Supernatural," *Society and the Holy*, 319.
5. Brown, "Society and the Supernatural," *Society and the Holy*, 313; Roberts, "Oaths, Autonomic Ordeals, and Power," 209; and Colman, "Reason and Unreason," 583, who does, however, acknowledge the predilection for the "rational": 577–578.
6. E. Adamson Hoebel, *The Law of Primitive Man* (Cambridge, Mass., 1954; reprinted, 1967), 290.
7. Binchy, "Celtic Suretyship," 357. Other treatments of *briduw* include *CU*, 80–81, §7; *Col*, pp. 64–65; Jenkins, *Cyfraith Hywel*, 85; Morfydd Owen, review of *Llyfr Colan*, *Llên Cymru* 8 (1964): 246–247; P. L. Henry, "Varia II: A Passage in *Scéla Cano Meic Gartnáin*," *Ériu* 20 (1966): 223–225; and, most recently, Huw Pryce, "Duw yn Lle Mach: Briduw yng Nghyfraith Hywel," *LAL*, 47–71. Pryce presents an English adaptation and summary of the latter article in his *Native Law and the Church in Medieval Wales* (Oxford, 1993), 53–65.

8. *Titi Livi ab vrbe condita*, 159–161, I.xxiv.4–7; Joseph Plescia, *The Oath and Perjury in Ancient Greece* (Tallahassee, 1970), especially 2–11, 73–74, 80–81; and Chevrier, *Du Serment Promissoire*, 11–14. See also Benveniste, *Le Vocabulaire des Institutions Indo-Européenes*, vol. 2, 173–175; and *Irish Kings*, 83, on similar oaths in Hittite texts of the second millenium B.C.E.

9. Plescia, *The Oath and Perjury in Ancient Greece*, 93–102.

10. See various versions of this story in "The *Bórama*," ed. Whitley Stokes, *RC* 13 (1892): 32–124 and 299, esp. p. 52, §40, (LL version); *Lebor na hUidre*, 9794 ff.; "Mitteilungen aus irischen Handschriften," 118, §25, (Rawl. B.502 version); and *AU* 462.

11. There are also many versions of this tale: see "The *Bórama*," 36–37, §2; *The Banquet of Dún na nGedh and the Battle of Mag Rath*, ed. J. O'Donovan (Dublin, 1842), 4–5; and references to other texts cited by Plummer, "Irish Miscellanies," *RC* 6 (1883–1885): 165 and note on p. 171. On the story of Tipraite Tírech see R. Thurneysen, "Morand's Fürstenspiegel," *ZCP* 11 (1917): 57, §§8–10.

12. "Quelques textes irlandais sur Saint Grégoire le Grand," ed. P. Grosjean, *RC* 46 (1929): 232; and "Cináed úa Hartacáin's Poem on Brugh na Bóinne," *Ériu* 7 (1914): 227, §61.

13. For example, the late prologue to *Cáin Adomnáin: CA*, 12–13, §22; Kuno Meyer, "The Expulsion of the Dessi," *Y Cymmrodor* 14 (1901): 112–113, §10; and J. H. Todd, *The Irish Version of the Historia Britonum of Nennius* (Dublin, 1848), 126–127, 140–141. Cf. also *The Tripartite Life of Patrick, with Other Documents Relating to that Saint*, ed. Whitley Stokes, 2 vols. (London, 1887, reprinted, 1965), vol. I, 48–51, two different interpretations of which can be found in Henry, "Varia. II," 224, and Binchy, "Varia. III: *Atomriug*," *Ériu* 20 (1966): 232–234.

14. Plescia, *The Oath and Perjury in Ancient Greece*, 5–8, and see note 15 below.

15. Ruairí Ó hUiginn, "Tongu do dia toinges mo thuath and Related Expressions," *Sages, Saints and Storytellers*, 339–340; but see also Calvert Watkins, "Some Celtic Phrasal Echoes," in *Celtic Language, Celtic Culture: A Festschrift for Eric P. Hamp*, ed. A. T. E. Matonis and Daniel Melia (Van Nuys, Calif., 1990), 48–52.

16. *CA*, 12–13, §22.

17. Thurneysen, "Morand's Fürstenspiegel," 57, §10.

18. "A Poem on the Airgialla," 181–183, §§24, 29, 40–41. The prologue to *CA* also distinguishes between the "personalized" gages used to guarantee the payment of the specific tribute owed to Adomnán and his community and the elemental and apostolic sureties who guaranteed the perpetual observance of the *cáin*: *CA*, 12–15, §§22–26. Compare also *The Poems of Blathmac*, 24–25, §§67–69.

19. *CIH* 42.28; 460.1–2 = *CU*, 66–67, §7; *CIH* 1371.16; and 2045.9 = *EICL*, 130–131, §5.

20. Pryce, "Duw un Lle Mach," *LAL*, 59–60. Gwilym Prys Davies suggested that *briduw* might have been created by southern canonists: "Rhwymedigaethau Cytundebol yn y Gyfraith Gymreig" (LL.M. thesis, University of Wales, 1952), 44–49. Pryce argues convincingly against this position, however (pp. 49, 51, and 59).

21. Arrian, writing in the second century C.E. about a treaty made between the Celts of the Danube and Alexander the Great, reports that when Alexander asked the Celts what they most feared in order that he might invoke this as a sanction for the treaty, they responded that their greatest worry was that "the sky might fall upon their heads." Alexander thought them dreadful braggarts, but if they spoke the truth, the suretyship of the elements could be very old indeed: *Arrian's Anabasis Alexandri*, ed. P. A. Brunt, 2 vols. (Cambridge, Mass. and London, 1976–1983), I.4.7–8, pp. 18–19. (The treaty was made several centuries before Arrian wrote, so his testimony is hardly conclusive.)

22. For example, the *aðsweord eorla* of *Beowulf: Beowulf and the Fight at Finnsburg*, ed. F. Klaeber (third edition, Lexington, Mass., 1950), line 2064. See also *Die Gesetze der Langobarden*, ed. F. Beyerle (Weimar, 1947), *L. Rothari* 269, 359, and 363; and *Lex Salica*, ed. K. Eckhardt, *MGH, Legum* Sectio I, *Leges Nationum Germanicarum*, vol. 4, pt. ii, 86.1–4 = *Pactus Legis Salicae* 50.1–4 (*Legum* Sectio I, vol. 4, pt. i). Other close parallels include the ascription *Deo testis*, which is found on certain Germanic charters, and the pledging of faith, on which see Louis Froget, *La Fides Facta aux époques Mérovingienne et Carolingienne* (thesis for the doctorate in law done for the Université d'Alger, 1932).

23. Even this reference is uncertain: see discussion below and, on connections between Ireland, Wales, and Brittany, see Fleuriot, "Un fragment en Latin"; and Pryce, "Early Irish Canons and Medieval Welsh Law."

24. See below on *godborg*.

25. *DwCol* 387.

26. *Ior* 68/9.

27. *CIH* 2044.21–2045.9 = *EICL*, 130–131, §5 clearly equates the *naidm soscélai*, "*naidm* of the Gospels," with the promissory oath. See also *CIH* 460.1–2 = *CU*, 66–67, §7; and "The Bórama," 106, §138. Other literary references are primarily to *rátha* instead of *nadmen*, another indication of their late date, since the *ráth*-surety was, by the Middle Irish period, the most common of all Irish guarantors.

28. *CIH* 42.28.

29. *CIH* 460.1–2 = *CU*, 66–67, §7. A text in *RC* 46, p. 232 speaks of an arrangement bound "on the honor of the Lord" (*ronaisgetar ar ínchuibh in Coimdhe fair*).

30. Lat B, Lat D, and Bleg are the exceptions. It is uncertain whether the term *briduw* itself was old or an invention of the lawyers: see Pryce, "Duw yn Lle Mach," *LAL*, 60.

31. *Bleg*, 184, note 41.10; *Col*, p. 64; Jenkins, *Cyfraith Hywel*, 85. Both T. P. Ellis in his *Welsh Tribal Law and Custom in the Middle Ages*, 2 vols. (Oxford, 1926), vol. II, p. 3; and Timothy Lewis in *A Glossary of Medieval Welsh Law Based upon the Black Book of Chirk* (Manchester, 1913), x, §45, had earlier argued that *briduw* represented a popular corruption of an oath taken *pro Deo*.

32. *PKM*, 57 and note on p. 240, and on law in the *Mabinogi*, see T. P. Ellis, "Legal References, Terms and Conceptions in the Mabinogion," *Y Cymmrodor* 39 (1928): 86–148.

33. Moreover, as Patrick Ford reminds me, the expression *e rof a Duw* is

ubiquitous throughout the *Mabinogi*, and seems in such instances to mean little more than our "honest to God!"

34. Pryce, "Duw yn Lle Mach," *LAL*, 60, and for a possible Irish parallel, see note 29 above.

35. See Pryce, "Duw un Lle Mach," *LAL*, 50–51, 59–61, and 64, note 28.

36. *DwCol* 387. Manuscript: *etneyt*; *edewyt* is the emendation proposed by the editor Dafydd Jenkins.

37. *Ior* 68/10, 97/6, and 99/1; *Col* 131; and see Pryce, "Duw yn Lle Mach," *LAL*, 57–58.

38. Pryce, "Duw yn Lle Mach," *LAL*, 61–62.

39. I here closely paraphrase Bronislaw Malinowski's formulation in *Magic, Science and Religion, and Other Essays* (Glencoe, Illinois, 1948), 38, 88.

40. *The Tripartite Life of Patrick*, 112–121 and 198–199. As Binchy points out, the tale about Patrick's hunger strike is a distortion of a much more mundane original: "Distraint in Irish Law," 35.

41. Baldwin, "The Intellectual Preparation for the Canon of 1215 Against Ordeals."

42. Peter Brown emphasizes the changes taking place between 1000–1200 in men's views on the relationship between the sacred and the profane in "Society and the Supernatural" (see note 3 above).

43. *Vitae Sanctorum Britanniae et Genealogiae*, 96–97, §34.

44. Keith Thomas, *Religion and the Decline of Magic* (London, 1971), 52–57.

45. *LAL*, 184–185, Cyfn 3 = *WML* 85.8–11.

46. *LTWL*, Lat D 369.1–3; *Bleg* 41.9–12; and Pryce, "Duw yn Lle Mach," *LAL*, 49.

47. *Ior* 68/1–10; *Col* 126–131.

48. Charles-Edwards, "The 'Iorwerth' Text," *LAL*, 158, note to 68/8.

49. Jenkins, *Cyfraith Hywel*, 85; Pryce, "Duw yn Lle Mach," *LAL*, 48–56, on denial procedures.

50. *LTWL*, Lat D 369.1–3; *Bleg* 41.10–12; *WML* 85.7–11 = *LAL*, 184–185, Cyfn 2–3.

51. *Ior* 68/1–6; *Col* 126–128. *Col* 128 remarks that compurgation is to be done *yn unwet a reyth mach*, "at the same time as the compurgation of a *mach*-surety."

52. *LTWL*, Lat B 217.38–218.1; Lat E 459.31–32 = *LAL*, 204–205, Lat E 25.

53. Pryce, "Duw un Lle Mach," *LAL*, 49.

54. *Die Gesetze der Angelsachsen*, ed. F. Liebermann, 3 vols. (Halle, 1903–1916; reprinted Aalen, 1960), vol. I, 66–67, Alf. 33 (and compare the *mennisc borg* of Alf. 1.8). See also Liebermann's commentary in vol. II, 332. Manuscript 7 has been spelled out as *and*.

55. The purpose of the fore-oath was to show that the plaintiff was not prosecuting the case out of malice: F. L. Attenborough, *Laws of the Earliest English Kings* (Cambridge, 1922), 197.

56. Jenkins, *Cyfraith Hywel*, 85; Pryce, "Duw yn Lle Mach," *LAL*, 51, 56.

57. *ALW* XIV.iii.12.

58. *ALW* XI.v.43.

59. *ALW* IX.xxxviii.10; XIV.xxii.1–4; and cf. XIV.xxxvi.4. Manuscript H is

written in court hand (Charles-Edwards, *The Welsh Laws*, 102). Perhaps its interest in *briduw* reflects a desire on the part of lord and court to ensure that such matters would proceed under their supervision.

60. *ALW* XIV.xxii.2; XIV.xli.31.
61. *ALW* XIV.i.10.
62. *DwCol* 383; and see *LTMW*, 229, note 24.33.
63. *ALW* XIV.xxii.1–2; XIV.xxxvi.4; IX.xxxviii.10.
64. *ALW* VI.i.40.
65. Interestingly, there is a confusion in the manuscript tradition here, with one text, Q, reading *nat oes cret namyn bri duö*, "there is no pledge of faith except *bri Duw*," and the other, K, *nat oes cret namyn brioödon*, "it is not a pledge of faith but bruised skin" (Owen's translation).
66. *Gwahard* was a common procedure in cases where land had been alienated or occupied. If the rightful owner did not object (*gwahard*) within a certain period of time, and thereby prohibit his rival from using the land until its ownership could be decided, he lost his right to the land: *Col* 612; *Bleg* 77.4–8; *WML* 51.11–13; *DwCol* 258. A "prohibition" could also be issued by a lord or his representative to force an offender to come to justice, as when Math fab Mathonwy sent out a "prohibition of food and drink" against Gilfaethwy and Gwydion to force them to compensate for the rape of Goewin: *PKM*, 74.
67. *LTMW*, 252, note 78.14–18; Pryce, "Duw un Lle Mach," *LAL*, 57.
68. Peter Brown, "The Rise and Function of the Holy Man in Late Antiquity," 103–152 in his *Society and the Holy*.
69. Although one late text remarks that the reason the bishop and the *déorad Dé* are equal in honor-price is that it is "just a change of pace" for a bishop to become a *déorad Dé*: *CIH* 686.31–32, and see also 2287.8; and Charles-Edwards, "The Social Background to Irish *Peregrinatio*," *Celtica* 11 (1976), 53–54.
70. *CIH* 2289.6–14 = *Br. Crólige*, 10–13, §12, and see note 12 on pp. 58–59; *CIH* 1966.28–30.
71. Normalized and translated by Binchy in *CU*, 66–67, §7 (= *CIH* 460.1–2), with a note on how his translation differs from that of Thurneysen on p. 81.
72. See below on *celebrad*.
73. For example, *The Liber Landavensis*, 152 (30); 212 (105); and 255 (144).
74. Pryce, "Duw yn Lle Mach," *LAL*, 62.
75. A passage in the Breton *Canones Wallici* might seem to provide recourse in secular law for contracts guaranteed through a religious suretyship, but there are so many textual problems with it that it is difficult to use:

> Si quis Deum fideiusorem inuocaverit et contempserit, a iudici condictione dampnetur. (Bieler, *The Irish Penitentials*, 156–157, §48.)
>
> If anyone invokes God as a surety and despises [Him], he shall be condemned by a decision of the court.

There are two recensions of this canon; Recension A is represented by five manuscripts, and Recension P by only one. The word *Deum* occurs only in the one manuscript of Recension P. But even if one assumes that this represents an omission rather than an interpolation on the part of P, it is not clear what meaning the term *condictio* should bear in this context. By the time of this canon, *condictio*, originally a technical term of Roman law, would have become a general legal action with little in common with the classical *legis actio* (Ernst Levy, *West Roman Vulgar Law: The Law of Property*, [Philadelphia, 1951], 202–208). The involvement of secular authorities is not necessarily implied.

76. *Vitae Sanctorum Britanniae et Genealogiae*, 94–97, §33.

77. *Ior* 68/9.

78. *Ior* 68/6; 71/10; and *WML* 29.5–7.

79. Pryce, "Duw yn Lle Mach," *LAL*, 50–51, 56, 62, and 64–65, note 30.

80. Compare Pryce, "Duw yn Lle Mach," *LAL*, 56.

81. Jenkins, *Cyfraith Hywel*, 85; *Col*, pp. 64–65, note to §128; *LTMW*, 252; and Davies, "Rhwymedigaethau Cytundebol," 44–49.

82. Pryce, "Duw yn Lle Mach," *LAL*, 53.

83. *Ior* 61/5; *Bleg* 41.14–15; *LTWL*, Lat A 125.35–36; Lat B 217.2–3; Lat D 369.3–4; Lat E 459.3 = *LAL*, 202–203, Lat E 13; and *LAL*, 196–197, Cyfn V 82 = *WML* 86.1–3.

84. *WML* 87.4–11 = *LAL*, 186–187, Cyfn 21–22; *LTWL*, Lat D 369.19–23; and *Bleg* 42.1–5.

85. *Ior* 59/3.

86. *Ior* 58–60; Pryce, "Duw yn Lle Mach," *LAL*, 53–55.

87. Jenkins, *Cyfraith Hywel*, 85; *Ior* 68/7.

88. *English Historical Documents, Vol. 1, c. 500-1042*, ed. Dorothy Whitelock (London, second edition, 1979), 413, note 6; Pryce, "Duw yn Lle Mach," *LAL*, 61.

89. *LTWL*, Lat B 217.33–218.4.

90. *Calendar of the Charter Rolls Preserved in the PRO: Henry III, 1226–1257*, vol. I (London, 1903), 164: "Notification that the king has made oath on the gospels and bound himself and his heirs . . . that he and they will faithfully, without fraud or guile . . . observe all the charters which he has granted to Margaret, countess of Kent . . . and for the better binding of himself he has made God his surety; so that if he or his heirs violate this oath . . . he subjects himself and his heirs to the Pope, renouncing all benefit of privilege or appeal, to be by him compelled to the observance of the said charters by sentence of excommunication, which shall not be removed, until the said countess has received satisfaction." Henry broke this oath only a few weeks after having made it.

91. *PKM*, 57.

92. *Topographia Hibernica*, ed. James F. Dimock, vol. 5 (London, 1867) of *Giraldi Cambrensis Opera*, ed. J. S. Brewer, J. F. Dimock, and G. F. Warner, 8 vols., Rolls Series (London, 1861–1891), 128–130, II.44–46. Gerald reports another such story in his *Gemma Ecclesiastica*, where a man borrowing from a Jewish lender gave St. Nicholas and his altar as his *fideiussor*. When the debtor attempted later to renege upon the debt, St. Nicholas brought him to an untimely end—to the amazement (and eventual conversion) of the Jew: 156–157, vol. II, Dist. I.52.

93. Hugh Kenner, Review of Patrick McGinley's *The Trick of the Ga Bolga*, *The New York Times Book Review*, July 21, 1985, p. 20.

94. *The Tripartite Life of Patrick*, 70–71, 76–79, 80–81, 112–113, 142–145, and 182–183.

95. Brown, *The Cult of the Saints*, 58–68.

96. *The Tripartite Life of Patrick*, 164–167, 234–235; *Lives of the Saints from the Book of Lismore*, ed. Whitley Stokes, *Anecdota Oxoniensia*, Mediaeval and Modern Series 5 (Oxford, 1890), lines 2504–2786; and *Adomnan's Life of Columba*, Book II, Chapters 22–25. Adomnán is careful to show Columba as foretelling rather than causing the death of these oppressors, but it is not difficult to imagine that such distinctions might frequently have become blurred in the minds of listeners.

97. *ECI*, 239; *Topographia Hibernica*, 137, II.55; and see also 131–137, II.48–50 and II.53–54; and 179, III.33. This is not to say that threatening or antisocial behavior was unique to Irish and Welsh saints. Recent work on general medieval sanctity demonstrates that liminal or eccentric actions were frequently interpreted as indications of sanctity.

98. *Itinerarium Kambriae et Descriptio Kambriae*, ed. James Dimock, vol. 6 (1868) of *Giraldi Cambrensis Opera*, 26–27, I.2.

99. *Vitae Sanctorum Britanniae et Genealogiae*, 90–97, §§29 and 33.

100. *ECI*, 241.

101. This issue has now been discussed by Pryce in his *Native Law and the Church*, 37–70.

102. *Berrad Airechta* exempts from the usual rules requiring two or three witnesses those who are "devout and believing": *CIH* 599.35–36 = *Bürgschaft*, 31–32, §84.

103. See, on relics, Pryce, "Duw yn Lle Mach," *LAL*, 51–53; and Pryce, *Native Law and the Church*, 41–44.

104. *Ior* 100/8; 106/9.

105. Binchy, *CU*, 81, note 7.

106. Binchy, *CU*, 66–67, §7.

107. *CIH* 594.36–37 = *Bürgschaft*, 14–15, §48.

108. *Topographia Hibernica*, 167, III.22 (translation by O'Meara, *The History and Topography of Ireland* by Gerald of Wales [1951; revised Harmondsworth, 1982], 108, §101). See also p. 89, II.7 for another such "barbarous rite, without rime or reason."

109. For example, *The Liber Landavensis*, 77 (9); 176 (58); 255 (144).

110. Binchy, "Distraint in Irish Law," 34–35; Binchy, "A Text on the Forms of Distraint," 75–76; and *GEIL*, 182–183.

111. *CIH* 466.22–24.

112. For example, Edward Harper, "*Hoylu*: A Belief Relating Justice and the Supernatural," *American Anthropologist* 59, no. 5 (1957): 808; and Edgar Winans and Robert Edgerton, "Hehe Magical Justice," *American Anthropologist* 66, no. 4 (1964): 745.

113. *CIH* 539.7–9. It is tempting to associate this type of *celebrad* with the formal curses and public humiliation of relics performed against offenders by representatives of the affected churches. The fearsome curses of the community of Armagh, for example, were enough to cause Hugh Tyrrell to return to them the

cooking pot he had stolen (unfortunately for him, however, the curses took effect despite his efforts to repay his crime: *Topographia Hibernica*, 133, II.50). Continental parallels to this procedure are discussed by Patrick Geary in his "Humiliation of Saints," in *Saints and their Cults: Studies in Religious Sociology, Folklore and History*, ed. Stephen Wilson (Cambridge, 1983; reprinted 1987), 123–140.

114. *ALW* IX.xvii.1; and *WML* 29.6–7.
115. *CD*, 166–167, §§6–7, lines 56–58 and 61–64; and see also *EJ*, 208, §29.
116. *ALW* XIV.xli.31.
117. Pryce's *Native Law and the Church* is happily now available.
118. Brown, "Society and the Holy," in Brown, *Society and the Holy*, 310–311, and 322–323.

Conclusion

1. *SD*.
2. *SD*, 77.
3. As argued by Jenkins in "The Significance of the Law of Hywel," 67–72.
4. Wormald, Review of *LTMW* and *Lawyers and Laymen*, 99.
5. Wormald, "Celtic and Anglo-Saxon Kingship," 157–170.
6. Wormald, "Celtic and Anglo-Saxon Kingship;" Ó Corráin, "Nationality and Kingship"; Gerriets, "Kingship and Exchange"; and Gerriets, "The King as Judge."
7. Sharpe, "Some Problems Concerning the Organization of the Church," and Sharpe, "Churches and Communities in Early Medieval Ireland."
8. Charles-Edwards, "*Cynghawsedd*: Counting and Pleading," and Charles-Edwards, *The Welsh Laws*, 53–67.
9. Stacey, "Law and Order in the *Very* Old West."
10. *The Dating of Beowulf*, ed. Colin Chase (Toronto, 1981).
11. Nelson, "Literacy in Carolingian Government," *The Uses of Literacy*, 262–272.

Notes to Diagram 3

1. The genealogies of the Loíchsi are to be found in *CGH*, 87–95 and 433–434. This table is selective; in other words, many persons and pedigrees recorded in *CGH* are not included in this diagram. Where birth order could not be determined from the pedigrees, I have entered sons in the order they are named in the Loíchsi book. Arrows indicate that the line continues in *CGH*.
2. *CGH*, 88, 126 b 49 (+Lec.); and 91, 127 a 32 (+Lec.).
3. The story of Barr mac Cáirthind's twelve sons and the family's relationship with Bishop Ibar is told in *CGH*, 90–93, 127 a 20 ff. I have listed only two of these sons here.
4. *CGH*, 90, 127 a 26 ff. claims that the Loíchse Raimne are the descendants of Fergus (+LL., Lec.) m. Bairr m. Cáirthind, and this is the relationship pictured

here. However, *CGH*, 88–89, 126 b 51–53 (+ Lec²) traces the Loíchse Raimne back to the Síl Senaich Móir.

    5. *CGH*, 93, 127 b 3 ff.

    6. According to Lec², the ultimate progenitors of the Loíchse Raimne; see above, note 4.

    7. *CGH*, 92–93, 127 a 43–44 and 127 b 10–11. Note the Loíchsi's claims of nobility vis-à-vis the Laigen in *CGH*, 25 and 79, 119 a 2 and 125 a 51 ff.; and *CGH*, 358, 318 c 7–10.

    8. The Síl mBeraich m. Mescill are termed "the royal race from which kings descend" in *CGH*, 92, 127 a 45.

    9. Appears only in the *Annals of the Four Masters*, where he is given an obituary of 886.

    10. Appears only in the *Fragmentary Annals*, where his obituary is listed as 913.

    11. Appears only in the annals, where the *Annals of the Four Masters* give his obituary as 906, and the *Fragmentary Annals* list it as 912.

    12. *CGH*, 433–434, 337 g 1 ff.

    13. *CGH*, 91, 127 a 31 ff., and note the Lec. addition that neatly ties the Síl mBairr in with this, the central line of the Loíchsi.

Bibliography

PRIMARY SOURCES

Adomnan's Life of Columba. Ed. A. O. Anderson and M. O. Anderson. London: Thomas Nelson and Sons, Ltd., 1961.
"Advice to a Prince." Ed. Tadhg O'Donoghue. *Ériu* 9 (1921–1923): 43–54.
"The Advice to Doidin." Ed. Roland M. Smith. *Ériu* 11 (1932): 66–85.
Ancient Laws and Institutes of Wales. Ed. Aneurin Owen. London: Public Records Commissioners, 1841.
Ancient Laws of Ireland. Rolls Series, 6 vols. Dublin and London: HMSO, 1865–1901.
Annála Rioghachta Éireann: Annals of the Kingdom of Ireland by the Four Masters, from the Earliest Period to the Year 1616. Ed. J. O'Donovan. 7 vols. Dublin: Hodges, Smith, and Co., 1848–1851; reprinted, 1856.
Annála Uladh: Annals of Ulster. Ed. W. M. Hennessy and B. MacCarthy. 4 vols. Dublin: HMSO, 1887–1901.
The Annals of Clonmacnoise, being annals of Ireland from the earliest period to A.D. 1408, translated into English, A.D. 1627, by Conell Mageoghagan. Ed. Dennis Murphy. Dublin: Annuary of the Kilkenny Archaeological Society, 1896.
The Annals of Inisfallen. Ed. Seán MacAirt. Dublin: DIAS, 1951.
The Annals of Loch Cé: A Chronicle of Irish affairs, 1014–1690. Ed. W. M. Hennessy. 2 vols. London: Longmans, Green, and Co., 1871; reprinted Dublin, 1939.
"The Annals of Tigernach." Ed. Whitley Stokes. *RC* 16 (1895): 374–419; *RC* 17 (1896): 6–33, 116–263, 337–420; *RC* 18 (1897): 9–59, 150–303, 374–391.
The Annals of Ulster (to A.D. 1131). Ed. Seán MacAirt and Gearóid Mac Niocaill. Dublin: DIAS, 1983.
Arrian's Anabasis Alexandri. Ed. P. A. Brunt. 2 vols. Cambridge, Mass. and London: Harvard University Press, 1976–1983.
Audacht Morainn. Ed. Fergus Kelly. Dublin: DIAS, 1976.
"Aus dem irischen Recht I-V." Ed. R. Thurneysen. *ZCP* 14 (1923): 335–394; *ZCP* 15 (1925): 238–296, 302–376; *ZCP* 16 (1927): 167–230; *ZCP* 18 (1930): 353–408.
The Banquet of Dún na nGedh and the Battle of Mag Rath. Ed. John O'Donovan. Dublin: Irish Archaeological Society, 1842.
Bechbretha: an Old Irish Law-tract on Bee-keeping. Ed. T. M. Charles-Edwards and Fergus Kelly. Early Irish Law Series. Vol. 1. Dublin: DIAS, 1983.
Beowulf and the Fight at Finnsburg. Ed. F. Klaeber. Lexington, Mass.: D. C. Heath and Company, third ed., 1950.

Berrad Airechta and Slán nAitire Cairde. See Thurneysen, *Die Bürgschaft im irischen Recht.*
Bethada Náem nÉrenn: Lives of Irish Saints. Ed. C. Plummer. 2 vols. Oxford: Clarendon Press, 1922; reprinted, 1968.
Bethu Phátraic: The Tripartite Life of Patrick. Ed. Kathleen Mulchrone. Dublin: Royal Irish Academy, 1939.
"The *Bóroma.*" Ed. W. Stokes. *RC* 13 (1892): 32–124 and 299.
Bretha Crólige. Ed. D. A. Binchy. *Ériu* 12 (1934): 1–77.
Bretha Déin Chécht. Ed. D. A. Binchy. *Ériu* 20 (1966): 1–66.
Bretha Nemed. See "An Old-Irish Tract on the Privileges and Responsibilities of Poets," "The Advice to Doidin," and "The First Third of *Bretha Nemed Toísech.*" Ed. Liam Breatnach. *Ériu* 40 (1989): 1–40.
Brut y Tywysogyon or The Chronicle of the Princes: Red Book of Hergest Version. Ed. Thomas Jones. Cardiff: University of Wales Press, 1955.
Die Bürgschaft im irischen Recht. Ed. R. Thurneysen. *Abhandlungen der preussischen Akademie der Wissenschaften* 2. Phil.-Hist. Klasse. Jahrgang 1928. Berlin, 1928. *Berrad Airechta* translated into English by Robin Chapman Stacey in "*Berrad Airechta*: an Old Irish Tract on Suretyship." In *Lawyers and Laymen.* Ed. Charles-Edwards, Owen, and Walters. Cardiff: University of Wales Press, 1986, 210–233.
C. Ivli Caesaris Commentariorvm pars prior et posterior. Ed. Rene DuPontet. Oxford: Clarendon Press, 1900–1901.
Caesar. *The Gallic War; with an English Translation by H.J. Edwards (De bello gallico).* Loeb Classical Library. Latin Authors 72. Cambridge, Mass.: Harvard University Press, 1917; reprinted, 1979.
Cáin Adamnáin: An Old-Irish Treatise on the Law of Adamnán. Ed. Kuno Meyer. *Anecdota Oxoniensia* Medieval and Modern Series 12. Oxford: Clarendon Press, 1905.
Cáin Aicillne. Ed. R. Thurneysen. "Aus dem irischen Recht I. Das Unfrei-Lehen." *ZCP* 14 (1923): 336–394.
Cáin Domnaig. Ed. Vernam Hull. *Ériu* 20 (1966): 151–177.
"*Cáin Domnaig*: I.—The Epistle concerning Sunday." Ed. J. G. O'Keeffe. *Ériu* 2 (1905): 189–214.
Cáin Éimíne Báin. Ed. Erich Poppe. *Celtica* 18 (1986): 35–52.
Cáin Lánamna. Ed. R. Thurneysen. In *Studies in Early Irish Law.* Ed. D. A. Binchy. Dublin: Royal Irish Academy, 1936, 1–80.
Cáin Sóerraith. Ed. R. Thurneysen. "Aus dem irischen Recht II. Das Frei-Lehen." *ZCP* 15 (1925): 238–260.
Calendar of the Charter Rolls Preserved in the PRO: Henry III, 1226–1257. Vol. I. London: HMSO, 1903.
Calendar of Various Chancery Rolls: Supplementary Close Rolls, Welsh Rolls, Scutage Rolls 1277–1326. Ed. H. C. Maxwell Lyte. London: HMSO, 1912.
Capitularia Regum Francorum. Ed. Boretius and Krause. *MGH, Legum*, Sectio II. 2 vols. Hannover: Hahnsche Buchhandlung, 1883–1897.
"The Celtic Ethnography of Posidonius." Ed. J. Tierney. *PRIA* 60 C (1959–1960): 189–275.

Chronicon Scotorum: A Chronicle of Irish Affairs from the Earliest Times to A.D. *1135, with Supplement, 1141–50.* Ed. W. M. Hennessy. Rolls Series. London: HMSO, 1866.
"Cináed úa Hartacáin's Poem on Brugh na Bóinne." Ed. L. Gwynn. *Ériu* 7 (1914): 210–238.
Coibnes Uisci Thairidne. Ed. D. A. Binchy. *Ériu* 17 (1955): 52–85.
Cóic Conara Fugill: Die fünf Wege zum Urteil. Ed. R. Thurneysen. *Abhandlungen der preussischen Akademie der Wissenschaften* 7. Phil.-Hist. Klasse. Jahrgang 1925. Berlin, 1926.
Collectio Canonum Hibernensis, See *Die irische Kanonensammlung*.
Corpus Genealogiarum Hiberniae. Ed. M. A. O'Brien. Vol. 1. Dublin: DIAS, 1962; reprinted, 1976.
Corpus Iuris Hibernici. Ed. D. A. Binchy. 6 vols. Dublin: DIAS, 1978.
Councils and Ecclesiastical Documents relating to Great Britain and Ireland. Ed. A. W. Haddan and W. Stubbs. 3 vols. Oxford: Clarendon Press, 1869–1878; reprinted 1965.
Críth Gablach. Ed. D. A. Binchy. Mediaeval and Modern Irish Series vol. 11. Dublin: DIAS, 1941; reprinted, 1979. Translated by Eoin MacNeill in "Ancient Irish Law: the Law of Status or Franchise." *PRIA* 36 C (1923): 265–306.
Cró 7 Díbad: "A Collation of *Críth Gablach*, and a Treatise on *Cró* and *Díbad*." Ed. Kuno Meyer. *Ériu* 1 (1904): 209–215, esp. pp. 214–215.
Cyfranc Lludd a Llefelys. Ed. Brynley Roberts. Dublin: DIAS, 1975.
Cyfreithiau Hywel Dda yn ôl Llyfr Blegywryd. Ed. Stephen J. Williams and J. Enoch Powell. Cardiff: University of Wales Press, second edition, 1961.
"Dál Caladbuig and Reciprocal Services between the Kings of Cashel and Various Munster States." Ed. J. G. O'Keeffe in vol. 1 of *Irish Texts*. Ed. J. Fraser, P. Grosjean, and J. G. O'Keeffe. 5 vols. London: Sheed and Ward, 1931–1933, 19–21.
Damweiniau Colan: Llyfr y Damweiniau yn ôl Llawysgrif Peniarth 30. Ed. Dafydd Jenkins. Aberystwyth: Cymdeithas Lyfrau Ceredigion, 1973.
Di Astud Chor. See *Early Irish Contract Law*.
Díre. See *Irisches Recht*, I. Ed. R. Thurneysen, pp. 1–37.
Early Irish Contract Law. Ed. Neil McLeod. Sydney, Australia: Centre for Celtic Studies, University of Sydney, 1992.
English Historical Documents, Volume 1, c. 500-1042. Ed. Dorothy Whitelock. London: Eyre Methuen, second ed., 1979.
"Epistle of Jesus." See *Cáin Domnaig*. Ed. O'Keeffe.
Expugnatio Hibernica: The Conquest of Ireland by Giraldus Cambrensis. Ed. A. B. Scott and F. X. Martin. Dublin: Royal Irish Academy, 1978.
"The Expulsion of the Déssi." Ed. K. Meyer. *Y Cymmrodor* 14 (1901): 101–135, and *Ériu* 3 (1907): 135–142.
Fled Dúin na nGéd. Ed. Ruth Lehmann. Dublin: DIAS, 1964.
Fragmentary Annals of Ireland. Ed. Joan N. Radner. Dublin: DIAS, 1978.
Frithfolaid tracts. See "Dál Caladbuig and Reciprocal Services."
Genealogical Tracts I. Ed. Toirdhealbhach Ó Raithbheartaigh. Dublin: Irish Manuscripts Commission, 1932.

Gesetze der Angelsachsen. Ed. F. Liebermann. 3 vols. Halle: Max Niemeyer, 1903–1916; reprinted Aalen, 1960.

Die Gesetze der Langobarden. Ed. F. Beyerle. Weimar: Hahnsche Buchhandlung, 1947.

Giraldi Cambrensis Opera. Ed. J. S. Brewer, J. F. Dimock, and G. F. Warner. Rolls Series, 8 vols. London: HMSO, 1861–1891.

Gúbretha Caratniad. Ed. R. Thurneysen. "Aus dem irischen Recht III. Die falschen Urteilssprüche Caratnia's." *ZCP* 15 (1925): 302–370.

Historia Francorum: Gregorii Turonensis Historiae Francorum Libri X. Ed. B. Krusch and W. Levison. *MGH, Scriptores Rerum Merovingicarum.* Vol. 1, second ed., Hannover: Hahnsche Buchhandlung, 1951. Translated by Lewis Thorpe in *The History of the Franks.* Harmondsworth: Penguin, 1974; reprinted 1977.

Historia Langobardorum. Ed. L. Bethmann and G. Waitz. *MGH, Scriptores Rerum Langobardicarum.* Hannover: Hahnsche Buchhandlung, 1878. Edited by Edward Peters and translated by William Foulke in *History of the Lombards* by Paul the Deacon. Philadelphia: University of Pennsylvania Press, reprinted 1974.

Die irische Kanonensammlung. Ed. H. Wasserschleben. Leipzig: Verlag Bernhard Tauchnitz, 1885; reprinted Aalen, 1966.

Irisches Recht. Parts I and II. Ed. R. Thurneysen. *Abhandlungen der preussischen Akademie der Wissenschaften* 2. Phil.-Hist. Klasse. Jahrgang 1931. Berlin, 1931.

Irische Texte. Ed. Windisch and Stokes. 4 vols. Leipzig: S. Hirzel, 1880–1909.

"The Irish Charters in the Book of Kells." Ed. J. O'Donovan. *Miscellany of the Irish Archaeological Society* 1 (1846): 127–158.

"Irish Miscellanies." Ed. C. Plummer. *RC* 6 (1883–1885): 162–172.

The Irish Penitentials. Ed. Ludwig Bieler. *Scriptores Latini Hiberniae.* Vol. 5. Dublin: DIAS, 1963; reprinted 1975.

The Irish Version of the Historia Britonum of Nennius. Ed. J. H. Todd. Dublin: Irish Archaeological Society, 1848.

Itinerarium Kambriae et Descriptio Kambriae. Ed. James F. Dimock, in vol. 6 (1868) of *Giraldi Cambrensis Opera.* Ed. J. S. Brewer, J. F. Dimock, and G. F. Warner. Rolls Series, 8 vols. London: HMSO, 1861–1891. Translated by Lewis Thorpe in *The Journey through Wales/The Description of Wales.* Harmondsworth: Penguin, 1978.

Latin Redaction A of the Law of Hywel. Translated by Ian Fletcher. Pamffledi Cyfraith Hywel. Aberystwyth: Centre for Advanced Welsh and Celtic Studies, 1986.

The Latin Texts of the Welsh Laws. Ed. Hywel Emanuel. Cardiff: University of Wales Press, 1967.

"The Laud Genealogies and Tribal Histories." Ed. Kuno Meyer. *ZCP* 8 (1912): 291–338.

The Laws of Earliest English Kings. Ed. F. L. Attenborough. Cambridge: Cambridge University Press, 1922.

The Laws of Hywel Dda (The Book of Blegywryd). Ed. Melville Richards. Liverpool: University Press, 1954.

The Law of Hywel Dda: Law Texts from Medieval Wales Translated and Edited. Ed. Dafydd Jenkins. The Welsh Classics, vol. 2. Llandysul: Gomer Press, 1986.
The Laws of the Kings of England from Edmund to Henry I. Ed. A. J. Robertson. Cambridge: Cambridge University Press, 1925; reprinted New York, 1974.
Lebor na hUidre, Book of the Dun Cow. Ed. R. I. Best and Osborn Bergin. Dublin: Royal Irish Academy, 1929.
Leges Alamannorum. Ed. Karl August Eckhardt. *Vol 1: Einführung und Recensio Chlothariana, Germanenrechte. Vol 2: Recensio Lantfridiana, Germanenrechte*. Göttingen, Berlin, Frankfurt: Musterschmidt, 1958 and 1962, respectively.
Leges Burgundionum. Ed. R. de Salis. *MGH, Legum* Sectio I. *Leges Nationum Germanicarum*. Vol. 2, part 1. Hannover: Hahnsche Buchhandlung, 1892; reprinted 1973. Translated by Katherine Drew in *The Burgundian Code*. Philadelphia: University of Pennsylvania Press, 1949; reprinted 1972.
Leges Henrici Primi. Ed. L. J. Downer. Oxford: Clarendon Press, 1972.
Lex Alamannorum. Second ed. Ed. K. Lehmann. *MGH, Legum* Sectio I. *Leges Nationum Germanicarum*. Vol. 5, part 1. Hannover: Hahnsche Buchhandlung, 1966.
Lex Baiwariorum. Ed. Ernst von Schwind. *MGH, Legum* Sectio I. *Leges Nationum Germanicarum*. Vol. 5, part 2. Hannover: Hahnsche Buchhandlung, 1926. Translated by T. J. Rivers in *Laws of the Alamans and Bavarians*. Philadelphia: University of Pennsylvania Press, 1977.
Lex Salica. Ed. K. A. Eckhardt. *MGH, Legum* Sectio I. *Leges Nationum Germanicarum*. Vol. 4, part 2. Hannover: Hahnsche Buchhandlung, 1969. Translated by T. J. Rivers in *Laws of the Salian and Ripuarian Franks*. New York: AMS Press, 1986.
Liber Landavensis: The Text of the Book of Llan Dâv. Ed. J. Gwenogvryn Evans and John Rhys. Oxford: Clarendon Press, 1893; reissued Aberystwyth, 1979.
The Life of St. Columba, founder of Hy; written by Adamnan. Ed. William Reeves. Dublin: University Press for the Irish Archaeological and Celtic Society, 1857.
Lives of the Cambro-British Saints. Ed. W. Rees. London: Society for the Publication of Ancient Welsh Manuscripts, 1853.
Lives of the Saints from the Book of Lismore. Ed. W. Stokes. *Anecdota Oxoniensia*. Mediaeval and Modern Series 5. Oxford: Clarendon Press, 1890.
Llyfr Blegywryd. See *Cyfreithiau Hywel Dda yn ôl Llyfr Blegywryd*.
Llyfr Colan. Ed. Dafydd Jenkins. Cardiff: University of Wales Press, 1963.
Llyfr Cyfnerth. See *Welsh Medieval Law*.
Llyfr Cynghawsedd. Ed. Aled Rhys Wiliam. *BBCS* 35 (1988): 73–85.
Llyfr Cynog. Ed. A. R. Wiliam. Pamffledi Cyfraith Hywel. Aberystywyth: Centre for Advanced Welsh and Celtic Studies, 1990.
Llyfr Gwyn Rhydderch: Y Chwedlau a'r Rhamantau. Ed. J. Gwenogvryn Evans and R. M. Jones. Cardiff: University of Wales Press, 1973.
Llyfr Iorwerth. Ed. Aled Rhys Wiliam. Cardiff: University of Wales Press, 1960.
"A London Municipal Collection of the Reign of John." Ed. Mary Bateson. *EHR* 17 (1902): 480–511, 707–730.

Medieval Handbooks of Penance: A Translation of the Principal Libri Poenitentiales and Selections from Related Documents. Ed. J. T. McNeill and Helena Gamer. New York: Columbia University Press, 1938; reprinted Octagon Books, 1979.

Medieval Irish Lyrics Selected and translated with The Irish Bardic Poet. Ed. James Carney. First published separately Dublin: Dolmen Press, Ltd., 1967. New edition in one volume, Dublin, 1985.

"Mitteilungen aus irischen Handschriften." Ed. Kuno Meyer. *ZCP* 8 (1912): 102–120.

"Morand's Fürstenspiegel." Ed. R. Thurneysen. *ZCP* 11 (1917): 56–106.

The O'Clery Book of Genealogies. Ed. Séamus Pender. *Analecta Hibernica* 18 (1951).

"An Old-Irish Tract on the Privileges and Responsibilities of Poets." Ed. E. J. Gwynn. *Ériu* 13 (1942): 1–60, 220–236.

Pactus Legis Salicae. Ed. K. A. Eckhardt. *MGH, Legum* Sectio I. *Leges Nationum Germanicarum*. Vol. 4, pt. 1. Hannover: Hahnsche Buchhandlung, 1962.

The Patrician Texts in the Book of Armagh. Ed. Ludwig Bieler. *Scriptores Latini Hiberniae*. Vol. 10. Dublin: DIAS, 1979.

Pedeir Keinc y Mabinogi. Ed. Ifor Williams. Cardiff: University of Wales Press, 1930; reprinted 1978.

Peniarth MS. 35, National Library of Wales.

"A Poem on the Airgialla." Ed. Máirín Ó Daly. *Ériu* 16 (1952): 179–188.

The Poems of Blathmac Son of Cú Brettan together with the Irish Gospel of Thomas and a Poem on the Virgin Mary. Ed. James Carney. Irish Texts Society vol. 47. Dublin: Irish Texts Society by the Educational Company of Ireland, 1964.

The Poetry of Llywarch Hen: Introduction, Text, and Translation. Ed. Patrick Ford. Berkeley, Los Angeles, and London: University of California Press, 1974.

"Quelques textes irlandais sur Saint Grégoire le Grand." Ed. P. Grosjean. *RC* 46 (1929): 223–251.

Remains of Old Latin. Ed. E. H. Warmington. 4 vols. Cambridge, Mass.: Harvard University Press, 1935–1940.

Rhigyfarch's Life of St. David. Ed. J. W. James. Cardiff: University of Wales Press, 1967. Translated by A. W. Wade-Evans in *Y Cymmrodor* 24 (1913): 1–73.

Ríagail Phátraic. Ed. J. G. O'Keeffe. "The Rule of Patrick." *Ériu* 1 (1904): 216–224.

"The Saga of Fergus mac Léti." Ed. D. A. Binchy. *Ériu* 16 (1952): 33–48.

Saint Patrick. *Confession et Lettre à Coroticus*. Ed. R. Hanson. Paris: Les Éditions du Cerf, 1978.

"The *Senbríathra Fíthail* and Related Texts." Ed. Roland Smith. *RC* 45 (1928): 1–92.

"Le siège de Druim Damhghaire." Ed. M. L. Sjoestedt. *RC* 43 (1926): 1–123.

The Statutes of Wales. Ed. Ivor Bowen. London: T. Fisher Unwin, 1908.

"Stories from the Law Tracts." Ed. Myles Dillon. *Ériu* 11 (1932): 42–65.

"Strata Marcella Documents." Ed. J. Conway Davies. *Montgomeryshire Collections* 51 (1949–1950): 164–187.

"A Text on the Forms of Distraint." Ed. D. A. Binchy. *Celtica* 10 (1973): 72–86.

Texte und Untersuchungen zur Geschichte der altchristlichen Literatur. Ed. S. Hellman. Series III, 4. Leipzig: J.C. Hinrichs, 1909.

Thesaurus Palaeohibernicus: A Collection of Old-Irish Glosses, Scholia, Prose and Verse. Ed. W. Stokes and J. Strachan. Cambridge: Cambridge University Press, 1901–1903; reprinted Dublin: DIAS, 1975.
"Three Poems in Middle-Irish relating to the Battle of Mucrama." Ed. Eoin MacNeill. *PRIA* 19 C, 3d series (1895): 529–563.
Titi Livi ab vrbe condita. Ed. W. Weissenborn and H. J. Müller. B. G. Teubner, 1898–1903.
Togail Bruidne Da Derga. Ed. Eleanor Knott. Mediaeval and Modern Irish Series vol. 8. Dublin: DIAS, 1936; reprinted 1975.
Topographia Hibernica. Ed. James F. Dimock. Vol. 5 (1867) of *Giraldi Cambrensis Opera.* Ed. J. S. Brewer, J. F. Dimock, and G. F. Warner. Rolls Series, 8 vols. London: HMSO, 1861–1891. Translated by John J. O'Meara in *The History and Topography of Ireland* by Gerald of Wales. Dundalk: Dundalgan Press, 1951; revised editions by Dolmen Press and Penguin Books, 1982.
Trioedd Ynys Prydein. Ed. Rachel Bromwich. Cardiff: University of Wales Press, 1961; reprinted, 1978.
The Tripartite Life of Patrick, with Other Documents Relating to that Saint. Ed. W. Stokes. 2 vols. London: HMSO, 1887; reprinted by Kraus Reprints, Ltd., 1965.
The Twelve Tables. Ed. Frederick Goodwin. London: Stevens and Son, 1886.
Uraicecht Becc. Translated by Eoin MacNeill in "Ancient Irish Law: the Law of Status or Franchise." *PRIA* 36 C (1923): 272–281.
Uraicecht na Ríar: the Poetic Grades in Early Irish Law. Ed. Liam Breatnach. Early Irish Law Series vol. 2. Dublin: DIAS, 1987.
Vita Sancti Columbae. In *Adomnan's Life of Columba.* Ed. A. O. Anderson and M. O. Anderson. London: Thomas Nelson and Sons, Ltd., 1961.
Vitae Sanctorum Britanniae et Genealogiae. Ed. A. W. Wade-Evans. Cardiff: University of Wales Press, 1944.
Vitae Sanctorum Hiberniae. Ed. C. Plummer. 2 vols. Oxford: Clarendon Press, 1910; reprinted, 1968.
The Welsh Assize Roll, 1277–1284. Ed. J. Conway Davies. Cardiff: University of Wales Press, 1940.
Welsh Genealogies, A.D. 300-1400. Ed. Peter Bartrum. 8 vols. Cardiff: University of Wales Press, 1974.
Welsh Medieval Law. Ed. A. W. Wade-Evans. Oxford: Clarendon Press, 1909; reprinted Aalen, 1979.

SECONDARY SOURCES

Arensberg, Conrad. *The Irish Countryman.* New York: Peter Smith, 1950.
Arensberg, Conrad, and S. T. Kimball. *Family and Community in Ireland.* Reprinted, Gloucester, Mass.: Peter Smith, 1961.
Baldwin, John. "The Intellectual Preparation for the Canon of 1215 against Ordeals." *Speculum* 36 (1961): 613–636.

Bannerman, John. "Notes on the Scottish Entries in the Early Irish Annals." In *Studies in the History of DalRiada*. Ed. Bannerman. Edinburgh: Scottish Academic Press, 1974, 9–26.
Bartlett, Robert. *Trial by Fire and Water: The Medieval Judicial Ordeal*. Oxford: Clarendon Press, 1986.
Bateson, Gregory. *Steps to an Ecology of Mind*. New York: Ballantine Books, 1972.
Bateson, Mary. "A London Municipal Collection of the Reign of John." *EHR* 17 (1902): 480–511, 707–730.
Bauman, Richard, ed. *Verbal Art as Performance*. Prospect Heights, Ill.: Waveland Press, Inc., 1977.
Bauman, Richard, and Charles Briggs. "Poetics and Performance as Critical Perspectives on Language and Social Life." *Annual Review of Anthropology* 19 (1990): 59–88.
Beckerman, John S. "The 40 Shilling Jurisdictional Limit in Medieval Personal Actions." In *Legal History Studies 1972: Papers presented to the Legal History Conference, Aberystwyth, 18–21 July 1972*. Ed. Dafydd Jenkins. Cardiff: University of Wales Press, 1975, 110–117.
Benveniste, Émile. *Le Vocabulaire des Institutions Indo-Européenes*. 2 vols. Paris: Les Éditions de Minuit, 1969.
Bergin, Osborn. "On the Syntax of the Verb in Old Irish." *Ériu* 12 (1934–1938): 197–214.
Beyerle, Franz. *Der Ursprung der Bürgschaft. Zeitschrift der Savigny-Stiftung für Rechtsgeschichte* 47 germanistische Abteilung (1927): 567–645.
Binchy, D. A. "Ancient Irish Law." *The Irish Jurist* 1, no. 1 (1966): 84–92.
———. "Bergin's Law." *Studia Celtica* 14/15 (1979–1980): 34–53.
———. "*Bretha Nemed*." *Ériu* 17 (1955): 4–6.
———. *Celtic and Anglo-Saxon Kingship*. Oxford: Clarendon Press, 1970.
———. "Celtic Suretyship, A Fossilized Indo-European Institution?" In *Indo-European and Indo-Europeans: Papers Presented to the Third Indo-European Conference, 1966*. Ed. G. Cardona and others. Philadelphia: University of Pennsylvania Press, 1970, 355–367. Reprinted in *The Irish Jurist* 7 (1972): 360–372.
———. "*Corpus Iuris Hibernici*—Incipit or Finit Amen?" In *Proceedings of the Sixth International Congress of Celtic Studies, 1979*. Ed. G. Mac Eoin. Dublin: DIAS, 1983, 149–164.
———. "The Date and Provenance of *Uraicecht Becc*." *Ériu* 18 (1958): 44–54.
———. "*De Fontibus Iuris Romani*." *Celtica* 15 (1983): 13–17.
———. "Distraint in Irish Law." *Celtica* 10 (1973): 22–71.
———. "*Féchem, Fethem, Aigne*." *Celtica* 11 (1976): 18–33.
———. "Indo-European $*Q^we$ in Irish." *Celtica* 5 (1960): 77–94.
———. "Irish History and Irish Law." *Studia Hibernica* 15 (1975): 7–36; *Studia Hibernica* 16 (1976): 7–45.
———. "The Linguistic and Historical Value of the Irish Law Tracts." *Proceedings of the British Academy* 29 (1943): 195–227. Reprinted in *CLP*, 71–107.
———. "Linguistic and Legal Archaisms in the Celtic Law Books." *Transactions of the Philological Society* (1959): 14–24. Reprinted in *CLP*, 109–120.

———. "MacNeill's Study of the Ancient Irish Laws." In *The Scholar Revolutionary: Eoin MacNeill (1867–1945) and the Making of the New Ireland*. Ed. F. X. Martin and F. J. Byrne. New York: Barnes and Noble, 1973, 37–48.

———. "The Pseudo-Historical Prologue to the *Senchas Már*." *Studia Celtica* 10/11 (1975–1976): 15–28.

———. "St. Patrick's 'First Synod.'" *Studia Hibernica* 8 (1968): 49–59.

———. "Secular Institutions." In *Early Irish Society*. Ed. Myles Dillon. Dublin: Colm Ó Lochlainn for the Cultural Relations Committee of Ireland, 1954, 52–65.

———. "Sick-Maintenance in Irish Law." *Ériu* 12 (1934): 78–134.

———. "Some Celtic Legal Terms." *Celtica* 3 (1956): 221–231.

———. "Varia. III: *Atomriug*." *Ériu* 20 (1966): 229–237.

Bitel, Lisa. *Isle of the Saints: Monastic Settlement and Christian Community in Early Ireland*. Ithaca, N.Y.: Cornell University Press, 1990.

Blair, John, and Richard Sharpe, eds. *Pastoral Care before the Parish*. Leicester, London, and New York: Leicester University Press, 1992.

Bohannan, P. J. "Anthropology and the Law." In *Horizons of Anthropology*. Ed. S. Tax. Chicago: Aldine Publishing Co., 1964; second ed., 1977, 290–299.

———. *Justice and Judgement among the Tiv*. London: Oxford University Press for the International African Institute, 1957; reprinted 1968.

Bossy, John, ed. *Disputes and Settlements: Law and Human Relations in the West*. Cambridge and New York: Cambridge University Press, 1983.

Breatnach, Liam. "Canon Law and Secular Law in Early Ireland: the Significance of *Bretha Nemed*." *Peritia* 3 (1984): 439–459.

———. "The Ecclesiastical Element in the Old-Irish Legal Tract *Cáin Fhuithirbe*." *Peritia* 5 (1986): 36–52.

———. "Lawyers in Early Ireland." In *Brehons, Serjeants, and Attorneys: Studies in the History of the Irish Legal Profession*. Ed. Daire Hogan and W. N. Osborough. Blackrock, co. Dublin: Irish Academic Press, 1990, 1–13.

———. "On Abstract Nouns from Prepositions in Irish." *Celtica* 15 (1983): 18–19.

———. "Some Remarks on the Relative in Old Irish." *Ériu* 31 (1980): 1–9.

Brett, Caroline. "Breton Latin Literature as Evidence for Literature in the Vernacular, A.D. 800-1300." *CMCS* 18 (Winter, 1989): 1–25.

Bromwich, Rachel, A. O. H. Jarman, and Brynley Roberts, eds. *The Arthur of the Welsh: a Collaborative Study of the Arthurian Legend in Medieval Welsh Literature*. Cardiff: University of Wales Press, 1991.

Bromwich, Rachel, and R. Brinley Jones, eds. *Astudiaethau ar yr Hengerdd: Studies in Old Welsh Poetry*. Cardiff: University of Wales Press, 1978.

Brown, Peter. *The Cult of the Saints*. Chicago: University of Chicago Press, 1981.

———. *Society and the Holy in Late Antiquity*. Berkeley and Los Angeles: University of California Press, 1982.

Brunner, H. *Deutsche Rechtsgeschichte*. 2 vols. Leipzig: Dunker and Humblot, 1887–1892. Third ed. with C. F. von Schwerin, Berlin, 1961.

Brynmor-Jones, Sir D. "The Brehon Laws and their Relation to the Ancient Welsh Institutes." *Transactions of the Cymmrodorion Society* (1904–1905): 7–36.

Buckland, W. W. *A Text-Book of Roman Law from Augustus to Justinian.* Cambridge: Cambridge University Press, 1921; third ed. revised by Peter Stein, 1963. Reprinted with additions and corrections, 1975.
Byrne, Francis John. *Irish Kings and High-Kings.* New York: St. Martin's Press, 1973.
———. *The Rise of the Uí Néill and the High-Kingship of Ireland.* Dublin: National University of Ireland, 1969.
———. "*Senchas*: The Nature of Gaelic Historical Tradition." *Historical Studies* 9 (1971): 137–159.
———. "Tribes and Tribalism in Early Ireland." *Ériu* 22 (1971): 128–166.
Campbell, James. *The Anglo-Saxons.* Ithaca, N. Y.: Cornell University Press, 1982.
———. *Essays in Anglo-Saxon History.* London and Ronceverte: Hambledon Press, 1986.
Carey, John. "The Two laws in Dubthach's Judgment." *CMCS* 19 (Summer 1990): 1–18.
Carney, James. "Three Old Irish Accentual Poems." *Ériu* 22 (1971): 23–80.
Carr, A. D. *A Look at Hywel's Law.* Whitland: Cymdeithas Genedlaethol, 1985.
Chadwick, Nora. *Celt and Saxon: Studies in the Early British Border.* Cambridge: Cambridge University Press, 1963.
Charles-Edwards, T. M. "Boundaries in Irish Law." In *Medieval Settlement: Continuity and Change.* Ed. P. H. Sawyer. London: Edward Arnold, 1976, 83–87.
———. "*Críth Gablach* and the Law of Status." *Peritia* 5 (1986): 53–73.
———. "Custom In Early Irish Law." *Recueils de la Société Jean Bodin* 52, part 2 (1990): 435–443.
———. "*Cynghausedd*: Counting and Pleading in Medieval Welsh Law." *BBCS* 33 (1986): 188–198.
———. "Early Irish Law." Unpublished article.
———. "The Heir-Apparent in Irish and Welsh Law." *Celtica* 9 (1971): 180–190.
———. "Kinship, Status and the Origins of the Hide." *Past and Present* 56 (1972): 3–33.
———. "NLW Peniarth MS. 35 (G)." Unpublished article.
———. Review of "The *Corpus Iuris Hibernici*." *Studia Hibernica* 20 (1980): 141–162.
———. "The Seven Bishop Houses of Dyfed." *BBCS* 24 (1970–1972): 247–262.
———. "The Social Background to Irish *Peregrinatio*." *Celtica* 11 (1976): 43–59.
———. "Some Celtic Kinship Terms." *BBCS* 24 (1970–1972): 105–122.
———. *The Welsh Laws.* Cardiff: University of Wales Press, 1989.
Charles-Edwards, T. M., Morfydd Owen, and Dafydd Walters, eds. *Lawyers and Laymen: Studies in the History of Law Presented to Professor Dafydd Jenkins on His Seventy-fifth Birthday.* Cardiff: University of Wales Press, 1986.
Chase, Colin, ed. *The Dating of Beowulf.* Toronto and Buffalo: University of Toronto Press in association with the Centre for Medieval Studies, 1981.
Chevrier, M. *Du Serment Promissoire en Droit Romain.* Dijon: Imprimerie de Thorey, 1921.
Clarke, H. B., and Anngret Simms, eds. *The Comparative History of Urban Origins in Non-Roman Europe: Ireland, Wales, Denmark, Germany, Poland, and Russia*

from the Ninth to the Thirteenth Century. BAR International Series 255 (i). Oxford: British Archaeological Reports, 1985.
Classen, Peter, ed. *Recht und Schrift im Mittelalter*. Vorträge und Forschungen 23. Sigmaringen: Thorbecke, 1977.
Collinet, P. "Droit Celtique et Droit Romain." *RC* 17 (1896): 321–336.
Collins, Roger. *Early Medieval Europe 300–1000*. New York and Basingstoke: Macmillan Education, 1991.
Colman, Rebecca: "Reason and Unreason in Early Medieval Law." *The Journal of Interdisciplinary History* 4 (1974): 571–591.
Comaroff, John and Simon Roberts. *Rules and Processes: The Cultural Logic of Dispute in an African Context*. Chicago: University of Chicago Press, 1981.
Cowgill, Warren. "The Etymology of Irish *guidid* and the Outcome of *g^wh in Celtic." In *Lautgeschichte und Etymologie*. Ed. Manfred Mayrhofer, Martin Peters, and Oskar Pfeiffer. Wiesbaden: Ludwig Reichert, 1978, 49–78.
Davies, Gwilym Prys. *Rhwymedigaethau Cytundebol yn y Gyfraith Gymreig*. LL. M. thesis, University of Wales, 1952.
Davies, R. R. *Conquest, Coexistence, and Change: Wales 1063–1415*. Oxford: Clarendon Press, 1987.
———. "Kings, Lords, and Liberties in the March of Wales, 1066–1272." *TRHS* 5th series, 29 (1979): 41–61.
———. "Law and National Identity in Thirteenth-Century Wales." In *Welsh Society and Nationhood*. Ed. R. R. Davies, Ralph Griffiths, Ieuan Gwynedd Jones, and Kenneth Morgan. Cardiff: University of Wales Press, 1984, 51–69.
———. "The Law of the March." *Welsh History Review* 5, no. 1 (June 1970): 1–30.
———. *Lordship and Society in the March of Wales, 1282–1400*. Oxford: Clarendon Press, 1978.
———. "The Survival of the Bloodfeud in Medieval Wales." *History* 54 (1969): 338–357.
———. "The Twilight of Welsh Law, 1284–1536." *History* 51 (1966): 143–164.
Davies, Wendy. "Clerics as Rulers: Some Implications of the Terminology of Ecclesiastical Authority in Early Medieval Ireland." In *Latin and the Vernacular Languages in Early Medieval Britain*. Ed. N. P. Brooks. Leicester: Leicester University Press, 1982, 81–97.
———. "Disputes, Their Conduct and Their Settlement in the Village Communities of Eastern Brittany in the Ninth Century." In *The Discourse of Law*. Ed. Sally Humphreys. *History and Anthropology* 1, part 2 (1985): 289–312.
———. *An Early Welsh Microcosm: Studies in the Llandaff Charters*. London: Royal Historical Society, 1978.
———. "Land and Power in Early Medieval Wales." *Past and Present* 81 (1978): 3–23.
———. "The Latin Charter-Tradition in Western Britain, Brittany and Ireland in the Early Mediaeval Period." In *Ireland in Early Mediaeval Europe*. Ed. Whitelock, 258–80.
———. *The Llandaff Charters*. Aberystwyth: National Library of Wales, 1979.
———. "On the Distribution of Political Power in Brittany in the Mid-Ninth Century." In *Charles the Bald: Court and Kingdom*. Ed. M. Gibson and

J. Nelson with D. Ganz. BAR, vol. 101. Aldershot: Variorum, 1981. Second ed., 1990, 87–107.
———. *Patterns of Power in Early Wales*. Oxford: Clarendon Press, 1990.
———. "Priests and Rural Communities in East Brittany in the Ninth Century." *Études Celtiques* 20 (1983): 177–197.
———. *Small Worlds: The Village Community in Early Medieval Brittany*. Berkeley and Los Angeles: University of California Press, 1988.
———. *Wales in the Early Middle Ages*. Leicester: Leicester University Press, 1982.
Davies, Wendy, and Paul Fouracre, eds. *The Settlement of Disputes in Early Medieval Europe*. Cambridge: Cambridge University Press, 1986.
(Contributions to A) Dictionary of the Irish Language. Royal Irish Academy. Dublin, 1913–1976. Compact edition, 1983.
Dillon, Myles. *Early Irish Society*. Dublin: Colm Ó Lochlainn for the Cultural Relations Committee of Ireland, 1954.
Diósdi, Gy. *Contract in Roman Law from the Twelve Tables to the Glossators*. Budapest: Akademiai Kiadbo, 1981.
Doherty, Charles. "Some Aspects of Hagiography as a Source for Irish Economic History." *Peritia* 1 (1982): 300–328.
Dumézil, Georges. *Mitra-Varuna: Essai sur Deux Représéntations Indo-Européenes de la Souveraineté*. Paris: Gallimard, second ed., 1948.
———. *Mythe et Épopée*. 3 vols. Paris: Gallimard, 1968–1973.
———. "Triadeste Calamités et Triades de Délits à Valeur Trifonctionelle Chez Divers Peuples Indo-Européens." *Latomus* 14 (1955): 173–185.
Dumville, David. "On the Dating of the Early Breton Lawcodes." *Études Celtiques* 21 (1984): 207–221.
———. "Sub-Roman Britain: History and Legend." *History* 62 (1977): 173–192.
Edwards, Goronwy. "The Historical Study of the Welsh Lawbooks." *TRHS* 12, 5th series (1962): 141–155.
———. "The Laws of Hywel Dda." In *Wales through the Ages*. Ed. A. H. Roderick. Llandybie: C. Davies, 1959–1960, 67–73.
———. Review of *Llyfr Iorwerth*. *Welsh History Review* 1 (1960–1963): 337–340.
———. "The Royal Household and the Welsh Lawbooks." *TRHS* 13, 5th series (1963): 163–176.
Edwards, Nancy. *The Archaeology of Early Medieval Ireland*. Philadelphia: University of Pennsylvania Press, 1990.
Ellis, T. P. "Legal References, Terms and Conceptions in the Mabinogion." *Y Cymmrodor* 39 (1928): 86–148.
———. *Welsh Tribal Law and Custom in the Middle Ages*. 2 vols. Oxford: Clarendon Press 1926.
Ellis Davidson, H. R. *Myths and Symbols in Pagan Europe: Early Scandinavian and Celtic Religions*. New York: Syracuse University Press, 1988.
Emania: Bulletin of the Navan Research Group 10 (1992).
Epstein, A. L. "The Case Method in The Field of Law." In *The Craft of Social Anthropology*. Ed. Epstein. London and New York: Tavistock, 1967.
Evans, D. Simon. *A Grammar of Middle Welsh*. Dublin: DIAS, 1976.

Evans-Pritchard, E. E. *Theories of Primitive Religion.* Oxford: Clarendon Press, 1965; reprinted, 1966, and Westport, Conn.: Greenwood Press, 1985.
———. *Witchcraft, Oracles, and Magic amomg the Azande of the Anglo-Egyptian Sudan.* Oxford: Clarendon Press, 1937.
Farnsworth, E. A. "The Past of Promise: An Historical Introduction to Contract." *Columbia Law Review* 69 (1969): 576–607.
Fleuriot, L. "Un fragment en Latin de très anciennes lois bretonnes armoricaines du 6ᵉ siècle." *Annales de Bretagne* 78 (1971): 601–660.
Foote, Peter. "Oral and Literary Tradition in Early Scandinavian Law: Aspects of a Problem." In *Oral Tradition, Literary Tradition: A Symposium.* Ed. Hans Bekker-Nielsen, P. Foote, and A. Haarder. Odense: Odense University Press, 1977, 47–55.
Ford, Patrick. *The Mabinogi and Other Medieval Welsh Tales.* Berkeley and Los Angeles: University of California Press, 1977.
Froget, Louis. *La Fides Facta aux époques Mérovingienne et Carolingienne.* Thesis for the doctorate in law, Université d'Alger, 1932.
Gagarin, Michael. *Early Greek Law.* Berkeley and Los Angeles: University of California Press, 1986.
Geary, Patrick. "Humiliation of Saints." In *Saints and their Cults: Studies in Religious Sociology, Folklore and History.* Ed. Stephen Wilson. Cambridge: Cambridge University Press, 1983; reprinted, 1987, 123–140.
Geertz, Clifford. "Ritual and Social Change: A Javanese Example." *American Anthropologist* 59, no. 1 (1957): 32–54.
Geiriadur Prifysgol Cymru. In progress. Cardiff: University of Wales Press, 1950–.
Gerriets, Marilyn. "Economy and Society: Clientship according to the Irish Laws." *CMCS* 6 (Winter 1983): 43–61.
———. "The King as Judge in Early Ireland." *Celtica* 20 (1988): 29–52.
———. "Kingship and Exchange in Pre-Viking Ireland." *CMCS* 13 (Summer 1987): 39–72.
———. "Money in Early Christian Ireland according to the Irish Laws." *Comparative Studies in Society and History* 27 (1985): 323–339.
Glob, P. V. *The Bog People: Iron-Age Man Preserved.* Translated by R. Bruce-Mitford. New York: Faber and Faber, Ltd., 1969; reprinted, 1977.
Gluckman, Max. *The Ideas in Barotse Jurisprudence.* New Haven and London: Yale University Press, 1965.
———. *The Judicial Process among the Barotse of Northern Rhodesia.* Manchester: Manchester University Press on behalf of the Rhodes-Livingstone Institute, Northern Rhodesia, 1955.
———. "The Peace in the Feud." In *Custom and Conflict in Africa.* Ed. Gluckman. Oxford: Basil Blackwell, 1955; reprinted, 1963, 1–26.
———. *Politics, Law and Ritual in Tribal Society.* Oxford: Basil Blackwell, 1965; reprinted 1977.
Goffman, Erving. *Frame Analysis: An Essay on the Organization of Experience.* New York: Northeastern University Press, 1974; reprinted, 1986.
Greene, David. "Archaic Irish." In *Indogermanisch und Keltisch.* Ed. Karl Horst Schmidt. Wiesbaden: Ludwig Reichert, 1977, 11–33.

———. "Miscellanea." *Celtica* 2 (1954): 337–339.

Gulliver, P. H. *Neighbours and Networks: the Idiom of Kinship in Social Action among the Ndendeuli of Tanzania*. Berkeley and Los Angeles: University of California Press, 1971.

———. *Social Control in an African Society; a Study of the Arusha: Agricultural Masai of Northern Tanganyika*. Boston: Boston University Press, 1963.

Gwynn, Aubrey. "Edward I and the Proposed Purchase of English Law for the Irish c. 1276–80." *TRHS* 5th series 10 (1960): 111–127.

———. "Ireland and the Continent in the Eleventh Century." *IHS* 8 (1953): 192–216.

———. Ireland and Rome in the Eleventh Century." *IER* 57 (1941): 213–232.

———. "Lanfranc and the Irish Church." *IER* 57 (1941): 481–500 and *IER* 58 (1941): 1–15.

———. "Pope Gregory VII and the Irish Church." *IER* 58 (1941): 97–109.

———. "St. Anselm and the Irish Church." *IER* 59 (1942): 1–14.

Hamnett, Ian. *Chieftainship and Legitimacy: An Anthropological Study of Executive Law in Lesotho*. London: Routledge and Kegan Paul, 1975.

———. *Social Anthropology and Law*. London and New York: Academic Press, 1977.

Hamp, Eric. "Varia: *Mech Deyrn*." *Études Celtiques* 21 (1984): 137–140.

Harding, Alan. "Regiam Majestatem amongst Medieval Law-Books." *Juridical Review* (1984): 97–111.

Harper, Edwards. "*Hoylu*: A Belief Relating Justice and the Supernatural." *American Anthropologist* 59, no. 5 (1957): 801–816.

Harrison, William. *The Old Historians of the Isle of Man*. Douglas, Isle of Man: Publications of the Manx Society, 1871.

Harvey, Anthony. "Early Literacy in Ireland: The Evidence from Ogam." *CMCS* 14 (Winter 1987): 1–15.

Henry, P. L. "Interpreting *Críth Gablach*." *ZCP* 36 (1977): 54–62.

———. "Varia. II.1: A Passage in *Scéla Cano Meic Gartnáin*." *Ériu* 20 (1966): 222–226.

Herbert, Máire. "The Preface to *Amra Coluim Cille*." In *Sages, Saints, and Storytellers*. Ed. Ó Corráin, 67–75.

———. "The World, The Text and the Critic of Early Irish Heroic Narrative." *Text and Context* (Autumn 1988): 1–9.

Hoebel, E. Adamson. *The Law of Primitive Man*. Cambridge, Mass.: Harvard University Press, 1954; reprinted, 1967.

Howells, Donald. "The Four Exclusive Possessions of a Man." *Studia Celtica* 8/9 (1973–1974): 48–67.

Huebner, Rudolf. *A History of Germanic Private Law*. Translated by Francis Philbrick. Continental Legal History Series 4. Boston: Little, Brown, and Co., 1918.

Hughes, Kathleen. "The Celtic Church and the Papacy." In *The English Church and the Papacy in the Middle Ages*. Ed. C. H. Lawrence. London: Burns and Oates, 1965, 3–28.

———. "The Celtic Church: Is This a Valid Concept?" *CMCS* 1 (Summer 1981): 1–20.

———. "The Church and the World in Early Christian Ireland." *IHS* 13, no. 50 (1962): 99–113.
———. *The Church in Early Irish Society*. London: Methuen and Co., Ltd., 1966; reprinted 1980.
———. *The Early Celtic Idea of History and the Modern Historian*. Cambridge: Cambridge University Press, 1977.
———. *Early Christian Ireland*. Ithaca, N. Y.: Cornell University Press, 1972.
Humphreys, Sally. "Law as Discourse." In *The Discourse of Law*. Ed. Humphreys. *History and Anthropology* 1, part 2 (1985): 241–264.
Huws, Daniel. "*Leges Howelda* at Canterbury." *National Library of Wales Journal* 19 (1975–1976): 340–344; and *National Library of Wales Journal* 20 (1977–1978): 95.
———. *The Medieval Codex with Reference to the Welsh Law Books*. Pamffledi Cyfraith Hywel. Aberystwyth: Centre for Advanced Welsh and Celtic Studies, 1980; reprinted 1982.
Hyams, Paul. "Trial by Ordeal: the Key to Proof in the Early Common Law." In *On the Laws and Customs of England: Essays in Honor of Samuel Thorne*. Ed. Morris Arnold, Thomas Green, Sally Scully, and Stephen White. Chapel Hill: University of North Carolina Press, 1981, 90–126.
The Hywel Dda Millenary Volume. *Aberystwyth Studies* 10 (1928).
Ifans, Dafydd. *William Salesbury and the Welsh Laws*. Pamffledi Cyfraith Hywel. Aberystwyth: Centre for Advanced Welsh and Celtic Studies, 1980.
Jack, R. Ian. *Medieval Wales*. Ithaca, N.Y.: Cornell University Press, 1972.
Jackson, K. H. *Language and History in Early Britain*. Edinburgh: Edinburgh University Press, 1953.
———. *The Oldest Irish Tradition: A Window on the Iron Age*. Cambridge: Cambridge University Press, 1964.
Jaffee, Martin S. "From Literary Tradition to Oral Torah: The Effective-History of *Halakhah* in Tannaitic Sources." Unpublished essay forthcoming as "*Halakhah* in Early Rabbinic Judaism: Innovation Beyond Exegesis, Tradition Before Oral Torah." In *Innovation and Religious Traditions: Essays in the Interpretation of Religious Change*. Ed. C. Cox, M. Jaffee, and M. Williams. Mouton de Gruyter.
———. "The *Taqqanah* in Tannaitic Literature: Jurisprudence and the Construction of Rabbinic Memory." *Journal of Jewish Studies* 41, no. 2 (Autumn 1990): 204–225.
Jenkins, Dafydd. *Cyfraith Hywel*. Llandysul: Gomer Press, 1970.
———. *Hywel Dda a'r Gwŷr Cyfraith*. Aberystwyth: Cymdeithas Lyfrau Ceredigion Gyf., 1977.
———. "Iorwerth ap Madog: Gŵr Cyfraith o'r Drydedd Ganrif ar Ddeg." *National Library of Wales Journal* 8 (1953): 164–170.
———. "Kings, Lords and Princes: The Nomenclature of Authority in Thirteenth-century Wales." *BBCS* 26 (1974–1976): 451–462.
———. *The Law of Hywel Dda: Law Texts from Medieval Wales Translated and Edited*. Llandysul: Gomer Press, 1986.
———. "The Lawbooks of Medieval Wales." In *The Political Context of Law: Pro-*

ceedings of the Seventh British Legal History Conference, Canterbury 1985. Ed. R. Eales and D. Sullivan. London and Ronceverte: Hambledon Press, 1987, 1—15.

———. "Llawysgrif Goll Llanforda o Gyfreithiau Hywel Dda." *BBCS* 14 (1950—1952): 89—104.

———. "The Medieval Welsh Idea of Law." *Tijdschrift voor Rechtsgeschiednis* 49, numbers 3—4 (1981): 323—348.

———. Review of *The Settlement of Disputes in Early Medieval Europe*. *CMCS* 15 (Summer 1988): 89—92.

———. "The Significance of the Law of Hywel." *Transactions of the Honourable Society of Cymmodorion* (1977): 54—76.

———, ed. *Celtic Law Papers Introductory to Welsh Medieval Law and Government: Studies Presented to the International Commission for the History of Representative and Parliamentary Institutions* 42. Brussels: Les Éditions de la Librairie Encyclopédique, 1973.

Jenkins, Dafydd, and Morfydd Owen, eds. *The Welsh Law of Women: Studies Presented to Professsor Daniel A. Binchy on his Eightieth Birthday, 3 June 1980*. Cardiff: University of Wales Press, 1980.

———. "The Welsh Marginalia in the Lichfield Gospels: Part I." *CMCS* 5 (Summer 1983): 37—66, and "Part II: The 'Surexit' Memorandum." *CMCS* 7 (Summer 1984): 91—120.

Jones Pierce, T. "The Laws of Wales—the Kindred and the Blood-Feud." *University of Birmingham Historical Journal* 3 (1952): 119—137. Reprinted in *Medieval Welsh Society*. Ed. Smith, 289—308.

———. Essays. See Smith, J. Beverly, ed. *Medieval Welsh Society, Selected Essays by T. Jones Pierce*.

Käser, Max. *Das altrömische Ius*. Göttingen: Vandenhoeck and Ruprecht, 1949.

Kelleher, John. "Early Irish History and Pseudo-history." *Studia Hibernica* 3 (1963): 113—127.

———. "The pre-Norman Irish Genealogies." *IHS* 16 (1968—1969): 138—153.

Kelly, Fergus. *A Guide to Early Irish Law*. Early Irish Law Series vol. 3. Dublin: DIAS, 1988.

———. "An Old-Irish Text on Court Procedure." *Peritia* 5 (1986): 74—106.

Kenner, Hugh. Review of Patrick McGinley's *The Trick of the Ga Bolga*. *The New York Times Book Review*, 21 July 1985, p. 20.

Kenney, J. F. *Sources for the Early History of Ireland: Ecclesiastical: An Introduction and Guide*. Addenda by Ludwig Bieler. New York: Octagon Books, 1966.

Kern, Fritz. *Kingship and Law in the Middle Ages*. Translated by S. B. Chrimes. London: Basil Blackwell, 1953.

Laistner, M. L. W. *Thought and Letters in Western Europe A.D. 500—900*. London: Methuen and Co., Ltd., 1931; revised edition London and Ithaca, N.Y.: Methuen and Cornell University Press, 1957.

Lapidge, Michael and Richard Sharpe. *A Bibliography of Celtic-Latin Literature, 400—1200*. Dublin: Royal Irish Academy, 1985.

Larson, G. J., C. Scott Littleton, and Jaan Puhvel, eds. *Myth in Indo-European Antiquity*. Berkeley and Los Angeles: University of California Press, 1974.

Leifer, Franz. "Zum römischen vindex-Problem." *Zeitschrift für vergleichende Rechtswissenschaft* 50 (1935): 5–62.
Levi, T. A. "The Laws of Hywel Dda in the Light of Roman and Early English Law." *Aberystwyth Studies* 10 (1928): 5–63.
Levy, Ernst. *West Roman Vulgar Law: The Law of Property*. Philadelphia: American Philosophical Society, 1951.
Lewis, Charlton, and Short, Charles. *A Latin Dictionary*. Oxford: Clarendon Press, 1975.
Lewis, Henry, and Pedersen, Holger. *A Concise Comparative Celtic Grammar*. Göttingen: Vandenhoeck and Ruprecht, 1937; reprinted with corrections and a supplement, 1961 and 1974.
Lewis, Timothy. *A Glossary of Medieval Welsh Law Based upon the Black Book of Chirk*. Manchester: Manchester University Press, 1913.
Littleton, C. Scott. *The New Comparative Mythology: an Anthropological Assessment of the Theories of Georges Dumézil*. Berkeley and Los Angeles: University of California Press, 1966; reprinted, 1973.
Llewellyn, K. N. and Hoebel, E. A. *The Cheyenne Way*. Norman: University of Oklahoma Press, 1941.
Lloyd, J. E. *History of Wales from the Earliest Times to the Edwardian Conquest*. 2 vols. Third ed., London: Longmans, Green, and Co., 1939.
———. *Hywel Dda 928-1928*. Cardiff: University of Wales Press, 1928.
Lloyd-Jones, J. *Geirfa Barddoniaeth Gynnar Gymraeg*. 8 parts. Cardiff: University of Wales Press, 1931–1963.
Mac Cana, Proinsias. *Celtic Mythology*. Feltham, Middlesex: Newnes Books, 1968; revised edition 1983.
———. "Conservation and Innovation in Early Celtic Literature." *Études Celtiques* 13 (1971): 61–118.
———. *The Learned Tales of Medieval Ireland*. Dublin: DIAS, 1980.
———. "Mongán mac Fiachra and *Immrain Brain*." *Ériu* 23 (1972): 102–142.
———. "The Three Languages and the Three Laws." *Studia Celtica* 5 (1970): 62–78.
———. "Varia." *Ériu* 20 (1966): 212–221.
Mac Niocaill, Gearóid. "Admissable and Inadmissable Evidence in Early Irish Law." *The Irish Jurist* 4 (1969): 332–337.
———. "Aspects of Irish Law in the Late Thirteenth Century." *Historical Studies* 10. Ed. G. A. Hayes-McCoy. Galway, 1976, 25–42.
———. "The "Heir-Designate" in Early Medieval Ireland." *The Irish Jurist* 3 (1968): 326–329.
———. "The Interaction of Laws." In *The English in Medieval Ireland*. Ed. J. Lydon. Dublin: Royal Irish Academy, 1984, 105–117.
———. *Ireland Before the Vikings*. Dublin: Gill and MacMillan, 1972; reprinted 1980.
———. "Notes on Litigation in Late Irish Law." *The Irish Jurist* 2 (1967): 299–307.
Maine, Henry Sumner. *Lectures on the Early History of Institutions*. London: John Murray, third ed., 1880.
Malinowski, Bronislaw. *Crime and Custom in Savage Society*. London: Routledge

and Kegan Paul, Ltd., 1926; reprinted Totowa, N.J.: Littlefield, Adams, and Co., 1972.

———. *Magic, Science and Religion, and other Essays*. Glencoe, Ill.: Beacon Press, 1948.

Mallory, J. P., ed. *Aspects of the Táin*. Belfast: December Publications, 1992.

Maund, K. L. *Ireland, Wales and England in the Eleventh Century*. Woodbridge, Suffolk: Boydell Press, 1991.

McCone, Kim. "Dubthach Maccu Lugair and A Matter of Life and Death in the Pseudo-Historical Prologue to the *Senchas Már*." *Peritia* 5 (1986): 1–35.

———. "Notes on the Text and Authorship of the Early Irish Bee-Laws." *CMCS* 8 (Winter 1984): 45–50.

———. *Pagan Past and Christian Present in Early Irish Literature*. Maynooth Monographs 3. Maynooth: An Sagart, 1990.

McKitterick, Rosamond. *The Carolingians and the Written Word*. Cambridge: Cambridge University Press, 1989.

———. "Some Carolingian Law-books and their Function." In *Authority and Power: Studies on Medieval Law and Government presented to Walter Ullmann on his Seventieth Birthday*. Ed. Peter Linehan and Brian Tierney. Cambridge and New York: Cambridge University Press, 1980, 13–27.

———. *The Uses of Literacy in Early Mediaeval Europe*. Cambridge: Cambridge University Press, 1990.

McLeod, Neil. "The Concept of Law in Ancient Irish Jurisprudence." *The Irish Jurist* 17 (1982): 356–367.

———. "Parallel and Paradox: Compensation in the Legal Systems of Celtic Ireland and Anglo-Saxon England." *Studia Celtica* 16/17 (1981–1982): 25–72.

———. "The Two *Fer Midboth* and their Evidence in Court." *Ériu* 33 (1982): 59–63.

Meillet, A. *The Comparative Method in Historical Linguistics*. Translated by G. Ford. Paris: Librairie Honoré Champion, 1967.

Melia, Daniel. "Review of *Lawyers and Laymen*." *Ius Commune, Zeitschrift für Europäische Rechtsgeschichte* 15 (1988): 292–295.

Meroney, Howard. "The Titles of Some Early Law-tracts." *Journal of Celtic Studies* 2 (1958): 189–206.

Meyer, Kuno. "Über die älteste irische Dichtung." *Abhandlungen der königlichen preussischen Akademie der Wissenschaften* 6, Phil.-Hist. Klasse (1913): 3–61.

Michel, J. H. "Reflexions sur quelques traits généraux du cautionnement archaïque à la lumière de l'ancien droit irlandais." *Recueils de la Societé Jean Bodin pour l'Histoire Comparative des Institutions. Les sûretés personnelles* 29, part 2 (1971): 383–397.

Milsom, S. F. C. *Historical Foundations of the Common Law*. London: Butterworths, 1969.

Moore, Sally Falk. *Law as Process: An Anthropological Approach*. London: Routledge and Kegan Paul, 1978.

Morris, William. *The Frankpledge System*. New York: Longmans, Green, and Co. for Harvard University Press, 1910.

Nader, Laura, ed. *The Ethnography of Law*. Special Publication of the *American Anthropologist* 67, no. 6, part 2. Wisconsin: 1965.

Nagy, Joseph Falaky. "Close Encounters of the Traditional Kind in Medieval Irish Literature." In *Celtic Folklore and Christianity: Studies in Memory of William W. Heist.* Ed. Patrick K. Ford. Santa Barbara and Los Angeles: McNally and Loftin, 1983, 129–149.

———. "Hierarchy, Heroes, and Heads: Indo-European Structures in Greek Myth." In *Approaches to Greek Myth.* Ed. Lowell Edmunds. Baltimore: Johns Hopkins University Press, 1990, 200–238.

———. "Oral Life and Literary Death in Medieval Irish Tradition." *Oral Tradition* 3/3 (1988): 368–380.

———. "Orality in Medieval Irish Narrative." *Oral Tradition* 1 (1986): 272–301.

———. "Representations of Oral Tradition in Medieval Irish Literature." *Language and Communication* 9, no. 2/3 (1989): 143–158.

———. "Sword as *Audacht*." In *Celtic Language, Celtic Culture: A Festschrift for Eric P. Hamp.* Ed. A. T. E. Matonis and Daniel F. Melia. Van Nuys, Calif.: Ford and Bailie, 1990, 131–136.

———. "Talking With and About the Past." Unpublished paper.

Nelson, Janet. "Legislation and Consensus in the Reign of Charles the Bald." In *Ideal and Reality in Frankish and Anglo-Saxon Society: Studies presented to J.M. Wallace-Hadrill.* Ed. Patrick Wormald with Donald Bullough and Roger Collins. Oxford: Basil Blackwell, 1983, 202–227.

Neusner, Jacob. *Oral Tradition in Judaism: The Case of the Mishnah.* New York: Garland Publishing, 1987.

———. *Rabbinic Traditions About the Pharisees Before 70.* Leiden: E.J. Brill, 1971.

Ní Chatháin, P., and M. Richter, eds. *Irland und die Christenheit: Bibelstudien und Mission/Ireland and Christendom: The Bible and the Missions.* Stuttgart: Klett-Cotta, 1987.

———. *Irland und Europa: Die Kirche im Frühmittelalter/Ireland and Europe: The Early Church.* Stuttgart: Klett-Cotta, 1984.

Ní Dhonnchadha, Máirín. "An Address to a Student of Law." In *Sages, Saints and Storytellers.* Ed. Ó Corráin, 159–177.

———. "The Guarantor List of *Cáin Adomnáin*, 697." *Peritia* 1 (1982): 178–215.

Oakley, T. P. "Mediaeval Penance and Secular Law." *Speculum* 7, no. 4 (1932): 515–524.

Ó Briain, Felim. "The Hagiography of Leinster." In *Féil-sgríbinn Eóin Mhic Neill.* Ed. J. Ryan. Dublin: The Sign of Three Candles, 1940, 454–464.

O'Brien, Bruce. *Studies of the "Leges Edwardi Confessoris" and Their Milieu.* Ph.D. diss., Yale University, 1990.

O'Brien, M. A. "Etymologies and Notes." *Celtica* 3 (1956): 168–184.

———. "Varia V." *Ériu* 11 (1932): 88–89.

Ó Buachalla, Liam. "Contributions towards the Political History of Munster, 450–800 A.D." *Journal of the Cork Historical and Archaeological Society* 56, part 1 (1951): 87–90; *JCHAS* 57, part 1 (1952): 67–86; *JCHAS* 59 (1954): 111–126; *JCHAS* 61, part 1 (1956): 89–102.

———. "Some Researches in Ancient Irish Law." *Journal of the Cork Historical and Archaeological Society* 52 (1947): 41–54, and 135–48; *JCHAS* 53 (1948): 1–12, and 75–81.

Ó Corráin, Donnchadh. "Historical Need and Literary Narrative." *Proceedings of the Seventh International Congress of Celtic Studies, Oxford, 1983.* Ed. D. Ellis Evans, John G. Griffith, and E. M. Jope. Jesus College, Oxford: Cranham Press, 1986, 141–158.

———. *Ireland before the Normans.* Dublin: Gill and MacMillan, 1972.

———. "Irish Law and Canon Law." In *Irland und Europa: Die Kirche im Frühmittelalter/Ireland and Europe: The Church in the Early Middle Ages.* Ed. Ní Chatháin and Richter, 157–166.

———. "Irish Origin Legends and Genealogy: Recurrent Aetiologies." In *History and Heroic Tale: A Symposium.* Ed. T. Nyberg, I. Pio, P. Sorensen, and A. Trommer. Odense: Odense University Press, 1985, 51–96.

———. "Irish Regnal Succession: A Reappraisal." *Studia Hibernica* 11 (1971): 7–39.

———. "Irish Vernacular Law and the Old Testament." In *Irland und die Christenheit: Bibelstudien und Mission/Ireland and Christendom: The Bible and the Missions.* Ed. Ní Chatháin and Richter, 284–307.

———. "Law and Society—Principles of Classification." In *Geschichte und Kultur der Kelten/ History and Culture of the Celts.* Ed. Karl Horst Schmidt with Rolf Ködderitzsch. Heidelberg: Carl Winter, 1986, 234–240.

———. "Legend as Critic." In *The Writer as Witness: Literature as Historical Evidence.* Ed. T. Dunne. Cork: Cork University Press, 1987, 23–38.

———. "Nationality and Kingship in Pre-Norman Ireland." In *Nationality and the Pursuit of National Independence.* Ed. T. W. Moody. Belfast: The Appletree Press, 1978, 1–35.

Ó Corráin, Donnchadh, Liam Breatnach, and Aidan Breen. "The Laws of the Irish." *Peritia* 3 (1984): 382–438.

Ó Corráin, Donnchadh, Liam Breatnach, and Kim McCone. *Sages, Saints and Storytellers: Celtic Studies in Honour of Professor James Carney.* Maynooth Monographs 2. Maynooth: An Sagart, 1989.

Ó hUiginn, Ruairi. "Tongu do dia toinges mo thuath and Related Expressions." In *Sages, Saints and Storytellers.* Ed. Ó Corráin, 332–341.

Ó Riain, Pádraig. "A Misunderstood Annal: A Hitherto Unnoticed *Cáin.*" *Celtica* 21 (1990): 561–566.

Otway-Ruthven, J. "The Request of the Irish for English Law, 1277–80." *IHS* 6, no. 24 (September 1949): 261–270.

Owen, Morfydd. "Y Cyfreithiau—(1) Natur y Testunau," and "Y Cyfraith—(2) Ansawdd Y Rhyddiaith." In *Y Traddiodiad Rhyddiaith yn yr Oesau Canol.* Ed. G. Bowen. Llandysul: Gomer Press, 1974, 196–244.

———. "Functional Prose." In *A Guide to Welsh Literature.* Vol. 1. Ed. A. O. H. Jarman and G. R. Hughes. Swansea: C. Davies, 1976.

———. Review of *Llyfr Colan. Llên Cymru* 8 (1964): 244–247.

Patterson, Nerys. "Brehon Law in Late Medieval Ireland: 'Antiquarian and Obsolete' or 'Traditional and Functional'?" *CMCS* 17 (Summer 1989): 43–63.

———. "Honour and Shame in Medieval Welsh Society: A Study of the Role of Burlesque in the Welsh Laws." *Studia Celtica* 16/17 (1981/1982): 73–103.

———. "Material and Symbolic Exchange in Early Irish Clientship." *Proceedings of the Harvard Celtic Colloquium* 1 (1981): 53–61.

Plescia, J. *The Oath and Perjury in Ancient Greece*. Tallahassee: Florida State University Press, 1970.
Pollock, F. and Maitland, F. W. *The History of English Law before the Time of Edward I*. Cambridge: Cambridge University Press, second ed. 1898; reissued with new introduction by S. F. C. Milsom, 1968.
Poppe, Erich. "The List of Sureties in *Cáin Éimíne*." *Celtica* 21 (1990): 588–592.
Pospisil, Leopold. *Kapauku Papuans and their Law*. New Haven: Yale University Press, 1958.
Powell, Enoch. "Floating Sections in the Laws of Howel." *BBCS* 9, part 1 (1937): 27–34.
Pryce, Huw. "Early Irish Canons and Medieval Welsh Law." *Peritia* 5 (1986): 107–127.
———. "Medieval Welsh Law." *Newsletter of the School of Celtic Studies* 4 (December 1990): 30–34.
———. *Native Law and the Church in Medieval Wales*. Oxford: Clarendon Press, 1993.
———. "The Prologues to the Welsh Lawbooks." *BBCS* 33 (1986): 151–187.
Radcliffe-Brown, A. R. "Primitive Law." *Encyclopedia of the Social Sciences* 9. New York: Macmillan Co., 1933.
———. *Structure and Function in Primitive Society*. London: Routledge and Kegan Paul, 1952.
Richter, Michael. *Medieval Ireland: The Enduring Tradition*. Translated by Brian Stone and Adrian Keogh. Originally published in German: Stuttgart, Verlag W. Kohlhammer, 1983; translation published New York: St. Martin's Press, 1988.
———. "The Political and Institutional Background to National Consciousness in Medieval Wales." In *Nationalism and the Pursuit of National Independence*. Ed. T. W. Moody. Belfast: The Appletree Press, 1978, 37–55.
Roberts, Brynley. *Early Welsh Poetry: Studies in the Book of Aneirin*. Aberystwyth: National Library of Wales, 1988.
Roberts, John. "Oaths, Autonomic Ordeals, and Power." In *The Ethnography of Law*. Ed. Nader, 186–212.
Roberts, Simon. *Order and Dispute: An Introduction to Legal Anthropology*. New York: St. Martin's Press, 1979.
Ronayne, Liam. "*Seandlithe na nGael*: an Annotated Bibliography of the Ancient Laws of Ireland." *The Irish Jurist* 17 (1982): 131–144.
Ruesch, Jurgen and Gregory Bateson. *Communication*. New York: Norton, 1968.
Sawyer, P. H. and I. N. Wood, eds. *Early Medieval Kingship*. Leeds: School of History, University of Leeds, 1977; reprinted, 1979.
Schapera, Ian. *A Handbook of Tswana Law and Custom*. London: Oxford University Press for the International African Institute, 1938; reprinted 1955.
Schneider, David. "Political Organization, Supernatural Sanctions and the Punishment for Incest on Yap." *American Anthropologist* 59, no. 5 (1957): 791–800.
Schröder, Franz. "Ein altirischer Krönungsritus und das indogermanische Rossopfer." *ZCP* 16 (1927): 310–312.

Sharpe, Richard. *Medieval Irish Saints' Lives: An Introduction to Vitae Sanctorum Hiberniae.* Oxford: Clarendon Press, 1991.
———. "Some Problems Concerning the Organization of the Church in Early Medieval Ireland." *Peritia* 3 (1984): 230–270.
Sheehy, Maurice. "Influence of Ancient Irish Law on the *Collectio Canonum Hibernensis.*" *Proceedings of the Third International Congress of Medieval Canon Law, Monumenta Iuris Canonici.* Series C, Subsidia 4. Vatican City: Bibliotheca Apostolica Vaticanae, 1971, 31–42.
Sheringham, J. G. T. "Les Machtierns." *Memoires de la Societé d'histoire et d'archéologie de Bretagne* 58 (1981): 61–72.
Smith, J. Beverly: "The Legal Position of Wales in the Middle Ages." In *Law-Making and Law-Makers in British History: Papers Presented to the Edinburgh Legal History Conference, 1977.* Ed. Alan Harding. London: Royal Historical Society, 1980, 21–53.
———, ed. *Medieval Welsh Society, Selected Essays by T. Jones Pierce.* Cardiff: University of Wales Press, 1972.
Smith, Julia. *Province and Empire: Brittany and the Carolingians.* Cambridge: Cambridge University Press, 1992.
Smith, Llinos B. "Disputes and Settlements in Medieval Wales: the Role of Arbitration." *EHR* 106, no. 421 (1991): 835–860.
———. "The Gage and the Land Market in Late Medieval Wales." *Economic History Review* 2nd series, 29 (1976): 537–550.
———. "The Gravamina of the Community of Gwynedd against Llywelyn ap Gruffydd." *BBCS* 31 (1984): 158–176.
Smyth, Alfred. *Celtic Leinster: Towards an Historical Geography of Early Irish Civilization A.D. 500-1600.* Blackrock, co. Dublin: Irish Academic Press, 1982.
———. "The Earliest Irish Annals: Their First Contemporary Entries, and the Earliest Centres of Recording." *PRIA* 72 C (1972): 1–48.
Stacey, Robin Chapman. "Law and Order in the *Very* Old West: England and Ireland in the Early Middle Ages." In *Crossed Paths: Methodological Approaches to the Celtic Aspect of the European Middle Ages.* Ed. Benjamin T. Hudson and Vickie Ziegler. Lanham, Maryland, and London: University Press of America, 1991, 39–60.
———. "Ties That Bind: Immunities in Irish and Welsh Law." *CMCS* 20 (Winter 1990): 39–60.
Stephenson, D. *The Governance of Gwynedd.* Cardiff: University of Wales Press, 1984.
———. *Thirteenth-Century Welsh Law Courts.* Pamffledi Cyfraith Hywel. Aberystwyth: Centre for Advanced Welsh and Celtic Studies, 1980.
Stokes, Whitley. "The Irish Ordeals, Cormac's Adventure in the Land of Promise, and the Decision as to Cormac's Sword." In *Irische Texte.* Ed. Stokes and Windisch, III, i. Leipzig: S. Hirzel, 1891.
Les sûretés personnelles. Recueils de la Société Jean Bodin pour l'Histoire Comparative des Institutions 28–30. Brussels: Les Éditions de la Librairie Encyclopédique, 1969–1974.

Thomas, Keith. *Religion and the Decline of Magic*. London: Weidenfeld and Nicolson, 1971; reprinted Harmondsworth: Penguin, 1973.
Thurneysen, R. "Allerlei Keltisches." *ZCP* 16 (1927): 267–278.
———. "Allerlei Nachträge." *ZCP* 19 (1933): 125–133.
———. "Aus dem irischen Recht I" [1. Das Unfrei-Lehen]. *ZCP* 14 (1923): 335–394.
———. "Aus dem irischen Recht II" [2. Das Frei-Lehen; 3. Das Fasten beim Pfändungsverfahren]. *ZCP* 15 (1925): 238–296.
———. "Aus dem irischen Recht III" [4. Die falschen Urteilssprüche Caratnia's; 5. Zur Überlieferung und zur Ausgabe der Texte über das Unfrei-Lehen und das Frei-Lehen]. *ZCP* 15 (1925): 302–376.
———. "Aus dem irischen Recht IV" [6. Zu den bisherigen Ausgaben der irischen Rechtstexte]. *ZCP* 16 (1927): 167–230.
———. "Aus dem irischen Recht V" [7. Zu Gúbretha Caradniad; 8. Zum ursprünglichen Umfang das Senchas Már; 9. Zu der Etymologie von irisch *ráth* "Bürgschaft" und zu der irischen Kanonensammlung und den Triaden; 10. Nachträge zur Bürgschaft]. *ZCP* 18 (1930): 353–408.
———. *Die Bürgschaft im irischen Recht*. *Abhandlungen der preussischen Akademie der Wissenschaften* 2, Phil.-Hist. Klasse. Jahrgang 1928. Berlin: Verlag der preussischen Akademie der Wissenschaften, 1928.
———. *Cóic Conara Fugill: Die fünf Wege zum Urteil*. *Abhandlungen der preussischen Akademie der Wissenschaften* 7, Phil.-Hist. Klasse. Jahrgang 1925. Berlin: Verlag der preussischen Akademie der Wissenschaften, 1926.
———. *A Grammar of Old Irish*. Translated from the German by D. A. Binchy and O. Bergin. Dublin: DIAS 1946; reprinted, 1975.
———. *Irisches Recht* [1. Díre. Ein altirischer Rechtstext; 2. Zu den unteren Ständen in Irland]. *Abhandlungen der preussischen Akademie der Wissenschaften* 2, Phil.-Hist. Klasse. Jahrgang 1931. Berlin: Verlag der preussischen Akademie der Wissenschaften, 1931.
———. "Nachträge zur Bürgschaft." See "Aus dem irischen Recht V," 375–408.
———. "Sochor." In *Féil-sgríbinn Eóin Mhic Néill*. Ed. John Ryan. Dublin: The Sign of Three Candles, 1940, 158–159.
———. "Über Zimmer, Nennius Vindicatus." *Zeitschrift für deutsche Philologie* 28 (1896): 80–113.
———. "Zu der Etymologie von irischen *ráth*, "Bürgschaft," und zu der irischen Kanonensammlung und der Triaden." See "Aus dem irischen Recht V," 364–375.
———, D. A. Binchy, and others. *Studies in Early Irish Law*. Dublin: Royal Irish Academy, 1936.
Toelken, J. Barre. "The 'Pretty Language' of Yellowman: Genre, Mode, and Texture in Navaho Coyote Narratives." *Genre* 2 (1969): 211–235.
Turner, V. *Schism and Continuity in an African Society*. Manchester: Manchester University Press, on behalf of the Rhodes-Livingstone Institute, Northern Rhodesia, 1957.

Vendryes, J. *Lexique Étymologique de l'Irlandais Ancien*. In progress. Paris and Dublin: DIAS and Centre National de la Recherche Scientifique, 1959–.

Vinogradoff, P. *Roman Law in Medieval Europe*. Second ed. edited by F. de Zulueta. Oxford: Clarendon Press, 1929.

Vollrath, Hanna. "Gesetzgebung und Schriftlichkeit: das Beispiel der angelsächsischen Gesetze." *Historisches Jahrbuch* 99 (1979): 28–54.

Walker, David. *Medieval Wales*. Cambridge: Cambridge University Press, 1990.

Wallace-Hadrill, J. M. *Early Germanic Kingship in England and on the Continent*. Oxford: Clarendon Press, 1971.

———. *The Long-Haired Kings*. London: Methuen and Co., Ltd., 1962; reprinted Toronto: University of Toronto Press in association with the Medieval Academy of America, 1982.

Walters, D. B. *The Comparative Legal Method: Marriage, Divorce and the Spouses' Property Rights in Early Medieval Welsh Law and Cyfraith Hywel*. Pamffledi Cyfraith Hywel. Aberystwyth: Centre for Advanced Welsh and Celtic Studies, 1982.

Watkins, Calvert. "The Indo-European Origin of English," and "Indo-European and the Indo-Europeans." *American Heritage Dictionary of the English Language* 19–20. American Heritage Publishing Co., 1975, 1496–1502 and endpapers.

———. *Indogermanische Grammatik*. Vol. III/1. Heidelberg, 1969.

———. "Preliminaries to a Historical and Comparative Analysis of the Syntax of the Old Irish Verb." *Celtica* 6 (1963): 1–49.

———. "Sick-Maintenance in Indo-European." *Ériu* 27 (1976): 21–25.

Watson, Alan. *The Evolution of Law*. Baltimore: Johns Hopkins University Press, 1985.

Watt, John. *The Church in Medieval Ireland*. Dublin: Gill and MacMillan, 1972.

Welsh History Review. Special Number devoted to the Welsh Laws (1963).

Whitelock, Dorothy, R. McKitterick, and D. Dumville, eds. *Ireland in Early Mediaeval Europe: Studies in Memory of Kathleen Hughes*. Cambridge: Cambridge University Press, 1982.

Wiliam, Aled. "Y Deddfgronau Cymraeg." *Cylchgrawn Llyfrgell Genedlaethol Cymru* 8 (1953): 97–103.

Winans, Edgar and Robert Edgerton. "Hehe Magical Justice." *American Anthropologist* 66, no. 4 (1964): 745–764.

Wormald, Patrick. "Aethelred the Lawmaker." In *Ethelred the Unready: Papers from the Millenary Conference*. Ed. David Hill. BAR British series 59. Oxford: British Archaeological Reports, 1978, 47–80.

———. "Celtic and Anglo-Saxon Kingship: Some Further Thoughts." In *Sources of Anglo-Saxon Culture*. Ed. Paul Szarmach with Virginia Oggins. Kalamazoo, Mich.: Medieval Institute Publications, 1986, 151–183.

———. "In Pursuit of Crime: The Early English Approach." Unpublished paper delivered to the British Legal History Conference at Oxford, 11 July 1991.

———. "*Lex Scripta* and *Verbum Regis*: Legislation and Germanic Kingship, from Euric to Cnut." In *Early Medieval Kingship*. Ed. P. H. Sawyer and I. N. Wood. Leeds: School of History, University of Leeds, 1977; reprinted, 1979, 105–138.

———. "*Lex Scripta* and *Verbum Regis*: A Retractatio?" Unpublished paper.
———. Review of *The Law of Hywel Dda* and *Lawyers and Laymen*. *CMCS* 16 (Winter 1988): 97–100.
———. "The Uses of Literacy in Anglo-Saxon England and its Neighbours." *TRHS* 5th series 27 (1977): 95–114.
Wylie, Diana. *The Center Cannot Hold: The Decline of the Ngwato Chieftainship 1926–1950*. Ph.D. diss., Yale University, 1985.

Index

Endnotes relating to specific texts or secondary authors have been indexed only when substantive discussion of their contents or views occurs there. Terms in languages other than English have been translated. Abbreviations are as follows: AS = Anglo-Saxon; Br. = Breton; Fr. = Frankish; G. = German; Ir. = Irish; L. = Latin; W. = Welsh.

Aberffraw, 13, 237 n.29
Achad Fobair, well of, 216
Adam, 7, 244 n.9
Adau, emadau (W.), "to promise" or "mutually promise," 171
Adomnán, 94, 264 n.77, 266–67 n.106, 294 n.18, 299 n.96. See also *Cáin Adomnáin*
Adoption, 67, 72, 80
Aí Cermna, 115, 277 n.107
Aicillne (Ir.), "base-clientship," 86–87, 109, 255–56 n.64. See also *Cáin Aicillne*; Clientship
Aicned (Ir.), "nature," 129–30, 137–38, 271 n.22, 276 n.77, 278 nn.113–14. See also Paths; *Recht n-aicnid*
Ailill Olom, 100
Aire coisring (Ir.), "*aire* [e.g., 'noble' or 'freeman'] of constraint," 73, 77–78, 123, 126, 255–56 n.64, 256 n.81, 258 n.106. See also Kindred; Lords
Aire désa (Ir.), "*aire* of a retinue," 252 n.7, 262 n.62
Airecht (Ir.), "court," 126–27, 129, 275 n.69
Airecht tract, 125–26, 130, 134, 136, 277 n.98
Airgialla, 92–93, 98–101, 107–8, 110, 202, 223, 265 n.95, 269 n.131
Airthir, 93
Aithech-thúath (Ir.), "rent-payer, plebeian tribe," 99. See also Clientship, tribal
Aitire (Ir.), 31–32, 82, 93–94, 96–97, 110, 116–17, 130, 132, 202, 218–19, 223, 245 n.18, 262 n.62, 263 n.72, 264 n.80; and *cáin*-law, 94–96, 187, 268 n.123; and *coir n-athcomairc*, 124–25; associations of freedom or high status with, 106–11, 262 n.62, 263 n.72; binding of, 88–90, 245 n.18; compensation of, 85, 91–93, 96, 259 n.17, 261–62 n.48, 262 n.54, 264 n.81; earlier hypotheses regarding, 83–84, 87–88, 97–98, 107, 260 n.26, 261 n.39, 268 n.123; of God, saints, or Gospels, 200, 203; office of, 96–98, 130, 260 nn. 26, 28, 261 n.39, 262 n.62, 264 nn. 81, 83, 268 n.123, 269 n.128, 275 n.64, 276 n.80. See also *Córus Aitire*; *Gíall*
Aitire chairdi (Ir.), "*aitire*-surety of a *cairde*," 90–93, 96, 262 n.54. See also *Cairde*; *Slán nAitire Cairde*
Aitire chána (Ir.), "*aitire* of a *cáin*," 187. See also *Cáin*
Aitire luigi (Ir.), "*aitire* of an oath," 90, 93–94, 96, 109. See also *Lugae*; Oath
Aititiu (Ir.), "acknowledgment," 67–68, 74, 92, 252 n.16
Alba, 201
Alexander the Great, 295 n.21
Alfred, King, 2, 13, 203, 208–9
Amalarius of Metz, 229 n.1
Amod (W.), "contract," 19, 169, 171–73, 175–76, 188, 210, 288 n.143; and *cyfnewid*, 172–75
Amod deddfol (W.), "legal contract," 173–76. See also *Amod kyfreithawl*
Amod kyfreithawl (W.), "legal contract," 288 n.149. See also *Amod deddfol*
Amodwr (W.), 116, 141–42, 188, 194, 198, 207, 209, 225, 279 n.7, 281 n.27, 287 nn. 123, 288 n.143; and *mach*, 171–78, 186, 287 nn. 124–25, 130, 132; and *tystion*, 170–72, 174; denial by debtor of, 170, 287 n.132; office

Amodwr (W.) (*continued*)
and duties of, 169–78, 287 n.130; origins of, 169, 175–78, 186, 194, 287 n.124. See also *Amod*; Contracts, Welsh; *Tyst*
Annals, Irish, 2, 14, 107, 109–10, 128, 263 n.69, 267 n.106, 269 n.128, 301 nn. 9, 11
Arberth, 204
Arddelw (W.), "claim, defense, warranty," 163–66, 210, 285–86 n.107, 286 n.112. See also Pleas, Welsh
Arglwydd (W.), "lord, ruler," 152, 156, 283 n.54. See also Lords, Welsh
Armagh, 92, 109, 216, 269 n.127, 299–300 n.113
Arrian, 295 n.21
Arthur, King, 290 n.27
Arwystli, 144
Asser, 2
Athchor (Ir.), "return of fief without financial penalty," 91–92, 100, 258 n.111, 262 n.56
Audacht Morainn, 138, 242 n.76
Augustine of Canterbury, 1
Aurradas (Ir.), "customary law," 69, 108

Bail, 291 n.30
Baldwin, John, 293 n.3
Bangor, 269 n.127
Barotse, 14, 25, 55
Barr m. Cáirthind, 265–66 n.98, 300–301 nn.3–4
Barr m. Sárbile, 265–66 n.98
Bartlett, Robert, 293 n.3
Battle of Brunanburh, The, 228
Bécc mac Cúanu, 93
Bechbretha, 126
Beowulf, 228, 295 n.22
Bergin's Law, 244 n.14, 273 n.38, 277 n.95. See also Language, Irish
Berrad Airechta, 31, 34, 36–37, 39, 41, 44, 47, 49, 51–53, 58–59, 65, 70, 72–73, 75, 79, 87–88, 90, 93, 96–97, 108–9, 116–17, 119–21, 128–29, 131, 133–34, 137–38, 140, 150, 218, 244 n.10, 246–47 n.37, 247 n.40, 247–48 n.58, 249 nn. 72, 80, 254 n.38, 259 n.17, 261 n.39, 262 n.55, 270 n.7, 272 n.35, 299 n.102
Béscnae (Ir.), "behavior," 69. See also *Córus Béscnai*
Betrothal, 177

Bible, 7, 30, 225. See also Gospels; New Testament; Old Testament; Scripture
Binchy, Daniel A., 62, 74, 76–77, 83–84, 86–88, 97–98, 129, 139, 169, 200–204, 241 n.67, 244 n.14, 259 n.17, 260 n.26, 261 n.39, 263 n.71, 268 nn. 116, 124, 126, 271 n.17, 275 n.64, 296 n.40, 297 n.71
Blathmac mac Con Brettan, 262 n.62
Bleddyn ap Cynfyn, 181–82, 184
Bluhme, F., 11
Bog burials, 234 n.7
Book of Leinster, 100
Book of Llandaff (also *Liber Landavensis*), 2, 14, 219, 237 n.29, 242 n.76
Boretius, A., 11
Bóruma, 201
Bothach (Ir.), "cottier, crofter," 121–23, 253 n.28, 273 nn.40–41
Bracton, 179, 185
Bratha Cai, 108
Brawdwyr o fraint tir (W.), "judges by virtue of land tenure," 23, 195. See also Judges, Welsh; *Ynad*
Breatnach, Liam, 19, 22, 112–13, 133, 231 n.15, 244 n.14, 277 n.95
Breen, Aidan, 112
Bretha Comaithchesa, 126. See also Neighbors
Bretha Crólige, 126–27, 254 n.38, 275 n.64. See also Sick-maintenance
Bretha im fuillema gell, 219. See also Gage; Gell
Bretha Nemed, 22, 40, 42, 57, 127, 236 n.15, 242 n.76, 257 n.90, 260 n.28. See also *Nemed*
Bri (W.), "strength," "honor," 202, 204–5
Briduw, 116, 171–72, 200–207, 222–23, 281 n.27, 291 n.32, 297 n.65; and *fides*, 205, 210–11; and *mechni*, 170, 186–87, 206–12, 214–15, 296 n.51; and promissory oath, 203–5, 295 n.27; binding of, 207, 281 n.29; curialization of, 210–14, 221; denial of, 206–9, 214; enforcement of, 211–17, 220; origins of, 203–6, 296–97 n.59, 294 n.20, 295 n.30. See also Suretyship, of God; Suretyship, of the elements
Brig, 139
Brithem (Ir.), "judge," 89, 127–28. See also Judges; Jurists; Lawyers
Brithem túaithe (Ir.), "tribal judge," 126, 135
Brittany, 6, 203, 223, 229–30 n.3, 231 n.12,

233 n.28, 239–40 n.52, 241 nn. 60, 63, 295 n.23, 297–98 n.75
Brown, Peter, 212, 216, 220, 293 n.4, 296 n.42
Brunner, H., 11
Búall River, 216
Bürgschaft im irischen Recht, Die, 82, 90, 244 n.10
Burgundian code, 234 n.7
Byrne, Francis John, 106, 110, 266 n.104, 269 n.131

Cadog, Saint, 213, 217, 282 n.40
Caesar, Julius, 2, 15, 21, 126, 129, 276 n.75
Caill Uallech, 216
Cáin (Ir.), "law," 86, 94–96, 103, 108–9, 259–60 n.19, 263 nn. 67, 69, 264 n.83, 266 n.100, 268 n.124, 269 n.127, 294 n.18. See also *Aitire*; *Cairde*; *Rechtgae*; and titles of specific *cánai* below
Cáin, (Ir.), "tax, tribute," 103–9, 266 nn.100–102, 269 n.127. See also *Cáin*, "law"
Cáin Adomnáin, 85, 92, 94–95, 103, 108–9, 202, 268 n.123, 294 n.18
Cáin Aicillne, 55–56, 67–68, 72, 85, 103, 127, 252 n.5, 255 n.51. See also Clientship
Cáin Domnaig, 86, 94–95, 103, 107, 219–20, 259 n.17
Cáin Éimíne Báin, 263, n. 69
Cáin Fhuithirbe, 263 n.69
Cáin Íarraith, 103, 254, n.38. See also Fosterage
Cáin Lánamna, 56, 60, 63, 103, 252 n.5, 254 n.35. See also *Lánamnas*; Marriage
Cáin Phátraic, 263 n.69
Cáin Sóerraith, 56, 103, 252 n.5. See also Clientship
Cairde (Ir.), "treaty," 90–94, 96, 98–100, 103, 106–9, 261 nn.45–46, 264 n.83, 266 n.100, 268 nn. 121, 124, 269 n.131. See also *Cáin*; Treaties
Cairpre Dam Aircit, 93
Cairpre Liphechar, 100–101
Cambray homily, 244 n.14, 245 n.15
Campion, 129
Canones Wallici, 239–40 n.52, 297–98 n.75. See also Law, canon
Capitularies, 14
Carae (Ir.), "kinsman," 98, 109. See also *Fine*; Kindred

Caratnia, 27, 118
Carolingian, 2, 8, 228
Case-law, 5, 14
Cashel, 99–100, 107, 265 n.95
Celebrad (Ir.), "celebrating," 117, 212, 218–19, 260 n.28, 271 n.20, 297 n.72, 299–300 n.113
Cenél Conaill, 216
Cenél nEógain, 110
Cenn (Ir.), "superior, head, chief," 59, 63, 70
Cerball of Ossory, 267 n.106
Cert (Ir.), "justice" (and curial path by that name), 44, 75, 88, 115, 119–21, 138, 249–50 n.80, 272–73 n.36. See also Gage; *Gell*; Paths; Procedure
Cétmuinter (Ir.), "primary wife, spouse," 58, 63
Champion's portion, 21
Charles-Edwards, T. M., 3, 120, 129, 136, 148, 162, 180, 182, 185, 235 nn.10–11, 238 n.44, 242 n.73, 243 n.87, 246 n.36, 249 n.71, 251 n.96, 270 n.8, 271 n.25, 272 n.35, 280 n.23, 281 n.32, 287 n.124, 289 nn. 14, 19, 293 n.58
Charters, 2, 14, 141, 212, 219, 237 n.27, 263 n.69, 278 n.1, 295 n.22
Chrenecruda (Fr.), "throwing of dirt," 245 n.23
Church, Irish, 1, 4, 81, 227, 232 n.20, 233 n.26; dues owed by, 79–80; dues owed to, 69, 74, 77–79, 255–56 n.64
Chwedyl Gereint vab Erbin, 290 n.27
Cianachta, 100
Ciarraige, 100, 106–7, 266 n.104
Cigfa, 204, 215
Cilmin Droetu, 23
Cín Dromna Snechta, 242 n.76
Cís (Ir.), "tax," 106–8
Clare (county), 79
Clergy, role in legal affairs of, 32, 136, 177, 211–21, 242 n.79, 276 n.83
Clientship, 27, 37, 56–57, 60–62, 67, 72, 74, 78–80, 86, 97, 103, 106, 109, 134–35, 253 nn. 23, 32, 255 n.47, 255–56 n.64, 260 n.21, 262 n.56, 265 n.95, 266 nn. 100, 103. See also *Aicillne*; *Cáin Aicillne*; *Cáin Sóerraith*; *Séoit turchluide*
Clientship, tribal, 99–100, 103, 109–11, 255–56 n.64, 258 n.111, 265 n.95,

Clientship, tribal (*continued*)
266 n.100, 267 n.107. *See also Aithech-thúath*; *Frithfolad*
Clonard, 269 n.127
Clonenagh, 266–67 n.106
Clonmacnois, 269 n.127
Coibnes Uisci Thairidne, 57, 71, 74–76, 203
Cóic Conara Fugill, 47, 97, 114–21, 123, 125, 129–33, 135–40, 141, 165, 249–50 n.80, 270 nn.7–8, 270–71 n.13, 271 n.17, 271–72 n.32, 272–73 n.35, 278 n.114. *See also* Curialization; Paths; Procedure
Coir n-athcomairc (Ir.), "suitability of inquiry" (and curial path by that name), 124, 132–33, 270 n.8. *See also Aitire*; Paths; Procedure
Collas, the three, 101
Collectanea, 118
Collectio Canonum Hibernensis, 118, 136, 148. *See also* Law, canon
Collins, Roger, 232 n.17
Colman, R., 293 n.5
Columba, Saint, 216, 299 n.96
Columban moccu Loígse, 266–67 n.106
Commentaries, Irish, 83–84, 107, 114
Common Celtic, 19, 141–42, 144, 202–3, 240 n.58. *See also* Language, Irish
Common law, 162, 180–81, 185, 227
Comnaidm (Ir.), "joint binding," 48, 52, 251 nn. 93, 96. *See also* Contracts, Irish
Compurgation, 148, 156–57, 160, 165–67, 170–71, 181, 208–9, 214, 224, 287 n.132, 296 n.51. *See also Raith*
Conall Corc, 100, 102
Conall mac Coelmáine, 94
Congal Cáech, 14
Conn Cétchathach, 27, 100–101
Connachta, 101
Constitution, American, 192
Consuetudo (L.), "custom," 185
Contract: Irish law of, 27–30, 32–33, 43, 45–54, 55–58, 65–66, 68, 76–78, 250 nn. 88, 92, 251 nn. 93–94, 96, 271–72 n.32; Roman law of, 29–30
Contracts, Irish: binding of, 30, 33–37, 47–49, 52–53, 76; cancellation of, 27, 44–54, 59–68, 76, 223, 250 n.83, 253 n.32, 257 n.94; challenges to the immunity of, 38, 44–54, 80, 119–21, 253 n.32, 257 nn. 94–95, 99, 271–72 n.32, 272 n.35; enforcement of, 38–43; guaranteed by supernatural guarantors, 202; made with the legally dependent, 60–68, 255 n.47; made with the legally incompetent, 58–61, 250 n.83, 252 n.18, 253 n.19; renegotiation of, 44–54, 119–21, 249–50 nn. 80, 85, 257 nn.94–95, 272 n.35; repayment of, 38–43; witnesses to, 36–39. *See also Cor mbél*; *Naidm*; *Ráth*; Suretyship, of God
Contracts, oral, 32–33, 119, 121, 138, 144. *See also Cor mbél*
Contracts, Welsh: binding of, 146–47, 157–58, 281 n.29; challenges to, 159–61, 163–68, 171, 175–78, 285–86 n.107; made with the legally dependent, 147–48, 191, 193; made with the legally incompetent, 147–48, 193. *See also Amod*; *Amodwr*; *Briduw*; *Mach*
Cor mbél (Ir.), "oral contract," 30, 72, 251 n.96. *See also* Contracts, oral
Cormac mac Airt, 101, 106
Córus Aitire, 245 nn.17–18. *See also Aitire*
Córus Béscnai, 56, 63, 69, 79, 250 n.85, 252 n.5, 255–56 n.64. *See also Béscnae*
Córus Fíadnaise, 31, 88, 245 n.17. *See also Fíadu*; *Fíadnaise*; Witnesses
Córus Iubaile, 244 n.6
Court, procedure in. *See* Curialization; Paths; Procedure
Crime, 118, 122, 187
Críth Gablach, 16, 64, 69–70, 83, 86, 93, 98, 107–10, 236 n.17, 243 n.87, 252 n.5, 254 nn. 38, 42
Cross, as guarantor, 215. *See also* Suretyship, of God
Crosses: in Irish law, 96, 215, 219–20, 264 n.82; in Welsh law, 153, 210, 213, 219–20
Curialization: Irish, 116–17, 125–40; Welsh, 134, 143–47, 150–68, 174–78, 179, 186–90, 210–11, 221–22, 286 n.112, 287 n.124, 290 n.25. *See also* Procedure, curial
Cyfnerth ap Morgenau, 23
Cyfnewid (W.), "exchange," 159, 172–75; and *amod*, 172–75
Cyfraith (W.) "law," 24, 151–52, 159, 161, 167, 181–82, 184–86, 188, 193. *See also Cyfraith Hywel*; *Mach ar gyfraith*
Cyfraith Hywel, 143, 153, 182–84, 190–91, 207, 211. *See also Cyfraith*; Hywel Dda; *Llyfr Hywel*

Cynaythuy, 206
Cyngaws (W.), "pleader," 163
Cynghawsedd (W.), "pleading," 14, 16, 20, 145, 157–66, 183–84, 189–90, 192, 197, 238 n.44, 289–90 n.22. See also *Llyfr Cynghawsedd*; Procedure, curial, Welsh
Cynnogyn (W.), "debtor," 159–61, 164, 284 nn. 75, 88. See also *Mach kynnogyn*
Cynyr ap Cadwgan, 23

Da dilis diuach (W.), "goods immune from claim without a surety," 148, 189, 243 n.88
Dadannudd (W.), "uncovering [the hearth as part of a ritual to claim land]," 4, 150
Dagda, 201
Damwein (W.), "eventuality," 14, 16, 152, 183–84, 238 n.44, 289–90 n.22. See also *Damweiniau Colan*; *Llyfr y Damweiniau*
Damweiniau Colan, 172–73, 176, 205. See also *Damwein*
Danube, 295 n.21
Davies, Gwilym Prys, 294 n.20
Davies, R. R., 144, 172, 179, 195, 236 n.15
Davies, Wendy, 2, 222–23, 233 n.28
De Salis, R., 11
De statu ecclesiae, 229 n.1
Debt, as social bond, 79–80, 148
Defod (W.), "custom," 184–85
Deheubarth, 17, 191
Delbna, 100
Déorad (Ir.), "stranger, exile," 58
Déorad Dé (Ir.), "exile of God," 212, 218, 297 n.69
Dharmasutras, 18
Di Astud Chor, 7, 30, 36, 45, 47–49, 51–53, 120, 134, 250 n.85, 251 n.96, 257 n.95, 272 n.35. See also Contracts, Irish
Di Chetharslicht Athgabála, 107, 115, 124, 270–71 n.13. See also Distraint
Di Gnímaib Gíall, 83, 85. See also *Gíall*
Díles (Ir.; also W. *dilys*; Br. *dilis*) "immune from claim," 19, 46. See also *Dílse*; Immunities; *Ruidles*
Dílse (Ir.), "immunity from claim," 34, 46. See also *Díles*; Immunities; *Ruidles*
Dinefwr, 237 n.29
Díre, 62, 103
Dispute settlement, 5, 9, 125–31, 141, 143–44, 222, 275 n.69
Distraint, 18, 39, 43, 96, 107–8, 115, 127, 133, 139, 147, 151–53, 219, 252 n.1, 261 n.39, 283 n.51, 283–84 n.62, 291–92 n.41. See also *Di Chetharslicht Athgabála*
Dliged (Ir.), "law," 40
Dliged (Ir.), "natural entitlement, fairness"; also "contractual entitlement" (and curial path by that name), 44, 46–47, 49, 75, 119–21, 129–30, 133, 137–38, 249–50 n.80, 250 nn. 88, 92, 258 nn.110–11, 271 n.22, 271–72 n.32, 276 n.77. See also Entitlement; Paths; *Naidm*; Procedure
Dliged (Ir.), "prerogative," 117, 127
Do Tuaslucud Rudradh, 244 n.6
Dochor (Ir.), "disadvantageous contract," 62. See also Contracts, Irish
Dóer (Ir.), "unfree," also "unfree person," 58, 253 n.28
Dowry, 71
Druids, 129, 131, 276 nn. 75, 83
Duel, judicial, 118–19
Dumville, David, 239–40 n.52
Dux (L.), 110
Dyfed, 204, 292 n.44

Echtra Cormaic, 131
Edern uab Nudd, 290 n.27
Edward I, King of England, 143, 179–81, 215, 226
Egypt, 201, 247 n.38. See also Law, Egyptian
Ellis, T. P., 295 n.31
Emain Macha, 92
Emly, 269 n.127
Entitlement, 44–49, 75, 80–81, 120, 127, 137–38, 173, 249–50 n.80, 250 nn. 88, 92, 251 n.94, 257 n.95. See also *Dliged*
Eochaid Finn Fuath nAirt, 266 n.105
Eochaid Mugmedón, 101
Eógan mac Níalláin, 93
Eógan Már, 100, 102
Eóganacht Chaisil, 102
Eóganacht Locha Léin, 99–100, 102, 106–7
Eóganacht Raithlind, 99, 100, 102
"Epistle of Jesus, The," 94–95
Éraic (Ir.), "(fixed) *wergild*," 40. See also Feud; *Wergild*
Érainn, 100
Etaim (Ir.), "interest paid by defaulting debtor [fine?]," 40–42
Eulogia (L.), "elements," 214
Exile, 149–50. See also *Déorad*; *Déorad Dé*

Index

Fásach (Ir.), "precedents," 23, 278 n.114
Fasting, 4, 18, 252 n.1. See also *Troscad*
Fathers, authority over sons, 57, 63–66, 80. See also Filial obligations; *Goire*; *Macc ingor*
Feichem (Ir.), "contracting parties," 31, 34
Fénechas (Ir.), "native law," 31, 114, 133, 270 n.8
Féni (Ir.), "native, free Irish," 22, 61, 68–69, 73, 137, 277 n.106
Fer midboth (Ir.), "man of middle huts," 64, 254 n.42. See also Fathers; Filial obligations
Fergus m. Bairr m. Cáirthind, 300–301 n.4
Fermanagh, 92
Festuca (L.), rod used in Frankish courts to show acceptance of judge's decision, 33, 245 n.23
Feud, 8, 74, 134, 284 n.78. See also *Éraic*; *Galanas*; *Wergild*
Fíadnaise, (Ir.), "eyewitness testimony," 275 n.64. See also *Córus Fíadnaise*; *Fíadu*
Fíadu, fiada (Ir.), "eyewitness," 73. See also *Fíadnaise*
Fideiussor (L.), 177, 288 n.143, 297–98 n.75, 298 n.92
Fides (L.), "faith, pledging of faith," 205, 210–11, 213, 295 n.22. See also *Briduw*; Oath
Fief, 60, 74, 91, 99, 134, 262 n.56; of an *aitire chairdi*, 92, 262 n.54. See also *Aitire chairdi*
Filial obligations, 64, 66, 68, 80, 254 n.41. See also Fathers; *Goire*
Fine (Ir.), "kindred," "kinsman," 61, 63, 66–67, 69–70, 72, 91, 256 n.73
Finian of Clonard, Saint, 216
Fir Rois, 216
Fír (Ir.), "truth, ordeal" (also curial path by that name), 115, 117–20, 122, 129, 137–39, 271 nn. 22, 25, 272–73 n.36, 276 n.77. See also *Fírgille*; Ordeal; Procedure
Fírgille (Ir.), "truth-gage, ordeal-gage" 118–19. See also *Fír*; Procedure
First Synod of St. Patrick, 136. See also Patrick, Saint
Flaith (Ir.), "lord," 61, 70, 85–86, 91, 95, 103, 107, 117, 255–56 n.64, 263 n.72, 275 n.64
Fland Febla, 109
Fleuriot, L., 239–40 n.52

Folad, folud (Ir.), "obligations, "considerations," 49, 73–74, 246–47 n.37, 250 n.88, 251 n.94, 257 n.94
Food-rent, 74, 86, 91–92, 99. See also Clientship
Ford, Patrick, 295–96 n.33
Formulas, 34, 36–38, 115, 245 n.18, 246 nn. 26, 30, 247 n.49. See also Contracts
Forngaire (Ir.), "supervision" 59, 67–68, 252 n.14, 254 n.36. See also Kindred
Fosterage, 56, 64–65, 74, 78, 80, 103, 254 n.38. See also *Cáin Íarraith*
Fothairt, 106, 266 nn.105–6
Fouracre, Paul, 222
Frankpledge, 290 n.27. See also Law, Anglo-Saxon
Freemen, serving as *naidm*-sureties, 70
Frithfolad, frithfolud (Ir.), "counterobligations," 80, 99, 107, 258 n.111. See also Clientship, tribal
Fuidir (Ir.), "semi-freeman," 121–23, 253 n.28, 266 n.100, 273 nn.40–41

Gáethíne m. Cináed, 267 n.106
Gage, 36, 55, 69, 77–78, 80, 91, 95–96, 108, 116–21, 151–52, 218–19, 248 n.64, 255–56 n.64, 256 n.81, 258 n.106, 261 n.45, 264 nn. 81, 83, 268 n.115. See also *Bretha im fuillema gell*; *Cert*; *Gell*; *Fírgille*; Pledge; *Smachtgille*
Gailenga, 100
Galanas (W.), "feud, *wergild* paid to end a feud," 242 n.71. See also Feud; *Wergild*
Gell (Ir.), "gage," 108, 219, 260 n.28. See also *Bretha im fuillema gell*; *Fírgille*; Gage; *Smachtgille*
Gemma Ecclesiastica, 298 n.92
Genealogies, Irish, 2, 100–106, 111, 266–67 n.106, 300 n.1
Genealogies, Welsh, 2
Genemain Aeda Sláine, 106
Gereint uab Erbin, 290 n.27
Gerriets, 264 n.88, 265 n.95, 266 n.100, 267 n.107
Gíall (Ir.), 223, 259 n.3; and clientship, 86–87; associations of subordination with, 106–11; compensation of, 85; earlier hypotheses regarding, 82–84, 97–98, 259 n.4, 268 nn. 115, 122–23; in *cáin*-law, 96, 268 n.123; office of, 84–87, 97–98, 107,

268 nn. 115, 122–23, 269 n.128. See also *Aitire*; *Di Gnímaib Gíall*; *Gorfodog*
Gifts, 55, 67, 69, 210
Gilbert of Limerick, 229 n.1
Gilfaethwy, 297 n.66
Giraldus Cambrensis, 216–18, 298 n.92
Glanvill, 179, 185
Glosses, on Irish law tracts, 16, 31, 84–86, 91–93, 108, 114, 238 n.40, 249 n.75, 259 n.6, 268 n.126, 272 n.34, 273 n.38, 274 n.48. See also H 3. 18
Gluckman, Max, 14, 25, 55
Godborg (AS), "divine surety," 208–9, 215, 295 n.24. See also Law, Anglo-Saxon
Gods, tribal, 201
Goewin, 297 n.66
Goire (Ir.), "filial piety," 66, 254 n.41. See also Fathers; Filial obligations; *Macc ingor*
Gorfodog (W.), 141, 187–88, 207, 281 n.27, 290–91 nn.25–28, 291 n.30, 292 n.51. See also *Aitire*; *Gíall*; *Mach goruodawc*
Gorfodogaeth (W.), "*gorfodog* suretyship," 170, 186–88, 290 n.27, 291 n.32. See also *Gorfodog*; *Mach goruodawc*
Gospel of Thomas, 7
Gospels, 203, 212, 257 n.86. See also Bible; New Testament; Scripture
Gospels of Gildas, 206
Gravamina (L.), "complaints," 177
Greece, 201, 247 n.38. See also Law, Greek
Gregory of Tours, 14
Gregory the Great, Pope, 1, 201
Gregory VII, Pope, 214
Gwahard (W.), "prohibiting [a person to make use of an object in dispute]," 211–13, 297 n.66
Gwenhwyfar, 290 n.27
Gwir (W.), "truth," 138
Gwydion, 297 n.66
Gwyn Gloew, 204
Gwynedd, 13, 16–17, 143, 145, 181, 195

H 3. 18 (manuscript held by Trinity College Dublin), 31, 72, 84–86, 91–93, 108, 238, 249, 259, 268 n.126. See also Glosses
Hamp, Eric, 241 n.60
Hands, grasping of to confirm agreement, 36, 146–47, 157, 170, 187–88, 207, 210, 224, 281 n.29. See also Contracts
Hawl (W.), "claim," 146, 159–60, 163

Hawlwr (W.), "claimant," 149, 159, 161, 287 n.132.
Head-hunting, 21
Henry III, King, 215, 298 n.90
Henry IV, Emperor, 214
Heptads, 65, 72, 74–75, 119, 249 n.75, 255 n.47, 255–56 n.64, 256 n.81
Herbert, Máire, 238 n.37, 242 n.72
Hincmar of Rheims, 230 n.5
Hoebel, E. Adamson, 200
Honor, 69, 148, 251 n.96, 253 n.20, 295 n.29
Honor-price, 40–41, 60–61, 103, 255 n.47, 259 n.17, 262 n.49, 266 n.103, 297 n.69. See also *Lóg n-enech*
Hostage-sureties, Roman, 82
Hostage-sureties, Irish and Welsh. See *Aitire*; *Gíall*; *Gorfodog*
Hugh Tyrrell, 299–300 n.113
Hywel Dda, 13, 16, 22, 143, 153, 180–83, 185–86, 190, 195, 198, 209, 225–26, 235 n.11, 289 n.14. See also *Cyfraith Hywel*; *Llyfr Hywel*

Ibar, Bishop, 300 n.3
Immliuch Sescainn, 216
Immunities, 73–80, 119, 134, 148, 151, 189, 223, 243 n.88, 246–47 n.37, 251 nn. 99, 103, 257 n.99, 257–58 n.101, 271–72 n.32, 283 nn. 54, 57. See also *Díles*; *Dílse*; *Da dílis diuach*; *Ruidles*
Indo-European, 1, 18–20, 88, 112, 169, 200–202, 230–31 n.12, 240 nn. 53, 55
Ine, King, 13
Inis Coel, 94
Iona, 109, 264 n.77
Iorwerth ap Madog, 23
Irluachair, 99
Iudex (L.), "judge," 128

Jenkins, Dafydd, 172, 204, 214–15, 239–40 n.52, 296 n.36
Jews, 298 n.92
Jonas of Orleans, 230 n.5
Jones Pierce, T., 242 n.71
Judges, Irish, 9, 22, 89–90, 95, 97, 115–17, 126–34, 136–37, 139–40, 236 n.13, 247 n.40, 271–72 n.32, 272 n.35, 275 nn. 58–59, 61, 69, 72, 276 n.84, 278 n.114. See also *Brithem*; Jurists; Lawyers, Irish
Judges, Welsh, 144, 146, 153, 156, 165, 167,

Judges, Welsh (*continued*)
174–75, 183, 188, 195–98, 214, 225, 237 n.30, 280 nn. 15–16, 18, 284 n.81, 292–93 n.56. See also *Brawdwyr o fraint tir*; Jurists; Lawyers, Welsh; *Ynad*

Jupiter, 201

Jurisprudence, Irish, consolidation of, 137–40

Jurists, 3, 7, 9–10, 15–16, 18, 21–26, 27, 30, 32, 34, 46, 48–49, 51, 53–54, 55, 68, 79, 81, 83–84, 87, 112–15, 123, 125, 128–31, 133–37, 139–40, 141, 144–45, 170, 172–73, 175–76, 180–82, 185, 187–90, 193, 195–96, 198, 205–7, 209–11, 220, 225, 227–28. See also *Brithem*; Judges; Law schools; Lawyers

Kelly, Fergus, 3, 124–25, 268 nn.115–16, 275 n.69, 276 n.84

Kenner, Hugh, 216

Kerennyd (W.), "kinship," 98

Kildare, 269 n.127

Kindred: and community, 69–73, 77–81, 148, 253 n.19, 256 nn. 65, 74, 263 n.75, 282 n.40; as sureties, 7, 37, 68–73, 77–78, 93–94, 96–97, 109, 123, 148, 187, 218–19, 246–47 n.37, 251 n.93, 252 n.7, 255–56 n.64, 256 nn.79–81, 259–60 n.19, 261 nn. 39, 46, 263 n.75, 274 n.46, 290 n.25; disputes within, 117–20, 131; economic cooperation within, 55–56, 62, 66–74, 255 nn. 48, 51–52; gage on behalf of, 77–78, 255–56 n.64, 256 n.81, 258 n.106; rights and obligations within, 7, 66–73, 80–81, 90–91, 148, 252 n.7, 255 nn. 48, 52, 56; status within, 56–57, 66, 80, 252 n.6. See also *Fine*; Kinship; *Ráth fine*; *Ráth forngartha fine*

Kings: dues owed to, 69, 74, 77, 226; Germanic, and law, 8, 11–13, 22, 131–32, 140, 226; Irish, role in law of, 94–96, 103, 108–9, 125–27, 135–36, 226, 236 n.13, 255–56 n.64, 261 n.45, 274 n.56, 275 n.58

Kingship: conceptualized as clientship, 99–103, 109–11; consolidation of, 1, 8, 110–12, 131–32, 135–36, 140–41, 143–44, 152–54, 176–78; ideology of, 12–13, 226; sacral, 1–2, 138, 212. See also Clientship, tribal; Kings; Lords

Kinship, 77, 174, 273 n.45, 284 n.78. See also *Fine*; Kindred

Laigin, 266–67 nn.105–6, 301 n.7

Lánamnas (Ir.), "pairing, partnership, marriage," 119. See also *Cáin Lánamna*; Marriage

Language, Irish, 2–4, 19, 34, 94, 115, 133, 238 n.41, 241 n.65, 244–45 nn.13–15

Latin A, 145, 191–92, 278–79 n.5, 283–84 n.62, 291–92 n.41

Latin B, 145, 149, 191, 194, 197, 206, 208, 211, 215, 283–84 n.62, 287 n.123, 292 nn. 45, 48, 52, 295 n.30

Latin D, 145, 160, 191, 206–7, 209–11, 281 n.32, 283–84 n.62, 287 n.123, 292 n.45, 295 n.30

Latin E, 145, 149, 152, 154, 191, 193–94, 197, 206, 208, 211, 278–79 n.5, 283 n.51, 283–84 n.62, 287 n.123, 292 nn. 48, 52

Latin redactions, 147–48, 169–70, 182, 187–98, 206, 281 n.30, 283 n.54, 283–84 n.62, 288 n.143, 291 n.40, 293 n.58 See also Latin A; Latin B; Latin D; Latin E

Law: Anglo-Saxon, 179, 188, 208–9, 255 n.61, 290 n.27; Babylonian, 247 n.38; canon, 13, 42, 148, 177, 191–92, 226, 239–40 n.52, 246 n.36, 248 n.65, 272 n.35, 292 n.45, 294 n.20, 297–98 n.75, 299 n.96; comparative, 5, 13–14, 18–20, 236–37 nn.19–23; Egyptian, 247 n.38; Germanic, 11–14, 18, 22, 224, 227, 234 n.7, 235 nn.8–9; Greek, 247 n.38; Hindu, 18; of Sunday (see *Cáin Domnaig*); of the March (*see* March); Old Testament, 13; "private," 7–10, 44, 50, 52–54, 114, 116, 126–29, 133–35, 140, 144, 153, 158, 162, 165, 176–78, 222–24; "public," 8–9, 44, 50, 52–54, 114, 126–29, 133–35, 140, 144, 153, 162, 165, 169, 176–78, 222–24, 249 n.78; Roman, 2, 16, 21, 29–30, 54, 136, 185, 192, 226, 280 n.23, 297–98 n.75, 297–98 n.75; Scandinavian, 18, 113, 188; Talmudic, 247 n.38; Visigothic, 278 n.118; written, 6, 12–26, 112–13, 125, 128, 135, 137, 140, 182–85, 188, 196, 234 n.7, 235 n.8, 289–90 n.22, 291–92 n.41. *See also* Frankpledge; *Godborg*; Law, Irish; Law, Welsh; Torah, Oral; *Stipulatio*; *Twelve Tables*, *Law of the*

Law, Irish: and kings, 94–96, 103, 108–9, 125–27, 135–36, 226, 236 n.13, 255–56 n.64, 261 n.45, 274 n.56, 275 n.58; archaisms in, 13, 15–16, 18–19, 21, 24, 34, 112–15, 133, 225,

231 n.14, 244–45 nn.13–15, 277 n.95; dating of, 14, 16, 18–20, 112–15, 133, 231 n.14, 241 n.65, 244–45 nn.13–15, 270 nn.8–10, 277 n.95; ecclesiastical elements in, 3, 13, 15–16, 21, 30–31, 42, 112–13, 136–37, 139, 231 n.14, 242 n.79, 249 n.75, 272 n.35; relationship to judicial process of, 22–26, 49–54, 59–73, 80–81, 113–14, 125–29, 139–40; style of, 5, 13, 15–16, 112–13, 133, 236 n.15, 242 nn. 76, 78, 244 n.12, 270 n.8. *See also* Jurists; Language; Law, written; Lawbooks, Irish; Law schools; Lawyers, Irish

Law, Welsh: and lords, 16, 143–46, 150–54, 161–63, 168–78, 179–82, 188, 192–93, 198, 211–21, 225–26, 289 n.11; archaisms in, 17–26, 142, 150, 181–98, 199–207, 222, 225, 238–39 n.47, 242 n.71, 279 n.9, 282 n.44, 291 n.41, 292 n.45; dating of, 14–18, 20–21, 241 n.68; influence of Roman law on, 21, 185, 192, 280 n.23; relationship to judicial process of, 23–26, 284 n.81; shaped by curial process, 162–168, 174–78, 189–90, 196, 210–11, 224. *See also* Jurists; Law, canon; Law, written; Lawbooks, Welsh; Law schools; Lawyers

Law schools, 3, 9, 15, 17, 22–25, 34, 128–29, 131, 242 n.76

Lawbooks: Irish, role played in teaching by, 21–26, 53, 113–14; Welsh, role played in teaching by, 21–26, 162; Welsh, textual tradition of, 17–18, 182–85, 190–98, 239–40 nn.48–52, 278–79 n.5, 282 n.44, 289 n.14, 289–90 n.22, 291–92 nn.39–41, 292 nn.44–45. *See also* Law schools; *Senchas Már*; Test Book

Laws of Country, 183

Laws of Court, 183

Lawyers, Irish: 3, 15–16, 18, 79, 81, 133–34, 139, 231 n.14, 236 n.13, 271 n.17, 276 n.84; law tracts shaped by priorities of, 7, 21–26, 49–54, 55, 81, 112–14, 121, 123, 125–40, 175, 225, 231 n.14, 236 n.13. *See also Brithem*; Judges; Jurists; Law, Irish; Law schools

Lawyers, Welsh: 18, 292–93 n.56; law shaped by priorities of, 7, 21–26, 145–46, 162–168, 172, 174–78, 179–98, 224–25, 292–93 n.56. *See also* Judges; Jurists; Law, Welsh; Law schools

Lebor na hUidre, 106

Legal dependency, 60–73, 193, 253 n.21; and *téchtae*, 121–23, 273 n.40. *See also* Clientship; Contracts; Fathers; Kindred; Kinship; Legal incompetency; Marriage

Legal incompetency, 58–61, 193, 253 n.19. *See also* Contracts; Fathers; Kindred; Kinship; Legal dependency; Marriage

Legislation and statute, 12–13, 143, 162–63, 166, 168, 181, 185, 225. *See also Cáin*; *Llunnyeith*; *Rechtgae*; Rhuddlan, statute of

Leinster, 99, 106, 110, 266–67 n.106

Leth Cam, 110

Leth-rí (Ir.), "joint-king, half-king," 110

Lethnaidm (Ir.), "one-sided *naidm*-surety," 35

Levites, 21

Lewis, Timothy, 295 n.31

Lex Salica, 245 n.23

Librán, 237 n.27, 254 n.41

Literacy, 3, 113, 144, 228

Llancarfan, 213

Llandinam, 144

Llunnyeith (W.), "ordinance," 182, 184. *See also* Legislation and statute

Llwyd fab Cil Coed, 204

Llwyn Gwyn, 284 n.81

Llyfr Blegywryd, 17, 145, 148, 151–52, 155–56, 160, 169, 182, 187–93, 195–98, 206–8, 211, 281 nn. 30, 32, 283 n.51, 283–84 n.62, 284 n.75, 287 n.123, 291 n.40, 293 n.58, 295 n.30

Llyfr Colan, 152, 164, 169–71, 173, 176, 187, 204, 206–8, 212, 287 n.132, 290 n.26, 291 n.32, 296 n.51

Llyfr Cyfnerth, 17, 23, 145, 147–48, 151–52, 155, 169–71, 176, 182, 184–85, 188–89, 191–93, 197, 204, 206–8, 211, 278–79 n.5, 282 n.44, 283 n.54, 283–84 n.62, 284 n.75, 287 n.123, 290 n.25, 291 n.39

Llyfr Cynghawsedd, 183–84, 196, 198, 280 n.23, 289 n.19, 289–90 n.22, 292 n.51, 292–93 n.56. *See also Cynghawsedd*

Llyfr Cynog, 280 n.24

Llyfr Hywel, 184. *See also Cyfraith Hywel*; Hywel Dda

Llyfr Iorwerth, 13, 17, 23, 142, 145–46, 148–49, 151–52, 154, 156–57, 164–65, 167–71, 173, 176, 183–84, 186–88, 190–97, 206–9, 211–14, 222, 278–79 n.5, 281 n.30, 282 n.44, 283 n.54, 283–84 n.62, 287 n.132, 291 n.32, 292 nn. 48, 51, 293 n.58

338 Index

Llyfr Prawf Ynaid, 183
Llyfr y Damweiniau, 183–84, 188, 198, 289–90 n.22
Llys (llyssu), "disqualification [e.g., of witnesses]," 156–57, 160–61, 284 n.78, 287 n.132
Llywelyn ap Gruffudd, 146, 177–79
Llywelyn ap Iorwerth, 17, 143, 181
Lóegaire mac Néill, 201
Lóg n-enech (Ir.), "honor-price," 39, 41. See also Honor-price
Loíchse (pl. Loíchsi), 103–6, 265–66 n.98, 266–67 nn.105–6, 300 n.1, 301 nn. 7, 13
Loíchse Raimne, 300–301 n.4, 301 n.6
Loíchse Réta, 105–6
London, merchants of, 215
Londonderry, 92
Lords, as sureties, 69, 123, 130–31, 148–49, 152–54, 188, 251 n.93, 255–56 n.64, 283 n.51, 292 n.52. See also Aire coisring; Arglwydd; Flaith
Lords, Welsh, and law, 16, 143–46, 150–54, 162–63, 170, 172, 176–78, 179–85, 188, 198, 211–21, 225, 283 n.51, 283–84 n.62, 284 n.69, 287 n.124, 290 n.25, 291 nn. 30, 33, 296–97 n.59, 297 n.66. See also Arglwydd
Lots, 118–19, 131. See also Ordeal
Lucifer, 244 n.9
Lugae, luige (Ir.), "oath," 88. See also Aitire luigi; Oath
Luigne, 100

Mabinogi, 295–96 n.33
Mac béoathar (Ir.), "son of a living father," 63–66. See also Fathers; Fer Midboth
Mac Cana, Proinsias, 230–31 n.12
Mac(c) (Ir.), "enforcing surety," 19, 36, 45, 76, 88, 133, 141, 277 n.95
Mac(c) ingor (Ir.; also W., mab anwar), "undutiful son," 19, 254 n.46. See also Fathers; Filial obligations; Goire
Mac-Cáirthind, 265–66 n.98
MacArddae's Synod, 106–7
Mach (W.), "enforcing surety," 19, 141, 207, 288 n.147; and amodwr, 168–78, 186, 287 nn. 125, 130; and Irish naidm, 144, 146–50; as type of plea, 150, 158–68, 186; denial by debtor of, 147–48, 151, 156–57, 160, 164–68, 170, 184, 189–90, 214–15, 224, 282 n.44, 285 n.105, 285–86 n.107; denial of obligation by, 166–68, 184, 224, 285–86 n.107; financial liability of, 142, 146–51, 155–56, 158–59, 161, 170, 191–94, 285–86 n.107, 292 nn. 45, 51–52; God functioning as, 203–4; identity with claim, 146–47, 150, 157–68, 189–90, 224–25, 285–86 n.107; role as witness of, 146, 154–58, 161, 224; role in enforcement of, 142, 146–47, 151–55, 157–59, 162, 170, 174, 191–93, 220, 224, 281 n.32, 283–84 n.62, 284 n.69, 285–86 n.107; social status of, 153–55, 166, 284 n.69. See also Amodwr; Briduw; Contracts; Mechni; Mechniaeth; Procedure, curial; and specific types of mach-surety listed below
Mach ar gyfraith (W.), "mach-surety to abide by law," 116, 153, 187, 193, 291 n.30
Mach ar heddwch (W.), "mach-surety to guarantee peace," 187
Mach goruodawc (W.), "gorfodog-surety," 187. See also Gorfodog; Gorfodogaeth
Mach kynnogyn (W.), "debtor-surety," 284 nn. 75, 88. See also Cynnogyn
Mach talu (W.), "paying mach-surety," 284 n.75, 285–86 n.107
MacNeill, Eoin, 277 n.106
Madog Goch Ynad, 23
Máel Bressail mac Máel Dúin, 93
Maelsechlaind mac Domnaill, 109
Mag Réta, 266–67 n.106
Magic, 205–6
*Makkos (Common Celtic), "macc/mach-surety," 141. See also Mac(c); Mach
Malinowski, Bronislaw, 13, 205
Manach (Ir.), "monk, monastic tenant," 70, 103, 253 n.28
Manawydan, 204, 215
March, Law of the, 143, 172
Margaret, countess of Kent, 298 n.90
Marriage, 18, 65, 68, 177, 237 n.30; and marital property, 57, 62–63, 223, 254 n.35, 255 n.48. See also Cáin Lánamna; Lánamnas; Nau Kynywedi Teithiauc
Martyrs, 200
Mass, 206, 214–15, 218
Math fab Mathonwy, 297 n.66
McCone, Kim, 112, 133
McKitterick, Rosamond, 235 n.9
McLeod, Neil, 45–46, 52, 138–39, 241 n.67, 246 n.36, 250 nn. 88, 92, 251 nn. 93, 96,

252 n.14, 253 n.28, 254 n.44, 257–58 n.101, 264 n.83, 268 n.116, 278 nn. 112–13

Mechni (W.), "suretyship," 146–48, 150, 153–56, 159, 161–65, 168, 170, 172, 178, 184, 187, 196, 198, 205, 220, 285–86 n.107; and *briduw*, 206–11, 214–15, 220, 296 n.51. See also *Mechniaeth*

Mechniaeth, "suretyship," 151, 154–55, 159, 161. See also *Mechni*

Mescill m. Mael-Aithcin, 267 n.106

Milsom, S. F. C., 162, 168, 224

Miracles, 199, 206, 212

Monaghan, 92

Mug (Ir.), "slave," 61

Mugdorna, 93

Muire (Ir.), "chief, lord," 85–86, 95–96. See also *Muiredach*

Muire fine (Ir.), "chief of a kindred," 259–60 n.19

Muiredach (Ir.), "chief, lord," 85, 90, 260 n.28, 261 n.46. See also *Muire*

Munster, 13, 99–100, 102, 106–7, 266–67 n.106

Mythology, comparative, 18

Nagy, Joseph Falaky, 125, 274 n.55

Naidm (Ir.), "binding," 58, 61, 250 n.87, 276 n.88

Naidm (Ir.), "enforcing surety," 44, 59, 69–70, 72–73, 89, 96, 119, 133, 141, 144, 148, 169, 218, 276 n.88, 277 n.95; and *aitire*, 87–88, 96–97, 260 n.28; and binding of contracts, 31, 34–37, 42, 88, 130, 146, 250 nn. 88, 92, 251 nn. 93–94, 96, 103; and curial path *dliged*, 119–21, 133; of God, saints, or Gospels, 200, 203, 212, 295 n.27; role as witness, 36–39, 42, 133–34, 146; role in enforcement, 39–40, 42–43, 88, 142, 247–48 n.58, 260 n.28; social status of, 70, 72, 130. See also *Aitire*; Contracts, Irish; *Dliged*; Entitlement; *Mac(c)*; Suretyship, of God

Narratio, "count," 162, 227

Nativist controversy, 238 n.37

Nau Kynywedi Teithiauc, 18. See also Marriage

Navaho, 246 n.28

Nawdd, "protection, sanctuary," 214

Neighbors, 56, 65, 77, 79, 126, 223. See also *Bretha Comaithchesa*

Nelson, Janet, 228

Nemed (Ir.), "dignitary," 108, 127. See also *Bretha Nemed*

New Testament, 199. See also Bible; Gospels

Nicholas, Saint, 298 n.92

Normans, arrival in Ireland, 2, 141

Ó Briain, Felim, 269 n.127

Ó Corráin, Donnchadh, 112, 141, 229 n.2, 241 n.63, 269 nn. 127, 130

Ó hUiginn, Ruairi, 201

O'Brien, M. A., 52–53

O'Mores, 266–67 n.106

Oath, 6, 89–90, 97–98, 119, 155, 159, 161, 171, 176, 199–201, 206, 208, 213–15, 217, 285–86 n.107, 287 n.132, 295 n.31, 296 n.55, 298 n.90; promissory, 6–7, 202–5, 211, 221, 295 n.27. See also *Aitire luigi*; *Briduw*; *Lugae*

Oath of Bromholm, 215

Old Testament, 199. See also Bible

Oral tradition, 2, 15, 21, 113, 125, 182, 185, 188–89, 230–31 n.12

Ordeal, 33, 118–19, 131, 199–200, 206, 217, 220–21, 271 n.25, 276 n.83, 293 n.3. See also *Fír*; *Fírgille*; Lots; Procedure

Orwell, George, 127

Ossory, 266–67 n.106

Owen, Aneirin, 183

Owen, Morfydd, 282 n. 44

Paruchia (L.), unit of ecclesiastical jurisdiction, 269 n.127

Paths, curial, definition of, 114–25, 137, 271 n.17. See also *Aicned*; *Cert*; *Coir n-athcomairc*; *Dliged*; *Fír*; Procedure; *Téchtae*

Patrick, Saint, 126, 128, 131, 143, 206, 216–17, 296 n.40. See also First Synod of St. Patrick

Paul, Saint and Apostle, 139, 278 n.113

Pecham, Archbishop, 180

Performance, as an element in law, 33–38, 43, 125, 129, 131–32, 140, 146, 222–23

Perjury, 151, 206, 213–14

Pleas, Welsh, 158–68, 186, 193–94, 198, 203, 210, 224, 280 n.23, 289–90 n.22. See also *Cynghawsedd*; *Llyfr Cynghawsedd*; Procedure

Pledge, 153, 291 n.30. See also Gages; *Mach ar gyfraith*

Poets, 15, 21, 74, 77–78, 93, 127, 129, 134, 136, 195, 216
Poppe, Erich, 263 n.69
Powell, J. Enoch, 204
Powys, 23, 181
Principalis debitor (L.), "principal debtor," 192
Prison, 153, 291 n.30
Procedure: curial, Irish, 114–37, 224, 271 n.17, 272 n.35, 276 n.84; curial, Welsh, 116, 145, 158–68, 189–90, 193, 224, 280 n.23, 285 nn. 103, 105, 285–86 n.107; extracurial, 116, 126–32, 144, 150–51, 166–68, 224, 281 n.32. See also *Cert*; *Coir n-athcomairc*; Curialization; *Cyngaws*; *Cynghawsedd*; *Dliged*; *Fír*; *Llyfr Cynghawsedd*; Paths; Pleas; *Téchtae*
Professional fees, 74, 77–78, 80, 120
Pryce, Huw, 180, 198, 205, 208, 215, 294 n.20, 299 n.101
Pryderi, 204

Raith (W.), "compurgation," 209. See also Compurgation
Rath (Ir.), "fief," 91–92, 258 n.111, 262 nn.53–55
Ráth (Ir.), "paying surety," 7, 32, 34–35, 45, 48, 59, 67–68, 71–73, 116–17, 131, 141, 150, 191, 202, 218, 247 n.49; and *aitire*, 87–88, 260 n.28, 263 n.64, 269 n.128; and curial path *téchtae*, 122–23; binding of, 37, 88–89, 245 n.18; compensation of, 39–43, 248 n.64, 249 nn. 72, 75, 256 n.79, 259 n.17; of God, saints, Gospels, or elements, 200–202, 295 n.27; payment of debt by, 38–43. See also Contracts; Suretyship, of God
Ráth airnisi (Ir.), "bound *ráth*-surety," 249, n.75
Ráth fine (Ir.), "*ráth*-surety of the kindred," 71, 256 nn. 79, 81, 274 n.46. See also *Fine*; Kindred; *Ráth forngartha fine*
Ráth forngartha fine (Ir.), "*ráth*-surety commanded by the kindred," 72. See also *Fine*; Kindred; *Ráth fine*
Recht n-aicnid (Ir.), "natural law," 138–39, 278 n.113. See also *Aicned*
Recht litre (Ir.), "law of Scripture," 278 n.113
Rechtaire (Ir.), "stewards," 95, 263 n.75
Rechtgae (Ir.), "royal ordinance," 108, 263 n.67, 268 nn. 124, 126. See also *Cáin*; Legislation and statute
Rechtsschule, 11
Relics, 202, 213–14, 217–18, 299 n.103, 299–300 n.113
Renaissance, Carolingian, 2
Rex (L.), "king," 110, 283 n.54
Rhiannon, 204
Rhuddlan, statute of, 143. See also Legislation and statute
Rhys ap Gruffudd, 181
Rí (Ir.), "king," 107, 110
Ríagail Phátraic, 263 n.69
Roach (Ir.), "witness," 250 n.85. See also Witnesses
Rome, 1, 2, 16, 29–30, 54, 94, 136, 185, 192, 201, 214, 216, 226–27, 280 n.23, 297–98 n.75
Rosc (Ir.), "poem," type of style associated with poetry, 20, 113, 125
Roscad (Ir.), "legal maxims," 23, 278 n.114
Ruidles (Ir.), "entirely immune to claim," "a transaction that is entirely immune to claim," 46, 73, 75, 134. See also *Díles*; Immunities
Rwym (W.), "binding," 210

Saint David's, 2
Saints, 2, 14, 200, 202–3, 216–18, 237 nn. 27, 30, 299 n.96. See also Cadog; Columba; Finian of Clonard; Nicholas; Patrick; Paul
Sárbile, 265–66 n.98
Sarhaed, "insult," "assault," "payment for insult or assault," 13, 210, 281 n.29, 284 n.69
Scandinavia, sources, 2, 113, 188–89; See also Law
Schools, druidic, 2, 15, 21
Scotland, 229–30 n.3
Scripture, 136, 278 n.113. See also Bible; Gospels; New Testament; Old Testament
Sencha, 139
Senchae (Ir.), "historian, custodian of the past," 122
Senchas (Ir.), "history, learning, tradition," 22, 242 n.76. See also *Senchas Már*
Senchas Már, 31, 125, 136, 143, 238 n.40, 270–71 n.13, 274 n.55, 278 n.113. See also Lawbooks; *Senchas*

Senchléithe (Ir.), "servile person," 121, 123, 253 n.28, 273 nn.40–41

Sensmúr cinad (Ir.), "old rust of crime, old offenses," 122–23. See also *Téchtae*

Séoit turchluide (Ir.), "chattels of submission," 60–61. See also Clientship

Sept, 93, 110, 263 n.65

Sharpe, Richard, 2, 5, 126, 133, 232 n.20, 275 n.69

Sick-maintenance, 4, 16, 18, 55, 126, 264 n.83, 275 n.64. See also *Bretha Crólige*

Siege of Druim Damhghaire, The, 106

Síl Chuind, 100

Síl mBairr, 100, 104–5, 265–66 n.98, 301 n.13

Síl mBeraich m. Mescill, 301 n.8

Síl nEchach, 100

Síl Senaich Móir, 300 n.4

Slán nAitire Cairde, 85, 90–91, 96, 107–8, 259 n.17, 260 n.28, 261–62 n.48. See also *Aitire Chairdi*; *Cairde*

Slige Dála, 266–67 n.106

Smacht (Ir.), "fine," 39, 41, 106

Smachtgille (Ir.), "penalty-gage," 121. See also Gage; *Gell*

Smyth, Alfred, 266–67 n.106

Sochor (Ir.), "advantageous contract," 62, 253 n.31. See also Contracts, Irish

Sons. See Fathers

St. Asaph's, Church of, 145, 177

Stacey, Robin Chapman, 282 n. 44

Stevenson, Jane, 278 n.1

Stipulatio (L.), type of Roman contract, 29. See also Law, Roman

Sureties. See *Aitire*; *Amodwr*; *Briduw*; *Gorfodog*; *Mach*; *Naidm*; *Ráth*; Suretyship, of God

Suretyship: definition of, 5; Germanic evidence on, 7; kin-based (*see* Kindred); of God, 7, 200–203, 205–9, 211–13, 215, 217–18, 222, 250 n.90, 257 n.86, 295 n.29, 297–98 n.75, 298 n.92; of the elements, 200–202, 295 n.21; Welsh, as active area of the law, 144–46

Surexit memorandum, 138

Syria, 212

Tafodiog (W.), "incontravertible witness," 146, 154–56, 170, 188, 281 n.30, 287 n.123. See also Witnesses

Tánaise (Ir.), "tanist, heir apparent," 92, 263 n.68

Tara, 14, 106

Tassilo, 237 n.24

Teachers, 57, 60, 74, 78, 80–81, 127

Téchtae (Ir.) "propriety" (also curial path by that name), 121–23, 138, 273 nn.40–41, 274 n.50. See also *Ráth*; Procedure

Teithi (W.), "duties characteristic [of the office of guarantor]," 149–50, 160

Tellach (Ir.), "entry," "procedure to claim land," 233 n.23, 252 n.1

Test Book, 183, 289 n.15. See also Lawbooks, Welsh

Theft, 75–76, 79, 135, 145, 151, 213, 299–300 n.113

Thomas, Keith, 206

Thurneysen, Rudolf, 35, 82–83, 85, 87, 90, 92, 94, 97–98, 107, 114–15, 117, 122, 132, 246–47 n.37, 248 nn. 64, 67, 69, 249 nn. 72, 75, 259 n.17, 261 nn. 33, 38–40, 264 n.81, 268 nn. 115, 122–23, 269 n.128, 271 n.17, 271–72, n.32, 273 nn. 38, 40, 44, 297 n.71

Tipraite Tírech, 201

Tírechán, 118, 131

Tmesis, 244 n.14

Torah, Oral, 113, 290 n.24, 269–70 n.2

Treaties, 85, 90, 94, 98, 103, 218, 295 n.21. See also *Cairde*

Trent, Council of, 177

Triads, 147–48, 188–90, 209, 253 n.28, 281 n.32, 283 nn. 54, 57, 62, 289 n.19

Tripartite Life of Patrick, 216–17

Troscad (Ir.) , "fasting," 219. See also Fasting

Túath (Ir.), "people, tribe, small kingdom," 89, 92, 258 n.110, 260 n.28, 261 n.40

Tuathal Techtmar, 201

Tudor, 266–67 n.106

Twelve Tables, Law of the, 82, 258–59 n.1. See also Law, Roman

Tŷ Gwyn, 180, 186

Tyllwedd (W.) , "concord," 210

Tyst (W.), "witness," 160, 170–71, 176. See also Witnesses

Uí Ailella, 101

Uí Bairrche, 267 n.106

Uí Briúin, 101, 136

Uí Buide, 267 n.106

Uí Chremthainn, 93, 110
Uí Enechglaiss, 266–67 n.106
Uí Failge, 266–67 n.106
Uí Fiachrach, 101
Uí Fidgenti, 99–100, 102
Uí Néill, 92–93, 98–101, 107, 110, 136, 202, 223, 265 n.95
Uí Nialláin, 93
Uí Thuirtri, 93
Uisnech, 216
Ulaid, 92
Ulster cycle, 21
Uraicecht Becc, 13, 23, 117, 120, 127, 129–30, 137–38, 140, 249–50 n.80, 252 n.5, 270 n.7, 271–72 n.32
Urchuilte Bretheman, 140, 275 n.61, 278 n.114

Virgin Mary, 262 n.62

Wallace-Hadill, J. M., 12
Watkins, Calvert, 246 n.29
Wergild, 12, 218, 220, 242 n.71
Wessex, 209
Whitelock, Dorothy, 215
Williams, Stephen J., 204
Witnesses, 36–39, 42, 157, 159–61, 163, 165–67, 170–72, 174–175, 217, 284 n.78, 285 nn. 103, 105, 287 n.132, 299 n.102. See also *Amodwr*; *Córus Fíadnaise*; *Fíadnaise*; *Fíadu*; *Mach*; *Naidm*; *Roach*; *Tafodiog*; *Tyst*
Women, 71, 139, 209, 239 n.51, 241 nn. 64, 67, 278–79 n.5, 284 n.78; legal and contractual capacity of, 20, 62–63, 142, 241 n.67
Wormald, Patrick, 12–13, 20, 226, 229–30 n.3, 232 n.18, 234 nn. 2, 4, 7, 235 n.8, 241 n.63, 277 n.101

Ynad (W.), "judge," 23, 143, 183, 195, 197, 280 n.16. See also Judges, Welsh

Zahlbürge (G.), "paying surety," 149
Zeumer, K., 11
Zuni, 28

University of Pennsylvania Press
MIDDLE AGES SERIES
Edward Peters, General Editor

F. R. P. Akehurst, trans. *The* Coutumes de Beauvaisis *of Philippe de Beaumanoir.* 1992

Peter L. Allen. *The Art of Love: Amatory Fiction from Ovid to the* Romance of the Rose. 1992

David Anderson. *Before the Knight's Tale: Imitation of Classical Epic in Boccaccio's* Teseida. 1988

Benjamin Arnold. *Count and Bishop in Medieval Germany: A Study of Regional Power, 1100–1350.* 1991

Mark C. Bartusis. *The Late Byzantine Army: Arms and Society, 1204–1453.* 1992

J. M. W. Bean. *From Lord to Patron: Lordship in Late Medieval England.* 1990

Uta-Renate Blumenthal. *The Investiture Controversy: Church and Monarchy from the Ninth to the Twelfth Century.* 1988

Daniel Bornstein, trans. *Dino Compagni's* Chronicle *of Florence.* 1986

Maureen Boulton. *The Song in the Story: Lyric Insertions in French Narrative Fiction, 1200–1400.* 1993

Betsy Bowden. *Chaucer Aloud: The Varieties of Textual Interpretation.* 1987

James William Brodman. *Ransoming Captives in Crusader Spain: The Order of Merced on the Christian-Islamic Frontier.* 1986

Kevin Brownlee and Sylvia Huot, eds. *Rethinking the* Romance of the Rose*: Text, Image, Reception.* 1992

Matilda Tomaryn Bruckner. *Shaping Romance: Interpretation, Truth, and Closure in Twelfth-Century French Fictions.* 1993

Otto Brunner (Howard Kaminsky and James Van Horn Melton, eds. and trans.). Land *and Lordship: Structures of Governance in Medieval Austria.* 1992

Robert I. Burns, S.J., ed. *Emperor of Culture: Alfonso X the Learned of Castile and His Thirteenth-Century Renaissance.* 1990

David Burr. *Olivi and Franciscan Poverty: The Origins of the* Usus Pauper *Controversy.* 1989

David Burr. *Olivi's Peaceable Kingdom: A Reading of the Apocalypse Commentary.* 1993

Thomas Cable. *The English Alliterative Tradition.* 1991

Anthony K. Cassell and Victoria Kirkham, eds. and trans. *Diana's Hunt/Caccia di Diana: Boccaccio's First Fiction.* 1991

John C. Cavadini. *The Last Christology of the West: Adoptionism in Spain and Gaul, 785–820.* 1993

Brigitte Cazelles. *The Lady as Saint: A Collection of French Hagiographic Romances of the Thirteenth Century.* 1991

Karen Cherewatuk and Ulrike Wiethaus, eds. *Dear Sister: Medieval Women and the Epistolary Genre.* 1993

Anne L. Clark. *Elisabeth of Schönau: A Twelfth-Century Visionary.* 1992

Willene B. Clark and Meradith T. McMunn, eds. *Beasts and Birds of the Middle Ages: The Bestiary and Its Legacy.* 1989

Richard C. Dales. *The Scientific Achievement of the Middle Ages.* 1973

Charles T. Davis. *Dante's Italy and Other Essays.* 1984

Katherine Fischer Drew, trans. *The Burgundian Code.* 1972

Katherine Fischer Drew, trans. *The Laws of the Salian Franks.* 1991

Katherine Fischer Drew, trans. *The Lombard Laws.* 1973

Nancy Edwards. *The Archaeology of Early Medieval Ireland.* 1990

Margaret J. Ehrhart. *The Judgment of the Trojan Prince Paris in Medieval Literature.* 1987

Richard K. Emmerson and Ronald B. Herzman. *The Apocalyptic Imagination in Medieval Literature.* 1992

Theodore Evergates. *Feudal Society in Medieval France: Documents from the County of Champagne.* 1993

Felipe Fernández-Armesto. *Before Columbus: Exploration and Colonization from the Mediterranean to the Atlantic, 1229–1492.* 1987

R. D. Fulk. *A History of Old English Meter.* 1992

Patrick J. Geary. *Aristocracy in Provence: The Rhône Basin at the Dawn of the Carolingian Age.* 1985

Peter Heath. *Allegory and Philosophy in Avicenna (Ibn Sînâ), with a Translation of the Book of the Prophet Muḥammad's Ascent to Heaven.* 1992

J. N. Hillgarth, ed. *Christianity and Paganism, 350–750: The Conversion of Western Europe.* 1986

Richard C. Hoffmann. *Land, Liberties, and Lordship in a Late Medieval Countryside: Agrarian Structures and Change in the Duchy of Wrocław.* 1990

Robert Hollander. *Boccaccio's Last Fiction: Il Corbaccio.* 1988

Edward B. Irving, Jr. *Rereading* Beowulf. 1989

C. Stephen Jaeger. *The Origins of Courtliness: Civilizing Trends and the Formation of Courtly Ideals, 939–1210.* 1985

William Chester Jordan. *The French Monarchy and the Jews: From Philip Augustus to the Last Capetians.* 1989

William Chester Jordan. *From Servitude to Freedom: Manumission in the Sénonais in the Thirteenth Century.* 1986

Richard Kay. *Dante's Christian Astrology.* 1994

Ellen E. Kittell. *From* Ad Hoc *to Routine: A Case Study in Medieval Bureaucracy.* 1991

Alan C. Kors and Edward Peters, eds. *Witchcraft in Europe, 1100–1700: A Documentary History.* 1972

Barbara M. Kreutz. *Before the Normans: Southern Italy in the Ninth and Tenth Centuries.* 1992

E. Ann Matter. *The Voice of My Beloved: The Song of Songs in Western Medieval Christianity.* 1990

María Rosa Menocal. *The Arabic Role in Medieval Literary History.* 1987

A. J. Minnis. *Medieval Theory of Authorship.* 1988

Lawrence Nees. *A Tainted Mantle: Hercules and the Classical Tradition at the Carolingian Court.* 1991

Lynn H. Nelson, trans. *The Chronicle of San Juan de la Peña: A Fourteenth-Century Official History of the Crown of Aragon.* 1991

Charlotte A. Newman. *The Anglo-Norman Nobility in the Reign of Henry I: The Second Generation.* 1988

Joseph F. O'Callaghan. *The Cortes of Castile-León, 1188–1350.* 1989

Joseph F. O'Callaghan. *The Learned King: The Reign of Alfonso X of Castile.* 1993

David M. Olster. *Roman Defeat, Christian Response, and the Literary Construction of the Jew.* 1994

William D. Paden, ed. *The Voice of the Trobairitz: Perspectives on the Women Troubadours.* 1989

Edward Peters. *The Magician, the Witch, and the Law.* 1982

Edward Peters, ed. *Christian Society and the Crusades, 1198–1229: Sources in Translation, including* The Capture of Damietta *by Oliver of Paderborn.* 1971

Edward Peters, ed. *The First Crusade: The* Chronicle of Fulcher of Chartres *and Other Source Materials.* 1971

Edward Peters, ed. *Heresy and Authority in Medieval Europe.* 1980

James M. Powell. *Albertanus of Brescia: The Pursuit of Happiness in the Early Thirteenth Century.* 1992

James M. Powell. *Anatomy of a Crusade, 1213–1221.* 1986

Jean Renart (Patricia Terry and Nancy Vine Durling, trans.). *The Romance of the Rose or Guillaume de Dole.* 1993

Michael Resler, trans. Erec *by Hartmann von Aue.* 1987

Pierre Riché (Michael Idomir Allen, trans.). *The Carolingians: A Family Who Forged Europe.* 1993

Pierre Riché (Jo Ann McNamara, trans.). *Daily Life in the World of Charlemagne.* 1978

Jonathan Riley-Smith. *The First Crusade and the Idea of Crusading.* 1986

Joel T. Rosenthal. *Patriarchy and Families of Privilege in Fifteenth-Century England.* 1991

Teofilo F. Ruiz. *Crisis and Continuity: Land and Town in Late Medieval Castile.* 1994

Steven D. Sargent, ed. and trans. *On the Threshold of Exact Science: Selected Writings of Anneliese Maier on Late Medieval Natural Philosophy.* 1982

Robin Chapman Stacey. *The Road to Judgment: From Custom to Court in Medieval Ireland and Wales.* 1994

Sarah Stanbury. *Seeing the* Gawain-Poet: *Description and the Act of Perception.* 1992

Thomas C. Stillinger. *The Song of Troilus: Lyric Authority in the Medieval Book.* 1992

Susan Mosher Stuard. *A State of Deference: Ragusa/Dubrovnik in the Medieval Centuries.* 1992

Susan Mosher Stuard, ed. *Women in Medieval History and Historiography.* 1987

Susan Mosher Stuard, ed. *Women in Medieval Society*. 1976
Jonathan Sumption. *The Hundred Years War: Trial by Battle*. 1992
Ronald E. Surtz. *The Guitar of God: Gender, Power, and Authority in the Visionary World of Mother Juana de la Cruz (1481–1534)*. 1990
William H. TeBrake. *A Plague of Insurrection: Popular Politics and Peasant Revolt in Flanders, 1323–1328*. 1993
Patricia Terry, trans. *Poems of the Elder Edda*. 1990
Hugh M. Thomas. *Vassals, Heiresses, Crusaders, and Thugs: The Gentry of Angevin Yorkshire, 1154–1216*. 1993
Frank Tobin. *Meister Eckhart: Thought and Language*. 1986
Ralph V. Turner. *Men Raised from the Dust: Administrative Service and Upward Mobility in Angevin England*. 1988
Harry Turtledove, trans. *The* Chronicle *of Theophanes: An English Translation of* Anni Mundi *6095–6305 (A.D. 602–813)*. 1982
Mary F. Wack. *Lovesickness in the Middle Ages: The* Viaticum *and Its Commentaries*. 1990
Benedicta Ward. *Miracles and the Medieval Mind: Theory, Record, and Event, 1000–1215*. 1982
Suzanne Fonay Wemple. *Women in Frankish Society: Marriage and the Cloister, 500–900*. 1981
Jan M. Ziolkowski. *Talking Animals: Medieval Latin Beast Poetry, 750–1150*. 1993

This book has been set in Linotron Galliard. Galliard was designed for Mergenthaler in 1978 by Matthew Carter. Galliard retains many of the features of a sixteenth-century typeface cut by Robert Granjon but has some modifications that give it a more contemporary look.

Printed on acid-free paper.